SEXING THE MAPLE

SEXING THE MAPLE
A CANADIAN SOURCEBOOK

edited by
RICHARD CAVELL AND PETER DICKINSON

broadview press

National Library of Canada Cataloguing in Publication

Sexing the maple : a Canadian sourcebook / edited by Richard Cavell and Peter Dickinson.

Includes bibliographical references.
ISBN-13: 978-1-55111-486-6
ISBN-10: 1-55111-486-0

1. Sex—Canada.   2. Sex—Canada—Literary collections.
I. Dickinson, Peter, 1968–   II. Cavell, Richard, 1949–

HQ18.C2S485 2006   306.70971   C2006-902349-2

Broadview Press is an independent, international publishing house, incorporated in 1985. Broadview believes in shared ownership, both with its employees and with the general public; since the year 2000 Broadview shares have traded publicly on the Toronto Venture Exchange under the symbol BDP.

We welcome comments and suggestions regarding any aspect of our publications – please feel free to contact us at the addresses below or at broadview@broadviewpress.com.

North America
Post Office Box 1243, Peterborough, Ontario, Canada K9J 7H5
Post Office Box 1015, 3576 California Road, Orchard Park, NY, USA 14127
Tel: (705) 743-8990; Fax: (705) 743-8353;
e-mail: customerservice@broadviewpress.com

UK, Ireland, and continental Europe
NBN International, Eastover Road, Plymouth PL6 7PY UK
Tel: 44 (0) 1752 202300   Fax: 44 (0) 1752 202330
e-mail: enquiries@nbninternational.com

Australia and New Zealand
UNIREPS, University of New South Wales
Sydney, NSW, 2052
Tel: 61 2 9664 0999; Fax: 61 2 9664 5420
email: info.press@unsw.edu.au

www.broadviewpress.com

Broadview Press gratefully acknowledges the financial support of the Government of Canada through the Book Publishing Industry Development Program for our publishing activities.

Typesetting and assembly: True to Type Inc., Mississauga, Canada.

PRINTED IN CANADA

for Jane Rule

and in memory of David Reimer

I am yours for your green sheathing,
strong because of your sweet breathing,
new restored by your achieving;
a dark flower opens past believing.

Douglas LePan, from *Leaves and Lyrics*

CONTENTS

ACKNOWLEDGEMENTS

First and foremost we would like to thank Don LePan, the genial spirit who presides over Broadview Press, for his support of this project, and Julia Gaunce for her patience with the manuscript and its editors. The University of British Columbia's Hampton Fund provided the wherewithal that supported research, compilation, and especially permission costs. Patricia Lackie and Angela Kajia of UBC's Department of English provided crucial help in dealing with Financial Services at different points in the life of this project. Jes Battis, Alessandra Capperdoni, and Alison McDonald, all of Simon Fraser University, were invaluable research assistants. Barbara Kuhne helped us with Press Gang permissions. Jesse Finkelstein of Raincoast Books, Nancy Grossman of McClelland and Stewart, Gilles Hurteau, Crown Copyright Officer, Penny Goldsmith of Lazara Press, Matie Molinaro of Canadian Speakers and Writers Services Ltd., and Amy Tompkins of Westwood Creative Artists were particularly helpful. We are happy to record our special gratitude to all the authors who so kindly gave permission to have their work reprinted here. Finally, Richard Cavell extends his special thanks to Peter Dickinson, who conceived of this project and nurtured it—and his co-editor—through the many visions and revisions that led to the volume that you now hold.

SEX AND CANADA: A THEORETICAL INTRODUCTION

> Sex is a national issue and nations depend on sex. Put another way, nations require particular sentiments of attachment, ones that often rest at least in part on the erotic. In the national anthem customarily sung before a Canadian hockey game, the libidinal affect that binds citizen to nation is called "true patriot love." ... Everyone has a sexuality, even those who don't practice it or those for whom the practice of it dictates not having it. In this way, sex just might be the ultimate in national belonging, that which is fundamentally shaped by gender, race, class and age, but also traverses across those divisions. We need to harness sex not to teach about nation—although sex is up for that—but to challenge how we "think Canadian."
>   —Steven Maynard, "The Maple Leaf (Gardens) Forever,"
>   *Journal of Canadian Studies* (2001)

True Patriot Love

When we sing the national anthem (or hear it sung) are we aware (as Steven Maynard suggests) that it contains an underlying discourse about sexuality? Perhaps not, yet the notions of birth, love, state fatherhood, mother country, and sons are all underpinned by sexual motifs, and one of the purposes of this book is to identify these motifs as they occur broadly in Canadian literature and to contextualize them through a range of critical articles. Ultimately, what connects sexual discourse with national discourse is the question of identity; as Arnold I. Davidson has remarked, "Sexuality individualizes, turns one into a specific kind of human being."[1] Analogously, the question of identity has been a constant in the discourse of Canadian nationalism, and it is on this question that we turn an unaccustomed light. Although the importance of sexuality as a category of social, political, and cultural analysis is broadly acknowledged, Karen Dubinsky noted in 1993 that "despite [this] growing international interest in the history of sexuality, Canadian historians are still silent on the topic.... We must now ... begin to rethink Canadian history as though sexuality mattered. At this point a national synthesis of the history of sexuality in Canada is difficult to imagine but delightful to speculate about."[2] *Sexing the Maple* moves such speculation into the classroom.

While teaching and research about Canadian history has increasingly sought to bring sexuality into its determinations over the last decade (though not without controversy; as Steven Maynard notes in the essay from which the epigraph to this introduction is taken, "there are those who believe that the writing of sexuality's past has torn asunder the story of Canada's national history"),[3] the literary field has been slower to do so. *Sexing the Maple* seeks to address this lack by raising issues of nationalism and sexuality through a broad historical range of literary texts, contextualizing them with additional pieces from law to medicine, from media to race. Its literary component allows it to be used in courses on Canadian literature; its contextual pieces provide a cultural studies orientation that makes it equally applicable for courses in sociology, women's studies, studies in gender relations, introductory law, sexuality studies, and so on. It is structured in such a way as to provide the basis for an interdisciplinary study of these issues in its anticipation of a number of contexts in which the book's various sections can be interrelated. These sections are comprised of works (some complete, some excerpted) which are often out of print, difficult of access, or generally unavailable in the context that we provide for them.

We should note at the outset, however, that the "turn" to sexuality does not imply that Canada's literature is somehow deficient and must thus be understood through other categories of knowledge production. As Nicholas Jenkins has recently written in an issue of the *Times Literary Supplement* with reference to the high cultural modalities of British literary modernism:

> The standard maps of modern literary history were drawn up during the Cold War period at a time when the academic mind was transfixed by the idea of national traditions and of warring, Us-and-Them poetic blocs (the "raw" versus the "cooked," ... manifesting the era's politically Manichean mindset). Modern British and American poetic histories suddenly became entities unto themselves, sealed off from foreign influences even as such rootless, ambiguous but central figures as Bishop, Pound, Auden and, in a minor way, Spender [the subject of Jenkins's review] were demonstrating the messier, more fluid realities of the most representative poetic lives.
>
> After half a century of the "national model," literary history desperately needs a new narrative for modern poetry [and for literature at large, we would suggest], if only to stop itself from falling asleep over yet one more account of "the Americanness" of Marianne Moore, or the "Englishness" of Larkin, or the "Irishness" of Yeats [or the "Canadianness" of Atwood?].[4]

Our anthology, however, does not seek to dispense with the national model as a way of understanding our literature; rather, we seek to enhance that understanding in critical terms by interrelating the national model with sexuality studies.

One of the few predecessors of our book is Jeremy Brown and Christopher Ondaatje's *The First Original Unexpurgated Canadian Book of Sex and Adventure*,[5] which is as interesting for its contents as for what it says about the time (1979) in which it was published. The book's frontispiece is a photograph of Margaret Trudeau dancing at Studio 54 (New York), and its first illustration labels athlete Diane Jones Konahowski "a great Canadian fantasy"; together they provide an apt introduction to the sexual politics of the period, which emerge with further clarity in the introduction by Brown:

> When I was growing up, Canada was very restrained and reserved. That was before the sixties when there was a lot of mystery and sanctimoniousness about the whole thing. Sex was something you identified gender with, not something you shared with a woman. The double standard was ever present. You were entitled to all you could get with a person of loose morals, but never, ever, with a candidate for marriage.[6]

Notions of sexuality have broadened in the intervening 25 years to include relations not contained by this heterosexualist, reproductivist discourse—the discourse produced by our national anthem—and these notions have become more discriminating as well in the use of terms such as "sex" and "gender." Many of these changes have been heralded by legal cases, and for this reason we devote a section to the topic of sex and the law.

Brown and Ondaatje's book is characterized by lists ("10 Great Sensual Quotations on Women," "10 Great Sensual Quotations on Men," "The 10 Most Sensuous Canadian Women," "Canada's Six Sexiest and Most Photogenic Women," and so on), perhaps an indication of the rather empirical approach taken towards sexuality in the period when they were writing (a legacy, no doubt, of Alfred Kinsey's famous reports on sexuality, which sought statistical foundations for its assertions).[7] Sexuality, in these terms, becomes comprised of "norms" that individuals either conform to or diverge from. Yet, as Gary Kinsman's pioneering work of exemplary scholarship, *The Regulation of Desire*,[8] has shown, it is precisely through the construction of such "normative" behaviour that sexuality becomes an instrument of social organization and governmentality that the state uses to control *both* "normal" *and* divergent sexuality—expressions of sexuality that undermine the way in which the state desires to represent itself. And clearly, one of the major ways in which the state desires to represent itself is through a specific discourse on sexuality.[9]

The notion of a sexual "discourse," or narrative, is founded upon the element of "constructivism"—the idea that sexuality is not a given but is actively constructed in social, literary, political, and even medical terms (see the excerpt from John Colapinto in "Sex and Medicine")—and thus provides a much more fluid basis for the understanding of sexual behaviour than one which assumes that sexuality is biologically determined. The notion of discourse also reminds us why narratives are so important in understanding sexuality. As Jeffrey Weeks has remarked, "We live in a culture of storytelling," and the stories we tell about our sexualities are one of the ways in which we articulate our sense of nationhood:

The most common narratives are stories which tell of discrimination, prejudice and empowerment, stories which tell of coming out as lesbian and gay or as a strong, independent woman, stories of victimization and of survival, stories of difference and similarity, stories of identity and stories of relationships. These new stories about the self, about sexuality and gender, are the context for the emergence of the sexual citizen because these stories telling of exclusion, through gender, sexuality, race, bodily appearance or function, have as their corollary the demand for inclusion: for equal rights under the law, in politics, in economics, in social matters and in sexual matters. They pose questions about who should control our bodies, the limits of the body, the burden of custom and of the state. They are stories which spring up from everyday life, but in turn place new demands on the wider community for the development of more responsive policies, in economics, welfare, the law, culture.[10]

One of the key areas through which these narratives enter the public sphere is literature, and hence it is the primary focus of this book.

A work often cited by Brown and Ondaatje is Benjamin Schlesinger's edited collection *Sexual Behaviour in Canada* (1977), the first such collection published in this country. The overall approach taken by the book's 31 authors (16 of whom are women) is physiological; as Schlesinger remarks in his introduction, "Sexuality plays an important part in the life cycle of every Canadian from birth to old age, and everyone has some claim on having a good and healthy sex life."[11] Schlesinger's introduction was written in the wake of Alex Comfort's *The Joy of Sex*,[12] which is in some ways the ultimate fulfilment of Kinsey's normative approach to sexuality, even though it is often cited as a significant moment in sexual liberation.[13] Despite Schlesinger's physiological approach, however, numerous cultural implications of sexuality emerge throughout his book. For example, in the contribution titled "Attitudes and Sexuality," F. Michael Barrett writes that, "[s]ince North Americans have traditionally viewed sexuality as a threat to social stability and therefore something to be controlled, it is not surprising that many of us were reared in a cultural setting that fostered sex-negative attitudes."[14] Barrett traces these attitudes to various sources, including religious strictures, the mind/body split, the work ethic, the subjugation of women, and taboos against aspects of the body. As another author remarks, these attitudes manifested themselves in an 1892 act of Parliament which not only prohibited obscene literature but also "every article or thing designed or intended for the prevention of conception or procuring of an abortion."[15] The act was justified with the comment made by a member of the government that "Nations enter upon their periods of decadence through effeminacy" (281), where "effeminacy" has to be understood as any deviation from the norms and goals of reproductive behaviour, thus revealing the gendered assumptions within normative sexuality. As a result of this act, information on contraception was banned in Canada for the next 77 years.

Equally prohibitory were publications such as the "Self and Sex" series (described by Michael Bliss in an article reprinted here in the section on "Sex and the Family"), which were deeply negative about non-normative forms of sexuality such as masturbation, which was said to lead to insanity. Similarly, Arthur Beall, in the "advanced purity lectures" he gave in the Ontario school system through the first 30 years of the twentieth century, discoursed on the "beautiful, wonderful *life glands*" but advised his youthful audiences to "Keep them clean and leave them alone."[16] Ironically, Beall's obsession with gonadal sexuality is present in Barrett's assessment as well, which focuses almost exclusively on heterosexual intercourse. However, the essays in *Sexual Behaviour in Canada* on lesbianism, homosexuality, and on the unfortunately titled "management of transsexualism" alter this pattern,[17] though the emphasis is still on "the uncommon deviant from the norm" ("Transsexualism" 162), and the term "management" identifies the utilitarian approach to sexuality which remains dominant in this period of apparent liberalization. Indeed, Beall's Victorian prudery is evident in various sections, such as Andrew I. Malcolm's definition of "aphrodisiac" as "any food or drug that excites to *venery*" (italics added),[18] a term as antiquated as it is euphemistic. The volume attributes the changes in attitudes in sexuality that it observes to ecology (diminishing resources mean that couples are opting to have fewer or no children at all, and thus sexual relations take on a non-reproductive orientation), automation (which has affected the physical labour that men and women may take on and thus their gender and sexual roles, a shift dramatically experienced during the Second World War), liberation movements, and birth control (the Pill having been legalized in Canada in 1963, thereby placing sexuality in the realm of technology, the implications of which Patricia Baird *et al.* deal with in the Royal Commission on Reproductive Technologies, excerpted here).

The sources of Brown and Ondaatje's *Canadian Book of Sex*, taken as a whole, are indicative of some of the changes that have occurred since its publication in the production of a discourse on sexuality in Canada. The Schlesinger anthology, and Schlesinger's other volume, *Family Planning in Canada*, together with Lyle Larson's *The Canadian Family in Comparative Perspective*, comprise the book's major "scientific" sources. The remainder of the *Canadian Book of Sex*'s information comes from magazine articles (in *Chatelaine, Homemaker, Quest, Maclean's*), newspapers (*Toronto Sun, Globe and Mail*), literary texts, the *Canadian Book of Lists*, Michelle Bedard's *Canada in Bed*, James Leslie McCary's *Sexual Myths and Fallacies*, Suzanne Cloutier's *How to Make Love*, Daniel Cappon's *Towards an Understanding of Homosexuality*, Claire Wallace's *Canadian Etiquette*, the *Canadian School Survey* for 1979, and a number of interviews. What these sources indicate is that sexuality was very much a "domestic" issue during the period that Ondaatje and Brown produced their anthology.

This domestic approach to sexuality derives in large part from the notion that sexuality is normative and thus "natural," taking place at home and preferably in the bedroom. Yet the changes in attitudes toward sexuality that became evident from the nineteenth century onward clearly demonstrated that sexuality was *in history*, that it was constructed according to certain social and political needs and constraints. Only with this realization did it become possible to perform an historical analysis of sexuality. As Arnold I. Davidson has remarked,

> It is not because we became preoccupied with our true sexuality that a sci-
> ence of sexuality arose in the nineteenth century; it is rather the emer-
> gence of a science of sexuality that made it possible, even inevitable, for us
> to become preoccupied with our true sexuality. Thus our existence became
> a sexistence, saturated with the promises and threats of sexuality. Historical
> epistemology attempts to show how this new form of experience that we
> call 'sexuality' is linked to the emergence of new structures of knowledge,
> and especially to a new style of reasoning and the concepts employed with-
> in it.[19]

What this means is that sexuality is constructed differently according to its context, which includes its historical moment, its geographical place, and its nationalist ideology. One need only watch a ten-year-old movie, or read descriptions of sexual encounters in novels published a decade ago, to under-stand the ways in which sexuality is very much embedded in history; what appeared "natural" ten years ago appears quaint or even laughable today—witness the excerpt from Gertrude Pringle's *Etiquette in Canada*, reprinted here in "Sex and the Family."

Another predecessor for our book is John Moss's *Sex and Violence in the Canadian Novel: The Ancestral Present*. Moss writes in the introduction to the book that "This is not ... a sociological report on sex and violence in the Cana-dian experience. It is a critical response to sex and violence in Canadian nov-els, in the Canadian novel. The first chapter presents the argument that gives the rest of the book its shape, relating sex to personal identity, violence to moral awareness, and showing the Canadian novel to draw, extensively, both form and content from the broad and brilliant spectrum between these sets."[20] Here the perennial Canadian question of national identity is given a new context, though the flexibility around identity that characterizes con-temporary discussions of identity—be those discussions about national or sex-ual identity—is absent. The reference to "form and content" and the dis-avowal of a "sociological" element to Moss's inquiry is likewise more indicative of the time when he was writing than it is of the time when we are writing, when disciplinary categories such as "literature" and "sociology" are becoming increasingly blurred.

Like Ondaatje and Brown's book, and like our own, Moss's book is redolent of the attitudes of its time, as is indicated by his comment that "in Canadian fiction at least, there is a proliferation of coquettes, a word that might best be updated as combining the attributes of cock-teaser and whimsical feminist" (12). A number of his book's sections, in fact, address feminism, reminding us of the enormous influence that the feminist movement has had on a large spectrum of social and cultural entities, including the academy. Indeed, historical moments in Canadian women's history are at once salutary and telling: while Canadian women were granted the vote in 1918 and the right to stand for Parliament in 1919, they were recognized as "persons" only in 1929. It was in 1967—the year of the national centennial—that Prime Minister Lester Pearson convened the Royal Commission on the Status of Women. The Commission's 1970 Report proposed the modernization of the Divorce Act and recommended increased access to abortion and birth control, the end of sexual stereotyping in textbooks, and the repeal of that section of the Criminal Code allowing police to arrest a woman for prostitution if she could not prove she had other means of supporting herself.[21] The Report further recommended pay equity (which, in 2006, women have still not achieved), 18 weeks' maternity leave, an end to practices in the pension system that discriminated against women, and the coverage by the employment insurance system of "traditional female jobs" as well as the opening up of "traditional male jobs" (such as bank managers) to women.[22] As Marlene Mackie has argued in *Gender Relations in Canada* (1991), the feminist movement in Canada, by altering gender role expectations, has had a profound influence upon the nation as a whole in terms of legislative changes with regard to employment equity, access to abortion and contraception, sexual harassment, maternity leave, and so on.[23] At the same time, early manifestations of the feminist movement have been criticized for their own normative assumptions about what "femininity" includes and excludes.

These issues emerge powerfully around discussions of pornography and obscenity, given that this is the domain *par excellence* of federal legislation on sexuality. As Mary Louise Adams discusses in *Love, Hate, and Fear in Canada's Cold War*, the post-Second World War period was especially concerned with returning to "normal" after the upheavals of the war, when men were thrust for long periods into homosocial environments and women took on the untraditional roles of head of the household and factory worker.[24] It was in this context that depictions in literature of lesbianism and homosexuality were severely punished. Currently in Canada there is an Obscenity Law in force which restricts "pornography" to representations of children—so-called "kiddie porn," as discussed by Stan Persky and John Dixon in the excerpt from their book of that title. The law itself is concerned with the corruption

of "public morals" and with "the undue exploitation of sex," although in practice what tend to prevail are contemporary standards of tolerance. Thus, the
1992 Supreme Court decision in the Butler case[25] argued that social harm
and not explicitness of depictions was the defining element of pornography
and that this element prevails over freedom of expression, although the
determination of "artistic merit" can find a defendant not guilty (an ambiguity around which Michael Turner's *The Pornographer's Poem* turns). As Bruce
Ryder has noted, the Butler decision allowed explicit sexual depictions to cir-
culate. At the same time, it did not fully reject the notion that exposure to
"bad" ideas would produce "bad" actions.[26] These contradictory notions have
been invoked in the various court cases convened to argue that Canada Customs has unfairly and unjustly blocked at the border books and videos destined for the gay, lesbian, bisexual, and transitional communities; these cases,
which involve bookstores such as Little Sister's in Vancouver (about which
Jane Rule writes in *Detained at Customs*, reprinted here in full) and Glad Day
in Toronto, are ongoing.[27]

Nationalisms and Sexualities

In his pioneering study, *Nationalism and Sexuality*, George L. Mosse writes that
"just as modern nationalism emerged in the eighteenth century, so the ideal
of respectability and its definition of sexuality fell into place at the same
time."[28] Mosse's focus is on the body, respectability, and the nation, a nexus
that Gary Kinsman (and others, such as Thomas Waugh) would rewrite in
terms of (moral) regulation. "Analyzing the relationship between nationalism
and respectability," writes Mosse, "involves tracing the development of some
of the most important norms that have informed our society: ideals of manliness ... and their effect on the place of women; and insiders who accepted the
norms, as compared to the outsiders, those considered abnormal or diseased"
(1). Sexuality was not just an index of moral behaviour, however; it was also
an aesthetic marker, and in this way the issues of sexuality, the nation, and literature become intertwined.

As Mosse's analyses consistently reveal, "What one regards as normal or
abnormal behaviour, sexual or otherwise, is a product of historical development, not universal law" (3), and this principle remains the guiding one of
sexuality studies within a nationalist context. Examining the history of sexuality in the context of the history of nationalism reveals a number of important conjunctions. For example, Mosse observes that the "nineteenth-century
struggle to control sex—beyond those controls already attempted by the various churches—was part of a larger effort to cope with the ever more obvious
results of industrialization and political upheaval" (9).[29] In an era of increasing secularism, the nation thus came to fulfil this "policing" function originally performed by the church (notions which Leonard Cohen intertwines

masterfully in *Beautiful Losers*). Mosse continues: "The two histories thus become enmeshed. Nationalism helped control sexuality, yet also provided the means through which changing sexual attitudes could be absorbed and tamed into respectability. In addition, it assumed a sexual dimension of its own, coming to advocate a stereotype of supposedly 'passionless' beauty for both men and women" while supporting a system of moral classification whereby the "appearance and character of each individual was classified as normal or abnormal: nervousness was supposedly induced by the practice of vice, while virility and manly bearing were signs of virtue. *Nationalism adopted this ideal of manliness and built its national stereotypes around it*" (10; emphasis added).[30] The true man sublimated his passion, transforming its energies into leadership of the home, through marriage, and the nation, through society; the nuclear family reflected the unified national state. This repressive paradigm was embodied by Greek culture as expressed in its statuary, which was seen as expressing ideals of abstraction, sublimation, and nobility (13–14); these qualities were especially useful in refuting any hint of the homoerotic that might be conveyed by the beauty of the Greek ideal of manliness. Women, on the contrary, "were represented through medieval symbols rather than by the lofty and harmonious spirit of Greece" (15). As Mosse is at pains to remind us throughout, these attitudes are directly linked to the fascism that led to the upheavals of the Second World War and the aftermath with which we are still living.[31]

What connects the elements of Mosse's analysis is *power*, and, as Joan Wallach Scott has argued, it is precisely power which is signified through the system of gender (and of sexuality, we would add).[32] Ian McKay has identified gender as one of the dimensions through which we might "think through the construction of the post-Confederation political and social order."[33] Quoting Joan Scott's definition of gender as "the social organization of sexual difference" (xv), McKay remarks on the significance of the patriarchal dimension of post-Confederation Canada: "Women were not seen as equals. In some respects, they were not even regarded as persons, with full possession of themselves.... Women were not invited as participants to the conferences in the 1860s that organized the Canadian constitution, whose key architects are now significantly called the '*Fathers* of Confederation'" (xv-xvi; emphasis in original).

Peter Dickinson's *Here is Queer: Nationalisms, Sexualities, and the Literatures of Canada* (1999) makes a similar argument for sexuality (while not unmooring it from issues of gender), bringing together the discourses of nationalism, literature, and sexuality in Canada by critiquing, or "queering," the assumption of heteronormativity in these domains. The title of the book indicates the general direction of its argument: it constitutes a riposte to Northrop Frye's famous question about Canadian identity, "Where is here?" by grounding that question in the historical (racial, ethnic, gendered) here and now of embodied experience, and it does this by expanding the key terms "nationalism," "sexuality," and "literature" beyond the univocal conceptions that tradition-ally regulate them into pluralized entities that flow into one another. Histor-ically, then, the "hereness" of Canada has always been "queered" through the multivalency of experiences that underpin it, including sexual experiences; at the same time, that queerness has been regulated so as to ensure the unin-terrupted transmission of patriarchal power (which gives quite a different inflection to the notion of "true patriot love"). As Dickinson writes in his introduction, "This is not to say that 'here' is only or ever 'queer,' nor that resistance to a heteronormative nationalism is always or exclusively homo-sexual; what ... this book does suggest, however, is that 'queer,' as a literary-critical category of an almost inevitable definitional elasticity, one whose inventory of sexual meanings has yet to be exhausted, challenges and upsets certain received national orthodoxies of writing in Canada."[34] Of particular importance to Dickinson's argument is the "homosocial" thesis of Eve Kosof-sky Sedgwick, whereby male-male desire (which is traditionally subject to heavy regulation) is triangulated, or expressed through, mutual declarations of love for a woman.[35] Within the colonial context, this homosociality is often configured as love for the land. "Canadian literature," Dickinson writes, "or at the very least *English*-Canadian literature, is riddled with male couples who displace their love for each other—and frequently their nation—across the 'body' of a woman, whom they symbolically share, or else onto a mythically feminized region or landscape, which they symbolically exploit" (5). And just as these triangulations undermine unitary notions of identity, so do questions of gender, race, ethnicity, and class undermine assumptions of who "a" Cana-dian is (as SKY Lee brings out in *Disappearing Moon Café*).

Sex in Theory: Foundational Notions

Sexuality was established as a discourse at about the same time that Canada was establishing itself as a nation—the last quarter of the nineteenth century. As Joseph Bristow remarks, "The word became common currency in late nine-teenth-century Europe and America when anthropological, scientific, and sociological studies of sex were flourishing as never before."[36] Bristow goes on to note that the words "heterosexuality" and "homosexuality" entered the Eng-lish language in 1892 through a translation of Richard von Krafft-Ebing's book, *Psychopathia Sexualis*. And it was in 1897—only two years after Oscar Wilde had been charged with "gross indecency"—that Havelock Ellis pub-lished *Sexual Inversion*, a detailed study of same-sex desire that was co-authored with literary critic and poet John Addington Symonds.[37] One of Krafft-Ebing's Vienna colleagues was Sigmund Freud, who began his own study of sexuality in 1876 with research on the gonads of eels. His first essay, on male hysteria, dates from 1886; a decade later he coined the term "psychoanalysis."[38]

Through the writings of Sigmund Freud, sexuality entered into the public domain in a way that it had not done before. As Freud makes clear in his *Three Essays on the Theory of Sexuality* (1905), his model of sexuality was normative; the *Three Essays* thus discuss sexual aberrations, sexual deviations, perversions, inversions, and neuroses.[39] His theories were also deeply misogynist in their proposal that women suffered from penis envy. Given the essentialist nature of Freudian sexuality, it is inevitable that he located the origin of sexual neuroses in childhood, hence his notion of "infantile sexuality" and "polymorphously perverse disposition," the latter referring to the idea that children are capable of experiencing erotic stimulation from organs other than the "normal" ones because they have not yet developed the "mental dams against sexual excesses" (268; the metaphor is important). One of the threats posed by this turbulence of the sexual drive as manifested in our unconscious is that it constantly threatens our conscious identity. Through repression the human consciousness seeks to control this turbulence; sexual regulation applies this model to the nation state. Freud also develops in these essays the notion of the "libido," or sexual drive, and its repression through the Oedipus complex and the fear of castration. The overall effect of his theories was to broaden the notion of sexuality from a reproductive model to a "pleasure" model while maintaining that such pleasure was beset by the need for civilizing control.

Freud's influence on our understanding of sexuality has been immense, whether in terms of those who have followed him or those who have sought to refute him. In both cases, those working in the field of sexuality after Freud have dislocated his emphasis on the physiological basis of neurosis to a more discursive basis, and chief among these theorists of sexuality are Jacques Lacan and Michel Foucault.

So powerful is the discursive element in Lacanian theory that Juliet Flower MacCannell feels justified in stating that, in Lacan, "Language ... replaces the body,"[40] such that the work of Freud, for Lacan, is a form of literature rather than a map of the road to the unconscious (2). As Joseph Bristow puts it, "Lacan's work completes one of the main tasks begun by Freud: to dissociate eroticism from biological mechanisms,"[41] which is to say: to speak about sexuality apart from reproduction. (One thinks here of the passage in Timothy Findley's *Not Wanted on the Voyage* where Japeth sees himself reflected in his shield, "and, before he could stop himself, his organ would rise into his hand and demand attention.").[42] Lacan extended his focus of inquiry to institutions such as marriage and love, which, he argued, function like languages— we exist through them and in them, just as we exist in and through language, a domain which he identified with the symbolic order. But Lacan's view of language (following from the linguistic theories of Ferdinand de Saussure) was that it never succeeded in communicating in any absolute sense—something is always left unsaid, or is miscommunicated or misunderstood, and it is at this point that language merges with desire. As Bristow puts it, "Identity, in Lacan's world, always remains precarious, and that is because the subject seeks to consolidate itself through processes of *mis*recognition" (84). According to Lacan, identity is conferred through the "mirror stage," in which the infant child first discovers an image (*imago*) of itself (as in a mirror); this image, of course, is an illusion, but the child's identification with it (albeit a form of *méconnaissance*) at least provides the child with a more coherent sense of self (ego). Bristow explains that "Such an image permits the 'I' to come together from fragmentary parts, to gain some stability, no matter how imaginary, in its development" (85–86); as such, this metaphor of selfhood and of sexual identity might also serve as a way of understanding the Canadian identity, which is less than one nation in its political strategy of multiculturalism and more than one nation historically, given the competing claims of the First Nations, the Anglos, and the *Québécois* (issues that Ian Rashid and Gregory Scofield grapple with in their different ways).[43]

In Lacanian theory, furthermore, the "I" is coterminous with the phallus, the patriarchal sign or signifier that authorizes selfhood and seeks to disguise its lack (precisely because it *is* a sign): "Like an omnipotent phantom or all-presiding deity, the phallic symbol of paternal authority retains [its] pre-eminence by hiding within the structures it governs."[44] And, like all effects of language, this act of signification is ongoing, processual, given that (according to the Saussurean theory of language employed by Lacan) language can never completely name its object—no one was ever bitten by the word dog, William James once said. As Joan Wallach Scott has written, "gender identification, although it always appears coherent and fixed, is, in fact, highly unstable. As meaning systems, subjective identities are processes of differentiation and distinction, requiring the suppression of ambiguities and opposite elements in order to ensure (create the illusion of) coherence and common understanding."[45] Jane Rule brilliantly exploits these ambiguities in "The Killer Dyke and the Lady."

Social institutions seek to make up for these absences in various ways. For example, the institution of marriage seeks to represent two people as if they were one, thus valorizing notions of "unity" and "sameness" but at the expense of denying the fundamental basis of relationships, which is the interhuman, as well as the basis of sexuality itself. In these terms, sexuality as an institutional norm can be understood as "hommosexuality," a Lacanian pun which combines the French word for man ("*homme*") with "sexuality."[46] Ironically, "normal" sexuality can be understood only in contradistinction to "abnormal" sexuality, and it is precisely this "otherness" that institutional relationships seek to mask. In Lacan's view, however, all communication, all social relationships, are directed toward the Other; meaning is possible only as an interhuman phenomenon, as a form of dialogue (or discourse), and never as an absolute, as something understood to be separate from all other phenomena. Meaning thus is never fully present to itself; it is always part of a relationship. "The signifier," writes MacCannell, "separates us from each other, disrupts any 'communication' we might have with each other. It also ... puts us on a 'route,' a path, that goes toward the Other."[47]

Desire, be it understood as sexual or discursive, is founded upon such an absence, such a lack: one desires because that desire can never be fulfilled (just as language can never adequately name its object). And because the Other is inaccessible, we tend to interact with institutions, rather than with individuals—with the idea of sex, the idea of love, rather than the thing itself. Hence the proliferation of cultural forms sexuality takes. Love, like sexuality, is a *cultural* form, not a "natural" one, and for this reason it has a history and can be analyzed as a form of cultural production, including the way in which a nation produces its culture. "Love," wrote Lacan, "is a sign that we are changing discourses."[48]

The ultimate institution in Lacan's theory is patriarchy (what he calls "the Name-of-the-Father"), which is functionalized through the signifying power of the phallus, and at this point psychoanalytical, sexual, and national discourses merge in what the Canadian anthem calls "true patriot love." Hélène Cixous has analyzed patriarchal values in terms of what she calls the "Empire of the Selfsame,"[49] which is similar to Lacan's notion of "hommosexuality" in that it values sameness over difference. Cixous argues that women's sexuality subverts this sameness because of its ability to overflow categories, its fluidity, as opposed to its rigidity (an aspect beautifully brought out by Dorothy Livesay in her poem "On Looking into Henry Moore"). This ability can be conveyed through *écriture féminine*, a form of writing that subverts the linearity of masculinist discourse, a form of writing practised by such Canadian writers as Daphne Marlatt (in her poetry as well as in works such as *Ana Historic*, excerpted here), Nicole Brossard, and others.[50]

The way in which patriarchal values tend to institutionalize aspects of sexuality is the focus of Michel Foucault's *History of Sexuality* (Volume One), which begins with two interrelated conundrums: why did the apparently repressed age of the Victorians (the era in which, as we recall, Canada was founded as a nation), known to have maintained a silence around sexual issues (even piano legs were kept clothed, for fear of offending the innocent), produce such a large discourse on sexuality? And doesn't our contemporary ease in discussing sexual matters indicate our liberation from that repression? Foucault's responses to these questions are startling: how could the Victorians be repressed if they produced such an enormous discourse on sexuality? And our proliferation of these discourses on sexuality simply continues this dislocation of sexuality from the body to discourse in what is anything but a form of liberation. "We need to consider the possibility," writes Foucault, "that one day, perhaps, in a different economy of bodies and pleasures, people will no longer quite understand how the ruses of sexuality, and the power that sustains its organization, were able to subject us to that austere monarchy of sex, so that we became dedicated to the endless task of forcing its secret, of exacting the truest of confessions from a shadow. The irony of this deployment," he concludes, "is in having us believe that our 'liberation' is in the balance."[51]

The key to Foucault's analysis is the notion of power and the way it permeates society through discourse (an aspect of his analysis that Joan Wallach Scott has developed). As Joseph Bristow puts it, "it is in his introduction to *The History of Sexuality* that Foucault's arguments ask us to contemplate, not only why sexuality became such a focus of concern in the past hundred years, but also how sexuality concentrated extremely potent transfers of power that have exerted considerable influence on the regulation of the social order" (169). Thus, Foucault's examination of the "repressive hypothesis" takes him to the institutional forms of sexuality through which the state exercises its power, such as medicine, education, and religion, all of which produced an explosion of discourses around sexuality starting in the 1600s in Europe (when Champlain was founding Montréal), and this discourse was imported by the wave of colonizers who came to North America at that time.[52] One of these was Father Joseph François Lafitau, whose *Moeurs des sauvages ameriquains, comparées aux moeurs des premiers temps* (1724), among the first works of comparative ethnography,[53] is based on the six years Lafitau spent in New France on the south shore of the St. Lawrence opposite Montréal. Deriving from his religious position and learning, Lafitau's ethnography sought to posit universals among peoples, based on a principle of origins from which fallen mankind had declined. "On matters of cultural similarity he was an extreme transmigrational diffusionist; on matters of diversity he relied on the doctrine of degeneration."[54] He is thus both gratified and appalled to observe polygamy among the Algonquian (1.6, 336) and concubinage among the Iroquois (352). While he is at pains to point out that "particular friendships" (361) among males are entirely free of the "monstrous vices" known to the Greeks (362), he does make the curious remark that "Among the North American Indians, these relationships of friendship carry no suspicion of apparent vice, although there is or may be much real vice. They are very ancient in their origin, very clear in their constant usage, *sacred, if I dare say so* [emphasis added], in the union which they form, the knots of which are as closely tied as those of blood and nature" (364). Clearly, what is "natural" is relative, and this cultural relativity makes Lafitau's work fascinating for a contemporary audience,[55] especially when read in the context of Gregory Scofield's *Thunder Through My Veins*.

Foucault understands the notion of sexual discursivity very broadly, examining the architectural layout of secondary schools in the 1700s and noting that enormous pains were taken to keep the students separate in their dormitories. He discusses how the Church particularized and extended the list of sexual sins that had to be spoken by the sinner in the confessional (and here we are reminded of *Beautiful Losers* again, as well as of *The Pornographer's Poem*). He demonstrates how medicine made sexuality into a pathology during this period, and did so in greater and greater detail. As he remarks, "we are dealing less with *a* discourse on sex than with a multiplicity of discourses produced by a whole series of mechanisms operating in different institutions."[56]

What Foucault demonstrates with these examples is that sex's "incitement" to discourse, contrary to what the repressive hypothesis would seem to suggest, did not occur apart from or counter to the central mechanisms of official power (in Victorian brothels and madhouses, for example), but, rather, right at the heart of them. In other words, for Foucault, sexuality was at once personally expressed and socially administered; it was both an individual "technique of the self" related to the corporeal body and a collective sense of "governmentality" related to institutions of the body politic. Sexuality thus provided the key element through which administrators (mayors, policemen, doctors, lawyers, psychiatrists, etc.) in the emerging nation-states of modern Europe (and their colonies in North America and elsewhere) could link one's individual—and intimate—experience of sex (as an act or as an identity) to laws, policies, and customs designed to regulate the productivity of an entire population and maintain social order. And this linkage continues today in Canada in discourses calling for a national registry of sex offenders and anxiety over same-sex marriage.

To speak in terms of the prohibition, censorship, and repression of sex, then, is counterintuitive according to Foucault. In representing something as unrepresentable (i.e., as a secret, something to be hidden, a taboo), one is still representing it; in saying that people shouldn't speak about something, one is paradoxically speaking of it. Confronted with this superabundance of *representation*, then, of the proliferation of discourse on sex, it makes more sense, when factoring power and knowledge into the equation, to think not in terms of repression but in terms of *regulation*. This regulation or "domestication" of sexuality, according to Foucault, is nowhere more evident than in the consolidation of monogamous reproductive sexuality as the respectable norm and arbiter of post seventeenth-century social organization in Western culture, one that carried with it all the *de facto* rights and privileges of citizenship and one, moreover, that could not be separated from the rise of industrial capitalism. (These issues hover compellingly behind the nuanced language of Alice Munro's "Family Furnishings.") Through these intersecting processes and modes of institutionalization, the family became a metonym of the nation precisely because non-procreative sexuality was incompatible with what Foucault termed the "work imperative."[57]

However, as Foucault further states, by codifying in law and naturalizing in discourse the regime of heterosexual monogamy and reproduction through the institution of marriage, all those sexualities "peripheral" to this privileged centre (such as promiscuity, polygamy, homosexuality, single motherhood, masturbation, prostitution, fetishism, voyeurism, fantasies, and so on) were simultaneously given a name for the first time and thus a space for their own elaboration. In other words, one cannot set up a norm without cataloguing what is not normal (i.e., what is a "perversion") and thus paradoxically bringing these excluded elements into discourse and thus into being. While these discourses were expressly catalogued or "implanted" for purposes of regulation, that is, to ensure that they remained peripheral to institutionalized forms of sexuality such as monogamy and reproductive sexuality, the operations of power nevertheless ensured that there would be space for resistance.

Sex in Theory: Contemporary Issues

Whereas earlier research (such as the Kinsey reports) sought to parse sexuality into categories, later research has sought to understand sexuality more fluidly, so that if categories haven't completely been eliminated, they are nevertheless understood as flowing into (and out of) one another. This broadening of categories can be observed in keynote works such as the 1966 Masters and Johnson report on *Human Sexual Response*, Kate Millett's *Sexual Politics* (1970), Jill Johnston's *Lesbian Nation* (1973), and the 1976 Hite Report. Current theories remain intent on coming to terms with the biases within studies of sexuality, especially around essentialist categories, be they of sex or gender. As Diane Richardson writes,

> Sexuality is a central feature of modern societies. It is the focus of major social and political issues that are global concerns [,] ranging from sexual violence, sex education, prostitution, trafficking in women, abortion and contraception, single parenthood, AIDS, divorce, the rights of lesbians and gay men, through to the organisation of social life through the institutionalisation of hetero(norms) [sic]. In the last thirty years [sexuality] has become a central aspect of global capitalism. From the use of sexual imagery in advertising and marketing, to billion dollar sex industries selling pornography and sexual services, to weddings, to mail-order brides, to international sex tourism, and so on: this is the political economy of sexuality. Sexuality is also a mechanism of social control and regulation. As a consequence, it is a focus of political struggle via the efforts of social movements concerned with sexual and reproductive issues.[58]

The 1960s, often known as the period of the "sexual revolution," saw a number of important changes in social attitudes in much of Europe and North America with reference to divorce, homosexuality, abortion, contraception, censorship, and the nuclear family. This was the era when Pierre Trudeau famously said that "there's no place for the state in the bedrooms of the nation"[59] (a comment which should be read in its full Foucauldian context). As Richardson notes, these changes gave rise, directly and indirectly, to political movements such as feminism and gay liberation, whether motivated by identity politics or concepts of sexual citizenship, and these movements were further politicized by the onset of AIDS. Yet there was a significant lag between these changes and the development of a discourse about sexuality which understood it less as something "natural" than as something that is socially and culturally "constructed," which is the position that dominates sexual theory today.

One of the prime targets of the construction position is the notion of "heteronormativity"—the idea that heterosexuality is natural, or normal, rather than institutional. It was in fact an American author of fiction, Adrienne Rich, who in 1980 proposed that heterosexuality was less of a natural choice than an ideology supported by labour markets and ideals of romance, in which we can include romance fiction.[60] The importance of heteronormativity in the national context has to do with the representation of the heterosexual couple as the bedrock of the social union (and here we can recall Lacan's analysis). This has had the tendency to make those social groups asking for equal (sexual) citizenship in the state to make their arguments in the form of "inclusion," as in the arguments that were made in Parliament around gay marriage. The question of "inclusion" raises the related notions of "public" and "private," as in Trudeau's statement, in which the social was associated with the public and the sexual with the private. However, this boundary is itself constructed; to this day, certain expressions of sexuality are permitted in public while others are severely regulated; heterosexuality, notably, "has ... been granted both more privacy and more public recognition than other sexualities."[61]

Yet it is possible to interrogate the legitimacy of heteronormativity along a number of avenues. One of these is "intersexuality"—the study of sexualities which do not fall easily into one gender category or another—and of those persons who are "transitional" in that they negotiate the spaces between and among sexualities. Anne Fausto-Sterling is one such theorist; in her book, *Sexing the Body: Gender Politics and the Construction of Sexuality*,[62] she draws on her experiences of having lived as a heterosexual, a lesbian, and as someone in transition, as well as on her immense reading in the area of sexuality (almost half of her 473-page book is comprised of notes and bibliography, many of which relate to the author's academic area of molecular biology). Fausto-Sterling focuses on "bodies that present themselves as neither entirely male nor entirely female. One of the major claims I make in this book is that labeling someone a man or a woman is a social decision. We may use scientific knowledge to help us make the decision, but only our beliefs about gender—not science—can define our sex. Furthermore, our beliefs about gender affect what kinds of knowledge scientists produce about sex in the first place" (3).[63] Whereas sex is commonly thought to differ from gender in the sense that sex is "physiologically determined" while gender is a psychological and social construction (3), Fausto-Sterling argues that sexuality is itself a socially produced category and that sex and gender are deeply intertwined. Once again the theme of regulation emerges: "By helping the normal take precedence over the natural, physicians have also contributed to population biopolitics. ... From the viewpoint of medical practitioners, progress in the handling of intersexuality involves maintaining the normal. Accordingly, there *ought* to be only two boxes: male and female" (8). Trish Salah brings a number of these issues together in the remarkable poem "Surgical Diary."

Elizabeth Grosz (one of the theorists quoted by Fausto-Sterling) takes a more complicated position. While not denying the body's materiality—its brain, muscles, sex organs, and so on—she argues that the relationship of these material bodily elements to cultural and experiential ones can be expressed by analogy to a möbius strip: "Culture and experience would constitute the outside surface. But, as the image suggests, the inside and the outside are continuous." This position places in question the general assumption that "sex and nature are real, while gender and culture are ... constructed.... [T]hese are false dichotomies."[64] Sexuality is also constructed, quite literally and materially, by medical practitioners and on a daily basis: surgeons regularly create sexual identifiers for newborns whose genitalia are not "normal." One of the reasons Fausto-Sterling seeks to challenge sexual binaries is that the sex-and-gender systems impose social, political, and economic hierarchies—at which point, the discourse of sexuality and of gender enters the terrain of the nation. As Donna Haraway has suggested, "biology is politics by other means."[65]

Haraway's comment foregrounds the public/private binary that plays itself out in discourses around sexuality and nationhood, as in Trudeau's famous remark. Nations, we must remind ourselves, are historically recent inventions. Indeed, as Benedict Anderson remarks in his book of that title, nations are "imagined communities." Anderson draws on Canadian theorist Marshall McLuhan's notion that nations are the invention of print culture and are directly related to the creation by book culture of "individuality"—hence the connection between personal identity and nationhood. However, as McLuhan noted in his 1951 book, *The Mechanical Bride* (whose title might also describe Atwood's post-apocalyptic Handmaid), such constructions are part of a libidinal economy and as such are both gendered and sexualized. McLuhan also theorized that electronic modes of communication would tend to break down these gendered and sexualized categories (the theme of Persimmon Blackridge's *Prozac Highway*) and with them the nation-state (which is the substance of his article reprinted below). Canada was paradigmatic for him, in this regard, and thus he referred to it as a "borderline case"—a software nation as opposed to one invested in nationalist hardware. Hence, it should come as no surprise that political resistance in the sexual camp has taken on the notion of nation as part of its battle cry, as in "lesbian nation" and "queer nation,"[66] as well as in works such as Lyndell Montgomery's "Border Crossing: On the Edge," reprinted below.[67] These "nations" define themselves in ways other than the heteronormative ones of reproduction and assimilation. Jeffrey Weeks suggests that the notion of "sexual citizen" reflects these post-national politics and "the new primacy given to sexual subjectivity in the contemporary world. The claim to a new form of belonging, which is what citizenship is ultimately about, arises from and reflects the remaking of the self and the multiplicity and diversity of possible identities that characterize the late-, or post-, modern world."[68] The emphasis on gay marriage, abortion, women's rights, and pornography in the 2004 federal election campaign lends considerable credence to Weeks's comment.

If we understand identity as coming into being by way of the Other, then sexuality, as the fundamental enactment of that relationship, is central to our understanding of identity at the personal or national level, as Tim Dean suggests in *Beyond Sexuality*.[69] However, it is crucial to note that understanding identity through the Other ultimately undermines notions of individuality and uniqueness that underlie both the State and identitarian politics. Thus, critics such as Dean seek to articulate a theory of sexuality that goes beyond "the ego, the individual, or the self" to "the impersonality of desire" (3). Dean draws heavily on Jacques Lacan, who "depsychologizes the unconscious by treating it as linguistic and thus as transindividual" (7); this linguistic element is of special significance for our book, as it provides the basic assumption for making the connection between sexuality, literature, and nationhood. In Canada's case, the multilingual and multicultural dimension of nationhood makes us at once less than one nation (in the sense of having one single identity) and radically multiple, a notion deeply supported by the readings in this anthology. Hence our use of the word "sexing" in the title, which implies that sexual identities in Canada are "in process" in ways parallel to that of the national process of becoming.

A Canadian Discourse on Sexuality

There is a geography of sexuality; a large part of the tourism industry thrives on it. As Karen Dubinsky remarks, "[l]ike classes, races, and genders, regions can bear distinct sexual reputations. Social divisions can acquire a spatial footing, and places often become associated with particular values or feelings."[70] These spatial expressions of sexuality reflect social and economic influences and are ultimately part of the process of nation-building. If it is possible at all (mindful of the need to avoid essentialisms) to speak of a *Canadian* discourse on sexuality, then that discourse might be said to have entered a watershed moment in the relationship of the Canadian Robert Ross (alluded to by Timothy Findley in his novel, *The Wars*) to Oscar Wilde. Ross was Wilde's lover, friend, and ultimately his literary executor. These relations of kinship—broadly defined—were becoming, at the end of the nineteenth century, as important as those such as "fascism" or "liberalism" to our understanding of nationalism, as Benedict Anderson has argued in *Imagined Communities*.[71] As the personal has increasingly become the domain of the political, issues such as pornography, abortion, sexuality, reproduction, marriage, morality, and family values have emerged more and more into the forefront of political debate at the national level in the United States, and they have done so as well in Canada.[72] Furthermore, the combined effects of decolonization and globalization have had a profound effect on traditional models of political organization. Add to this the current concerns about changes in global climate patterns and fears (post-9/11) about threats to nationhood that do not emerge from traditional national configurations and we have a conceptual (as well as social, cultural, and political) need to rethink the very concept of "nation."

Eve Sedgwick cites a telling (if humorous) example of how the boundedness of nations makes less sense within a globalized awareness: that of the weather maps that appear in newspapers. While the *New York Times* and *USA Today* ritually print maps that show weather patterns abruptly halting at the 49th parallel, the "*Globe and Mail*, and indeed every other Canadian newspaper I have seen, runs a weather map that extends southward at least as far as the Mason-Dixon Line in the United States. There is no presumption that the Toronto reader would (as it were) identify more with the fog over Vancouver than with the blizzard approaching Detroit. Does this mean that Canada does not have 'nation-ness'? Or instead that its nation-ness, having a different history from that of the United States, may well therefore have a structure different enough to put into question any single definition of the quality 'nation-ness'?" Sedgwick concludes from this that "it may be that there exists for nations, as for genders, simply no normal way to partake of the categorical definitiveness of the national, no single kind of 'other' of what a nation is to which all can by the same saturation be definitionally opposed."[73]

Sedgwick sees these complexities coalescing in the career of Wilde as an Irishman writing in a colonial context. "Indeed, the consciousness of foundational and/or incipient national *difference* already internal to national *definition* must have been part of what Wilde literally embodied" (242). This dynamic of difference and similarity was as crucial to Wilde's understanding of his nationality as it was to his understanding of his sexuality. Here is where the colonial histories of Ireland and Canada come into play. As Ronald Hyam has argued in *Empire and Sexuality* "sexual dynamics crucially underpinned the whole operation of British empire and Victorian expansion."[74] In late Victorian Britain—the imperial period most directly connected to Canada's formal establishment as a nation—these sexual dynamics were complicated: while British imperialists trafficked freely in sexuality, they were also governed by a "Purity Campaign" (launched in 1869) which sought to reduce sexual interaction between rulers and ruled out of "fears of imperial decline and alarm about the degeneration of the imperial race" (65), which were precisely the terms that informed Lafitau's ethnographical discourse in the previous century. These dynamics can be observed at work in the early history of the Hudson's Bay Company, where there was a long tradition of interracial marriage. While the company may have preferred that its factors remain celibate, they recognized the practical need to form unions with the Aboriginal population, and especially with the women, whose knowledge of traditional crafts and abilities as interpreters were vital to the success of the Company. Subsequently, there was a preference among British employees of the Company for mixed-race women, and the practice of taking Aboriginal women as wives became far less common, an attitude encouraged by the missionaries.

Further complicating the sexual dynamics of the period was the notion of sublimation, the idea that "love's loss is empire's gain,"[75] a concept which takes on interesting overtones when understood in theoretical terms through the notion of "triangulation," as developed by Sedgwick, whereby male-male desire (which profoundly informed imperialist sexualities, as the various cases of Rudyard Kipling and Cecil Rhodes illustrate)[76] is "normalized" by being expressed through a "traffic in women," and the word "traffic" here can be read as shorthand for the economic model of the imperialist enterprise.[77] The prevailing metaphors of this enterprise were mechanical ones, and revolved around the spending and conserving of energies, out of which Freud's theses emerged as well.[78] These metaphors were fully congruent with the economic models of the period; hence the enormous energies that were directed toward the elimination of masturbation.[79] In all cases, it was believed that energies must be preserved in order to be spent at the right moment and in the right way—and very often this meant in fighting wars. As a result, "All was reduced to the exclusive promotion of reproductive, adult marital sexuality."[80] This was the era in which homosexuality was named and outlawed with increasing severity and in which Britain was increasingly vigilant about pornography,[81] which it defined very broadly—Havelock Ellis's *Sexual Inversion* (1898) was banned in 1908. And this was the era in which swimming costumes were increasingly urged upon men and women alike.

During this same period, there was a change in the ways in which "manliness" or masculinity was expressed, from a sort of spiritual manliness as exemplified in the muscular Christianity of Ralph Connor's novels[82] to much more physical manifestations of manliness, especially those taking the form of athletics. The covert and overt connections of masculinity to patriotism (via the military, which has always loomed large in the life of nations; recall Wellington's comment that the battle of Waterloo had been won on the playing fields of Eton) was thus opposed to expressions of effeminacy and, interestingly, to the "excessively intellectual.... The need to experience pain was held to be a necessary preparation for the self-reliance and wretchedness of the imperial frontier."[83]

Anna Laura Stoler makes an argument similar to Hyam's, but much more rigorously theoretical, in *Carnal Knowledge and Imperial Power*, where her main theme is that "dictates of who could be intimate with whom, and in what way, were central to imperial politics."[84] Stoler is much more sensitive to issues of gender than Hyam; as she writes, "European women in these colonies [Dutch, French, and British] experienced the cleavages of racial dominance and internal social distinctions very differently than [sic] men precisely because of their ambiguous positions, as both subordinates in colonial hierarchies and as agents of empire in their own right" (41). It is this double vision that emerges most powerfully in works such as Susanna Moodie's *Roughing It in the Bush*, in which Susanna increasingly takes on the role traditionally played by the man of the house. As Carol Shields has written in her study of "Mrs. Moodie, and Sexual Reversal," a "panoramic look at the writings of Susanna Moodie uncovers one rather startling feature: the women figures in her work tend to be strong, moral, and aggressive, while the males, almost without exception, are weak, easily corrupted, and malleable. Furthermore, the interaction of males and females frequently leads to the progressive feminization of men and the elevation of women to the position of rescuer."[85] This notion of sexual reversal is important in understanding how colonization both extended the colonizers' sexual norms and mores and undermined them. In this sense, the geographical element long posited as crucial to Canadian identity takes on a sexualized role.

Nowhere is this eroticization of the landscape to be observed more starkly than in the romantic discourse that has grown up around Niagara Falls. In *The Second Greatest Disappointment*, Karen Dubinsky takes Oscar Wilde's mordant observation about honeymooning at Niagara Falls ("Niagara Falls must be the second greatest disappointment in marriage" he noted on his Canadian tour) as her starting point for a study of "love, nature, and nation."[86] Arguing from the principle that "[p]laces have a sexual, as well as political and economic, dimension" (13), Dubinsky examines the way in which Niagara encapsulates changes in the histories of heterosexuality and homosexuality.[87] Ironically, it was that great nationalist outpouring, Expo 67, that spelled the end of Niagara's reign as the supreme Canadian destination for sexual travel. By this time, premarital sex was making the honeymoon outmoded, the changing sexual mores (such as the decriminalization of "buggery" in 1969) paralleling the changes in the way the nation was understanding itself.

These changes were part of a much larger shift in what Ian McKay has termed "the shifting boundaries of the self." McKay sees these shifts as representative of the broader uncertainties inherent within modernity and its "institutionalization of doubt."[88] What is important to note is that such changes alter the way we understand heterosexuality as well as homosexuality, as Atom Egoyan suggests in his film *Exotica*, where the domain of the exotic is represented by traditional family life (a theme which Katherine Monk places in its broad filmic context in the excerpt from *Weird Sex and Snowshoes*) and as Bert Archer indicates in his book, *The End of Gay (and the Death of Heterosexuality)*. What interests Archer in this book is the establishment of "a sort of interzone"[89] in sexuality that is not readily identifiable by the traditional labels of straight, gay, transgendered, and so on. This interzone is not subject to binary thinking about sexuality—that if there is a gay category, then there must be a straight category, which makes third categories, such as bisexual, unthinkable, as Marjorie Garber has brilliantly demonstrated in *Vested Interests*.[90] What upsets these binaries are Archer's first sexual experiences as an openly gay man: of the first four men he has sex with, only half are self-identified as gay. This leads Archer to imagine a society in which "sexual habits" didn't figure in "list[s] of priorities and character assessments, didn't ... get swirled into a pre-set world of In and Out, Gay and Straight, in which every sexual act is seen as a denial of identity."[91] "Identity" is the key word here and remains the point of articulation for many of our current discussions of sexuality, including in the political domain.

While the sexual politics of the 1960s and 1970s was clearly identitarian, current debates around sexuality are much more integrationist, as the controversy about gay marriage in Canada suggests. Indeed, writers such as Jane Rule are opposed to gay marriage precisely on the grounds that it is *too* integrationist; Rule argues that lesbians and gays did not fight their identitarian battles only to become merged with the very culture whose sexual politics they opposed. Archer makes a similar point, stating that "[g]ay is not dead yet, of course. It is, in fact, trying to evolve into something that can survive, ... trying to appeal to ever-broader audiences and in the process obviating whatever special attraction and use it once had" (21–22).[92] In effect, Archer supports an "evolutionary" model of sexuality while authors such as Rule argue for the need to avoid political complacency. The key moment in this evolution, for Archer, is the separation of sexuality from reproduction, thus liberating sexuality into the realm of pleasure and, in doing so, liberating it, as well, from identitarian issues. Everyone, according to this argument, both seeks pleasure and experiences it equally; thus, the specific form of pleasure achieved is immaterial. This is not to deny that different sorts of sexual experiences exist; rather, "[i]t means that sex, though far more pervasive than we generally assume it to be, is also far less necessarily profound, far less universally significant, and far more open to incidental enjoyment than our current monolithic treatment of it would imply" (34). And the same sort of argument can be made for gender, which Archer sees as "a continuum, and not the static, binary system most of us automatically presume it to be" (37).

What authors such as Rule would insist on, however, is that these issues be understood in their institutional contexts—that even pleasure is politicized and that, while gender and sexuality may occupy a continuum, there are institutional forces in whose interests—interests which are ultimately those of the State—that continuum will be compartmentalized in various ways. This is not to say that Archer's desire "to get through the politics and into the pleasure" (249) lacks merit; it is simply to say that it might describe a process rather than a goal, which is to identify an interzone in which politics and pleasure merge. This interzone is currently labelled as "queerness," but Archer suggests that we "stop calling it queerness.... As long as we call it queerness, it sounds like something other, stranger people do. Let's try calling it sexuality," he concludes, "something we all do" (263).

Criteria for Choices

One of the most important aspects of sexuality studies, as Graham L. Hammill has suggested, is its ability to think beyond itself—"to think about sexuality in order to think beyond sexuality."[93] In this spirit, we have tried to avoid making this book "representative," since what emerges from these selections is that there is no essential category of sexuality that *can* be represented. We likewise rejected a purely historical approach and its concomitant suggestion of completeness and of evolution. Rather, we wanted to supply some specific directions for our readers in our choice of subject areas that together comprise, not a complete picture of sexuality in Canada (even if such a picture were possible or desirable) but a map for a discourse on sexuality that is one of the ways in which Canada identifies itself. As the book makes clear, this discourse is present in a broad range of cultural production in Canada—so broad that what you see here is a very small part of our original set of readings, which were beyond the capacity of a single volume such as this one—and for that reason we also rejected a specifically generic approach. If nationalism is related to sexuality, as the national anthem implies, then one way to understand Canada is through the sexual discourses it has produced. It is the discovery of these discourses (including the complete works from which extracts are cited)—and their own place in it—that awaits the users of this volume.

Notes

1   Arnold I. Davidson, *The Emergence of Sexuality: Historical Epistemology and the Formation of Concepts* (Cambridge, MA: Harvard University Press, 2001) 21.

2   See Karen Dubinsky, *Improper Advances: Rape and Heterosexual Conflict in Ontario, 1880–1929* (Chicago, IL: University of Chicago Press, 1993) 6, 167. Her comment is echoed in the preamble to the entry on Canada in *The International*

Encyclopedia of Sexuality 1, ed. Robert T. Francoeur (New York: Continuum, 1997): "there have been no large-scale studies of adult sexual behavior in Canada.... While sexological research in Canada has grown significantly over the last twenty years, it is still a new field" (222); "[t]here have been few large-scale studies of gay male sexual behavior in Canada and none of lesbian sexual behavior" (277).

3   Steven Maynard, "The Maple Leaf (Gardens) Forever: Sex, Canadian Historians and National History," *Journal of Canadian Studies* 36.2 (2001): 72.

4   Nicholas Jenkins, "Under-Exposure," review of *Stephen Spender*, by John Sutherland (London: Viking, 2004) and of *New Collected Poems*, by Stephen Spender (London: Faber, 2004), *Times Literary Supplement* (13 August 2004): 6. It is interesting to note on the same page an advertisement for Stanley Wells's *Looking for Sex in Shakespeare*, published by Cambridge University Press.

5   Jeremy Brown and Christopher Ondaatje, *The First Original Unexpurgated Canadian Book of Sex and Adventure* (Toronto: Pagurian Press, 1979).

6   Brown and Ondaatje 7.

7   Alfred C. Kinsey, *Sexual Behavior in the Human Male* (Philadelphia, PA: Saunders, 1948), and *Sexual Behavior in the Human Female* (Philadelphia, PA: Saunders, 1953). See also Angus McLaren, "'Surveying Sex': From Alfred C. Kinsey to Hugh Hefner," in *Twentieth-Century Sexuality: A History* (Oxford: Blackwell, 1999) 143–65.

8   Gary Kinsman, *The Regulation of Desire: Homo and Hetero Sexualities* (1987; rev. Montreal: Between the Lines, 1996). To date, Kinsman's study remains the most comprehensive analysis of the institutions of sexuality as instruments of social organization and governmentality in Canada; we reprint a chapter in the section on "Sex and the Law."

9   See also Angus McLaren, "'Compulsory Heterosexuality': Eugenicists, Fascists and Nazis" in *Twentieth-Century Sexuality: A History* (Oxford: Blackwell, 1999) 124–42; and Adrienne Rich's classic essay, "Compulsory Heterosexuality and Lesbian Existence," in *Culture, Society and Sexuality: A Reader*, ed. Richard Parker and Peter Aggleton (London: University College London Press, 1999) 199–225.

10   Jeffrey Weeks, "The Sexual Citizen," *Theory, Culture and Society* 15.3–4 (1998): 35–52; these quotes 46–47.

11   Benjamin Schlesinger, ed. *Sexual Behaviour in Canada: Patterns and Problems* (Toronto: University of Toronto Press, 1977) ix.

12   Alex Comfort, *The Joy of Sex: A Cordon Bleu Guide to Lovemaking* (New York: Crown, 1972).

13   As Foucault remarks at the end of *The History of Sexuality 1: An Introduction* (1976; New York: Vintage, 1990), "The irony of this deployment [of sexual discourses] is in having us believe that our 'liberation' is in the balance" (159).

14   F. Michael Barrett, "Attitudes and Sexuality," in Schlesinger, *Sexual Behaviour in Canada* 4.

15 Cyril Greenland, "Is There a Future for Human Sexuality?," in Schlesinger, *Sexual Behaviour in Canada* 281.

16 Among Beall's publications we find *The Living Temple: A Manual on Eugenics for Parents and Teachers* (1933).

17 Susan Hanley, Benjamin Schlesinger, and Paul Steinberg, "Lesbianism: Knowns and Unknowns," in Schlesinger, *Sexual Behaviour in Canada* 126–47; "Male Homosexuality," from *Operation Socrates Handbook* (University of Waterloo, 1973) in Schlesinger, *Sexual Behaviour in Canada* 148–61; and J. Hoenig, "The Management of Transsexualism" reprinted from the *Canadian Psychiatric Association Journal* 19.1 (1974): 1–6, in Schlesinger, *Sexual Behaviour in Canada* 162–70.

18 Andrew I. Malcolm, "The Influence of Drugs on Sexual Behaviour," reprinted from *Medical Aspects of Human Sexuality* [Canadian ed.] 3.11 (1973): 30–33, in Schlesinger, *Sexual Behaviour in Canada* 170–74.

19 See Davidson xiii. See also Joan Wallach Scott's classic essay, "Gender as a Useful Category of Historical Analysis," reprinted in Parker and Aggleton, *Culture, Society and Sexuality* 57–75 (originally published in 1986); and Robert A. Padgug, "Sexual Matters: On Conceptualizing Sexuality in History" in Parker and Aggleton, *Culture, Society and Sexuality* 15–28.

20 John Moss, *Sex and Violence in the Canadian Novel: The Ancestral Present* (Toronto: McClelland and Stewart, 1977) 5. Title and subtitle appear reversed in the book, and the relationship between its contents and its index is often more violent than sexual.

21 In 1985, the Fraser Committee, convened by the federal government to investigate prostitution and pornography in Canada, recommended that the quagmire of laws around prostitution be clarified and that the economic circumstances of sex trade workers be addressed. The legislative result was the 1985 Communicating Law, in which communication "for the purpose of engaging in prostitution" was made illegal. It is noteworthy that street solicitation accounts for about 5 per cent of the sex trade currently and that most prostitutes work for themselves. See Chris Gudgeon, *The Naked Truth: The Untold Story of Sex in Canada* (Vancouver: Greystone, 2003) 153 and 155, drawing on the research of Frances Shaver. Gudgeon's book makes an important contribution to the history of sexuality in Canada, though its humour often interferes with its many serious points, and vice versa.

22 As quoted by Gudgeon 92; see his summary pages 91–92.

23 See Marlene Mackie, *Gender Relations in Canada: Further Explorations* (Markham, ON: Butterworths, 1991). The key moment in this history was the 1967 Royal Commission on the Status of Women.

24 Mary Louise Adams, "Margin Notes: Reading Lesbianism as Obscenity in a Cold War Courtroom," in *Love, Hate, and Fear in Canada's Cold War*, ed. Richard Cavell (Toronto: University of Toronto Press, 2004): 135–58.

25 Donald Butler ran a video store in Winnipeg which also stocked dildos, lubricants, and flavoured condoms; in 1987, police raided the store, seized its con-

tents, and charged Butler on 250 counts of obscenity. The Supreme Court argued that Butler's right to freedom of expression had been breached and ordered a new trial. See Gudgeon 182–83 and 204, where he notes that the Little Sister's Bookstore challenge to Canada Customs' persistent seizure of printed materials destined for their store included a challenge to the Butler decision. The 1996 decision on the bookstore's case refused to strike down the Butler decision and upheld the discriminatory powers of Canada Customs, although it did note that Little Sister's had been unduly targeted. Little Sister's has issued a further challenge of a 2002 seizure of materials and has requested that the Butler decision be reviewed once again. In 2005, the bookstore's lawyer asked that the Supreme Court grant "Advance Costs" to the bookstore as the case proceeds. For the Court to grant such funding, the defendants must demonstrate how their case is important to all Canadians. The Supreme Court was to hear this appeal in April 2006.

26 Ryder is quoted by Gudgeon 184–85.

27 See the brief overview presented in part C of the section on Canada in the *International Encyclopedia* 296–99. Gudgeon wittily brings out the paradoxes of Canadian laws on pornography: "it is legal to have sex with a fourteen-year old, but illegal to look at a picture of a twenty-five-year-old pretending to be a seventeen-year-old having sex" (Gudgeon 162).

28 George L. Mosse, *Nationalism and Sexuality: Middle-Class Morality and Sexual Norms in Modern Europe* (Madison, WI: University of Wisconsin Press, 1985).

29 In this regard see Richard Cavell on the Eulenburg scandal in late nineteenth-century Germany and its determining influence on the career of the author who was to transform himself into canonical Canadian writer Frederick Philip Grove: "Felix Paul Greve, the Eulenburg Scandal, and Frederick Philip Grove," *Essays on Canadian Writing* 62 (1998): 12–45.

30 This paradigm was easily racialized, the sexual outsider often coinciding with the racial outsider.

31 Mosse's analysis is more convincing than the one, long current in studies of Canadian literature, that our attitudes toward sexuality are the legacy of our "puritan" heritage, a term whose application to Canada is historically inaccurate. See, however, *The Puritan Origins of American Sex: Religion, Sexuality, and the National Identity in American Literature*, ed. Tracy Fessenden *et al.* (London: Routledge, 2001), in which one chapter discusses Jane Rule's *Desert of the Heart* as a displaced version of *Pilgrim's Progress*.

32 See Scott 53–75.

33 Ian McKay, "Introduction" to *The Challenge of Modernity: A Reader on Post-Confederation Canada*, ed. Ian McKay (Toronto: McGraw-Hill Ryerson, 1992): ix-xxvi.

34 Peter Dickinson, *Here is Queer* (Toronto: University of Toronto Press, 1999) 5.

35 Compare Moss's discussion, in *Sex and Violence*, of "trisexuality": "Trisexuality, in literature at least, usually involves two men and a woman, and it usually exploits traditional gender stereotypes. The focal centre is a passive male, self-conscious

and unsure of his own identity. The other male is aggressive, assertively masculine. The female is self-effacing, sensitive and loving, the traditional feminine
cliché. The responses of these three to one another are complex.... Both male
and female stereotypes are drawn to the neutral male in response to his need
for them. To the female, his vulnerability allows her to express her sympathetic
nature without being threatened, as she would be by the more forceful male.
The latter, for his part, is attracted empathetically to the neutral male in whom
he can see a more sensitive or humane or vulnerable version of himself" (Moss
85).

36 Joseph Bristow, *Sexuality* (London: Routledge, 1997) 2.
37 Both Ellis and Symonds have been the subjects of biographies by Canadian his-
    torian Phyllis Grosskurth; see *John Addington Symonds: A Biography* (London:
    Longmans, 1964) and *Havelock Ellis: A Biography* (New York: Knopf, 1980).
    Grosskurth has also written *Margaret Mead* (London: Penguin, 1988); *Melanie
    Klein: Her World and Her Work* (Toronto: McClelland and Stewart, 1986); and *The
    Secret Ring: Freud's Inner Circle and the Politics of Psychoanalysis* (Toronto: Macfar-
    lane, Walter and Ross, 1991).
38 See the full chronology in Sigmund Freud, *The Freud Reader*, ed. Peter Gay (New
    York: Norton, 1989): xxxi-xlvii.
39 See the excerpted selection in Freud 239–93.
40 Juliet Flower MacCannell, *Figuring Lacan: Criticism and the Cultural Unconscious*
    (Lincoln, NB: University of Nebraska Press, 1986) xiii.
41 Bristow 7.
42 Timothy Findley, *Not Wanted on the Voyage* (New York: Viking, 1984) 232.
43 Note Homi Bhabha: "Once the liminality of the nation-space is established, and
    its 'difference' is turned from the boundary 'outside' to its finitude 'within,' the
    threat of cultural difference is no longer a problem of 'other' people. It
    becomes a question of the otherness of the people-as-one.... Minority discourse
    sets the act of emergence in the antagonistic *in-between* of image and sign, the
    accumulative and the adjunct, presence and proxy. It contests genealogies of
    'origin' that lead to claims for cultural supremacy and historical priority. Minor-
    ity discourse acknowledges the status of national culture—and the people—as a
    contentious, performative space of the perplexity of the living in the midst of
    the pedagogical representation of the fullness of life.... The postcolonial space
    is now 'supplementary' to the metropolitan centre; it stands in a subaltern,
    adjunct relation that doesn't aggrandize the *presence* of the west but redraws its
    frontiers in the menacing, agonistic boundary of cultural difference that never
    quite adds up, always less than one nation and double." Homi Bhabha, "Dissem-
    iNation: Time, Narrative, and the Margins of the Modern Nation," in *Nation and
    Narration*, ed. H. Bhabha (New York: Routledge, 1990): 301, 307, 318.
44 Bristow 95; note the metaphors of state and governance here.
45 Scott 63.
46 See MacCannell 44.

47 MacCannell 9.

48 Quoted in MacCannell 167.

49 Hélène Cixous, "Empire of the Selfsame" in *Sorties,* as discussed by Bristow 113.

50 See the groundbreaking anthology, *A Mazing Space: Writing Canadian Women Writing,* ed. Shirley Neuman and Smaro Kamboureli (Edmonton: NeWest, 1987).

51 Foucault 159.

52 This was also the time, as Chris Gudgeon notes, when France was luring male settlers to its North American colonies and sending young women from orphanages and workhouses "as marriage fodder" (Gudgeon 55).

53 Joseph François Lafitau, *Customs of the American Indians Compared with the Customs of Primitive Times,* ed. and trans. William N. Fenton and Elizabeth L. Moore, 2 vols. (Toronto: Champlain Society, 1974).

54 Fenton and Moore, "Introduction," in Lafitau, *Customs of the American Indians* xlvii.

55 For a gloss on these issues see Louis Montrose, "The Work of Gender and Sexuality in the Elizabethan Discourse of Discovery" in *Discourses of Sexuality: From Aristotle to AIDS,* ed. Domna C. Stanton (Ann Arbor, MI: University of Michigan Press, 1992): 138–84.

56 Foucault 33. A most useful aspect of Foucault's studies, especially when one seeks to apply them to an understanding of "nations," is the series of connections he draws between eugenics, racism, and fascism. As Bristow writes, "both incest and racial miscegenation were issues of enduring concern during this period [the late nineteenth century]. These two practices were systematically outlawed to uphold sexual purity and respectability, thereby maintaining class and racial power" (Bristow 180).

57 Foucault 6.

58 Diane Richardson, *Rethinking Sexuality* (London: Sage, 2000): 14–15.

59 Pierre Trudeau, 21 December 1967, as quoted in Gudgeon 199.

60 Richardson 22; Rich 199–225.

61 Richardson 24, 33.

62 Anne Fausto-Sterling, *Sexing the Body: Gender Politics and the Construction of Sexuality* (New York: Basic Books, 2000).

63 If anyone in an arts faculty ever wanted an argument for the fundamental importance of discursive inquiry into scientific practice, this is it.

64 Fausto-Sterling 24, 27.

65 As noted by Fausto-Sterling 255.

66 This is the point of departure for Terry Goldie's essay, "Queer Nation?" in *In A Queer Country: Gay and Lesbian Studies in the Canadian Context,* ed. Terry Goldie (Vancouver: Arsenal Pulp Press, 2001) 7–26.

67 Note also Brett Josef Grubisic and Carellin Brooks, eds., *Carnal Nation: Brave New Sex Fictions* (Vancouver: Arsenal Pulp Press, 2000).

68 Weeks 35.

69 Tim Dean, *Beyond Sexuality* (Chicago, IL: University of Chicago Press, 2000) 1.

70 Karen Dubinsky, *Improper Advances: Rape and Heterosexual Conflict in Ontario, 1880–1929* (Chicago, IL: University of Chicago Press, 1993) 9.

71 Anderson's comments are productively analyzed by Eve Kosofsky Sedgwick in her article "Nationalisms and Sexualities in the Age of Wilde," in *Nationalisms and Sexualities*, ed. Andrew Parker, Mary Russo, Doris Sommer, and Patricia Yaeger (New York: Routledge, 1992): 235–45; see especially p. 238.

72 Lauren Berlant, *The Queen of America Goes to Washington City: Essays on Sex and Citizenship* (Durham, NC: Duke University Press, 1997) 1. The major difference in the way these personal issues have emerged into the political domain of national politics in the United States and Canada has to do with the enshrinement of personal rights in the United States as opposed to the more socially oriented arena of debate in Canada.

73 Sedgwick 240–41.

74 Ronald Hyam, *Empire and Sexuality* (Manchester: Manchester University Press, 1990) 1. This book should be used with caution, given its anti-feminist stance and its reliance on "normative" categories of sexual behaviour, despite its opening protestations to the contrary.

75 Quoted by Hyam 10.

76 Note in this regard the Canadian novel *Who Look in Stove* by Lawrence Jeffery (Toronto: Exile, 1993).

77 Hyam in fact comments that the "nineteenth-century empire was a distinctly masculine affair" (Hyam 38).

78 As MacCannell comments, "For Freud,... civilisation demands the limitation of sexuality to heterosexuality for the purposes of reproduction, the union of sex-opposed persons to form another one. In addition, ... culture gains the surplus value of the excess libidinal energy that has been cut off by this limitation" (MacCannell 44).

79 As George Mosse comments, "Masturbation was thought to be the root cause of all loss of control, indeed, of abnormal passion in general. It was said to reflect an over-heated imagination, inimical to bourgeois sobriety, and was supposed to induce nervousness and loss of energy. Not only did it put forward a stereotype opposed to all that was manly and virile, or womanly and chaste, but masturbation was considered an anti-social act. The masturbator practices a lonely vice, we hear over and over again; he loves no one and is dead to the call of family, nation, and humanity." See Mosse 11.

80 Hyam 57.

81 Hyam 66–71.

82 See W.H. New, "Muscular Christianity," *Encyclopedia of Canadian Literature* (Toronto: University of Toronto Press, 2002) 774.

83 Hyam 72, 73.

84 Anna Laura Stoler, *Carnal Knowledge and Imperial Power: Race and the Intimate in Colonial Rule* (Berkeley, CA: University of California Press, 2002) back cover.

85 Carol Shields, *Susanna Moodie: Voice and Vision* (Ottawa: Borealis, 1977) 34; Chapter Two is on sexual reversal.

86 Karen Dubinsky, *The Second Greatest Disappointment: Honeymooning and Tourism at Niagara Falls* (Toronto: Between the Lines, 1999) 1.

87 These changes also emerge, hilariously, in Catherine Ann Gildiner's *Too Close to the Falls* (Toronto: ECW Press, 1999).

88 Ian McKay, "The Shifting Boundaries of the Self: Transformations of Gender, 1940–1990," in McKay, *The Challenge of Modernity* 406–45. The quotation is from the "Introduction," McKay, *The Challenge of Modernity* xi; the phrase is from Anthony Giddens.

89 Bert Archer, *The End of Gay (and The Death of Heterosexuality)* (Toronto: Doubleday, 1999) 7.

90 Marjorie Garber, *Vested Interests: Cross-Dressing and Cultural Anxiety* (New York: Routledge, 1992).

91 Archer 14.

92 Archer also quite explicitly states: "Far better to win rights and privileges for newly expanded notions of partnership and human relationships.... And without disenfranchising anyone—there's no need for marriage to actually disappear—it would improve the lot of a much larger sector of society than the staid gays whom gay marriage would benefit the most" (Archer 196).

93 Gordon L. Hammill, *Sexuality and Form: Caravaggio, Marlowe, and Bacon* (Chicago, IL: University of Chicago Press, 2000) 169. Hammill identifies this as "One of the fundamental contributions of queer theory" but we have taken him at his word and tried to think beyond queer theory as well. The subtitle of his book provides one—copious—indication of the breadth of research supported by sexuality studies.

⇒⊢ SEX AND THE FAMILY ⊣⇐

The idea of the family mediates the normative dimension of sexuality within the nation, and "family values" remain a major platform of Canada's political parties. As Mariana Valverde notes, the state (here, the province of Ontario) actually declared itself the parent of the famous Dionne quintuplets, usurping their natural parents in a bid to control the money generated by the spectacle of the babies' birth. This already puts in question the assumed norm of the nuclear heterosexual family. Current demographic statistics challenge the family norm further: single-parent families are very common, and same-sex parenting is on the rise. Ivan E. Coyote complicates this picture in another direction in the story of a transgendered father and his "freak family." A historical examination of the idea of the family in Canada demonstrates how the familial "norm" has in fact changed over the years. Gertrude Pringle's *Etiquette in Canada*, first published in 1932 and given a postwar revision (from which we quote here), is noteworthy not only for the gulf separating normative behaviour of the 1940s from our own but also for her sense of how values had shifted in the decade and a half between the book's first publication and its second edition. As she remarks in the "Preface to the Second Edition," "[f]ifteen years have elapsed since *Etiquette in Canada* first appeared, and these intervening years, which produced a stock market crash, a world-wide depression, and a great war, were not without their effect upon the social patterns of our times" (v). It is into this world of rapidly shifting values that Alice Munro takes us in "Family Furnishings." From its opening lines, the story stresses ambiguity rather than normativity—the old furnishings don't quite fit their new room. Like Pringle, Alfrida—known as Freddie and writing often as Flora—is a professional giver of advice, in a newspaper column advising brides what sort of china to choose for their trousseaus. The patent falseness surrounding Alfrida's advice-giving is subtly mapped by Munro onto the narrator's family, such that the "norm" for their behaviour—"proper married [sex]"—appears to recede further and further into the distance, leaving in its wake "queers, man-made bosoms, household triangles." The attempt to contain these non-normative sexualities is traced by historian Michael Bliss, who

1

notes that the sex manuals of the early twentieth century all proclaimed the "nobility" of sex while prohibiting its every manifestation, particularly that of masturbation, to which intercourse outside marriage (the open secret of Munro's story) was not seen as an alternative. These manuals describe a world comprised of passive females and "husbanding" males, rigidly structured by class-based assumptions about sexual mores and presided over by the reticence which Munro makes her ironic stock in trade.

"Family Furnishings," *Hateship, Friendship, Courtship, Loveship, Marriage* (2001)

Alfrida. My father called her Freddie. The two of them were first cousins and lived for a while on adjoining farms. One day they were out in the fields of stubble playing with my father's dog, whose name was Mack. That day the sun shone, but did not melt the ice in the furrows. They stomped on the ice and enjoyed its crackle underfoot.

How could she remember a thing like that? my father said. She made it up, he said.

"I did not," she said.

"You did so."

"I did not."

All of a sudden they heard bells pealing, whistles blowing. The town bell and the church bells were ringing. The factory whistles were blowing in the town three miles away. The world had burst its seams for joy, and Mack tore out to the road, because he was sure a parade was coming. It was the end of the First World War.

Three times a week, we could read Alfrida's name in the paper. Just her first name—Alfrida. It was printed as if written by hand, a flowing, fountain-pen signature. Round and About the Town, with Alfrida. The town mentioned was not the one close by, but the city to the south, where Alfrida lived, and which my family visited perhaps once every two or three years.

Now is the time for all you future June brides to start registering your preferences at the China Cabinet, and I must tell you that if I were a bride-to-be—which alas I am not—I might resist all the patterned dinner sets, exquisite as they are, and go for the pearly-white, the ultra-modern Rosenthal ...

Beauty treatments may come and beauty treatments may go, but the masques they slather on you at Fantine's Salon are guaranteed—speaking of brides—to make your skin bloom like orange blossoms. And to make the bride's mom—and the brides aunts and for all I know her grandmom—feel as if they'd just taken a dip in the Fountain of Youth ...

You would never expect Alfrida to write in this style, from the way she talked.

She was also one of the people who wrote under the name of Flora Simpson, on the Flora Simpson Housewives' Page. Women from all over the countryside believed that they were writing their letters to the plump woman with the crimped gray hair and the forgiving smile who was pictured at the top of the page. But the truth—which I was not to tell—was that the notes that appeared at the bottom of each of their letters were produced by Alfrida and a man she called Horse Henry, who otherwise did the obituaries. The women gave themselves such names as Morning Star and Lily-of-the-Valley and Green Thumb and Little Annie Rooney and Dishmop Queen. Some names were so popular that numbers had to be assigned to them—Goldilocks 1, Goldilocks 2, Goldilocks 3.

Dear Morning Star, Alfrida or Horse Henry would write,

> *Eczema is a dreadful pest, especially in this hot weather we're having, and I hope the baking soda does some good. Home treatments certainly ought to be respected, but it never hurts to seek out your doctor's advice. It's splendid news to hear your hubby is up and about again. It can't have been any fun with both of you under the weather ...*

In all the small towns of that part of Ontario, housewives who belonged to the Flora Simpson Club would hold an annual summer picnic. Flora Simpson always sent her special greetings but explained that there were just too many events for her to show up at all of them and she did not like to make distinctions. Alfrida said that there had been talk of sending Horse Henry done up in a wig and pillow bosoms, or perhaps herself leering like the Witch of Babylon (not even she, at my parents' table, could quote the Bible accurately and say "Whore") with a ciggie-boo stuck to her lipstick. But, oh, she said, the paper would kill us. And anyway, it would be too mean.

She always called her cigarettes ciggie-boos. When I was fifteen or sixteen she leaned across the table and asked me, "How would you like a ciggie-boo, too?" The meal was finished, and my younger brother and sister had left the table. My father was shaking his head. He had started to roll his own.

I said thank you and let Alfrida light it and smoked for the first time in front of my parents.

They pretended that it was a great joke.

"Ah, will you look at your daughter?" said my mother to my father. She rolled her eyes and clapped her hands to her chest and spoke in an artificial, languishing voice. "I'm like to faint."

"Have to get the horsewhip out," my father said, half rising in his chair.

This moment was amazing, as if Alfrida had transformed us into new people. Ordinarily, my mother would say that she did not like to see a woman smoke. She did not say that it was indecent, or unladylike—just that she did not like it. And when she said in a certain tone that she did not like something it seemed that she was not making a confession of irrationality but drawing on a private source of wisdom, which was unassailable and almost sacred.

It was when she reached for this tone, with its accompanying expression of listening to inner voices, that I particularly hated her.

As for my father, he had beaten me, in this very room, not with a horsewhip but his belt, for running afoul of my mother's rules and wounding my mother's feelings, and for answering back. Now it seemed that such beatings could occur only in another universe.

My parents had been put in a corner by Alfrida—and also by me—but they had responded so gamely and gracefully that it was really as if all three of us— my mother and my father and myself—had been lifted to a new level of ease and aplomb. In that instant I could see them—particularly my mother—as being capable of a kind of lightheartedness that was scarcely ever on view.

All due to Alfrida.

Alfrida was always referred to as a career girl. This made her seem to be younger than my parents, though she was known to be about the same age. It was also said that she was a city person. And the city, when it was spoken of in this way, meant the one she lived and worked in. But it meant something else as well—not just a distinct configuration of buildings and sidewalks and streetcar lines or even a crowding together of individual people. It meant something more abstract that could be repeated over and over, something like a hive of bees, stormy but organized, not useless or deluded exactly, but disturbing and sometimes dangerous. People went into such a place when they had to and were glad when they got out. Some, however, were attracted to it—as Alfrida must have been, long ago, and as I was now, puffing on my cigarette and trying to hold it in a nonchalant way, though it seemed to have grown to the size of a baseball bat between my fingers.

My family did not have a regular social life—people did not come to the house for dinner, let alone to parties. It was a matter of class, maybe. The parents of the boy I married, about five years after this scene at the dinner table, invited people who were not related to them to dinner, and they went to afternoon parties that they spoke of, unselfconsciously, as cocktail parties. It was a life such as I had read of in magazine stories, and it seemed to me to place my in-laws in a world of storybook privilege.

What our family did was put boards in the dining-room table two or three times a year to entertain my grandmother and my aunts—my father's older sisters—and their husbands. We did this at Christmas or Thanksgiving, when it was our turn, and perhaps also when a relative from another part of the province showed up on a visit. This visitor would always be a person rather like the aunts and their husbands and never the least bit like Alfrida.

My mother and I would start preparing for such dinners a couple of days ahead. We ironed the good tablecloth, which was as heavy as a bed quilt, and washed the good dishes, which had been sitting in the china cabinet collecting dust, and wiped the legs of the dining-room chairs, as well as making the jellied salads, the pies and cakes, that had to accompany the central roast turkey or baked ham and bowls of vegetables. There had to be far too much to eat, and most of the conversation at the table had to do with the food, with the company saying how good it was and being urged to have more, and saying that they couldn't, they were stuffed, and then the aunts' husbands relenting, taking more, and the aunts taking just a little more and saying that they shouldn't, they were ready to bust.

And dessert still to come.

There was hardly any idea of a general conversation, and in fact there was a feeling that conversation that passed beyond certain understood limits might be a disruption, a showing-off. My mother's understanding of the limits was not reliable, and she sometimes could not wait out the pauses or honor the aversion to follow-up. So when somebody said, "Seen Harley upstreet yesterday," she was liable to say, perhaps, "Do you think a man like Harley is a confirmed bachelor? Or he just hasn't met the right person?"

As if, when you mentioned seeing a person you were bound to have something further to say, something *interesting*.

Then there might be a silence, not because the people at the table meant to be rude but because they were flummoxed. Till my father would say with embarrassment, and oblique reproach, "He seems to get on all right by hisself."

If his relatives had not been present, he would more likely have said "himself."

And everybody went on cutting, spooning, swallowing, in the glare of the fresh tablecloth, with the bright light pouring in through the newly washed windows. These dinners were always in the middle of the day.

The people at that table were quite capable of talk. Washing and drying the dishes, in the kitchen, the aunts would talk about who had a tumor, a septic throat, a bad mess of boils. They would tell about how their own digestions, kidneys, nerves were functioning. Mention of intimate bodily matters seemed never to be so out of place, or suspect, as the mention of something read in a magazine, or an item in the news—it was improper somehow to pay attention to anything that was not close at hand. Meanwhile, resting on the porch, or during a brief walk out to look at the crops, the aunts' husbands might pass on the information that somebody was in a tight spot with the bank, or still owed money on an expensive piece of machinery, or had invested in a bull that was a disappointment on the job.

It could have been that they felt clamped down by the formality of the dining room, the presence of bread-and-butter plates and dessert spoons, when it was the custom, at other times, to put a piece of pie right onto a dinner plate that had been cleaned up with bread. (It would have been an offense, however, not to set things out in this proper way. In their own houses, on like occasions, they would put their guests through the same paces.) It may have been just that eating was one thing, and talking was something else.

When Alfrida came it was altogether another story. The good cloth would be spread and the good dishes would be out. My mother would have gone to a lot of trouble with the food and she would be nervous about the results— probably she would have abandoned the usual turkey-and-stuffing-and-mashed-potatoes menu and made something like chicken salad surrounded by mounds of molded rice with cut-up pimientos, and this would be followed by a dessert involving gelatin and egg white and whipped cream, taking a long, nerve-racking time to set because we had no refrigerator and it had to be chilled on the cellar floor. But the constraint, the pall over the table, was quite absent. Alfrida not only accepted second helpings, she asked for them. And she did this almost absentmindedly, and tossed off her compliments in the same way, as if the food, the eating of the food, was a secondary though agreeable thing, and she was really there to talk, and make other people talk, and anything you wanted to talk about—almost anything—would be fine.

She always visited in summer, and usually she wore some sort of striped, silky sundress, with a halter top that left her back bare. Her back was not pretty, being sprinkled with little dark moles, and her shoulders were bony and her chest nearly flat. My father would always remark on how much she could eat and remain thin. Or he turned truth on its head by noting that her appetite was as picky as ever, but she still hadn't been prevented from larding on the fat. (It was not considered out of place in our family to comment about fatness or skinniness or pallor or ruddiness or baldness.)

Her dark hair was done up in rolls above her face and at the sides, in the style of the time. Her skin was brownish-looking, netted with fine wrinkles, and her mouth wide, the lower lip rather thick, almost drooping, painted with a hearty lipstick that left a smear on the teacup and water tumbler. When her mouth was opened wide—as it nearly always was, talking or laughing— you could see that some of her teeth had been pulled at the back. Nobody could say that she was good-looking—any woman over twenty-five seemed to me to have pretty well passed beyond the possibility of being good-looking, anyway, to have lost the right to be so, and perhaps even the desire—but she was fervent and dashing. My father said thoughtfully that she had zing.

Alfrida talked to my father about things that were happening in the world, about politics. My father read the paper, he listened to the radio, he had opinions about these things but rarely got a chance to talk about them. The aunts' husbands had opinions too, but theirs were brief and unvaried and expressed an everlasting distrust of all public figures and particularly all foreigners, so that most of the time all that could be gotten out of them were grunts of dismissal. My grandmother was deaf—nobody could tell how much she knew or what she thought about anything, and the aunts themselves seemed fairly proud of how much they didn't know or didn't have to pay attention to. My mother had been a school-teacher, and she could readily have pointed out all the countries of Europe on the map, but she saw everything through a personal haze, with the British Empire and the royal family looming large and everything else diminished, thrown into a jumble-heap that was easy for her to disregard.

Alfrida's views were not really so far away from those of the uncles. Or so it appeared. But instead of grunting and letting the subject go, she gave her hooting laugh, and told stories about prime ministers and the American president and John L. Lewis and the mayor of Montreal—stories in which they all came out badly. She told stories about the royal family too, but there she made a distinction between the good ones like the king and queen and the beautiful Duchess of Kent and the dreadful ones like the Windsors and old King Eddy, who—she said—had a certain disease and had marked his wife's neck by trying to strangle her, which was why she always had to wear her pearls. This distinction coincided pretty well with one my mother made but seldom spoke about, so she did not object—though the reference to syphilis made her wince.

I smiled at it, knowingly, with a foolhardy composure.

Alfrida called the Russians funny names. Mikoyan-sky. Uncle Joe-sky. She believed that they were pulling the wool over everybody's eyes, and that the United Nations was a farce that would never work and that Japan would rise again and should have been finished off when there was the chance. She didn't trust Quebec either. Or the pope. There was a problem for her with Senator McCarthy—she would have liked to be on his side, but his being a Catholic was a stumbling block. She called the pope the poop. She relished the thought of all the crooks and scoundrels to be found in the world.

Sometimes it seemed as if she was putting on a show—a display, maybe to tease my father. To rile him up, as he himself would have said, to get his goat. But not because she disliked him or even wanted to make him uncomfortable. Quite the opposite. She might have been tormenting him as young girls torment boys at school, when arguments are a peculiar delight to both sides and insults are taken as flattery. My father argued with her, always in a mild steady voice, and yet it was clear that he had the intention of goading her on. Sometimes he would do a turnaround, and say that maybe she was right—that with her work on the newspaper, she must have sources of information that he couldn't have. You've put me straight, he would say, if I had any sense I'd be obliged to you. And she would say, Don't give me that load of baloney.

"You two," said my mother, in mock despair and perhaps in real exhaustion, and Alfrida told her to go and have a lie-down, she deserved it after this splendiferous dinner, she and I would manage the dishes. My mother was subject to a tremor in her right arm, a stiffness in her fingers, that she believed came when she got overtired.

While we worked in the kitchen Alfrida talked to me about celebrities—actors, even minor movie stars, who had made stage in the city where she lived. In a lowered voice still broken by wildly disrespectful laughter she told me stories of their bad behavior, the rumors of private scandals that had never made it into the magazines. She mentioned queers, man-made bosoms, household triangles—all things that I had found hints of in my reading but felt giddy to hear about, even at third or fourth hand, in real life.

Alfrida's teeth always got my attention, so that even in these confidential recitals I sometimes lost track of what was being said. Those teeth that were left, across the front, were each of a slightly different color, no two alike. Some with a fairly strong enamel tended towards shades of dark ivory, others were opalescent, shadowed with lilac, and giving out fish-flashes of silver rims, occasionally a gleam of gold. People's teeth in those days seldom made such a solid, handsome show as they do now, unless they were false. But these teeth of Alfrida's were unusual in their individuality, clear separation, and large size. When Alfrida let out some jibe that was especially, knowingly outrageous, they seemed to leap to the fore like a palace guard, like jolly spear-fighters.

"She always did have trouble with her teeth," the aunts said. "She had that abscess, remember, the poison went all through her system."

How like them, I thought, to toss aside Alfrida's wit and style and turn her teeth into a sorry problem.

"Why doesn't she just have them all out and be done with it?"

"Likely she couldn't afford it," said my grandmother, surprising everybody as she sometimes did, by showing that she had been keeping up with the conversation all along.

And surprising me with the new, everyday sort of light this shed on Alfrida's life. I had believed that Alfrida was rich—rich at least in comparison with the rest of the family. She lived in an apartment—I had never seen it, but to me that fact conveyed at least the idea of a very civilized life—and she wore clothes that were not homemade, and her shoes were not Oxfords like the shoes of practically all the other grown-up women I knew—they were sandals made of bright strips of the new plastic. It was hard to know whether my grandmother was simply living in the past, when getting your false teeth was the solemn, crowning expense of a lifetime, or whether she really knew things about Alfrida's life that I never would have guessed.

The rest of the family was never present when Alfrida had dinner at our house. She did go to see my grandmother, who was her aunt, her mother's sister. My grandmother no longer lived at her own house but lived alternately with one or the other of the aunts, and Alfrida went to whichever house she was living in at the time, but not to the other house, to see the other aunt who was as much her cousin as my father was. And the meal she took was never with any of them. Usually she came to our house first and visited awhile, and then gathered herself up, as if reluctantly, to make the other visit. When she came back later and we sat down to eat, nothing derogatory was said outright against the aunts and their husbands, and certainly nothing disrespectful about my grandmother. In fact, it was the way that my grandmother would be spoken of by Alfrida—a sudden sobriety and concern in her voice, even a touch of fear (what about her blood pressure, had she been to the doctor lately, what did he have to say?)—that made me aware of the difference, the coolness or possibly unfriendly restraint, with which she asked after the others. Then there would be a similar restraint in my mother's reply, and an extra gravity in my father's—a caricature of gravity, you might say—that showed how they all agreed about something they could not say.

On the day when I smoked the cigarette Alfrida decided to take this a bit further, and she said solemnly, "How about Asa, then? Is he still as much of a conversation grabber as ever?"

My father shook his head sadly, as if the thought of this uncle's garrulousness must weigh us all down.

"Indeed," he said. "He is indeed."

Then I took my chance.

"Looks like the roundworms have got into the hogs," I said. "Yup."

Except for the "yup," this was just what my uncle had said, and he had said it at this very table, being overcome by an uncharacteristic need to break the silence or to pass on something important that had just come to mind. And I said it with just his stately grunts, his innocent solemnity.

Alfrida gave a great, approving laugh, showing her festive teeth. "That's it, she's got him to a *T*."

My father bent over his plate, as if to hide how he was laughing too, but of course not really hiding it, and my mother shook her head, biting her lips, smiling. I felt a keen triumph. Nothing was said to put me in my place, no reproof for what was sometimes called my sarcasm, my being smart. The word "smart" when it was used about me, in the family, might mean intelligent, and then it was used rather grudgingly—"oh, she's smart enough some ways"—or it might be used to mean pushy, attention-seeking, obnoxious. *Don't be so smart.*

Sometimes my mother said sadly, "You have a cruel tongue."

Sometimes—and this was a great deal worse—my father was disgusted with me.

"What makes you think you have the right to run down decent people?"

This day nothing like that happened—I seemed to be as free as a visitor at the table, almost as free as Alfrida, and flourishing under the banner of my own personality.

But there was a gap about to open, and perhaps that was the last time, the very last time, that Alfrida sat at our table. Christmas cards continued to be exchanged, possibly even letters—as long as my mother could manage a pen—and we still read Alfrida's name in the paper, but I cannot recall any visits during the last couple of years I lived at home.

It may have been that Alfrida asked if she could bring her friend and had been told that she could not. If she was already living with him, that would have been one reason, and if he was the same man she had later, the fact that he was married would have been another. My parents would have been united in this. My mother had a horror of irregular sex or flaunted sex—of any sex, you might say, for the proper married kind was not acknowledged at all—and my father too judged these matters strictly at that time in his life. He might have had a special objection, also, to a man who could get a hold over Alfrida.

She would have made herself cheap in their eyes. I can imagine either one of them saying it. *She didn't need to go and make herself cheap.*

But she may not have asked at all, she may have known enough not to. During the time of those earlier, lively visits there may have been no man in her life, and then when there was one, her attention may have shifted entirely. She may have become a different person then, as she certainly was later on.

Or she may have been wary of the special atmosphere of a household where there is a sick person who will go on getting sicker and never get better. Which was the case with my mother, whose symptoms joined together, and turned a corner, and instead of a worry and an inconvenience became her whole destiny.

"The poor thing," the aunts said.

And as my mother was changed from a mother into a stricken presence around the house, these other, formerly so restricted females in the family seemed to gain some little liveliness and increased competence in the world. My grandmother got herself a hearing aid—something nobody would have suggested to her. One of the aunts' husbands—not Asa, but the one called Irvine—died, and the aunt who had been married to him learned to drive the car and got a job doing alterations in a clothing store and no longer wore a hairnet.

They called to see my mother, and saw always the same thing—that the one who had been better-looking, who had never quite let them forget she was a schoolteacher, was growing month by month more slow and stiff in the movements of her limbs and more thick and importunate in her speech, and that nothing was going to help her.

They told me to take good care of her.

"She's your mother," they reminded me.

"The poor thing."

Alfrida would not have been able to say those things, and she might not have been able to find anything to say in their place.

Her not coming to see us was all right with me. I didn't want people coming. I had no time for them, I had became a furious housekeeper—waxing the floors and ironing even the dish towels, and this was all done to keep some sort of disgrace (my mother's deterioration seemed to be a unique disgrace that infected us all) at bay. It was done to make it seem as if I lived with my parents and my brother and my sister in a normal family in an ordinary house, but the moment somebody stepped in our door and saw my mother they saw that this was not so and they pitied us. A thing I could not stand.

I won a scholarship. I didn't stay home to take care of my mother or of anything else. I went off to college. The college was in the city where Alfrida lived. After a few months she asked me to come for supper, but I could not go, because I worked every evening of the week except on Sundays. I worked in the city library, downtown, and in the college library, both of which stayed open until nine o'clock. Some time later, during the winter, Alfrida asked me again, and this time the invitation was for a Sunday. I told her that I could not come because I was going to a concert.

"Oh—a date?" she said, and I said yes, but at the time it was not true. I would go to the free Sunday concerts in the college auditorium with another girl, or two or three other girls, for something to do and in the faint hope of meeting some boys there.

"Well you'll have to bring him around sometime," Alfrida said. "I'm dying to meet him."

Towards the end of the year I did have someone to bring, and I had actually met him at a concert. At least, he had seen me at a concert and had phoned me up and asked me to go out with him. But I would never have brought him to meet Alfrida. I would never have brought any of my new friends to meet her. My new friends were people who said, "Have you read *Look Homeward Angel?* Oh, you have to read that. Have you read *Buddenbrooks?*" They were people with whom I went to see *Forbidden Games* and *Les Enfants du Paradis* when the Film Society brought them in. The boy I went out with, and later became engaged to, had taken me to the Music Building, where you could listen to records at lunch hour. He introduced me to Gounod and because of Gounod I loved opera, and because of opera I loved Mozart.

When Alfrida left a message at my rooming house, asking me to call back, I never did. After that she didn't call again.

She still wrote for the paper—occasionally I glanced at one of her rhapsodies about Royal Doulton figurines or imported ginger biscuits or honeymoon negligees. Very likely she was still answering the letters from the Flora Simpson housewives, and still laughing at them. Now that I was living in that city I seldom looked at the paper that had once seemed to me the center of city life—and even, in a way, the center of our life at home, sixty miles away. The jokes, the compulsive insincerity, of people like Alfrida and Horse Henry now struck me as tawdry and boring.

I did not worry about running into her, even in this city that was not, after all, so very large. I never went into the shops that she mentioned in her column. I had no reason ever to walk past the newspaper building, and she lived far away from my rooming house somewhere on the south side of town.

Nor did I think that Alfrida was the kind of person to show up at the library. The very word, "library," would probably make her turn down her big mouth in a parody of consternation, as she used to do at the books in the bookcase in our house—those books not bought in my time, some of them won as school prizes by my teenaged parents (there was my mother's maiden name, in her beautiful lost handwriting), books that seemed to me not like things bought in a store at all, but like presences in the house just as the trees outside the window were not plants but presences rooted in the ground. *The Mill on the Floss, The Call of the Wild, The Heart of Midlothian.* "Lot of hotshot reading in there," Alfrida had said. "Bet you don't crack those very often." And my father had said no, he didn't, falling in with her comradely tone of dismissal or even contempt and to some extent telling a lie, because he did look into them, once in a long while, when he had the time.

That was the kind of lie that I hoped never to have to tell again, the contempt I hoped never to have to show, about the things that really mattered to me. And in order not to have to do that, I would pretty well have to stay clear of the people I used to know.

At the end of my second year I was leaving college—my scholarship had covered only two years there. It didn't matter—I was planning to be a writer anyway. And I was getting married.

Alfrida had heard about this, and she got in touch with me again.

"I guess you must've been too busy to call me, or maybe nobody ever gave you my messages," she said.

I said that maybe I had been, or maybe they hadn't.

This time I agreed to visit. A visit would not commit me to anything, since I was not going to be living in this city in the future. I picked a Sunday, just after my final exams were over, when my fiancé was going to be in Ottawa for a job interview. The day was bright and sunny—it was around the beginning of May. I decided to walk. I had hardly ever been south of Dundas Street or east of Adelaide, so there were parts of the city that were entirely strange to me. The shade trees along the northern streets had just come out in leaf, and the lilacs, the ornamental crab apple trees, the beds of tulips were all in flower, the lawns like fresh carpets. But after a while I found myself walking along streets where there were no shade trees, streets where the houses were hardly an arm's reach from the sidewalk, and where such lilacs as there were—lilacs will grow anywhere—were pale, as if sun-bleached, and their fragrance did not carry. On these streets, as well as houses there were narrow apartment buildings, only two or three stories high—some with the utilitarian decoration of a rim of bricks around their doors, and some with raised windows and limp curtains falling out over their sills.

Alfrida lived in a house, not in an apartment building. She had the whole upstairs of a house. The downstairs, at least the front part of the downstairs, had been turned into a shop, which was closed, because of Sunday. It was a secondhand shop—I could see through the dirty front windows a lot of non-descript furniture with stacks of old dishes and utensils set everywhere. The only thing that caught my eye was a honey pail, exactly like the honey pail with a blue sky and a golden beehive in which I had carried my lunch to school when I was six or seven years old. I could remember reading over and over the words on its side.

All pure honey will granulate.

I had no idea then what "granulate" meant, but I liked the sound of it. It seemed ornate and delicious.

I had taken longer to get there than I had expected and I was very hot. I had not thought that Alfrida, inviting me to lunch, would present me with a meal like the Sunday dinners at home, but it was cooked meat and vegetables I smelled as I climbed the outdoor stairway.

"I thought you'd got lost," Alfrida called out above me. "I was about to get up a rescue party."

Instead of a sundress she was wearing a pink blouse with a floppy bow at the neck, tucked into a pleated brown skirt. Her hair was no longer done up in smooth rolls but cut short and frizzed around her face, its dark brown color now harshly touched with red. And her face, which I remembered as lean and summer-tanned, had got fuller and somewhat pouchy. Her makeup stood out on her skin like orange-pink paint in the noon light.

But the biggest difference was that she had gotten false teeth, of a uniform color, slightly overfilling her mouth and giving an anxious edge to her old expression of slapdash eagerness.

"Well—haven't you plumped out," she said. "You used to be so skinny."

This was true, but I did not like to hear it. Along with all the girls at the rooming house, I ate cheap food—copious meals of Kraft dinners and packages of jam-filled cookies. My fiancé, so sturdily and possessively in favor of everything about me, said that he liked full-bodied women and that I reminded him of Jane Russell. I did not mind his saying that, but usually I was affronted when people had anything to say about my appearance. Particularly when it was somebody like Alfrida—somebody who had lost all importance in my life. I believed that such people had no right to be looking at me, or forming any opinions about me, let alone stating them.

This house was narrow across the front, but long from front to back. There was a living room whose ceiling sloped at the sides and whose windows over-looked the street, a hall-like dining room with no windows at all because side bedrooms with dormers opened off it, a kitchen, a bathroom also without windows that got its daylight through a pebbled-glass pane in its door, and across the back of the house a glassed-in sunporch.

The sloping ceilings made the rooms look makeshift, as if they were only pretending to be anything but bedrooms. But they were crowded with serious furniture—dining-room table and chairs, kitchen table and chairs, living-room sofa and recliner—all meant for larger, proper rooms. Doilies on the tables, squares of embroidered white cloth protecting the backs and arms of sofa and chairs, sheer curtains across the windows and heavy flowered drapes at the sides—it was all more like the aunts' houses than I would have thought possible. And on the dining-room wall—not in the bathroom or bedroom but in the dining room—there hung a picture that was the silhouette of a girl in a hoopskirt, all constructed of pink satin ribbon.

A strip of tough linoleum was laid down on the dining-room floor, on the path from the kitchen to the living room.

Alfrida seemed to guess something of what I was thinking.

"I know I've got far too much stuff in here," she said. "But it's my parents' stuff. It's family furnishings, and I couldn't let them go."

I had never thought of her as having parents. Her mother had died long ago, and she had been brought up by my grandmother, who was her aunt.

"My dad and mother's," Alfrida said. "When Dad went off, your grandma kept it because she said it ought to be mine when I grew up, and so here it is. I couldn't turn it down, when she went to that trouble."

Now it came back to me—the part of Alfrida's life that I had forgotten about. Her father had married again. He had left the farm and got a job working for the railway. He had some other children, the family moved from one town to another, and sometimes Alfrida used to mention them, in a joking way that had something to do with how many children there had been and how close they came together and how much the family had to move around.

"Come and meet Bill," Alfrida said.

Bill was out on the sunporch. He sat, as if waiting to be summoned, on a low couch or daybed that was covered with a brown plaid blanket. The blanket was rumpled—he must have been lying on it recently—and the blinds on the windows were all pulled down to their sills. The light in the room—the hot sunlight coming through the rain-marked yellow blinds—and the rumpled rough blanket and faded, dented cushion, even the smell of the blanket, and of the masculine slippers, old scuffed slippers that had lost their shape and pattern, reminded me—just as much as the doilies and the heavy polished furniture in the inner rooms had done, and the ribbon-girl on the wall—of my aunts' houses. There, too, you could come upon a shabby male hideaway with its furtive yet insistent odors, its shamefaced but stubborn look of contradicting the female domain.

Bill stood up and shook my hand, however, as the uncles would never have done with a strange girl. Or with any girl. No specific rudeness would have held them back, just a dread of appearing ceremonious.

He was a tall man with wavy, glistening gray hair and a smooth but not young-looking face. A handsome man, with the force of his good looks somehow drained away—by indifferent health, or some bad luck, or lack of gumption. But he had still a worn courtesy, a way of bending towards a woman, that suggested the meeting would be a pleasure, for her and for himself.

Alfrida directed us into the windowless dining room where the lights were on in the middle of this bright day. I got the impression that the meal had been ready some time ago, and that my late arrival had delayed their usual schedule. Bill served the roast chicken and dressing, Alfrida the vegetables. Alfrida said to Bill, "Honey, what do you think that is beside your plate?" and then he remembered to pick up his napkin.

He had not much to say. He offered the gravy, he inquired as to whether I wanted mustard relish or salt and pepper, he followed the conversation by turning his head towards Alfrida or towards me. Every so often he made a little whistling sound between his teeth, a shivery sound that seemed meant to be genial and appreciative and that I thought at first might be a prelude to some remark. But it never was, and Alfrida never paused for it. I have since seen reformed drinkers who behaved somewhat as he did—chiming in agreeably but unable to carry things beyond that, helplessly preoccupied. I never knew whether that was true of Bill, but he did seem to carry around a history of defeat, of troubles borne and lessons learned. He had an air too of gallant accommodation towards whatever choices had gone wrong or chances hadn't panned out.

These were frozen peas and carrots, Alfrida said. Frozen vegetables were fairly new at the time.

"They beat the canned," she said. "They're practically as good as fresh."

Then Bill made a whole statement. He said they were better than fresh. The color, the flavor, everything was better than fresh. He said it was remarkable what they could do now and what would be done by way of freezing things in the future.

Alfrida leaned forward, smiling. She seemed almost to hold her breath, as if he was her child taking unsupported steps, or a first lone wobble on a bicycle.

There was a way they could inject something into a chicken, he told us, there was a new process that would have every chicken coming out the same, plump and tasty. No such thing as taking a risk on getting an inferior chicken anymore.

"Bill's field is chemistry," Alfrida said.

When I had nothing to say to this she added, "He worked for Gooderhams."

Still nothing.

"The distillers," she said. "Gooderhams Whisky."

The reason that I had nothing to say was not that I was rude or bored (or any more rude than I was naturally at that time, or more bored than I had expected to be) but that I did not understand that I should ask questions—almost any questions at all, to draw a shy male into conversation, to shake him out of his abstraction and set him up as a man of a certain authority, therefore the man of the house. I did not understand why Alfrida looked at him with such a fiercely encouraging smile. All of my experience of a woman with men, of a woman listening to her man, hoping and hoping that he will establish himself as somebody she can reasonably be proud of, was in the future. The only observation I had made of couples was of my aunts and uncles and of my mother and father, and those husbands and wives seemed to have remote and formalized connections and no obvious dependence on each other.

Bill continued eating as if he had not heard this mention of his profession and his employer, and Alfrida began to question me about my courses. She was still smiling, but her smile had changed. There was a little twitch of impatience and unpleasantness in it, as if she was just waiting for me to get to the end of my explanations so that she could say—as she did say— "You couldn't get me to read that stuff for a million dollars."

"Life's too short," she said. "You know, down at the paper we sometimes get somebody that's been through all that. Honors English. Honors Philosophy. You don't know what to do with them. They can't write worth a nickel. I've told you that, haven't I?" she said to Bill, and Bill looked up and gave her his dutiful smile.

She let this settle.

"So what do you do for fun?" she said.

A Streetcar Named Desire was being done in a theater in Toronto at that time, and I told her that I had gone down on the train with a couple of friends to see it.

Alfrida let the knife and fork clatter onto her plate.

"That filth," she cried. Her face leapt out at me, carved with disgust. Then she spoke more calmly but still with a virulent displeasure.

"You went *all the way to Toronto* to see that filth."

We had finished the dessert, and Bill picked that moment to ask if he might be excused. He asked Alfrida, then with the slightest bow he asked me. He went back to the sunporch and in a little while we could smell his pipe. Alfrida, watching him go, seemed to forget about me and the play. There was a look of such stricken tenderness on her face that when she stood up I thought she was going to follow him. But she was only going to get her cigarettes.

She held them out to me, and when I took one she said, with a deliberate effort at jollity, "I see you kept up the bad habit I got you started on." She might have remembered that I was not a child anymore and I did not have to be in her house and that there was no point in making an enemy of me. And I wasn't going to argue—I did not care what Alfrida thought about Tennessee Williams. Or what she thought about anything else.

"I guess it's your own business," Alfrida said. "You can go where you want to go." And she added, "After all—you'll pretty soon be a married woman."

By her tone, this could mean either "I have to allow that you're grown up now" or "Pretty soon you'll have to toe the line."

We got up and started to collect the dishes. Working close to each other in the small space between the kitchen table and counter and the refrigerator, we soon developed without speaking about it a certain order and harmony of scraping and stacking and putting the leftover food into smaller containers for storage and filling the sink with hot, soapy water and pouncing on any piece of cutlery that hadn't been touched and slipping it into the baize-lined drawer in the dining-room buffet. We brought the ashtray out to the kitchen and stopped every now and then to take a restorative, businesslike drag on our cigarettes. There are things women agree on or don't agree on when they work together in this way—whether it is all right to smoke, for instance, or preferable not to smoke because some migratory ash might find its way onto a clean dish, or whether every single thing that has been on the table has to be washed even if it has not been used—and it turned out that Alfrida and I agreed. Also, the thought that I could get away, once dishes were done, made me feel more relaxed and generous. I already said that I had to meet a friend that afternoon.

"These are pretty dishes," I said. They were creamy-colored, yellowish, with a rim of blue flowers.

"Well—they were my mother's wedding dishes," Alfrida said. "That was one other good thing your grandma did for me. She packed up all my mother's dishes and put them away until the time came when I could use them. Jeanie never knew they existed. They wouldn't have lasted long, with that bunch."

Jeanie. That bunch. Her stepmother and the half brothers and sisters.

"You know about that, don't you?" Alfrida said. "You know what happened to my mother?"

Of course I knew. Alfrida's mother had died when a lamp exploded in her hands—that is, she died of burns she got when a lamp exploded in her hands—and my aunts and my mother had spoken of this regularly. Nothing could be said about Alfrida's mother or about Alfrida's father, and very little about Alfrida herself—without that death being dragged in and tacked onto it. It was the reason that Alfrida's father left the farm (always somewhat of a downward step morally if not financially). It was a reason to be desperately careful with coal oil, and a reason to be grateful for electricity, whatever the cost. And it was a dreadful thing for a child of Alfrida's age. (That is—whatever she had done with herself since.)

If it hadn't 've been for the thunderstorm she wouldn't ever have been lighting a lamp in the middle of the afternoon.

She lived all that night and the next day and the next night and it would have been the best thing in the world for her if she hadn't 've.

And just the year after that the Hydro came down their road, and they didn't have need of the lamps anymore.

The aunts and my mother seldom felt the same way about anything, but they shared a feeling about this story. The feeling was in their voices whenever they said Alfrida's mother's name. The story seemed to be a horrible treasure to them, something our family could claim that nobody else could, a distinction that would never be let go. To listen to them had always made me feel as if there was some obscene connivance going on, a fond fingering of whatever was grisly or disastrous. Their voices were like worms slithering around in my insides.

Men were not like this, in my experience. Men looked away from frightful happenings as soon as they could and behaved as if there was no use, once things were over with, in mentioning them or thinking about them ever again. They didn't want to stir themselves up, or stir other people up.

So if Alfrida was going to talk about it, I thought, it was a good thing that my fiancé had not come. A good thing that he didn't have to hear about Alfrida's mother, on top of finding out about my mother and my family's relative or maybe considerable poverty. He admired opera and Laurence Olivier's *Hamlet*, but he had no time for tragedy—for the squalor of tragedy—in ordinary life. His parents were healthy and good-looking and prosperous (though he said of course that they were dull), and it seemed he had not had to know anybody who did not live in fairly sunny circumstances. Failures in life—failures of luck, of health, of finances—all struck him as lapses, and his resolute approval of me did not extend to my ramshackle background.

"They wouldn't let me in to see her, at the hospital," Alfrida said, and at least she was saying this in her normal voice, not preparing the way with any special piety, or greasy excitement. "Well, I probably wouldn't have let me in either, if I'd been in their shoes. I've no idea what she looked like. Probably all bound up like a mummy. Or if she wasn't she should have been. I wasn't there when it happened, I was at school. It got very dark and the teacher turned the lights on—we had the lights, at school—and we all had to stay till the thunderstorm was over. Then my aunt Lily, well, your grandmother—she came to meet me and took me to her place. And I never got to see my mother again."

I thought that was all she was going to say but in a moment she continued, in a voice that had actually brightened up a bit, as if she was preparing for a laugh.

"I yelled and yelled my fool head off that I wanted to see her. I carried on and carried on, and finally when they couldn't shut me up your grandmother said to me, 'You're just better off not to see her. You would not want to see her, if you knew what she looks like now. You wouldn't want to remember her this way.'

"But you know what I said? I remember saying it. I said, But she would want to see me. *She would want to see me.*"

Then she really did laugh, or make a snorting sound that was evasive and scornful.

"I must've thought I was a pretty big cheese, mustn't I? *She would want to see me.*"

This was a part of the story I had never heard.

And the minute that I heard it, something happened. It was as if a trap had snapped shut, to hold these words in my head. I did not exactly understand what use I would have for them. I only knew how they jolted me and released me, right away, to breathe a different kind of air, available only to myself,

She would want to see me.

The story I wrote, with this in it, would not be written till years later, not until it had become quite unimportant to think about who had put the idea into my head in the first place.

I thanked Alfrida and said that I had to go. Alfrida went to call Bill to say good-bye to me, but came back to report that he had fallen asleep.

"He'll be kicking himself when he wakes up," she said. "He enjoyed meeting you."

She took off her apron and accompanied me all the way down the outside steps. At the bottom of the steps was a gravel path leading around to the sidewalk. The gravel crunched under our feet and she stumbled in her thin-soled house shoes.

She said, "Ouch! Goldarn it," and caught hold of my shoulder.

"How's your dad?" she said.

"He's all right."

"He works too hard."

I said, "He has to."

"Oh, I know. And how's your mother?"

"She's about the same."

She turned aside towards the shop window.

"Who do they think is ever going to buy this junk? Look at that honey pail. Your dad and I used to take our lunch to school in pails just like that."

"So did I," I said.

"Did you?" She squeezed me. "You tell your folks I'm thinking about them, will you do that?"

Alfrida did not come to my father's funeral. I wondered if that was because she did not want to meet me. As far as I knew she had never made public what she held against me; nobody else would know about it. But my father had known. When I was home visiting him and learned that Alfrida was living not far away—in my grandmother's house, in fact, which she had finally inherited—I had suggested that we go to see her. This was in the flurry between my two marriages, when I was in an expansive mood, newly released and able to make contact with anyone I chose.

My father said, "Well, you know, Alfrida was a bit upset."

He was calling her Alfrida now. When had that started?

I could not even think, at first, what Alfrida might be upset about. My father had to remind me of the story, published several years ago, and I was surprised, even impatient and a little angry, to think of Alfrida's objecting to something that seemed now to have so little to do with her.

"It wasn't Alfrida at all," I said to my father. "I changed it, I wasn't even thinking about her. It was a character. Anybody could see that."

But as a matter of fact there was still the exploding lamp, the mother in her charnel wrappings, the staunch, bereft child.

"Well," my father said. He was in general quite pleased that I had become a writer, but there were reservations he had about what might be called my character. About the fact that I had ended my marriage for personal—that is, wanton—reasons, and the way I went around justifying myself—or perhaps, as he would have said, weaseling out of things. He would not say so—it was not his business anymore.

I asked him how he knew that Alfrida felt this way.

He said, "A letter."

A letter, though they lived not far apart. I did feel sorry to think that he had had to bear the brunt of what could be taken as my thoughtlessness, or even my wrongdoing. Also that he and Alfrida seemed now to be on such formal terms. I wondered what he was leaving out. Had he felt compelled to defend me to Alfrida, as he had to defend my writing to other people? He would do that now, though it was never easy for him. In his uneasy defense he might have said something harsh.

Through me, peculiar difficulties had developed for him.

There was a danger whenever I was on home ground. It was the danger of seeing my life through other eyes than my own. Seeing it as an ever-increasing roll of words like barbed wire, intricate, bewildering, uncomforting—set against the rich productions, the food, flowers, and knitted garments, of other women's domesticity. It became harder to say that it was worth the trouble.

Worth my trouble, maybe, but what about anyone else's?

My father had said that Alfrida was living alone now. I asked him what had become of Bill. He said that all of that was outside of his jurisdiction. But he believed there had been a bit of a rescue operation.

"Of Bill? How come? Who by?"

"Well, I believe there was a wife."

"I met him at Alfrida's once. I liked him."

"People did. Women."

I had to consider that the rupture might have had nothing to do with me. My stepmother had urged my father into a new sort of life. They went bowling and curling and regularly joined other couples for coffee and doughnuts at Tim Horton's. She had been a widow for a long time before she married him, and she had many friends from those days who became new friends for him. What had happened with him and Alfrida might have been simply one of the changes, the wearing-out of old attachments, that I understood so well in my own life but did not expect to happen in the lives of older people—particularly, as I would have said, in the lives of people at home.

My stepmother died just a little while before my father. After their short, happy marriage they were sent to separate cemeteries to lie beside their first, more troublesome, partners. Before either of those deaths Alfrida had moved back to the city. She didn't sell the house, she just went away and left it. My father wrote to me, "That's a pretty funny way of doing things."

There were a lot of people at my father's funeral, a lot of people I didn't know. A woman came across the grass in the cemetery to speak to me—I thought at first she must be a friend of my step-mother's. Then I saw that the woman was only a few years past my own age. The stocky figure and crown of gray-blond curls and floral-patterned jacket made her look older.

"I recognized you by your picture," she said. "Alfrida used to always be bragging about you."

I said, "Alfrida's not dead?"

"Oh, no," the woman said, and went on to tell me that Alfrida was in a nursing home in a town just north of Toronto.

"I moved her down there so's I could keep an eye on her."

Now it was easy to tell—even by her voice—that she was of my own generation, and it came to me that she must be one of the other family, a half sister of Alfrida's, born when Alfrida was almost grown up.

She told me her name, and it was of course not the same as Alfrida's—she must have married. And I couldn't recall Alfrida's ever mentioning any of her half family by their first names.

I asked how Alfrida was, and the woman said her own eyesight was so bad that she was legally blind. And she had a serious kidney problem, which meant that she had to be on dialysis twice a week.

"Other than that—?" she said, and laughed. I thought, yes, a sister, because I could hear something of Alfrida in that reckless, tossed laugh.

"So she doesn't travel too good," she said. "Or else I would've brought her. She still gets the paper from here and I read it to her sometimes. That's where I saw about your dad."

I wondered out loud, impulsively, if I should go to visit, at the nursing home. The emotions of the funeral—all the warm and relieved and reconciled feelings opened up in me by the death of my father at a reasonable age—prompted this suggestion. It would have been hard to carry out. My husband—my second husband—and I had only two days here before we were flying to Europe on an already delayed holiday.

"I don't know if you'd get so much out of it," the woman said. "She has her good days. Then she has her bad days. You never know. Sometimes I think she's putting it on. Like, she'll sit there all day and whatever anybody says to her, she'll just say the same thing. *Fit as a fiddle and ready for love.* That's what she'll say all day long. *Fit-as-a-fiddle-and-ready-for-love.* She'll drive you crazy. Then other days she can answer all right.

Again, her voice and laugh—this time half submerged—reminded me of Alfrida, and I said, "You know I must have met you, I remember once when Alfrida's stepmother and her father dropped in, or maybe it was only her father and some of the children—"

"Oh, that's not who I am," the woman said. "You thought I was Alfrida's sister? Glory. I must be looking my age."

I started to say that I could not see her very well, and it was true. In October the afternoon sun was low, and it was coming straight into my eyes. The woman was standing against the light, so that it was hard to make out her features or her expression.

She twitched her shoulders nervously and importantly. She said, "Alfrida was my birth mom."

Mawm. Mother.

Then she told me, at not too great length, the story that she must have told often, because it was about an emphatic event in her life and an adventure she had embarked on alone. She had been adopted by a family in eastern Ontario; they were the only family she had ever known ("and I love them dearly"), and she had married and had her children, who were grown up before she got the urge to find out who her own mother was. It wasn't too easy, because of the way records used to be kept, and the secrecy ("It was kept one hundred percent secret that she had me"), but a few years ago she had tracked down Alfrida.

"Just in time too," she said. "I mean, it was time somebody came along to look after her. As much as I can."

I said, "I never knew."

"No. Those days, I don't suppose too many did. They warn you, when you start out to do this, it could be a shock when you show up. Older people, it's still heavy-duty. However. I don't think she minded. Earlier on, maybe she would have."

There was some sense of triumph about her, which wasn't hard to understand. If you have something to tell that will stagger someone, and you've told it, and it has done so, there has to be a balmy moment of power. In this case it was so complete that she felt a need to apologize.

"Excuse me talking all about myself and not saying how sorry I am about your dad."

I thanked her.

"You know Alfrida told me that your dad and her were walking home from school one day, this was in high school. They couldn't walk all the way together because, you know, in those days, a boy and a girl, they would just get teased something terrible. So if he got out first he'd wait just where their road went off the main road, outside of town, and if she got out first she would do the same, wait for him. And one day they were walking together and they heard all the bells starting to ring and you know what that was? It was the end of the First World War."

I said that I had heard that story too.

"Only I thought they were just children."

"Then how could they be coming home from high school, if they were just children?"

I said that I had thought they were out playing in the fields. "They had my father's dog with them. He was called Mack."

"Maybe they had the dog all right. Maybe he came to meet them. I wouldn't think she'd get mixed up on what she was telling me. She was pretty good on remembering anything that involved your dad."

Now I was aware of two things. First, that my father was born in 1902, and that Alfrida was close to the same age. So it was much more likely that they were walking home from high school than that they were playing in the fields, and it was odd that I had never thought of that before. Maybe they had said they were in the fields, that is, walking home across the fields. Maybe they had never said "playing."

Also, that the feeling of apology or friendliness, the harmlessness that I had felt in this woman a little while before, was not there now.

I said, "Things get changed around."

"That's right," the woman said. "People change things around. You want to know what Alfrida said about you?"

Now. I knew it was coming now.

"What?"

"She said you were smart, but you weren't ever quite as smart as you thought you were."

I made myself keep looking into the dark face against the light.

Smart, too smart, not smart enough.

I said, "Is that all?"

"She said you were kind of a cold fish. That's her talking, not me. I haven't got anything against you."

That Sunday, after the noon dinner at Alfrida's, I set out to walk all the way back to my rooming house. If I walked both ways, I reckoned that I would have covered about ten miles, which ought to offset the effects of the meal I had eaten. I felt overfull, not just of food but of everything that I had seen and sensed in the apartment. The crowded, old-fashioned furnishings. Bill's silences. Alfrida's love, stubborn as sludge, and inappropriate, and hopeless—as far as I could see—on the grounds of age alone.

After I had walked for a while, my stomach did not feel so heavy. I made a vow not to eat anything for the next twenty-four hours. I walked north and west, north and west, on the streets of the tidily rectangular small city. On a Sunday afternoon there was hardly any traffic, except on the main thoroughfares. Sometimes my route coincided with a bus route for a few blocks. A bus might go by with only two or three people in it. People I did not know and who did not know me. What a blessing.

I had lied, I was not meeting any friends. My friends had mostly all gone home to wherever they lived. My fiancé would be away until the next day—he was visiting his parents, in Cobourg, on the way home from Ottawa. There would be nobody in the rooming house when I got there—nobody I had to bother talking to or listening to. I had nothing to do.

When I had walked for over an hour, I saw a drugstore that was open. I went in and had a cup of coffee. The coffee was reheated, black and bitter—its taste was medicinal, exactly what I needed. I was already feeling relieved, and now I began to feel happy. Such happiness, to be alone. To see the hot late-afternoon light on the sidewalk outside, the branches of a tree just out in leaf, throwing their skimpy shadows. To hear from the back of the shop the sounds of the ball game that the man who had served me was listening to on the radio. I did not think of the story I would make about Alfrida—not of that in particular—but of the work I wanted to do, which seemed more like grabbing something out of the air than constructing stories. The cries of the crowd came to me like big heartbeats, full of sorrows. Lovely formal-sounding waves, with their distant, almost inhuman assent and lamentation.

This was what I wanted, this was what I thought I had to pay attention to, this was how I wanted my life to be.

Ivan E. Coyote

"Just Like My Dad," *Boys Like Her* (1998)

I was lying on his bed, watching him button his black jeans. His pressed white shirt, black belt and black leather vest were all laid out, ready for him to slide into. The equivalent of dress blues for a lesbian. He used to be a lesbian.

"I don't miss them a bit, not a bit." His voice was warm honey rolling over gravel, and his small-for-the rest-of-him hands kept returning to the still-angry scars on his chest, like a tongue to a missing tooth.

He stands taller, since his breasts were removed, because his honey-gravel voice and sparse mustache now match the rest of him.

"Look at you," he rumbled, so I looked down at my stretched-out self. "You're built like a teenage boy that grew tits by accident. And you're too thin. We'll have to fatten you up."

He grins and then bares one of his eye teeth at me, a friendly predator. His shirt is buttoned up, belt buckled, vest on, he is ready to take that girl out for dinner. He kisses the top of my head and is gone, just the smell of him is left in the room with me.

I have known him for five years, and he is my surrogate father, my queer dad, the head of my freak family. He calls me his son, and I am proud of this. He was already my dad back when he was a she.

I can't explain this, so I'll just use words:

Sometimes, I want to be just like my dad when I grow up, but without the scars.

Gertrude Pringle

from *Etiquette in Canada* (1949)

BRINGING OUT A DAUGHTER

A generation ago a Canadian girl usually made her bow to society at the age of eighteen, and if her parents were well-to-do they gave a house dance for her; for this was the day of large, stately mansions set in ample grounds. Many were the preparations made for such a dance.

Verandahs were enclosed with awnings and hung with coloured lanterns to form sitting-out places. The glittering floor was reflected in long mirrors. There was a profusion of lovely hothouse flowers, and the three-piece orchestra was stationed behind a barricade of palms. The supper itself would need a whole chapter to do it justice. It began with oyster soup, which was followed by cold turkey, ham, or chicken salad. The sweets included charlotte russe, jellies and ice-cream, while claret and punch were available throughout the evening.

Many a girl, however, made her formal début at a large, crowded afternoon reception. On such an occasion, with the daylight shut out and all the lights turned on, the débutante stood beside her mother and was presented to her friends.

The coming-out dance or tea was then an event second only in importance to being married and was eagerly looked forward to during the last year at school. But a change has taken place. With the many interesting careers now open to young women, making a formal début has become a rather secondary matter.

For one thing, the routine of society offers no particular novelty nowadays. From the age of sixteen, girls attend 'not-out' dances and theatre parties. Rather more alluring indeed does a career seem. And so some pursue the higher learning in university halls. Sororities and college organizations and activities have a social emphasis. Others study abroad. Later on perhaps they may plan to take a whirl in society before going on with the serious business of life. Thus today girls are older when they come out—anywhere from nineteen to twenty-three.

In the larger cities each year's output of débutantes is numerous, and much entertaining is done for them. For this reason the girl who has been out for two years (certainly one in her third season unless she has unusual personality) finds she has to retire in favour of the newcomers. By this time she has formed friendships and joined various clubs, and these with some of the milder forms of social entertainment fill her time.

In England, girls belonging to the nobility and county families are presented at court, this constituting their formal presentation to society.

In the United States the coming-out of a daughter of the fashionable class is marked by elaborate preparations and a vast amount of enthusiasm. Scores of bouquets are sent to a débutante. Here wardrobe, and the large dance held in her home or at a hotel, at which she is the bright and shining star, are minutely described in the local newspapers to the extent of many columns. Her picture in the Sunday edition may occupy a full half page, and she is sometimes interviewed.

In Canada we steer a middle course. More than a thread of the thoughtful Scottish runs through our social fabric, as well as strands of conservative English customs. If a Canadian girl belonging to a socially prominent family is introduced at a dance, her picture may appear in the papers among those of other débutantes, and her party be briefly described, but her début will be given no more than the moderate publicity of any other social event.

Her name very likely will be on the invitations her mother has sent out; she will have an exceedingly pretty frock for her début. The ballroom will be beautiful with flowers, the floor in perfect condition, the orchestra good and the men and girls personable, well-bred young people. She will take her place beside her mother and receive with her, standing farthest from the entrance to the room, so that the guests shake hands first with her mother and father, and then with her. And perhaps not until supper time will she be free to leave her post of duty and enjoy a dance.

A large dance given in a house or hotel ballroom is quite the most approved way of introducing a daughter to society, and it is also the most costly way. Girls who are unable to come out at a dance of their own often make their formal début at a friend's dance.

At every large coming-out party there are always a number of such débutantes. A dinner usually precedes the dance, and the group goes on to it afterwards. A wise mother with a girl in her first or second season always arranges a dinner party for the evening of a dance, so that her daughter has the advantages of a partner and men of her own group on which to depend.

THE WELL-BRED GIRL

A girl who has good sense and dignity will avoid the extremes of dress and make-up in which so many young women indulge. To resemble a chorus girl with rouge thickly plastered on, eye shadow and exaggerated red mouth, is far from attractive and has a cheap effect. The only purpose in using make-up is to gain a natural effect. Blood-red finger nails are in bad taste; a delicate pink is the colour nature bestows on healthy nails.

There are certain rules of conduct which a well-brought-up girl observes. When a man accompanies her home after a party, she must never invite him to come in, but bid him good-night at the door. Even if the man is her fiancé, it does not alter the rule, although it is nowadays more honoured in the breach than in the observance.

Another even more stringent rule is that a girl must never go alone to a man's bachelor apartment. This rule is *absolute*, and any girl that disobeys it runs the risk of losing her good name.

For a girl in her first or second season to dine or take supper after theatre alone with a man in a restaurant is not correct behaviour. Nor should she accept attentions from a married man, or go with him to theatre or restaurant.

Self-control and self-respect are the result of being well-brought-up. Such a girl's sense of honour will not allow her to speak unkindly of those she knows, or to say anything in their absence which she would not say in their presence. She will always treat with deference her parents and seniors. When an elderly woman who is standing addresses her, the girl if sitting, will rise. When entertained at dinner she will always be punctual.

One of the greatest drawbacks is an inability to remember faces and names. A débutante should give all her attention to those she meets and endeavour to fix their features and names on her mind. It is a great aid to popularity to be able to recognize people quickly.

The wise girl does not force herself upon any man's attention by frequently telephoning him, and showing eagerness for his companionship. Men always prize most that which is difficult to win, and the more reserved type of girl is the one they admire rather than the free and easy one.

Michael Bliss

"'Pure Books on Avoided Subjects': Pre-Freudian Sexual Ideas in Canada,"[1] *Historical Papers* (1970)

Books purporting to contain facts and wisdom about human sexuality were common in North America long before Dr. Reuben, *Human Sexual Response*, the Kinsey Reports, or even the Freudian revolution. The best-selling "sex" manuals in Canada between about 1900 and 1915 were the eight volumes in the "Self and Sex Series," published in Philadelphia and distributed in Canada by William Briggs, official publisher for the Methodist Church. The Self and Sex books for males were *What a Young Boy Ought to Know, What a Young Man Ought to Know, What a Young Husband Ought to Know,* and *What a Man of 45 Ought to Know.* Their author and publisher was the Rev. Sylvanus Stall, a Lutheran Minister. Dr. Mary Wood-Allen, a popular lecturer and writer on sex education, contributed *What a Young Girl Ought to Know,* and *What a Young Woman Ought to Know* to the series; and Dr. Emma F. Angell Drake completed the symmetry with *What a Young Wife Ought to Know* and *What a Woman of 45 Ought to Know.* The first "ought to know" book was issued in 1897; by 1908 the publisher claimed sales of one million copies of the series in English and the books had been translated into the leading European as well as eight Asian languages. No Canadian circulation figures have been recorded, only the claim that they outsold all other books of their kind. The individual volumes, all in common format, were accompanied by glowing commendations from prominent clergymen, medical experts (including, in later editions, the Canadian Dr. Amelia Yeomans of Winnipeg), popular writers such as Charles M. Sheldon and Margaret Warner Morley, and other public figures including Josiah Strong, W. T. Stead, Elizabeth Cady Stanton, and Anthony Comstock. Advertisements for the series in Canada were headed "Pure Books on Avoided Subjects."[2]

The Self and Sex books are a compendium of orthodox sexual knowledge and precept in late-Victorian and Edwardian Canada. It is true that they are American sex manuals. But the few works by Canadians that do exist on the subject are both derivative from and in complete agreement with foreign writers. In this field, as in so many others, Canadians initially relied on a kind of cross-fertilization from the United States. Assuming, then, the relevance of the Self and Sex series for the study of sexual thought in Canada, I will try to do three things in this paper: outline the fundamental ideas expressed in the Self and Sex books, attempt to explain the background of some of these ideas in North American medical and popular thought, and finally note some additional evidence of the spread of this approach to sexuality in Canada as well as suggest directions for further research.

I

There was no rejection of sex per se in the Self and Sex series. On the contrary, Sylvanus Stall advised his readers that "Sexuality has been strongly marked in all the great men who have risen to eminence in all departments of life. Without it man would be mean, selfish, sordid and ungracious to his fellow-men and uncivil to womankind.... No other part of his being so much assists him in the development of that which is highest, noblest and best in his nature."[3] He argued that the sex act itself was meant to bring "pleasure and a sense of satisfaction", and criticized those women who proclaimed utter indifference to marital intercourse.[4] Similarly, Dr. Wood-Allen told young women that their womanhood was "the mental, moral and physical expression of sex ... a glorious, divine gift, to be received with solemn thankfulness".[5]

The major theme of every book in the series, however, was the difficulty that the fact of sexuality created for boys, girls, men, women, husbands, wives, and the elderly.

By far the most persistent and pernicious difficulty for the unmarried was the temptation to indulge in the habit of the secret vice, the solitary vice, self-pollution, self-abuse, onanism, or masturbation. After a few pages on plants and fishes, the Self and Sex books for boys and girls became little more than anti-masturbation tracts. The subject was introduced as a misuse of sexual parts that could be learned innocently enough by sliding down banisters, climbing trees, and wearing tight clothes, or not so innocently from other children and nurses. However commenced, the act rapidly led to a grim series of consequences:

The health declines. The eyes lose their lustre. The skin becomes sallow. The muscles become flabby. There is an unnatural languor. Every little effort is followed by weariness. There is a great indifference to exertion.... (The victim) complains of pain in the back; of headache and dizziness. The hands become cold and clammy. The digestion becomes poor, the appetite fitful. The heart palpitates. He sits in a stooping posture, becomes hollow-chested, and the entire body, instead of enlarging into a strong, manly frame, becomes wasted, and many signs give promise of early decline and death....

If persisted in, masturbation will not only undermine, but completely overthrow the health. If the body is naturally strong, the mind may give way first, and in extreme cases imbecility and insanity may, and often do come as the inevitable result Where the body is not naturally strong, a general wasting may be followed by consumption, or life may be terminated by any one of many diseases.[6]

Boys were told of how parents often resorted to drastic measures to stop the insidious habit, including tying children's hands behind their backs, to bed posts, or to rings in a wall, or simply wrapping the whole child in a straight-jacket.[7] The books for mothers and fathers did not actually advise any of these methods; but in *What a Young Wife Ought to Know* Dr. Drake called on mothers to be "Argus-eyed" in watching their babies, to keep young children from sleeping in the same bed or playing together without an adult's presence, and to teach them right attitudes at the earliest possible age.

> While yet very young, they can be taught that the organs are to be used by them only for throwing off the waste water of the system, but that they are so closely related to other parts of the body that handling them at all will hurt them and make them sick. Tell them that little children, sometimes when they do not know this, form the habit of handling themselves and as a result they become listless and sick, and many times idiotic and insane, or develop epileptic fits. This will so impress them that they will not fall easily into the bad habit.[8]

Single young men who avoided the curse of self-pollution (the results of which in their book also included "the dwarfing and wasting of the organ itself")[9] were nonetheless bedeviled with the problem of nocturnal emissions or "wet dreams". The Rev. Stall rejected the views of those experts who taught that any and all sexual emissions were indications of coming imbecility—discounting in passing the old story that Newton had never lost a drop of semen in his life—and reassured his readers that even the most continent men often experienced emissions every ten or fourteen days as a "safety-valve". Nevertheless, it was "relatively" true that nocturnal emissions were debilitating to the system—and "few men can suffer emissions more frequently than once in two weeks without serious physical loss". With proper physical and mental habits it should be possible to avoid nocturnal emissions entirely.[10]

Resorting to sexual intercourse outside of marriage was not an acceptable substitute for onanism. Chapters IV, V, and VI of *What a Young Man Ought to Know* were each entitled "Evils to be Shunned and Consequences to be Dreaded" and composed a sixty-one page warning of the horrors of venereal disease. It was claimed that more than 25% of the population was infected with this "leprosy of lust", a sad comment on a society which inoculated its cattle against contagious diseases, but left its own young men and women in total ignorance "to be crushed beneath the Juggernaut of lust, disease and death, as its gory wheels roll from ocean to ocean ... in the rising dawn of the Twentieth Century".[11] Even the young woman of good social standing who had innocently allowed a young man of dubious reputation to kiss her one night on the doorstep had fallen prey to syphilis; today she bore the loathsome disfigurement in consequence. "I do not need to multiply such cases", Dr. Wood-Allen wrote. "You can be warned by one as well as by a hundred."[12]

The chaste young couple who had enjoyed a quiet wedding and wisely foregone an exhausting bridal tour were now legally and morally free to indulge themselves, but not exactly physiologically free. For they now had to deal with the major sexual problem of married life—excess.

Do not wait (Stall warned) until you have the pronounced effects of backache, lassitude, giddiness, dimness of sight, noises in the ears, numbness of fingers and paralysis. Note your own condition for the next day very carefully. If you observe a lack of normal, physical power, a loss of intellectual quickness or mental grip, if you are sensitive and irritable, if you are less kind and considerate of your wife, if you are morose and less companionable, or in any way fall below your best standard of excellence, it would be well for you to think seriously and proceed cautiously.[13]

It was not entirely clear how frequently sexual intercourse could be enjoyed with safety. Some physicians were inclined to recommend once a month, but the Rev. Stall was slightly more permissive, suggesting that a couple in average health who stayed within the bounds of once a week would not be in danger of having entered upon "a life of excess".[14] On the other hand, the theory that absolute continence except for the purpose of reproduction was the ideal married state had some "very strong arguments" in its favor. Unfortunately, it required a degree of self-denial "far beyond the possession of the great mass of humanity".[15]

Nature had, however, placed a beneficial check on the natural sexual aggressiveness of males by making women sexually passive, in fact rather disinclined to participate in sexual relations at all. Husbands were to understand this diffidence in their wives, and above all to respect it. Far too many marriages were little more than legalized prostitution or arrangements by which husbands turned the right to enjoy sexual intercourse into a form of legalized rape.[16] "Be guarded, O husband!", Dr. Drake warned lustful men, "It is a woman's nature to forgive, but there comes a time when love and forgiveness have reached their limit, and love struggles vainly to rise above disgust and loathing." At the same time, though, she advised wives not to allow "little carelessnesses and thoughtless acts" to "invite attentions" which they would afterward repel. Best to preserve "womanly modesty" and "innate dignity" at all times.[17]

When men and women reached approximately age 45, the activity of the sexual organs would cease. Accordingly, two volumes of the Self and Sex series were designed to explain to the aging the impact of the menopause. Its main effect on sexual behaviour was flatly to rule out any further intercourse. The increased lassitude or weariness that a man of 45 would feel after the act was a warning from nature to avoid any further use of a secretion "which can now ill be spared". Sexual indulgence from now on would merely be throwing so many pellets of earth upon his coffin. Women, too, would find that sexual relations during and after the menopause would be positively harmful, and they also had to be particularly careful during this period not to arouse their husbands.[18] But in both cases nature offered returns that fully compensated for what had been lost. Not the least of these was "the grateful sense of relief" that "the stress of the sexual impulse is gradually passing away".[19]

Before the menopause men and women of all ages could take special measures to reduce the "stress of the sexual impulse", and thereby stave off the urge to fall into one of the several kinds of sexual excess. Physical exercise was recommended for everyone, particularly bicycling, horseback riding and calisthenics, as well as the use of dumbbells and Indian clubs by males. Cold baths or showers every morning, followed by a brisk rub-down with a coarse towel, were always helpful, especially for young men worried about excessive nocturnal emissions. A right diet throughout one's life was an essential complement of this regime, one which minimized the consumption of stimulating foods, such as spices, and animal foods, particularly meat. Regular evacuation of the bowels also seemed to reduce sexual propensities and contributed to general physical well-being. Further, the Rev. Stall advised that no young man troubled with sexual weakness could hope to attain entire relief while sleeping on or under bedclothes stuffed with feathers.[20] If none of this worked for a troubled young man, he could try tying a towel around his waist with a hard knot opposite the spine; by preventing him from lying on his back it would inhibit nocturnal emissions. If that failed, a footnote in *What a Young Man Ought Know* advised that the Sax Company, 105 South Broad St., Philadelphia, offered for 50¢ "An effective and satisfactory device, to prevent lying on the back and its attendant evils".[21]

More important, sexual propensities could only ultimately be reduced by a rigid avoidance of stimulating thoughts. "No man can look upon obscene pictures without the danger of photographing upon his mind that which he might subsequently be willing to give thousands of dollars to obliterate", Stall advised young men, after earlier warning them that "The appeal to the amative and sexual nature is so universal in novels that ... no young man or young woman should be permitted to read a novel before they arrive at the age of twenty-five".[22] The Roman Catholic confessional had revealed that nineteen out of every twenty fallen women confessed the beginning of their sad state to the modern dance, and the "debasing influences" of the theatre plunged more young men into vice and sin "than it would be possible accurately to imagine".[23] The more direct carnal temptations of the married state could and should be reduced by the use of separate beds, preferably separate bed-rooms, and by avoiding "the sexual excitement which comes daily by the twice-repeated exposure of dressing and undressing in each others presence".[24] Alcohol and tobacco were condemned throughout the series as both unhealthy in general and as sexual stimulants in particular.

Many other problems peripherally related to sexual behaviour were considered in the Self and Sex books, including the need for women's dress reform to avoid the destructive effects of the "corset curse" on feminine reproductive organs, the desirability of taking a healthy and normal view of both menstruation and the curious side-effects of the menopause in women,[25] the six-to eight-week period of total confinement necessary for mothers after giving birth, and methods of caring for prostate trouble in older men (a problem on which Stall advised from his own experience). Various theories of the sex determination of children were considered, the authors leaning to the belief that children conceived early in the menstrual cycle were girls, later in the cycle, boys.[26] Abortion was condemned as infanticide, the mere desire for which might cause the birth of a monstrosity or a potential murderer.[27] Too frequent child-bearing was recognized as a problem, but the use of birth-control devices as both ineffective and injurious. The authors did delineate the "safe" of the menstrual cycle when conception was unlikely, but generally felt that continence was the surest contraceptive (we may hope that concerned readers followed the latter advice because the recommended timing for the "safe" period was exactly wrong). Marriage was a divine institution; divorce was sanctioned only for adultery and on the condition that divorcees never remarry.[28]

The most important and most emphasized of the subsidiary themes was the role of heredity in human reproduction and development. The "Law of Heredity" doomed men and women to inherit both their physical structure and all their character traits from their ancestors. All physical deformities, most kinds of insanity, venereal diseases, proclivities to sexual excess, and potential addictions to alcohol, nicotine, and masturbation passed from parent to child. So, too, did the mental impressions felt by the pregnant woman, thus making it possible for women to shape the characters of their unborn children by thinking beautiful and uplifting thoughts during pregnancy, and also making it necessary for mothers to avoid upsetting experiences such as the sight of the physically deformed for fear of transmitting the same deformity to the infant in the womb.

Fortunately, the Law of Heredity was meliorated by the "Gospel of Heredity", the divine provision by which humans could overcome many, if not all, of the less fortunate effects of heredity and then transmit better qualities to succeeding generations. The Gospel of Heredity indeed held out the promise of infinitely improving the species through right physical and sexual living. In fact it was this fundamental duty to conserve and improve one's health for the sake of future generations that the authors of the "ought to know" books for women, both doctors, returned to repeatedly as the ultimate moral imperative that should bind their readers. By contrast, the Rev. Sylvanus Stall, in his books for men, was more concerned with salvation and the afterlife.[29]

Before attempting to place the ideas of the Self and Sex series in the context of North American thought on these subjects it may bear repeating that in 1915 the Methodist Church publishing house claimed these had been the best-selling books of their kind in Canada.

II

The Self and Sex series was reviewed in the *Canadian Journal of Medicine and Surgery* by Dr. B. E. McKenzie, Surgeon to the Toronto Orthopedic Hospital, Surgeon to the Out-Patient Department, Toronto General Hospital, and Assistant Professor of Clinical Surgery, Ontario Medical College for Women. He found that while the books had been written for non-medical readers, "yet they throw much needed light upon subjects that the medical practitioner is called to deal with constantly, and upon which he may profitably consult this excellent series". He took issue with the question of whether conception during a state of intoxication would produce alcoholic offspring, but without further quibbling concluded that "Every book of the series may be confidently recommended ... as containing the very best statement of the important information which should be supplied to every young man and woman, every boy and girl, entering upon the duties and responsibilities of life."[30]

This is not a surprising review, inasmuch as "Leading Canadian Medical Men" were at approximately the same time supplying exactly similar information on sexual problems to the Canadian public in the pages of one of the few native-Canadian home medical encyclopaedias, *The Family Physician, Or, Every Man His Own Doctor*. Here, too, masturbation destroyed beauty and manhood, leading to "absolute idiocy or a premature and most horrible death"; frequent nocturnal emissions were very harmful; children had to be shielded from late hours, sensational novels, questionable pictorial illustrations, love stories, the drama and the ball-room, all to avoid unnaturally hastening puberty; and engaged couples were commanded to exercise "caution and reserve" in their ordinary embraces because one impure, indelicate, or low word uttered in the ear of a truly chaste and virtuous woman may be destructive of her true happiness for all time to come".[31]

Clearly, then, there was little in the complex of sexual beliefs and maxims popularized by the Self and Sex series that Canadian doctors found objectionable.

On the simplest level much of this ready medical acceptance of what now seems to be quaint, ludicrous, and/or harmful can be explained by reference to the state of medical and scientific research in the late Nineteenth

Century. Doctrines of prenatal influences or "maternal impressions", for example, rested in large part on medical confusion about the physiological bond between mother and foetus during gestation. Doctors did not know the extent to which mental and physical shocks to a mother's system were transferred along with food and oxygen through the wall of the placenta. Lacking this basic physiological knowledge they had to pay attention to the many current stories about monstrosities and geniuses being the products of maternal impressions. Nineteenth Century medical journals are laced with reports of such cases.[32] Similarly, the key problem in the field of evolutionary thought—the questions of the inheritance of acquired characteristics—would only be finally clarified at the beginning of the Twentieth Century by the discovery of the mechanism of genetic transmission. Until then there was no basic contradiction between Darwinian thought and the "Law" and "Gospel" of Heredity.[33]

On the crucial issue of masturbation the medical profession had long been aware of the seemingly empirically-based conclusions of the first medical personnel to observe uncontrolled masturbation among large groups of people—the superintendents of asylums for the mentally ill. In a classic application of the *post hoc propter hoc* fallacy, these well-intentioned doctors (influenced as well by Eighteenth Century preconceptions) concluded that as much as fifty percent of mental illness stemmed from masturbation. In their concern they penned horrifying descriptions of the effects of the practice that were often copied from their reports by the authors of popular sex manuals. Two Canadian doctors, Joseph Workman and Daniel Clarke, successive superintendents of the Toronto Asylum for the Insane, contributed mightily to the Nineteenth Century masturbation scare in their respective 1865 and 1877 annual reports, anticipating everything that would be said about masturbation in the Self and Sex books. In fact, Workman's 1865 observations about the secret vice found a prominent place in one of the most popular post-Civil War American sex manuals, and were being reprinted in popular literature at least as late as 1911.[34] Although Canadian medical attitudes towards masturbation began to change gradually by the mid-1880's,[35] the up-to-date medical student of 1909 would still find in the seventh edition of William Osler's *The Principles and Practice of Medicine* that "sexual excess, particularly masturbation" was an important causal factor in hysteria, and that sexual excesses were in a number of instances responsible for neurasthenia or nervous exhaustion.[36]

By far the most influential factor shaping medical and popular attitudes towards sexuality was the persistence of vitalist concepts in physiological thought throughout the Nineteenth Century. Until late in the Century any systematic theory of the human organism almost by definition implied the belief in some vital force or vital principle uniting its parts and enervating it in its totality. This could be just simple "vital force" or "life force", or in some of the more esoteric medical systems it could be any or all of magnetism, electricity, galvanism, animal heat, nervous energy, or nerve force. Sexual activity was the function of the human system most obviously connected with transmitting forces vital to human existence—it was the activity that transmitted life itself. Accordingly, the identification of vital energy with sexual energy was made by virtually all writers on sexual problems in the Nineteenth Century.[37]

This was done in two basic ways. Those writers who followed the system of the Swiss doctor S.A. Tissot (whose 1758 book on onanism was a classic in the field) taught that male semen was pure condensed vital energy, secreted from the blood for the purpose of creating a new life—a concept summarized in the engaging phrase *totus homo semen est.* The other system, first popularized in North America by Sylvester Graham in the 1830's, saw the sex act as involving an enormous release of nervous energy, a force akin to electricity. This latter view, a variation of which became physiological orthodoxy in the last third of the Century, had among other things the merit of restoring the idea of some sexual sensitivity to women. Most sex manuals, however, including the Self and Sex books, mixed the two theories indiscriminately, and were generally muddled, usually dubious, about female sexuality.[38]

Whether male semen was pure vital force or whether sexual energy was simply another form of nervous energy, its expenditure was obviously a drain on the limited amount of vital energy in the human system. This is the heart of the matter. All the prohibitions and restrictions on sexual activity follow. Masturbation, nocturnal emissions, sexual intercourse itself, all represented outpourings of vital energy, the preservation of which was absolutely essential to the well-being of the human organism. As Sylvanus Stall told young men with emphasis, "Nature has provided us not only with the sacs for the retention of seminal fluid, but *its retention is necessary in order that this vitalizing and life-giving fluid may be reabsorbed into the system, and become the vitalizing and strength-giving source of added physical and intellectual power.*"[39]

Here, then, is what might be called the doctrine of creative sexual repression. Because sexual energy is vital energy, or life force, it is too important to the whole physical economy to be expended in autoerotism or mere sexual intercourse without procreation! Far better to repress urges to waste the energy in basically animal activities and instead use it for truly human, truly creative, intellectual and aesthetic purposes. In themselves sexual energy and man's sexual nature were good, and the act of propagating a new life by the transmission of life force was one of the great creative achievements open to man. The only thing evil or harmful about sexuality was the way it could be misused, abused, or indulged in irresponsibly, in other words wasted in noncreative activities.

(It appears that one of the implications of these vitalist physiologies was the belief that the second most demanding drain on vital energy was intellectual activity; thus the mind suffered most when vital force was expended in sexual activity. Therefore, idiocy was thought to be an even more common consequence of masturbation than death. Further, the idea of a competition between sex life and intellect as the major consumers of vital force seems to have provided the physiological underpinning for several Nineteenth and Twentieth Century popular beliefs: that the nervous, intellectual child or man was the most liable to have sexual problems; that negroes, who were obviously short of mental ability, must have enlarged sexual inclinations by way of explanation or compensation; that as civilization grew ever more complex, requiring the expenditure of ever more intellectual force, the stock of vital energy available for reproduction would be diminished—hence the falling birth rate in the most advanced western civilizations and fears that the most advanced "races" would be swamped by simpler peoples who had more energy available for copulation and reproduction. A.R.M. Lower's 1943 article, "*Two Ways of life: The Primary Antithesis of Canadian History*", seems to contain a representative expression of these latter fears in a Canadian setting, the physiological bases assumed.)[40]

The Self and Sex manuals were late products of a long North American tradition of home advice on sexual problems. Dozens of books on anatomy, physiology, marriage, parenthood, masturbation, etc., were churned out in the United States from the 1830's, most of them written by members of health cults or medical sects, including vegetarians, phrenologists, homeopaths, and hydropaths.[41] These authors and medical practitioners were stepping into a sort of medical vacuum created by the retreat of orthodox doctors into a medical eclecticism which for a time seemed to offer neither cures nor explanations of illness.[42] The new cultists were drawn to sexual problems partly because of orthodox medicine's reluctance to deal with them at all, partly because their systematic physiologies, usually throw-backs to the vitalism of earlier medical thought, seemed to lead directly to dislocations of vital energy as a basic cause of illness. Gradually, the regular medical profession stepped back into the field, but in so doing accepted and reinforced many of the ideas of the cultists. The influences of vegetarianism and the hydropathic (or "water-cure") system of medicine on sexual theories seem to have lingered on in the Self and Sex series' concern with reducing sexual passion by eliminating meat from the diet and by frequent bathing (and to this day Canadians continue to enjoy other legacies of the vegetarian-sexologists—the foods named after Sylvester Graham and the corn flakes and peanut butter invented by John Harvey Kellogg to make vegetarian dishes palatable at his Battle Creek Sanitarium. Kellogg's establishment was the great North American health-cure institute of the late Nineteenth Century, having enjoyed its first popularity catering to the young men and women terrified of the consequences of sexual excess portrayed in the director's best-selling sex manual, *Plain Facts for Old and Young*).[43]

The doctrine of creative sexual repression was intensely idealistic. Philosophic idealism was at the basis of the vitalist physiology that provided the foundations of the doctrine. Practical idealism was inherent in the work of the medical sectarians whose systems appealed to those who hoped for a medical millennium at a time when the orthodox profession was wallowing in uncertainty. The whole movement for physiologic and sexual reform was in every way connected with the outpouring of idealism in the form of a secularized evangelicalism that caused the ferment of reform movements in the United States in the 1840's and 1850's. The evangelists of sexual repression had extremely close links with antislavery work, the public health movement, the movement to liberate women—often, indeed to liberate them from male sexual tyranny—and with Utopian "perfectionists" such as the Shakers and John Humphrey Noyes' Oneida Community. As S.W. Nissenbaum has shown, even the founders of the American free love movement, the most radical product of "freedom's ferment" in the mid-Nineteenth Century, were imbued with the idealism of sexual repression; freedom to love, they taught, could be safely enjoyed about once every two years. In the post-Civil War years the institutionalized "Purity" movement—in which the Self and Sex authors were deeply involved—was the crystallization of this basic idealism, the determination to purify human life of everything that tempted or conduced to harmful mental and physical practices.[44] Further, it was precisely the metaphysical idealism of these new Puritans, stressing the ability of mind to "amputate matter," that led them to advocate the most rigid forms of state thought-control in order to protect young men and women from powerful ideas that would stimulate the material, animal passions of the body. Censorship was a form of idealistic reform. After all only a good idealist would believe that a young woman really could be ruined by a book.[45]

If this account seems to be becoming a bit thin on purely Canadian sexual thought, consider the work of Alexander Milton Ross, a Belleville boy who was introduced into American reform circles in the 1840's by the exiled Reformer Marshall Spring Bidwell. Ross took a medical degree in hydropathy in the United States, was led from friendship with leading abolitionists into active work in the South encouraging negroes to flee to Canada, was a close friend of reformers ranging from Garibaldi to John Brown, and was employed by Lincoln as a special agent in Canada during the Civil War. After the War he became one of the most renowned Canadian naturalists, was president of the vegetarian Food Reform Society of Canada, worked for temperance, women's suffrage and women's dress reform, took credit for securing Garibaldi a pension from the Italian government, and led the anti-vaccination crusade in Montreal in 1885 (on the ground that vaccination for smallpox was a deadly ruse on the part of the Establishment to avoid its moral and social responsibility for public health). In the midst of all these activities Dr. Ross concluded from studies of insane asylum reports that fully "ONE-THIRD" of all the insane had brought the curse upon themselves by "indulgence in an unphysiological habit practised in ignorance of the results". Finding that no voice of alarm was being raised in Canada about this "worm eating at the core of society, and doing more injury than all other diseases combined", Ross resolved to do his duty. In the quarter century after Confederation he distributed, he claims, 600,000 pieces of literature alerting the Canadian public to the evils of masturbation.[46] Crusading for sexual enlightenment was then, as it is now, a necessary part of the work of any thoroughgoing reformer dedicated to the perfection of the human condition.

III

The Self and Sex books were advertised extensively through the Methodist Church publishing house for at least fifteen years. It seems reasonable to assume at a minimum that they were standard reference works for Methodist ministers concerned with their own and their congregations' sexual problems (the Methodist minister, for example, who wrote Sir Wilfrid Laurier about the plight of a young lady whose husband had gone insane through self-abuse and abandoned her).[47] The series was also widely circulated by the ladies of the Canadian Woman's Christian Temperance Union, whose Department of Social Purity was specifically designed to promote the doctrine of sexual repression in all of its manifestations.[48] Dr. Ross's flood of anti-masturbation literature was supplemented by Dr. Daniel Clarke's circulation of 600 copies of his own 1877 report on masturbation and insanity. The letters from educators and clergymen included in Ross's autobiography suggest widespread, semi-underground fears of and campaigns against the secret vice in the two generations after Confederation.[49] So, too, do the notes on new cures for onanism and nocturnal emissions routinely printed in Canadian medical journals—such as the 1869 suggestion of Dr. George Wood that the application of a strip of isinglass adhesive plaster "worked like a charm" in cases of incurable masturbation (after tying the hands, using hair gloves, croton oil linament, moral suasion, and many other methods had failed).[50] In addition, anyone who has browsed through Nineteenth Century Canadian newspapers will have noticed the hundreds of brands of compounds, pills, tonics, magnetic and electrical devices offered by quack doctors, to cure, among other things, "sexual weakness", "unnatural drains", "failing manhood", and "diseases peculiar to women". The fact of these ads indicates that a large market existed; their language suggests a general belief in the basic equation of sexual energy and vital energy.[51]

Research into the activities of Y.M.C.A. groups, youth movements such as the Boy Scouts, and possibly certain religious denominations like the Salvation Army would almost certainly locate more evidence of the work of purity reformers in Canada before World War I. From 1906 to at least 1915 there existed a formal purity organization, the Canadian Purity-Education Association, staffed mainly by doctors and operating out of Toronto. In 1914 it sponsored 56 lectures on aspects of social purity, probably largely on the evils of venereal disease and masturbation. It distributed literature across Canada and in the United States, and reported in 1915 that its speakers were in great demand for mothers', girls' and women's meetings.[52]

In his recent book of memoirs, *Never Sleep Three in a Bed*, Max Braithwaite has finally broken the tacit conspiracy of silence about sexuality in Canadian history by describing his own sex education in Saskatoon in the 1920's. It featured books like *The Young Husband's Guide to Married Sex*, a horrifying tract on *The Solitary Vice*, and an earnest drill and hygiene teacher who with "jaw out-thrust" and "eyes flashing" lectured to young boys on the dangers of losing their manhood. "Take it out in good manly sport—such as boxing, wrestling, club-swinging and the rest", he told his pupils. "I was so ashamed I couldn't look at him", says Braithwaite.[53] Undoubtedly, there are similar stories to be told in memoirs yet unwritten.

We also know that in Ontario between 1905 and 1911, 13,463 public school boys received the "advanced" purity lectures given by the Ontario W.C.T.U.'s "Purity Agent", one Arthur W. Beall, a former missionary and teacher in Japan who had returned to Canada after suffering a nervous breakdown.[54] The main theme of these special talks was the danger involved in young boys bleeding away the "LIFE FLUID" from the "MALE PART". It had been secreted from the "LIFE GLANDS" and was needed to feed the brain and the nervous system. Repeated draining of this fluid would occasionally lead to death, but usually to something "ten thousand times worse than dying"—the fate of Henry, the farm boy from Perth County whose evil habits had led to hospitalization in the insane asylum. Nevertheless, Henry continued to bleed away the precious "LIFE FLUID", "until one day the doctors came along and cut off the two LIFE GLANDS just to keep the miserable dregs of a miserable existence from all being frittered away". The Henry incident was told in Lesson Nine of Mr. Beall's trail-breaking classes in sex education. The same lesson ended a few moments later with the boys all repeating after him, "The more you use the penis muscle, the weaker it becomes; but the less you use the penis muscle, the stronger it becomes."[55]

In 1911 the W.C.T.U. arranged to have the Ontario Department of Education take over this work and appoint Beall as a Special Lecturer.[56] He continued to lecture to Ontario pupils all through the 1920's and well on into the 1930's. The Department took no official notice of his work in its reports. But acquaintances of mine remember with no little vividness this little white-haired man, dressed in a flowing red-and-blue cloak, the expression on his face of a "benign Hindenburg", striding about their classrooms delivering what he now called his "eugenics" lectures in the 1930's—interesting young boys, it is thought, in masturbation for the first time in their lives.[57] When Arthur Beall died in 1939 the *Globe and Mail* hailed him as "one of the best informed men on educational matters in Canada."[58]

The doctrine of creative sexual repression represented the orthodox, even the "enlightened," sexual attitudes of those English-speaking Canadians who read about such problems before World War I. Indeed it was sexual orthodoxy throughout much of the Western world, and therefore I would be very surprised to find any significant variation of these attitudes in whatever literature in the French language on these questions that may have circulated in Canada.[59] In this paper I have tried to explain the doctrine of creative sexual repression and explore its paternity in medical and popular thought. This has been only a discussion of the *ideas* of sexuality held by well-informed Canadians of the period. It will be up to future research to correlate these ideas with the actual sexual *behaviour* of all Canadians. Such research might include studies of prostitution through police records, court cases, and army records, as well as analyses of illegitimacy rates, birthrates, and the time-lag between marriage and the birth of a first child. Probably Canadian sexual behaviour will be shown to be related to social class, and historians should be able to apply psychological and sociological tools to explain why some classes accepted extremely repressive ideas of sexuality both in theory and practice while others did not. When we finally know who believed what and which groups acted on their beliefs, then perhaps psychologists can explore the effects of various sexual attitudes on the people who held them or were exposed to them. As a preliminary observation I think we can safely say that the doctrine of sexual repression added somewhat to the anxieties of middle class Canadians.[60]

Whatever emerges from more sophisticated and detailed future studies, I would like to urge Canadian historians to take this esoteric form of social history seriously. It has been ignored in our literature to the point where our readers might well conclude that sex simply hasn't been a factor in Canadian life. Yet who can deny that the problem of coming to terms with the fact of sex has caused Canadians more concern than the activities of all their politicians combined?

Notes

1 I would like to record my debt for support in this and other work to my brother, the late Dr. James Quartus Bliss.

2 For further biographical information on Stall and Wood-Allen, see *Who's Who in America*, v. 2 (Chicago, 1901–02), 1072, 1260; on Drake, *Woman's Who's Who of America*, 1914–15 (New York, 1914), 258. The circulation claim is contained in the frontispiece of the 1908 revised edition of *What a Young Wife Ought to Know*. The best-selling claim is contained in the Briggs advertisement in *The Canadian Women's Annual and Social Service Directory* (Toronto, 1915), 325. The series was also regularly advertised in the *Christian Guardian* beginning in 1902. About 1908 most of the books in the series were slightly revised; in the late 1920s they were considerably rewritten and watered down. The Ryerson Press still distributed the series in Canada in the 1930s. All quotations are from the first edition.

3 Sylvanus Stall, *What a Young Man Ought to Know* (Philadelphia, 1897), 23.

4 Sylvanus Stall, *What a Young Husband Ought to Know* (Philadelphia, 1897), 125, 127.

5 Mary Wood-Allen, M.D., *What a Young Woman Ought to Know* (Philadelphia, 1898), 116.

6 Sylvanus Stall, *What a Young Boy Ought to Know* (Philadelphia, 1897), 104–05.

7 Ibid., 107.

8 Emma F. Angell Drake, M.D., *What a Young Wife Ought to Know* (Philadelphia, 1901), 239.

9 *Young Man*, 56–57.

10 Ibid., 72–77.

11 Ibid., 98, 140. Also 121: "It has for years been a serious question in our mind whether, for the protection of the pure, the government should not brand upon the forehead those who have this disease, so that they could always be recognized."

12 *Young Woman*, 230.

13 *Young Husband*, 95–96.

14 Ibid., 95.

15 Ibid., 87–88.

16 Ibid., chs. II, III, IX, X. Especially 49: "With rare exceptions, both of person and of instances, in married life all the sexual aggressiveness is with the male. Wives seldom seek the closer embraces of their husbands. They are generally indifferent; often absolutely averse. With the husband, while in perfect health, the conditions are quite the opposite; and the wisdom of the Creator is manifest in the fact that were the wife equally quickened by the same amative tendencies, the male nature would be called into such frequent and continuous exercise that the power of reproduction would be either totally destroyed or so impaired that the race would degenerate into moral, intellectual and physical pigmies. God has made the passivity of the wife the protection of her husband and a source of manifold blessing to her children.

"Upon the other hand, her uninterrupted and entire neglect of the sexual relation is wisely overcome, to the advantage of the wife, by her husband's greater sexual activity,..."

17 *Young Wife*, 84–85.

18 Sylvanus Stall, *What a Man of 45 Ought to Know* (Philadelphia, 1901), 78, 84; Emma F. Angell Drake, *What a Woman of 45 Ought to Know* (Philadelphia, 1902), 148, 157–58.

19 *Man of 45*, 60.

20 *Young Boy*, Part IV; *Young Man*, ch. III; *Young Woman*, chs. III, VIII, IX; feather beds, *Young Man*, 54.

21 *Young Man*, 89.

22 Ibid., 241, 33.

23 Ibid., 243, 245.

24 *Young Husband*, 100; *Young Wife*, 85.

25 Women were thought to exhibit such extraordinary behaviour during the menopause—dim vision, loss of voice, spitting of blood, hysteria, melancholia,

loss of religious interest, etc.—that Stall took pains to convince their spouses not to have such women removed to insane asylums. *Man of 45*, chs. XVI-XVIII.

26 *Young Husband*, 288. Discussing "signs of fruitful conjunction," i.e., conception, Stall noted that "with some women the act of conception is attended with great emotion, a sense of unusual pleasure, and even of a tremor, in which all parts of the body may participate. Sometimes it is followed by a sense of weakness." Ibid., 95. This is the only hint that the authors of the series were aware of the female orgasm.

27 Ibid., 159.

28 All of Stall's thought was permeated with Christian verbiage. Early in his book for husbands he pleaded with his readers to practice Christianity, outlining in passing his remarkable sociology: one should divide society into two classes, "and then the result is seen at a glance. In the one class you have the defiers of God and man. To this class belongs every man who staggers, reels and falls into the gutter, every tramp who walks the road, and nine-tenths of all persons who fill our almshouses. It includes, with scarcely an exception, every man and woman who fill our prisons and reformatory institutions; those who crowd the great tenements and live in filth and squalor in the slums of our cities; those whose bodies reek with physical and moral rottenness—these, and many others, constitute the class of the ungodly, and no attentive person can fail to observe that this is the character of that portion which the ungodly have in this world.

"Now, turn to the other class. Walk up and down the streets where you find the most comfortable homes, the largest dwellings, and abodes of the most affluent and respectable in any city, and then answer the question, whether or no the wealth of the nation is not to-day largely in the hands of Christian men and Christian women? These are the people who have the best credit, who can draw checks for the largest amounts. Among this class you will find the most influential in business, the owners of our largest mercantile establishments. Men who direct and control the commerce of the world. Men who are at the head of our largest banking institutions, railroad and other corporations. But not only so. These are the people who dwell in the best homes, who eat the best food, who have the largest amount of material comforts. They are the people who enjoy the best health, who have the brightest minds, who produce the best books, the most helpful literature. They have the brightest eyes and the strongest bodies, and when cholera and plague come and sweep away men and women by the thousands, it scarcely ever crosses the line which separates these from the intemperate and the vicious, who go down before these scourges like grass before the sickle. Truly, my dear friend, if you are to look at it only from the lowest plane of present good and material comfort, godly living will bring to you the promise of life that is *to come*,..." *Young Husband*, 71–73. This passage was reprinted without alteration in the 1933 revision of the book.

29 On heredity see *Young Husband*, ch. XVII; *Young Women*, chs. XXVIII-XXX; *Young Wife*, ch. XI. On maternal impressions, *Young Husband*, ch. XVIII; *Young Wife*, ch. VIII.

30 *Canadian Journal of Medicine and Surgery*, XII, 2, Aug. 1902, 147–48.

31 *The Family Physician* (Musson, Toronto, n.d.), 328, 164, 319, 332. Medical librarians have been unable to date this book; internal evidence suggests 1890–1905. The publishers deliberately left it undated to maintain the aura of up-to-date authority.

32 In *Aedoelogy, A Treatise on Generative Life* (New York, 1892), Dr. Sydney Barrington Elliott includes a list of several hundred articles on prenatal influences. For Canada, see J. Draewiecki, "The Influence of Maternal Impressions Upon the Foetus," *Canada Lancet*, 24, Dec. 1891, 110–13, in which it is concluded, "I am thoroughly convinced that different psychical and physical defects ... are in most instances the results of moral impressions derived from the surroundings of the mother."

33 Mark H. Haller, *Eugenics: Hereditarian Attitudes in American Thought* (New Brunswick, New Jersey, 1963), 59–61. Haller notes that the new theories denying the inheritance of acquired characteristics seriously distressed social reformers, who were now told that the achievements of one generation would not be passed on to the next. For this reason the Self and Sex authors also rejected the new doctrine that had just been proclaimed. See Wood-Allen, *Young Man*, 236–37.

34 *Report of the Inspectors and the Medical Superintendent of the Provincial Lunatic Asylum, Toronto, for the Year 1865* (Toronto, 1866), 35–43; *Report of the Medical Superintendent of the Asylum for the Insane, Toronto, 1877* (Toronto, 1878), 18–26. Workman's report was initially reprinted in John Cowan, M.D., *The Science of a New Life* (New York, 1869) and as part of the excerpts from Cowan in *The Education of Sex: A Compilation From the Writings and Teachings of Many Eminent Physicians and Authorities ... Forming a Textbook on the Physiology of Marriage, the Phenomena of Life, Existing Social Evils and their Needed Reforms* (Philadelphia, 1911). For a definitive account of medical attitudes towards masturbation see E.H. Hare, "Masturbatory Insanity: The History of an Idea," *Journal of Mental Science*, 108, January 1962, 1–25.

35 Stephen Lett, "The Relationship of Insanity to Masturbation," *Canada Lancet*, 19, August 1887, 360–63, argued that masturbation was more a symptom than a cause of mental disorder; the practice was so widespread that it could not possibly cause insanity. See also Hare, "Masturbatory Insanity." As Prof. Frank MacKinnon pointed out in the discussion at the initial presentation of this paper, other doctors seem to have held similar common-sense attitudes to the phenomenon.

36 (New York, 1909), 1077, 1087.

37 Among numerous other sex manuals that have been consulted the most representative are Cowan, *The Science of a New Life*, J.H. Kellogg, *Plain Facts for Old and Young* (Burlington, Iowa, 1879; revised edition, 1886); Diocletian Lewis, *Chastity, or Our Secret Sins* (Philadelphia, New York, Boston, Cincinnati, Chicago, 1875); George H. Napheys, *The Transmission of Life* (Philadelphia, 1870). At an indeterminate later date the Hunter, Rose Co. of Toronto published an "Enlarged and Revised" edition of Napheys. It is slightly more technical and moderate than the Self and Sex books, but not significantly different. The Cowan book, copies of which circulated in Canada, represents the extreme of Nineteenth Century sexology: it calls for total vegetarianism to repress sexual desires and marital intercourse no more frequently than every two years—for the sole purpose of conception.

38 On Graham and Tissot see S.W. Nissenbaum, "Careful Love: Sylvester Graham and the Emergence of Victorian Sexual Theory in America, 1830–40" (unpublished Ph.D. thesis, Wisconsin, 1968), esp. ch. 6. The Latin phrase is quoted in Lewis, *Chastity*, 245. For more orthodox concepts of nervous energy, neurasthenia, and the belief in the conservation of energy see Charles F. Rosenberg, "The Place of George M. Beard in Nineteenth-Century Psychiatry," *Bulletin of the History of Medicine*, 36, 3 (1962), 245–59; Rosenberg, "Science and American Social Thought," in David Van Tassel and Michael G. Hall, eds., *Science and Society in the United States* (Homewood, Illinois, 1966).

39 *Young Man*, 75. Also Cowan, *Science of a New Life*, 91–92; Lewis, *Chastity*, 25, 245–; Kellogg, *Plain Facts*, 277.

40 This concept also seems to have been popularized by Tissot. In *De La Santé Des Gens de Lettres* (Lausanne, 1770) he claimed that excessive mental activity resulted in the same disorders as masturbation. On the later ideas of industrial society as consumer of nervous energy see Rosenberg, "The Place of George M. Beard in Nineteenth-Century Psychiatry," and John Duffy, "Mental Strain and 'Overpressure' in the Schools: A Nineteenth-Century Viewpoint," *Journal of the History of Medicine and Allied Sciences*, XXIII, I (June 1968), 63–79. For fears of the impact of education on reproduction, see Arthur Wallace Calhoun, *A Social History of the American Family* (Cleveland, 1919), v. III, 92–93. There is a clear statement of the myth of negro sexuality in Eugene S. Talbot, *Degeneracy: Its Causes, Signs, and Results* (London, 1898), 60. The best statement of the general concept of the problem is in W.H. Walling, *Sexology* (Philadelphia, 1904), 97: "A learned author has said that one must choose between leaving to posterity works of genius or children." The Lower article is reprinted in C.C. Berger, ed., *Approaches to Canadian History* (Toronto, 1967).

41 American historians are just beginning to investigate this body of literature. Nissenbaum, "Careful Love," is invaluable—and includes a comprehensive bibliography of primary sources. See also Sidney Ditzion, *Marriage, Morals and Sex in America* (New York, 1953), and Eric John Dingwall, *The American Woman: A Historical Study* (London, 1956). Gerald Carson, *The Cornflake Crusade* (New York, 1957), ostensibly a study of the breakfast food industry, is an excellent survey of the health cults, unfortunately omitting the sexual emphasis.

42 Richard H. Shyrock, *The Development of Modern Medicine* (Philadelphia, 1936), chs. IX-XIII; Joseph K. Kett, *The Formation of the American Medical Profession: The Role of Institutions, 1780–1860* (New Haven, 1968), 65 ff.

43 On the Kelloggs and Battle Creek see Carson, *Cornflake Crusade*; Ronald M. Deutsch, *The Nuts Among the Berries* (New York, 1961); and Horace B. Powell, *The Original Has This Signature—"W.K. Kellogg"* (Englewood Cliffs, New Jersey, 1956). Although these authors ignore Kellogg's sex manuals the inference about the growth of the Sanitarium is reasonable in view of Kellogg's discussion of masturbation and his work with its victims in *Plain Facts*. His methods of treatment ranged from circumcision and the use of metal cages through suturing the male foreskin shut and applying pure carbonic acid to the female clitoris. *Plain Facts*,

294–96. Kellogg also argued that nocturnal emissions in males were no more necessary than vomiting. Consistent with his theories he remained continent throughout his life although he was married and adopted several dozen children; Mrs Kellogg was active in purity work with the W.C.T.U.

44 Nissenbaum, "Careful Love"; on the purity movement see David J. Pivar, "The New Abolitionism: The Quest for Social Purity, 1876–1900" (unpublished Ph.D. thesis, University of Pennsylvania, 1965). The best published discussion and interpretation of "freedom's ferment" is still Gilbert Seldes, *The Stammering Century* (New York, 1928, reissued, 1964). See also Carson, *Cornflake Crusade*, and the discussion of the Shakers and the Oneida Community in Lewis, *Chastity*.

   Noyes' doctrine of "male continence" involved complete *coitus reservatus*; male incontinence, or sexual intercourse to orgasm, was nothing more than masturbation. Vital forces would only be expended for the purpose of procreation. Although conservative sexologists were repelled by the Oneida community's adoption of communal marriage and distrusted the idea of male continence, the doctrine lived on and ultimately came to Canada in the form of Dr. Alice Stockham's book on *Karezza* (orign. pub., 1896, rev. ed., 1905) or "a controlled sexual relation." When properly practised Karezza represented sexual "expression" rather than "repression" and was also an effective method of contraception. *Karezza* was given a most enthusiastic review at the 1896 Dominion Convention of the Canadian W.C.T.U. by the Superintendent of the Department of Purity in Literature, Arts and Fashion, who recommended that it "should be put into the hands of every young man before marriage." *Report of the Ninth Convention of the Dominion Woman's Christian Temperance Union, 1896* (Montreal, 1897), 63. In 1911 McClelland and Goodchild published a Canadian edition of Dr. Stockham's earlier *Tokology* (first edition, 1883), a book on the "science of midwifery" which advocated painless child-birth through dress reform and vegetarian dietetics. *Tokology* is also one of the clearest demonstrations of the link between the women's rights movement and the doctrine of sexual repression.

45 Popular idealism, the belief in the supremacy of mind over matter, permeated North American popular culture in the late Nineteenth Century. See, for example, Donald Meyer, *The Positive Thinkers* (New York, 1965), and Richard Weiss, *The American Myth of Success* (New York, 1969). Doctrines of "thought power" and the "mind cure" reached their apogee in Christian Science. Their sexual implications came to their logical culmination in 1890 when Josephine Curtis Woodbury, a Christian Scientist, announced that she had had a virginal conception (the child was named "Prince of Peace"). The Self and Sex books for women stressed thought power to the point where denials had to be made that they were preaching Christian Science doctrine.

46 Alexander Milton Ross, *Memoirs of a Reformer* (Toronto, 1893); for his anti-masturbation work see 215–1, 261–65. Further biographical data is in H.J. Morgan, *The Canadian Men and Women of the Time* (Toronto, 1898), 883–84.

47 P.A.C. *Laurier Papers*, 62267–69, Rev. W.J. Waddell to Laurier, Feb. 1, 1902.

48 See the *Reports* of Dominion W.C.T.U. Conventions, 1890–1911.

49 Ross, *Memoirs of a Reformer*, 261–65.
50 "A Prevention for Priapism, due to Onanism," *Canada Medical Journal* Nov. 1869, 246–47. This suggestion was reprinted in Napheys, *The Transmission of Life*. For a suggestion of suturing with silver wire see "The Prevention of Masturbation," *Canadian Journal of Medical Science*, Nov. 1876, 394. On the application of blisters and tonics to cure seminal emissions see "The Treatment of Seminal Emissions," *Canada Lancet*, July 1889, 340.
51 Phrases taken from advertisements in the Toronto *Globe*, Sept. 1, 6, 9, 1899. The quacks did their best business playing on the fears of venereal disease ("blood poisoning"), impotence, and sterility. One of the curious implications of the doctrine of sexual repression was that too much sexual activity led to the inability to perform at all, vital energy having been exhausted. Accordingly, the less one performed the better one performed. The Self and Sex books repeatedly warned their readers against falling into the hands of quacks, particularly those who offered to cure venereal disease. To some extent, of course, the sex writers were competing in the same market with the quacks.
52 *The Canadian Woman's Annual and Social Service Directory*, 273.
53 Max Braithwaite, *Never Sleep Three in a Bed* (Toronto, 1969), 148.
54 Figures compiled from *Reports* of Ontario W.C.T.U. Conventions, 1902–1912. For biographical data on Beall see the Toronto *Globe and Mail*, Nov. 11, 1939, and H.J. Morgan, *Canadian Men and Women of the Time* (Toronto, 1912), 72.
55 Arthur W. Beall, *The Living Temple: A Manual on Eugenics for Parents and Teachers* (Whitby, 1933), 62–65, 67. This little book is a word by word account of Beall's lessons.
56 *Report of the Minister of Education, Province of Ontario, for the Year 1911* (Toronto, 1912), 269.
57 Interview with the Rev. Harold Hendershot, April 1970.
58 Nov. 11, 1939.
59 Particularly because of the affinity of the doctrine with Roman Catholic sexual thought and ultimately the ideas of St. Paul. Although Nineteenth Century science challenged Christian ideology in many fields, in the area of sexual thought it obviously reinforced Christian beliefs. This is probably the chief reason why liberalism came to sex so much later than to other fields of human activity.
60 In chapter one of *The Other Victorians* (New York, 1966) Stephen Marcus attempts a general explanation of Nineteenth Century sexual orthodoxy (as mirrored in Dr. William Acton's popular writings) as functions of an "essentially mechanical," "primitive form of materialism," that relied heavily on an economic model of scarcity, specifically the equation of male semen with money. This is largely incorrect. The doctrine of sexual repression was permeated with idealism. While the analogy with capitalism does hold, there is no evidence of a causal relationship. The economics of sexual scarcity arose out of the Newtonian concept of the universe and the second law of thermodynamics and were thus independent of the economics of capital scarcity.

Mariana Valverde

"Families, Private Property, and the State: The Dionnes and the Toronto Stork Derby," *Journal of Canadian Studies* 29.4 (1994–95)

In the middle of the Great Depression, a number of state institutions in Ontario (the legislature, the judiciary, the Attorney-General's office) felt called upon to administer two sets of "problem" families. One was the Dionnes, the other those competing in the Toronto Stork Derby. The former "group" was perceived by the Hepburn government as two distinct families: the Quintuplets on the one hand, and their five siblings and parents on the other. In 1934, the Ontario government declared itself the true parent of the newborn Quintuplets and made a complete physical as well as legal separation between them and their kin. Eventually the Quints were legally and physically reunited with the other Dionnes, at a time when their fame and fortune had in any case been rather exhausted, and control over their trust fund was no longer a source of wages to many retainers and of tourist revenue to the province. A close analysis of the government documents of the Dionne case reveals that the Quintuplets were not dealt with as children in need of state protection: the Children's Aid Society was not involved.[1] Rather, they were managed as natural resources or scenic wonders requiring nationalization. In other words, the guardianship of the five little girls had very little to do with child welfare or family policy; rather, it became an aspect of provincial economic policy. Just as the "natural beauty" of Niagara Falls has been sold to tourists and exploited by Ontario Hydro, so too the apparently priceless Quintuplets were economically exploited by their legal father, the government of Ontario.

The unusual degree of government intervention in the Dionne case stands in contrast to the more laissez-faire position taken by the same government in another regulatory dilemma, namely the so-called Toronto Stork Derby of 1926–38. The Stork Derby was occasioned by an eccentric lawyer's will leaving a very large amount of money to the Toronto woman giving birth to the largest number of children over the subsequent 10 years. Immediately after the will was probated, in December of 1926, the Conservative government at Queen's Park attempted to declare the Stork Derby clause invalid on the grounds that it was "disgusting" and against the public interest. However a public outcry, mostly from women's groups, managed to reverse the government's decision: both Premier George Henry's government and the subsequent Hepburn government let the various mothers and other potential heirs fight the case out in the courts, with little political interference. The courts, concerned with safeguarding the principle of the autonomy of property owners, decided to uphold the will against the claims of distant relatives, but only after resolving tricky issues regarding the moral and legal status of both children and mothers.

A comparison of these two cases raises some interesting questions about the role of the state in the administration of reproduction. The relationship between the state and mothers and children is always analyzed under the rubric of family policy or social policy, but the present study shows that at least some children and mothers were managed and administered through processes normally associated with the regulation of the economy. Property, rather than family, is the central category in both the Dionne and the Stork Derby cases, casting some doubt on historians' generalizations about the 20th century's view of childhood as a sentimental, non-economic category. At a theoretical level, this study shows that instead of assuming the family and the economy to be fixed realms with unchanging boundaries, they might be better regarded as categories in flux, which the state can invoke with astonishing flexibility.[2] What is and is not a family question and, even more surprising, what is or is not a child, turns out to be largely a matter of which administrative techniques are brought to bear on a particular situation.

"A HUMAN GOLDMINE TO THEIR PROVINCE": THE PATERNAL STATE AND THE DIONNE QUINTUPLETS

Elzire Dionne, a 25-year-old francophone farm woman living in the village of Corbeil near North Bay, Ontario gave birth to five identical girls in May of 1934. The attending anglophone doctor, Dr. Allan R. Dafoe, did not believe the tiny babies would survive, and most probably neither did the parents. Oliva Dionne, their father, signed a contract—which the mother, extremely sick as she was, refused to co-sign—with Chicago World Fair promoters, promising to let the girls be exhibited if and when they were sufficiently healthy. In the late 20th century public displays of unusual human beings have virtually disappeared under the weight of ideas about "privacy," but such displays, either in freak shows or in the sanitized displays of modern science, were still relatively common in the 1930s. Nevertheless, both Canadian and American press reports painted the parents as ruthless baby-sellers. The negative publicity prompted the Ontario government to obtain a judicial order taking the children away from their parents' custody and control. The *Globe* reported: "Acting in his function as *parens patriae*—father of the people— [Attorney-General] Mr. Roebuck has obtained ... a judicial order appointing guardians for the quintuplets, and so defeated the 'perfidious contract.'" Roebuck, posing as the chivalrous defender of a feminized Canadian nation, stated that "If exploiters from American cities come to Canada to pull off this sort of racket, they need not expect the Attorney-General's office or the courts to stand idly by."[3]

The guardians named were all male and all Liberal, and included Dr. Dafoe but excluded both parents. The records of this first guardianship were removed from the government records by then Minister of Public Welfare, David Croll.[4] That extant evidence, however, clearly shows that Dr. Dafoe behaved as if he were the only guardian, signing commercial contracts involving the Quintuplets as well as his own increasingly famous self.

The government had a shiny new hospital built across the road from the Dionne farm. The babies were placed there under the care of nurses, and Dr. Dafoe put very strict restrictions on the Dionne family's right to visit them. Louise de Kiriline, Dafoe's second in command, later admitted that she had treated the parents and five older Dionne siblings as nothing but unhygienic nuisances.[5] The parents complained that they had to put on surgical masks when in attendance, while famous visitors, including provincial politicians, were photographed holding the babies without any fear of germs.

The hospital's widely publicized medical equipment, including the new reproductive technology of incubators, created the impression that the children were very delicate and needed to be away from the family home, when in fact the babies had survived their crucial first weeks with minimal technology. To polish even further its paternal image, the government claimed that it had spent $20,000 on the hospital, when in fact the funds had come from the Red Cross and private donations.[6]

In March of 1935, when the Quintuplets were 10 months old, the government sought to regularize the guardianship through a special law making the girls wards of "His Majesty," with the Crown's authority vested in David Croll, head of the new Ministry of Public Welfare. The crucial clauses of the law were No. 4, by which the province assumed direct control over any commercial contracts involving the Quints (thus marginalizing the enterprising Dr. Dafoe), and No. 6, by which the estates of the Quintuplets were vested in the minister of welfare.[7] In a change of policy, however, the father was also named as a guardian, though his opinion was to be subject to "the jurisdiction and direction of the said Minister." The mother was not included, either at the time or later when she requested that she and the other mothers be added to the board of guardians.

During the debate on this bill, the government revealed that it was by no means rejecting the father's original idea of displaying the sisters: "the government is also considering improvements to the Dafoe hospital that may include a large glass-covered solarium where tourists and visitors would be liable to see the quintuplets."[8] The solarium eventually expanded to include a whole complex of buildings, complete with a parking lot for 1000 cars and several souvenir shops (one owned by the midwives who had attended the Quintuplets' birth, and one owned by Oliva Dionne).[9] Quintland, as this attraction was predictably named, soon drew as many tourists as Niagara Falls. Speaking before the Canadian Association of Tourist and Publicity Bureaus, Dr. Dafoe boasted that his "winsome charges" had attracted 400,000 tourists to North Bay in 1938 alone, whereas the snowy peaks of the Rockies had only managed to draw 200,000 to Banff.[10] The Quintuplets were exhibited to tourists twice a day. The crowds were supposedly contained behind one-way glass, but the girls later said that although the glass did not allow them to see their visitors well, they were aware of them and "performed" accordingly. It is, of course, not possible to generalize about the motives of the hundreds of thousands of people who used the relatively new leisure activity of motoring to visit Quintland.[11] One can nevertheless speculate that the Quintuplets offered North American middle-class families on holidays a certain Shirley Temple cuteness combined with a uniquely Canadian emphasis on scenic rural ruggedness (symbolized by the stained logs covering the exterior of the nursery building).

In addition, Quintland seemed to have functioned as a post-Christian fertility shrine. Every day in the summer, trucks from the Ontario Department of Public Works delivered pebbles from nearby Lake Nipissing to Quintland. Made available to tourists as "stones from the quints' playground," these seem to have been popularly regarded as fertility amulets.[12]

Misleading information about public funds spent on the hospital was part of a larger government strategy. Very few people seemed to know that the doctor, the parents, the nurses, the business manager and the security guards were all paid out of the Quints' own money (the trust fund controlled first by the minister of public welfare and later by the official guardian, P.D. Wilson). The business manager was the highest paid employee of the trust fund, which reveals something of the guardianship's character. The trust fund's function as a fiscal goose laying golden eggs, reversing the usual flow of welfare state expenditures on children, is further demonstrated by the fact that quite a number of provincial officials, including the Ontario Provincial Police posted in Quintland, were paid out of the children's money, instead of the government payroll. The government's records contain many letters from Ontarians hoping to obtain employment in the privately funded but publicly controlled Quint enterprise. People offering their services as teachers or general help often mentioned their commitment to the Liberals as a job qualification, in keeping with the patronage practices of the time.

During the relatively profitable year of 1938, expenses billed to the trust fund included $8737 for administrative salaries, $4900 for legal fees, $2918 for medical fees, $4748 as parents' allowance, and $4019 paid to private security and public police. Although complete financial records do not exist for every year, there are enough records to suggest that the 1938 level of expenditures was typical. (For comparison purposes, the excess of revenue over expenditures for 1935–36 was $162,969, and for 1936–37 was $359,524; the largest source of revenue was Hollywood movie contracts.)[13]

In later years, this pork-barrel effect was compounded by the curious fact that both the judge who oversaw the trust fund's accounts and the official guardian decided to pay themselves for going over the accounts.[14] P.D. Wilson clearly had become used to seeing the Quints' trust fund as the province's, and hence his own, money. Every conceivable expense, from trips to New York to meet with legal counsel to the fish and chips Wilson regularly ate in North Bay hotels, was charged not to his government department but to the trust fund. Despite this reality, David Croll misled the legislature about the direction of the flow of dollars, reassuring the opposition that the government was not squandering public money on the Quints: "We regard what the province has done as a whole-hearted contribution from all the people of the province."[15]

The trust fund paid for at least some of the expenses of Canada's leading child psychologist, Dr. William Blatz, whose research assistants studied the girls' physical and behavioural characteristics in obsessive detail. Billing one's research subjects is, needless to say, not a common practice among psychologists, but once again powerful men did not hesitate to dip into the fund set up for the "protection" of the girls.[16] Blatz's actions were not, however, simple researcher's greed. In his view they were fully justified by the Quintuplets' status as servants of science. In a remarkable passage in his popular book on the girls, he expresses pleasure at the fact that in the management of the Dionne family, "no petty consideration of individual rights" has been allowed to intrude. The whole passage is worth quoting as an example of the discourses—scientific in this case, but similar to those employed by the media and by the government—that constructed the girls as indebted to the very people who exploited them. Using the language of capital investment in a way that would have warmed the business manager's heart, he wrote:

> It will be their responsibility to show some day that the care and effort that is expended on childhood returns dividends in the form of a happily adjusted adult. This is the first price which the children have to pay. It is needless to emphasize the responsibility of the Guardians in this connection. Happily, to date no petty consideration of individual rights have been permitted to interfere with the carrying out of this trust.[17]

It is curious that, in Dr. Blatz's narrative, the five children are envisaged as turning into one "happily adjusted adult," rather than five adults. And indeed, neither Blatz's management of scientific objects nor the official guardian's practices reveal any concern for the psychological growth of the girls as individuals. In the thousands of pages of documents in the official guardian's files, it is difficult to discover the Quintuplets' names. They are always treated as a single entity—with the significant exception of the "Income tax" file (by far the fattest in the collection). Wilson thought that if the girls were considered to be individuals for income tax then the trust fund would be subject to a lower rate of income tax. He fought a long battle with Ottawa on this point, since Ottawa considered the fund a single income. Eventually Wilson won: the five identical income tax returns filed every year are the only official document in which they are consistently individuated.[18]

Unconcerned with the effect on the girls of always showing them as a group and never for a moment separating them, the guardians were equally unconcerned about the possible ramifications of their "performer" status. When some press reports suggested that the daily exhibitions of the girls might not be good for their mental health, the guardians quickly called in Canada's leading pediatrician, Dr. Alan Brown. After playing with the girls for a short time he had no hesitation in submitting a very brief and very general report stating that the girls were psychologically healthy. No stranger to the commercial world since leading a team that invented the baby cereal Pablum, the chief physician of Toronto's prestigious Hospital for Sick Children wrote: "the showing of the children under the present plan appears to have had no effect upon them either mentally or physically, and in fact, I believe that if necessary the time could be extended to one hour."[19] Dr. Brown's advice appears to be a prescription to improve the health of Ontario's tourist industry rather than to benefit the girls.

The most graphic evidence of the government's perception of the Quintuplets as a godsend for the provincial coffers is found in the documents regarding the province's effort to have the federal parliament pass a special "Quintuplet" trade mark law in early 1937. This act to copyright the word "Quintuplet," its synonyms and French translations, was sought in order to prevent manufacturers from using references to the Quints in advertising without paying royalties to the trust fund. Expensive lawyers in the United States as well as on Bay Street concurred that the peculiar law, effectively copyrighting a common noun, would not stand judicial scrutiny, since only names of products could be trademarked. The lawyers had to tell the guardians that the Quintuplets were not exactly products in the eyes of the law.

Nevertheless, the provincial Attorney-General's department, acting on the assumption that even if the Quintuplets were not legally products they could be administered as such without political repercussions, proceeded to obtain from Ottawa a badly drafted law. In this the provincial government was influenced by legal opinions highlighting the scarcely legal but importantly symbolic value of making the children into products with registered trade marks. New York lawyer Arthur Garfield Hays put it frankly:

The obtaining of some trade-marks, the licencing of the names and the reputation of the Quintuplets has resulted in a general public belief that these terms should be regarded as a monopoly. Business men hesitate to infringe when threatened with a law suit. We have on occasion been hard put to it to lay a foundation for legal rights when we have been squarely faced with the question, but we have not yet failed in persuading any such user to cease his unfair use. The argument that a law suit for infringement would publicize the user as one who is attempting to take money from babies, has usually been effective as a deterrent.[20]

Meanwhile, of course, Mr. Hays himself was collecting thousands of dollars from the babies' trust fund.[21] Like so many other people, most of them professional men, he was no doubt glad to obtain such credit-worthy customers in the middle of the Depression.

The final irony is that the government's attempt to protect its monopoly over the valuable word "Quintuplets" was couched in the language of chivalrous protection. The Quintuplet copyright act read: "hereas it has been, by petition, represented that it is in the interests of the above named quintuplets and of the people of Canada that a special Act be passed to protect the said quintuplets against exploitation...."[22]

There is evidence that by the early 1940s some people began to suspect that the rhetoric of state benevolence was but a cover for public greed. In an influential article in an American magazine, Lillian Barker noted in 1941 that the Government of Ontario could not have foreseen "that such human mites would soon become a human gold mine to the province."[23] But by then, the government's paternal image was in any case tarnished due partly to the efforts of Catholic leaders in both the US and Canada to "reunite the family," and most importantly to Oliva Dionne's ultimately successful mobilization of Franco-Ontarian interests on his behalf. Oliva Dionne began to work closely with the Association Canadienne-Française de l'Education de l'Ontario (ACFEO), and found in this association a useful ally in his battle against Dr. Dafoe for control of the girls. The ACFEO in turn saw the Quintuplets, and specifically their education, as an important site for the ongoing battle for francophone education rights. But what was for the ACFEO an issue of language politics appears, in the minutes of the guardians' meetings, as a purely financial issue. Business manager Keith Munro, expressing no opinion at all on the merits of French vs. English education, constantly reminded the guardians that the commercial value of the children would be raised considerably if they learned to speak English. The other guardians, including Oliva Dionne, quite agreed. On one occasion Munro deplored the "loss of revenue" that was taking place due to the girls' poor English, and so Oliva Dionne agreed to cooperate with his adversary Dr. Dafoe in writing the government yet again to request an English teacher.[24] From outside the guardianship, Munro was supported and pressured by manufacturers holding Quintuplet contracts, as shown in a letter from the American Grocers' Association: "Everyone with whom I talked tells me that the children are going to be much more valuable from an advertising standpoint after they have learned to speak English.... This is straight from the shoulder, Keith. But they [advertising executives] informed me: 'Get these kids speaking English, and they'll have great advertising value!'"[25] The government also wanted to increase the advertising and tourist value of the Quintuplets, but Dionne's actions as a committed Franco-Ontarian (as distinguished from his rather different actions as a guardian) had caused political headaches at Queen's Park. Eventually Wilson resigned himself to losing some potential financial benefits for the sake of political peace. His resistance worn down by constant harassment from Dionne and from the ACFEO's legal counsel, Wilson wrote an exasperated memo to the Attorney-General recommending that the Quints' education be entrusted to French-speaking nuns, since "the parents would, perhaps, be more amenable to their authority, or at least more amenable to them than to any other authority."[26]

In any case, by 1940–41 the commercial value of the Quintuplets was on the wane. Even if the business agent had been able to maximize their modest acting talents and their fluency in English, this would not have sufficed to maintain the previous level of revenues. The children were no longer babies, but rather ordinary looking girls; they were no longer associated with the "medical miracle" imagery which defined their identities as babies; and the war had turned the public's attention to other matters. Thus, the campaign by francophone groups to return the Quintuplets to their parents could be allowed to succeed without serious harm to the provincial treasury, and with some benefit to the provincial government's legitimation problems vis-à-vis francophones. The Depression was in any case over, and many of those who had fed from the Quintland trough moved on—business manager Keith Munro, for instance, set up his own advertising firm on Madison Avenue.

By 1942 Wilson worried that the Quintuplets might lose their commercial value altogether: "It must ever be kept in mind, in view of the general conditions, of the possibility of the earning power of the quintuplets falling below their necessary expenditures. In other words, the time will come when the capital will have to be drawn upon for their maintenance...."[27] Until then, the fund had generated so much revenue every year that capital accumulated despite the numerous drains on the fund. After reaching somewhat over half a million dollars, however, revenues began slowly to decline. The prospect of financial decline gradually led Wilson to accept the plan of returning the girls to their parents, which was done through the 1940s.[28]

The government went so far as to build a large new home for the parents and both sets of siblings. At a high-level meeting to plan a site for this home, the Attorney-General stressed that the parents had the duty to continue to foster tourism. Wilson stated that the government was quite willing to give up guardianship rights as long as the children were still used "by way of attracting tourists to the province."[29]

In the protracted power struggles between the biological father, the doctor, the provincial government, and other "paternal" claimants such as the media and the scientific establishment, maternal voices are conspicuously absent. This was not due to any reticence or passivity on Elzire Dionne's part.[30] On several occasions she mobilized political support for her claims as a mother as successfully as a rural francophone woman speaking little or no English could be expected to do. In 1935, the Federation des Femmes Canadiennes-Françaises happened to be meeting in North Bay, and Mrs. Dionne attended this meeting to plead her case: "Mrs. Dionne said she is anxious the board of guardians include herself and two other women, both mothers, who could understand her longing to be with the babies as much as possible." Since there were three active guardians at this time, the addition of three women would have created gender parity. The politics of this request are thus quite sophisticated, and go beyond a simple "mother's plea." The federation's president supported Mrs. Dionne, but the North Bay convention, possibly unwilling to antagonize the Liberal government given traditional French and Catholic support for the Liberal Party, merely expressed pious hopes that Mrs. Dionne would soon be able to spend more time with her daughters.[31] (It is interesting, incidentally, that the recent film *Million Dollar Babies* paints a sexist portrait of Elzire Dionne as a weak and passive character with no connection to women's organizations.)

Having lost the fight to become guardian to her children, Mrs. Dionne still tried to retain some control and some maternal dignity. Two years later, she managed to obtain the support of the provincial ruling party's own women's wing for a new demand: equal schooling for her non-famous children. Mrs. M.J. Poupure, French vice-president of the Ontario Women's Liberal Association, met with Mrs. Dionne and wrote a long and eloquent report that caused discontent at Queen's Park. Mrs. Poupure began by covertly attacking the male guardians' authority by describing her talk "in my own language as a French woman, as one Northener to another, and as one mother to another." She stated that Mrs. Dionne appreciated the educational opportunities being given to the Quintuplets, but complained that her other children were "getting a rural education without any opportunity of gaining culture, and in the French language only, when English too is imperative." Thus the Quints' better education would "create a barrier between the two family groups. It might make for an inferiority complex on the part of her other children...." Mrs. Poupure then movingly described Mrs. Dionne's exclusion from the maternal tasks of putting children to bed, having them say their prayers, and choosing their clothes, and concluded by putting her finger on the delicate question of revenue, saying "when we think how much the Province of

Ontario gained from tourist trade by the publicity the Quints have given the province [Mrs. Dionne's] request for a private school for her family would be only a small consideration."[32] Contrary to the newspaper's portrayal of her as a peasant with purely instinctual mothering practices, Mrs. Dionne clearly wanted her other children to share the benefits of the sudden modernity foisted on the Quintuplets, and was able and willing to engage in sophisticated political tactics.

Mrs. Dionne's political efforts were all unsuccessful. This could be attributed to the fact that francophone interests tended to rally behind their own image of a patriarchal family, while most of the women who might have had influence at Queen's Park probably shared the media's contempt for the "peasant" woman who had had 10 children by age 26 and had only a grade 3 education. Excluded from public power struggles, Elzire Dionne was reduced to very undignified battles with the Dafoe-appointed nurses for control over the daily details of her nursery, from prayers to hair styles. A log kept by a Dafoe Hospital nurse during the summer of 1939 records painful and almost daily squabbles between the mother and the nurses, squabbles in which the children seemed to have played one woman off against another.[33] The mother's visits to her children often ended in tears. Blamed by the nurse for interrupting the children's highly orchestrated activities, Mrs. Dionne must have been perpetually anxious about her children's loyalty.

The exclusion of Mrs. Dionne, and the relative absence of an outcry by women, is in contrast to the Stork Derby case, which saw a successful protest by organized and unorganized women against the province's attempt to invalidate Charles Millar's will and hence deprive mothers of numerous children of their share in the eccentric lawyer's estate. One wonders to what extent the Quintuplets' *sui generis* status as a scenic wonder, compounded by their media presentation as medical rarities, disqualified them for child status altogether, hence disqualifying their mother from motherhood. As we shall see below, the Stork Derby mothers could only qualify as legitimate mothers if their children met a number of specifications, among which being a *legal* child was the primary one. The disjunction between natural and legal children is one of the key features of the Stork Derby case. The Dionne Quintuplets, whose legitimacy was never in doubt, ran no risk of being construed as "natural" in the sense of illegitimate or legal; on the contrary, they verged on the supernatural. They were celebrities, medical miracles, and tourist attractions, and as such members of categories superseding childhood.

The Dionne Quintuplets' tragedy is that, while their mass-produced photographs are still considered to be the ideal representation of 1930s childhood, they were not themselves considered to be children. Like Mickey Mouse in Disneyland (who represents animals but is not an animal), the girls in Quintland were icons of "modern" childhood who were not treated as children. Therefore, they were not seen as requiring a mother, and nobody thought it odd that they were cared for by a series of nurses under Dafoe's paternal eye.

To continue the analysis of the ways in which "natural" mothers and "natural" children might or might not be certified as such by legal and media discourses, let us then turn to the Toronto Stork Derby.

VALUABLE BABIES AND ILLEGITIMATE MOTHERS: THE TORONTO STORK DERBY, 1926–38

A study of newspapers and judicial decisions reveals that, for the men generating both the "expert" and the media opinions, the issues involved in the Stork Derby case did not include the situation of mothers with numerous offspring during Canada's worst economic depression.[34] Rather, the themes outlined in dominant discourses were the following: the right of testators to defy common sense in the disposition of their property, the right of the government to interfere with private property, the eugenic theme of poor mothers having "excess" offspring and, finally, the norms of reproductive conduct. When focusing on reproductive morality, the prime object of discussion was the dubious morality of poor women, accused of recklessly getting pregnant for the sake of a prize; but moral aspersions were also cast on the male lawyer whose will produced the spectacle in the first place.

From the legal standpoint, morality was a side issue; the case centred more on the respective rights of testators and government regulatory authorities. The judgements, from the lowest to the highest court, were consistently included in the *Dominion Law Reports* for the sake of clarifying the situation of unusual wills, and were apparently regularly taught in wills and estates courses in Ontario law schools for decades afterwards. Nevertheless, to discuss the case simply as an interesting precedent in the history of estate law would be to miss some very important social dimensions. The state's right to regulate private property (the estate) was in this case inextricably linked to the moral and legal regulation of family and reproduction. That private property, family and the state should be so intertwined (as Frederick Engels pointed out in a different context) meant that many Toronto women and children had their lives organized by a peculiar combination of the law of wills and estates and the dominant norms regulating reproductive conduct.

When Charles Millar's will was probated in November of 1926, the clause leaving most of the estate to the Toronto mother who would have the most children in the 10 years after his death caused much consternation. A headline in the *Toronto Star* raised the possibility that the controversial clause might be judged to be "not in [the] public interest," hence invalidating the will. Unnamed people questioned the immorality implicit in Millar's wording, particularly since it did not specify that the prize ought to go to a married woman with the most number of children, although as a lawyer he knew full well the difference between married and unmarried mothers.[35] But the neglected distant relatives, who had a financial interest in declaring the will against the public interest, took almost a year to get organized to contest the will and claim their share of over $300,000 in the estate. The story simmered, and the *Toronto Star* tried to keep it alive by sending reporters to hunt down possible prizewinners and sign them up for exclusive interviews.[36]

The first set of long-lost cousins launched a case in November of 1927, with their lawyer arguing "... that the said clause is void on the ground that it is against public policy and the provision therein contained tends to the propagation [sic] of illegal children and promotes competition among the women of Toronto in sexual matters and tends to place a premium on immorality...."[37] This case was thrown out, not because of the appalling grammar and logic of the lawyer's argument, but because the cousins launching the suit were not next of kin. This initial attempt to brand certain children as illegal and certain mothers as immoral, however, was to be continued by others in later years.

A recently deceased half-aunt was in fact the next of kin, and the executor of her estate now made a more credible attack on the will. Even though the nationality of the executor (who was also a partial heir) was of course legally irrelevant, his status as a US citizen harmed his claim, in the opinion of a patriotic and Depression-ridden public, and an equally patriotic and equally Depression-ridden provincial government. The Attorney-General, William Price, introduced a bill to "escheat" or invalidate the Millar estate and give the money to the University of Toronto, which had been the main beneficiary in an earlier Millar will.[38] The government's actions may have been prompted by a desire to keep the money in the country. It may also have been influenced by the kind of sentiment expressed by the distant cousins' lawyer regarding the immorality of reckless breeding: the spectre of the eugenically unfit was repeatedly applied to the Millar estate case by a clergyman leading the publicly visible movement for birth-control clinics.[39] (The last judicial decision in the Derby case was made in the middle of the much-publicized Dorothea Palmer birth-control case.)

The *Star*, whose reporters had combed the city of Toronto for possible winning mothers, chivalrously leaped to the defence of wounded motherhood. A mother of 27 philosophically said, "Maybe it's just as well if we don't get the money.... If we were rich, some[one] might kidnap little Jean... here, like they did with Lindbergh's baby."[40] But other women, whether participating in the contest or not, were less resigned to seeing the prize money disappear. Women of the Liberal Party said the government had "cheated," and the *Globe* reported that women were threatening to make the will an election issue.[41] The same day, the *Globe* took the opportunity to chastise the government on the Millar will issue. In keeping with the newspaper's politics, its main complaint was the right of testators to dispose of their money at will, not the raised hopes of poor women:

The Ontario government will have serious difficulty in convincing the people of the Province that it has any justification whatsoever for setting aside, by legislation, the will of a wealthy citizen, and diverting the proceeds of the estate to provincial purposes.... It is a dangerous precedent for any Province to set up in these days when the right to hold and dispose of property is being challenged in many quarters.[42]

Faced with this anti-statist, anti-regulatory sentiment, the Attorney-General quickly withdrew the contentious bill and allowed the courts to dispose of the estate.

Despite the *Globe*'s attempt to make property the central issue, the unusual activism of women forced the conservative newspaper to acknowledge women's role in the reversal (though in a somewhat offensive tongue-in-cheek prose). The *Globe*'s headline was: "Women Halt Millar Estate Escheatment Attempt," and the article is worth quoting at length:

Womanhood—indignant, outspoken womanhood—asserted itself in the political arena yesterday.... Both yesterday and the day before the articulate indignation of women could be heard in every phase of daily life. On the street cars they could be overheard denouncing as "thievery" the proposed action of the government in escheating the half million dollar estate.... In the department stores and from the small corner grocers the feminine customers raised their voices in an equally protesting vein. Newspaper offices were bombarded with salvos of feminine protestations [43]

The following day the *Star*, taking its cue from the earlier *Globe* editorial decrying state intervention in the economy, accused Attorney-General Price of "resort[ing] to Communism in the raw when he contemplated, regardless of the courts, to set aside a man's last will and testament by statute."[44] Price, who had been responsible for the jailing of Communist leader Tim Buck, was probably infuriated by this editorial, as well as by a *Star* editorial cartoon a few days later portraying him taking a bag marked $500,000 from a woman pushing a pram full of babies. From this moment on, no provincial politician, however distasteful he found the contest, dared to interfere with the judiciary's decisions.

In October 1936, newspaper readers with an interest in reproduction could have followed two high-profile stories running in the front pages of the Toronto press: the closing days of the Stork Derby, and the Dorothea Palmer birth-control trial. At issue in the trial was not so much women's right to control their own bodies as the fear that the poor and "unfit" were reproducing more than the middle classes. The eugenic views of A.R. Kaufman, a Kitchener manufacturer sponsoring the birth-control clinic being prosecuted, have been outlined in detail by Angus and Arlene McLaren and need not detain us here.[45] What should be noted is that expert witnesses in favour of population control literally went from one courtroom to another and related the two cases in interesting ways. The Stork Derby was ominously cited by the magistrate in the birth-control trial as an example of the consequences of unregulated reproduction. He went on to invoke the spectre of fascist pro-natalist policies in order to justify finding Dorothea Palmer not guilty despite the fact she had clearly broken the law banning contraceptive information.[46]

Meanwhile, back at the Stork Derby trial, the pro-eugenic expert witnesses borrowed from the contraception case did not manage to persuade the courts to declare the will invalid, but they heaped moral and social stigma on the contesting mothers. Their eugenic views were at this time widely accepted: in the fall of 1936 the Ontario Liberal Party passed a resolution in favour of the compulsory sterilization of the "feeble-minded."[47]

Eugenic fears were clearly fuelled by the fact that many of the contesting mothers (and most of the ultimate winners) were on welfare. Nevertheless, some people offered a different interpretation of the eugenic gospel, arguing that pro-natalism was useful to make sure that Ontario anglophones were not overtaken by the French in Quebec. A bachelor writing to the *Star* stated that "The shade of Theodore Roosevelt could delight in the pictures of large healthy families, rather than race suicide. Is Ontario to suffer in comparison to Quebec? There large families are very common."[48] The fact that several of the leading contestants had Italian names probably diminished the popularity of this writer's selective pro-natalism. Although the newspaper coverage does not make explicit reference to the women's ethnicities, the over-representation of Italians or Italian-Canadians had to be, given the context, yet another sign that the Stork Derby babies were not the kind of "stock" favoured by ruling groups. Even those who favoured giving the Millar money to poor mothers did not always view them as deserving. Some of the people writing to the government to express their views opined that although the mothers should never have been encouraged to have so many babies, the money should be apportioned out among them in order to support the Derby babies, described by one writer as "victims of avarice."[49]

While prevalent views about population control, about the worthiness of the poor, and about sexual morality could not suffice to overturn the will in the face of a strong sentiment against government regulation of private property, they did have some influence on judicial decisions about exactly which mothers were entitled to the money. The Derby officially ended 10 years after Millar's death, on Halloween night 1936. A few days later, a senior judge about to retire, Justice Middleton, was called upon to adjudicate the prize. Undaunted by affidavits against the will filed by Rev. Charles Silcox of the Social Service Council of Canada (who had just testified in favour of population control at the Palmer birth-control trial), and by a prominent obstetrician who believed that the will encouraged dangerous numbers of births,

Middleton said: "I don't see that the reproduction of the human race is contrary to public morals."[50]

But Middleton now had to make decisions that would give precise legal content to the suddenly vague words "mothers" and "children." In respect to children, Middleton did not hesitate to specify that despite the indiscriminate wording of Millar's will, only legitimate children could be counted. As we shall see shortly, there were various ways in which the line between having a child and not having a child could be blurred, but the most important distinction made both by Middleton and by subsequent higher courts was that between the legitimate and the illegitimate.

There were no "really" illegitimate children in the contest. One of the leading contenders, however, had had five children by her husband and five by another man. Although she was still married, and hence her second set of children was by the letter of the law legitimate, Middleton eventually disqualified the mother on the basis that some of her children had been conceived in "open adultery."[51] Having made this questionable ruling on the children's legitimacy status, Middleton then proceeded to the most questionable feature of his decision. In a judgement later endorsed by the Supreme Court of Canada, Middleton argued that although it was the mothers, not the children, who were inheriting (and hence it should have been the mothers' own legitimacy status that counted, not that of their children), the children's status somehow rubbed off on their mothers: "'Children,' when used in any testamentary document, always means legitimate children and I can find no foundation for the contention that this is only in gifts to the children. I think it applies equally, perhaps *a fortiori*, to gifts to the mother of the children."[52] The mother of the 10 children by two different biological fathers, Mrs. P.C., was thus branded as an illegitimate mother by Middleton. The Court of Appeal agreed that to include illegitimate children in the head count would be "against public policy," and this was reaffirmed by the Supreme Court.[53]

By the beginning of 1938 when the case, having gone up to the Supreme Court, was referred back to Middleton for the adjudication of the prize among various possible winners, the issue of legitimacy had been settled. But this did not put an end to the difficulties of specifying exactly who counted as a legal child. There were two further issues which made a difference to some of the contesting mothers. One was the distinction between stillbirths (which according to Middleton did not count as children) and live births of children who died very quickly. Many of the mothers, from whose point of view a child born dead was still a child, took a dim view of the ruling; one of the top contenders, Mrs. H.G., wrote to Premier Hepburn that she had had a child born dead five years earlier, and that she found it odd that a minister had now ruled that the dead child did not count.[54] In court, Middleton listened to lengthy medical testimony on the fine line separating babies who do not breathe at birth and are not baptized and those who die but appear to have been born alive. Although the court was cleared during the medical testimony, the doctors' graphic descriptions of the births, the efforts to make the babies breathe, and the death throes of the newborns were reported at length in the newspapers.[55]

The second point of contention between mothers and the law was that women believed that all physical children counted, whereas the state insisted that only babies whose births had been legally registered counted. Not surprisingly, some of the women with the most children had not complied with the requirement of registering all births within the time limit. A Mrs. K., for example, had two unregistered children as well as nine registered ones, and since she expected to give birth a day or two before the will's deadline, she was counting on walking away with the prize (no other mother had more than 10 eligible children).[56] The birth registrar's official records were deemed more authoritative than her experience and she was disqualified. As Elizabeth Wilton points out in her thesis on the topic, the mother's lawyer tried to get the provincial government to register retroactively the children, something which was commonly done when parents suddenly experienced the need for official documents. But the government, undoubtedly aware of the fact that Mrs. K. was Italian and her husband was Irish Catholic, refused to issue the certificates, hence throwing Mrs. K. out of the competition.[57]

Finally, on Mar. 19, 1938 Middleton ruled that the prize money should be divided between four mothers who all had nine eligible children. The prolific Mrs. K. was disqualified because she had had two stillbirths and two unregistered children, while Mrs. C., whose last five children were fathered by her new commonlaw husband rather than by her legal husband, was also disqualified in a slanderous ruling that intimated that Mrs. C. may have been sleeping with both men simultaneously.[58] Subsequently, however, counsel for Mrs. K. and Mrs. C. pressed Middleton and the executors of the will, and were able to obtain a kind of consolation prize of $12,500 for each of their clients.

The municipal welfare department, in a move of questionable taste as well as dubious legality, sent out a press release showing that 11 of the Stork Derby finalists had received a total of $28,956 in relief and medical care. The names of all these people, losers as well as winners, were published, and the city insisted that the winners should repay them. Two out of the four winners had been on relief, and pressure was put upon them to repay, which they did. Mrs. C., who had received one of the small consolation prizes, thought better of it and simply disappeared with her money.[59]

The winners enjoyed a brief moment of celebrity. In a pale reflection of the Dionne Quintuplets' fame, three out of the four winning families appeared in advertisements for corn syrup and signed various contracts to appear in public. Earlier on, three hopeful mothers had done a vaudeville tour in the US.[60] The mothers, however, were not simply exploiting the situation; there is plenty of evidence to suggest that although they certainly enjoyed both the money and the fame, they also showed remarkable solidarity with one another. Mrs. H.G. (an early leader eventually disqualified) asked Premier Hepburn to divide the money equally rather than to force a competition, a sentiment echoed by other mothers. Mrs. G. also gave blood for the baby of another contestant.[61] The *Star* recorded various acts of sisterly solidarity among the women, particularly those on relief, and remarked on "the spirit of camaraderie which has lately grown up among the maternity contest mothers" even though this spirit undermined the horse-race metaphor promoted by the newspapers.[62] Although the mothers obviously saw a need to maintain an image of respectability and good citizenship (as evidenced in the voluntary payback of relief money to the city), they nevertheless stood their ground and made their views known, going so far as to defy Premier Hepburn when he publicly described the Stork Derby as "disgusting and revolting." "Mothers of Big Families Don't Agree with Hepburn" was, perhaps, the headline that pointed to the heart of the Stork Derby controversy.[63]

CONCLUSION: DILEMMAS IN STATE REGULATION

The Stork Derby ended up financially benefitting some Toronto mothers. Unlike the disenfranchised Elzire Dionne, at least some of the Toronto mothers obtained a reward—although the money was won at the cost of having the details of private lives, from medical histories to finances, publicly broadcast, as well as the less direct cost of further stigmatizing poor mothers of large families. The reason for their somewhat tarnished victory was, however, that their cause happened to be tied to the interests of private property. The *Star* expressed the dominant opinion: "it may have been a foolish will, but in law a man has a perfect right to do foolish things as concerns the disposition, in life or in death, of his property."[64]

Mrs. Dionne, by contrast, was not able to appeal to the right of "a man" over his property in order to buttress her case. She tried to invoke the accepted idea that mothers have a natural relationship to their children, but this appeal to biology and to natural right was no match for the state's desire to control the estate of the Quintuplets. The Quints had in any case been constructed by the media as peculiar entities located at the intersection of tourism and science, having nothing in common with ordinary children.

Thus, one can see that the fortunes of motherhood depend not only on the social and legal standards regulating motherhood and family life at any particular time. They can also depend to a large extent on other factors—the interests of private property, for instance—which may appear as external but which become internal organizing principles for at least some women's experience of motherhood.

And what can one say about the role of the state in the regulation of childhood? We saw that Attorney-General Arthur Roebuck had declared himself to be the legal father of the Quintuplets in his capacity as *parens patriae*, although why the paternal qualities of the state ought to devolve on the Attorney-General in particular was never explained. In the Derby case, Roebuck was moved to repeat the high-sounding phrase: "I am watching in my capacity as *parens patriae*, a term which literally means father of the people, but which actually means more or less official guardian."[65] Roebuck was clearly torn between his parental/patriarchal desire to regulate, on the one hand, and the laissez-faire principles of estate law and property on the other. The structural contradiction between the two opposing principles (paternalism and liberalism) manifested itself as political wavering, as is obvious in the following report:

> Attorney-General Arthur Roebuck was understood to be lukewarm to any legislative tampering with the will, but yesterday pointed out that the Government had stepped in to save the Dionne quintuplets from harm.... If the Dionne case is taken as precedent, the Government may see fit to split the prize money, set it up in a trust fund, or otherwise act for the public welfare.[66]

Whatever the noble intentions of this statement, the precedent of the Quintuplet trust fund suggests that the well-being of poor children and mothers would not have been the government's first priority if it had taken over the half-million-dollar Millar estate. The publicity and commercialism decried by Premier Hepburn, when engaged in by parents, would not have been so distasteful if the estate had been nationalized by the province as the Quintuplets had been.

Both Roebuck and his predecessor were forced to take a more laissez-faire attitude in the Derby case than with the Dionnes, since the right of a man over his property was deemed by the courts to be the overriding factor in the case. And yet, the requirements of a capitalist marketplace, though tending to uphold the validity of the Millar will, do not suffice to explain the specific outcome. In order to adjudicate the prize Justice Middleton had to make a series of extra-economic decisions about the legal and moral legitimacy of both children and mothers. Moral regulation, economic regulation, and certain local political questions (such as the issue of francophone rights, which ultimately weighted the balance against the state in the Dionne case) were all involved in determining the fates of the two sets of people whose administration is analyzed here. In future studies of cases involving families and the state it may therefore be useful to avoid the assumption that what is at stake is the history of child welfare or the relation between the public state and the private family. The social world is not always best understood through taken-for-granted, mutually exclusive categories dividing economics from sexuality, estate law from birth control, tourism from family policy. Why certain children were treated by the state as though they were not children is perhaps as important a question as determining the state's policy toward official children. Examining the "exceptional" cases can provide new insights into the ways in which categories such as "child welfare" (or for that matter "children") were constructed. Revealing the fractures in the exercise of power, the slippages from one category to another is as important as outlining the basic lines of the development of economic regulation or family policy.

Notes

1 In keeping with Pierre Berton's *The Dionne Years,* her main source, Veronica Strong-Boag portrays the Dionne parents as victims of an interventionist state and a powerful group of experts. (V. Strong-Boag, "Intruders in the Nursery," in J. Parr, ed., *Childhood and Family in Canadian History* [Toronto: McClelland Stewart, 1982], esp. 173–78). Strong-Boag's general thesis on the growth of government and professional regulation of family relations is undoubtedly correct, but I want to show here that the Dionne case and the Stork Derby case make it clear that not all children being regulated by the state are regulated as children.

2 For a relevant theorization of the family / market / state triad, see Frances E. Olsen, "The Family and the Market: A Study of Ideology and Legal Reform," *Harvard Law Review* 96 (1983), 1497–1578.

3 "Roebuck breaks Chicago Contract," *Globe,* 27 July 1934. The next day's *Globe* had an editorial praising Roebuck's action. The text of the contract between Mr. Dionne and the Chicago Fair promoters can be found in "Agreement between Oliva Dionne and Chicago World's Fair Promoters," dated 31 May 1934, in vol. 1, series C, Dafoe Papers, Public Archives of Ontario (This collection will be cited simply as Dafoe Papers).

4 When the second guardianship was established under the provincial official guardian, P.D. Wilson, he made repeated requests to Croll for the files on the first guardianship, even visiting Croll in his Windsor law office. But Croll refused, writing to one of the later guardians: "I cannot possibly let you have the quintuplet file...." (Croll to K. Munro, 7 July 1937; letter in Croll file. Box 2 of Dionne Quintuplet Guardianship papers, RG 4, Series 4–53, Public Archives of Ontario [This 12–box collection will be cited simply as DQG papers]).

5 See Berton, *The Dionne Years* (Toronto: McClelland and Stewart, 1977), 71–73.

6 For the government's claim see "Province plans full care for the whole Dionne family," *Toronto Star* 27 March 1935, 23. But the documents in the "Reports of the Official Guardian" file, Box 8 DQG papers, show that the Dafoe Hospital was built by the Red Cross with $5000 of its own money plus an equal amount from private donations. The government may have paid the $4000 that was later given to local landowners in compensation for land expropriated for the Quintland complex, but Queen's Park specifically refused to pay for the buildings; David

Croll said the government had "done plenty" (undated report c. late 1938, "Reports of the Official Guardian," Box 8 DQG papers).

7 An Act Respecting the Guardianship of the Dionne Quintuplets, 1st session, 19th legislature of Ontario, 25 George V, 1935.

8 "Dionne family to get care," *Mail and Empire* 27 March 1935, 11.

9 For a full description of Quintland and of the tourist industry it sparked in nearby towns, see Berton, *The Dionne Years*, chapter 10.

10 For Dafoe's speech, see clipping in "New site and reunion of family" file, Box 7, DQG; the Niagara Falls comparison is from Berton, *The Dionne Years*, 9.

11 On Quintland see Berton, *The Dionne Years*, 5–9; see also the ghost written autobiography by James Brough, *We Were Five* (New York: Simon and Schuster, 1965).

12 Berton, *The Dionne Years*, 6.

13 See auditor's reports in "Reports of the Official Guardian" file, Box 8, DQG papers.

14 Detailed financial information is in the file marked "Surrogate Court Audits" in Box 9, DQG papers. Copies of annual expense reports for the early years also exist in Vol. 2, Series C of the Dafoe papers.

15 "Dionne Bill Being Aimed at Chisellers," *Globe*, 12 March 1935.

16 For Blatz's expenses, see minutes of the guardianship for January 1938, in "Minutes" file, Box 5, DQG papers.

17 William Blatz, *The Five Sisters* (Toronto: McClelland and Stewart, 1938), 203.

18 See "Income Tax" file, Box 4, DQG papers.

19 Dr. Alan Brown, report dated 2 July 1938, in "Reports" file, Box 8, DQG papers.

20 A.G. Hays to P.D. Wilson, 28 Jan. 1938, "Trade Mark" file, Box 9, DQG papers. This file also contains information about the province's negotiations with the Ottawa office in charge of trade marks.

21 From July 1937 to July 1938, Hays's firm in New York billed the guardianship for $5815 (information from the "Minutes" file, Box 5, DQG papers).

22 An Act for the Protection of the Dionne Quintuplets, 2nd session, 18th parliament, 1 George VI, 1937.

23 Lillian Barker, "Dionne wins back the Quints," *America*, 25 October 1941, 65.

24 Minutes of January 1940 meeting of guardians, "Minutes" file, Box 6, DQG.

25 Darius Benham Inc., NY, to Keith Munro, 11 July 1941, general correspondence file, Box 2, DQG papers.

26 Wilson's memo (probably to Attorney-General) of 20 June 1941, Reports of the Official Guardian file, Box 8, DQG papers.

27 Wilson to Munro, 19 Jan. 1942, "Paramount" file, Box 8, DQG papers.

28 There is no reliable information on how the remaining trust fund money was spent. The surviving Quintuplets have consistently claimed that they never got their rightful share of the fund upon reaching the age of majority, and on occasion have made allegations against both their father and the Ontario government. No legal case for fraud or misappropriation of funds has ever been heard, however.

29 See Wilson's "Memo of a discussion re guardianship on 7 March 1941," in "Religious" file, Box 8, DQG papers.

30 Pierre Berton consistently portrays Elzire Dionne as a simple-minded woman with no political savvy whatsoever; he even writes that "childbearing was for her as natural a process as eating" (*The Dionne Years*, 24).

31 "Mother of Quints voices complaints," *Globe*, 28 March 1935, 12.

32 "Looking into the future with Mrs. Dionne," Report in "Mrs. Dionne" file, Box 2, DQG papers.

33 Nurse's log, June-September 1939; unnumbered file, Box 11, DQG papers. See also "Mrs. Dionne" file in Box 2 for complaints from the mother transmitted to Queen's Park via the ACFEO's lawyer, Henri St-Jacques.

34 A similar point is made by Elizabeth Wilton in her MA thesis on the Stork Derby (Dalhousie University, History Department, 1994). I thank Elizabeth Wilton for allowing me to read a draft of her thesis.

35 The question of married vs. unmarried mothers is raised in a front-page article, "Attempt may be made to break Millar's will," *Star*, 7 Dec. 1926, 1 and 8; for information about the estate see *Globe*, 7 Dec. 1926, 1 and 17.

36 See Mark M. Orkin, *The Great Stork Derby* (Don Mills: General Publishing, 1981), 77. Orkin's book is an uncritical exposé, focusing mainly on the careers and personalities of the legal personnel involved in decision-making, but providing some useful information.

37 Quoted in Orkin, *The Great Stork Derby*, 86.

38 Orkin, *The Great Stork Derby*, 91–93; and two stories in the *Star*, 24 March 1932, 2.

39 The Rev. A.H. Tyrer, quoted in "Millar will is withdrawn by Price," *Star*, 24 March 1932, 2.

40 "Mother of 27 children proposes legal fight," *Star* 23 March 1932, 2; articles referring to the kidnapping of US aviator Charles Lindbergh's small child appeared around this time in the *Star*, and in this same issue of the *Star* there was an article reporting a sighting of the Lindbergh baby.

41 "Legatee 'Cheated,' say Liberal Women," *Globe*, 24 March 1932, 1.

42 Editorial, *Globe*, 24 March 1932, 4.

43 "Women halt Millar estate," *Globe*, 25 March 1932, 1–2.

44 Editorial, *Star*, 26 March 1932, 4.

45 Arlene and Angus McLaren, *The Bedroom and the State* (Toronto: McClelland and Stewart, 1986), chapter 5.

46 See especially "Eastview charge reduced by court," *Mail and Empire*, 28 October 1936, 1–2; but also stories in all Toronto papers during the month of October.

47 *Globe*, 7 November 1936, 1.

48 Letter, *Star*, 31 October 1936, 6; as part of the same discussion on reproductive politics, another letter writer opined that Millar should have left his money to a birth-control clinic (*Star*, 29 October 1936, 6).

49 Public Archives of Ontario, Hepburn papers, RG3, Box 259, unnumbered file. There appear to be no records of public input into the earlier government deci-

sions of 1926 and 1932, but the records of all decisions in the Attorney-General's department are very badly documented up to 1935.

50 "Judge refuses to agree frequent births an evil," *Star*, 16 November 1936, 1–2; for Dr. Silcox and Dr. Hendry's affidavits, see "Two affidavits," *Globe*, 13 November 1936, 1, section 2.

51 Middleton, quoted in "Four mothers share," *Star*, 19 March 1938, 1 and 3.

52 Re Millar, Ontario Supreme Court, Middleton J.A., Nov. 16, 1936; Dominion Law Reports (1937), 135.

53 For Appeal Court ruling, see "Appeal Court rules," in *Star*, 23 February 1937; for Supreme Court, see "Legitimate children alone are eligible," *Star*, 22 December 1937, 1. The Supreme Court ruling is: Re Millar (Estate of), (1938) S.C.R. 1; it is almost wholly concerned with the question of the rights of testators, and on issues concerning legitimate or illegitimate mothers it simply confirms Middleton's decision.

54 Mrs. H.G. to Premier Hepburn, 28 October 1936, in Public Archives of Ontario, Hepburn papers, Box 259, "Millar" file.

55 "Babies didn't breathe though heart beat," *Star*, 25 February 1938, 1–2.

56 "Mrs. K. expects baby's birth today," *Star*, 29 October 1936, 1.

57 Elizabeth Wilton, "The Toronto Stork Derby."

58 See the details of Middleton's judgement in Orkin, *The Great Stork Derby*, 297–99.

59 Orkin, *The Great Stork Derby*, 301–02; also "Two Stork Derby winners will gladly repay city," *Star*, 21 March 1938, 2.

60 See for instance ad for Edwardsburg Corn Syrup, including the statement "Money can't buy a more healthful food," in *Star*, 21 March 1938, 7; for vaudeville tour, see *Globe*, 14 November 1936, 1.

61 Letter from H.G. to Hepburn, 28 October 1936, in Public Archives of Ontario, Hepburn papers, Box 259, "Millar" file; see also "Millar will contenders offer one another aid," *Star*, 23 October, 1,2.

62 "Millar will contenders offer one another aid," *Star*, 23 October, 1.

63 "Mothers of big families," *Star*, 24 October 1936, 2.

64 Editorial, *Star*, 26 March 1932, 4.

65 *Star*, 23 October 1936, 3.

66 *Star*, 24 October 1936, 1, section 2.

═══╬ SEX AND MEDIA ╬═══

Within the canon of Canadian poetry, Irving Layton's career was most closely associated with themes of sexuality. To read his *Collected Poems* (1971) is to be reminded that he saw these themes as integral to his depiction of broader social concerns. "The Improved Binoculars" was, in fact, adopted by Northrop Frye as the title of a chapter in *The Modern Century* (1967), his wary assessment of modern society as it appeared in Canada's centennial year. Frye's allusion to Layton highlights a major theme of that poem: how progress is double-edged, bringing alienation along with improved social conditions. The artist as maker escapes the cycle of consumerism by turning technology to his own ends, a notion explored by Marshall McLuhan as well. Like Layton, McLuhan understood media as participating in a libidinal economy, a vast desiring-machine of consumerism. This notion of bio-technology, a hallmark of his groundbreaking theories on media, is reflected explicitly in his musings on "The Future of Sex," the title of which suggests that sexuality is historically inflected; indeed, some of the observations here will inevitably strike us as dated. Similar notions underscore other works by McLuhan, including *The Mechanical Bride* (1951), which examines ways in which advertising displaces sexuality onto consumer objects, and *Understanding Media* (1964). In this book, McLuhan suggested that media function as both extensions and amputations of our bodies and of consciousness itself. Persimmon Blackridge puts these notions to the test in *Prozac Highway*, in which she examines the implications for human relationships as they are enacted through email dating—"long-distance sex"—where the borderline between real life and the Internet becomes increasingly blurred. Nicole Markotić provides us with the historical prequel to these concepts in her novella about Alexander Graham Bell's invention of the telephone and the way in which the improved communication it promised (for the deaf, in this case) was likewise conceived of as an enhanced way of reaching out and touching someone through the kiss of communication. Katherine Monk's survey of "weird sex" in Canadian cinema returns us to Layton's preoccupation with sexuality and social issues. Here, Layton's voyeur figure is represented by David Cronenberg, whose films include the McLuhanesque *Videodrome,* where watching a video becomes increasingly sexually charged, and *Crash,* where sex is experienced prosthetically by crashing cars into each other—a darkly witty realization of the mechanical bride. Monk's research suggests that the enormous guilt around sexuality that she sees in Canadian cinema reflects the Canadian identity crisis. Rather than a cinema characterized by "phallonationalism," Canadian films are filled with strong-willed women, and the characters in these films slide easily along a continuum of gender "norms."

Irving Layton

"The Improved Binoculars,"
Collected Poems (1971)

Below me the city was in flames:
the firemen were the first to save
themselves. I saw steeples fall on their knees.

I saw an agent kick the charred bodies
from an orphanage to one side, marking
the site carefully for a future speculation.

Lovers stopped short of the final spasm
and went off angrily in opposite directions,
their elbows held by giant escorts of fire.

Then the dignitaries rode across the bridges
under an auricle of light which delighted them,
noting for later punishment those that went before.

And the rest of the populace, their mouths
distorted by an unusual gladness, bawled thanks
to this comely and ravaging ally, asking

Only for more light with which to see
their neighbour's destruction.

All this I saw through my improved binoculars.

from *Prozac Highway* (1997)

8:30 A.M. on Tuesday, two hours till it's time to write Fruitbat. Check mail. The usual overnight gang. Terry is preparing a formal complaint about the executive/asshole. D'isMay says Gina should present it to the board because she won't get mad and blow it. Terry says thanks for the vote of confidence. D'isMay says know thyself, and Gina says she's sure Terry will do fine. Terry says maybe Gina *should* do it and Gina says okay. Then the east coast wakes up, but no Fruitbat. She's being cool, waiting for me to make the next move. Or she's forgotten. Parnell talked to Junior. Says he's doing all right, out of solitary and on a ward with a couple of old friends from last time. Trying to be good, not yell, get out. So far no one's talking shock.

9:00, the midwest is in full swing. Someone at the Paradise wants info on Zoloft, someone in Chicago says it saved their life, someone in England says it nearly killed them.

9:30. Time to start my note.

```
from: Jam
to: Fruitbat
re: Life, etc.
Hey Fruitbat, you around?
```

It's kind of short. Sounds anxious, too. Come on, you took small talk lessons, you can do this. The weather. Yes. Open the blind, god it's bright. Close the blind.

```
It's summer outside, blazing on last night's rain, wet streets
steaming. This is a city of flowers, coming in waves for months
now: snow drops, forsythia, cherry blossoms, clematis, magnolia,
honeysuckle, on and on. If you're going to be depressed, Vancou-
ver is a great city to go down in.
```

Maybe a bit florid. Depends on what Baltimore is like. People from Saskatchewan don't mind when you talk like that because then they can talk about the big sky and Prairie sunsets. But people in industrial Ontario get huffy and call you names.

```
Of course in the winter it rains all the time.
```

People in Ontario often forgive you if you mention that. As long as you don't say you like the rain or prefer it to freezing your ass for five months out of the year.

    I have no idea what Baltimore is like. I know it's in Maryland.
    Does that mean it's hot? Do people have those southern US accents?
    Do *you* have a southern accent, my god I didn't think of that,
    I'll have to start reading your email differently.

Good enough. Light yet personal. 9:45. Wait another forty-five minutes then send. Fashionably late.
    9:50.
    Check mail. George is going to be one of four witnesses talking about the Squeegee at the Senate Labour & Human Resources Committee Hearings on July 27. George? Oh right, he's the director of some enormous mental health consumer group. George. Wow. He'll be the only c/s/x there (of course). And the only formerly homeless person too, no doubt. He wants feedback for his presentation.
    9:58. No new mail.
    10:05. Howard snarking Lucy. Lucy biting back.
    10:10. Sarah with three pages of advice for George's testimony. Parnell with five pages. Cyber Joe with eight.
    10:11. Okay, mail the goddamn Fruitbat note and do something useful with the rest of your life.
    Send. Check mail. Fruitbat.
    from: Fruitbat
    to: ThisIsCrazy
    re: George at the Squeegee
    Congratulations, George! It's good to know *someone* will be
    there. How much time will you have? Who else is speaking? I will
    definitely put some thought into what I dislike about outpatient
    commitment and why homeless people shouldn't be rounded up and
    drugged. I'll probably be able to come up with a reason or two <g>.

Writing to the list, the cool bitch. Why why why didn't I wait longer? Okay, I'm not sitting by the phone like some teenager. I'm way too old for this. I should be pursuing my important career. Close Eudora, open Word. Write something brilliant and then go to a cocktail party and name-drop. First line ...
    Close Word, open Eudora. Check mail. Fruitbat.

    from: Fruitbat
    to: Jam
    re: life, etc.

Hey, there you are, from sunny Vancouver to cloudy Baltimore.
Yes, it's hot. Southern accent? Meaning California? Texas? Geor-
gia? None of the above. I just have a regular Baltimore accent.
And you probably have one of those cute Canadian accents (grin,
duck and run, as you sophisticated net-types say).

Now what? Answer, bozo.

from: Jam
to: Fruitbat
re: life, etc.
Yes, my accent is very cute. So how's life in the library?

Send. Regret. I can't believe how dumb that was. Have I ever written two
more gooney sentences in my life? Wait an agonizing three minutes, and then
her reply arrives.

Fruitbat
Life in the library is air conditioned. Other than that it's pretty slow. How's life in the basement?

Jam
Life in the basement is very cool. And incredibly lively. It's
only 10:20 and already I've drunk three cups of coffee. Looked
out my window and checked my email twelve times.

You can't send that. Start over.

Jam
Life in the basement is very cool. And incredibly lively. It's
only 10:20 and already I've had twelve mainstream publishers
offering me book contracts and five Hollywood stars begging for
a part in the movie-version of my life story. I'm holding out for
Margot Kidder.

Better. Which isn't saying much.

Fruitbat
Margot Kidder, good choice. Have you ever read _The History of
Shock Treatment_ by Leonard Roy Frank? I just started it.

This conversation is falling apart. I can't think of a thing to say and I haven't
read *The History of Shock Treatment.* Come on, come on, you can do this.

```
Jam
I never read it, but I heard him speak once. Are you liking the
```
book?

Here I am, discussing literature. John-the-psychologist would be proud of me.

```
Fruitbat
Yeah, it's good. Did you know that the guy who invented shock
treatment got the inspiration from watching pigs being shocked
in a slaughterhouse?
```

```
Jam
No, I didn't know that.
```

Come on, come on, you can do better than that. We're having a pleasant conversation about shock treatment. This is how people talk, get with the program.

```
Jam
This is a perfectly normal conversation and I can't seem to man-
age it. It's probably a symptom.
```

No no no. You're not supposed to say things like that. You're supposed to ask about her hobbies and move your eyes around. I can't do it. **Send.** You fool, you stupid fool! No new mail, no new mail, no new mail. She's probably talking to Parnell, I bet *he's* read *The History of Shock Treatment.* I don't care, people are too much work. Go put the kettle on. I should eat something. Open the fridge. Close it again. Food is too much work. Go back and check my mail.

```
Fruitbat
If it's a symptom, the goddamn thing is contagious.
```

Takes me a minute to work that one out.

```
Jam
Yeah, it's kind of awkward all of a sudden.
```

```
Fruitbat
You aren't kidding.
```

```
Jam
So is this a date?
```

Another bad move, but I send it anyway. I don't care. The kettle is whistling. I don't care.

Fruitbat
Maybe. I guess so. Awkwardness is one of the big signs of dating.

Jam
Yeah, I read that somewhere. In a pamphlet, "The Twelve Warning
Signs of Dating."

The kettle is still whistling. Just a minute hold on *shut up.*

Fruitbat
So what can we do about it?

Jam
Be awkward, I guess. I'm real bad at faking it these days.

Fruitbat
I noticed that.

Jam
You're not so shit-hot either.

Now it's stopped whistling, which probably means the water's all boiled away,
and the kettle's about to melt and set the kitchen on fire.

Fruitbat
True. And I'm trying so hard. But at least you're an experienced
net-dyke. I've never been on an email date before. I have no idea
what you're supposed to do.

Run to the kitchen no fire *excellent* turn off the stove run back.

Jam
I could make up all sorts of arcane rules and astound you with
my sophistication but the truth is I've never been on an email
date either.

Fruitbat
How can you have an email date anyway? What's the point? Oh baby,
you have such beautiful typing. It doesn't make sense. How can
you be attracted to someone you've never met?
   And if you were, what would you do about it?

Jam
Hey look, you're the one that asked me on this date-thing. So
you tell *me* what the point is. Was.

Fruitbat
Is. I don't know. The point is maybe it was a dumb idea. But, ok, I like you.

Jam
Ok, I like you too.

Fruitbat
Ok, now what?

Jam
In my experience of Meatworld dating (which is vast, it's true) this is the moment when we either die of embarrassment or start kissing. Do you kiss on the first date?

Fruitbat
Yes, but I've never kissed on the computer.

Jam
Me neither. I'm trying to imagine kissing you. I don't know what your lips look like. How do you kiss invisible lips? You make it up, I guess. We're sitting side by side on a couch, our awkward first date, and you just said you like me. So I move closer, put my arms around you. You don't feel like anyone else, you don't smell like anyone else. I don't really know you but I want you. I put my mouth on yours. Your lips are soft.

Fruitbat
Wait a minute. Are you saying you're attracted to me? In real life.

Jam
I'm saying I'm attracted to you. In real life. And I'm kissing you. In real life. On the computer.

Fruitbat
Good. I'm attracted to you too. Whoever you are.

... I finally write to Lucy for advice. I know hip urban lesbians shouldn't look to sixty-eight-year-old Christian ladies in rural Virginia for etiquette lessons, but there's no one else.

How do you ask someone for a favour when you haven't returned their phone calls for two and a half months?

Her reply comes a few hours later.

Many people would return one or two phone calls and then ask the favour, but that's a form of lying—which adds to your isolation, which is your problem in the first place. And it's sleazy. Just ask her.

Just ask her? Thanks, Lucy. How do I just ask her?

Ring. Ring. Ring. Maybe she's not home. Ring.

"Hello?"

"Hi, Cynthia."

"Jam, hi, how are you?"

"Good, how're you?"

"Somewhere on the road between tragedy and ecstasy. You know. So what's up?"

Just ask her. "I ... have a question. Kind of a long question."

"Great. I love to show off my vast and peculiar knowledge."

"Well actually ..." Spit it out. "It's about phone sex."

"You want to do phone sex? Hey, that would be fabulous! I could put in a word with my boss. You would be perfect. Lots of older women work the lines."

"No, it's not about a job, it's ... it's a little hard to explain. I'm kind of involved with this woman." How to describe Fruitbat? Better not to.

"Anyone I know?"

"No, that's the problem. She lives in Baltimore and I've never even met her, but I think we're, you know, like, doing it."

"Hey that's great!"

"But I've never done that kind of long-distance sex-thing before and well, I thought you could help. Like ... tell me what to do."

"Doing it with someone you know is pretty different from working."

"But I don't really know her, and I've never really ... I don't know." I'm ready to hang up now, but Cynthia's just getting started.

"I've never heard you so flustered. Must be love!"

"It's just—"

"It's so cute!"

"Come on, are you going to help me or not?"

"Anything for love, honey. What do you want to know?"

What do I want to know? I want you to write a script for my life. "How do you start? Like, there you are at work and the phone rings. What then?"

"Let me see. The first thing is to find out what they want. Sometimes they just tell you, 'Suck my cock,' or whatever. Or they'll ask you, 'Are you a blonde,' and you know that means they want a blonde, so you say, 'Yes, I've got long blonde hair.'"

"What if they hate blondes and they're just checking to make sure you're not one?"

"It doesn't work like that. Whatever they ask about, it's what they're looking for. If they say, 'What kind of shoes are you wearing?' you know it's a foot fetish. Sometimes you need to dig a bit. You can say, 'What do you like to do for fun,' and that tells you what to be. Something they can have fun with. If they say, 'I like hiking,' you can say, 'So do I. I like to go way up in the mountains where there's no one else around. The sun is so hot I have to take off my Helle Henson hiking shirt. All I have on is a flimsy, black lace brassiere and my cut-offs. And then I see you walking down the path toward me.' Like that. You follow the cues."

"What was the cue for the black lace brassiere?"

"Listen, they all want black lace lingerie."

"What next?"

"It really depends on what they're into. What's this girl of yours like? What does she do?"

"She spends a lot of time in the library."

"Ah, the intellectual type. Intellectuals like to figure things out, look below the surface. So tell her, 'I walk into the library wearing a pearl-grey suit. Underneath I have black lace lingerie.' You could take her down into the stacks and read obscure poetry to her."

"Then what?"

"What do you mean, then what? You're an artist, use your imagination. On the phone lines *you're* working on *their* fantasy, and you're also trying to keep them on for as long as possible because they pay by the minute. But in real life it's supposed to be fun. Loosen up!"

"I guess I am nervous."

"This is not like you. Jam. How long has it been since you've dated anyone?"

"Since Alex. Eight months."

"Oh right, Alex. You gave user-friendly a whole new meaning when you took up with her. Forget Alex, you've got better fish to fry. It'll be great. Relax. Sex is like riding a bike. As soon as you get back on, your body remembers everything."

"Sure, every bike accident you ever had comes vividly to mind."

"That too."

After we hung up I sat there looking at the phone. Fun, loosen up, relax.

Nicole Markotić

from *Yellow Pages: A Catalogue of Intentions* (1995)

THE THOUGHT BOOKS OF A. GRAHAM BELL

November 2nd, 1872. Boston
Watson has proven himself a godsend, yet I don't trust the man. He is a good worker but eternally tired. I have caught him napping several times this past week, asleep with his arms wrapped around his ears. Oblivious. There's work to be done, I say loudly enough, but sometimes even that won't rouse him. He sleeps in his chair and on my work table, and once he fell asleep in the middle of fixing a leaky pipe. I strode into the kitchen in search of black tea and discovered his legs sticking out of my cupboard. He could have been a dead body. He has yet to offer me an explanation or apology.

Watson loves the deafness of sleep too much.

November 13th, 1872. Boston
Rather than taking the train back to Salem every night, Watson has been sleeping on my floors. Watson is handy and young. His head brims with ideas that help my own, my mechanical man-Friday, tho' his yearning for magic leads him away from the path of science. Watson believes electricity to be an occult force and listens, fascinated, to what he calls the music of static.

But I cannot bear living with a man so mannerless. He shovels food down his throat without stopping his conversation. He rolls his sleeves up and turns chairs wrong side around in order to dine. He holds his knife in a fist, stabs at his food, then pokes the whole thing into his mouth. He eats as if he has never been introduced to a fork. I am disgusted every meal. What can I do?

Yesterday I burst out: Were you born in a barn? And without pause or hesitation, he replied: Yes, my father ran the stables.

What can I make of that? Watson slips food inside his mouth with a dexterity that comes from necessity. Too busy swallowing, he lacks conversation skills at the table. I, too, increase the speed of my food intake and soon enough we are back in the attic speaking to each other through metal and wires.

November 28th, 1872. Boston
I can't fathom Hubbard's motives. He sponsors my scientific endeavors financially, sends his daughter to me, assuming I can perform a miracle of speech

with her, yet directs and manipulates my experiments, understanding nothing. Money, of course, but there is more money to be had in creating a machine that can talk than in merely encouraging simultaneous telegraphs. Hubbard pushes so hard for the telegraph invention, and it is, after all, his funding that pays for the equipment and for the attic suite and for Watson, but I cannot bear to be the first person to develop a contraption only to watch it turn obsolete in days.

Invention is about voice and where I can send it. Hubbard, a businessman, doesn't understand this seduction's about changing the future. Being original doesn't count for much; Hubbard should know that. What counts is the forward leap. The hesitation between connections.

The multiple telegraph is obsolete already, yet Hubbard insists I spend hours a day searching for ways to invent the thing. Fool.

I want to trap the human throat inside a box. I want to speak to Watson without tolerating his body in the same room. I want Mabel Hubbard to implant my device inside her ear.

The future, I have discovered, is no longer what it used to be.

December 23rd, 1872. Boston
The best kiss I ever had I can't remember.

Marie and I walking—no hiking—I felt so sorry for her limp, for her inability to climb rocks or scale mountains.

Marie always endeavored to scale mountains.

I followed her footsteps on the steep path then increased my gait so I could accompany her bad leg. An injury or birth defect, she never said. And I wanted so wickedly to help, to offer a bent elbow, to wrap an arm around her waist. To lift.

Really, I wanted to touch her, her lameness the excuse I invented. But Marie refused to understand her lameness. She hobbled and scrambled over that difficult path more eager than I. She turned, and I froze my arm against my chest in order not to reach for hers. I wanted to touch her. My fingers consumed with desire to stretch out against skin. My body, caught between its own longing and her resistance, unable to follow either path.

She kissed me then. While my hand hesitated solo above her unafraid arm, she kissed me open mouthed and full against my greedy surprise.

I kissed her back, of course, her tongue sensational and confident beneath my own. I pulled her inside my lips and tried to trap her breath there beneath my tongue. I can't remember, but the dynamite persuasion of her mouth against mine resonates inside my body.

An explosion.

My body reminds me it was too convenient, Marie's kiss, and too much hoped for. A kiss I will try to memorize all my life. The best kiss I ever. The best I ever.

January 3rd, 1873. Boston

Mabel's mouth smells of apples and birch trees. A New England mouth twists around *k*s and *t*s and breathes out even and confident. Mabel claims she can read my lips, but I don't believe her. I mouth: I-love-you-I-love-you-I-love—. She can't hear. She turns away from my overzealous lips and cradles the caraway seeds on the windowsill. Look, she says into the glass, the shells are invisible.

I used to breathe words against my mother's forehead. My mother couldn't decipher a single sound except by me pressing my lips against her receptive temple. My mother, who has never heard my father speak her name, has heard her one remaining son sing churchly hymns, expound on the Great Beyond. Although no lover of religion, I plucked sermons and diatribes from the air above my mother, pushed them into her head. Her skull remembers what she can no longer hear. My mother stares at the minister every Sunday— every Sunday for forty-one years with only one change of country in between—but cannot discern what his lips trace. She misses the singing, my mother says. She misses the long hollow words retreating into exile.

Mabel claims she has no need to hear. She turns from the clear glass, lowers her eyes, stares at the motion of my lips.

I lean my shoulders forward:—love-you-I-love-you-I-love-you-I—my lips rehearse silently, so Watson in the next room can't hear. Mabel can't hear. The final -I- catches in my throat, and I choke on the words that even I can't hear.

Mabel concentrates on my lips and sees sound. What sort of hearing, then, can I put into her eyes? Or might Watson outline from across the room where I don't notice?

Mabel claims she can read lips, but I say differently.

January 31st, 1875. Boston

I can't stand this infernal heat. How is it possible to be suffering from sweat in the middle of winter? Even Ontario makes more sense than this country.

Watson and I enter the attic, strip down to our trousers and bare skin, and immediately begin to overheat. We keep the windows closed so the air doesn't disturb the passage of sound through wires. It gets so bad, we go down to the kitchen just to breathe to the bottom of our lungs. Watson finds it impossible to stay awake for large spaces of time when working in the attic. I usually send him down to make the tea. Otherwise, when I return with a boiling pot of chamomile or Earl Grey, I'll find him slumped over the connectors, drowsing into an amplifier. It's too hot to drink the stuff, but I send Watson anyway. He slumbers against the counter until the kettle's whine wakes him, then comes back upstairs refreshed.

The logistics of this thing wind round and round my head. I can't grab hold of the angles. Hubbard wants his telegraph. Father wants me to continue with his Visible Speech system. I've yet to hear of Father using his method to teach his own wife.

Mabel claims that lipreading is possible. To Mabel, anything is possible. Why doesn't Mother think that way? Mabel stares at my lips, which frees me to stare at her. For someone so young, Mabel is tough. Her parents never let her grow up Deaf, so she isn't; she's a hearing person gone deaf. She is the shining example I show off to my other deaf pupils' parents. Look, I tell them. If this girl can learn to speak, so can your daughters, so will your sons.

And they believe me.

Those with money entrust their children to me, but I no longer make personal time for instructing such individuals. I feel like a circus entertainer whose juggling balls rest on the ground. What happened to my delicate balance?

Mabel arrives early for her lesson and flirts with Watson until I send him away. They are both children, still.

HUSHA-HUSHA

Recite one of your old nursery rhymes, Aleck lips at Mabel. Perhaps memory will trigger in this girl the urge to speak normally. She is his most promising and most difficult student. The years and years her parents have invested in her articulation have turned her against the beauty of sound.

Children, Aleck knows, need encouragement.

Sing to me, he says to her again and opens his own mouth wide as if in accompaniment. She believes he is singing with her. Astounded, Aleck hears Mabel repeat flawlessly the lilt and cadence of Ring Around the Rosy. Her voice, harsh and untrained and forgotten, startles him with its accuracy. She can no longer pronounce rhymes, but the idea of the melody resides in her memory.

Mabel, had she not gone deaf with scarlet fever, would have a perfect ear. Childhood tunes beat beneath her skull. Another, he says to her when the song ends. One more, one more, each time she closes her lips.

Mabel has never met anyone who likes the noise her throat makes.

Aleck's fingers twitch against the sides of his legs as if he must restrain himself from reaching out and plucking her voice out of air. Mabel opens her lips and sings. Another. And another. She stares at Aleck's hands and makes stories out of the thick workman fingers and the chipped and gritty nails. From his hands, she knows he is more than a teacher or statesman.

Mabel's voice wavers along the walls and ceilings; her hands rest on Aleck's undulating fingers. His is their first lesson together where he hasn't worn gloves.

Mabel tells Aleck that except for her immediate family she talks to no one. She writes this down so that he will understand her exactly. Aleck wonders if she writes notes to the grocer and to delivery boys. He multiplies her opportunities for befriending.

Perhaps Mabel has met Watson before. Perhaps in hiring Watson, her father employed a family acquaintance, a man Mabel must surely have met previously? Mabel's index finger traces Watson's forearm. She removes her white gloves one finger at a time and reaches her hand to the sleeping Watson, a man consumed by the urge to close his eyes in front of strangers.

Child's play, Aleck thinks, observing the two of them. Watson and Mabel remember games and toys too well. Both are on the other side of twenty from Aleck. Watson thinks the task of invention jolly good fun; Mabel deigns to receive the benefits of speech for the sake of her father. Two children, Aleck thinks.

Mabel has invented the art of reading lips. And Watson has invented layers upon layers of improved defunct telephones.

For the duration of the invention of the telephone, Watson must fit his life into Aleck's. Watson is his and his alone. That Watson has a full-time position as a mechanic in someone else's shop is an irritation to Aleck. Watson works in the attic before he goes to the shop, after he goes to the shop. In the middle of the night, he arrives from Salem and works until morning. Watson sleeps on the train, he sleeps on the trams to and from Aleck's home, he sleeps on the desk when a space of five minutes opens up and Aleck is late with a deaf student. His day is divided into snatches of naps, sections of dreams that never reach their end. He wakes from a twenty-minute snooze, his hands already wrapped around the base of a telegraph wire. His body, pushed and strained, prepares to steal seconds of night.

Asleep or awake, Watson is the same person.

Aleck walks into the apartment, stares at his young assistant's lanky legs, sprawled between two rooms, oblivious to the approaching day.

On his one day off a month, Watson doesn't ride home to Salem, doesn't retreat to his bunk to sleep the sleep of twenty-nine days of never enough sleep. No. On his only free day, on this one day in thirty that he can designate his own, Watson takes the train out of Boston.

When the train passes over Lynn marshes, Watson focuses his attention outside the car window. He should shut his eyes. He should lean back and rest his head against the window and invest these few moments of his free day in healing his exhausted body. But Watson is a young man, practically a boy. The risk of the day still tastes fresh in his lungs.

When they first met, Aleck told Watson his name was Graham Bell, and that's what Watson called him for weeks. Watson now wishes he'd offered his own middle name, Augustus, as fair exchange. Watson hadn't understood Aleck's obsession with titles. Aleck had a nickname for Mabel that Watson can't bear to repeat: Adored One. Luckily, Watson thinks, Mabel can't hear the sugar tones reverberate inside the cracks of the inventor's lips. She reads Joan of Arc there, or she shuts her eyes.

The sun low on the horizon, Watson stares at the liquid shimmer of the field. The train's shadow bends and darts about the creases in the landscape, and Watson locates his own shadow inside its trace. He focuses on an elongated glow, a little brighter than the sunlight on the grass, that marks where he's seated. He changes seats, and the wavering halo follows him. He walks the length of the car until he stands at the train's end platform. The glow is there, too. Watson is astounded. Is this a flag of today's foolhardiness or some divine communication? The halo surely streams from his head! He returns to his seat to see whether any of the other passengers have a glow attached to their shadows. There is only one halo, and it remains attached to Watson.

Watson hesitates in a meadow of daisies, the white heads, the yellow hearts up to his knees. He breathes in their smoky pollen and coughs. The train has long retreated into the day. Watson walks to the farmer's pond—there is always a farmer's pond—rounds the marshy land until he discovers some rotting boards jutting into the middle of this murky water. He strides down the length of this dilapidated dock. When he reaches the end, he steps over.

Breathes.

Watson breathes thick water into his body, and his lungs protest. They sputter and contract, begin to sink inside his chest cavity. He feels his arms go numb. Watson flings his shoulders out of the water, and heaves his body onto the barely floating wooden dock. Gasps and gasps and gasps.

Sometimes a man needs to half drown in order to find out he's alive at all. Watson is very much alive.

Watson derives pleasure from each device he brings to life. Aleck proclaims another miraculous idea, and Watson fiddles with metal shavings and glue. With string and long sheets of paper. With inflection. Every week, Aleck requests another impossibility, and Watson produces results out of air. Two tuning forks that vibrate in sympathy. A speaking tube connected to a diaphragm. A human ear.

At first, Aleck cannot bear to touch the thing, severed as it is from a fresh cadaver. So he imagines. He breathes into the shriveled, gray appendage, unsure how to make it register what comes out of his lungs. Aleck discovers that the membrane of the ear, light as tissue paper, controls the machinations of bones. Build me this, he tells Watson. Make a machine where a paper-thin reed can power its metal components.

Watson nods, continues winding cord along the attic walls and down through the banister of the staircase. When Mabel arrives, she can follow the humming wire with her fingers; a vibrating arrow. When Mabel arrives, Aleck will tell her that the ear is from a run-over pig. Watson, unwilling to hear such nonsense, goes to sleep under the table.

Mabel can't tell for sure, but it looks as if her teacher is shouting into the ear, fluttering indifferently on the workbench. Melly-Melly-Melly, Aleck shouts. Melly-Melly, she sees his lips pronounce.

Oh Aleck: the first ache in her chest.

Mabel wants to reach inside the eardrum and pull out a multilayered kerchief, an egg or a yellow feather. Instead, she points his attention to the pinprick of collapsed skin at the center of the ear's lobe.

A woman, she says to Aleck. She can't hear you.

The Attic has become the world. At the very least, a country. Aleck and Watson set up the cities of North America in the loops and crannies of their low-ceilinged existence. They spend their days transmitting messages to hypothetical cities. Watson phones Aleck from Boston to New York; Aleck replies from San Francisco to Los Angeles. They dash from one corner of the attic to another making as many calls as possible. The trick is to encourage the machine's worst problems now. Both shout or yell or sing into the mikes. The cities receive only half a voice. When Aleck sends a message to Portland, a portion of his sentence gets relayed to Detroit. Watson's out-of-tune songs scatter themselves among Miami, Winnipeg, Houston, and Yellowstone. They decided that the telegraph apparatus cannot accommodate this new idea of sound that is more than clicks. Their voices splay across this constructed country, they trip their mouths into funneled tubes, they dive their ears toward opposite ends. These frenzied scrambles are their best mistakes.

The two of them perform the victory dance: Aleck's traditional throb of celebration. Hooting and hollering, they crash about the attic, their arms waving above their heads, the chairs around them plummeting. They don't hear their landlady pound on her ceiling. They think the bang, bang, bang is their feet on the wooden floor. They don't hear Mabel arrive for her lesson. Aleck thumps Watson across his shoulders. Watson coughs the names of cities into the air: Grand Forks, St. Louis, New Orleans, Salt Lake City. They point at each other in glee. They hop over wire runners that crisscross the attic floor. They toss quartz and gypsum stones back and forth between them. They stuff their mouths full of fingers and make a popping noise. Mabel can't hear a thing, but she sees two crazy men.

Aleck and Watson exhausted, pleased, dripping with perspiration. We reached L.A. today, they tell her. They point at the map that is the room, that obscenely expands cities, dwindles the rest of the country. Mabel walks from city to city in two steps or less, laughs every time she crosses a state border.

Tag, she shouts when she touches the table that represents New York. Tag, she says to Washington. The final *g* slurs into the back of her throat. Her toes nudge wires. Not It, she declares to the two men. Watson slides his hand across Aleck's tense shoulder. You're It. Aleck joins in, lunges for Mabel.

They play all the rest of the afternoon. Two inventors: chasing Mabel.

PLATYPUS LOVE

Yesterday:
They began in the attic. Two men stroking words as if they were parts of a body.

Not my body.
Which had flung itself into a chair at the opposite end of Aleck's worktable. I was waiting for my lesson. For my speech therapy. I couldn't touch their fingers or their words. I couldn't decipher a single sentence. The table sliced the room. The attic brimmed with electronic gadgets, wood shavings and other masculine clutter. They began with a verbal agreement that left me out, that also entangled me. The two men held up a model of love across the room, and I reached out. I missed. They promised love from more than one angle. They promised each other.

Two men: voicing a trialogue.
They told a story I couldn't refuse. I can't refuse. But they left me out. Told the story as if I were a character living inside their foregone conclusion.

I turned away. Blanked out the expectations, the geometric possibilities of three. I walked downstairs, announcing my decision to wait in Aleck's kitchen. Surely a disciplined and eager student was as important as the toys they tinkered with up there in that bachelor's attic? I turned away from the offer they couldn't even whisper into my mute ears.

I met a boy yesterday in Boston Public Gardens. The day after those two men in the attic offered up their triangular affection. Mother didn't see me slip down to the musky stagnant pond. I sat on wet grass and threw crumbs to the grubby swans our city imports every spring. She assumes I can't speak to anybody new.

I can't speak to anybody new.
But this boy sat next to me and initiated a dialogue. Couple talk. Investing in the power of two. Oh, arithmetic is so much simpler than geometry! He had unusual hands, that boy in the park, twisted and gnarled like an old woman's. He let me stroke them alive. I rubbed the creases between his fingers, charmed his still-emerging calluses. Tingle, he said, you make them tingle, and he opened his hands slowly, stretching each finger. His words brushed against my lips. My eyes inhaled them. And when he smiled, I saw my body's fresh impression beneath me in the grass.

That boy in the park was an equation I could believe in.
But a couple is easy to disrupt. Triangles don't break in half. The pull of that unspoken invitation became too strong a temptation. Those two men, whose words couldn't grab, spoke to me. The complexities of their story intrigued me. I can't hear promises; I can't hear lies. But I read lips across darkened attic rooms. Those two men, boys really, inserted their hands inside my own, closed their fingers against my palms. Tight. Their lips, loose and suggestive, articulated versions of a trinity.

Whereas the gnarled hand I massaged belonged to only one body.

Mother called and called for me. Of course I heard nothing. My sisters sat far away on another hill and couldn't report her words. She headed home exasperated, knowing I'd soon grow tired of having no one to talk to.

I have no one to talk to.

For that boy in the Gardens, I massaged and massaged, but his body remained singular, his hands only one pair. I clasped my palms together, trapped his one hand between my own two. And there it was: an ending to this beginning.

Now I anticipate a dusty cluttered attic filled with the doubled image of two bodies longing.

That first day, as soon as he noticed I'd deserted his precious attic, Alex returned downstairs, asked me to rehearse speech for him. Whatever I wanted. Say whatever words you feel most comfortable pronouncing, he instructed. I kissed a boy, once, I told him, and left, swinging the gate on the way out. The slam of its metal against wood finished my sentence.

I travel at times with a boy whose name is Odysseus. He lives inside the pages of a book but wants more. I want no less. We sit on the lip of his boat, drag our toes in the slippery green of ocean. We plan feasts of goat's cheese and papayas and fried octopus, which we'll consume when we hit shore. Elixirs we'll drink through crazy straws that bend and twist the fluid into our mouths. I sing to the dolphins and hear them sing back.

Odysseus, though, has a tendency to bind his arms to solid masts whenever he suspects a seditious voice. He taught me about the Sirens and how men drown in their liquid throats. How Sirens use his name as bait to tempt him out of his skin: Odysseus-Odysseus-Odysseus.

A boy on a quest to hear his own name sung and not die in the process. He lashes his body to wood rather than stuff his ears with cotton. The other sailors drown inside a language they can only see. Odysseus claws his own flesh in an effort to consume the treacherous reverberations of female seduction. Then blames his bleeding wounds on mythical beings who are all voice and no body.

Creatures of desire.

Fault lines of pure sensation.

The other sailors ignore his desperation. Bored by his antics, they stuff silence inside their heads, read each other's signs and signals efficiently. Forget him. Odysseus screams on, not devoured whole. He's been trained by the gods to expect devotion. If not from the ship's sailors, then from fish he's schemed into women. I leave him strapped to the ship's mast. Fingernails gouging his rib cage. Praying to the Sirens to release his name from their witchery.

There are two ways to build a triangle, mathematical and mythological. Math requires too much faith for me to follow; numbers are such difficult magic. Mother says too much reading rots your brain, but that's because she was fed poetry that's always a trick or puzzle. Miss-True-the-governess buys me thick books, the heavier the better, and I sink inside their weight. Perhaps Mother does know best, but since I can't hear, what other way is there to rehearse this language? And she does so want me to learn the King's English.

Myth is more reliable than science, although both come packaged inside the covers of books. Most numbers I've met are imaginary. Places across the world rest side by side on my shelves. The friends I choose live under rocks or beneath lakes or inside someone else's body. I hold hands with Thomas and Alex at the same time, although they will expect me, eventually, to choose.

Eventually is a country I've never been to.

The country I live in is called the bedroom of Boston proper. Boston is made up of parks and slums, Mother says. Boston is made up of rebels and reformers, Father says. Of lovers and the overly cautious, I say.

I indulge a boy who has yet to inherit his own pleasure. Our bodies grasp each other, then depart at strange angles.

I ache for a girl who drops pennies into cracks in the road. She insists such minute treasures shout their own muted acoustics.

I anticipate a boy whose hearing replaces his sight. The double joint of his eyebrows offers me more than just memory. He is his own vision, unfolding.

My lips belong to Alex who stares at them more than my breasts or ankles or wrists. Thomas can have the rest. He demands nothing short of excess. Thomas rubs the tiny triangle of skin just above my earlobe till my kneecaps quiver. He grazes my neck with the tip of his tongue. He strokes my skin so lightly I feel a ripple all the way up my scalp.

Thomas is all cartilage and raised muscle and hair follicles. I creep up behind him while he sleeps, and his body wakes to mine. Before he hears a step. He closes his eyes again, an invitation to stroke his eyelids, to catch his lashes inside the grooves of my index finger.

Alex leaves the room when Thomas and I play these games with our bodies. We two become the undulating current Alex hopes to capture. This isn't dignified, he tells me, but I reject dignified the way Thomas rejects the supremacy of fork tines and gaps over the simple basin of a spoon.

I stand at one point of the triangle, watching the other two. A version of the double. Alex says I live in the center, but he projects a linearity not one of us believes. We believe, instead, in the bent and sweaty contortion of our original geometric figure, flexed equally between three points. I think Alex distrusts equality. Now that these two men have invented the triangle, Alex wants to conflate it back into a smooth line—with those two at each end and me in the middle. Then he can write our story with Thomas at the beginning and himself as ending. He doesn't see there is no middle, only space made precious by our joint enclosure.

Will Electric Speech be faster than lipreading? Will I see the telephone flash across computers and highways? These are questions not possible to articulate.

Thomas says that when we die we slip into another body. Those who feel awkward or uncomfortable inside their own skins haven't learned to live with others. I am becoming a specialist of the other. Alex declares Thomas's stories to be preposterous. Alex attends lectures by men preaching a medicine of knives inserted below ribs. A science that ties a deaf girl's hands together with her mother's scarf. His father spent a lifetime transcribing sounds that grow out of our lungs, out of our mouths, but Alex believes words commence at the tip of the tongue. He thinks thoughts reside in the brain. That the body functions only as a useful column for the head. And that nobody lives in Alex's body but Alex.

Thomas believes we're either saints or angels.

Boston, my Boston, for all its advances, will remain faithful to the habit of Oralism. Boston never moves. Only those arriving by water approach Boston with any decency. The city is too trapped in its constructions and reconstructions to recognize the debris collecting in North End Square, in South End, to the west of the Neck. Our city fathers drained the marshes, then left the oyster shells, gravel and street garbage to rot in the sun. Beacon Hill used to be an actual hill till they took off its top. And they poured gravel and street sweepings and oyster shells into Mill Pond. Leveled the surrounding hills to fill the waters north of Causeway Street. Demolished Father's house in the process. At twenty-eight cents a shovelful, demolished the land's curves, inverted the earth's valleys.

The geologist's sense of time is more spatial than the historian's. Turn down Cow Lane and get lost in a maze of alleys and burnt down shacks from before the great fire. Cross Mystic River Bridge, and the city recedes in fog. Wander past the Bunker hill obelisk till Winter Street turns into Summer. The distance between Boston and the rest of America is filled with cultural mistrust. Boston is an island located under water. We rarely swim to the surface to breathe. Instead, we trap air bubbles escaping from doomed explorers' nostrils. We have a passion for righteousness. I embrace that passion, though I am deaf to its sermon.

I love the word femur. On my tongue. This is why I lick your leg, and why I lick your leg. I want to taste the murmur within bone. In love with your body wrapped around the hum of this word. And your body. Flesh I embody with my tongue. And with my tongue.

One of you privileges the mind. One privileges the body. Why name you? I am the eager lover of both, that much I know. You worship the body, already a saint. And you, a secular angel, beatific with longing.

You two leave me out. Already. There are two of you, one of me. Convention suggests a *menage à trois* is in my favor, but I know better. Two penises are better than one, you tell me, but you tell me so many lies I can't say which I desire to believe. Every time I reach my palm toward one forehead, I should also touch the other. Otherwise, you tell me, this machine won't function. But I don't think so. We've made this love story in too many directions.

But one of us could disappear, and the other two could continue. Would continue. We've made this triangle so tight, even the loss of one angle wouldn't subtract its energy.

So. We may each be seduced by invisibility, but my desire is ubiquitous. Look: I stroke both hands toward your temples.

There are many rules I'll break but intimacy isn't one. People use sound as a barrier against connection. They say a person's name and then don't have to touch or be touched, though they long for both. That's why you want me to speak. Sound, when it escapes the body, leaves the idea of the body behind. And I have left too much of myself behind to settle for a disembodied caress.

I know a boy who rolls marbles under his tongue. Two, three, six, he plops between his lips, sucks back inside his cheeks. Jawbreakers that refuse to melt, slippery against his teeth. Smooth against the inside ridges of his mouth.

The laws of gravity throw objects to the ground before we notice they've abandoned our fingers. Words have a density that hearing people don't recognize. I see them spill from Alex's lips and gather in a puddle at his feet. Thomas is hearing, but he's also Deaf. We rub our arms together in conversations that endure for hours. Skin against skin, our hands rhyme each other's thoughts.

Alex is either hero or thief. The legacy of the hero is a people stronger than their best weakness. The legacy of the thief is loss, the excuse for a lack of precious possessions. Alex will steal the voice of an entire community: a language spoken with arms outstretched. Even a reaching hand frightens Alex with its implication of grammar and syntax. He will steal their language. Only a great thief could perform such a prank. Only a hero.

I taste a boy who sucks lollipops till his lips rainbow. His throat a tunnel breathing sugar. When I lick him my mouth borrows red, blue, mango. I dream ice cream out of his lips. He explodes ice cubes with simple execution of a smile.

My own eyes lick the air dry. I breath: in-out, in-out, shallow pockets of oxygen push through my tear ducts. Alex and Thomas play that the world is a toy. They hide countries in the attic and shout messages from one city to another. I never hear what they're saying but witness their laughter when words connect. Thomas has designed a digital counting system, which he demonstrates to me across the room. Alex doesn't see; he shouts out each success and failure, even when his back is turned from me. He never questions how I manage to gather the score. Between the three of us rest layers of loyalties. Where to begin unraveling? Thomas halts his rampage to hold up three fingers, one bent at the knuckle. I don't want to be so happy I can't remember straining to make my brain hear. I don't want to be content.

Alex bought me a diary for my birthday. He gifts me with pages blank of words.

The body is only as reliable as we expect. My father believes that I emerged—fully formed, perfect even down to the delicacy of my eardrums—out of his forehead. Birth through the vagina for other children.

How does Father explain my loss of hearing? Other senses accompany me, and besides, it's mothers who are responsible for fevers and prolonged delirium. Father says if he'd been with me I never would have caught the scarlet fever that invaded my ears. Father delivered a daughter out of his eye. No wonder I've got perfect vision. No wonder I'm not frightened by malaria or spring fever. But Father never lets himself sneeze in case his body releases an afterbirth.

What I can't hear, I write in my diary. Make nothing into words, make sound visible. I write down "birds" and right away the *b* curls the shape of a flying animal whose bones are hollow. Alive on the page. Mother says she wakes up mornings on account of singing birds. I don't believe her. I remember singing. Lyrics. *Blackbird sittin in* ... In church or on the front porch before bedtime. Mama singing in my ear 'cuz that's where words go.

Where words used to go.

Now they just disappear. Till I catch them in my hands and put them on the page. I read faster than Thomas. We sit on the attic roof, Alex searching for both of us and we read. Same book, same page. We turn each leaf together till I get impatient and rush past. Then I hold the page halfway between its flip and lean into what happens next. Even holding paper between where Thomas is and where I've come to, I get lost. When I'm inside a book, I hear again.

Words in a book travel in straight lines.

It must have been a deaf person who invented writing. The need to see sound. Who else would understand how a person loses herself inside the image of a word? Inside its vision?

Thomas chuckles and I look over the pages dividing us to see where he is. His finger gestures to the word "diaphragm," and I leap two pages back. To singing opera at midnight. Then I remember what hasn't happened yet, and I'm off to the next morning, the pages gathering between us. Thomas will never catch up, he'll never.

The attic roof is all slope and angle. Thomas shows me the opening in the ceiling. Every time we climb up, Thomas says we have to reinvent gravity. Every time we climb up, he says, we create a need for ledges, a need for the temptation to fall. Thomas says he's been falling most of his life, from his childhood into his job as a laborer, from carpentry into mechanics, from electronics into the hands of Alex, the mad inventor.

Except he doesn't say mad inventor. Only I tease Alex about madness and edges. They both assume Alex will be the climax of our story. They have forgotten to trust madness and blurred edges. Thomas loves Alex more than he loves himself. Thomas believes he has already lost, although no contest has been declared.

Truth is, he'd rather lose than win. Thomas wouldn't know how to beat Alex, not even when he's better, so much better, at touch, at knowing when to close his eyes. Alex doesn't trust the world enough to close his eyes except when sleep forces them shut. Nor does he trust his body. Thomas trusts his limbs so thoroughly he never questions their science. He lets his blood pump as fast as it needs to, steps out into the sky when his skin demands blue on blue on blue.

The English language has no proper future tense. But I can pronounce tomorrow. On our wedding night, Alex will offer me a wire from an instrument that mechanically conveys human voice. I will hold in my hand what I cannot hold inside my ears.

Alex carried me on his back today. I am too old for such games, but I ran toward his body and leapt onto his hips, and he embraced my legs in a backward hug. Then he walked forward tirelessly, my chin hooked over his crown. He walked till he reached a hill, then descended. I looked down from a great height with no fear of falling. As long as Alex carries me, I will always be able to see the road ahead. When we returned to the attic, Thomas kissed me on the forehead. He stared at the path I'd just coasted. That kiss, the intersection we three arrive at. An ending of sorts. A beginning. We play the telephone game: I speak into Thomas's ear, Thomas into Alex's and Alex into mine. The game ends there. Sometimes your whole life is decided by a detail. I haven't kissed Thomas again.

I love a boy whose lips were designed by his other lover. Who's kissed and kissed him till his mouth is all anticipation, his longing mere memory. I myself am recovering from a drop of great heights, from a love that I slipped on and that is called falling.

Really, I was thrown.

He crawls inside my damaged arms but won't stay long enough to heal his mind. Or his yearning. I've lost both, of course, for the mind is a paltry substitute once the heart has been stimulated.

Some prefer the loneliness of sanity.

He disappears through the gaps between my fingers, that boy. Wanders lost and upside down in a world that doesn't recognize hunger is an emotion. His want includes his chest and his thighs, but his lips continue to refuse my dialect. Instead, he anticipates the past. He travels to the Arctic, unhinges his tongue from the back of his throat, leaves it to freeze. It lingers there, immobile, awaiting a promised taste of thaw.

And my own body parts?

I have repaired and sewn them back together so often I am all seams. My body a spiderweb of scars. A reminder.

Oh, not of him. Too many lovers have worn through these limbs for any single one to impress my skin with more than a trace of indelible ink. No, the scars testify that once I could be hurt. Once I was whole enough to be broken.

The scars remind me that I used to ignore the ground beneath my feet. And I lament my forgotten talent for stepping—blind—into open air.

I'll marry the boy my father designed for me. Handsome, in love with ideas and soon wealthy from them. A boy who doesn't know his own limitations. Thomas, in love with the idea of Aleck, thinks I make my father's choice. Perhaps, I do. The deaf girl and the boy shouting devotion into a telephone receiver. Irony is the invention we all succumb to. When Aleck plays the piano, he expects me to hold my palms against the wood so I can feel sound. He believes he can guess my wants. Really, they are not so contained by rooms and music. My lover's love. The last boy I want.

Alex's hands belong to parlor rooms and piano playing soirees. His veins behave inside his skin. Even weeks and weeks of grease and metal grit and hammer bruises won't convert his fingers to anyone else's phonetics.

Thomas's arms crawl with veins. I rest my palms in the crease inside his elbow and feel the throb of his body pushing outward. His fingers hint at the world. Once I saw Thomas rub the bellyside of his forearm along the bellyside of Alex's. Alex jumped aside.

As if he'd never felt such softness.

Thomas wanted to stroke hairless against hairless, wasn't prepared for Alex's fear. What hasn't been written down is harder for me to believe. Eyes shut, Thomas traces fingernails past the inside of my elbows. Alex leaves the room. His eyes open.

Once he's gone, the stroking ceases. If Alex would close his eyes, he'd see the entire planet strung round and round with stovepipe wire, transporting voices. Thomas closes his eyes and sees a trail of discoveries Alex hasn't yet had time for. When I close my eyes, I see the same as when they're open, imprinted on the backs of my lids, instead of on air.

They leave me out, these men with their games. The undersides of my arms are too much like the rest of my body, and predicting the future is a simile for predicting the past. I have no camouflage.

Boston. My Boston. A city cracked with love and leftover corpses. I live in Cambridge; this bridge captured inside a city inside another city. The bridge connects inner and outer. Boston has two faces, one corrupt, one exuberant. The division is one between those who, having sworn off claret, turn finally to whiskey.

Boston's inhabitants become real by wearing a mask. Masks. The only code needed to unlock this city is the code of triumph. That's why Alex is the true Bostonian, and Thomas will forever be a man from Salem. Boston is two cities. And I embrace both.

Alex prefers kisses that begin with his lips closed. Sealed with a kiss, he mouths at me. He takes these catchphrases seriously. Sometimes a moment in a person's life will rhyme with an event gone past. Or one still to come. Thomas kisses me with his whole body.

I used to live in the ocean but grew weary of raw fish and seaweed, of soggy handshakes and slow-motion waltzes. Even the idea of fire can be drowned. In water, it is impossible to remember dust or old age. Most people need to believe in wrinkles, although their reflection frightens. Looking at water from beneath its surface contradicts the possibilities of a mirror. Every time I stared through the ocean's rim out into air another vision of my face evaporated. Narcissus in reverse.

The ocean swallows men whole then spits them back again when women begin a lavish ritual of combing blood from their skulls. Their graying scalps shaved with stones decorated red.

I grew gray hair when I lived in the ocean and emerged from that water with no memory of what I looked like and with a head the color of moon.

Thomas dives into lakes on his days away from the city. Nothing every catches between his teeth. The trick, he tells me, is not to care. He never closes his mouth or holds his nose, but opens both and lets his body absorb what it will. As long as his lungs are closed, he cannot drown. As long as he locks his lungs shut, the Sirens leave him alone. They want his name but not its container. But what if you *want* to swallow water? I question him. What if catching a mermaid's tale between your teeth is part of the trick? He smiles and repeats: The trick is not to care. Alex sees only container; he doesn't understand the body can be wrapping as well. He stares at my face when I speak and thinks he sees me.

Sometimes he does.

Mostly he witnesses my eyes performing miracles my lips can't fathom. But I am from Boston, and there is always more than one solution to becoming invisible.

I invent a boy who has hair the color of cinnamon. And a body so full of grace I dare not touch him. His mind brims with prairie love and how to swim to China on the back of a horse. I'll find him in books I haven't read yet. Yet: his favorite word. His voice is the length of my bead necklace, and as circular. He rejects the acquisition of knowledge. He says the principals of property and merchandise oppose learning. His mind is too cluttered with broken primary color crayons that he eats like worms with graphs of the underworld charting the devil's progress as misunderstood bystander.

This boy carries butterflies on the crests of his shoulder blades. He weighs more naked than he does when burdened by the costume of personality and social disguise.

You live inside a book I want to read.

I travel often to when I first meet Alex. He: so expectant, the impulse to teach imprinted on his forehead. Sometimes, I attempt to change the order of my appearance into his life. Or his into mine. I try to meet him in the street instead of that confounded attic, try to meet by accident, instead of Father's prearranged tutoring. I grab his sleeve and whisper my guttural words into his well-tuned ears. But each time I steal into the past, I recognize his face: anticipation. For his brave new deaf girl. For his wife-to-be. Much as I prefer to shake up our story, I am unable to deny him this.

When I travel forward I don't change anything. Why distort tomorrows today? Arrows pointing, tensed to release. My hands reach out to stroke scalp beneath thick strands of hair. Thomas will bow out and Alex will win the lottery. We know this script already, but the two of them never speak, trusting, as they must, in spontaneity. If only there was more at hand than this counterclockwise chase.

If only Thomas didn't love Alex so much.

They think I'm deaf, but I remember the feel of sound trapped inside my rib cage. I used to eat words when I was a child, before sickness eroded my vocal cords. Before sickness changed other people's hearing. Alex says he likes my voice. He strokes my hair when I speak hesitation. My words stumble and trip over themselves. Alex doesn't ever smile.

Thomas hears me whether I speak or not. The choice is mine. Thomas insists on reincarnation, that we three who are now together will be again. Not necessarily born into the same language. This appalls Alex, the man of science. But Alex doesn't need visions, at least not this one. His voice will live forever.

I hold a girl whose fingertips are fire. She talks with flames that reach from her fingernails to air. She sleeps with buckets of water beside her bed. In the morning, her arms swim in empty buckets. The flames devour the slight hairs on her wrists. On her forearms. I can only believe in her at noon, when the sun eclipses her body's perfect desire.

Thomas has promised to teach me the art of conversation. Skill, he tells me, has nothing to do with it. Patience is a myth. Listening is more about the tilt of the head than about which sounds tickle healthy earlobes. Conversation, Thomas tells me, is a simple conjuring trick of any amateur magician. Pull a word out of a hat, he says, and they'll see a live rabbit.

Those of us from Boston live in two time periods at once. My parents chose the present and some forgotten time buried in thirteenth century England. I live inside the nineteenth and twentieth, but unlike Alex, I'll travel both directions.

I imagine a girl who speaks with both hands. Only the Deaf can understand her. My parents never let me near another deaf child, fearing Dumbness might rub off. Alex, self-proclaimed champion of The Deaf, pushes me in the direction of lips I can't read, ears that can't unscramble the thick words on my tongue. I can't speak this Deaf girl's language, even though her ears rhyme with mine. My parents don't understand: I am more than my disability. And Alex will never see: I am also so much less.

Wherever I wander, speech defines me. Labels other people hang from my skirts. But I know how to live inside a disguise that masks silence. Even a diary is only one clue. The trick to passing as Hearing is to learn as many tricks as possible. Memorize what other people listen to: the scales of a piano, the national anthem. A line of a poem blown back in my face.

I run away from the boy who thinks passion is an apricot pit he could choke on. He bites into fruit gingerly or first splits it open with his fingers. It's not that he doesn't like surprise, he just can't allow himself to rely on astonishment. I used to rub his cheekbones, the bottom of his jaw leading to his chin, kiss the hairs on the back of his neck when he wasn't looking. He thought my passion was aimed at him, but really it was my own body I coaxed alive. My lips wander everywhere except where he fears. He waits for my fingers to abandon his skin so he can turn around and refuse to kiss me.

We climb trees together and hang upside down. Our knees wrap around bark, and our heads brush the grass tips. This boy wants love to be surprising and permanent. Or neither. I don't tell him that you can have no depth without surface, that the air is so thin and stretched here on the surface that breathing becomes dangerous.

So it should be.

My lungs contract and expand, and my blood beats at its own pace. Fast. Even upside down, kisses end up in the belly. But they begin on the stretched surface of skin outlining the mouth. A kiss is neither easy nor expected. Unless you crack it open with your knuckles first. Unless you dissect it before it is born.

Platypus love. Alex and Thomas explain to me that we are a bridge holding hands over water. They discuss the implications of letting go. Men like to believe in drowning as a solution to love. But winter announces itself outside the attic window. The river chokes on ice and snowdrifts. I play with long division and with the buttercups Thomas has stored in Alex's apartment. The river grumbles from below unattached floes that crack its jagged edges. By spring we won't need the yellow blossoms. But for now we cater to their near-invisible petals.

How can you two men not understand that seasons change?

Alex and Thomas play ping-pong on their giant maps. They have cleared all the wires to one side and aim the ball at the center. The trick is not to hit the ball onto the same city twice. They play within, beside, against the rules. Thomas lacks the desire for competition. But Alex can taste the future. He is so close. So close. If they could see beneath my eyelids, they would drop their game, run to embrace me. One in delight. One in fear. Not that my vision is so startling, but uncertainty is one game neither has learned how to embrace. Yet they play on. They play on.

These men will invent the twentieth century.

I prefer to disregard the hierarchy of the apex. A triangle can be a wheel, turning within the turning within. Passion and exclusion and multiplication. And *and* and *and* and *and.*

I laugh with a girl whose hair is plastic snakes braided red, yellow, pink, green, orange. She lives inside the future where she writes books containing pages made from water. I'll meet her, someday, when the path of my remembering and her forgetting cross the same century.

Sometimes, a moment in life rhymes with its future. My father has chosen an appropriate husband; who am I to say otherwise? My lover would agree. Thomas believes Alex the better man because he is right and proper and genius. Thomas appears to me with no flaws except his own trusting kindness. Alex presumes that when he speaks a kiss into the telephone I will receive it. In my future, I will need to fall in love with flaws, with kisses I cannot hear.

How does the future fit our triangle? A man can go his whole life without a climax, die in a state of anticipation. But he must believe in phantom rewards, must pursue what he considers eternal compensation.

Most men live inside the climax that just happened, its echo still throbbing their fingertips. These men lust after today.

A man who climaxes only once—and early—walks a path that leads away from memory. He hopes for a Second Coming to blast away the present. Hope: the emotion rooted in past triumphs. He longs for the explosion that will release him from his life's extended denouement.

The sun set twice tonight. Once it dipped below the horizon, and once it disappeared into my mouth. The first sunset followed nature's law of cycle and expectation; the second hid from the first but not from me. Both Alex and Thomas think it is when the sun sets that the moon becomes possible. But there it is: triumphant in the sky, hours before the sun risks approaching the lip of horizon.

A woman who climaxes only once has been interrupted.

Marshall McLuhan and George B. Leonard

"The Future of Sex," *Look Magazine* (1967)

"Well, it finally happened," Michael Murphy of California's Esalyn recently said. "A young person came up to talk with me, and I couldn't tell if this person was a man or a woman. Now, I've seen plenty of young people of both sexes dressed in slacks, sweater and long hair, but I'd always been able to find *some* sexually distinguishing clue. This time there was *no way for me to tell.* I admit it shook me up. I didn't know exactly how to relate. I felt it would take a new kind of relating, no matter if it were a boy *or* a girl."

This episode is extreme, but it points to a strong trend. In today's most technologically advanced societies, especially urban Britain and America, members of the younger generation are making it clearer—in dress and music, deeds and words—just how unequivocally they reject their elders' sexual world. It is tempting to treat the extremes as fads: perhaps many of them are. But beneath the external symptoms, deep transforming forces are at work.

Sex as we now think of it may soon be dead. Sexual concepts, ideas and practices already are being altered almost beyond recognition. Marriage and the family are shifting into new dimensions. What it will mean to be boy or girl, man or woman, husband or wife, male or female may come as one of the great surprises the future holds for us.

We study the future to better understand a present that will not stand still for inspection. Today, corporations, foundations and governments are asking a new breed of experts called "futurists" to tell them how things are going to be. These futurists tend to limit their predictions to things rather than people. Their imaginations and their computers fight future wars, knit future systems of economies, transportation and communication, build future cities of fantastic cast. Into these wars, systems and cities, they place people just like us—and thereby falsify all their predictions. By default rather than design, most futurists assume that "human nature" will hold firm. They ignore the fact that technological change has always struck human life right at the heart, changing people just as it changes things.

This may be especially true of sex. A history of mankind in terms of sexual practices would make wildly variegated reading. Many ancient civilizations, for example, encouraged varying degrees of incest, and the Ptolemies, successors to Alexander the Great, practiced marriage between brother and sister for some three hundred years with no obvious ill effect. Modern anthropologists have brought back stories of present-day primitive tribes whose sex customs confound our traditional notion that there is only one "natural" pattern of relationship between the sexes.

In early man, just as in most of the higher mammals, males and females lived rather similar lives, with little specialization except where child-bearing and child rearing were concerned. Life for every member of a primitive hunting tribe was integral, all-involving; there could be no feminist movement, nor any special class of homosexuals or prostitutes. But when mankind turned from hunting to farming, and then to creating cities, empires, pyramids and temples, men and women were split apart in ways that went far beyond biology. Many men became specialists—kings, workers, merchants, warriors, farmers, scribes—in the increasingly complex social machine. Most women fell heir to less specialized, but separate, domestic tasks.

With the coming of writing, it was the manly virtues that were recorded and extolled. As Charles W.F. Ferguson points out in *The Male Attitude*, men have kept the records of the race, which may explain why history is a chronicle of war, conquest, politics, hot competition and abstract reasoning. "What survives in the broad account of the days before the modern era," Ferguson writes, "is a picture of a humankind full of hostility and inevitable hate." (*LOOK* researchers were surprised to find that, until relatively recent times, female births and deaths often were not even recorded.) Ancient writers exaggerated the biological as well as the social differences between the sexes, with the female coming off very badly indeed.

The Romans invented the word *sexus*, probably deriving it from the Latin verb *secare*, to cut or sever. And that is exactly what civilization has done to man and woman. The cutting apart of the sexes rarely has been more drastic than in the industrial age of Europe and America, the period that was presaged by the invention of printing around 1460, and that is now changing into something new right before our eyes.

Throughout the Middle Ages, there had been less separateness between men and women. Privacy, for example, was unwished. Houses had no hallways; bedrooms served as passageways and sleeping places for children, relatives and visitors, along with married couples. Under such circumstances, the sexual act merged easily with the rest of life. Language now considered intimate or vulgar was part of ordinary conversation. Childhood did not exist as a separate category. At about age seven, children simply moved into the grown-up world; paintings of that day depict the young as scaled-down adults, even to the matter of clothing,

After printing, however, human life became increasingly visual and compartmentalized. Architecture took up the idea of visual enclosure, with private rooms connected by hallways. It was only when this happened that childhood separated out from the rest of life. At the same lime, sexual activity went underground. Hidden and mysterious, it receded into a realm apart from ordinary existence, becoming more and more fraught with a special intensity, a vague anxiety. Indecency, pornography and obscenity came into being as a result of specialist stress on separate parts of the body. By the time of Queen Victoria, the split between sex and proper life was complete. Any wedding night, after a five-to-ten year engagement, was likely to be a trauma.

Freud flushed sex up out of the underground, but he, like his contemporaries, saw it as an explosive, a possible threat to whatever held civilization together. In his time—and even up to the present—the forces of life seemed constantly at odds with one another; since the Renaissance, it has seemed necessary to pen them up in separate compartments. The industrial age built more than its share of these boxes. It split class from class, job from job, profession from profession, work from play; divorced the self from the reality and joy of the present moment; fragmented the senses from the emotions, from the intellect; and, perhaps most importantly of all, created highly specialized and standardized males and females.

The ideal male of the industrial age was "all man." He was aggressive, competitive, logical. This man of action was also an apostle of the abstract. And he feared to show much emotion. The ideal woman, for her part, was emotional, intuitive, guilefully practical, submissive. Maleness and femaleness were separate territories; man and woman shared only a tiny plot of common humanity. The wonder is that the two could get together long enough to continue the race.

When sex—under the influence of Freud, factories, the automobile and world wars—came out into the open to become SEX, a peculiar thing happened; people were *supposed* to be free and frequent with their sexual activity. Women were *supposed* to turn from Victorian propriety to passionate responsiveness. And yet the basic ideals of maleness and femaleness continued unchanged. It was like a revolution without popular support: a lot of slogans, shouting and confusion, but not much revolution.

The only real attempt at change up until the present turned out to be abortive. Women of the feminist persuasion, viewing the action and the power over there in the arena of aggressiveness, specialization and hot competition, tried to take on those attributes of maleness. How ironical! They may have been heading in the wrong direction. When the Victorian novelist George Meredith wrote, "I dare expect that Woman will be the last thing civilized by Man," he was unknowingly describing her fitness for the *post*-civilized Electric Age. Where the old technology split people and the world apart, demanded human fragmentation, the emerging technology is putting Humpty Dumpty back together again. It is most doubtful, in the new age, that the rigidly "male" qualities will be of much use. In fact, there may well be little need for standardized males or females.

Trying to define a new sexuality in the industrial period, D.H. Lawrence placed his characters against a backdrop of factories, mines, smokestacks. His most successful sexual hero (in *Lady Chatterly's Lover*) was a gamekeeper; he may be viewed as the closest Lawrence could get to the primitive hunter. In a sense, the man of the future will be a hunter, an adventurer, a researcher—not a cog in a social machine. The coming age, linked by all-involving, instantaneous, responsive, electronic communication, may seem more "tribal" than "industrial." The whole business of sex may become again, as in the tribal state, play—freer, *but less important.*

When survey-takers "prove" that there is no sexual revolution among our young people by showing that the frequency of sexual intercourse has not generally increased, they are missing the point completely. Indeed, the frequency of intercourse may decrease in the future because of a real revolution in attitudes toward, feelings about, and uses of sex, especially concerning the roles of male and female. What are those young men with long, flowing hair really saying? In what may seem a ludicrous overstatement, they are sending a clear message to all who will listen; "We are no longer afraid to display what you may call 'feminine.' We are willing to reveal that we have feelings, weaknesses, tenderness—that we are human. And, by the way, we just may be ridiculing all of those up-tight movie males with cropped hair and unflinching eyes. We're betting they can't touch our girls."

Indeed, the long-haired boys' appeal is not aesthetic, but sexual; not private, but corporate. Bear in mind that the Beatles' dazzling early success, long before their remarkable musicianship became clear, was conferred upon them by millions of young *females* who were transported by those pageboy hairdos and those sensitive faces.

And the Beatles were not the first in a modern lineage of girl-movers. A younger, slenderer, tenderer Frank Sinatra, and then a hip-swiveling Elvis Presley, had reduced earlier sub-generations to squeals and moans. It takes a particularly obstinate blindness not to realize that an ability to free emotions, and not a fragmented "all-maleness," provides today's most compelling erotic appeal.

We might also confess that our reading of the new teen-age "conformity" of dress and hairdo fails to consider the social ritualism of these forms. They express the new desire for depth involvement in social life rather than egotistic eccentricity.

The trend (perhaps without the exaggerated hair style) seems likely to continue. The all-sensory, all-pervasive total environment of the future may be no place for the narrow-gauge, specialized male. Emotional range and psychic mobility may be valued. Heightened intuition may be required. The breed of hombre generally portrayed by John Wayne is already an anachronism. "Be a man!" the hombre bellows, and the more perceptive of our young laugh.

And if the narrow-gauge male is not laughed out of existence, he may, literally, *die* out. Specialized, competitive man is particularly susceptible to the maladies of the involuntary muscle, nervous and vascular systems. A U.S. male's life expectancy now is seven years less than a female's. Figures on earlier times are impossible to verify, but one thing is sure: the gap has never been greater. Men who operate inside the boxes of regimented civilization—whether bus driver, production-line worker, professional specialist—die off at an alarming rate from the heart and gut diseases. Figures for the peptic ulcer are particularly revealing: deaths for white men are four times that for white women in the U.S. But the female death rate, as women have started pushing into the man's world, has been rising. And what about today's younger generation, those under 25? Here are the children of TV and science fiction, the pioneers of the Electric Age, the first humans to sample, even briefly and incompletely, the less fragmented, less competitive, more involving future. What of these tentatively retribalized young men? We may predict that their ulcer rate will decline.

No surprise. In the most isolated primitive tribes, those whose members still operate as free-roving hunters, digestive disorders are practically unknown and the usual civilized heart troubles are rare. Significantly, these people make little distinction between the identities of male and female. As the noted British anthropologist Geoffrey Corer writes concerning the peace-loving Pygmies of Africa, the Arapesh of New Guinea and the Lepchas of Sikkim: "Men and women have different primary sexual characteristics—a source of endless merriment as well as more concrete satisfactions—and some different skills and aptitudes. No child, however, grows up with the injunctions, 'All real men do' or 'No proper woman does...,' so that there is no confusion of sexual identity; no cases of sexual inversion have been reported among them. The model for the growing child is one of concrete performance and frank enjoyment, not of metaphysical symbolic achievements, or of ordeals to be surmounted. They do not have heroes or martyrs to emulate, or cowards or traitors to despise ... a happy, hard-working and productive life is within the reach of all."

It would seem that "being a man" in the usual, aggressive Western sense is, if nothing else, unhealthy. To live an ordinary peacetime life in the U.S.—as a recent Army study of the "nervous secretions" of combat soldiers in Vietnam shows—is as bad or worse for your gut, heart and nervous system as facing enemy bullets. But the present fragmented civilization seems on its way out, and what "being a man" means could swiftly change.

Extremes create opposite extremes. The specialized, narrow-gauge male of the industrial age produced—in ideal, at least—the specialized woman. The age stressed the visual over the other senses; the fast development of photography, and then movies, helped pull femaleness up from the context of life, of actuality, and make it something special, intense, "hot."

Grotesque and distorted extremes tend to pop out just at the end of any era, a good example being the recent rash of blown-up photographic nudes. The foldout playmate in *Playboy Magazine*—she of outsized breasts and buttocks, pictured in sharp detail—signals the death throes of a departing age.

Already, she is beginning to appear quaint, not sexy. She might still be possible for a while in a wide-screen, color movie (another hot medium). But try to imagine her, in that same artificial pose, on the intimate, involving, "cool" television set in your living room.

Don't throw away your Playboy foldouts, however. Sooner than it may seem possible, those playmate-size nudes may become fashionable as collectors' items, having the same old-timey quality for future generations that cigar-store Indians and Victorian cartoons have for us. This is not to say that nudity is on its way out. On the contrary, it will most likely increase in the neo-tribal future. But it will merge into the context of ordinary living, becoming not so much lurid and sexy as natural and sensuous.

Already, new "sex symbols" poke fun at the super female. Notable among them is the boyish and gentle young model known as Twiggy. Sophia Loren, for example, is to Twiggy as a Rubens painting is to an X-ray. And what does an X-ray of a woman reveal? Not a realistic picture, but a deep, involving image. Not a specialized female, but a *human being*.

It is toward a common humanity that both sexes now tend. As artificial, socially-imposed distinctions disappear, the unalterable essentials of maleness and femaleness may assume their rightful importance and delight. The lusty Gallic salute, *Vive le difference!*, rings truer about biology than about mores, mannerisms and dress. Even fashion speaks. "Glamour" was a form of armor, designed to insulate, to separate. The new styles, male and female, invite dialogue.

The Pill makes a woman a Bomb

While both sexes will probably change, most men will have farther to go than most women in adjusting to the new life. In an unspecialized world of computers and all-enveloping communications, sensitive intuition and openness will win more prizes, if you will, than unfeeling simplistic logic. Right now, it is impossible to guess how many companies are being held together by intuitive and sensitive executive secretaries. Fortunate is the enterprise that has a womanly woman (not a brittle, feminist dame) as a high-level officer. Many forward-looking corporations, especially in the aerospace industry, already are engaged in sensitivity-training sessions for their male executives. The behavior encouraged in these sessions would make a John Wayne's character wince: Manly males learn how to reveal their emotions, to become sensitive to others, to weep openly if that is what they feel like doing—all this in the pursuit of higher profits. Sensitivity works. The new technology—complex, interrelated, responsive—demands it.

The demands for new male and female ideals and actions are all around us, changing people in many a subtle and unsuspected way. But there is one specific product of modern technology, the contraceptive pill, that can blow the old boundaries sky high. It makes it possible for sexual woman to act like sexual man. Just as the Bomb instantly wipes out all the separating boundaries essential to conventional war, the Pill erases the old sexual boundaries in a flash. The Pill makes woman a Bomb. She creates a new kind of fragmentation, separating sexual intercourse from procreation. She also explodes old barriers between the sexes, bringing them closer together. Watch for traditions to fall.

Romantic love seems a likely victim. As a specialty, romance was an invention of the late Middle Ages, a triumph of highly individualistic enterprise. It requires separation, unfulfillment. The chase is everything—the man aflame, the maiden coy. Sexual consummation bursts the balloon of yearning. As in the romantic movies, the significant embrace can hardly be imagined without "The End" printed over it. Indeed, what we have called sex in recent decades may be viewed as the lag end of Romantic Love.

As a way of selecting a spouse, romance ("In all the world, you are the only girl for me") never worked very well. Back in the 18th century, Boswell may have felt some shock at Dr. Johnson's answer to his question: "Pray, sir, do you suppose there are fifty women in the world, with any one of whom a man may be as happy as with any woman in particular?" Johnson replied, "Aye, fifty-thousand." The future may well agree with Dr. Johnson. It is difficult to play the coy maiden on a daily diet of contraceptive pills. And the appeal of computer dating suggests that young people are seeking out a wide and quite practical range of qualities in their mates—not just romance or high-intensity sex appeal. Here, in fact, may be the electronic counterpart of arranged marriage.

The great mystics have always perceived Romantic Love as somehow defective, as a double ego that selfishly ignores other people. Today's youngsters have a different way of putting it: "Our parents' generation is hung up about sex."

YOUTHFUL SEXUALITY IS COOLING DOWN

As Romantic Love fades, so may sexual privacy. Already, young people shock their elders by casually conversing on matters previously considered top secret. And the hippies, those brash pioneers of new life patterns, have reverted—boys and girls together, along with a few little children—to the communal living of the Middle Ages or the primitive tribe. It is not uncommon to find a goodly mixture of them sleeping in one room. Readers who envisage wild orgies just don't get the picture. Most of the hippies are not hung up on sex. To them, sex is merely one of many sensory experiences. It is available when desired—therefore perhaps not so desperately pursued.

Today, sex is returning to the adult world just as childhood is once again becoming enmeshed in grown-up matters. The dream girl or dream guy is becoming as odd an idea as the dream house in a world of integral urban design. Sex is becoming secondary to the young. At the same rate that it becomes accessible, it is cooling down. A couple of teenagers like Romeo and Juliet would now have some of their most dramatic moments deciding on the kind of education they want for their children, plus a second career for Romeo in middle age.

In future generations, it seems most likely that sex will merge with the rest of life, that it will settle down and take its place within a whole spectrum of experiences. You might not think so, what with the outpouring of sexed-up novels and plays since World War II. But these, like the slickly pictured play-mates, bring to mind the death of an era. When a novelist like Norman Mail-er contends that man is boxed-in by civilized constraints, he is quite right. But when he goes on to say that the free human spirit can now assert itself most-ly through sex and violence, he is being merely Victorian.

The more that modern writers present sexual activity as a separate, highly delineated, "hot" aspect of life, the more they hasten the death of SEX. Most "literary" novelists have not yet discovered the present, much less glimpsed the future, which is one reason why so many of the brighter college students have turned to anti-novels and, in spite of its questionable literary reputation, science fiction. Robert Heinlein's *Stranger in a Strange Land*, a popular under-ground book, tells of an attempt to set up Martian, rather than the usual human, relationships here on earth. In these relationships, what we term sex is communal and multisensual. There is no sharp, artificial distinction between male and female roles. Sex blends with other activities that might be called mystical. And there is even the need for a new word (Heinlen calls it "growing closer") for this demi-erotic mode of relating. Many young people see something of their own aspirations in the Heinlen book and others simi-lar to it. Norman O. Brown (*Life Against Death, Love's Body*) strikes an equally sympathetic response with his thesis that civilized man has even fragmented his physical person. According to Brown, many people can feel sexual plea-sure only in the sex organs themselves: the rich sensory universe of the rest of the body has been deadened.

Just as the Electric Age, with its multitudinous communication aids, is extending the human nervous system *outside* the body, it is also creating a new desire for exploration inside the self. This inner trip seeks ways to awaken all the senses, to find long-lost human, capacities, to discover turn-ons beyond the narrowly sexual. One instance of this new drive for depth-involvement is the growing national interest in Oriental religion and philosophy; another, riskier one is increasing use of LSD and marijuana among young people. The drugs, the experimentalists claim, very quickly "blow your mind," that is to say, they knock out the old partitions within the self, allowing new connec-tions to be made. Some theorists also say that the new rock music with psy-chedelic light effects can aid the inner traveler.

Serious researchers are looking for means of accomplishing even more without the use of drugs. In several centers throughout the U.S. they are working out techniques for awakening the body and senses, especially those other than the purely visual, and for helping people achieve the unusual psychic states described, for example, in the literature of mysticism. The future will likely demonstrate that *every* human being has capacities for pleasure and fulfillment beyond sex that the present barely hints at.

In this rich context, those reports on the death of the American family may turn out to be premature. Actually, the family may be moving into a Golden Age. With so much experiment possible, marriage may come later in life than ever before. Future family units may not be separated from each other in little capsules, but may join together in loosely organized "tribes." As it is now, the capsular family often has nowhere to turn for advice or encouragement when in need, except to professional counselors or organization. The informal tribes of the future can provide a sounding board and a source of support for each of its families, far more responsive and more loving than any professional helper.

HOMOSEXUALITY MAY FADE OUT

With marriage coming later in life, it may also become a more serious matter—perhaps as serious as divorce. Some couples may even wish to write up a legally binding separation agreement (to be revised when their financial and parental situation changes) as a precondition to marriage. Thus, in a sense, marriage becomes "divorce." With all this unpleasant business anticipated and accomplished even before the nuptial vows are spoken, divorce becomes far easier—and probably far less likely. In any case, the divorce rate will probably fall.

Marriage—firmly and willfully welded, centered on creative parenthood—may become the future's most stable institution. The old, largely discredited "togetherness" was based on stereotyped concepts of each family member's role. The new family, integral and deeply involving, may provide the ideal unit for personal discovery, for experiment and the seemingly infinite possibilities of being human. Each new child can provide a new set of perceptions for all the family. Each develops rapidly, urges change in parents and other children alike. It is possible that the family of the future may find its stability in constant change, in the encouragement of what is unique in each of its members; that marriage, freed from the compulsions and restrictions surrounding high-intensity SEX, can become far more *sensual*, that is to say, more integral.

What about homosexuality and prostitution? Lifelong, specialized sexual inversion has baffled many researchers. But may it not be viewed simply as a response to sexual overspecialization? Just as men in our society are far more specialized than women, so male homosexuality is far more prevalent. To "be a man" in the narrow sense has often proven difficult and dehumanizing. In certain stressful and ambiguous family situations, some young men have not been able to pull it off. So they flip-flop over to the coin's reverse side, the mirror image of hyper-maleness—even more specialized, even more limiting. If a new, less specialized maleness emerges, it is possible that the need to turn to specialized homosexuality will decrease. There is a striking absence of it among the communal-living young people of today.

As for prostitution, if it is the oldest profession (or, if you will, service industry), it is also one of the most ancient specialties—an early consequence of the creation of man-in-the-mass. Armies, merchant fleets, work forces: Men without women demanded Woman, or at least one aspect of her. So long as men are massed and shipped away from home, this female specialist will likely follow. But, like homosexuality, prostitution may also be looked upon as a response to a certain kind of hyper-femininity. When men, as in the Victorian Age and long after, require sexually-inhibited wives, they create an equal and opposite demand for sexually-uninhibited partners-for-pay. As the first requirement fades, so does the second. Already, call girls are becoming game for the aging. The whole notion seems somewhat ridiculous to the young.

Indeed, the future may well wonder why there has been so much fuss about sex over all these years. Sex may well be regaining some of its traditional cool. It is still a three-letter word, despite the efforts of its four-letter relatives to hot it up. This is not to say the future will be sexless. Far from it, generations yet to come may very well find all of life far more erotic than now seems possible.

Those who try to puzzle out any single sexual way for the next age will probably find their efforts in vain. Rather, it seems, the future holds out infinite variety, diversity. The search for a new sexuality is, after all, a search for a new selfhood, a new way of relating. This search already is well under way. What it turns up will surprise us all.

Katherine Monk

from *Weird Sex and Snowshoes* (2001)

GETTING HOT (AND STAYING COLD)

... A lot has been said about all the kinky, dark, quirky and obsessive sex in Canadian film. From David Cronenberg's violent body collisions in *Crash* to the necrophilia of Lynne Stopkewich's *Kissed,* Canadian film has explored more sexual quirks on screen than Canadian society has ever had the courage to talk about out loud. This is probably no accident. As Canadians, we have an apparent cultural aversion to sharing the details of our bodily functions with others, and when it comes to the sex act itself—well, the less said the better. Not only does the state have no business in the bedrooms of the nation (thanks to the closest thing this country ever had to a sex symbol: the vaguely androgynous Pierre Elliot Trudeau), but no one else does either. We're repressed on both sides of the linguistic border. The French-Canadian soul is haunted by the Gothic complications of sex and the Catholic church, while the English-Canadian soul is burdened by Victorian codes of physical denial. Sex = Guilt in Canadian society, no matter which way you undress it.

Part of this guilt reflects our lingering institutional past—as represented by both the church and government. In the late 1990s, there was a wonderful example of this tightly sphinctered sexual approach when a parliamentary backbencher threw a political fit about the film *Bubbles Galore* (1996). This Cynthia Roberts feminist take on pornography featured a very long orgasm sequence featuring porn star Annie Sprinkle, and several other graphic porn movie devices. It also received government funding, which sparked a small brushfire in Parliament as right-wing members spouted off about the evils of the taxpayer paying for a bombastic but educational film about women and sex. (Lord knows, the average taxpayer doesn't waste money on pornography.) Not one of the members had even seen the film, but the very fact that it featured frank depictions of sex was offensive enough to merit a thrashing in the House of Commons. Clearly it's a natural reaction to be embarrassed when watching something as raw and animal-like as fornication. The guilt comes because we generally want to watch anyway. Whenever someone balls up enough courage to let a screaming sex demon fly in this society, we find ourselves transfixed and settle into a voyeuristic groove—which only makes us feel guiltier.

The rest of the guilt may very well be a function of our survivor guilt. Both survival and sex are normally considered life-affirming acts, and both cause the Canadian psyche to outwardly shrivel. We've already suggested some of the causes of survivor guilt in previous chapters, namely the burden of knowing that others died, and the non-socialist, non-pluralistic connotations of the "survival of the fittest" moral code. As Canadian actor Peter Outerbridge told me when I interviewed him on the set of *Marine Life*, a project he started just after appearing as a Russian rocket scientist in Brian DePalma's *Mission to Mars*: "The difference between Canadians and Americans is that they believe in survival of the fittest and we believe the strong should take care of the weak. I think we have to take care of others. It's the right thing to do, if only because it's really boring to think and talk about yourself all the time. We might look like capitalists on the surface, but deep down, we're socialist."[1]

Socially spurred survival guilt, or plain perversion? In this chapter, we'll focus on sex—lots of sex—and all its many perverse manifestations in Canadian film. Lord knows, there is no shortage of weird sex in our celluloid closet, and when I say closet—I mean it. We're as quiet about sex in general as other cultures are about homosexuality, which in itself affirms the guilt that sex has historically carried in Canadian culture. It also offers a clue as to why there is almost as much gay sex in Canadian film as there is heterosexual copulation. We'll deal with all of this later in greater depth in the rest of the chapter. First, though, we'll look at gay sex, straight sex and all the variations therein. We'll also survey the major shifts that have taken place in the cinematic boudoir over the last few decades, and what's become of our long-voyaging guilt valise. We'll dissect and discuss our take on gender roles and look at how they, in turn, affect the types of sexual unions we see on screen. Finally, we'll take a broad view of the whole sweaty business and look at sex as the great Jungian metaphor for personal integration and where that leaves us as a culture.

THE DIRTY DEED

"I'm always so scared of being abnormal."
—*Le Déclin de l'empire américain*

One of the beautiful things about not talking about sex with any great regularity is the way it makes all sex uniformly "dirty." There is no distinction between what's "normal" sex and what's truly "kinky" sex when we barely acknowledge the act exists at all. This idea turned out to be one of the main comic engines in Denys Arcand's *Le Déclin de l'empire américain* (Decline of the American Empire), in which a group of upwardly mobile, educated professionals begin talking about their sex lives only to find out that "normal" doesn't exist. One is in the midst of a near-anonymous sadomasochist relationship with a biker type. Another is sleeping with every spouse in the house. "Whenever he talks about sex, he makes it sound ridiculous," says the wife about her husband, unaware of the fact that he's sleeping with her confidante. Similarly, the yuppy couple in David Cronenberg's *Crash* (James Spader and Deborah Kara Unger) appear to be the very model of conformity with their minimalist concrete apartment and luxury automobiles when in fact they are suicidal sexual thrill-seekers desperate to experience a symbolic mutual orgasm with their automobiles. I could go on at length, but the truth about Canadians is, you just never know what their sexual habits are going to be because they are so seldomly discussed out loud. We are a sexually closeted culture.

The late critic Vito Russo wrote an entire book on the subject of closets. In his book and the subsequent documentary, *The Celluloid Closet*, Russo dealt with the latent signs of homosexuality on the American silver screen—essentially arguing that even though there are no overt homosexuals in Hollywood, the gay figure emerges one way or other, between the cracks—no pun intended. If we analyze what Russo says about why America felt this need to hide the whole gay issue, we may be able to apply a similar logic to why Canada feels this need to repress sexuality in general, gay or straight.

As Russo writes under the title "Who's a Sissy?":

> The predominantly masculine character of the earliest cinema reflected an America that saw itself as a recently-conquered wilderness ... Men of action and strength were the embodiment of our [American] culture, and a vast mythology was created to keep them in constant repair. Real men were strong, silent and ostentatiously unemotional. They acted quickly and never intellectualized. In short, they did not behave like women ... The idea of homosexuality first emerged on screen, then, as an unseen danger, a reflection of our fears about the dangers of tampering with male and female roles.[2]

From what Russo gleaned on the subject of repression and the national identity with regards to our oh-so-potent southern neighbours, he makes a direct link between sexual identity and the national ideal. Reaffirming the logic behind the idea of "phallonationalism," America is generally a nation of masculine strength, not of hesitating girly-men who blur the boundary between the genders. If America wanted to ensure its beefy masculine image to propel the idea of the conquering wilderness hero, then the Canadian propensity for complete sexual denial could be reflecting our continuing national insecurity complex. We don't want to assert anything, in either official language, lest we upset the precarious balance of Confederation.

SEXUAL REALISTS

Despite our reticence to talk dirty in public, the Canadian psyche simply revels in sexual imagery on screen. Nothing graphic, mind you. Heaven forbid. Sex is more of a mental than physical occupation on Canadian screens, and a very popular one at that. If we scan back to early films, we could easily call ourselves sexual realists: people who are constantly contradicting, de-mythologizing and cerebrally deconstructing sex like some latter-day Gulliver, stumbling across a giant breast that is just too big, too real, too porous and too visibly hairy to see it as anything but a blob of human tissue—not some mythic globe of the great goddess.

Filmmaker Lynne Stopkewich observed: "The real difference between Canadian and American mainstream film can be summed up in an ad I saw when I was last in Los Angeles for 'Laser Vaginal Rejuvenation.' That, to me, is so completely bizarre. Canadians are constantly being labelled as sexually perverse or dysfunctional, but what could be more unnatural than getting cosmetic surgery to fix a natural process?" she asks. "That whole idea of correcting, perfecting and manipulating what is natural—to the point where it's unrecognizable—is so much a part the American psyche that they don't even see it as strange anymore … But we, or at least I, do."[3] Stopkewich doesn't say it in so many words, but her comment echoes a common feeling among most Canadians that we have a more grounded approach to all areas of romance. Think about it: Where are all the great Canadian romantic comedies? All our sexy, melodramatic tear-jerkers about falling in love? There aren't many, but we're getting there. The year 2000 witnessed the premieres of such bona fide romantic comedies as Richard Roy's *Café Olé* and Clement Virgo's poignantly funny, *Love Come Down.*

In the past, we made comedies that include sex, as well as comedies that suitably deconstruct it. Films such as Yves Simoneau's *Perfectly Normal* (1990), which included this idea of a Canuck come-on: "It looks like you want to cover him with Mazola oil and ride the luge with him." Bruce McDonald's *Roadkill* and *Highway 61* are "comedies" that include romance, while John Hamilton's *Myth of the Male Orgasm* (1993) was a sassy precedent to Neil Labute's much harsher *In the Company of Men* (1997), which, according to Hamilton, "aimed to demystify the way men really talk about sex and women—without pulling any punches."[4]

When that movie was released—it was made without government funding—Hamilton said that he believed it would be popular with Canadians. "Why wouldn't it be? It's talking about sex. And it's talking about sex in a way that most people will be able to identify with." The movie had a respectable Canadian run, but it was hardly a testament to the romance in our hearts, which, despite much filmed evidence to the contrary, is something I believe we carry with us in great quantities—but we bury beneath bitter layers of emotional permafrost as a result of our dysfunctional national family.

We've already looked at some of the reasons for this cool approach. Fortunately, the sixties didn't pass us by, nor did feminism, nor did the swarms of people who showed up to watch Robert Lantos' landmark scandal, *In Praise of Older Women*, at the *Toronto Festival of Festivals* in 1978. From a society that was completely closed on the subject of sex, we're slowly opening up and letting all those wily sexual demons loose. Not surprisingly, the first such demons were dissected under the realist, documentary lens and dealt with things that should not be done. We witnessed the release of one of the most noted NFB documentaries of its day, the award-winning *Not a Love Story*, Bonnie Sherr Klein's verité look at the hidden world of exotic dancers and prostitutes that introduced an articulate stripper who, after taking part in the exposé, realized she could no longer continue in her field. (Lindalee Tracey later chose broadcast journalism). Other public-service oriented movies followed, such as *Sexual Abuse—The Family: Sexual Abuse of Children: A Time for Caring*, and *Feeling Yes, Feeling No* (1984), a sexual abuse prevention workshop series for school kids. Another film to make some waves was Vancouver film-maker Peg Campbell's *Street Kids* (1985), which used a docudrama approach that blended talking-head documentary segments intercut with dramatized scenes.

Other sex-demystifying docs followed with Aerlyn Weissman and Lynne Fernie's investigation into the secret history of lesbian courtship, *Forbidden Love* (1993), Penelope Buitenhuis' candid look at the life of Canadian hostesses in Japan, *Tokyo Girls* (2000), and perhaps the very epitome of the clinical Canadian documentary dealing with sex and gender roles, *Two Brides and a Scalpel: Diary of a Lesbian Marriage* (1999), Mark Achbar's non-fiction look at a cross-gendered man who wants to marry a lesbian, as a lesbian. The film not only shows the legal marriage, but it also shows the surgical removal of the penis and the inversion of the penile sheath into the abdomen to create a vagina. (Now that's what I call a perfect example of our resistance to phallonationalism.) It's a wild ride, but what makes it enlightening instead of simply sensationalist is the way Achbar dissects the anatomy of gender from an emotional as well as clinical perspective.

Granted, we're still pretty clinical when it comes to sex. We've got Sue Johanson's *Sunday Night Sex Show*—a TV broadcast that features a postmenopausal woman posing wooden puppets to give us pointers on hot positions with all the rev and rumble of a mechanic talking about your fuel pump. We also have sex-oriented call-in shows, so anonymous sufferers can discuss their innermost sexual shortcomings with an audience of thousands. Although Canada is the birthplace of Pamela Anderson, Dorothy Straiten, Carrie-Anne Moss, Keanu Reeves, Natasha Henstridge or countless other sex symbols with all the va-va-voom of Neve Campbell and hairy-chest charisma of William Shatner, trying to find a "positive" or "normal" image of sexual coupling in Canadian film is very difficult—but not impossible.

COMING OF AGE

While twisted, perverse and generally dysfunctional sex has been part of the Canadian artistic landscape for quite some time—and no wonder, considering how repressed we've been—it was in the closing decade of the 20th century that we woke up, collectively, to smell the sex. "Puritan filmgoers, brace yourselves, the Canadian portion of the 1994 Toronto International Film Festival is going to be hot," read Jane Stevenson's advance newser on the festival lineup for Canadian Press. "This year Perspective Canada is about sex. All kinds, all approaches, whatever makes life worth living. We've had some pretty sexy movies here in the past, but this year it's rampant," said Perspective Canada programmer Cameron Bailey, pushing the tried, tested and proven big red sex button to raise festival awareness for that year. Included in the 1994 lineup was Atom Egoyan's *Exotica*, a film about a man struggling to cope with the death of his daughter by developing an obsessive interest with a stripper; *Eclipse*, Jeremy Podeswa's debut feature that looks at the sex lives of several people on the eve of a solar eclipse in Toronto; *Super 8 1/2*, by Bruce LaBruce, which stars LaBruce himself as a burnt-out porn house star. By the time David Cronenberg's *Crash* came out two years later, our reputation as kinky Canucks was already well-established. And then came *Kissed* (1996), Lynne Stopkewich's tender coming-of-age story about a young necrophile, to forever cement the image of the quiet Canadian awash in sexual quirks.

Where does all this dark, twisted sexual imagery come from? If you're a Freudian, you naturally believe in all the Electra/Oedipal problems suffered by us poor Canadians. As an ex-pat Canadian who worked as a cultural attache in Los Angeles once told me: "Canadian films are about nothing but smoking pot and sleeping with your mother." In a Freudian analysis, then, our sexual repression is the result of missing fathers and powerful mothers, or in the case of the Quebecois tradition, it's the result of the Catholic church's perceived emasculation of the male figure, leaving priests looking like women, or as *Parti Pris* editor Pierre Maheu said in 1964, *"pères en jupes"*[5]—fathers in skirts. If you're a Jungian, you could point the finger at the "shadow"—the repressed subconscious desperate for release. If you're a person who prefers a common sense approach, Canadian film's fascination for the darkly perverse could be seen as little more than a titillation tactic aimed at seducing the reluctant masses with the oldest trick in the book. I believe it's probably a combination of all these things. But what matters more than the root cause, at this particular point in narrative time, is the images themselves. It's one thing to agree that there's something perverse about the way sex is treated in Canadian film; it's quite another to look, at the perversions themselves, which can tell us a great deal more about what's been repressed than any surface, historical dissection.

A quick survey of Canadian film on both sides of the linguistic border reveals a few common images in our collective sexual cellar, such as May-December couples, homosexuality, sexual displacement, incest, prostitution, sexual abuse and mental, if not literal, necrophilia:

Maelstrom (2000), dir. Denis Villeneuve: Bibi (Marie Josée Croze) is a young woman suffering from an image problem. Suffocated by her mother's fame and her brother's perfection, the film opens with Bibi getting an abortion, then getting drunk to assuage her guilt. She drives home, kills someone with her car, and then tries to escape using the only means she knows how: through anonymous sex with a stranger. From the blank expression on her face during the act, we can assume this is bad sex, and that for Bibi, the whole purpose behind sexual encounters is self-effacement, even self-destruction.

Crash (1996), dir. David Cronenberg: A cast of scarred characters gets a sexual charge from car crashes and particularly the mutilated flesh of wreck survivors. We see images of James Spader licking a long scar on the inside of Rosanna Arquette's leg, and more of him going down on Elias Koteas in the back seat of his car. Those are just a few examples. The whole movie is about revving your physical engine into oblivion with a carload of partners.

Kissed (1996), dir. Lynne Stopkewich: Sandra Larson (Molly Parker) shuns the attention of a good-looking, kind-hearted Matt (Peter Outerbridge) in favour of exploring the "other side" through the flesh of dead bodies. For her, sexual climax can only be achieved through necrophilic encounters. Similarly, in Stopkewich's second film, *Suspicious River* (2000), the lead character (once again played by Molly Parker) subjects herself to several violent sexual encounters with men in the motel where she works. In both cases, the sex seems to be a vehicle of emotional empowerment for the woman because she put herself in that place, with those partners, of her own free will.

New Waterford Girl (1999), dir. Allan Moyle: Our hero Mooney (Liane Balaban) is an aspiring artist who desperately wants to leave the small, oppressive Cape Breton community she calls home. After going over all the escape routes, she decides the only way to set herself free is to get pregnant—or at least, pretend to get pregnant. Up to this point the only chaste girl in the entire town, Mooney gives everyone the impression she's a complete slut—even though she doesn't have sex at all. In this Tricia Fish script, the only way for a woman to escape and pursue her creative destiny is to get "knocked up."

Live Bait (1995), dir. Bruce Sweeney: Our confused hero Trevor MacIntosh (Tom Scholte), is sexually unavailable to women his own age. There's something holding him back—and we're led to believe it's his own mother (Babz Chula). However, once he sets his eyes on an older female sculptor (a Louise Nevelson type played by Micki Maunsell, who looks at big hunks of metal and says things such as "We have to open this up a bit"), he realizes a sexual relationship with her and is emotionally healed. The movie ends on an undeniably upbeat note as he leaves his lover's bed, saunters back home, and smiles at his mother. Similar themes return in Sweeney's second feature, *Dirty* (1998), but this time the sex is far more obsessive, as the lead character can't let go of his infatuation for an older, drug-dealing woman. In the first movie, sex has healing powers—even if the bigger sexual picture is rather unorthodox. In the second film, sex is the disease, not the cure.

Careful (1992), dir. Guy Maddin: In this Gothic fairy tale, sex is the root of all evil. Carnal lust forces a young man to kill himself after drugging his mother and fondling her while she was sedated. It leads to one sister killing another because she's so in love with her father that she can't stand the idea of sharing his love with anyone. Sex also leads to the death of the supposed hero after he kills his mother's lover in order to win the heart of the same scheming woman who killed her own sibling.

Le Polygraphe (1996), dir. Robert Lepage: A multifaceted tale that revolves around the murder of a young woman in which everyone is using sex as a means of escape. A young actress heads home with a man she does not know, because she just witnessed a suicide on the Metro tracks. She and the man have sex. Later, we discover she auditioned for the role of the dead woman in a dramatization of the murder, and that the man she has sex with is a leading forensic examiner. Once again, sex, death and obsession are part of the same picture.

Ginger Snaps (2000), dir. John Fawcett: In this adventurous take on teen horror, we watch two late-blooming sisters undergo a transformation. At first, they are outcasts who amuse themselves by taking pictures of their own staged suicides. Later, after sister Ginger (Katharine Isabelle) begins to menstruate, she slowly turns into a werewolf with an insatiable sexual appetite and literally eats her partners alive. The functioning allegory here is that sex equals a complete lack of control, which has typically been one of the most frightening things for the control-freak Canadian psyche to deal with. Also, we see the same themes of sex and death revisited with the same grim results.

Exotica (1994), dir. Atom Egoyan: A tax accountant (Bruce Greenwood) begins to develop an obsessive interest in a young stripper (Mia Kirshner) who reminds him of his dead daughter. At first we think the man's a bit of a pedophilic freak. Then we realize that he is obsessed with this woman. His compulsion eventually pushes him to break through the non-contact barriers of the sex trade and talk to her as a human being because it reunites him with the spirit of his dead loved one. Egoyan's other films, particularly *The Adjuster* and *Family Viewing* (and in lesser ways in *The Sweet Hereafter* and *Speaking Parts*) deal with similar ideas of using sex as means of connectedness—a vehicle to escape from a state of complete alienation. Sadly, for all these haunted souls, sex provides no relief. It only makes the heart ache more for the things it can never hold again.

Cold Comfort (1989), dir. Vie Sarin: We watch as Paul Gross is saved from a blizzard by an odd tow-truck driver (Maury Chaykin), only to be held captive by his saviour and his equally odd daughter (Margaret Langrick), who appear to be romantically connected.

Lilies (1996), dir. John Greyson, **Le Confessionnal** (1995), dir. Robert Lepage, **Hanging Garden** (1997), dir. Thom Fitzgerald, **Better Than Chocolate** (1999), dir. Anne Wheeler: These are just a few examples of Canadian films where the camera assumes a queer point of view. This does not mean the films show us "weird sex" because they show gay mating. It means these movies push the viewer to alter his or her own "frame" around notions of homosexuality. This alteration of context is the essence of these films' inherent "weirdness."

The inventory could go on for pages and pages. There are so many images of weird sex in Canadian film that we can assume if sex is there at all, it's going to be a downer: a symptom of a socially rooted disease—not a happy communion of two souls who can't wait to explore each other's private parts.

If we turn our minds back to the theories of Carl Jung, who believed sex in dream imagery was a barometer of psychic health (because it integrates a person with his or her anima or animus, the creative impulse in the human spirit), then all the weird sex manifested in Canadian film suddenly makes a lot of sense, because it's not so much about sex at all, but about identity.

SEX & IDENTITY

Sex (particularly heterosexual sex) is the ultimate symbol of unity and birth, but it is also a reminder of our death, as we reach the grand climax—experience brief transcendence—then collapse into a jiggling bundle of nerves and sweat and clammy dampness that does nothing but remind us of our physical essence. It brings opposites together in a physical embrace. The empty vaginal void is filled, the vulnerable phallus finds a safe harbour, and the force of nature itself is reaffirmed without any interference from that stubborn, and oh-so-distracting cerebellum. I know it's a reach, but if we translate this idea to film—which is a type of dream state in its own right, and quite literally a shadow world—then we can compare the dysfunctional sex in Canadian cinema to our fractured and continually frustrated national psyche.

In this respect, sex becomes a mirror to reflect the things we feel about ourselves as Canadians, but can't—for whatever reason—express. As Jung said, the "shadow" is not the whole of the unconscious personality—it only represents the parts that no one wants to talk about. "Whether the unconscious comes up at first in a helpful or a negative form, after a time the need usually arises to readapt the conscious attitude in a better way to the unconscious factors—therefore to accept what seems to be "criticism" from the unconscious."[6]

We've already established the fact that as Canadians, we're generally private, quiet and repressed on the subject of sex, just as we are quiet on the subject of national unity. Politicians are often looking to stir up a fear of "the other"—whether it's the evil English establishment, the flag-stomping PQ-istes, the "Asian invasion," or myriad other conveniently manufactured enemies. But in the real world—or at least the private world of most Canadians—national unity may well be a big concern, but it's not something you go around blabbing about ad nauseam.

Perhaps, then, we are using sexual imagery in film as a means of healing our inner "anima-animus" tensions. Maybe we are merely finding symbolic ways of integrating our national self. If we are, then we aren't so screwed up after all. In order to get to the root of the matter and figure out what's really going on with our anima-animus/yin-yang teeter-totter, we'll begin with an investigation into gender and dissect the assigned roles given to each sex in Canadian cinema. This exercise should shed some light on the larger relationship between the anima-animus, as well as offer up some clues as to why the unions between men and women in Canadian film tend to be so strange.

WOMEN: STRONGER, FASTER, SMARTER

"Like mother earth, women are the givers of life—and that makes them the most powerful of all."
—Alanis Obomsawin

One of the most notable new universals in both French and English New Canadian Cinema is the appearance of the strong-willed, highly competent and generally intellectually superior female character. The modern Canadian female protagonist bears little physical resemblance to the overabundance of "crones" that Atwood discussed 30 years ago in the pages of *Survival.* Back then, Atwood noted that most of the women in Canadian literature were over the age of 50. Not only were they "old" (she was in her twenties, remember), but they were a "tough, sterile, suppressed granite-jawed lot" who lived their lives "with intensity, but through gritted teeth and they were often seen as malevolent, sinister or life-denying." In archetypal terms, Canadian literature suffered a strange lack of Venus-like goddesses, but had an over-abundance of crones. Pointing to characters like Margaret Laurence's crochety crone Hagar in *The Stone Angel* and the diseased mother in Alice Munro's *The Peace of Utrecht,* Atwood spotted an entire "Angry-Granny" group of "powerful, negative old women" in the pages of CanLit. She was absolutely right, of course. But just as these crones filled the pages of the burgeoning Canadian canon, another type of heroine was emerging on screen.

Before Laurence or Munro were even conceived, Nell Shipman was reinventing the Canadian female on screen. A sassy lass from Victoria, British

Columbia, Shipman (*nee* Helen Barham, b.1892) was born to a family of limited means but turned herself into an accomplished actress by the age of 16, eventually winning the attentions of Lothario impressario Ernest Shipman. The two married in 1910 and became a creative team, with Nell ensuring she had a starring role. In 1914, she directed and starred in her first film, *The Ball of Yarn* (1914). Then came *God's Country and the Woman* (1915), a film based on a James Oliver Curwood story about a woman who could traverse the arctic tundra with sled dogs, a character in whom Nell found her ideal alter ego. The movie was a commercial success, and when Ernest and Nell returned to Canada in 1919 to make *Back to God's Country* (1919), they were one of filmdom's most successful couples, thanks in large part to Nell's outgoing and creative energies.

The young, vital women Shipman plays have little in common with the "crones" on the pages of CanLit. Shipman created female versions of the romantic male hero, but cast in a feminine eye, because these heroines are at one with nature. The difference between the page and the film images could suggest that the film medium itself presented a whole new way to frame the female experience—one that allowed for complete recreation without gender-role expectations.

Back to God's Country featured Shipman (also the screenwriter) as a young woman living in the North who was at home on the frozen tundra. She could trap, canoe and snow-shoe. She even goes so far as to save her ailing husband from certain death while singlehandedly dealing with a bunch of no-goodniks. Shipman's character is the equivalent of the archetypal American male, with two crucial differences: She is not a man, and she is not a real conqueror; she gains her strength and mental advantage over the enemy by living in harmony with the natural world around her.

Film historian and Toronto film festival programmer Kay Armatage explored Shipman's heroic proportions in her article, "Nell Shipman, A Case for Heroic Femininity."[7] In it, Armatage establishes Shipman's unique approach to depicting the natural world as empathetic, not hostile: "Shipman routinely shifted the protagonist's position from the dog to the woman, and effected concomitant shifts in the working of the narrative as well. Thus into this circuit of commercial cinema, popular genre, animals and nature, Shipman inserts the new variable: Heroic femininity." As Dolores, the heroine in *Back to God's Country*, Shipman literally comes to the rescue of the abused dog (and saviour) Wapi, who is transformed into a gentle beast by a simple touch. "A new miracle of understanding," read the title card, "roused by the touch of a woman's hand." Armatage writes: "... Shipman played the leading role, always of the heroic stamp. Husbands or lovers were either absent or incapacitated: they fell ill, were injured, or were simply 'artistic.' Nell invariably had to save the day ... Her great sense of moral justice, and the instinctive connection with animals and nature: these are the signs of her essential femininity and simultaneously the source of heroism which allows her to resist the conventional narrative inscriptions of the woman protagonist as victimized and rescued."[8]

BEYOND GOD'S COUNTRY

Threads of Shipman's character continue to run through the contemporary tapestry of Canadian film. While the tax-shelter films of the seventies were as exploitative of the female form as their producers were of tax laws, the idea of the dominant female remains an integral part of the Canadian imagination. Even the work of expatriate James Cameron reverberates with the ghost of his formative years. His most interesting and well-rounded characters tend to be women: Linda Hamilton in the *Terminator* series, Sigourney Weaver in *Aliens*, Kate Winslet in *Titanic*, Jamie Lee Curtis in *True Lies*. For Canadian filmmakers who remain in Canada, the female character is even stronger— and generally less oppressed by a dominant, terminating, male force.

The most obvious shift from our crone-prone days has been the discovery of the autonomous Venus character. Not only is the modern Canadian female decidedly youthful, generally benevolent, physically attractive and outward looking, she is also fecund—physically and intellectually. She can bear children, even if she frequently decides not to. She's just as headstrong as her foresisters, but in an age where many of the women on the big screen are used as silicone-injected set decor, the Canadian female is one of the most realized characters in any film tradition going.

The power centre for these women is the empty, but potentially creative void within them: the uterus. Not only is this fist-sized organ a perfectly portable and altogether symbolic empty void that plays into our "negative space theory," but it is a blatant symbol of one's creative potential. As New Age guru Deepak Chopra says: "We spring forth out of nothingness; nothing is the womb of life." In order to make the most of that nothing, one must possess self-knowledge. Then, and only then, will the act of creation be positive and constructive instead of a burden to those who made it. In this respect, there is a great deal of revolutionary power in empty space. An idea can change the world just as a child can change the nature of a relationship. All of these things give the female character an unprecedented amount of power in the distilled fictional universe of film. I think it's important to specify that it is the "character" and not the filmmaker that we are talking about here, because both male and female filmmakers in this country tend to give women similar attributes, which I find quite intriguing.

We can explain the rise of the powerful female character in Canadian film by using our handy-dandy negative space theory. Let me explain. If the average Canadian male character appears to be in the "sensitive-New-Age-guy" category because he's comfortable with ambiguity and "the hole inside," then it's only logical that the female whose own void mirrors that of the vast, empty Canadian landscape will be more in harmony with the natural world, and she will potentially be able to exercise more control, or at least have a more empowered attitude, to the world around her. One look at what happens when someone or something tries to invade that hole with an unwanted "positive appendage," and the whole equation becomes absolutely clear: she rebels against it until either the unwanted cargo, or the unwanted appendage backs down. In a situation where she is forced to carry the cargo, or allow entry to an unwanted appendage, she will either turn into the hardened crone or destroy herself. What follows is an exploration of some noteworthy films that deal with the woman and her womb.

The Handmaid's Tale

The most obvious example of this symbolic relationship between women, the womb and the locus of social control is in Margaret Atwood's *The Handmaid's Tale*, a novel that was turned into a film by German director Volker Schloendorff, from a script by Harold Pinter. When the book was written in the 1980s, America was in the midst of a cyclical return to the political right. Ronald Reagan had been elected president and there was a lot of talk about so-called "family values." Women were once again encouraged, thanks to Nancy Reagan's role-modelling, to reassume their matriarchal duty of maintaining the home and nurturing the family while men went off to do a variety of industrial, manly things. In Atwood's book, our main character Offred (even her name has been supplanted by that of the man's: "Of Fred") is one of the few remaining women in the fictional Republic of Gilead with a working womb. While other women have been rendered sterile as a result of toxic pollution, Offred can conceive, and so, when she is apprehended in the midst of an escape attempt from Gilead with her husband and daughter, she is forcibly turned into a handmaid—a woman whose womb will be appropriated by a wealthy woman who desires children. Offred has no control or say in the matter. She is now a human farm field, who will be tilled and sown as "The General" and his wife, Serena Joy, see fit. Without giving away the entire plot of the worthy film, it's safe to say that Offred rebels against the oppression—but in her very own way. The ending of the movie is highly ambiguous, but there's the suggestion that things work out for poor Offred. At the very least, her inner void is never taken over by a hostile force.

Parsley Days

Contrary to Atwood's dystopian vision, maritimer Andrea Dorfman's bittersweet relationship comedy *Parsley Days* (2000) deals with similar issues—only without all the hard edges. In this release, which toured festivals with solid success but was later panned by some Toronto critics (which almost prevented its national run), Dorfman tells us the story of Kate and Ollie. Kate is a bike mechanic who teaches outreach classes, and her longtime boyfriend, Ollie, is "the king of contraception"—a public health worker charged with handing out condoms and touring schools to teach birth control.

As the film opens, we see someone handling a strip of multicoloured condoms as Kate's voice-over tells us: "I think a relationship is a lot like a condom: You look out at the world outside from behind your transparent shield and feel safe and snug. Your relationship is strong ... your relationship is the one that won't break." Just as the last words are uttered, one of the pretty condoms is pierced with a safety pin. Bam. Suddenly Kate finds herself pregnant and her world starts falling apart piece by piece. She realizes her safe relationship may be little more than an escape device. She might not love Ollie anymore. She's attracted to one of her bike students—the slow one. She is torn: should she stay with Ollie, the nicest guy in town, because she's safe and happy? Or should she come clean about the affair and see what happens? Or should she break up with Ollie and have an abortion?

Yes, that's right: abortion. The United States rarely uses that word in any popular media—let alone a comedy, but up here in the Great White North, women have what's called free choice. In this country, where tolerance is hailed as the most important social virtue, women have complete autonomy over their own bodies, and so for Dorfman—as it is for most Canadians—abortion is simply part of the natural landscape.

In this case, it's also a part of the metaphorical landscape, because as Kate tries to solve her dilemma in a way that will have the least impact on others, she turns to her lesbian herbalist pal who tells her of parsley's "menses-inducing" properties. Kate is told she can induce her own naturopathic abortion if she ingests several kilos of parsley a day ... which she does, to great comic effect but absolutely no clinical effect. As the guilt builds within her, Kate finally snaps. She has to tell Oilie what's happened. She has to "be an honest person again." It's not the guilt of the affair that seems to be bugging Kate most, but the sad fact that she knows—if she is truly honest with herself—that she is going to break Ollie's heart. (We know this because as she comes home, tormented about facing the music, she hears a newscast on the TV about a rash of "people dying of broken hearts.") In the end, Kate isn't just completely honest with Oilie, she tells him that she is no longer in love with him. She also has the abortion in the final frames of the film.

What makes this movie such a beautiful experience, and such a moving one, is the way it toys with our expectations. As Kate and Oilie sit there in the backyard, in the—what else, eh?—red canoe that is the running symbol of their love affair, we almost expect them to kiss and make up. And let's face it, most of us have been so programmed by the Hollywood romance formula (where opposites fight, then fall in love) that we find it impossible to conjure a love story where people simply fall out of love for no good reason at all. Affairs can end in Hollywood romances too, but usually only after someone meets an all-too tragic end in a plane crash, car crash, drowning, from AIDS, cancer ... whatever. The films where love affairs end not because someone has died but because people have grown apart, contradict the norm, and that negation of expectation is certainly one of the main ingredients in good drama.

Parsley Days is a good movie because it contradicts expectation without bending over backward to do so. Moreover, it's a good movie because it articulates the sense of loss we feel when a relationship ends—that sickening feeling of elation and sadness all at the same time.

New Waterford Girl

Mooney lives in Nowheresville (AKA New Waterford) Cape Breton. She knows everyone in town. She lives in a curtained "room" at the top of the stairs in the home she shares with her many brothers and sisters. Her mother, played by Mary Walsh (of *This Hour Has 22–Minutes-Codco* fame) is the dominant matriarch and her father, played by Nicholas Campbell (*DaVinci's Inquest*), is a deflated dreamer whose sole creative outlet is baking cakes. With these two parents as role models, the last thing Mooney wants is to end up trapped in the same procreative hell as her mom and dad. When the film opens, we learn that Mooney is a talented artist who has a chance of going to art school in the big city but there's no money to facilitate the escape, so Mooney is left with few options. Either she can get pregnant and take the next train out of town like all the other gals who have been "knocked up" before her, or she can play the prude and exempt herself from the whole breeder business. Mooney sees no salvation in either scenario, until she meets Lou, the outsider from New York City.

Lou (Tara Spencer-Nairn) is a feisty young woman who appears out of nowhere with her leopard-print sporting mother (Cathy Moriarty). Voluntary exiles in Cape Breton, the two are trying to escape the mom's dead-beat, abusive, boxing boyfriend back home. Within a few frames, Mooney (the outsider from within) and Lou (the outsider from New York) bond over their alienation and come up with a plan that may free Mooney from her destiny as a tethered baby-making machine: pretend to get pregnant, catch the train out of New Waterford, and never return. Suddenly the body part that was her biggest liability—the empty womb—becomes her biggest asset as Mooney borrows urine from pregnant friends and turns the town upside down with her sudden character swing.

The key to Mooney's empowerment is the way she takes control of her own reproductive organs. She isn't passively waiting for some boy. Both of these women take the proverbial bull by the horns and recreate their femininity in androgynous space. For instance, Lou's a girl—and second, she can punch the boys out cold. With Lou's help, Mooney goes out and controls the opposite sex to realize her own personal goals. This is a definite shift from the early models of women in Canadian Lit, who were victimized by their wombs and their creative abilities. Without autonomy over their own nature and control over the open and highly creative space inside, these women evolved into bitter crones. Now, it seems, women in Canadian film are using the mere potential for creation to their advantage. This does not mean children—it means a realization of one's inner, creative self.

Maelstrom

In the case of Maelstrom, our conflicted heroine Bibiane is awash in guilt over a recent abortion. Mentally eclipsed by her mother's fame and depressed by the failure of her own business at the hands of her nasty and zealously rational, know-it-all brother, Bibi finds herself free-floating. She is overcome and is now emotionally paralyzed. At first, she looks for comfort in the arms of an anonymous sexual partner she picks up at a rave. But because she doesn't really care about anything anymore, they have bad sex and she becomes even more fatalistic, more shut down and more alienated from herself. Making things worse, she drives home drunk, runs a man down, then leaves the scene. When she meets the son of the Norwegian fisherman she killed with her car, she sees a possibility for healing. On the surface, she is looking for forgiveness from the man who was hurt most by her irresponsible act. But if we go a little deeper (which this movie is wont to do, as it is swimming in deep water imagery), we can see that the budding relationship between Bibi and Evian (Jean-Nicolas Verreault) is not just about forgiveness, it's about spiritual integration: these two people are both lost souls. Together they are found. Together, they have meaning. The only problem is Bibi's bad deed—a fact that director Denis Villeneuve drives home symbolically when Evian throws the ashes of his dead dad all over Bibi as she lies in bed, the same bed the two of them made love in the night before. Death, sex, guilt—it's all here.

Perhaps had Villeneuve made this movie at another time—or come from another generation (he was born in 1967)—he would have ended his surreal love story with a downer ending, the way most of us might have expected. But Villeneuve resists. Not only does he depart from our linear, four-walled tradition of realism in the very first frames—when he opts for fantasy and uses an ancient fish as the narrator—but he goes the extra creative mile and gives us a morally ambiguous but romantically sound "happy ending." The mise-en-scene of the film remains highly realistic, at least on the surface, but Bibi and Evian are courageous and creatively open enough to explore beneath the surface. They let the love in—which proves to be stronger than any of the negative energy around them.

Such romantic healing is a true novelty in Canadian film, seen only on the rarest occasions in such movies as *Last Night* (which is a bit more ambiguous) and *New Waterford Girl*—both of which are relatively new films from young filmmakers. Is it fair to suggest this new courage bodes well for our psychic future, not just as individuals, but as a nation?

Villeneuve might have a problem with it. The filmmaker considers himself "a confused separatist" who yearns for a new, positive start. However, in an interview at the Toronto International Film Festival, where *Maelstrom* premiered in 2000, Villeneuve also said he felt Canada was essentially "a battle between two cultures out to reject the other."

In order to heal the desire for mutual destruction, Villeneuve said the only solution was separation, "because at least that way, the two cultures could grow and flourish on their own."[9] I don't dispute the sincerity of Villeneuve's comments. But as we've just seen, the larger message of his film could be interpreted as being quite the opposite. It could very well be a shadow message of hope. Then again, it might just be sex—in which case, the very fact that we're talking about it at all is reason enough to rejoice.

There are a great many more examples of these new Canadian heroines who maintain control of their own inner space. She can be seen in everyone from Valerie Buhagiar's self-possessed characters in Bruce McDonald and Don McKellar's road movies, to the pregnant strip club owner (Arsinee Khanjian) in Atom Egoyan's *Exotica*. She is a ubiquitous feature at this point in Canadian film, and she has sprung from the cerebral loins of both genders.

If we see the female as the embodiment of our vast, empty landscape, then this new feisty femme fecund could attest to our changing attitude to the world around us. No longer foreign, cold and barren, she is able to give life— but only when she wants to. She can create, but only if she feels love. Now it's in her hands, not those, of the predominantly male establishment. This, clearly, represents progress.

If we view the female as half the Jungian anima-animus equation of Self, then we can assume we are moving toward increased artistic expression, but, by the same token, a potential psychic imbalance as the female "anima" may well overpower the "masculine" animus. In order to get the full picture, we'll look now at the fate of men in Canadian film.

THE CANADIAN MALE

"Canadian men are nice guys."
—*Jeopardy* host, and proud Canadian, Alex Trebek

Some people, myself among them, have looked at the Canadian male on screen and felt pity. Pity these poor saps who don't get to carry guns and rescue maidens in distress. Pity these losers whose girlfriends would rather sleep with dead men, such as Peter Outerbridge's character in *Kissed*. Pity those freaks who need uniforms to make them feel big and powerful, like Tom McCamus in *I Love a Man in Uniform*. Pity even that hunky Paul Gross who is held captive by a crazy tow truck driver (Maury Chaykin) after being hauled, half frozen, out of his half-entombed car in a snowstorm in *Cold Comfort*.

To people who have been trained to view heroism as the art of being bulletproof, the Canadian hero barely rates as a sidekick. He has no special powers, no clear insight into the ways of the heavens, no code name ... not even a special piece of snap-on technology that can turn him into a superhero at the push of a button. To outsiders, we've been lucky enough to coast on the manly red serge coat-tails of the RCMP, but we know they don't wear those cool uniforms unless they are on diplomatic duty, or out to impress tourists. It's all about appearances, and as Canadians, we tend to take a jaundiced view of anything that appears too perfect, or in the case of the RCMP, anything too institutional and earnest. Every once in a while, you get a movie like *Map of the Human Heart*, where the hero is an Inuit fighter pilot who falls in love with a Metis girl at the tuberculosis hospital in Montreal—but again, the man is hardly a winner in the classic American sense of the word hero. He dies a nobody on an ice floe.

In Atwood's decryption, the Canadian male is someone who cannot be redeemed by a heroic death, usually because he dies accidentally (by freezing or drowning). Certainly we could say the same still holds true in many cases. Canadian film is full of men who die accidentally, from the man who freezes to death in an outdoor bathtub at the beginning of *Highway 61* (because "he was no longer insulated from the harsh reality of the world around him"), to the conflicted hero in *Careful* who falls asleep in the snow cave, to the missing father figure in *Surfacing* who drowns looking for petroglyphs.

MEASURING OURSELVES

> "Quite often I've noticed that Canadians always have the doughnut hole as the hero. He's not doing anything—he's the empty space in the middle. You'd never have an American hero like that. Not ever."
> —Guy Maddin

If you just look at the surface of Canadian film, our boys don't quite measure up to the sizeable expectations surrounding the male hero myth propagated by the American movie industry, but as Atwood hypothesized, the very comparison may be a lingering symptom of our colonial past. If we look at the Canadian male in isolation, he doesn't look so wimpy at all. In fact, his very humanity and willingness to embrace ambiguity may render him far more heroic than anything we can see from the buff heroes in Hollywood.

The American mythology that we've been trained to absorb rhapsodizes about the achievements of the hero—concrete actions that not only affirm the man's place in the universe but also have the ability to transform the universe, even subdue and tame it with a human hand. As Russo said, "They did not behave like women."

In Canada, we clearly aren't so threatened by the idea of gender bending. Our women are often "manly" and our men are often "effeminate." In our universe, people are simply creatures who carry both "male" and "female" traits. As we've noted elsewhere, we are a cerebral culture, meaning sexual body parts may come second to brain. We distrust a clearly defined, and rather arrogant, approach to the cosmos because we are all too aware of how vulnerable we really are. We are all to apt to "drown or freeze" to death.[10] We are puny, near-powerless and ultimately subject to the forces of nature. Can you see a Canadian version of *Gladiator*? Hardly. But does that mean our men are weak and geeky? Hardly.

When I approached male Canadian actors at the 2000 Toronto International Film Festival with the geek theory, it became clear that the men who play these characters were for the most part opposed to the geek conclusion. At first, I figured it was just denial. But the more we talked, the more obvious it became that the whole geek theory had one giant hole in the middle.

The first misconception is to assume that these men are even trying to be larger than life. In other words, we shouldn't compare Hollywood's phallo-nationalist heroes with the Tim Horton doughnut-hole of a Canadian male—nor should we use the phallo-nationalist model as a measure of our identity, because we are, as we shall prove, a sexually ambiguous kind of people. Where they give us imported beefcake like Tom Cruise, Arnold Schwarzenegger and Russell Crowe, our hardest working male actors are people such as Don McKellar, who played the likes of an introverted, ambiguously sexual exotic bird breeder in *Exotica*; Tom McCamus who played a passive brain in a bottle in *Possible Worlds*, Bruce Greenwood, who in *The Sweet Hereafter* was forced to watch his kids die before his eyes, and Saul Rubinek, who plays a variety of atypical hero types in both Canadian and American movies. Let's not forget Jay Brazeau, who played the undertaker in *Kissed*, and Maury Chaykin, who played the chubby, dysfunctional musician in *Whale Music*. On the surface, it's probably all right to say that we fall on the goofier, negative side of the equation, but that's about the only thing we can say—safely—because the Canadian male is actually a great deal stronger than the American male once you get past the packaging and look at the contents.

"The men I have played [in Canadian movies] are incredibly strong," said Bruce Greenwood when I approached him on the geek theory. "If you look at *The Sweet Hereafter* or *Exotica*, the characters are in so much pain—but they move through it because they are strong. They are not denying their feelings. They are trying to live with them. They adapt [with] some strange coping mechanisms, but they are strong enough to feel ... and I think that's psychically far more healthy than picking up a gun and blowing someone away. Don't you?" Indeed. Beneath the so-called "wimpy" or "passive" exterior, these are men who are comfortable, or at least willing, to explore their emotional or feminine side. They do not feel an inherent need to conquer the wilderness and assert their destructive power, and as such, they stand in direct contrast to the all-conquering archetypal American hero myth. They are real human beings capable of great acts of bravery—only on a human scale.

According to Tom McCamus—who played the vivisected George Barber in *Possible Worlds*, the nerdy bank employee with the secret cop persona in *I Love a Man in Uniform*, and the father who has an incestuous relationship with his daughter in *The Sweet Hereafter*—the males he portrays are not weak, they are "vulnerable"—and there's a distinct difference between the two. A weak person is ineffectual and easily crushed, but a vulnerable person is someone who is able to open up and expand his field of experience.

"The thing about us [Canadians] is that we apologize all the time. I think that reflects a certain vulnerability," said McCamus in a 2000 interview. "That's what directors are usually asking for, vulnerability. As a result, my character is not a guy who you'd look up to, but someone we can identify with. That doesn't mean to say we are wimps, perhaps it just means we have become more confident—that we can show a vulnerable side. I know George is an Everyman—in some ways, quite literally because he has this ability to process the thoughts of others in his disembodied state. He is many people all at once, and he is vulnerable, and vulnerability is a quality several Canadian lead males that I've played have."[11]

BEYOND THE MACK JACKET

In addition to vulnerability, if we pull the Canadian male apart, trait by trait, the Canadian "hero" generally possesses one or more of the following:

> An inner longing that he may be unable to articulate. Good examples of this can be seen in characters like Renzo (Michael Riley), the hockey player and beer-plant employee who dreams of being an opera singer in *Perfectly Normal*; the perpetually unsatisfied grocer (Simon Webb) in John Pozer's *The Grocer's Life*, or the unemployed and perpetually unsatisfied Christophe (Paul Ahmarani) in Philippe Falardeau's *La Moitié gauche du frigo*.
>
> An ambiguous sexuality. Examples include Don McKellar's pet store owner in Atom Egoyan's *Exotica*; the bisexual James Dean wannabe played by Elias Koteas in *Crash*; Jeremy Irons' twins in *Dead Ringers*, and the lost Marc in Robert Lepage's *Le Confessionnal*. In the notes for Egoyan's *Speaking Parts*, he even specifies that Lance is "strikingly beautiful ... almost androgynous."[12]
>
> A submissive relationship with women. Witness the run of male characters befuddled, and often threatened, by female sexual power: In Reg Harke-

ma's *A Girl is a Girl*, a nice guy finds himself striking out with one woman after another because he just can't get a handle on the female experience. In Blaine Thurier's *Low Self-Esteem Girl*, a young woman is demonized by members of a Christian Youth group because she is too sexual and could very well seduce the strong and virtuous, sending them all straight to Hades. Other submissive male models can be seen in Anne Wheeler's *Marine Life*, where a younger man Robert (Peter Outerbridge) plays second fiddle to a few ex-husbands and a bunch of kids; Clement Virgo's *The Planet of Junior Brown* shows us a boy forced into submission by his mother and his unhinged piano teacher (Margot Kidder), and in Peg Thompson's script for *Better Than Chocolate*, the man is fully concealed in the cross-gendered character of Judy/Jeremy.

A distrust of the physical world and the outward manifestations of "reality." My favourite example, and there are many, is the Ted Pikul character played by Jude Law in Cronenberg's *eXistenZ*. Pikul fears being disconnected to "civilization," and at one point, cries out for his "pink phone," which he keeps firmly tucked in his trousers. Of course the Allegra Geller character (Jennifer Jason Leigh) is in control and chucks the knobby pink phone out of the car window the minute it makes an appearance. (You have to love Cronenberg's gift for sexual imagery in every nook and flesh fold.)

A potentially menacing other side. Witness the dad (Maury Chaykin) in Vie Sarin's *Cold Comfort*, who seems like the nicest goof until you see him forcibly confine Paul Gross in his gas station home, or Tom McCamus' mild-mannered bank teller who takes on the persona of a cop in David Wellington's *I Love a Man in Uniform*. Even Jeff Goldblum in *The Fly* fits the description when he begins to metamorphose into an insect, as does Larenz Tate's drug-addicted character Neville in *Love Come Down* when he loses control under the influence.

Taken together, these might not seem like particularly "heroic" traits—or add up to anything remotely resembling the classic hero myth. Rather, the resulting image of the typical Canadian male character is someone steeped in confusion, distrustful of others, potentially dangerous and ultimately subject to the will of the women around him. No wonder we think our guys are wimps. But if we go back to Atwood's last point and think about this man in isolation from other expected notions of masculine power, we can see a lot of "positive" elements in this rather "negative"—or anti-macho—male.

First, because he is ambiguously sexual and subject to the desires of women, he is symbolically in tune with the negative landscape around him. Standing in harmony with nature automatically lends him a power the conquering male could never hope to have as he spends all his energies effacing the feminine and controlling her "natural" ways. By contrast, the Canadian male can spend his time and energy pursuing more "creative" pursuits himself, such as learning how to sing opera (as Renzo did in *Perfectly Normal*) or perfecting a stand-up routine (as Neville did in *Love Come Down*) or playing trumpet (like Pokey Jones in *Highway 61*).

In some cases, there is such a desire to commune with nature that the male comes up with absurd creative concepts, such as the grizzly-proof suit we see in the NFB documentary, *Project Grizzly*. The suit's a great idea, but it inevitably proves to be too cumbersome to be of any pragmatic use in the proverbial bush. This brings to mind another interesting element in the treatment of the male identity in Canadian film: if a man is trying to assume classical heroic proportions in the American mould, he is generally rendered ridiculous, if not completely insane. Again, this suggests that we know who we are, and it has little in common with the mythology we've been trained to assimilate through the Hollywood model. The Canadian man is more of a thinker than a doer, and as men are constantly referred to as slaves to their sex organ, the Canadian male's distinct separation from his reproductive system can be seen as nothing but a psychic liberation.

Director Reg Harkema hit the nail on the proverbial head when he talked about the process of making *A Girl is a Girl*: "When I started making *A Girl is a Girl*, I had no idea I was formulating a male response to evolving female sexuality, but that's kind of what happened. Men have been trapped by these historical and corporate ideas about women, as typified by fashion-magazine images. We actually bought into it, but now women are saying 'Fuck you, buddy!' And thank God. None of it is real ... Unfortunately, a lot of men never get over that. And that's too bad because they are missing so much of what relationships are all about—two people trying to understand each other."[13]

LONG-NECKS VS. STUBBIES

In a typical Freudian analysis, the Canadian male's acceptance of a female point of view would be interpreted as "our men have no balls—or are castrated" because they do not priapically assert themselves. They are not eager to fill every vessel with a bit of themselves. In this analysis, the man would be marked by an unmistakable feminine edge. Once again, since the dominant culture in this society has determined that muscle cars, big tall skyscrapers, monster trucks, long-necked Buds, cigars, baseball bats and Fender Stratocasters are the Biggy Meal du jour, it's not surprising that the Canadian male has been the object of derision among men who identify more with an American way of thinking—and believe in the phallo-nationalist model. It's also not surprising that Egoyan is often criticized for his "cold," "passive" characters—after all, the more they are in harmony with the bleak, frigid landscape that surrounds them, the more they assume a feminine perspective.

If we take the Freudian analysis a bit further, then we can say the cold has shrunk our collective manhood into the proportions of a squirrel. Is this a bad thing? Only if you're intent on having sex in the snow or waving yourself around like a flagpole. Most of us aren't. What's so wrong with showing that we are, indeed, subject to the forces of nature? When it gets cold, the thing shrinks, and so the man must either accept the fact and think of something other than his member, or make a fire. This places us in stark contrast to the likes of the sexually omnipotent James Bond, who can rescue a rich heiress from an avalanche one minute and have sex with her the next. As sexual realists, we clearly don't buy into that manufactured nonsense. We are only too well aware of nature's overwhelming force, which I think makes us more honest, more apt to survive, and far more open to the forces of creativity as they are embodied by nature herself.

One of my favourite barometers of manhood is the hunt motif. The traditional domain of men, and only men, the hunt is one of the most primitive, and therefore immediately telling, measures of manhood. Almost every man in American film is a hunter of some sort: he walks around with a gun, and shoots at the people who threaten his survival. In Canadian film, it's difficult to even find a gun, and when you do, its manly function is rendered absurd. Take the case of Noah Render (Elias Koteas), the title character in *The Adjuster*, who shoots his quiver of arrows into a giant billboard of a nuclear family at the entrance to his barren housing development. Another image can be seen in Jean-Claude Lauzon's *Night Zoo*, where the son and father reconcile over their last great adventure by breaking into the zoo and shooting a caged elephant. Certainly there isn't much of a macho challenge in killing an animal behind bars, but you can see other men do something similar in *Highway 61*, when the rock star character played by Art Bergmann decides to release a chicken in the mansion and issues revolvers to all his guests. While other cultures may see the indoor chicken hunt as a manly activity, it's clear that McKellar has deflated the thick, hard, gun-barrel aesthetic with the prick of a small needle.

COPULATION

How do these dissections of the Canadian female and the Canadian male translate into screen sex? Metaphorically, of course. Despite our desire to talk about sex and our unending fascination with exploring the most rugged of sexual terrains, we don't actually show the sexual act as much as most American films do. We are all familiar with the Hollywood drill: the saccharine strains of some Kenny G-soundalike generally flare up for the foreplay, settle into a slow rhythm, then explode in a tinny solo at the climax. The images are usually bathed in orange and red gels and the actors' body parts are shot in close-up isolation—a saliva-covered lip, the dart of a tongue, a clenched hand grabbing at the sheets in ecstasy. Clearly this is done to make the scenes look as sexy and as graphic as possible without risking an Adult, or NC-17 rating, but the final effect is something like watching sex in an abattoir: body part by body part.

Canadian sex is just as fragmented, but because it's used mostly for symbolic and not sensationalist purposes, the fragmentation takes place beneath the surface. Take *In Praise of Older Women* (1978) as a case in point. This scandalous Robert Lantos project is clearly one of the most graphically sexual films to emerge from Canada. It features Tom Berenger making love to a variety of willing women (played by the likes of Karen Black and Helen Shaver). There are plenty of wide shots and full frontal nudity, and the sex itself is rather "normal." There is nothing kinky about this coitus, but the lack of real emotional intimacy and a sense of commitment between Berenger and his coterie of female admirers is our hero's main struggle. He loves sex, but he's also a romantic searching for the one woman who will complete him—an older woman and mother figure who will hold him close to her bosom and relieve his existential angst.

Once *In Praise of Older Women* opened the floodgates, more sexual imagery poured through the system, seeping up from the storm drains and the kitchen sink—just like the poo-shaped parasite in *Shivers* (1975), which crawled through the pipes of a Montreal apartment building a few years earlier and entered a variety of hosts, boosting their libidos to Bacchanal extremes. In *Shivers* and in *In Praise of Older Women*—as in just about every film worth mentioning—the woman is in control of the union. Cronenberg's other films also give the women the dominant role. Check out the psycho ex-wife figure in *The Brood*, who transforms into a morbid she-wolf, spawning litters of deformed children that she pulls from her loins and licks in front of her horrified ex-husband, or the mind-screwing game developer Allegra Geller in *eXistenZ*, who ensures the male, Pikul, is penetrated at the base of his spine with her very own version of reality. Even the gender-bending in *M. Butterfly* gives the "female" the dominant role as the French attaché (Jeremy Irons) surrenders to her "feminine" powers, even though she is actually a man. Once again, we have gender confusion, anima-animus imbalance and a potent female.

It only follows logically then that if we ever see images of the act, the woman is usually on top. In Don McKellar's Canadian Film Centre short, *Blue*, he cuts between an older woman reminiscing about her days as a blue movie star and an uptight, mild-mannered carpet-store owner (David Cronenberg) addicted to hardcore pornography. The older woman talks about how much "fun" she had acting the femme fatale, but she also says "my breasts hung better naturally, so I always tried to get on top." In the end, we find out the two are aunt and nephew, but neither one has a clue about the other's hidden sex life—affirming elements of fragmentation and repressed sexuality. More women on top can be seen in *Kissed*, where we watch Molly Parker mount several stiffs on the embalmer's table, or *Lulu*, where we watch the depressed Vietnamese mail-order bride attempt to make her impotent husband hard by rolling around on top of him—without success. Even Arsinee Khanjian's character in *The Adjuster* assumes a dominant position with regards to male sexuality when she bootlegs the porn films she is supposed to censor, then brings them home to her sister—essentially subverting "the institution" of the film classification office, as well as regaining the lost power of the gaze when she refilms the images of the "victimized" women in the porn industry with her very own camera.

Taping porn, mounting dead bodies, rolling around on flaccid male members: these are not what one might call images of healthy coupling. Something is broken in the symbolic bedroom of the nation: We can't seem to come together.

Things look different in the homosexual arena. There, both partners tend to share an equal sexual footing without necessarily buying into and following the heterosexual pattern. In the case of the gay male couple in *Lilies*, or the lesbian couple in *Better Than Chocolate*, there's a lot of rolling around and role-playing, but there's no dominant sexual partner. Ironically—and let's face it, we're good at irony—the gay sex tends to be "healthier" psychically than the heterosexual unions we see in Canadian film—perhaps because it doesn't demand an embrace of "other." Gay sex unites sameness—only on the outskirts of the mainstream perspective. We'll bring the binoculars to the queer peep-hole later on, but for now, we'll press our face to the fishbowl of the dominant, heterosexual society for the real freak show and see that almost all straight sex in Canadian film is downright bent.

PROCREATION DENIED

As the inventory shows, the attempt at sexual union in Canadian film is undermined, either through endemic disease or through an act of will. As a result, there is a peculiar lack of progeny in a lot of Canadian film. Understanding why the procreative act is denied usually says a lot about a relationship, so we can expect it also says something about our Canadian psyche. So let's return to Jung—who understood the psyche and divided it into two opposing, but linked, halves. We see men and women struggling to understand each other: anima and animus desperate for mutual recognition. In Jungian terms, dysfunctional heterosexual unions indicate a symbolic schism between male and female traits within the self. The non-visible, and often repressed, female traits within a man (anima) are all about intuition, superstition, irrational thought and emotion. If the anima is repressed or denied, she can quickly turn into a femme fatale—a demon of death who threatens to undermine all that hard, cerebral work the man has put into creating his reality. A perfect example of the gender imbalance can be seen in Cronenberg's *Naked Lunch*, where the cerebral Dr. Benway (Roy Scheider) is revealed as a woman, Fadela, who peels off her breasts and face to show her hairy, man's chest.

In Jung's theory, if a man fails to meet the challenges posed by his anima, he'll be in for big trouble: "These anima moods cause a sort of dullness, a fear of disease, of impotence, or of accidents. The whole of life takes on a sad and oppressive aspect."[14] Hmmm. Accidents, lethargy, alienation, gender confusion, erectile dysfunction? Thus far, it describes the Canadian male in film perfectly.

The animus within the woman works in much the same way: it represents typically male characteristics such as reason, conviction and authority. Should the woman choose to deny her inherent masculinity, then she too will find herself facing down a death demon—a dark, dangerous stranger who will either rob her, rape her, kill her—or all three. "A strange passivity and paralysis of all feeling, or a deep insecurity that can lead almost to a sense of nullity, may sometimes be the result of an unconscious animus opinion."[15]

Once again, we can see a parallel between the way people see Canadian film and the way Jung describes the effects of an animus imbalance.

Given that we are a country steeped in historic tension between our two founding European cultures, between Upper and Lower Canada, evidence of psychic tension should come as no surprise. Our collective imagination has stunted any chance at mundane, missionary-style sexual union. As a result, we have a history of film that offers little in the way of a future. The children in Canadian film who are born, are often killed off (*The Sweet Hereafter*) or are declared missing (*The Five Senses*) or are aborted before they become children at all (*Nô, Parsley Days, Maelstrom*). If we relate this to the gap theory, then we can see "missing children" as a recurring motif symbolic of what could be seen as a latent or subconscious desire for unity.

We can see a concrete translation of this idea in Robert Lepage's award-winning feature, *Nô*. The film opens with, Sophie (Anne-Marie Cadieux), a Quebec actress at the Osaka World's Fair, getting the news that she's pregnant from a doctor (with her best friend, a blind Japanese translator). Lost and confused about what to do, she calls her partner Michel in Montreal. It's four o'clock in the morning and he's tired. It's also October, 1970, and just as Sophie is about to uncork the news to Michel, there's a banging on the door of Michel's basement apartment. It's his buddies—FLQ boys on the lam. Michel hangs up the phone. Sophie sits in her Japanese cubicle of a hotel room, oozing frustration. Sophie's stress about the growing fetus is mirrored by larger, external issues such as the long-term future of Michel and Sophie's relationship and the future of the nation as a whole. The fetus represents a world of possibilities, but it also symbolizes a potentially unwanted occupation of someone's private space—like a bunch of soldiers with guns in their hands standing on the street corners of your hometown. The film ends on a decidedly ambiguous note as Lepage fast-forwards to the 1980 referendum, when the people of Quebec were asked whether they wanted to remain in Confederation or opt for a symbolic divorce. The results were far from conclusive, and simply led to more referenda—and more relationship tension—down the road.

GAY SEX

"I like the politicalness of film. I think sex is great. I don't know why people get upset about sex with two women. Sex is a wonderful thing. Love is not a relationship between two people, it's a state of being. I aspire to being in a loving State."
—Anne Wheeler

For all the dysfunction on the straight sex front, things look different when we look at the manner in which homosexual unions are portrayed on screen. Let's consider a few of the many relatively positive depictions of gay sex in Canadian film:

Outrageous!: This cutting-edge 1977 movie starring female impersonator Craig Russell features a psychotic (Liza McLaren) who leaves a mental institution to live with her gay hairdresser friend. The two outsiders find meaning and companionship together, which proves to have a positive, if temporary, anti-psychotic effect.
Better Than Chocolate: Anne wheeler's film shows us two young, good-looking women who fall in love and have great sex. The sex is not destructive, despite one character's latent guilt and fear of disclosure. In fact, in this film (which is one of a few films to use nudity in an erotic way), the women find their creative powers are enhanced by the union, as we can see in the sex scene that has them painting each other with chocolate and rolling around on blank canvases.
The Hanging Garden and **Beefcake**: in the first feature from Thom Fitzgerald, *The Hanging Garden*, he shows us the path to accepting a gay identity as he brings a gay man home, where he encounters the ghost of his former, dysfunctional self. This film not only has a happy ending, it's one of the few Canadian films that ends on a note of closure and healing. In his second film, *Beefcake*, Fitzgerald dramatizes the life of an early beefcake photographer in the fifties. The film feels really twisted in the way it makes the boys into sex slaves exploited by older men, but the sex itself is happy, escapist and altogether jubilant. They are proud gay men in a world that refuses to even acknowledge homosexuality as a reality in the world of muscle-building.

I've Heard the Mermaids Singing and **When Night Is Falling**: In Patricia Rozema's first film, *I've Heard the Mermaids Singing*, Polly (Sheila McCarthy) is an idiot-savant artist who develops a crush on a gallery owner (Paule Baillargeon) because she believes the curator knows the inner secrets of art. When she discovers the gallery owner has her own lesbian lover (Anne-Marie MacDonald), she feels the pain of jealousy ... but as destructive as the emotion is, it eventually leads to a catharsis and bonding between the three women. Similar images of "good sex"—or at least sexy sex—can be found in Rozema's *When Night Is Falling*.

Lilies: John Greyson's adaptation of Michel Marc Bouchard's Quebecois play, *Lilies*, shows us a gay couple who fulfill the full romantic cycle: they fall in love as children, fight for their love together as teens, then tragically lose each other at the hands of a jealous peer—who is so threatened by their devotion and commitment that he destroys one of them in a fire and leaves the other to rot in prison, wrongly incarcerated for the death of his true love. It might not have a happy ending, but the relationship between the two men is healthy and sincere, affirming all the positive elements of love and bonding. Gender, in this case, is a universal because all the parts are played by men—even those of the women—because the film is set in a prison, where the inmates put on a play to force the aging criminal (now a priest) to confess his guilt.

Being at Home with Claude: As it opens with the corpse of a murdered gay lover, this Jean Beaudin effort appears to break the "positive image" rule, but for all the pain and homicidal misery in the movie, there is no doubt how much the two men love each other. They are passionate about their affections. They are connected in ways far beyond the surface, and it's their connection, not their difference, that finally leads to the Romeo and Juliet ending.

There are other positive examples of gay sex to be found in Canadian cinema, and while they all deal with the same Samsonite luggage of repression and self-loathing, they tend to assert a more "positive" sense of self-worth in the final frames. Why gay sex gets a better shake than straight sex should be easy to explain at this point because it reaffirms, symbolically, what we've already come to understand about the larger systems at work in Canadian cinema—particularly our attempts to reconcile all the varying manifestations of "other" that occur in Canadian society at large. With difference all around us, alienating us at every turn, isn't it only natural to gravitate to sameness?

In Jung's mind, the real reflection of self could be found in a dream character of the same gender. "It is particularly in contacts with other people of the same sex that one stumbles over both one's own shadow and those of other people. Although we do see the shadow in a person of the opposite sex, we are usually much less annoyed by it."[16] In other words, a homosexual encounter in a dream is not a homosexual encounter at all, but a confrontation, and potential reconciliation with the repressed shadow self ... or, in the case of Canadian film, a confrontation and eventual reconciliation of repressed notions of identity.

In Rozema's *I've Heard the Mermaids Singing*, we can take the symbolism to a surface level because one woman is Quebecoise, the other is Ontario Anglo. On the symbolic level, we can see the frequency and relative health of homosexual couplings as a sign of psychic healing, because it reflects an understanding of selfhood—and we all know we can't love someone else until we've learned to love ourselves, eh?

Notes

1 Interview by author, 1999.
2 Vito Russo, *The Celluloid Closet*, pp. 5–6.
3 Interview by author, 2000.
4 Interview by author, 1993.
5 Maheu, "L'oedipe coloniale," *Parti Pris*, 1964. This article is cited at length in Bill Marshall's book *Quebec National Cinema*. I heard about it for the first time as a result of reading Marshall's text, so for any readers with an academic bent, I highly recommend it as supplementary reading.
6 Carl Jung, *Man and his Symbols*, p. 168.
7 Kay Armatage, *Gendering the Nation*, "Nell Shipman: a Case for Heroic Femininity," p. 17–38. (For those seeking a separate look at women in Canadian film, the book is a wonderful academic anthology on the subject.)
8 Ibid. p. 35.
9 Interview by author.
10 Margaret Atwood, *Survival*, pp. 170–72.
11 Interview by author.
12 Atom Egoyan, *Speaking Parts*, from the introduction to the screenplay.
13 Interview by author. Fragments of this interview appeared in *The Vancouver Sun*, in the article "Harkema's Girl Trouble Led To Insight," Oct 5, 1999, p. C5.
14 Jung, *Man and his Symbols*, p. 178.
15 Ibid. p. 191.
16 Ibid. p. 169.

⇒ Sex and Medicine ⇐

The field of medicine presents itself as the realm of sexual certainty in Derek McCormack's "Stargaze," as certain as the configuration of stars in the sky. Dr. Vine knows what "normal" sexuality is (homosexuality was still officially considered an abnormality by the psychiatric profession at the time the story is set) and uses his medical knowledge to "adjust" the narrator's sexuality accordingly. Ironically, the very fact that sexuality can be manipulated in this way takes it out of the biological realm and puts it into the technological domain. The other readings in this section are variations on this theme. Trish Salah brings out the assumptions about sexuality and race that emerge through her diary account of the surgeries she undergoes during her transition to a "body which is less truth than occasion," a "fantasy" of the sort that McCormack's narrator constellates at the fairground. Salah unflinchingly interfaces this realm of fantasy with the brutal details of her surgeries—fantasies of another sort, reminding us that the origin of the word "sex" is *secare*, meaning "to cut." The technical language in Patricia Baird's report on reproductive technology extends this theme. Canada's legalization of the birth control pill in 1963 was a defining moment in the medical technologizing of sexuality that reaches back to nineteenth-century studies by sexologists such as Krafft-Ebing. Baird's report makes explicit the role of the state in the regulation of sexuality and the heteronormative assumptions around that regulation (in its assertion, for example, that most Canadians want to have children). Anomalously in this section, the excerpt from John Colapinto's account of the life of David Reimer appears to argue *against* the "primacy of environment over biology," as Colapinto puts it. Reimer, born a male, was surgically altered to a female after a botched genital operation, but eventually sought to regain his male identity. Yet what emerges most powerfully from Colapinto's harrowing narrative are the enormous environmental pressures that impinge on Reimer at every stage of his life and the gendered assumptions around these social categories. The fluidity of Reimer's sexual identities is thus all the more remarkable, especially when understood in the context of the regulatory culture that seeks to contain those identities in stereotypes. David/Brenda Reimer committed suicide in 2005.

Derek McCormack

"Stargaze," *Dark Rides* (1996)

From Peterborough I took the Greyhound. I checked into Toronto General Hospital. My room was a bed, a chair, a closet. A barred window. Streetcars sparked past in the night.

* * *

First thing in the morning I was sitting in Dr. Vine's office.

"Age?" he said.

"Eighteen," I said. "Sir."

He scribbled on my chart. "How long have you been aware of your inversion?"

I breathed deep. "Eighteen years."

In the examining room I stripped and stretched out on a gurney. He girded my shins and arms, rolled an electric generator up to me. Taped electrodes to my penis and scrotum.

He said, "I'd like you to describe your fantasies involving men."

I shut my eyes. I spoke about kissing Gary Cooper's lips and nipples and stomach and—

Dr. Vine shocked me.

Back in my room I cupped my balls in my palm. Legs cramped. After a couple hours I signed out at the nurses' station and went down to the street.

The July sun. I shuffled north, past Queen's Park and Victoria University. At the Royal Ontario Museum I bought a ticket and wandered into an auditorium where people sat in dentists' chairs under a plaster dome. The usher seated me as the house lights died.

Over loudspeakers: "Welcome to the Milky Way."

Constellations brightened overhead—the Pleiades, Cepheus, Andromeda—

The auditorium seemed to spin. I gasped.

* * *

Come morning Dr. Vine strapped me down and hooked me up and showed me photographs of naked hulks with brush-cuts flexing their biceps.

I glanced from them to him. He was drumming his fingertips against the pictures, nails yellow, uncut. My penis limp.

145

"You're not concentrating," he said. He lined the pictures up on an easel. He ripped the electrodes off my privates and pressed them to my temples.

I blacked out.

* * *

I walked to the planetarium. Sat near the projector. It was dumbbell-shaped, fifteen feet long. Lying lengthwise it projected the night skies of the northern and southern hemispheres. Then it tilted. At a twenty-degree angle it shot out images of the planets. It tilted again and suddenly the sun filled the dome.

* * *

In the morning in Dr. Vine's office. I took off my clothes.

"You're extremely tense," he said. "Can you tell me why?"

"Because you really hurt me yesterday," I said.

"You're generalizing." He wheeled the generator closer. He wired my temples. "Your behaviour," he said. "Your behaviour is what hurts. Isn't that so?"

"Yes but I'm not sure—"

He ordered me to think men. Nude men.

"I can't, I'm too nervous."

"Close your eyes *now!*"

* * *

I came to in my room, my pillow bloody. I'd bitten my tongue.

At the Greyhound depot I bought popsicles. My lips were grape when I pulled into Peterborough.

I tramped home to bed. Clouds blanking out the stars.

* * *

Didn't catch a wink till dawn. My alarm went off and I ignored it. Sometime after noon the telephone rang. I picked it up.

It was Dr. Vine. "Admitting told me you'd checked out," he said.

My legs cramped.

"I'm expecting you bright and early tomorrow."

"No it's okay," I stammered. "I think I'm cured."

"If you're not here in the morning I'll be forced to contact your parents. Or the police."

I threw on some clothes and dashed downstreet. The bookstore had nothing. Likewise Hampton's Novelty Shop. At Turnbull's Department Store

I snatched up a celestial map and a copy of *The Amateur Astronomer's Guide*.

"You been to the Ex?" the saleslady said. She showed me a flyer for the Peterborough Exhibition. Listed among the attractions—"Science Fair and Planetarium."

I hopped the next bus to the fairgrounds. I tore into the Recreation Centre. Representing Science were an ant farm and a model of Peterborough's hydraulic liftlock. A papier-mâché sun dangled from a ceiling fan. Nine styrofoam orbs twirled around it.

The solar system.

"That's it?" I said punching my hip. "That's it?" I trudged out into the midway. Wall-to-wall people. Kids swarming the Haunted House, The Caterpillar, The Chairplane. The moon a fingernail clipping.

I staggered up against a cotton candy stand and shut my eyes. When I opened them I saw a dumbbell tilting in midair. It was cherry red, studded with lights. Instead of weights it had cages full of screaming people.

I fell onto my back, hands pillowing my head, heavenly bodies whirring across the sky.

Trish Salah

"Surgical Diary,"
Wanting in Arabic (2002)

Oct. 15, 2000

This is A's hand writing, not mine: *(not quite)*

For reduction of bruising, swelling and muscle/tissue soreness:
arnica homeopathic encapsulates   undertongue, you will want daily
may vary your intake while you heal
will help you notice
you'll heal daily
arnica tincture as liquid applied directly to your skin on sores

For reduction of scarring:
lavender essential oil after tissue is closed, you are closed, not weeping in
your skin vitamin e is also effective, after you're tissue healing, it goes in
closing
after it is

Icepacks feel terrible applied directly to you to your skin go
directly on swollen tissue where you are bruised
immediately after surgery for three to four days
directly applied will significantly reduce swelling

A humidifier might be useful
you'll have a hard time breathing
you'll heal dry

(A's curls fall in the finely knotted leather of a flail, the red of blood welts,
remembering
her voice is crackling sugar, where normally as smooth as warm maple.
More than most A's face both composes and conceals the designs of beauty.
Today, she is generous with a history she suffered.)

Oct. 16, 2000

I had my last consult today. Three surgeries in two hours. I can't believe it. I'm not sure what we agreed.

I said: *I don't want you to make my nose too small.*
He laughed.
I said: *I don't want to look like a white girl. My nose is an Arab nose.*
He said: *It's unusual, but ... but you want to be pretty? To look like a woman.*
I said: *Yeah, but I can be Arab and be pretty? A woman? My sister has the same nose.*
There was a pause.

He smiled: *Many Arab women enjoy having a smaller, more delicate nose.*

* * *

Yael's got everyone's email. They're making a schedule for the first week at least, and then we'll see. I'm going to be well taken care of. I tell myself I do need this. I won't be able to make my own food, maybe I won't be able to stand up. How do you know yourself in the midst of such loving care?

Oct. 23, 2000

I think we're going to go on strike. I wonder if it will all be done by the time I'm walking again. Among our more controversial demands: medical leave for transitioning transsexuals, financial assistance for sex reassignment surgeries.

Millot writes that we transsexuals make a demand upon the Real, for its adjustment. Just so.

Oct. 26, 2000

The question is how I can here try to rewrite this body which is less truth than occasion, which is making a bargain not with a fantasy but with fantasy, all the distortion that entails.

That's a lie, the second to last thing. The fantasy is specific, singular. (Having been a serious marxist boy, and a good feminist, I may have a hard time living it down. Or out.)

Oct. 29, 2000

Tomorrow, incisions. And something fuller. 375ccs of saline in a silicone
shell. If my skin will stretch that far. Apparently there are instruments that
can tell. Submuscular, so my tits won't ripple like a pond and pebble
collision. The incisions (tomorrow) under my arms, how much of a stretch,
to get them all the way in? I'm hoping my nipples won't point outward,
we'll see. I expect my breasts will be bigger than I expect because
everything is imaginary and ideal right now.

I couldn't make the party last night. My friends are so loving, there are no
words for it—
They're curious inevitably. But it would have been too much to see that
many people so soon before. I kind of felt I should though, given them a last
look at the pre-surgery body. There's something seductive and strange about
imagining my body as public property. Why?

It's just going out to party, being part of *the scene,* you know ...

*(I say that particularly in the habit of antiphony. And hard now not to feel
(your) absence as anything other than conspicuous. A space of whiteness
very near the centre, I might be very nearly staining what is seen (obscene).*

*I have these flashes, I have to confess, where none of this is my doing, where
it is all me being done to, at the behest of someone unknowable and
undeniable. It's a story you've come across before.)*

Nov. 1, 2000

Going in and under was easy, science fiction, because for years I used to lie
in bed and imagine my surgery and it was the future. It was early in the
morning when we left.

There was a waiver to sign. I felt calm changing into the paper gown. The
nurse took some photos, and I walked into the theatre, which felt very small.
I lay down and my arms were restrained, so I wouldn't shake the drip. The
drip knocked me out, better than those old ether masks. Passing out was
from childhood too. I don't know how many times I went under as a kid. It's
always their talking while you fade that is most warm and scary.
I don't remember the trip home.

Nov. 2, 2000

When he drew the packing out of my nose, I was afraid the blood would get everywhere. He said my lips were already healing and that I needed to come back in a week for him to check my nose and my breasts. He decided to make my breasts larger. He said they looked too small and that he knew I wouldn't want that. I made a show of being outraged.

We had trouble getting my meds. The pharmacist said she couldn't fill the prescription because the name on it was different from what was on my insurance. Yael took care and explained everything. The pharmacist understood perfectly. She refused to call the clinic to confirm Yael's story. Yael was near to tears, she was so furious. At the next pharmacy Yael pretended she was me and paid for the meds out of pocket.

Inside, my chest tears and pulls the lengths of my arms. Every motion has a measure of pain, that is almost calculated (somewhere else) in the time between motion and sensation. The mind is more quickly trained by this severe and immediate flesh than I am.

I cannot believe he wanted me to do this without codeine.

Yael's catching some sleep on the couch now, while I sip my soup.

Nov. 3, 2000

Gender Dysphoria (dysphasia)

I used to think dysphoria meant falling,
to fall out of, or even, within,
Not unbearable and so I used to be
Falling out of   not just
Bearing with the difficulty   of mine
Of being a place and its erasure.

Nov. 5, 2000

Mostly today, I am floating, bodiless, and I am an eleven year old at Christmas or home sick. It's time for ice cream and soup. Though soon ... Odd that reading children's fantasy now would evoke such old consolations and escape routes, just days after the surgeries which should have answered that longing once and for all. As if—

I can walk to the couch on my own now, and it doesn't hurt much so long as I am careful. It's not as if every upper body gesture doesn't rip at or through something inside, but there are other muscles. Still all my metaphors have closed in on my body, and the world is contracted to the smaller square of this basement. I like the amber of the walls. I really dread ever having to go outside again.

My breasts seem strangely high, distortions of chest, rather than resembling ... It's normal, I'm told, but it makes me nervous. I cannot lift my arms high enough to see where the skin is sutured, under the arms and disappearing inward. But I itch inside and out.

Yael is holding me together. My brother and sister-in-law should be by soon, with their newborn.

Nov. 7, 2000

scared girl
she would sleep next to me, here,
me, anxious of every touch
there is no word for *hers*
she put her skin, there, on the outside

i keep thinking this is forever
like when you're to be married.

Nov. 9, 2000

Questions for the Doctor:

how to tell healing yellow from?
what are acceptable fluid emissions?
how soft or firm should they be?

(is it strange to ask? what do I know of breasts?)

when do I get unstitched, or will they melt?
I can't feel my lips or nose, for how long?
how long before sex?

Nov. 13, 2000

Woke up with dreams still pulling, and so the day is hazy, not quite in
focus. Could be the meds. Could be the lack of light. Dreamt the scene in
Passion of the New Eve, where Eve meets Tristessa, discloses what
we've maybe known all along, that Tristessa, paragon of cinematic
femininity, is transsexual, or at least Angela Carter's imagining thereof.
Funny to be returning to this book, the one that opened for me the
thought of surgery, having just been operated.

The inscription on the book, *from Dana* is *to Patrick;* so loving, and from
when I so needed that, the world had ended mostly and I was gone. I
remember one day though, Dana and I were in a café in Little
Italy—maybe on Clinton Street—scribbling poems to one another. Like
this entry the poems were nostalgic, sentimental. Nonetheless, they
allowed the future.

Nov. 17, 2000

It will be six months before my body settles into shape.
How many hours of knit before this is not a body and its change?

Don't be deceived.
No, I've not, not yet. I'm not, not there. Or there, or—
Though I can feel something move as if across a great distance.

I keep catching at a length of a rope descending, the slip
Returns your questions.
I think they are your questions.

If desire is always a ruse, why this time or shape?
Why this cut, here?

Patricia Baird, et al.

Proceed with Care: Final Report of the Royal Commission on New Reproductive Technologies: Summary and Highlights (1993)

Having children and ensuring they are healthy are fundamentally important goals to most Canadians, but some people cannot reach these goals without help. As a caring society, Canada should respond to these deeply held aspirations, but the technology used to help can also be misused, and have harmful consequences both for individuals and for society. National action is needed to ensure new reproductive technologies are not misused, but used with care. It is the responsibility of the federal government, on behalf of society, to set boundaries around the technologies prohibiting those that contravene Canadian ethical and social values, and to put in place regulation to ensure that only legitimate, beneficial uses occur. Only the federal government has the power to put in place a system to manage the technologies. In the interest of protecting Canadian citizens, the federal government has the responsibility to do so.

Internationally, no other inquiry into new reproductive technologies had such a broad and far reaching mandate, and no other looked at these issues from a uniquely Canadian viewpoint. The commission examined the issues from within the context of Canada's unique values and attitudes, social make-up, geography, institutions, health and social systems. The scope of our recommendations and the breadth of our final report will set an international precedent, will complement other international efforts in the area, and will urge the Canadian government to take the lead internationally to protect society from unethical and unsafe uses of new reproductive technologies.

Within the clearly specified boundaries of what is ethically acceptable, the technologies must be offered only in a safe, fair and accountable way. For example, it is unethical to offer as services unproven procedures or treatments. and it is irresponsible to devote public resources for health care to them. Few existing treatments have been conclusively proven beneficial, and many need to be evaluated in research. Canada needs a regulatory and monitoring system to protect Canadians and ensure that only safe and effective treatments are offered as service, that appropriate record-keeping and informed consent mechanisms are in place, and that useful and beneficial research is conducted.

Strong provincial and professional participation and leadership is also required within the proposed national system for it to serve the interests of

Canadians. There is a need for a rational approach to health care management with coordinated decisions about resource allocation and what services will be offered, in the light of an evidence-based approach to medical practice. Only this approach will allow us to keep and maintain our system of universal access.

New reproductive technologies are evolving. Canada's response to emerging and future issues must reflect inclusive, informed, broad-based input, and must be consistent with the values of Canadians. The structure we have recommended will ensure public input and accountability, and ensure future technologies are used only in a beneficial and ethical way.

How the commission went about its work

In completing the task of coming to recommendations about how new reproductive technologies should be handled in this country, the Commission consulted with and listened to Canadians from all sectors of society and carried out research and critical analysis of information and evidence on the technologies. The work was organized into two major streams—consultations and communications with Canadians, and research and evaluation of the technologies and the issues surrounding them.

Consultations and Communications
The commission listened to Canadians across the country, and helped inform the public about the issues contained in our mandate. The following activities were undertaken as part of the consultations and communications program:

- Public hearings in 17 centres across Canada (2,000 participated)
- Toll-free telephone lines (6,000 individuals left their views)
- Information meetings with national groups interested in the technologies;
- National surveys exploring Canadians' values and attitudes (15,000 participated);
- The release of 14 research studies on varied topics to inform and educate Canadians, and to stimulate public interest and debate around the issues;
- Distribution of more than 50,000 copies of our newsletter, *Update.*
- Distribution of over 250,000 pieces of information, such as information kits, brochures, and information for use by journals, newspapers, and television networks.

Research and Evaluation
Research and analysis efforts involved more than 300 scholars and academics representing 70 disciplines, 21 Canadian universities and 27 hospitals and other institutions. The program culminated in 130 research projects available in 15 published volumes. They include:

- Analysis and inquiry into the prevalence, risk factors and prevention of infertility, methods of assisted reproduction, prenatal diagnosis and genetics, research involving human zygotes, the use of fetal tissue, and their social, ethical and other implications.
- Analysis of the experiences of other countries dealing with technologies.
- Understanding the current context within which the technologies exist, including the values of Canadians and the societal systems that interact with reproductive issues such as health, education, and legal systems and other institutions.
- An evaluation of relevant areas of law and ethics.

Through these two streams of work, the Commission was able to provide, for the first time, a picture of infertility and new reproductive technology use in this country, and substantive social, ethical, and legal analysis of the implications of using or not using the technologies. Our recommendations were reached relying on three considerations: explicit ethical principles, Canadian values as expressed to us in our consultations and through our surveys, and a conviction that decisions about offering medical procedures should be evidence based. In the next pages we give the most important points about the main topics we addressed—what we found, what we concluded, and what we recommend relevant to each.

RESPONSIBLE REGULATION: THE NATIONAL REPRODUCTIVE TECHNOLOGIES COMMISSION

In light of the evidence collected and assessed according to an ethical framework, the commission concluded that some reproductive technologies and some uses of the technologies are unethical and contrary to the values of Canadians—they should be prohibited. Others are potentially beneficial, if they are used ethically and responsibly. This means a system is needed to oversee, license and monitor activities in this field.

The Commission recommends the federal government establish a regulatory and licensing body, the NRTC, to oversee research, technologies and practices. There is a need of urgent action in a rapidly evolving technological field, for comprehensiveness and similarity of approach across the country, and for public accountability in managing the technologies. It is the only way to ensure that the appropriate mix of resources, skills and experience is brought to the technologies in all their dimensions: ethical, social, legal, scientific and medical. Only the federal government can set up such a system, and it is important that the government fulfill its responsibility to protect citizens and society by doing so.

Several requirements are common to all the technologies: the need for reliable information to guide policy and practice; the need for standards and guidelines for the organization and provision of services; the need for effective means to ensure compliance; and the need for accountability. The approach we propose builds on the best standards and practices of the medical specialties involved which already are in use in some Canadian clinics. These standards should be expanded, and should be embodied in a licensing system.

We recommend the NRTC be composed of 12 members representing a broad range of experiences and perspectives. Consultation activities should be undertaken to further enhance public input and involvement. Women should make up a substantial proportion of the Commission's membership, normally at least half.

To ensure wide public input into the working of the system and to deal with setting policy as new issues evolve, we recommend membership in the proposed NRTC should always include persons knowledgeable about the interests and perspectives of those with disabilities, those who are infertile, and those who are members of racial minorities. A range of expertise should be represented, including reproductive medicine, ethics, law, and social sciences.

We recommend the NRTC have five areas of regulatory responsibility in which the provision of services would be subject to compulsory licensing through five sub-committees established for that purpose. They are:

- sperm collection, storage and distribution, and the provision of assisted insemination services.
- assisted conception services, including egg retrieval and use.
- prenatal diagnosis.
- research involving human zygotes (embryos).
- the provision of human fetal tissues for research or other specified purposes.

License hearings would be public, a license would be conditional on compliance with certain standards and conditions of license. The major functions in these five areas of regulatory authority are as follows:

- to license, set standards and monitor practices in the area.
- to collect, evaluate, disseminate and store information.
- to consult, help coordinate and facilitate intergovernmental cooperation in the area.
- to monitor future technologies and practices and set policies.

In addition we recommend a sixth subcommittee with primary responsibility in the field of infertility prevention. Its responsibilities would include the compilation and evaluation of data pertaining to the causes of infertility, the promotion of cooperative research efforts in Canada and internationally, and the regulatory, public education or other options for preventing or reducing the incidence of infertility.

National action is necessary, but not sufficient. Strong provincial and professional leadership and participation is also needed. Cooperation from all parties will ensure that the system serves the interests of Canadians.

NEW REPRODUCTIVE TECHNOLOGIES AND THE HEALTH CARE SYSTEM

The health care system is a source of national pride for Canadians. It is a tangible way in which our society expresses mutual support and caring for its members. It is important to manage the system responsibly, and not to overburden it with functions or responsibilities that should lie elsewhere.

Having children is important to most Canadians, and if effective, safe techniques exist to achieve that goal, it is appropriate that they are offered as part of the health care system in a non-discriminatory way; for example, prenatal diagnosis for serious disorders, IVF for blocked fallopian tubes, and doctor insemination if there is no fertile male partner. However, it is unethical to offer as services unproven procedures or treatments, and it is irresponsible to devote public resources to them. Procedures without good evidence of effectiveness should be considered research, and regulated as such. Health care resources are limited, and the continued provision of unproven, ineffective, expensive technical procedures undermines the system by using resources without evidence of benefit. In fact, an evidence based approach taken throughout the health care system would allow society to better use existing health care resources, and manage the system better.

Decisions about resource allocation, access and practice should be made in light of outcomes—that is, practice should be evidence based. The commission's recommended NRTC will play a valuable role in establishing, administering and exemplifying this approach by requiring data on outcomes that will be used to shape practice at licensed centers.

ETHICAL FRAMEWORK AND GUIDING PRINCIPLES

A broad ethical orientation was used in Commission deliberations—an ethic of care—which gives priority to the mutual care and connectedness between people and communities, and attempts to prevent conflict instead of resolving conflicts that have already occurred. Within that orientation, a set of guiding principles were used to assess how a technology's use should be viewed, and what conclusions should be made. They were:

Individual Autonomy: People should be free to choose how to lead their lives, particularly with respect to their bodies and fundamental commitments such as health, family, sexuality and work. This freedom must be limited if others are harmed, forced or coerced, or if social stability is undermined.

Equality: Every member of the community is entitled to equal concern and respect. This precludes any practice that reflects or perpetuates the idea that some lives are worth less than others.

Respect for Human Life and Dignity: All forms of human life and tissues should be treated with sensitivity and respect. Although the law does not treat embryos as persons, they are connected to the community by their origins and potential.

Protection of the Vulnerable: In the case of power imbalance where one party is open to exploitation, this should be given special consideration. This can arise from socioeconomic status, membership in a minority group, or disability, and society has a responsibility to safeguard individuals who are vulnerable.

Non-commercialization of Reproduction: Human beings, their reproductive capacities or tissues should not be treated as commodities to be traded for money or other goods.

Appropriate Use of Resources: There are many needs yet finite resources, so we need to use resources wisely. Public resources should not be used on ineffective treatments, and evaluation of technology is needed to manage resources.

Accountability: Those who hold power, whether personally or because of their role in government or other fields, are responsible for the way they use it.

Balancing Individual and Collective Interests: Neither individual nor collective interests take automatic precedence; each must be taken into consideration in any decisions made about new reproductive technologies. The Commission endorses a strategy that encompasses both individual and collective interests and maintains a necessary awareness of both, remembering that the Charter of Rights and Freedoms expresses the Canadian stance on the relationship between the individual and the collective.

THE PREVALENCE OF INFERTILITY

The commission conducted the first Canadian survey to determine the prevalence of infertility in this country in couples in which the woman was aged 18–44. It found that 8.5% or 300,000 couples who have been married or living together for at least one year at the time of the survey were infertile. Seven percent or 250,000 couples married or living together for at least two years were infertile.

This estimate is useful for the following reasons:

- for public policy decisions regarding planning of infertility prevention programs and infertility treatment programs;
- for use as a baseline figure for future studies to determine if the rate of infertility is rising or declining in Canada;
- for comparison with other countries and communities.

STDs AND INFERTILITY

Preventing STDs, specifically gonorrhea and Chlamydia, must become a greater priority in Canada if we are to reduce the prevalence of infertility in the future. STDs cause pelvic inflammatory disease (PID) and an estimated 20% of all infertility among couples can be traced to damage to the woman's fallopian tubes that has resulted after PID.

STD prevention should be focused on by school health programs to educate young people about risks to their fertility and how to protect against these risks. Other programs should be targeted to reach sexually active young people at high risk who are not in school. More attention should also be given to the role of physicians and other health care workers in STD prevention.

Research on the incidence of STDs and on the evaluation of prevention strategies is very important. The proposed NRTC subcommittee's role is to facilitate and promote a focus on policies that will be effective in prevention of infertility.

SMOKING AND INFERTILITY

There is mounting evidence that heavy smoking reduces fertility as well as increasing risks to the developing fetus during pregnancy. The evidence on fertility reduction, while not conclusive, is enough to justify counseling couples to quit smoking before they try to conceive. Success rates of assisted conceptions may be lower in smokers, so individuals considering using these should be counseled to stop smoking and receive support to do so.

Preventing smoking is as important as helping smokers to quit. Because the majority of smokers begin in their teens, prevention efforts should be targeted at young people, and public "no smoking policies" and restrictions on tobacco advertising should be in place.

AGE AND INFERTILITY

Women's fertility declines with age because of two factors; cumulative exposure to risk factors affecting fertility, and the natural aging of the reproductive system. On average, a woman in her mid to late 30s will take longer to conceive than a woman in her twenties.

From a biological perspective the ideal time for a woman to have children is in her twenties. This may not be practical or desirable for many women for many reasons. Steps must be taken to reduce the impediments to earlier child-caring, including lessening the financial and opportunity costs of interrupting a career to raise children by introducing family-friendly workplace strategies such as flex-time, paid leave, job sharing, and permanent part-time employment to allow women to continue in the workforce. Strategies to encourage men to assume more responsibility for child and home care are needed.

Women should have information on the biological realities of aging so they may factor this into decisions about when to have children. Information incorporated into school programs and information provided by health care workers can help them become aware of this.

EXPOSURE TO HARMFUL AGENTS IN THE WORKPLACE AND THE ENVIRONMENT AND INFERTILITY

This field is characterized by a lack of information. Data clearly show that in a sufficient dose a number of agents in the workplace and environment can delay conception or reduce fertility (by affecting the menstrual cycle, sperm production or quality, reducing interest in sexual activity, or causing spontaneous abortion), but evidence about the effect of more common levels of exposure does not exist. A rational and effective prevention strategy must be based on knowledge, so research should be a priority. The task is one facing all nations, and Canada should take a lead role to organize cooperative and coordinated international efforts in the research and data analysis needed. We recommend the NRTC Infertility Prevention Subcommittee work toward facilitating and developing such an initiative.

Past and current prevention strategies have been fragmented, and have concentrated on removing at-risk workers (usually women) from positions where they are exposed to agents that could be harmful. A single approach is not sufficient; an integrated approach using exposure standards, regulatory measures, education of workers, and improved health and safety legislation is likely to be more effective in preventing reproductive harm. The focus should be to develop a knowledge base that provides a solid foundation for further definitive preventive action.

Environmental health hazards are emerging as a focus in public policy and legislation, but aspects related to reproductive health are often ignored. We recommend that reproductive health experts be involved as advisors to any environmental protection legislation, particularly existing and proposed regulations under the Canadian Environmental Protection Act, to ensure protection of human reproductive health is included in planning.

PREVENTING INFERTILITY

Canada needs a national infertility prevention strategy so that aspects of current programs can be integrated for a greater focus on protecting fertility. Such a strategy should be aimed at reducing and preventing STDs and smoking, and at increasing awareness of the effects of delaying childbearing, and workplace and environmental risks to fertility.

Cooperation between federal, provincial/territorial and private bodies currently administering health, education, counseling and outreach programs is crucial. A central body such as the proposed NRTC Infertility Prevention Subcommittee is needed to stimulate and coordinate such cooperation, provide useful information and educational materials, and encourage legislative changes where needed. Research into what programs or initiatives are effective in infertility prevention should be a priority.

ADOPTION

Our review showed that the number of children available for adoption has dropped markedly, so that adoption is no longer a feasible alternative for most couples, and even less likely for single people or those in non-traditional relationships. In 1990 there were eight people waiting to adopt for every infant in Canada. The current system is not structured in the best interests of the child, meeting the needs of other parties involved (such as adoptive parents and birth mothers), access to adoption, cost, record keeping and disclosure, counseling and consent.

How international adoptions are handled is an important aspect for review.

International adoptions are problematic from an ethical standpoint if protections and policies are not in place, as they may contribute to commodification of human beings and possible coercion and exploitation of women in other countries. Regulations governing these adoptions should be reviewed. A priority for all levels of government should be harmonizing provincial regulations and practices.

The current status of private adoptions in Canada raises concerns about non-commercialization and non-commodification of children, equality and non-discrimination in access. It should be reviewed and changes made.

FERTILITY DRUGS

Drugs to induce ovulation are very commonly used in treating infertility. It is therefore important to collect information on short-term and long-term effects of their use. Their widespread prescription by physicians outside clinics makes it difficult to collect information on outcomes. Fertility drugs are not alone in this regard—there are problems with existing mechanisms governing all evaluation of outcomes in an ongoing way after a drug has been approved for use in Canada. The Commission has made recommendations that will help assure Canadians that citizens are protected from unethical, unproven, or unsafe drug use at licensed centers, and that will help the profession more generally to follow better prescribing practices for these drugs.

The Commission found questionable treatment practices, such as drugs used for unapproved uses or at unapproved dosages, that put patients at risk yet are not in the context of research trials. There is a need to protect patients from experimental or unproven drug therapies by putting in place regulations and guidelines to ensure that only drugs meeting standards of effectiveness and safety are used in practice at licensed clinics. Licensed centers should offer others only in the context of multicenter clinical trials where standards of ethical research are adhered to. Use of some drugs should be discontinued altogether. Full information for patients is a crucial component.

Most fertility drugs, apart from clomiphene citrate used in approved dosages, should only be prescribed where monitoring and appropriate clinical and laboratory expertise for following the patient is available. This means it is inappropriate to provide them outside infertility treatment clinics.

ASSISTED INSEMINATION

The Commission's investigation found that AI is the most commonly used method for women without a fertile male partner to form families. Far more children are born from this each year than are adopted in Canada, and children born this way are 5–10x more common than IVF children. This means AI is worthy of much more scrutiny, assessment and policy attention than it has been afforded in the past.

We found insemination is being offered under widely varying clinical conditions, sometimes in a dangerous fashion; technical variations of the procedures are being performed with no evidence of their benefit; some practitioners are not adhering to the standards physicians have set for themselves as a profession; access criteria differ from clinic to clinic, with single women and lesbians being excluded in some.

Forming a family is of great importance to people. Provided standards are adhered to, DI is a safe and very effective way to have a child. Therefore, the Commission recommends DI be available through the publicly supported health care system. Unless there is evidence that the well being of resulting children will be harmed, DI should be equally available to all women. The available evidence does not show different outcomes in children born to or raised by lesbians or single women when compared to children born to heterosexual women and couples, in similar circumstances. Thus the best interests of the child cannot be used as a reason to deny access. If a service is available, women should be treated equally, unless there is good evidence that the best interest of the child will suffer.

The experiences of adoptees and their families have indicated the importance of information about biological origins, and access to medical and social information about genetic parents. Inadequate or absent record keeping by DI practitioners have made it impossible to meet the current and future needs of existing AI children and their families. We have recommended an integrated, reliable record-keeping system to ensure their needs are met.

Regulation and licensing is needed to standardize practices and safeguard the health of citizens. Neglecting to enforce regulations and adequate monitoring of the practice of AI endangers the health of AI recipients, their partners and children.

Family law has not kept pace with the realities created by DI. As a result, DI families and sperm donors could be vulnerable to challenges to custody, access, inheritance and support for DI children. This vulnerability encourages secrecy around DI, which is not in the best interests of DI children or families. We recommend changes to family law to reflect DI realities.

Commissioners are strongly opposed to commercializing human reproduction, as are Canadians generally. No profit should be made from the selling of any reproductive material, including sperm, because of ultimately dehumanizing effects. Current commercial practices in storage and distribution of donor sperm contravene these values, and we recommend a licensed, non-profit system.

In vitro fertilization

IVF is currently offered in a way that is unacceptable. In about half of cases in Canada it is used for indications for which there is not good evidence it is effective, yet it is offered in these cases as a treatment, not as research. As well, there are marked differences in how services are offered, often without clear or understandable information for patients. Record keeping is unsatisfactory and insufficient to be able to assess outcomes—even such critical aspects as the number of children born. Voluntary guidelines developed by practitioners for practice are not routinely adhered to. The situation of voluntary regulation in the treatment community has led to practice ranging from excellent to completely unacceptable.

Medical procedures should move from the realm of research to that of treatment only if they can be demonstrated to be effective and beneficial, and only if information on their risks and effects is available. To date, IVF has been proven effective for only one category of infertility disorders—those involving complete blockage of the fallopian tubes. Only for this category of cases is it a treatment proven to be of benefit and therefore a candidate for provincial health-insurance coverage. For all other uses, there is a pressing need to find out for what indications IVF is effective. Until that information is available, IVF for indications other than tubal blockage should be offered only in the context of well designed clinical trials.

Some uses of IVF technology contravene Canadian values, and are unethical, thus they should be banned. These include IVF in support of preconception arrangements and IVF for post-menopausal women, IVF as a profit-making venture, and experimental uses of IVF offered as treatment.

A nationally administered, regulated, standardized system is needed to ensure adherence to rigorous standards of practice and care, useful and standardized record-keeping, access to adequate information and counseling for patients, analysis of any long-term effects, and ongoing monitoring and policy-making.

There is a good opportunity to put in place a well regulated system to provide assisted conception services in Canada. There is a history of voluntary cooperation in the field, and only a relatively small and clearly indefinable number of such facilities and concerned professional organizations.

HANDLING OF EGGS AND EMBRYOS

Egg and embryo donation can be beneficial for some infertile individuals and couples, but it is also possible to misuse the technology. Some uses would violate Canadian values and are unethical when viewed through the Commission's ethical framework. These include designated donation of eggs and zygotes, which raises the issue of potential coercion, egg retrieval solely for the purpose of donation, which puts women at risk without benefit, donation to women who have experienced menopause at the usual age, storage of embryos for more than five years or after the death of either partner, and the implantation of eggs from female fetuses.

The autonomy of donor women and couples must be respected by having detailed standardized information and consent to fertilization, donation or disposition. Guidelines and standards as conditions of license will ensure this consent is given before eggs are retrieved, and that eggs and embryos will only be used and disposed of in accordance with the wishes of the donor.

As in DI, the health of women recipients and the children that result should be protected by testing donors for infectious diseases that could be transmitted to recipients. Families need non-identifying social and medical information about donors, so standardized records need to be kept to allow this. Coded, recorded information will allow research on outcomes. NRTC licensing requirements for facilities will ensure these standards are met.

EMBRYO RESEARCH

Some knowledge about reproduction particularly relevant to the treatment of infertility, can be gained only through research using human embryos or zygotes. Such research is an essential part of ensuring safety and quality of medical treatment in this field. However it is also essential to ensure that zygotes be treated with respect because of their connections to the human community.

Research on human zygotes in Canada to date has been conducted without clear legal and public policy direction. It is important to put in place boundaries, and to regulate within these boundaries to ensure that only ethically acceptable, accountable use of human zygotes in research is made. In view of our ethical principles, research in human zygotes is acceptable only if it occurs within certain boundaries, and to ensure this, any facility doing such research will be required to be licensed.

Conditions of license will include: the goal of the research is knowledge about human health and treatment of disease; there is no other way of gaining the knowledge other than using human zygotes; it occurs prior to 14 days after fertilization. Strict and standardized protocols of informed consent are required when zygotes are donated for research, and retrieving eggs solely for fertilization and use in research is not permissible.

PRECONCEPTION ARRANGEMENTS

A preconception agreement is where a woman agrees to conceive and carry a pregnancy in order to hand over the child to a commissioning person to raise. Our review of the evidence shows that the potential benefits to a few individuals are far outweighed by the harm to others and to society. Commissioners believe strongly that preconception arrangements are unacceptable and should not be encouraged. Preconception arrangements commodify reproduction and children, they have the potential to exploit women's vulnerability because of race, poverty or powerlessness and leave women open to coercion. Thus they contravene the Commission's ethical principles.

The most appropriate ways to discourage commercial preconception arrangements are by criminally prosecuting those who act as intermediaries, and by making payments for preconception arrangements illegal.

To be effective, prohibitions against preconception must be national in scope and equally enforced in all areas of the country, so federal regulation is necessary. We also recommend that Canada take a lead in discouraging such practices internationally.

We recommend the interests of children born through non-commercial preconception arrangements should be protected by establishing that a child's legal mother is the woman who gives birth to the child. We recommend that the best interests of the child predominate in any dispute over custody.

COMMERCIAL INTERESTS

New reproductive technologies may bring benefits but they also have potential harms to individuals and society if misused. This means the development and dissemination of new reproductive technologies cannot be left to market forces or corporate goals. A regulatory framework that ensures the profit motive is not the deciding factor in the development or provision of the technologies is essential, and the government, as guardian of public interest, must put legislation in place to set this up. If commercial interests continue unregulated, they could lead to inappropriate, unethical or unsafe use of technology. However, within a regulated context, commercial interests have a useful role—for example, in the development of drugs.

The technologies should not be used in any way that commodifies human beings, commercializes reproduction, or otherwise offends Canadian values and our ethical principles. Among the activities that are ethically unacceptable and that we recommend not be permitted are: the buying and selling of gametes, zygotes, embryos and fetuses for-profit provision of assisted insemination and conception services, the use of financial incentives in preconception or adoption arrangements, and the patenting of medical treatments or of human gametes, zygotes, embryos or fetuses.

In the open market it is assumed that consumers can protect their own interests—in the field of health care they cannot, and they are vulnerable. We recommend specific policies to limit commercial interests so that vulnerable interests are protected including: licensing only non-profit service provision with required standards of quality control and provision of objective information to prospective patients; monitoring the promotional activities of pharmaceutical firms; strengthening the procedures governing the testing of new products and services and approving them for use; and ensuring ethical review of industry-funded research.

PRENATAL DIAGNOSIS FOR CONGENITAL ANOMALIES AND GENETIC DISEASE

Some people are at increased risk of having congenital anomalies or a genetic disease in their children. A large majority of Canadians think PND should be available to such individuals. PND provides choices for at-risk couples, and allows them to have healthy children, and, if used for serious disorders with fully informed choices, is beneficial. Nevertheless there are risks if PND is misused, and a regulatory system is needed to ensure adherence to rigorous standards of practice and care, and to ensure that practice continues to evolve in line with Canadian values.

We found a major difference in the likelihood a woman would have access to testing by being referred to a genetics centre—a more than four-fold difference between provinces, although women's attitudes to PND varied little regionally. It is imperative that the choice to use PND be made by the woman, not by the physician.

Not enough attention has been given to how patients view the PND experience and how the public perceives genetics. There is a great deal of misinformation about PND, and there is a need for accurate, unbiased, accessible information in this field. It is important that all eligible women be informed of the service and that their wishes to use or not use the technology be respected.

A regulated licensing system for facilities providing prenatal diagnosis is recommended to ensure continued adherence to standards of practice, record keeping, adequate information and counseling for patients. The structure we have recommended for this system will ensure that a wide representation of views is included in policy-setting as the field continues to evolve. It will also report publicly on current and future developments so Canadians will be reassured that all activities are open and accountable.

PRENATAL DIAGNOSIS FOR LATE ONSET SINGLE-GENE DISORDERS

Presymptomatic prenatal diagnosis for late-onset disorders raises issues in addition to those raised by PND for congenital or early onset problems. If a couple does not consider termination an option, the benefits of prenatal testing are outweighed by potential harm to the child. Women and couples, when given complete and accurate information, are capable of making enlightened and appropriate decisions for themselves and their children. Appropriate counseling should be available to ensure parents are aware of negative and positive aspects of such prenatal testing and possible outcomes.

There has been no demand for the development and provision of prenatal testing for genes that increase susceptibility to common multifactorial disorders. Such testing at this time is unable to provide any useful or reliable information about the likelihood of a person becoming ill. This means prenatal testing for such disorders would not be an effective or responsible investment of scarce health care resources.

We recommend continued and ongoing monitoring of developments in this field and a mechanism, in the form of the NRTC Prenatal Diagnosis Subcommittee, to ensure policy responses take into account public input to ensure future technologies are used in a beneficial and ethical way.

SEX SELECTION FOR NON-MEDICAL REASONS

The practice of PND and sex-selective abortion, simply because one sex is preferred over the other, is contrary to the Commission's guiding principles and incompatible with Canadian values. It violates the principles of respect for human life and dignity, protection of the vulnerable, and appropriate use of resources.

For the same reasons, sex-selective zygote transfer is also inappropriate if used simply because of a preference. Licensing of IVF practitioners will ensure that pre-implantation diagnosis for non-medical reasons will not be done in licensed centres.

Sperm treatments and sex-selective insemination does not violate the principle of respect for human life. Although evidence suggests that the great majority of Canadians do not have a gender bias with respect to the sex of their children and would consider using this technique only with the aim of having at least one child of each sex, additional factors must be taken into consideration:

• it reinforces the idea that the sex of a child is important, and encourages the view that families with all boys or all girls are less than ideal.
• it could make existing children in the family feel that their own sex was lacking in some way.
• it would involve an inappropriate use of resources.
• the technique is unproven and research to determine its effectiveness and safety is not of sufficient value to devote scarce research resources to it.

These considerations led us to conclude that sex-selective insemination services should not be available in Canada for reasons of sex preference. We recommend such services be provided only where there is a medical indication such as an X-linked disorder, and only in licensed settings with requirements for informed consent, data collection, and reporting.

GENE THERAPY AND GENETIC ALTERATION

Several applications of DNA technology, such as gene therapy and alteration, are relevant to human reproduction and all are highly experimental.

Somatic cell gene therapy involves the insertion of genetic material into the non-reproductive cells of an individual for the purpose of correcting a genetic disease. Technical limitations mean that only a small fraction of single-gene disorders are presently amenable to gene therapy. Use of this therapy in children or even adults may be appropriate if it is the only treatment available for severely affected individuals. In the prenatal context, use of gene therapy poses risks to both the woman and the developing zygote or fetus. A two-part mechanism for review of any proposed gene therapy research involving prenatal treatment is recommended. The Medical Research Council and the NRTC would both assess any such project before approval to proceed could be given.

Germ-line genetic alteration refers to the introduction of corrective genetic material into germ cells (gametes or zygotes) so that the resulting genetic change is passed onto offspring in subsequent generations. There is no situation where this is the only way to avoid having affected offspring, and the risks are significant. Therefore we recommend such research should not be conducted in Canada. The practice is inconsistent with the Commission's guiding principles and there are many potential harms, without clear benefit to any individual.

Non-therapeutic genetic alteration involves the insertion of a gene into an already healthy structure in order to improve or enhance a known characteristic, such as intelligence, height, or longevity. Genetic enhancement carries social and medical risks disproportionate to any benefit, and involves opportunity costs by diverting scarce financial and professional resources away from real medical problems. No research into this are should be permitted or funded in Canada.

JUDICIAL INTERVENTION

Judicial intervention into pregnancy and birth has increased in part because of technological and medical advancements allowing the fetus to be seen as a separate entity from the pregnant woman. This has positive consequences— increased awareness of risks to the fetus with avoidance of harmful exposures and treatment of disease in utero. It also has the potential to establish an adversary relationship in which a pregnant woman's autonomy is compromised. This has serious, negative implications for all women who become pregnant.

Society has an interest in promoting the health and well-being of the fetus, but not at the expense of the basic components of the woman's human dignity. To coerce and compel by judicial intervention is also unlikely to be effective in protecting the fetus. The instruments available to the courts are blunt and unsuited to the goal of promoting anyone's well-being.

A better alternative to judicial intervention in reaching the goal of fetal well being is care and assistance to the pregnant woman: this respects the life and dignity of both the woman and fetus. The woman's consent and cooperation are needed to ensure a positive outcome for the fetus. Judicial intervention should not be permissible, instead steps should be taken to maximize the health of the woman and fetus through information, education, culturally appropriate outreach, counseling and support.

USES OF FETAL TISSUE

On the basis of the evidence reviewed by the Commission, there is a real possibility that research involving the use of fetal tissue could result in considerable alleviation of human suffering. At present, elective abortion provides the only practical source of fetal tissue. Research carried out under the controlled conditions we have specified may benefit human health and is respectful of human dignity.

The controlled conditions for obtaining and using fetal tissue include safeguards against coercion, commercialization and unethical use of fetal tissue. We recommend: prohibition of giving or receiving payment for fetal tissue; consent to use of tissue obtained separately from and subsequent to the decision to have an abortion; standards of information disclosure; and the method of abortion to be chosen for the woman's safety and health only. We recommend licensing by the NRTC of any provider of fetal tissue, with conditions of license to ensure that fetal tissue is obtained in accordance with the above licensing requirements and is only provided for use in research directed to understanding biologic mechanisms with potential relevance to treating disease.

Commission research found that placentas are being sold to a firm that uses them to make pharmaceutical products used in the diagnosis and treatment of disease. This material is a byproduct of birth and would be incinerated otherwise, so we do not view this as unethical. However, the consent of the woman is not currently being obtained. We recommend that this be done and that she may choose disposal if she does not wish the placenta to be used in this way.

CONCLUSION

As we have shown, having children and healthy families are centrally important life goals for most Canadians. Commissioners therefore believe that a caring society should help people attain these goals, but always in the context of guarding against larger harms, whether to individuals or to society. As guardian of the public interest and on behalf of individual citizens, the federal government has a responsibility to prevent harms. This means clear limits and boundaries must be placed around the use of reproductive technologies, and that only ethical and accountable use of permissible technologies be allowed within these boundaries. The approach we propose will do this, will allow input from a wide range of interests in society, and will allow a continuing response to evolving issues.

Commissioners have set out a blueprint for how Canada, with its unique institutions and social make-up, can deal with new reproductive technologies, regulate their use, and ensure that future developments or use are in the public interest. Our blueprint involves the leadership of the federal government but needs the participation and commitment of provincial governments and many sectors of society. The approach we propose is feasible and practical, and we have laid out a detailed plan for how it can be accomplished.

The reasons for such action are compelling: the potential for harm to individuals and the need to protect the vulnerable interests of individuals and society. Adopting our recommendations will enable this protection, but will also allow scientific knowledge to be used to better the lives of many Canadians. Implementing the blueprint will demonstrate that we care about each other's well-being and recognize collective values with respect to the importance people attach to having children. At the same time, it will ensure that only ethical and accountable use of technology is made, and demonstrate that Canadians have wisdom, humanity, and compassion in the way they choose to use technology.

The Commission has done its work, and indicated the path we believe should be taken. It is now up to the Government and the people of Canada to decide if they will take it.

John Colapinto

from *As Nature Made Him* (2000)

At thirty-one years of age David Reimer could have passed for more than a decade younger. Partly it was the sparseness of his facial hair—just a few blond wisps that sprouted from his jawline; partly it was a certain delicacy to his prominent cheek-bones and tapering chin. Otherwise he looked and sounded like what he was: a blue-collar factory worker, a man of high school education, whose fondest pleasures were to do a little weekend fishing with his dad in the local river or to have a backyard barbecue with his wife and kids. He was the kind of rough-edged but affable young man whose conversation ran to such topics as his tinkering with his car engine, his work woes, or the challenges of raising three kids on less than forty thousand a year.

I had come to Winnipeg to learn all I could about David Reimer, but my chief interest was in his childhood—a subject that, when I raised it, brought an immediate and dramatic change in him. Gone was the smile on his face and the bantering tone in his voice. Now his brows gathered together above his small straight nose, his eyes began to blink with startled rapidity, and he thrust his chin forward like someone who'd just been challenged to a fight. His voice—a deep, burred baritone—took on a new pitch and rhythm, an insistent, hammering rhythm, which for all its obvious aggrievement and anger also carried the pleading edge of someone desperate to communicate emotions that he feared others could never understand. How well even *he* understood these emotions was not immediately clear. I noticed that when David described events that had occurred prior to his fifteenth birthday, he tended to drop the pronoun I from his speech, replacing it with the distancing you—almost as if he were speaking about someone else altogether. Which, in a sense, he was.

"It was like brainwashing," he was saying as he lit the first in an unbroken chain of cigarettes. "I'd give just about anything to go to a hypnotist to black out my whole past. Because it's torture. What they did to you in the body is sometimes not near as bad as what they did to you in the mind—with the psychological warfare in your head."

He was referring to the events that had begun to unfold on an April morning three decades earlier when, at eight months of age, he lost his entire penis to a botched circumcision. As a result of that irreparable injury, his parents had taken him to see a famed expert in sex research at the renowned Johns Hopkins Hospital in Baltimore where they were convinced to submit their son to a surgical sex change. The process involved clinical castration and other genital surgery when he was a baby, followed by a twelve-year pro-

173

gram of social, mental, and hormonal conditioning to make the transformation take hold in his psyche. The case was reported in the medical literature as an unqualified success, and he became one of the most famous (though unnamed) patients in the annals of modern medicine.

It was a fame that derived not only from the fact that his medical and surgical metamorphosis from boy to girl was the first infant sex reassignment ever reported on a developmentally normal child, but also from a stunning statistical long shot that lent special significance to the case. He had been born an identical twin. His brother and sole sibling provided to the experiment a built-in matched control—a genetic clone who, with penis and testicles intact, was raised as a male. That the twins were reported to have grown into happy, well-adjusted children of opposite sex seemed unassailable proof of the primacy of environment over biology in the differentiation of the sexes. Textbooks in medicine and the social sciences were rewritten to include the case, and a precedent for infant sex reassignment as standard treatment in cases of newborns with injured or irregular genitals was established. The case also became a touchstone for the feminist movement in the 1970s, when it was widely cited as proof that the gender gap was purely a result of cultural conditioning, not biology. For Dr. John Money, the medical psychologist who was the architect of the experiment, the so-called "twins case" became the most publicly celebrated triumph of a forty-year career that in 1997 earned him the accolade "one of the greatest sex researchers of the century."

But as the mere existence of the young man who sat in front of me on that morning in June 1997 would suggest, the experiment was a failure—a fact not publicly revealed until that spring, in the medical journal *Archives of Pediatrics and Adolescent Medicine*. There, authors Dr. Milton Diamond, a biologist at the University of Hawaii, and Dr. Keith Sigmundson, a psychiatrist from Victoria, British Columbia, had documented how David had struggled against his imposed girlhood from the start and how, at age fourteen, he had reverted to the sex written in his genes and chromosomes. The paper had set off shock waves in medical circles around the world, generating furious debate about the ongoing practice of infant sex reassignment (a procedure more common than a layperson might think). The paper also raised troubling questions about the way the case had been reported in the first place, why it had taken almost twenty years for a follow-up to reveal the actual outcome, and why that follow-up was conducted not by Dr. Money or Johns Hopkins, but by outside researchers. The answers to these questions, fascinating for what they suggest about the mysteries of sexual identity, also brought to light a thirty-year rivalry between eminent sex researchers, a rivalry whose very bitterness not only dictated how this most unsettling of medical tragedies was exposed, but also may have been the impetus behind the experiment in the first place.

...

It was Ron's custom to pick Brenda up in the car after her weekly sessions with Dr. McKenty. The afternoon of 14 March 1980 was no exception. The only difference was that when Brenda climbed into the car, Ron said that instead of driving straight home, they would get an ice cream cone.

Immediately Brenda was suspicious. "Usually when there was some kind of disaster in the family, good old dad takes you out in the family car for a cone or something," David says. "So I was thinking, Is mother dying? Are you guys getting a divorce? Is everything OK with Brian?"

"No, no," Ron said to Brenda's nervous questioning. "Everything's fine."

It was not until Brenda had bought her ice cream and Ron had pulled the car into the family's driveway that he found the words he needed.

"He just started explaining, step by step, everything that had happened to me," David says. "He told me that I was born a boy, and about the accident when they were trying to circumcise me, and how they saw all kinds of specialists, and they took the best advice they had at the time, which was to try to change me over. My dad got very upset." It was the first time Brenda ever saw her father cry. She remained dry-eyed, however, staring straight ahead through the windshield, the ice cream cone melting in her hand.

"She just sat there listening, real quiet," Ron says, almost two decades after this extraordinary encounter between father and child. "I guess she was so fascinated with this unbelievable tale that I was telling her."

Today David says that the revelations awoke many emotions within him—anger, disbelief, amazement. But one emotion overrode all the others. "I was relieved," he says. "Suddenly it all made sense why I felt the way I did. I wasn't some sort of weirdo. I wasn't *crazy*."

Brenda did have a question for her father. It concerned that brief charmed span of eight months directly after her birth, the only period of her life when she ever had been, or ever would be, fully intact.

"What," she asked, "was my name?"

...

Brenda's decision to revert to the sex of her biological makeup was immediate. "When I'm eighteen I'll be what I want," she told McKenty in her first therapy session after learning the truth. "I'll go from girl to boy." The question was how to do it without creating gossip. She considered disappearing to Vancouver for a while and then returning as a male who had come to stay with the Reimer family. But there was an obvious drawback to this plan: "I look like Brian," she said to McKenty. "People will know." Then Brenda raised a still more agonizing problem. Trained her whole life to behave like a girl and to hide her impulses and feelings, Brenda wondered how her parents would take it when she revealed her true self. "What will they say," she asked McKenty, "if I go out with a girl?"

A month and a half later, the Reimers attended a large family gathering to celebrate Janet's youngest brother's engagement. Still living socially as a girl, Brenda had no choice but to go to the party in female attire: a dress, red shoes, panty hose, makeup, and a stylish, short, imitation white mink coat which Janet had bought specially for the occasion—and, perhaps, as a last inducement to Brenda to remain in the sex they had chosen for her. But the humiliation of parading herself publicly as a girl, now that she knew the truth, was too much for Brenda. Having vowed to change sex in three years, she now moved up the deadline. "In *two* years," she told McKenty a day after the party, "I want to look like a boy. I'd like a mustache."

At her next session, Brenda again moved up the deadline for becoming a boy. She wanted to do it now, and she told McKenty that she had been thinking about a boy's name for herself. She did not want to revert to her birth name, Bruce, which she considered a name for "geeks and nerds." She'd come up with two options. She liked Joe because it had no pretensions; it was a name for Everyman. She also thought of calling herself David, after the biblical king and giant-slayer. "It reminded me of the guy with the odds stacked against him," David says, "the guy who was facing up to a giant eight feet tall. It reminded me of courage."

Brenda left the final decision up to her parents, who chose the name David. Ron says it was easy to make the transition from calling their child Brenda and he cannot recall ever accidentally calling his son Brenda after that. Others, too, found Brenda's transformation to David easier to accept than they had anticipated. David's tutor, Dorothy Troop, says that she had initially been nervous when notified of the change, but when David arrived for his first tutoring session, Troop found that his maleness was far from an obstacle between them. Brenda had always been a sullen, depressed, angry child; as David, everything was different. "He was happier," Troop says, "far more settled and alive to what was going on around him." Troop gave David a chain with his new name on it. In return, David gave his tutor a gift: the imitation mink jacket he had worn to the family party. "He seemed to want to get rid of anything that reminded him of when he was Brenda," Troop recalls.

That August, one week after his fifteenth birthday, David made his big public debut as a boy among his extended family. The occasion was the wedding ceremony and reception of his uncle Dale. Using tape to flatten the breasts that still protruded from his chest, David donned a starched white dress shirt, a dark tie, and a charcoal gray suit identical to his brother Brian's. It was not easy, David says, to step out as a boy for the first time in front of aunts, uncles, grandparents, and friends. He knew that the whole family had been informed long ago about his sex reassignment as a baby, but this knowledge did not make it any easier for him, trained for so long to play the little lady in front of relatives. Still, determined to get up in front of the crowd, he danced with the bride and several of her bridesmaids. "Happy," Dr. McKenty wrote in her session notes with David two days later, "wedding a success."

David began to receive injections of testosterone. He soon boasted a growth of peach fuzz on his cheeks and chin, and he grew over an inch in height. On 22 October 1980 he underwent a double mastectomy, an intensely painful procedure that left him in agony for weeks afterward. He decided to wait until the following summer—until he finished tenth grade—before having any further surgery.

In the intervening months, he fell to brooding on the accident that had set his life on its bewildering course. "At that stage in his life," Dr. Winter says, "all he wanted was a gun to kill the doctor who had done that to him." As the dismal Winnipeg winter progressed, David's fantasies of revenge began to take on the contours of reality. With two hundred dollars saved from his paper route money, David bought an unlicensed 1950 Russian Luger on the streets of downtown Winnipeg. One February day he went to the Winnipeg clinic where Dr. Jean-Marie Huot had an office.

"I had the gun in my pocket," David says. "I opened the door to his office. He looked at me and says, 'Yes, what can I do for you?' I said, 'Do you remember me?' He said, 'No. Should I remember you?' I said, 'Take a good look.' Then he knew who I was. He nodded his head. I was intending to pull out the gun and blow his brains out, but he started crying. I felt sorry for him. He had his head down. I said, 'Do you know the hell you put me through?' He didn't say anything, just sat there, crying. I walked out. I could hear him behind me saying, 'Wait! Wait!' But I left. I sat by the river, crying."

David smashed the gun with a rock and threw it into the Red River. A few days later he admitted to McKenty that he had gone to Huot's office and "blasted him about the accident." He did not say he had been carrying a gun in his pocket.

I contacted Dr. Huot in the summer of 1997. He refused to speak about this encounter. "That was seventeen years ago," he said, "a very long time ago." Nor did he care to discuss the incident that had brought the murderously depressed fifteen-year-old boy to his office in the first place. Asked about the circumcision accident, Huot said in his heavy French-Canadian accent, "I'm not in a situation to start talking about that now, for sure, for sure, for *sure.*"

On 2 July 1981, a month before his sixteenth birthday, David underwent surgery to create a rudimentary penis. Constructed of muscles and skin from the inside of his thighs, the penis was attached to the small stump of remaining penile corpora under the skin. False testicles, made of light-colored plastic, were inserted into his reconstructed scrotum. The sensation of a penis hanging between his legs was odd and unfamiliar. And he soon learned the drawbacks to phalloplasties. Over that first year, he was hospitalized eighteen times for blockages and infections in his artificial urethra. He would continue to be hospitalized regularly over the next three years.

Meanwhile, David tried to come to terms with his new life, and to prepare for reentering the world. In some respects, he says, this proved less difficult than he had feared. For apart from her fleeting friendships with Heather Legarry and Esther Haselhauer, Brenda had suffered severe social rejection; this, along with her almost annual changes of school, had guaranteed that no one ever got close enough to her to remark on her sudden vanishing—and David's sudden materialization. Still, after his reversion to his biological sex, David (fearing that he might run into someone who would recognize him as the former Brenda) took the precaution of lying low in his parents' basement. He watched TV, listened to records, and mulled all that had happened to him, trying to absorb and process it. This period would ultimately extend to nearly two years, until gradually, around the time of his eighteenth birthday, he began to emerge from the house, hanging out at local fast-food joints, roller rinks, and bars with Brian and his friends. Brian's buddies immediately accepted David as one of the guys, but there were inevitably kids who vaguely recalled that Brian had once had a sister named Brenda.

Together the twins dreamed up a story to explain Brenda's disappearance. They claimed she had gone to live with her boyfriend in British Columbia and had died in a plane crash. David was Brian's long-lost cousin. As for David's frequent hospitalizations, the twins said that they were to treat injuries sustained in a motorcycle accident.

"We all knew they weren't telling us the entire truth," says Lyle Denike, one of Brian and David's friends from that era. "But we didn't want to push things too far. We knew we were dealing with something very personal."

Heather Legarry, Brenda's friend from sixth grade, also had doubts. In July 1983 she was working for the summer at her brother's Go-Cart track after completing her freshman year of college. "I was selling tickets," Heather says. "Suddenly there was a familiar face at the counter. It was Brian Reimer—or so I thought. I said hi, but instead of smiling, he flushed and stammered, then stepped away and pointed at this other guy. Up steps the real Brian. I asked, 'Who was that? He looks just like you.' Brian said, 'That's my cousin David.' I wondered if it was Brenda, but I just brushed it off, telling myself, If he says it's his cousin, it's his cousin."

"I couldn't say anything to her," David says of this encounter with the one person from his childhood whom he had considered a true friend. "It would take too long to explain everything. It was easier just to avoid people."

Later that summer, when David turned eighteen, he reached another milestone, for it was then that he came into possession of the money that had been held in trust for him since he was two and a half years old—money awarded to him when St. Boniface Hospital settled out of court with Ron and Janet for a sum of sixty-six thousand dollars in 1967. This was far less than the millions that some had predicted they would receive in compensation for their son's penile ablation. But then urgently in need of funds, and warned by their lawyer that a judge might overturn a large jury award, the young couple had accepted the hospital's offer. In 1960s dollars, it had seemed a considerable sum to Ron, who at the time had an annual income of only six thousand dollars. Placed in trust for David, the settlement money was to be used by Ron and Janet only for treatment associated with David's injury and had financed the family's annual trips to Johns Hopkins. By 1983 the money had grown to over a hundred and seventy thousand dollars—a sum that instantly made David one of the best-heeled young men in his peer group. In the hopes of "lassoing some ladies" (as he would later tell Diamond), he bought a souped-up van. Equipped with a wet bar, TV, and wall-to-wall carpeting, it was quickly dubbed "The Shaggin' Wagon."

David did not do any shagging in the van, however. Indeed it was in his relations to girls that he felt the worst complications of his transition—complications that were only exacerbated by the fact that by age eighteen he was not merely a passably attractive young man, but an arrestingly handsome one. His sudden popularity with what was now the opposite sex introduced a terrible dilemma, because he knew his penis neither resembled nor performed like the real thing (it was incapable of becoming erect). "How do you even *start* dating?" David says, recalling this period of his life. "You *can't.* You're in such an embarrassing situation."

Eventually he did date a girl two years his junior, a pretty but flighty sixteen-year-old. For David there was an ever-present anxiety. "I would think, What the hell is going to happen when she wants to go further than a kiss? How am I going to handle *that.* He developed a strategy for stopping their sexual encounters before they became too intimate: he would drink a lot and then say, *I'm tired, I'm going to pass out now.* But one evening he miscalculated and truly did drop unconscious after drinking too much. When he woke in the morning, his girlfriend was beside him in the bed, and he could tell from her expression that she had looked between his legs. He had no choice now but to tell her. He explained that he had suffered an "accident." Within days, he says, everyone knew. Just as in his childhood, he was suddenly the object of muttered comments, giggling, and ridicule. For David, this proved unbearable. The next day, he swallowed a bottle of his mother's antidepressants and lay down on his parents' sofa to die.

Ron and Janet discovered him unconscious. "Me and Janet looked at each other," Ron recalls, "and we were wondering if we *should* wake him up."

Janet remembers saying to Ron, "I wonder if we should just leave him, because that kid has done nothing but suffer all his life. He really wants to die." Within seconds, however, she had made up her mind, and they lifted him and rushed him to the hospital, where his stomach was pumped. On his release one week later, he tried it again, ingesting another bottle of his mother's antidepressants, then running a bath with the intention of drowning himself. "I was thinking, *When you're dead you don't feel anything, no pain in your heart, no pain in your body, no humiliation—nothing*, but I couldn't make it to the bathtub. Every step was like I had a hundred-pound weight on each foot." With the overdose beginning to suck him under, he lay down on the sofa and dropped unconscious. This time Brian saved him.

David withdrew from the world. He spent sojourns of up to six months at a time alone in a cabin in the woods near Lake Winnipeg. By now he refused to see even Dr. McKenty, but she had convinced him to bring a tape recorder with him to the cabin and to speak his thoughts into it. One night in January 1985, he did so.

"This is David Reimer," he began, his voice slurred with alcohol. "I'm nineteen. Soon I'll be turning twenty. I'm halfway through grade twelve. What I plan to do in my life is"—after a pause, he continued in a new tone—"OK, by the time I'm twenty-five, I should be all fixed up. I don't plan to marry until I'm in my thirties, because I'm just not the—not the type to get married." He rambled for a few minutes before returning to the subject that was preying obsessively on his mind. "I want to marry a chick that's sort of shy," he said. "Not too shy. And I would prefer her to have kids of her own. Because I want to have kids. And I can't have kids." This statement seemed to trigger a new set of associations. "Oh yeah," he said, "I got some money, about a hundred grand, because of an accident I had a long time ago. When I was small." He paused again, as if trying to decide whether he had the energy, or inclination, to speak about this part of his life. He did not. "Well, that's just about it," he said. "I hope everybody out there has a great life." He turned off the recorder and never made another tape.

It was not until almost a year after David had retreated to his cabin, that two friends of his, Harold Normand and Ron Mandel, talked him into leaving the woods and indeed getting far from frigid mid-winter Manitoba. Given subsequent events, there was an irony in the destination the three young men chose: Hawaii. On 11 January 1986 they flew to Honolulu, where they stayed for a week in the Outrigger Hotel not ten minutes drive from Milton Diamond's house. The trip had a salubrious effect on David, but it was an incident in the airplane on the way to Hawaii that suggested he was finally coming out of his depression and beginning to come to terms with the secrets of his past.

In the plane over the Pacific Ocean, he turned to Harold. "He said to me, 'I always wanted to tell you about that sister of Brian's,'" Harold recalls. "I said, 'You don't have to. I already know.'"

Harold had heard the truth three years earlier when he first met David. Immediately suspicious about the tale of the twin sister who had died in a plane crash, Harold mentioned the mystery to his parents. They instantly recalled the short newspaper item from 1967 about a twin boy who had lost his penis while being circumcised at St. Boniface Hospital. They had later learned through the grapevine that the family was named Reimer and had even heard whispers that the boy had been raised as a girl. "My parents put two and two together," Harold recalls. A uniquely private person himself, Harold had never gossiped about David's secret among their friends and had never revealed to David that he knew the truth.

In the months after their trip to Hawaii, David confided much to his friend that he had never told anyone except Mary McKenty. "He said to me that he never felt like a girl, so that when he found out he was a boy, his mind was made up to switch back," says Harold. "Either that, or he was going to be a lesbian. Because that was his biggest problem when he was growing up. He had feelings about girls."

After his return from Hawaii, David heard from his doctor about a new type of artificial penis, one that would, the doctor said, be a vast improvement over his current one. His new penis would resemble the real thing, and through the use of advanced microsurgery could be supplied with sensation. Shortly before his twenty-second birthday, David underwent a second phalloplasty. In a twelve-stage operation, which took three surgeons thirteen hours to perform, David underwent a procedure known as microvascular right radial artery forearm flap reconstruction of the penis—an operation in which the flesh, nerves, and an artery from his right wrist to elbow were cut away and formed into a tube to build the new urethra and main body of his penis, and a segment of cartilage was grafted from one of his left ribs to give structural support to the organ. Despite the long recovery time, David was delighted with the results, which were immeasurably better than his former phalloplasty. "I was driving down the street afterward," David says, "and I just started crying."

Despite the marked improvement in both appearance and sensation of his new penis, it would be two more years before David used it for sex. The delay had less to do with his feelings of confidence about his penis, he says, than with the legacy of what had been done to him in the operating room at Johns Hopkins Hospital when he was twenty-two months old—his castration. "I kept thinking, What am I going to say to the woman I meet who I want to marry?" David remembers. "What am I going to say to her when she says she wants children and I can't give her children?" Even if he did meet a woman who said she did not want to have children, she might change her mind later in life and then resent him. "I thought it would be unfair for me to do that to somebody I love," David says.

Still, David could not put thoughts of marriage and children out of his mind. His brother had married at the age of nineteen, and by the summer of 1988, Brian was twice a father—and possessed everything David wanted for himself. "I got so terribly lonely," David says. "I did something I'd never done before. I wound up praying to God. I said, 'You know, I've had such a terrible life. I'm not going to complain to You, because You must have some idea of why You're putting me through this. But I could be a good husband if I was given the chance; I think I could be a good father, if I was given a chance.'"

Two months later, Brian and his wife introduced David to a young woman of their acquaintance. Twenty-five years old, Jane Fontane was a pretty woman with blue eyes and shoulder-length strawberry blond hair. At five feet one and one hundred and eighty pounds, she was sensitive about her weight, but she carried her generous size easily, and to those who knew her, it seemed merely a natural adjunct to her nurturing personality. When I first met Jane in the summer of 1997, her combination of unflappability, affectionate friendliness, and infectious laughter reminded me of no one so much as the central character in Joyce Cary's comic novel *Herself Surprised*—the unsinkable Sara Monday, the picaresque mother of five children, a woman whom Cary describes as a kind of force of nature, a woman whose earthy goodness and fundamental optimism see her through every scrape life can throw at her—including her own youthful poor judgments.

Like Sara, Jane possessed a guilelessness and innocence that helped to explain how, by the time she met David, she was herself the single mother of three children—by three different fathers. Unworldly to a fault, Jane was a lifelong nonsmoker and nondrinker, a homebody who did not go to bars and didn't approve of "cursing." Her chief flaw was a certain neediness, a result perhaps of her difficult childhood in Winnipeg, where she was raised by her mother and stepfather.

Jane was sixteen when she joined the civilian cadets—an army program offered at her school as an extracurricular activity. There she met Robert, a cadet a few years older than her. "He was the first guy I ever fell in love with," she says. Robert suggested that they leave Winnipeg and move across the country to his hometown of Bancroft, Ontario. To her parents' chagrin, Jane agreed to the plan. The couple stayed with Robert's parents for the summer, then moved on to Quebec, where Jane soon learned that she was pregnant. Robert talked about marriage, but then he started taking off. "He'd go out for cigarettes—and he wouldn't come back for six hours," Jane recalls. One day she saw him on the street holding hands with another girl. Shortly after that, she left and returned home to Winnipeg on the train.

Her parents were furious to learn that she was pregnant, but she was jobless and broke and had no choice but to stay with them. Her daughter was born in 1982. Jane was twenty years old. She was an excellent mother, surrounding her daughter with the love that she felt she had never received from her own parents. Jane eventually moved out to a small apartment in the city's West End, where a friend of a friend introduced her to Dean, a handsome, dark-haired young man who worked as a security guard. They started dating, but he was too young to settle down, even when Jane discovered that she was pregnant again. Their daughter was born in 1984. Dean helped out financially when he could, but his visits gradually grew less frequent and finally stopped altogether. With two infants at home, Jane could not work, but eventually she got a job through a government program and started making money. Life was looking up. Then she met a young man who lived across the way. His name was Raymond. "Our apartment block was right across from each other," Jane says. "He said, 'If you ever want to use my washer and dryer . . .'" Jane took him up on this offer, and more besides.

"I'm not proud of it," Jane says. "But I was really looking for love in all the wrong places. I wanted a relationship. I wanted someone to love me." When Raymond learned that Jane was carrying her third child, he told her about his "common-law wife" who happened to be returning soon from British Columbia. "That's how I lost Raymond," Jane says. Her son was born in the early spring of 1988. Jane was at the lowest point in her life.

Three weeks after her son's birth, Jane got a call from her mother. Anne had some news. Lately she had been keeping house for a young woman recuperating from surgery. Anne had mentioned to this woman Jane's difficult situation, saying that she would probably never find someone to marry her now that she was saddled with three children. The woman had mentioned that she knew a young man who might like to meet Jane: he was her brother-in-law, the identical twin of her husband, Brian.

Jane had little hope for this long-shot matchmaking effort, but she gave the woman a call. Brian's wife told Jane all about David's accident and how he had received a substantial sum of money as a settlement. "She said he's got this van and a convertible. I said, 'Does it really matter how much money he has or what he has between his legs? If he's not good to me or the kids, he can go his own way.'"

The two women arranged a day when Jane would go to Brian's house and meet David. The two hit it off right away. David, who was probably the more nervous of the two, says, "She had such a true heart."

The foursome made plans for a double date and that weekend went to a restaurant. At the end of the night, David held Jane's hand, and they made a date to meet each other alone. Soon they were dating regularly, and as they fell increasingly for each other, David began to worry about when, and how, to tell Jane about his injury. He finally got up the nerve one day while they were driving in his van up to his cabin in the woods. He had not got more than a few words out when Jane stopped him. She told him she already knew, and she didn't care about it. "She said that she had known all that time and she didn't want to tell me because she figured it would bother me," David recalls. "That's when I knew it was the real thing; I knew that she cared for me."

Asked her feelings about knowing her husband was raised to age fifteen as a girl, Jane treats it as a fact less to be marveled at than one to inspire outrage.

"When I saw those pictures of him as Brenda, I just shook my head and thought, Poor child. He didn't look like a girl to me. He looked like Dave. I thought, Going to school must have been the hardest thing."

In the fall of 1989, they moved into an apartment together. David's phalloplasty allowed him to have sex with Jane. "You know how it is when you get into a relationship," Jane laughs. "You do it a lot in the first year."

David sold his "Shaggin' Wagon"—emblem of the reckless, oats-sowing youth that he had never actually had. With the money, he bought a diamond ring.

"I remember," Jane says, "he came into the bedroom and he said, in a very serious voice, 'I want to talk to you.' We were sitting on the bed. He took out this box and opened it up. There was a ring inside. My eyes were like saucers. He said, 'Will you marry me?'"

On 22 September 1990, two years and four months after they first met, David Peter Reimer and Jane Anne Fontane were married at a ceremony in Regents Park United Church in the city of Winnipeg. Jane's two daughters were bridesmaids. David wore a white tuxedo; Jane wore a white dress. Standing before the congregation of some one hundred and thirty guests, made up of friends and family, on an unseasonably warm fall morning, David and Jane spoke the vows that they had written for one another.

"Jane," David said, "I take you to be my wife; to laugh with you in joy, to grieve with you in sorrow, to grow with you in love, to be faithful to you alone, as long as we both shall live."

And Jane said to him, "David, I choose you to be my life's partner. I promise to respect you, to encourage you, to forgive you and instill hope in you. I give you my love for this day, and for all the days to come."

...

Milton Diamond says that he cannot recall what spurred his decision to refocus his attention on the twins case at the dawn of the 1990s. He says that he had simply grown impatient with the silence around the experiment. "My thinking at that time was, This person has to be an adult now," Diamond says. "We should be able to write an article about this."

Further incentive for returning to the subject was soon provided by Money himself, who in 1991 published *Biographies of Gender and Hermaphroditism in Paired Comparisons*, a career-summing monograph on his forty years of work at the Psychohormonal Research Unit. Presenting his largest collection to date of "matched pairs" the book was Money's latest defense of his theory that social learning overrides biological imperatives in the shaping of human sexual identity. Missing from the text was mention of the definitive test for his thesis—his ultimate matched pair: the sex-changed twin and her brother. In the book's introduction, Money explained the mysterious absence of the case from this otherwise comprehensive volume—an absence that he insinuated owed something to the machinations of his longtime challenger, Milton Diamond.

"On the international academic scene," Money wrote, "doctrinal rivalry regarding the origins of gender identity led to an alliance with an unscrupulous media"—here he inserted a parenthetical reference to Diamond's 1982 paper on the troubled case—"that prematurely terminated a unique longitudinal study of identical twins. A BBC crew of television sleuths, incited by the prospect of airing a doctrinal dispute, traced the whereabouts of the twins and their family and unethically invaded their privacy for programming purposes." Money provided no information about Brenda's 1980 decision to become David, and this brief reference, with its hint that Diamond was somehow connected to the case's premature termination, marked Money's last published comment on the case.

Perhaps understandably, Diamond was disinclined to allow this innuendo-steeped passage to stand as the final historical word on the twins experiment. That the academic community at large accepted Money's version of events was clear from yet another book published that year: *John Money: A Tribute*, a collection of essays written on the occasion of Money's seventieth birthday. Replete with paeans to Money's scholarship from longtime acolytes, including Anke Ehrhardt and June Reinisch, the volume also included a fulsome tribute from Dr. John Bancroft, a psychiatrist and clinical consultant at the Royal Edinburgh Hospital in Scotland, who is now director of the Kinsey Institute. A behaviorist who was a believer in the primacy of rearing over biology in sexual orientation, Bancroft had taken this nurturist view to its logical conclusion in his clinical work. As a sex therapist in Great Britain, he had experimented with trying (in vain) to convert adult homosexuals to heterosexuality through aversion therapy. In his tribute to Money, Bancroft referred with tart disapproval to the "recurring attack from Diamond" and went on to cast doubts on the veracity of the information Diamond had reported from the BBC about the psychological difficulties Brenda had suffered.

"Money has reported her development at various stages, consistent with his theoretical expectations," Bancroft wrote. "However, since the prepubertal stage, the scientific community has received no further authoritative reports, but rather rumors (not from Money) of troubled developments." He moved on to defend Money's decade-long silence on the case, casting it as evidence of Money's scrupulous care for the emotional health of his research subjects. "In a case such as this," wrote Bancroft, "when the attention of the scientific community (and in this case the media also) is focused on a particular individual, it is easy to see the need to withdraw and be silent to protect that individual; it must be, extremely difficult to be the living test of a controversial theory!"

With his own academic integrity now being questioned, Milton Diamond did not have the luxury of withdrawing and being silent. Since the late 1970s and through the '80s, he had made periodic inquiries (and placed at least one ad) seeking information from endocrinologists and psychiatrists about the case. But now he resolved to redouble his efforts to learn the fate of the twin.

Through the BBC, Diamond found the name of a psychiatrist who had worked on the case—Dr. Doreen Moggey. That spring, he called her.

It had been fourteen years since Moggey terminated therapy with Brenda. She told Diamond that she did not know the final outcome of the experiment. She did, however, offer to give Diamond a phone number for the man who had overseen Brenda's psychiatric treatment: Keith Sigmundson.

"I remember the first words Sigmundson said to me when I called," Diamond recalls with a chuckle. "It was to the effect of 'I was wondering how long it would take for you to get here.'"

By that time Sigmundson was living in Victoria, British Columbia, where he had become head of the province's Division of Child Psychiatry. "Mickey said, 'Keith, we gotta do this,'" Sigmundson remembers. At first Sigmundson tried to beg off, but Diamond, he says, "kept on badgering me a little bit."

As someone who had seen firsthand the results of a reportedly successful sex reassignment, Sigmundson was inclined to agree with Diamond's thesis that the procedure of turning baby boys into girls was wrongheaded. Still, Sigmundson had been warned by colleagues that Diamond was a "fanatic" with an ax to grind. Further conversations with Diamond and a reading of his journal articles convinced Sigmundson otherwise. "I came to see that Mickey is a serious researcher and a caring guy who really believed that Money's theory had caused—and was continuing to cause—great harm to children." Sigmundson agreed to contact David Reimer and ask if he would be willing to cooperate with a follow-up article on his life.

"I wasn't sure what it was all about," David says about the call he received that spring from Sigmundson. At that time David had been married for less than a year and wanted nothing more than to put his tortured past behind him. Sigmundson was persistent, however, and David finally agreed to meet Diamond and see what happened.

Diamond flew to Winnipeg to meet David. Over lunch at a local diner, David learned for the first time about his own fame in the medical literature and how the reported success of his case stood as the precedent upon which thousands of sex reassignments had since been performed—and continued to be performed. "There are people who are going through what you're going through every day,'" David recalls Diamond telling him, "'and we're trying to stop that.'"

David was staggered. "I figured I was the only one," he says. "And here Diamond tells me they're doing all these surgeries based on *me*. That's why I decided to cooperate with Mickey." And there was another reason: David sensed in Diamond one of those people whose response to his sufferings was not purely detached and clinical. "When I told him a few things about my life," David says, "I saw that Mickey had tears on his cheeks."

Over the course of the following year, David and his wife and mother recounted to Diamond and Sigmundson the story of David's harrowing journey from boy to girl and back again. Using these interviews plus the detailed clinical records that had accumulated at the Child Guidance Clinic, Diamond set out, as the paper's lead author, to write up the results. He had promised the Reimers anonymity, agreeing to obscure their location, to omit the names of the local physicians, and to refer to David by pseudonym—or rather pseudonyms, since Diamond was faced with the narrative problem of retelling David's double life as both he and she. He settled on the solution of calling David variously Joan (for when he was Brenda) and John (following his switch back to his genetic sex). Only in a conversation with me two years later did Diamond notice that he had bestowed on John/Joan the Christian names of Money's two most important collaborators: Drs. John and Joan Hampson— an act that Diamond assured me was purely unconscious.

Written over the winter of 1994, the paper cast David's life as living proof of precisely the opposite of what Money had said it proved. Citing the Kansas team's classic work from the late 1950s, Diamond wrote that David's case was evidence that gender identity and sexual orientation are largely inborn, a result of prenatal hormone exposure and other genetic influences on the brain and nervous system, which set limits to the degree of cross-gender flexibility that any person can comfortably display. Diamond argued that while nurture may play a role in helping to shape a person's expressed degree of masculinity or femininity, nature is by far the stronger of the two forces in the formation of a person's private inner sense of self as man or woman, boy or girl.

Powerful as the paper was in presenting anecdotal evidence of the neurobiological basis of sexuality, it also served as a clear warning to physicians about the dangers of surgical sex reassignment for all newborns—not just those like David who are born with normal genitals and nervous system. Diamond argued that the procedure was equally misguided for intersexual newborns, since physicians have no way of predicting in which direction the infant's gender identity has differentiated. To change such children surgically into one sex or the other, he argued, was to consign at least half of them to lives as tortured as David's.

Accordingly, Diamond and Sigmundson offered a new set of guidelines for management of babies with ambiguous genitalia. Recognizing that a child must be raised as either a boy or a girl, they recommended that doctors continue to assign a firm sex to the baby—but only in terms of hair length, clothing, and name. Any irreversible surgical intervention, they said, must be delayed until the children were old enough to know, and be able to articulate, which gender they felt closest to. Or as Diamond put it to me, "To rear the child in a consistent gender—but keep away the knife."

Diamond was aware that writing the paper would inevitably raise the specter of a personal vendetta against Money. To minimize this danger, he removed from David's quoted utterances all reference to the famous psychologist. "In fact," Diamond says, "Money's name is only mentioned once. I didn't want it to be an argument ad hominem. I wanted it to be a theoretical discussion."

Nevertheless it took Diamond and Sigmundson two years to find someone willing to publish their paper.

"We were turned down by all these journals that said it was too controversial," says Sigmundson. "*The New England Journal, The Journal of the American Medical Association.*" The article was finally accepted by the *American Medical Association's Archives of Pediatrics and Adolescent Medicine* in September 1996, with publication set for March 1997. In the intervening months. Diamond and Sigmundson felt considerable apprehension as they waited for their bombshell to go off. "We were basically telling all these physicians that they'd been doing the wrong thing for the past thirty years," Sigmundson says. "We knew we were going to be pissing a lot of people off."

Some critics, as expected, attempted to dismiss the paper on the grounds that Diamond was simply using David's history to embarrass a scientific rival, but at least one physician who saw a prepublication copy of the paper was inclined to agree strongly with its conclusions. Dr. William Reiner had two years earlier launched the first comprehensive long-term follow-up study of patients who had been sex reassigned. Trained as a pediatric urologist, Reiner had actually spent the first eighteen years of his medical career in California performing "normalizing" genital surgeries on intersexual children. It was early in his career that Reiner had his first glimmer of doubt about the Johns Hopkins treatment model. "I got babies and two-year-olds and four-year-olds and eight-year-olds and sixteen-year-olds," he says. "So I really saw a longitudinal view of all these urological conditions—all these birth defects—and I was therefore able to visualize in a relatively short period of time the kinds of effects that these conditions have on the lives of these kids and their families." Then, in 1986, Reiner met a patient who changed his life.

She was a fourteen-year-old girl—a Hmong immigrant—who had announced that she was dropping out of high school because she was "not a girl." To all outward appearances an anatomically normal female, she had nevertheless always rejected girls' play and had insisted on wearing gender-neutral clothes. At puberty she had arrived at the unshakable conviction that she wanted to change sex and live as a male. Referred to Reiner to discuss the possibility of reconstructive surgery, she was threatening suicide unless her wishes were met.

"I had a complete medical workup on the child done," says Reiner. Tests revealed that "she" was biologically a he—a 46XY male who suffered from a rare chromosomal condition that prevents masculine differentiation of the genitals. Reiner performed sex change surgery, after which the former girl effortlessly assumed the sex written in his DNA. The case convinced Reiner of what he had suspected for years: that the biological underpinnings for psychosexual identity are not so easily overridden by social and environmental rearing as he (and every other pediatric urologist, endocrinologist, psychiatrist, and psychologist) had been taught. This further forced Reiner to the uncomfortable conclusion that he had been doing the wrong thing in his surgical career in helping to steer intersexual children into one sex or the other at birth. In a 1996 edition of the *Journal of the American Academy of Child and Adolescent Psychiatry*, Reiner published a paper on the Hmong case, along with a warning to his fellow physicians about the long-accepted theory that rearing prevails over biology in shaping human sexuality.

Reiner also did something else. After eighteen years as a surgeon, he put down his scalpel. He began to retrain as a child psychiatrist specializing in psychosexual development and intersexual conditions. In 1995 he was hired by Johns Hopkins as an assistant professor in psychiatry. There he launched his study on the long-term psychosexual implications of sex reassignment. Reiner set out to follow sixteen patients, focusing particularly on six genetic males who were born without penises and as a result were castrated and raised as girls. Two years into his study, he noted that all six sex-changed boys were closer to males than to females in attitudes and behavior. Two had spontaneously reverted to being boys without being told of their male (XY) chromosome status.

"These are children who did not have penises," Reiner told me, "who had been reared as girls and yet knew they were boys. They don't say, 'I wish I was a boy' or 'I'd really rather be a boy' or 'I think I'm a boy.' They say, 'I am a boy.'" Reiner stressed the parallels between the children he was studying and David Reimer, who also "knew," despite his rearing as Brenda, that he was not a girl. Reiner wrote a supportive editorial in *Archives of Pediatrics and Adolescent Medicine* to accompany Diamond and Sigmundson's John/Joan paper.

Today Reiner says that both David's case and the trend in his own study support the findings that have emerged on the primacy of neurobiological influences on gender identity and sexual orientation. He cites the now-classic study done at Oxford University in 1971, which showed anatomic differences between the male and female brain in rats. Six years later, at UCLA, researchers narrowed these differences to a cluster of cells in the hypothalamus. A study done in the mid-1980s in Amsterdam located the corresponding area in the human hypothalamus, noting that it is twice as large in homosexual as in heterosexual men. Further studies have supported this finding. In 1993 and again in 1995, researcher Dean Hamer announced that in two separate studies of gay male brothers, he had found a certain distinctive pattern on their X chromosomes. The finding suggested that sexual orientation may have a genetic component.

Although Hamer's studies have failed to be replicated by other scientists, few sex researchers today dispute the mounting evidence of an inborn propensity for acting as, and inwardly identifying with, a particular sex. "It's quite clear that the vast majority of boys born with functioning testicles have masculine brains," Reiner says. He endorses Diamond and Sigmundson's recommendation to delay surgery in cases of penile loss or intersexuality and to impose only a provisional assignment that can be changed should the child voice a strong desire to live as the other sex. Reiner suggests that this treatment model is diametrically opposed to the one pioneered at Johns Hopkins by Money and his colleagues, in which a sexual identity is imposed on a child through unshakable fiat of physicians, and any doubts or confusions the child may express about the assignment are denied by caregivers. Reiner says that on the basis of David's case and the others he has studied, the decades-old Johns Hopkins treatment model needs to be reevaluated. "We have to learn to listen to the children themselves," he says. "They're the ones who are going to tell us what is the right thing to do."

Before Diamond and Sigmundson's journal article appeared in the *Archives of Pediatrics and Adolescent Medicine* in March 1997, the American Medical Association's public relations department alerted the media that something explosive was coming. On the day of the article's publication, the New York Times ran a front-page story headlined SEXUAL IDENTITY NOT PLIABLE AFTER ALL, REPORT SAYS, in which writer Natalie Angier described David's life as having "the force of allegory." Twenty-four years after publishing news of the case's success, *Time* magazine ran a full-page story declaring, "The experts had it all wrong." Similar news accounts appeared around the world—and soon Diamond and Sigmundson were deluged with calls from reporters in several countries seeking an interview with the young man now known simply as John/Joan.

David agreed to appear on two television newsmagazine programs. He was shown in darkened silhouette on ABC-TV's *Primetime Live* and with his face obscured in a Canadian Broadcasting Corporation documentary. It was during the latter taping, which took place in New York City in June 1997, that I was introduced to David by Diamond and Sigmundson. The researchers had passed along to David the names of the many reporters who had requested an interview with him, but David (a rock 'n' roll fan) had chosen the reporter from *Rolling Stone*.

At that first meeting with me, David was nervous and guarded. He explained that his childhood had made it difficult for him to trust strangers, but later, over a beer at the Hard Rock Cafe, he grew more relaxed. He spoke about how his parents and brother had been crucial supports in a childhood that he described as "a pit of darkness." I soon learned that a formidable sense of humor had also played a role in his survival. Describing the physical differences between himself and his heavier, slightly balding twin, he shouted over the pounding music, "I'm the young *cool* Elvis. He's the fat *old* Elvis."

But the strongest impression I was left with was of David's unequivocal masculinity. His gestures, walk, attitudes, tastes, vocabulary—none of them betrayed the least hint that he had been raised as a girl. And indeed, when I asked whether he thought his extraordinary childhood had given him a special insight into women, he dismissed the question. David had apparently never been a girl—not in his mind, where it counts. He insisted that his conversion from Brenda at age fourteen marked nothing more than a superficial switch in name—as if the double mastectomy, two phalloplasties, and lifelong course of testosterone injections he needs to compensate for his castration were mere details. "I've changed over," David said, "but mainly by name. The rest was all cosmetic. I just had repaired what was damaged. That's all."

⋙ SEX AND GENDER ⋘

The word "gender" entered the English language as a grammatical term referring to the status of a noun as masculine, feminine, or neuter. Gender was thus in discourse from its first usage, and, as the Oxford English Dictionary (second edition, revised) reminds us, the word "is only very loosely associated with natural distinctions of sex." Also pertinent to this volume of essays as a whole is the origin of "gender" in the Latin word *genus*, meaning "birth, family, nation." While, in contemporary usage, the word "sex" is used to refer to biological differences and "gender" to social or cultural ones, the texts in this section tend to complicate that distinction, reminding us that biological categories are ultimately cultural ones. Jane Rule's "The Killer Dyke and the Lady" plays brilliantly on this ambiguity, its shifting narrative perspectives drawing on the cultural codes that identify a "lady" as a gendered term and a "dyke" as a sexed one. "But take a good look, ladies and gentlemen, because in a moment you may not be able to tell one from the other." Dorothy Livesay's poem invokes similar ambiguities but in an apocalyptic mode. Here, differences coincide as expressions of a being that can only be one when it unites its maleness and femaleness in an "all-one-ness" that goes beyond such categories. Lyndell Montgomery is likewise interested in the transgression of boundaries but sets these concerns in a context as grounded as Livesay's is ecstatic. An unpleasant encounter with border guards provokes questions about whether they are "trained" to be aggressive or "pre-programmed in the womb," questions which are complicated further by the issue of "power" and by the regulatory domain gestured to by the Canada-U.S. border. Daphne Marlatt's concern with "trespassing across an old boundary" is similar to Livesay's, that of "end[ing] up as girls were meant to be," which is to say as gendered stereotypes would have them be. To overwrite gender with sexuality is thus seen as a prime way of liberating the self, and one of those modes of liberation is writing—*Ana Historic* never ceases to remind us how gender is fundamentally encoded in language (even in one as apparently uninflected for gender as English): "tomboy, her mother said. tom, the male of the species plus boy. double masculine, as if girl were completely erased." Roberta Hamilton is concerned with other aspects of the gender system, such as work. As she puts it, "women and men are likely to think of themselves in ways that make some kinds of work, activity, and behaviours more appropriate for them than others simply because of their sex." Her particular focus in the section of her book excerpted here is how representation overlaps with subjectivity, producing a system whereby "[w]omen were to look at; men were to look." Hamilton makes an important critique of gender polarity—the idea that one is either masculine or feminine—and demonstrates how this polarity permeates private and public domains alike.

"On Looking into Henry Moore,"
Collected Poems (1972)

I

Sun, stun me, sustain me
Turn me to stone:
Stone, goad me and gall me
Urge me to run.

When I have found
Passivity in fire
And fire in stone
Female and male
I'll rise alone
Self-extending and self-known.

II

The message of the tree is this:
Aloneness is the only bliss

Self-adoration is not in it
(Narcissus tried, but could not win it)

Rather, to extend the root
Tombwards, be at home with death

But in the upper branches know
A green eternity of fire and snow.

III

The fire in the farthest hills
Is where I'd burn myself to bone:
Clad in the armour of the sun
I'd stand anew, alone.

Take off this flesh, this hasty dress
Prepare my half-self for myself:
One unit, as a tree or stone
Woman in man, and man in womb.

Jane Rule

"The Killer Dyke and the Lady,"
Outlander (1981)

If you're a killer dyke into leather, into aggressive visibility, it takes a lot of consciousness-raising along with a basic social conscience to call one of those expensively pant-suited, family-jeweled, narrow-nosed women "sister," particularly when her voice is pitched as low as yours but has enough breathy melody to be perfectly acceptable anywhere or almost anywhere. I wonder, shaking Dr. Ellen Compton's hand, the answering grip as firm as my own but not as assertive, why her sort of confidence is always attractive, whether for raping or for taking gentler advantage of for the advantage she has over me, Fay McBride with no title but Mac. We are peers, however, about to address together this room full of well-meaning heterosexists who will have less trouble being tolerant of me than of her. She could pass if she wanted to, easily, never mind the voice and the long bones. I could not. Oh, I have my own confidence, even arrogance; but there's no way I could condescend to this crowd as she does, just by being here, an aristocrat with impeccable professional credentials. If that makes me mean, imagining only a cleft palate could house all those silver spoons in her mouth, it can make this crowd meaner. But, as my leather belt creaks around my increasing Archie Bunker belly, I wonder if she has any sympathy at all for me. The woman introducing us to this conference of social workers spends longer on the short list of my accomplishments than on the long list of hers. I don't like the fact that we are the same age, and take only small comfort in knowing that she looks older than I do, the skin at her throat along her fine jaw loose with the flesh that has melted away—probably because I find that attractive, too. I won't look any different at sixty, "applecheeked," "sunny." Only my guts age. Just as the silence falls for my beginning, her elegantly panted thigh touches my tight blue jeans and finally there is something to do with all this mounting energy. I look out at the bland courtesy of a hundred faces, and as my deep voice hits them with honesties they'd like to endure, I put my hand, perfectly visible, over hers, which is warm and full of pliant bones and tame as a domestic creature. Sister.

"That felt good," I say, as we sit in the hotel bar having a drink before the banquet. She's changed for the evening's entertainment, still in pants but autumn leaves now cover her breasts, and through the filmy sleeves her arms are beautiful. There are new rings on her fingers. If I hadn't held her hand through most of the public afternoon, my good humor balancing her charm, her authority in service to my assertions, I would have wanted to make a remark about those rings or those leaves falling, killer dyke screwing the upper classes.

"Very good," she says, sipping, of course, a martini.

I'm drinking whiskey, neat, instead of the beer I want. Other people from the conference stop at the table. A man or two finds it necessary to lean a hand on my shoulder. She has her cigarette lighted for her, distinctions which, because they seem to amuse her, amuse me. You don't go to these conferences to be hostile. But I know, if one of them laid a hand on her, a look in his eye to suggest, "Lady, all you need...," I'd let him know there's not much difference between his fraternity and my sorority. Still, she knows how to take care of herself. Those rings are her brass knuckles. She can put out an eye without raising a finger. I don't admire that kind of brutality, but, damn it, it does become her.

As we walk over among the others to the banquet hall, she takes my arm at the curb, smiles, and says, "My first pair of bifocals. The curb keeps coming up at me."

They separate us then, but she's at the head of a table where I can easily watch her attending to this second-class meal with her first-class manners, and I wonder why I doubted even for a moment her reception among these mild enemies of ours, these knee-jerk liberals. She's one of them; and because they're all as upwardly mobile as a bunch of new-suited skiers, she's enviable there on the high slopes, but not envied ... admired. And I'm as bad as the rest of them. I want to take those rings off her fingers, those expensive bifocals away from those ancestrally intelligent eyes, and expose those subtly braless breasts, and ... and what? Eat the flesh? Sweet Jesus, meek and mild, let's put her through the eye of a needle.

"If someone's *disturbed* about her sexual orientation, don't you think ... ?"

"Along with the American Association of Psychiatrists ... ?" I interrupt the nervous heterosexist sister on my right. "No, all she needs is a good lay, with me or you. But that's not therapy enough to change her politics any more than it would yours..."

"I'm not really sure I understand sexual politics, and of course politics of any sort in a ..."

"It takes a long time for a woman not to let herself be oppressed, in bed or out of it."

"But if she becomes simply an oppressor instead .... I don't like the language any better from a woman than I do from a man."

"A poem would suit you better:

      'That ye resist not
      evil' falling
      limp into the arms
      of the oppressor

he is not undone
by the burden
of your righteousness
he has touched you.[1]

"I agree with that," the man on my right says heartily. "It was no answer to Hitler; and until oppressed people, whether they're Jews or women or homosexuals or Indians, I don't care what, stop cooperating in their oppression ..."

That's the right rhetoric, brother, but there's one obvious difficulty with it coming out of your mouth. You happen to be the oppressor. You don't confuse or anger me, however. It is my sister there, across the room, against whom all my desire and all my revenge sing. Jacob and his angel were the same sex, too. I have done my social duty today. Sweet lady, enemy of the people, lift that fine, aging face of yours and see me here, wanting to eat your flesh. You're the only real meal in the room, and you know it.

Finally I am next to her again. "Let's get out of here," I say. "I've undone most of the good work of the afternoon."

Her eyebrows lift above her glasses in question.

"Let's do the bars," I suggest.

"A brandy back at the hotel, maybe," she says. "That's about all I'm good for."

She doesn't take my arm this time; so I put a hand under her elbow and help her across the street, but if I did not want her, I would not be so sure she is moving away. The caste of politeness is bone-deep.

"You don't go to the bars," I say, this time having my beer.

"No," she says.

"Just not your taste, or aren't you allowed?"

"Allowed?"

"By whoever..."

"Don't you live with someone?" she asks.

"Would that make any difference to you?"

"In what way?"

I have to laugh. We are both good at asking questions, neither of us about to answer any. Around us, the social workers are drinking and parrying, too, reluctant as she is to go off to more blatant climates. Having the two of us around, whether they call us "resource persons" or not, is as much of mixing with their "clients" as they can risk.

"Don't you think all of them would be more comfortable? Don't you think we'd be more comfortable somewhere else?" I ask.

"I'm still on Toronto time, and the only place I'm going to be comfortable tonight is in bed, but don't let me keep you ..." she says, all graciousness.

"You're not keeping me. This is my town, after all. I thought you might like to see the sights, that's all."

"That was a great afternoon, Mac," a familiar, drunken voice says just behind my right ear. "They knew it would be, and that's why you came before the discussion about battered wives; you'd have seemed too good a solution."

She's by now leaning on my shoulder and leering at Dr. Ellen Compton.

"Betty Hall, Dr. Compton."

"*Formal*," Betty says, straightening to manage a stupid curtsey. "And *you* probably don't beat your wife, Dr. Compton, but I'm not sure Mac wouldn't. You can't convince me that belt's just for holding up your jeans."

"Betty's here as a resource person for the discussion on battered wives," I explain. "She's going to demonstrate the sort of woman who asks for it."

"Ver-y funn-y," Betty says, threatening to slump into the extra empty chair at our table. "Actually, Dr. Compton, though Mac looks like the toughest bull dyke in the block, she's really just a marshmallow; aren't you, Mac?"

"Just a marshmallow," I agree, knowing the only hope of getting rid of her is to be agreeable. She's at that stage of the night when only an argument will hold her attention.

"But seriously," Betty says, "violence is a matter of class, not sex, don't you think? The only reason my husband doesn't beat the shit out of me is that he doesn't think it's 'nice,' and if Mac wanted to beat the shit out of me, she would; but everybody here, including Mac, is so nervous about being racist, sexist, classist, nobody's going to admit how anything really works. It was cute of you to rub thighs with Mac this afternoon, Dr. Compton, and that holding-hand bit was really sweet, but you wouldn't go to bed with Mac, would you? Or even to a gay bar, I bet. You don't need your consciousness lowered. Even being here is a bit of slumming for you, isn't it? And maybe Mac doesn't like the taste of your licked boots in her mouth either, but, as I've heard her say before, 'You don't go to these things to be hostile,' right, Mac?"

"And you can see how successful a teacher I am," I say to Dr. Ellen Compton. Betty's like having a drunken puppet on your knee, full of all the farts and belches you thought you could suppress.

"Why *are* you here?" the lady asks the puppet.

"To learn, to learn," Betty says, "and you've been very educational, thanks ..." She's smiling at the next table. There must be someone there more interesting to harass.

Ellen Compton doesn't ask a question, even with her eyebrows.

"I've known her for twenty years," I try to explain anyway. "We went to school together ... on the wrong side of the tracks."

"Would you beat her?" she asks, smiling.

"Would you?"

For just a moment, it's a game we're playing together and liking it.

Then she signals for the bill, and when the waiter brings it, she gives me a smile any dentist would be proud of and says, "May I?"

"If you're sure you won't have to hock your diamonds," I answer.

Because she is as quick with a retort as I am, I know she chooses to say nothing, which puts me at an unfair disadvantage.

"It would be polite to be rude," I say, "unless you want to make me feel like a clod."

"I don't like double negatives," she says directly. "I have my sorts of protections, and you have yours."

"Quite right," I say, standing up as she does. "Do you go tomorrow?"

"Yes, in the morning. That's why I'd like to stay on Toronto time if I can manage it."

We go in opposite directions, I toward the street exit, she toward the lobby. As I turn out the door, I see she has stopped at a table to please its occupants with her good looks and good manners. Why would I want to take a woman like that to a gay bar? To flaunt her in front of my younger, more radical friends; to rattle her confidence in the minority she thinks she represents; to keep tasting the peculiar flavor of being with a woman of my own age. The oldest lesbian I know around here is ten years younger than I am. I realize, before I am half a block from the hotel, that I don't want to go to the bar myself, but I'm not ready to go home to my own company either. Will it look silly if I go back? I don't really care, as long as I find easy company for another beer or two. As I wait for the light to change to re-cross the street, I see her on the opposite side, waiting to come toward me.

"I wanted some air," she says simply.

I don't ask to join her. I simply turn around and take her arm. After we've walked several blocks in silence, she asks, "Am I not safe?"

"With me?"

"Alone," she says.

"Relatively, but you look ... too expensive."

And wish I'd said something like "too vulnerable," which is all I mean. Again she chooses not to reply. I want to say to her, "Apparently tonight I don't want just a good lay; I want you." As we turn to walk back to the hotel, I dread being dismissed again, gently, politely, but I have no idea how to avoid it. I don't hesitate at the door; I go in with her and walk to the desk where she asks for her key. There is no point in telling her I owe her a drink. She doesn't want another, and neither do I. I stand with her waiting for the elevator, a dumb brute, refusing to look at her, refusing to give her the opportunity to say no. When she steps in, I follow. Is she allowing this because she feels challenged to make some kind of democratic gesture? I don't know. I am beyond rape fantasies myself. I remember her thigh against mine, her hand quiet in the cage of mine, her arms naked inside those transparent sleeves. I want to make love with her.

She is in my arms the moment the door has closed behind us. We kiss, slowly, curiously. I take off her glasses. She reaches for my belt.

"And now, ladies and gentlemen, exhibit A and exhibit B are going to show you what lesbians actually do in bed," she says, pulling my belt off. "First, however, they have to remove their armor. It comes in two styles," she explains, as she removes the rings from her fingers, "killer dyke and lady. But take a good look, ladies and gentlemen, because in a moment you may not be able to tell one from the other."

She is angry, very angry, but not at me, at them, and the undressing is not at all seductive; it's a hostile act against that day-long audience. Only when we are, in fact, naked, standing before each other like creatures ready for the gas chamber, does she say quietly, almost timidly. "You see?"

Her body is younger than her face. I shelter it with my own, appalled by her vulnerability.

"They don't matter," I say into her hair. "They don't matter at all."

"They matter very much. That's why we were there."

"That, sure," I say, "but not to hurt you."

I have a reputation for being a great talker in bed, I often don't realize I'm doing it because words are then as much acts as any other touching, sucking, entering. I can hear my voice against her rib cage, taste the tenderness of sound in my mouth. When we finally lie quiet, I can't think why I didn't know from the moment her thigh touched mine that this was how the day would end. She is already asleep, in Toronto time where she will be tomorrow.

Note

1   Poem by Phyllis Webb.

Daphne Marlatt

from *Ana Historic* (1988)

Who's There? she was whispering, knock knock. in the dark. only it wasn't dark had woken her to her solitude, conscious alone in the night of his snoring more like snuffling dreaming elsewhere, burrowed into it, under the covers against her in animal sleep, he was dreaming without her in some place she had no access to and she was awake, now she would have to move, shift, legs aware of themselves and wanting out. a truck gearing down somewhere, the sound of a train, in some yard where men already up were working signals, levers, lamps, she turned the clock so she could see its blue digital light like some invented mineral glowing, radium 4:23. it was the sound of her own voice had woken her, heard like an echo asking,

who's there?

echoes from further back, her fear-defiant child voice carried still in her chest, stealing at night into the basement with the carving knife toward those wardrobes at the bottom of the staircase. wardrobes. wordrobes. warding off what? first the staircase with its star scrawled on the yellow wall and COMRADE, an illicit word never heard upstairs but known from Major Hoople's talk about those sleazy reds who were always infiltrating from some foreign underworld and threatening to get under or was it into the bed. nobody ever erased or painted over the scrawl and nobody seemed to see it but her, like some signal blinking every time she had to go downstairs with the knife. Comrade / would she really kill? she who was only a girl but even so the oldest in her family recently settled in cold-war Vancouver of the Fifties—a cold country, Canada, her mother said, people don't care. would she kill if she had to? after all she was responsible for her younger sisters sleeping innocent above while she, their guardian on those nights (babysitter wasn't quite the word), conscious and awake, unable NOT to hear, tiptoed after those suspicious noises—what if he were hungry, starved even, and so desperately from outside he would kill to get what he wanted, as afraid even as she, to get what he needed, while she who had her needs met, secure (was she really?) in her parents' house, trembling and bare-armed (in nightie even), she was merely in his way—no, he was in the wrong if he were there at all he meant to do them harm, and she would resist, righteously, she stood in front of the darkest of the six-foot wardrobes, teak, too big to place upstairs, big enough to hide Frankenstein, stood feeling her fear, her desperate being up against it, that other breathing on the other side of the door she could almost hear, would take him by surprise, her only real weapon, kick it open

flashlight weaving madly yelling (don't let me see! don't let me!)
Who's There?

empty. it always was. though every time she believed it might not be. relief, adrenalin shaking her legs. she had chosen the darkest first and must go to each in turn, confronting her fear (for what if he were there, in one of the others, waiting til she had her back turned, absorbed and vulnerable and never thinking he would leap on her from behind?), wishing, even, that what she knew could be there would be there and she be taken, lost, just to show them. who? her parents who went out leaving her alone to defend the house.

her mother who ...

my mother (who) ... voice that carries through all rooms, imperative, imperious, don't be silly. soft breast under blue wool dressing gown, tea breath, warm touch ... gone. I-na (the long drawn calling out at night for a drink of water, one more story, one last hug, as i experimented with attracting your attention, Mum-my, Mom-eee, Mah-mee ...)

I-na, I-no-longer, i can't turn you into a story. there is this absence here, where the words stop. (and then i remember—

i was two perhaps, you told me often enough, hurry up Annie, we have to go now, while i went on playing, paying no attention, Annie, hurry up! i'm going now! playing with your attention, delaying, and then there was silence, the whole house filled with it. Mummy, i cried, Mummy? and you said in a low distant voice i didn't recognize (i did but i knew i wasn't meant to): your Mummy's gone. i burst into tears, don't be silly, darling, i'm here, you see how silly you are—as if *saying* it makes it so. but it does, it did. you had gone in the moment you thought to say it, separating yourself even as you stood there, making what wasn't, what couldn't be, suddenly real.

and now you've made your words come true, making it so by an act of will (despair). gone. locked up in a box. frozen in all the photographs Harald took. the worst is that you will never reappear with that ironic smile, don't be silly, darling. pulling through. the worst is that it's up to me to pull you through. this crumbling apart of words. 'true, real.' you who is you or me. she. a part struck off from me. apart, separated.

she, my Lost Girl, because i keep thinking, going back to that time with you (and why weren't there Lost Girls in Never-Never Land, only Lost Boys and Wendy who had to mother them all, mother or nurse—of course they fought the enemy, that's what boys did) and what i did when i was she who did not feel separated or split, her whole body trembling with one intent behind the knife. and it was defense (as they say in every war). no, it was trespassing across an old boundary, exposing my fear before it could paralyse me—before i would end up as girls were meant to be.

who did my Lost Girl think might be there in that house on the side of a mountain on the edge of a suburb surrounded by private laurels? what did she think would come staggering out of the woods? those woods men worked in, building powerlines and clearing land for subdivision. those woods the boys on the rest of the block had claimed as theirs.

except for that part directly behind the garden, that part she and her sisters called the Old Wood, moulted and softened with years of needle drift, tea brown, and the cedar stump hollow in the middle where they nestled in a womb, exchanging what if's, digging further with their fingers, sniffing the odour of tree matter become a stain upon their hands like dried blood.

what if the boys came down from their fort in the Green Wood with slingshots and air gun? would their own string bows and crookedly peeled arrows hold them off? standing on the rockery for practice, shooting at the bull's-eye in the field (a stone in an empty lot), she despaired of herself, her sister-archers, her camarades—their arrows fell off the string, plopped on the dirt like so many cowpies. who cares? they said. they hurt their thumbs, they got tired, they went off to read Little Lulu (not even Sheba, Queen of the Jungle). but what if the boys ... what if the men tried to bulldoze their woods? so what could *we* do? her little sister shrugged.

do, do. she my Lost Girl, my Heroine, wanted something to do not something that might be done to them. the refrain of a rainy afternoon: there's nothing to do! do something useful, her mother said, clean up your room. but she wanted out, in the fresh wet smell of cedar and rain.

tomboy, her mother said. tom, the male of the species plus boy. double masculine, as if girl were completely erased. a girl, especially a young girl, who behaves like a spirited boy—as if only boys could be spirited. who read Robin Hood, wore scarlet, identified with Lancelot and the boy who wanted to join the knights of St. John (all trespassers, law-breakers in the guise of saviours. what did 'useful' mean to them?)

the trouble was you gave me a sense of justice—your 'fair play,' Ina, your mother's instinct distributing things equally between us. but you would never admit it wasn't 'fair' that girls weren't allowed to do the things boys did.

escape the house, 'home-free'—not home, but free in the woods to run, nameless in the split-second manoeuvre of deadfalls, bush blinds, ghost stumps glowing in the twilight, spirit(ed), filled with it, the world of what was other than us, torn as in thrum as in bullfrog sound, or the sudden awful drumming of a grouse.

it wasn't tom, or boy, it wasn't hoyden, minx, baggage, but what lay below names—barely even touched by them.

'Douglas fir and red cedar are the principal trees. Of these, the former—named after David Douglas, a well-known botanist—is the staple timber of commerce. Average trees grow 150 feet high, clear of limbs, with a diameter of 5 to 6 feet. The wood has great strength and is largely used for shipbuilding, bridge work, fencing, railway ties, and furniture. As a pulp-making tree the fir is valuable. Its bark makes a good fuel.'

clear of limbs? of extras, of asides. tree as a straight line, a stick. there for the taking.

Mrs. Richards, who stood as straight as any tree (o that Victorian sensibility—backbone, Madam, backbone!) wasn't there for the taking, i imagine her standing slim in whalebone at the ship's rail as it turns with the wind, giving her her first view of what would become home as she imagined it, imagining herself free of history. (black poplin. useless baggage.) there is a story here.

Arrival at Hastings Mill

She stood at the rail as the ship hove to, holding her bonnet against the wind and looking every inch a lady, lady-teacher that is, come to her first post. Would she look too young to them, too inexperienced for this outpost?—bush settlement, mill town (she would learn their terms, she would learn them as if from a book). Her dark skirt went suddenly slack in the loss of wind as they turned, edged by the tug in a slow momentum toward the wharf.

'Well, Mrs. Richards,' the captain's wife patted her hand, 'what do you think of your destination? A pretty harbour, is it not?'

She gazed at the piles of lumber, the heavy smoke, the low sprawling sheds. So many men, so foreign-looking, dressed in such an outlandish assortment of clothes. They were shouting to those on board in a great bustle of hawsers and fenders—the oddest English she had ever heard.

'Where do they come from?' she gestured at the wharf. The captain's wife had visited many ports.

'Some of them will be Kanakas from the Pacific Islands I expect—they jump ship often enough. Some of them will be natives, of course. And then there are always those roustabouts—Italians, Portuguese, Irish—you know what the Irish are like, my dear—who have drifted around the world to end up at this unlikely spot. Adventurers they call themselves.'

and was she not one also?

no, we don't know how she came. we know only that she was appointed teacher for the second term of the mill school's first year, a widow, they said (a safe bet), she would have been educated, she would have spoken a proper English, the Queen's they said. after all this was *British Columbia,* 1873.

The day was frosty still in places where the sun, blocked by buildings, by the massive bulk of trees, of mountains even, had failed to penetrate. A subtle white sparkle, ethereal as powder. And everything else legible, easily read: the rawness of new wood, the brashness of cleared land, of hastily built houses, outhouses, leantos. And beyond them, the endless green of woods, a green so green it outgreened itself, hill after hill. When she turned she could see the mountains behind her hanging close, close and yet aloof. Beautiful, she thought, or perilous. But not pretty. Well-versed in the Romantics, she had arrived with images of the Alps inside her eyes. Yet she knew this was not Europe and Mary Shelley's monster would never speak his loneliness here.

---

i learned to stay in the house as a good girl should. i am still in the house i move around in all day in the rain, the kids in school, Richard at it, at school as he calls the campus, reducing it to the scale of Mickey's elementary, why? they all do it, all the faculty, as if belittling, and maybe it is, the forced rote of teaching the same course year after year. when i go there i see library, see centuries of hidden knowledge, wealth, see romance—like you in this, Ina, how you used to enter the North Van library as if entering a medieval cloister, sssh, you warned, as if trespassing, pulling me into the smell of dust, of breath bated between plastic covers, heading immediately for the shelf of historical novels, family history with its lurid stretches shaping the destiny of a nation. consoled by this, that the familial, the mundane, could actually have historic proportions? kings and queens in bed with you of an afternoon. rain, rain.

you might as well learn some history, you said, handing me *The Old Curiosity Shoppe* (both volumes), *The Scarlet Pimpernel,* drawing distinctions between trash and literature. you might as well learn, you said, and blamed me later for becoming a 'blue-stocking—I can't even *talk* to you,' when i got my degree (BA only, mind you, ending my graduate career by getting pregnant and marrying Richard). 'i'm marrying my history prof,' i said, hoping to shock you. but you were pleased. trained to exhibit a 'good mind,' but only 'within reason'—reason being utilitarian, education as part of 'attractiveness' leading to marriage—i ended up doing what i was meant to, i followed the plotline through, the story you had me enact.

and now you're dead, Ina, the story has abandoned me. i can't seem to stay on track, nor can my sentence, even close its brackets, you didn't teach me about asides, you never told me the 'right track' is full of holes, pot-holes of absence (sleeping pills and social smiles, 'i'm fine, fine,' hanging on.) i don't even want to 'pull yourself together,' as Richard urges (myself? yourself? theirself), 'after all, grieving can't bring her back, you've got your own life to lead, you've got us.' true. (that reasonable word again.) but something isn't.

i've been moving around the house all day in the rain, in the growing dark outside, far from leading my own life or my life leading anywhere (goodbye, hero), i feel myself in you, irritated at the edges where we overlap. it occurs to me you died of reason (thunder far off on the edges of town and always i think it's missiles going off): i mean explanation, justification, normal mental state—that old standard.

the dictionary, your immigrant weapon, Ina, saves me when the words stop, when the names stick... real? you said, what is 'real cute'? Canadians don't know how to speak proper English, real is an adjective, look, and you showed me in the dictionary: true, actual. true cute? it doesn't make sense, you can say it's either true or cute, but not both. too true.

was dying a way of stopping all those words, all those variable terms, true or not? because it's hopeless ('hopeless,' you said, 'you'll never learn'), this task of trying to muffle them to one. true: exactly conforming to a rule, standard, or pattern; trying to sing true. by whose standard or rule? and what do you do when the true you feel inside sounds different from the standard?

i want to talk to you. (now? now when it's too late?) i want to say something. tell you something about the bush and what you were afraid of, what i escaped to: anonymous territory where names faded to a tiny hubbub, lost in all that other noise—the soughing, sighing of bodies, the cracks and chirps, odd rustles, something like breath escaping, something inhuman i slipped through. in communion with trees, following the migratory routes of bugs, the pathways of water, the warning sounds of birds, i was native, i was the child who grew up with wolves, original lost girl, elusive, vanished from the world of men ...

but you, a woman, walked with the possibility of being seen, ambushed in the sudden arms of bears or men. 'never go into the woods with a man,' you said, 'and don't go into the woods alone.'

we knew about bears, sometimes they would raid our garbage cans at night and the phones would ring all up and down the block, there's a bear at the Potts', keep the dogs and kids inside, excitement, peering through the windows out at streetlight pooling gravel. so they were real then? shambling shadows, garbage-eaters, only a little larger than the Newfoundland next door. but with something canny in them, resistant to attempts to scare them off, looking over their shoulders with contempt, four-footed men in shaggy suits intent on a meal.

'if a man talks to you on the street, don't answer him,' you said. 'but what if he wants directions? what if he wants a dime?' we asked, 'just keep walking,' you said. but we saw you fish for quarters when the men shambled up to you on the street outside department stores. we watched you in your trim black coat, well-tailored, your little hat, we watched you scrambling around in your purse for change, and it was true, you didn't say a word, though you did respond, awkward and flushed, when we asked if that's what you meant, you said it wasn't that.

skid row was a name we learned. rape was a word that was hidden from us. 'but what would he do?' 'bad things you wouldn't like.'

our bodies were ours as far as we knew and we knew what we liked, laughing exhausted and sweaty in our fort or wiping bloody knees with leaves and creek water. without history we squatted in needle droppings to pee, flung our bodies through the trees—we would have swung on vines if there had been any, as it was we swung on vine maples. always we imagined we were the first ones there, the first trespassers—

if you go down in the woods today you'd better go in disguise. it was bears' territory we entered, or cedars'. it was the land of skunk cabbage. it was not ours and no one human, no man preceded us.

'The red cedar, unequalled as a wood for shingles, comes next to the fir in importance. Because of its variety of shading, and the brilliant polish which it takes, it is prized for the interior finishing of houses. As the cedar lasts well underground it is used for telegraph poles and fence posts ... Well can this wood be called the settler's friend, for from it he can with simple tools, such as axe and saw, build his house, fence his farm, and make his furniture.'

without history or use, sitting in the middle of the rain forest, an immigrant school teacher wrote: 'To touch the soft fingerlings of Fir, the scaly fronds of Cedar!—Underfoot, a veritable pelt of needle droppings. If Earth be sentient here, then Man with his machinery, his noisy saw, his clanking chain and bit, is afterall dwarf in such green fur, mere Insect only.—It comforts me.'

well-read. she must have been. writing with a touch of the sublime, that nine-teenth-century sense of grandeur, in her immaculate teacher's handwriting.

you would never write like that. not just because of your blunt sprawled hand, so impossible to read, huge words that took up all the space on the scraps of paper you left: '2 homo pls. 2 brown,' but because of the grade-school scribbler you hid under your bed and which you showed me once, family stories for *The Reader's Digest*, 'Laughter is the Best Medicine,' stories that lost their humour in description, faded away in proper sentences, 'tell me the truth: they're terrible, aren't they?' you who could outtalk, outname, outargue me anytime.

Mrs. Richards wrote for herself, her English self she wanted to lose in the trees, trees we have already lost. trees so big men lay inside the gash their axes left and the tree still standing, still joined to part of itself. so big men balanced on boards wedged in the trunk to cut it down, or had pictures made of themselves standing victorious on top of the fallen length, oxen waiting to haul it away.

and though we didn't know it then in the 1950s when we came, we saw only second growth, the mountain logged off long ago to feed Moody's mill, or Stamp's (no, where we were was Moody's territory—they were jealous of their territory, those lumber-barons). we didn't know that then, penetrating under-growth thick with fern and salal (itself a sign), salmonberry, thimbleberry, all the berry bushes obscuring trails long over-grown.

we couldn't have imagined the world Mrs. Richards walked into, a man's world of work, of mud the odd boardwalk covered. a world of leantos and lanterns, of sudden accident, of jokes and brawls to punctuate long hours of labour. by 1873 she is there, named in the pages of history as 'Mrs. Richards, a young and pretty widow' who fills the suddenly vacated post of school teacher.

when she arrived she walked into sawdust, a sprawling conglomeration of sheds alive with dogs, pigs, chickens. 'what is the meaning of this agglomera-tion of filth?' Captain Raymur had thundered through his Protestant Halifax whiskers in 1869. in 1873, though it still shuts down for several days when there's a gambling game and though Raymur hasn't been able to stop the traffic down the two-plank walk to Granville saloons—'a lovely walk on a hot day'—the mill boasts a brand new school, a post office in its store, a few front parlours, several ladies now in residence. ('ladies'?) listen, there is even the sound of a piano tinkling through the smoke of clearing fires. someone is playing Chopin ...

—now you're exaggerating.

—how would you know?

—you always did. you should've gone into theatre, not history.

—i mean how would you know what this place was like? you never read about it, you were never interested in any past outside of England's.

—well think about it. who would play Chopin in a grimy little milltown? who would even appreciate it? no one appreciates good music here, they think it's snobbish, what do they call it? uppercrust. and this is supposed to be a city!

—there you go, always criticizing this place for its lack of culture. as if we were living somewhere out in the bush.

—we may as well be, and it's only provincialism that stops you from seeing it. we should've packed you off to boarding school in England long ago. then you'd know something about culture.

the smoky glass swan drifting in a pool of tears. les sylphides. the forlorn Soho flowergirl haunting the blue wall of the room i practised and practised in. music meant the moonlight sonata, meant someplace else, not history (i thought vaguely of the plaster busts lined up on Mrs. Pritchett's grand piano—Beethoven looking burgherish, Mozart looking slightly mad, they meant nothing to me), it wasn't the music i escaped to but the aura of tears, of blue walls, of infinite lemon layers of furniture polish. polish, everything said, in the grace is the promise. (that lie you spent hours perfecting.) i breathed it like incense after the hot betrayals of locker rooms, the ridicule of notes, of whispered gossip. my difference i was trying to erase. my English shoes and woolly vests. my very words.

impasse: 'my very words' were yours.

woollies and sweeties, hotties and hermits for tea, honey-bunch. all the comforts of home when the world of school, the public world (not private—that was another confusion), the schoolyard world of who likes / who cuts who, got to be too much. Miss Goody-Two-Shoes, stuck-up, i knew those words too. just as i knew gah-gah and common. sweater's such a common word, darling, can't you say woolly, say cardigan? say, who do you think you are? (yes, who? who?) you think you're really something, don't you? but you're weird (different, foreign), eating that stuff! (curry tarts in my lunchbox) looks like . . puke! i'd vomit too if i had to eat hot dogs. Hot Dog, the creep talks! and niggerbabies and chickenbones. that's just candy. it's sweets, boiled or not. it's what you buy with pocket money. at least we had pennies in common. but who else said, do you want to spend a penny? meaning, go to the washroom. i mean the lavatory, i mean the loo. the ladies, let's say. at least you asked for the ladies as we stood embarrassed by you in department stores. two languages. two allegiances.

impasse: impossible to exit. dead end. when the walls close down. the public / private wall. defined the world you lived inside, the world you brought with you, transposed, onto a Salish mountainside. and never questioned its terms. 'lady.' never questioned its values. English gentility in a rain forest?

o the cultural labyrinth of our inheritance, mother to daughter to mother ...

—and i suppose you see me as the monster hidden at the heart of it?

there *is* a monster, there is something monstrous here, but it's not you. i saw you as something else when i was running down the road late for school. i could hear the bell ringing, the sound of thundering feet, the jostling, giggling. could smell tomato-rice soup already reeking from the closed kitchen, mixed with the smell of sweat, of pencil shavings, hear the clock ticking in the Principal's Office. late again. the sound of the word DETENTION, pink slip like a flag in my hands as i opened the door and all those faces slowly turned to eye me, ascertain my fear in the pause before Miss Skalder's words would send me to my seat. the road so quiet, long, my feet so slow, i wondered what you did in the empty house alone, one in a row of houses settled in the sunlight, dreaming. all the housewives absent, their curlerheads, their still mops on their knees in the aftermath of storm, endless morning stretched before them, tendrils of quiet crept in their windows, hours of nothing slipped through their doors. bathrobe sleeping beauties gone in a trice, a trance, embalmed, waiting for a kiss to wake them when their kids, their men would finally come home. how peaceful i thought, how i longed for it. a woman's place. safe. suspended out of the swift race of the world.

the monstrous lie of it: the lure of absence, self-effacing.

Lyndell Montgomery

"Border Crossing: On the Edge,"
Boys Like Her (1998)

We are all sitting on cold cement blocks at the Canada/U.S. border crossing. We are being detained and our car is being searched. It's not a terribly cold day (Anna is wearing a kilt), though when you're nervous, the elements always seem more acute. We sit, we stand, sit again, pace a bit, talk anxiously amongst and to ourselves. Ivan is smoking a cigarette, another sign of nervousness. The two ex-marines ripping our car apart notice our nervousness, so they slow their pace even more and begin to take articles of clothing, books, make-up cases, etc., out of the car.

I stroll over, trying to appear nonchalant in my approach. "Excuse me, guys. There's a violin in the back of the trunk that is worth a lot to me. If you decide to take it out, please let me do it for you. I'd be happy to open the case, anything you want, just please let me handle the violin." They respond with grunts, both their heads buried in the contents of our trunk.

I return to my place on the cold pillar. The gang demands to know what I said, so I tell them and we fall silent, watching strange hands touch personal objects, hold up sex toys, flip through journals and writing material, stopping to read.

I'm pissed and justifiably so. Zoë echoes my anger with her own spoken thoughts. "Are border guards specifically trained to be as fucking rude as these guys? Are they so threatened by people like us that the only way they can gain any sense of worth is by trying to make us feel like shit? Or are they pre-programmed in the womb to end up ripping lives apart and degrading others?"

Our voices are rising, the talk is about power imbalances and a sense of importance tied to something as fucking stupid as being able to wear a jacket that says Police. Our discussion is heated and easily heard by the goons holding the power right now. The words "assholes" and "swollen cock" litter the air around us. Anna tells us to shut up and launches into a speech about us giving them what they want by acting like we are. Like kids who've been grounded we slink to the cement block and sit down. Mouths shut. Anna informs us of the time she was crossing the border only to be detained and strip searched, thick gloved fingers shoved in and up orifices. I'm raging. So what if we look like freaks, so fucking what. I hate the fucking border, it's an obvious reminder that human nature and the desire to feel superior has kept us from evolving as a whole species. Right now I find it hard to believe that the nineties are liberating.

"The fuckers, what do they think they're doing?" I shout. Anna and Ivan grab my arms, Zoë stands in front of me. My violin lies sprawled on the ground as cars which have successfully avoided interrogation drive by. "Let go of me, that's my fucking violin lying there and they're ripping my fucking case apart. I told them I'd be happy to do anything they wanted with it and the fucks ..."

Anna stares into my reddened face. "Lyndell, calm the fuck down right now. Stop thinking about yourself. I'm not wearing any underwear. I have a kilt on with no underwear. Can you understand why I'm not feeling very lippy right now? Sit down and shut up so we can get the hell out of here."

My arms are still being held and Ivan begins telling me that they've been reading his writing and he's not flipping. Zoë mentions that they've rooted through everything in her bag, writing included. I open my mouth again to defend my anger. Anna says, "No underwear, Lyndell, remember that."

The goons look in our direction. "You can go," one of them says.

"Thank you very fucking much," I reply with the hatred of an erupting volcano. We repack clothes and journals and my violin. I put her back into her velvet case, the velvet pulled and stretched, detached from the case itself, and all for what, I wonder. So every time I open it I will be reminded of exactly how small I am and how big the ocean I swim in is.

"Fuck," I say, snapping the case shut. "Another example of white collar crime has just been witnessed here."

"Testify," Ivan belts back.

Zoë salutes to the north. "Canada," she says and sighs. Anna tells me how lucky I am that she didn't get strip searched. I make a mental note to buy her underwear and lots of it for Xmas. We pile into the car and drive onward.

This is the truth, the entire truth. Not a version of it. It has not been altered or adapted in any way.

Roberta Hamilton

"Representation and Subjectivity: Women as Sexual Objects," *Gendering the Vertical Mosaic: Feminist Perspectives on Canadian Society* (2004)

The last chapter was about work. Work is a simple word; its meaning seems self-evident. Yet we saw that feminists expanded its definition to include the kind of activity women have done in the home, as well as community service and social action. Anthropologists report that the earliest form of the division of labour was based on sex. Historically, in Western societies, all forms of work have been deeply gendered; work is implicitly, and more often explicitly, perceived as "women's work" or "men's work" or at the least, more suitable to one sex than the other. More generally, not just work, but most forms of activity and behaviour are similarly gendered. I mean this in two interrelated ways. First, activities and behaviourism in every aspect of social life, are represented verbally and pictorially, as gendered. During World War II, government recruitment posters geared to attracting women were careful to depict conventional femininity. In case the point was lost, one poster showed a mother with a photograph of her daughters who had joined the service, with a caption that read "my girls are the real glamour girls" (Pierson 1986, 142–43). Second, women and men are likely to think of themselves in ways that make some kinds of work, activity, and behaviours more appropriate for them than others simply because of their sex. Old rationales for gendered employment ghettos—women's physical weakness, greater manual dexterity (good for typing), and raging hormones—are still summoned on occasion. Moreover, as Karen Messing (1987) has documented, keeping women away from equipment for the purposes of protecting their fertility and their foetuses provides new grounds for exclusion. She argues that this rationale is used selectively by employers for their convenience and ignores the effects of exposure for men's fertility.

What we do, how we see ourselves and are portrayed, and who we think we are are all interconnected. Feminists have explored each of these three aspects of social life, trying to figure out how they are related to each other and how, together, they shape relations of domination and subordination between the sexes. What motivates this analysis is a commitment to social change. But, strategically speaking, how do we go about changing society? Is it more important to expand women's and men's options for the sorts of work they choose? To change the ways in which they are represented? Or is social

214

change well nigh impossible until women and men—that is we ourselves—are changed?

For analytical purposes, we could think of these three questions as reflecting three areas of social life: activity, representation, and subjectivity. The focus of the last chapter was on activity—in particular, work. In this chapter, the focus shifts to the last two parts of this trilogy. First, how are men and women represented in this culture? What are the dominant ways in which men and women are portrayed in the media, in law, in educational institutions and texts, in virtually any social location Second, how and in what ways do human infants become men or women in social terms? What does it mean to be a man or woman in this culture? What are the connections between the ways in which people feel themselves to be men or women and come to behave as men or women, and the representations of men and women that they see in their social worlds?

My approach, once again, will be historical and theoretical. Such discussions immerse us in feminist debates about what is more important for women's liberation, how the various issues are connected, what sort of explanations are most useful for analyzing the relations between men and women, and which strategies are most likely to transform those relations I am going to start with a dramatic feminist protest in the late 1960s and use the issues it raised to set the terms of the discussion in this chapter. That protest was about the sexual objectification of women, and this has been an enduring theme of feminist activism and scholarship ever since.

On September 1968, the media reported that a group of women had disrupted the Miss America Beauty Pageant in Atlantic City. For many people, this protest, together with reports that some women had publicly burned their bras, not only marked the beginning of the women's movement but also became its lasting symbol. Bra-burning feminists: for many, the words were forever linked. The image amused, threatened, and outraged. Its meaning was pliable: on the one hand it was used to ridicule—this was what women were struggling for? How trivial! How absurd! But, if bra burning and beauty pageant protests were that trivial, why was so much sustained attention given to them? What did it mean when women protested against time-honoured beauty pageants and made the brassiere an optional garment? Why all the ridicule and why all the fuss?

First, the question of ridicule. Among the many and interrelated social movements of the last half of the twentieth century, the women's movement was surely alone in eliciting an early and predominant response of ridicule from the media. Women's protest, whatever it was about, made people chortle. Women could not be taken seriously even when they were rebelling. During the hearings of the Royal Commission on the Status of Women, Peter Newman noted that "most editors seemed to think there was something uproariously funny about the whole idea of women contemplating their navels" (1969, 23). Women's rebellion was ridiculous, and this ridicule helped legitimate continued subordination: this was an early insight that would be taken up more elaborately in later feminist cultural and poststructural analysis.

Second, if women's protests were so ridiculous, why so much attention? For the media, the protests provided great copy and good footage. But the level of interest betrays, I would argue, considerable anxiety. What did it mean to have women refusing the role of beauty queen? What did it mean when women insisted that they did not want to be represented as sexual objects? Taken together with feminist critiques of compulsory motherhood and demands for free abortion and access to contraception, feminists appeared to be pulling the rug out from under the whole social order. Protesting a beauty pageant was a protest against a system that judged men by their intellectual and physical achievements and women by their appearance. It was a protest against a single standard of beauty that measured women against each other and found almost all of them wanting.[1]

When we look back at the protests against beauty pageants, it is possible to tease out many of the substantive and theoretical issues that became important within feminist activism and scholarship. What were the forms, the extent, and the impact of sexual objectification on women's lives? What were the links between representing women as sexual objects and how women thought about themselves, how they treated others, and how they chose courses of study and work? More succinctly, what were the links between how women were portrayed and who women really were?

The insight that women are expected to present themselves, and be treated, as sexual objects contributed to an exploration of the ways in which women are represented in all aspects of social life. Feminists subjected advertisements, television programming, school textbooks, and pornography to searing critique and often mass protest. They went on to unmask how women were represented in family law, rape law, laws about contraception and abortion, and in the assumptions underwriting the development of reproductive technologies.

The issue of beauty and sexual objectification contributed to exploring issues around women and health. Feminists argued that the cultural standards of beauty demanded that women treat their bodies as enemies to be pummelled and starved into submission. Plastic surgery on parts of the body deemed too big or too small, constant dieting, and other "beauty" techniques that contribute to ill-health have been central feminist concerns.[2]

The question of sexual objectification became elaborated into more general reappraisals of sexuality. Defining women as sexual beings in their own right, criticizing the double standard of sexual behaviour, launching a full-scale critique of "compulsory heterosexuality," debating the meanings and consequences of pornography: all this captured the attention of feminists in many social and theoretical locations. Was sexuality a terrain of danger, pleasure, or both for women? What would it take for women to have the power to define and pursue their own desires?

The feminist analysis that presented women's oppression as intricately wrapped up with their sexual objectification was subsequently challenged, from many quarters, for its apparent claims to universality. All women were not treated as actual or potential sexual objects, and certainly not in the same ways. Racialized women, women with disability, older women, and lesbians, among others, wrote thoughtful and often stinging rebukes of the assumptions of what they came to call white, middle-class, ageist, and able-ist feminist assumptions.

Let us look back in more detail at the issue of sexual objectification and some of the related questions that this concept helped to mobilize and then at some of the critiques that have been offered of this analysis.

WOMEN AS SEXUAL OBJECTS

Until the late 1960s, beauty contests were a regular feature on university campuses. My 1962 Carleton University Yearbook includes full page pictures of Frosh Queen, Arts Queen, and Winter Weekend Queen. They received their titles by garnering the highest number of votes in a student plebiscite, after nomination by the specific dance committee. Pictures of all nominees flooded the campus in the days prior to the vote, and the winner was duly crowned at the dance. Only heterosexual couples attended the dance. "Girls" waited for an invitation—no invitation, no dance. Single men and women did not attend, nor did lesbians and gays. Indeed, there were no out lesbians or gays on campus. The dances were exquisitely heterosexual events; for women, attendance was a sign of their acceptability by at least one member of the opposite sex. Election as queen of the dance represented the epitome of more general appreciation.

Working women were also encouraged to participate in beauty contests. During the 1950s and 1960s, the Recreation Association (RA), catering exclusively to federal government employees, sponsored interdepartmental contests for Miss Civil Service. As the contest advertisement for 1952 pointed out, "Your Department has as much chance as the next one. All you need is a good-looking girl. From what we can see there are a lot of good-looking girls in the Civil Service. And your Department has its quota" (quoted in Gentile 1995). Patrizia Gentile has argued that these beauty contests served at once to legitimate women's growing presence in the civil service and to reinforce almost perfect occupational segregation, hierarchically arranged.[3] The Civil Service Commission's method for keeping women down (and often out) was simple: women were hired as 'stenographers' and 'typewriters' while men became 'general clerks,' who, incidentally, climb the administrative ladder while 'typewriters' could not" (Archibald 1973, 15). There was a place for typewriters to compete, however, and that was at the "Night of the Stars." How well did they represent the "typical government girl"? Winners were "preferably single with no children, heterosexual, well-groomed, tall, thin and 'beautiful'—with shiny hair." Their height, weight, and measurements were published in *The RA News* (Gentile 1995, 29–30).

Looking back, it is easy to see why feminists attacked beauty contests.[4] That beauty contests were such an intrinsic aspect of university and working life indicated how pervasive was the system of judging women by their racial features and the shape of their bodies, rather than by academic accomplishments or even athletic prowess.[5] Women were to look at; men were to look. But of course women looked too—at each other and at themselves. Every day could be a re-enactment of the beauty contest, as women judged themselves harshly and surveyed other women as potential competitors. A beautiful woman with much male attention was assumed to have it all. Her penalty was often the hostility of other women. Such reaction wasn't supposed to matter. Women who saw their own opinions as mattering little, and their own physique as inadequate, assumed that they did not have the power to hurt a more beautiful and popular woman. In the late 1960s the beauty pageant appeared to feminist protestors as a straightforward case of men using women as sexual objects. The language varied, but feminists depicted the women who participated as falsely conscious or brainwashed. Deprived of their own desire, they strutted on stage to satisfy the voyeuristic pleasures of men. Underneath the eager-to-please exterior, feminists argued, lay the genuine woman, awaiting emancipation so that she might pursue her own projects and pleasures. This interpretation may be described as part of the development of radical feminism. Men's power over women was blatant and easy to identify; feminists had to confront such power directly; men had to be prevented from continuing to wield this power over women. Once this happened, women would be free to exercise their own will and develop their own capacities and talents. Women would stop obeying men and begin to please themselves. Clearly this would involve an end to beauty pageants. But such contests were only a symbol of the problem: women dressed to please men; used cosmetics to please men; had sex with men in order to please men; and shaped their bodies in a myriad of ways to please men.

The radical feminist analysis was far-reaching in its critique, and many of the issues were taken up, disputed, and elaborated upon from, other feminist positions. In *Sexual Politics*, an early text of second-wave feminism, Kate Millett cast the situation of women—the beautiful and the not-so-beautiful—into sharp relief:

The continual surveillance in which she is held tends to perpetuate the infantilization of women even in situations such as those of higher education. The female is continually obliged to seek survival or advancement through the approval of males as those who hold power. She may do this either through appeasement or through the exchange of her sexuality for support and status. (1971, 54)

Millett succinctly captured the dilemma of women, thrown into competition with each other on the basis of their appearance. Treated as mindless, deprived of power, set against each other, women internalize the lack of esteem in which they are held and "despise both themselves and each other" (ibid., 55). Millett presents a more complicated picture than some radical feminist positions that suggested that lurking beneath women's outward capitulation to male power was their real self, a self capable of self-love, love for other women, and the capacity for realizing their own projects. In Millett's understanding, misogyny—the hatred of women—far from being a prerogative of men, is also lodged deep in women's own psyches.

Novelist Margaret Atwood has created female characters who may be seen in the light of Millett's conceptualization. Atwood's riveting portrayal of Cordelia and Elaine in *Cat's Eye* (1988) resonates with many female readers. Cordelia is everlastingly mean to her vulnerable friend Elaine, catching her off-guard, offering enough reward to sweep her back into her orbit whenever she demonstrates the will to escape:

"There's dog poop on your shoe," Cordelia says.
I look down. "It's only a rotten apple."
"It's the same colour though, isn't it?" Cordelia says. (1988, 71)

With so much capacity to influence others, will Cordelia grow up to run a corporation, a university, or a family? No, by mid-life Elaine finds Cordelia living at the Dorothy Lyndwick Rest Home, "a discreet, private loony bin ... the sort of place well-off people use for stowing away those members of their families who are not considered fit to run around in public" (ibid., 354). By then, Elaine has realized how she had internalized the contempt that Cordelia had projected: "There is the same shame, the sick feeling in my body, the same knowledge of my own wrongness, awkwardness, weakness; the same wish to be loved; the same loneliness; the same fear. But these are not my own emotions any more. They are Cordelia's; as they always were" (ibid., 419). Elaine and Cordelia were raised in the 1940s and 1950s, growing up to be women in a man's world. In their world of the relatively powerless, they jockeyed for position, humiliated others as a strategy for self-survival, and, at the limits destroyed the other—emotionally and physically. All this was the stuff of ongoing daily interactions.

This is the conundrum that psychoanalytic feminists have addressed. What are the differences between growing up female and growing up male? How are the relations of domination and subordination lodged in the psyches of the next generation? This is not only the work of men subjecting women to their will, as the radical feminist position tends to suggest; this is also the work of girls and women, the Cordelias and the Elaines. In *The Bonds of Love,* Jessica Benjamin argues that this is relational work, that it takes two to tango. The powerful are equally dependent upon the powerless, although their inability to acknowledge this dependence leads to tyranny. Meanwhile, the powerless make a last-ditch attempt to save their egos by identification with the powerful (1988, 85–132). This is what conventional heterosexual romance and marriage has been about. Simone de Beauvoir reckoned that "when woman gives herself completely to her idol, she hopes that he will give her at once possession of herself and of the universe he represents" (1952, 717).

Cordelia's mother cannot affirm her daughter because she has not affirmed herself; she cannot take her daughter's projects seriously because her own life is about facilitating her husband's. Nine-year-old Elaine, from a more unconventional family, is getting the picture from her friends:

> Something is unfolding, being revealed to me. I see that there's a whole world of girls and their doings that has been unknown to me, and that I can be part of without making any effort at all. I don't have to keep up with anyone, run as fast, aim as well, make loud explosive noises, decode messages, die on cue. I don't have to think about whether I've done these things well, as well as a boy. All I have to do is sit on the floor and cut frying pans out of the Eaton's Catalogue with embroidery scissors, and say I've done it badly. Partly this is a relief. (Atwood 1988, 54)

Elaine is learning to be surveyed and found wanting; she is also learning that girls grow up to be women who are inordinately interested in domestic life. In her research on working-class high school students in Vancouver in 1977, sociologist Jane Gaskell confirmed the corollary: boys are not interested in things domestic. As one of her female respondents put it, "I just couldn't picture my husband doing it—cleaning, making beds, making supper. I guess it's picturing my brother and dad." Most of the boys in the study agreed with her: "If I marry my girlfriend, I'd help her out. I don't like doing it. If someone doesn't ask me, I won't do it" (1988, 154–55).[6]

In the 1950s, sociologist Talcott Parsons (1959) had noted that growing up female in America was a tricky business, though he stopped short of thinking that anything should be done about it. Girls had to present themselves as sexy in order to catch a man who would be willing to marry them. Once married, however, they were expected to shun the role of sexual object for a thoroughly domestic existence. Feminists pointed out that it was more complicated than this. Even beauty queens were to present themselves as sexual objects—to be gazed upon—not as sexual subjects with their own desires.

Contestants were expected to be virgins; having already had a child, for example, was not just a disqualifier, it was a monumental blot on one's character.[7] So it was with all girls. Be sexy enough to keep boys interested, but never go "all the way." Girls who didn't get that message not only risked becoming pregnant (which was only the girl's fault), they could count on a reputation as "bad girl" and a lifetime sentence of singledom.

Feminists have linked the two symbols—woman as sexual object (always perilously close to whore) and woman as mother (hopefully as close to virgin as possible). Neither type is expected to feel or exhibit her own sexual desires. Although "the image of woman is associated with motherhood and fertility," Jessica Benjamin explains, "the mother is not articulated as a sexual subject, one who actively desires something for herself—quite the contrary. The mother is a desexualized figure" (1988, 88). Many students in my introductory class laugh nervously at the very notion that their fathers, or indeed any man, let alone woman, might have once (hopefully not now) seen their mothers as sexy. But sexy for women does not mean having sexual desire. As Benjamin continues, "the sexy woman—an image that intimidates women whether or not they strive to conform to it—is sexy, but as object, not as subject. She expresses not so much her desire as her pleasure in being desired." Benjamin confirmed through psychoanalytic analysis the discoveries of early second wave feminists that "neither the power of the mother nor that of the sexy woman can ... be described as sexual subject" (ibid., 89).

Being a sexual subject is part and parcel of being a *subject*—that is, the author of one's own life script, one who directs energy into her own projects and not just into facilitating those of others. In her research with teenagers at a Toronto shopping mall in the 1980s, Elaine Batcher found that "whether it is an individual skill like breakdancing, or a group talent in football or basketball, boys are more likely to be found doing things, and girls found cheering them on" (1987, 154). The groups that Batcher observed "centre around boys who like power and girls who like boys" (ibid., 155). One of Gaskell's teenage male respondents expressed it this way: "there's a difference between raising kids and looking after them. The woman might spend more time with the kids, but the father has the authority" (1988, 161). Psychoanalytic feminism explores the links between sexual desire and desirability and these broader questions of autonomy and dependence. What is the relation between the sexual object and sexual subject? What are the processes through which cultural notions of proper femininity and masculinity are internalized and resisted in the course of psychosexual development?

For Benjamin, the enormous social, cultural, and psychic consequences of relations of domination and subordination between the sexes are rooted in the psychosocial construction of gender polarity: one is *either* masculine *or* feminine. This gender polarity goes far beyond individual expressions of masculinity and femininity because it pervades the structuring of both private and public worlds and their separation from each other. The public world is supposed to be governed by notions of *instrumental rationality*—that is, the emphasis is on the most technically efficient means of reaching goals. Whether in the realm of bureaucracy, public policy, or multinational corporations, the preoccupation with this narrow form of rationality marks the public world as a stereotypical expression of "masculinity."[8] All emotion, love, intimacy, caring, and nurturing are relegated to the private world of family and friendship, where they are marked as the special domain of women. Sociologists Reginald Bibby and Donald Posterski found these gendered differences reflected in their 1992 survey of Canadian teens. Girls placed greater importance on integrity and civility and a higher value on human relationships. *Globe and Mail* columnist Michael Valpy wrote that these findings "limn a society of dominant and subordinate constituencies—with feel-good, physically stronger, bellicose males on top... They suggest Canadians should think again about all the contemporary rhetoric of gender equality" (1992, 2).[9]

In her research on World War II, Ruth Pierson found that people perceived (appreciatively) that life in the army made men more masculine, but feared that military life threatened women's femininity (1986, 140). Similarly, women who reach beyond the glass ceiling in corporations or government bureaucracies report that they take great care in not presenting themselves as too feminine while at the same time steering clear of any behaviours that might be perceived as masculine. This is not an easy business. These women's clothes must give the message that their wearers should be taken seriously but that they carry no threat to male authority. Women's behaviour must negotiate the thicket between deference and assertiveness. *Globe and Mail* business reporter Kimberly Noble asks: "Ever tried confronting a guy who says something suggestive about your face or your legs or your breasts? The remark will pass unnoticed at a dinner party or in a roomful of people or on the street; if you get angry, however, you can ruin an evening, shock a crowd into embarrassed silence and be labelled as a bitter, aggressive ballbreaker who probably can't get dates" (1991, A18). Rick Salutin, a columnist for the same paper, marvelled

at the hostility and ridicule [politician Sheila Copps] provokes from other politicians and the media. *Sun* columnist Doug Fisher on "her relentless bloodymindedness"; *Maclean's* Alan Fotheringham on "her rpms turned up too high"; The *Globe's* Jeffrey Simpson saying she's "never seen a microphone into which she could resist shrieking." Why shrieking? Would he use that word about a male MP? Would he even comment on the tendency? What's bugging them? (1993, C1)

It's a double bind: men must be protected from aggressive—strident, bitchy, shrill—women; but deferential women clearly don't merit success.

Decisions in the public world are supposed to be made without considerations of emotion, nurturance, or care. This tendency not only promotes the maintenance of male-only spaces—or, at the very least, male-only behaviours—in the lofty confines of major decision making, but also legitimates creating and sustaining a world that fails to take account of the needs, desires, and dreams of most people. The consequences for the private world, as feminists have observed, are no less devastating. There, the knowledge that human beings are interdependent is hidden from view by the relations of domination and subordination between the sexes. As long as women provide for men without insisting upon acknowledgment, men can have their cake and eat it: they can have their needs met without having to acknowledge their dependence on those who meet them. For their part, girls who grow up without receiving recognition for themselves as people whose own desires and projects matter may identify with those who assume that they are—and should be—the centre of their world. Such girls and women consciously or unconsciously say, "I will strive for personhood by identifying with a man who assumes that he is a person, and I will seek visibility (to myself) by furthering his needs and wishes." Such asymmetry in relationships is both product and cause of relations of domination and subordination.

Listen to conversations about boys, men, and love among girls and women, and you can detect certain themes. There is often an assumption that boys and men are unreliable: they pull you into involvements, and then? Consider David Caravaggio in novelist Michael Ondaatje's *The English Patient*: "He is a man in middle age who has never become accustomed to families. All his life he has avoided permanent intimacy. Till this war he has been a better lover than husband. He has been a man who slips away, in the way lovers leave chaos, the way thieves leave reduced houses" (1992, 116). Not that Ondaatje's female characters accept men's behaviour without resistance. The English patient himself asks Katherine Clifton, his colleague's wife:

"What do you hate most?"
"A lie. And you?"
"Ownership," he says. "When you leave me, forget me."
Her fist swings towards him and hits hard into the bone just below his eye. She dresses and leaves. (ibid, 152)

Shulamith Firestone, writing in 1970, argued that

The very structure of culture itself is saturated with the gender polarity. ... But while the male half is termed all of culture, there is a female "emotional" half: They [men] live it on the sly.... The question that remains for every male is, then, *how do I get someone to love me without her demanding an equal commitment in return?* (127, 137)

Feminist psychoanalytic approaches provide answers to this question by focusing on the *gendered* nature of psychosexual development and subjectivity. When women are nothing more than the objects of men's desire—that is, they are not recognized as full human beings in their own right—the way is cleared for their invisibility to others in their life, whether husbands, lovers, boyfriends, or children. If mothers are those who do for you, without thanks, acknowledgment, or any claim on reciprocity, if children learn how to be male or female from those who mother them, if boys grow up believing in their own autonomy and that any sign of dependence is a sign of weakness, then men will seek control at all costs because dependency causes such anxiety and threats to their (imagined) autonomy, and therefore their precarious sense of self.

Control may be wrought by means psychological, emotional, and physical. The 1994 Statistics Canada's survey, *Violence Against Women*, reported that "three-in-ten women currently or previously married in Canada have experienced at least one incident of physical or sexual violence at the hands of a marital partner" (Rodgers 1994, 1).[10] Over 20 percent of those abused by a marital partner reported that they were assaulted during pregnancy, and 40 percent of these women stated that the abuse began during their pregnancy (ibid., 12).

Since the early 1970s, with the growing realization of the extent of men's violence towards women, feminists have been in the business of developing explanations for these behaviours. All these explanations deal with power, men's power over women. Sometimes the exercise of this power is taken for granted, as in the phrase "men assault women because they can." This has undoubtedly been so. Men are often stronger; they have held control in households and in every area of society; until recently their behaviour was likely to go unnoticed except by the women subjected to their violence, and it was usually unpunished; male power and violence are represented as heroic and exciting in the media. But to say that men can use violence does not explain why so many men do use violence or, for that matter, why so many do not and, indeed, may not even be able to imagine themselves doing so. We might want to use an analogy here. All parents are stronger than their children. Many parents do use violence against their children, often or occasionally. But their ability to use violence is not sufficient explanation, for it begs the question, what about all the rest who could but do not?

There has been speculation that violence towards women increases with women's growing assertiveness. From this perspective, the feminist movement has been tagged as contributing to the increase in such violence (Phillips 1995). But, from a feminist psychoanalytic perspective it is important to understand that the person seeking absolute control cannot bear to acknowledge that the other person is not just an extension of himself. The other person's separateness provides constant reminders of his dependence upon her.

He may be the dominant partner, but he needs her, the less powerful, less valued person in the relationship (and in the culture more generally). Dominance is a strategy to avoid acknowledging vulnerability, and violence is one common technique in that never-ending struggle. Never-ending because, since internal vulnerability is the problem, control of the other can never be the solution. When a man murdered thirteen women at the Ecole Polytechnique on 6 December 1989, he then turned the gun on himself, as do many men after killing their partners. Eradicating the other is intricately related to eradicating oneself, whether physically, psychologically, or emotionally.

The evidence from the violence against women survey indicates that women may be at risk both when they resist and when they comply. Assault occurs when women leave partners—although it usually does not begin then (Rodgers 1994, 12)—and when they stay quiet and remain with abusive partners. Twenty-two percent of the respondents had never before told anyone that they had been assaulted—not police, doctor, clergy, friends, or family. Ten percent of these women had at some point feared for their life (ibid., 20). Yet the *Globe and Mail* could still provide space in its feature guest column on 10 November 1995 to air the views of a man who believed that the way to eradicate violence against women was for women to "stage a strategic retreat to the ostensible subservience of times past." David Phillips concluded that "as long as there is a rough parity between the sexes, violence and victimhood will be woman's lot" (A22).

I have been discussing the relations of domination and subordination as if they coincided with the relations between men and women. A good deal of feminist writing, including psychoanalytic writing, proceeds in this way. Language promotes unreflexive use of these categories. Common sense observations seem to support them, as does much research into male and female behaviour. What is important to remember, however, is that *in social terms* human beings become gendered *after* they are born. Not only are the classifications of biological sex "fundamentally social productions" (Findlay 1995, 46), but sociological gender has for a long time been recognized as a postnatal development by anthropologists, historians, and certainly by generations of feminists.

There are two considerations for feminists seeking to explain the development of gendered subjectivity. One explores how human beings become social beings who vie for domination or must tolerate subordination. The second focuses on the ways masculinity and femininity are constructed and represented as discrete categories. The behaviour of women in boardrooms may be similar to the behaviour of men. But it may well be perceived differently because of the (perceived) sex of the biological body who is behaving. Similarly, seeking control in relationships may well be seen as masculine, but this doesn't mean that only (biological) men want to control. Research on relationships between men, and between women, whether of love or friendship, reveals that the power dynamics do not always tend towards reciprocity and symmetry. Some lesbians have written bitterly about their experiences of being turned away from shelters for battered women because their assailants were women (Elliot 1991).[11] We seem stuck with a vocabulary and a discourse that equates masculinity with activity and dominance, and femininity with passivity and subordination.

This is part of the conundrum that feminist poststructuralists have taken on energetically and insightfully. Their challenges to the discussions of sexual objectification, representation, and gender attend to the discourses through which assumptions about masculinity and femininity are created and transformed. Feminists working with poststructuralism and deconstruction have argued that the focus of attention should not be the gendered individual per se, but rather the ways in which specific historical discourses produce gender and gendered representations both explicitly and implicitly. The reference here is not to a gendered individual, but rather to the ways in which representations of gender are part of a continuing production of language. The concept of *subjectivity* speaks to the ways in which individuals are constituted—in a myriad of continually shifting ways—through discourse. *Gendered subjectivity* refers to the ways in which masculinity and femininity are integral aspects of the production of subjectivity in any discourse.

Such interpretations do not distinguish between subjectivity and representation but rather see them, if you like, as *both* sides of the same coin. Gendered subjectivity is always a representation, never an actual reproduction or reflection. This is because language can never reproduce an already existing reality, but is always engaged with producing interpretations. Those interpretations then become the object for (poststructural) analysis. Representation once referred mainly to images—what women see reflected back at them in paintings, films, or advertisements. The concept is now used to refer to visual, literary, documentary, and oral depictions. In poststructural analysis, the focus is upon what the viewer or reader makes of those representations. The goal is no longer to determine what the author or painter or advertising copywriter intend to say. The focus is rather on the text or image itself and the interpretations (or readings) of the observer, reader, or person in the audience.

In poststructural approaches, close attention is paid to the meanings and hidden meanings in the text or image. Representations produce meaning only by suppressing other meanings. In her article on the poetry and fiction of Michael Ondaatje, Lorraine York asks, "Why don't we have a gender criticism of Ondaatje in the nineties?" (1994, 71) She hypothesizes that "feminist critics shied away from Ondaatje because they assumed that there wasn't much to write about" or that they would end up simply cataloguing various "victim positions" of women that appear in his work. While she insists that such indictments of male authors have a place—she approvingly cites Kate Millett's *Sexual Politics* (1971) for its "energizing, astringent effect on women readers and critics who ... [henceforth felt] that they had a right to a dissenting voice"—York has a different aim. She seeks to reveal that Ondaatje shows increasing awareness of issues of gender, "especially as they relate to ownership: the poet's ownership of the material, the patriarch's ownership of the female, and the imperialist's ownership of the colonized" (1994, 75). In other words, she demonstrates that gender and gender assumptions infuse Ondaatje's politically complex texts, and not just in those places where he is speaking specifically about victimized women or the "male chaotic" (1994, 76).

Feminists using poststructuralism have shown how to read texts—from foreign policy documents to corporate law to university lectures—as gendered discourses. The old expression "appearances may be deceiving" receives new meaning in the hands of poststructuralists. The previous theoretical positions we have considered present gendered and sexual identities as relatively fixed realities: fluid up to a point, socially constructed in time and place, but nonetheless integral to a person's self, personality, or character. Such theoretical formulations tend to confirm everyday understandings. We assume a correspondence between what we see and hear—that is, how people represent themselves and who people really are in gendered and sexual terms. The poststructuralist shifts the focus to the production of gender as a continuing one of discourse: hence the special interest in the text.

CRITIQUES OF SEXUAL OBJECTIFICATION

Many women have disputed the link that feminists made between women's oppression and their representation as sexual objects for men's desire. Dominant standards of beauty—as represented in criteria for beauty contests, modelling, advertisements, or film—are rigid, with only a small fraction of women eligible. Nor have standards of beauty become more flexible since early feminist protests. Naomi Wolf reports that, in 1970 the average model weighed 8 percent less than the average American woman; twenty years later, she weighed 23 percent less (Wolf 1990, 184). If real women had measurements proportionate to the ubiquitous Barbie Doll—40–18–32—they would not have enough body fat to menstruate regularly. Older women continue to be represented as desexualized. Racialized women point out that they never met the standards of beauty of the dominant culture. Women with disability have raised the only apparently contradictory situation that they are more likely than able-bodied women to be the objects of sexual assault (Rodgers 1994, 6) yet are unlikely to be perceived as meeting the standards for sexual objects. There are many rich, nuanced, and historically and culturally specific analyses of traditional feminist views of sexual objectification, and we will look at some examples that deal with intersections between sexism and racism, able-ism, ageism, and sexual identities and desires.

ANTI-RACIST CRITIQUES

In 1979, Toronto writer Makeda Silvera took part in a protest with other black women against the Miss Black Ontario Pageant (1985, 69). The protest was ridiculed in the black community newspapers and, as she put it, "we were not given space in our newspapers to articulate our position on the issue." Such pageants were a response to the exclusion of black women from existing competitions. The 1960s slogan "black is beautiful" proved a powerful message of resistance to dominant cultural representations in which whiteness was a necessary, though not sufficient, condition of beauty. But in a patriarchal society, the slogan was parlayed into different meanings for men and women. Men would still gaze; women would be the object of the gaze. Adopting white sexist practices such as beauty competitions sidestepped the different ways in which racism shaped the lives of men and women, compounded the oppression of black women, and perpetuated heterosexism.

A black beauty contest did little to interrupt black-white hierarchies that made white women appear more desirable than black women to men generally. It also extended rather than challenged the treatment of black women as sexual objects that was rooted in its most brutal form in the political economy of slavery in North America. Such contests also had a different impact upon black men than upon white men. In the slavery and post-slavery days in the United States, black men were constructed as hypersexualized and were subjected to savage retribution for the mere charge that they had gazed upon a white woman. White men, on the other hand, raped white and, particularly, black women with legal and social impunity. The messages suggested, then, by a black beauty contest for the (gazing) black man appear complex and contradictory. Did such a contest suggest that black men might gaze on black women—but only black women—with impunity? Did the image of the gazing black man resonate with social constructions of hypersexualization, thus leaving white men—with their history of licensed assault—constructed as normally sexed?[12]

Black feminists have pointed out that black women had been portrayed as sexual objects, though not as beautiful sexual objects. At the same time, they were denied the other model of appropriate femininity open to white women, that of the good mother. The good mother was the mother who stayed home with her children, looked after by a good husband and father. Long before most white women sought waged work, black women worked, mainly as domestics in the homes of others, to support their families.[13] With black men in Canada generally relegated to jobs as porters and janitors (with a few in the entertainment industry), the family wage never reflected either reality or ideal for most black families (Brand 1984; 1991; Sadlier 1994). The experiences of black women—raising and supporting families, active in their communities, and struggling against discrimination—not only remained outside dominant representations, but also were not captured by feminist analysis. At the same time, writing by black women was rejected by white publishers (including feminist publishers) who were unable "to comprehend how the work resonates or illuminates the condition of women of colour" (Silvera 1985, 71).

Aboriginal women have a different critique of the feminist equation of women as sexual object with women's oppression. Beth Brant, an Indian lesbian writer, wants to dispel the prevailing idea "that Indian women are not sexual.... It really is a stereotype that we are not, that we just give birth to kids without a process, or that we're only interested in planting corn or something. This really angers me and I think that Indian lesbians are the ones who are going to be talking about sex" (1985, 59). Brant seeks to distinguish the stereotypes of the Indian woman "and all these things that we have been called as squaw" from "a truth that we are poor, that we often have to exist in substandard ways." The writings of Aboriginal women not only challenge dominant representations but also present a range of experiences, images, dreams, and desires that confirm the dilemmas inherent in any attempts to represent woman or Indian woman or Indian lesbian, as though one image would do for all who might be so categorized.

Beth Brant expresses the constraints and possibilities not only of images, but of the language in which she writes. The "language of our enemy," a language with

> new words that do not exist in our own language.
> RAPE, MURDER, TORTURE, SPEECHLESSNESS, INCEST.
> POVERTY, ADDICTION.
> These obscene words that do not appear in our language.

She asks, "If love could be made visible, would it be in the enemy's language?" And answers:

> It is the only weapon I hold: this pen, this tool, this knife, this language. The writer has to know how to tell. It is the weapon I know how to use. (1991, 16–17)

DIS/ABILITY AND OBJECTIFICATION

When I turn to look at the writing of "women with disability," I am struck by the impossibility, the distortion, even the deception involved in any attempt to represent them as though one image would do for all who might be so categorized. Not long ago, while facilitating a panel on women and diversity, I asked a panelist if she had seen a particular television program. "It's been a long time since I've seen any television program," she retorted sharply but with humour in her voice. Kristin is blind; for some public purposes, she calls herself a lesbian with a disability. She tires of raising the question of accessibility at all gatherings, feminist and otherwise, but feels compelled to do so when no one else does. As a result, she represents herself often, and may be perceived, as a "one-issue candidate." In any case, other people will categorize her as "woman with disability," along with women who—for reasons ranging from conditions attendant at birth through impairment suffered in accidents or from abuse to effects of chronic and progressive illnesses—may not be able to walk, talk, or read. If anything unites all these women, it is not their disabilities as such but rather both their treatment by a society that disadvantages them and their collective resistance to that treatment (Russell 1989).

Kristin's sharp retort to me, following my casual assumption about seeing, breaks with dominant representations of women with disability as "victim," as "needy," as "grateful," or even as "quiet and nice." My reaction—of embarrassment, some enjoyment that others were laughing at my expense, and admiration—resembled the "click" made famous in early issues of *Ms.* magazine to describe any moment when the penny dropped, when one had a consciousness-raising moment related to one's treatment as a woman. This time I was the one who had the click, certainly, and it resulted from this very public transformation in my perspective. My language had betrayed my assumption about what was natural and shared, and this assumption was shattered by Kristin's response.

Francine Odette has critiqued the feminist assumption that "identifies women's alienation from themselves and their bodies" with "the objectification of the female body" (1992, 42). Growing up with a physical disability may take one out of the running altogether as someone who elicits attention as an attractive person. The problem is not sexual objectification but exclusion from the possibility of the appreciative gaze. Recently, I saw a young woman with long blond hair who was modelling a sweater in an advertising brochure. She was sitting in a wheel-chair. The presence of this image clearly resulted from the pressure for inclusion of those with disabilities in the range of images presented by TV programming, advertising, school textbooks, everywhere. This is surely a victory. In this culture, most girls spend considerable time on their appearance: they care about how they are perceived, whether they fit in, whether they look cool. As Odette notes, "for young girls with disabilities, the invisibility of our lives becomes reinforced by the fact that popular advertising suggests the 'normal' body is that which is desirable" (ibid., 42).

Feminists with disabilities critique the socially constructed notions not only of "the body beautiful" but also, in Odette's words "the notion of the 'body perfect'" (ibid., 42–43). Such challenges reveal the ways in which the lives, experiences, and fears of women with disabilities are similar to the lives of all women[14] and also how an attention to "differentness" extends the previous feminist cultural critiques. For example, although Odette raises an issue from the particular perspective of women with disabilities, the issue bears on the lives of all those who require medical consultations. While "the way in which women's bodies are portrayed as commodities in the media may not be a reality for many women labelled 'disabled,' ... our bodies become objectified for the purposes of domination ... as part of the medical process" (ibid., 42). In hospitals, people's bodies are often used as a teaching tool as though they were detached from the thinking, feeling, meaning-creating human beings seeking control over what happens to them.

AGE AND SEXUAL OBJECTIFICATION

Second wave feminists who launched the critiques of sexual objectification and the unreachable standards that represented female beauty and sexiness were mostly in their twenties and thirties. They tended to share the presumptions of their peers expressed in the 1960s slogan "You can't trust anyone over thirty." Only members of a society seriously denying the process of aging could develop a slogan that propelled one into the arena of the bad guys for no better reason than the onset of one's thirty-first year on earth. But as second wave feminists inevitably crossed the line into their thirties, they began critiquing the partiality of their earlier formulations. In this process, growing old(er) was not only reclaimed as a universal human process, but the gendered consequences of aging became an important focus for feminist analysis and activism (Carpenter 1996).

In this process, one of the great taken-for-granted assumptions of cultural life was subjected to scrutiny and was rejected: namely, women could be beautiful and sexy only when young, while men could gain in sexual power and attractiveness their whole life through. Canadians had a very public example of this truism: in 1971 Prime Minister Pierre Trudeau, aged fifty-one, married Margaret Sinclair, a woman twenty-nine years his junior. Everyone—including Sinclair's father, a one-time cabinet minister in Lester Pearson's government—expressed great pleasure upon this occasion. But what if a woman in public life—or any woman, for that matter—had married a man almost young enough to be her grandson? Such an act would evoke more than social ridicule; it would be almost against nature: a man marrying a woman *old enough to be his mother*? Indeed, as Judy LaMarsh reported in her autobiography, just travelling with a younger man on cabinet business "although I was always careful never to travel with just one young man," became the subject of media scrutiny and was reflected in articles teeming with rumour and innuendo (1968, 304). That she was targeted for travelling with younger men during the same decade in which Trudeau contracted his marriage illustrates the gendered story of love, sex, and age in the 1960s and beyond. Why did the eye rolling and tongue clicking only happen when women were associated with men younger than themselves?

Feminists point to two related explanations. First, the mere suggestion of sexual encounters between older women and younger men may create a generalized anxiety because such relationships threaten the sexual hierarchy. The advantages of age may confound the advantages of sex. In relationships men were supposed to take the initiative, make the important decisions, certainly be the more experienced sexual partner. But when the woman was older, wouldn't *she* know more? Have more experience? Perhaps be less willing to be the subordinate partner? When a man is widowed or divorced, he has traditionally not only been free to remarry but free to choose from among women who are younger, including the young and never married. But women, enjoined to marry only men older than themselves, have had fewer choices. No longer sexual objects, they are not acceptable as sexual subjects either. Wouldn't she dominate her partner? Would this not be against the laws of god and nature? The perspectives of older women reveal the dense nature of patriarchal relations, practices, and attitudes in all arenas of social life.

Second, women are positioned as sexual objects not sexual subjects, and then only when they are young and beautiful. Older women may be portrayed, but only as mothers, harridans, or caregivers. Relationships between older women and younger men raise the question: Can she be old(er) and sexy? Certainly the representations in popular culture provide one answer: a resounding no! The stereotypical explanation held that a younger man interested in an older woman was only after her money.

That older lesbian couples, in particular, escaped public scrutiny in so many communities in the days prior to women's liberation and beyond may be attributed in part to the assumptions discussed above. First, if women were sexual objects (for men's desire), not sexual subjects, then the question of sexuality remained publicly invisible when there was no man present. When Judy LaMarsh travelled with younger women, this was not news. Second, as women aged, any suggestion that they were sexual beings faded commensurately. Recently I asked my mother about Celine and Edith, friends she had in the 1950s:

"What was the nature of their relationship?" I asked.
"Well, they were friends."
"Just friends?"
"Yes."
"Did they live together?"
"Yes, for years and years."
"How many bedrooms did they have?"
"One."
"How many beds?"
"One."

My point here is not to draw conclusions from my number-of-beds-in-the-house research! There is much evidence that many married couples, for example, sleep in one bed without sharing an explicitly sexual life. But if my mother had known a man and a woman living in a similar arrangement, she might well have assumed that they were more than friends.[15]

HETEROSEXISM AND SEXUAL OBJECTIFICATION

The story of Celine and Edith draws our attention to one of the critiques offered by lesbian activists and scholars to feminist analysis of the sexual objectification of women by men. Put simply, the cultural stereotypes—however pervasive—that only young women are beautiful, that women are only sexual objects not sexual subjects, or women care whether they attract male attention have served to hide more than they reveal. What they hid was the risky, often dangerous lives of women who loved women, of women who dressed to attract women, who—not to put too fine a point on it—couldn't care less if they attracted male attention except insofar as men might have been decoys for their interest in women. The National Film Board's *Forbidden Love* (Weissman and Fernie 1993) weaves together interviews with lesbians talking about their strategies for living and loving in decades after World War II with a dramatization of a typical lesbian pulp novel of the period. One woman explained, with evident satisfaction, how dating gay men provided a front, diverting the attention of family and friends from her intimate life. Such creative acts of subterfuge reveal some of the limitations of reading the history of contemporary culture in terms of the sexual objectification of women by men.

Cultural stereotypes are steeped in heterosexist assumptions and, since the dawn of feminism's second wave, lesbians openly challenged much feminist writing for buying into those assumptions even as they aimed to transform them. The cultural stereotypes say little about who appears beautiful, desirable, or sexy to whom or why. Long-time peace activist Kay Macpherson revealed in her autobiography that "for a long time I clung to the conviction that a married woman who had a relationship with another woman wasn't really being 'unfaithful' to her husband" (1994, 148). The culture's heterosexism filtered out any understanding of sex and love that did not fit the preconceived categories. Women and men, lesbian, bisexual, and heterosexual, live lives that confound and oppose the stereotypes, and only by understanding this can we understand the origins of the social movements for sexual liberation of the last decades. These social movements not only provide locations from which to wage the right to live and love publicly, but they also occasion a profound questioning of the past. That human beings historically and cross-culturally engaged in a range of sexual practices, heterosexual and homosexual, is not at issue. But when and how do women and men forge identities, create communities, carve out space within hostile environments to find, attract, and live with those of their own sex?

Researchers have used such questions to reread the historical record: diaries, letters between friends, newspaper articles, advertisements, court records, and novels from the classics to pulp fiction. They conducted many interviews, and women have told their own stories (Chenier 1995; Ross 1995; Weissman and Fernie 1993). In this process, many divergent and overlapping paths for exploring "forbidden love," bestowing affection, creating space, and sharing time, households, and beds with other women have been made visible. A rich history of intimate female friendships and long-term coupling challenges conventional history. Lesbians carved out urban spaces such as bars and clubs where liaisons with those similarly minded could be wrought in comparative safety, and they developed a range of signs for ascertaining who might be interested in one's interest in them. All these practices challenged, whether openly or secretly, the dominant order.

Reinterpretations of lesbian histories, identities, and practices have not, of course, rendered irrelevant the cultural stereotypes that girls are judged not by their desire but by their desirability and that girls are interested in boys not girls. Coming-out stories are richly diverse and often funny, at least in retrospect. One woman writes about arriving at the Alberta farm of her Roman Catholic parents and making this announcement at the dinner table: "I've changed my name to Gillean Chase, the name I'll use when I'm published. I've converted to Judaism and I'm a lesbian" (Chase 1996, 62). Often there is relief, as with Joy McBride:

> Before my sister came out to me, I had never met anyone who was out. This isn't surprising, considering how hard I had worked to isolate myself socially. I had grown up with the theory that I was unlovable, and this stuck with me as an adult so strongly that it never occurred to me to think that I might instead be a lesbian—one who had been brought up in a world that hadn't taught me how to recognize or cherish myself. (1996, 183)

Surely no one, at least in contemporary culture, navigates the route from childhood through adolescence to adulthood without experiencing unrequited love; but those who have lived unremittingly as heterosexuals might stop to think how much more complicated this is when there are few, if any, ways of telling whether the object of your affections—or anyone else—even shares your desire for other women, let alone an interest in you. Some things have changed. In the 1950s, girls danced with each other at school dances: we awaited invitations and, when they weren't forthcoming, we remained "wallflowers," a status that brought neither prestige nor fun. But young people growing up report that high school culture continues to normalize expressions of heterosexual affection, discussion and ritual, while ostracizing and policing the same activities when formed by lesbians and gays. Indeed, activities like school dances, once the prerogative of high school students, are now events in primary school. Explicit and public priming for a heterosexual adulthood appears to start earlier and earlier. Becki Ross estimates that "nine-tenths of the 'lesbian population' continue to live in fear of disclosure and the attendant loss of family, friends, jobs and the custody of children" (1995, 9). Of course, it is not just children who come out to their parents. Parents also come out to their children, and sometimes they come out with each other:

> Sharing one's sexual identity with one's mother and sister is the norm if one is heterosexual. This is not the case if one is lesbian and living in St John's Newfoundland. As far as I know, we are truly unique. We [the writer, her mother, and sister] thus tend to be fairly conspicuous, as the three of us, with or without our respective lovers, enter the gay bar or the bimonthly women's dance. I have heard various kinds of comments, ranging from "Here comes the cute family" to "Do I have to get your mother's permission to dance with you?" (Yetman and Yetman 1996, 214)

MALE/FEMALE; MASCULINITY/FEMININITY

Discussions in this chapter on representation of women and femininity presuppose, of course, a discourse on men and masculinity, and I want to deal with this more directly now. The assumption in early second wave feminism was that the problem of women's subordination was femininity (its attributes, dress, characteristics), restricted roles, and sexual objectification by men. The corollary was that women should give up feminine trappings—high-heeled shoes, make-up, skirts and dresses—for more sensible attire; they should abandon nurturing for self-actualization; they should train themselves for male-dominated professions and jobs; and they should refuse sexual objectification in favour of asserting their own sexual needs and desires. Although the explicit goal is not so much to become like men, but rather that women should share power and resources equally with men, there was a subtext that suggested that women, not men, had to change. But masculinity—its characteristics, attributes, aims, and hubris—was on the threshold of scrutiny from many quarters.

Radical and cultural feminists began to insist that the problem was not women's activities and characteristics but men's behaviour and psychology. Women should not strive to share the power that men wielded; rather, that power should be dismantled at the psychic and social level. Men have waged war; women have made peace. Men have been systemically violent; women and children have been their victims. Men are sexual predators; women are nurturing and affectionate. In short, women aren't the problem; men are. At a descriptive level, at the level of accumulated evidence, it's a hard case to refute. But satisfactory explanations for these gendered differences in power, behaviour, and experience are harder to come by, and not only because the generalizations can be shown not to apply to all men or all women.

The most obvious explanation—that the problem must be laid at the doorstep of biology—is rejected by almost all feminists and feminisms. Notice this response in the *New York Times Book Review* from radical feminists Catharine MacKinnon and Andrea Dworkin to the charge that they blame biology: "Biological determinism is the complete antithesis of everything either one of us has written and done for the last quarter-century. We have each explicitly and repeatedly denounced systems of inferiority and superiority based on biology" (1995, 47). If it's not biology, most feminists reason, it must be social. Something has to happen after birth to explain gender differences, to explain how ideas of masculinity and femininity appear most of the time as givens of social life. This understanding is captured in theories that explicate, in a variety of ways, two interrelated concepts—power and social construction. Relations of power inform, indeed saturate, the social relations between the sexes, socialization practices, and especially how such practices are received and internalized as children grow up.

Socialist feminists, especially those engaging with psychoanalytic formulations, launched a critique of the construction of masculinity, arguing that "normal" masculinity was constituted by denial of emotion and by subsequent aggression and violence, underpinned by deep psychic anxiety, self-hatred, and insecurity. In *Beyond Patriarchy*, Michael Kaufman (1987) discusses the masculine trilogy of violence against self, against other men, and against women. Boys growing up in this society must dis-identify with their mothers, their less powerful parent, in favour of identification with their fathers. The consequences are deep-seated, long-lasting, and extensive. Given that women are the only legitimate repository for nurturing, care, emotion, and attention to relationships, boys must repress their emotions, their love, and their feelings of dependence upon others in order not to be like their mothers. The vulnerability boys feel as small and dependent people goes underground; bravado and bullying take its place. But that vulnerability returns to be projected onto those perceived as vulnerable—girls and women. Hence the scorn, the repudiation, what psychoanalyst Ruth Brunswick called "the normal male contempt for women" (1948). The result, according to feminists, is not a good recipe for living in a social world, and it's certainly not been good news for women and children. The boy in the schoolyard who does not demonstrate success in this endeavour is called a sissy. A sissy is a boy who acts like a girl. Here we see early training for misogyny. If boys who act like girls are contemptible, what does this say about girls, the model for this contempt?

Many feminists challenge the view that masculinity is constituted through a set of social and linguistic practices that repeats and consolidates an apparently uncontested division between the sexes. They suggest that we could have a masculinity that was clearly linked with male bodies but did not share in this repudiation of femininity. This would amount to an analytical and objective distinction between sex and gender. Could such a distinction be sustained? Lately, some poststructuralists who have coined the term *queer theory* have been questioning the assumption that male and female bodies are givens, waiting to be filled, as it were with socially constructed gendered and sexual identities. As Kathleen Pirie Adams explains:

> By arguing that all gender identity involves the impersonation of an abstract (gender) ideal, and, by continually remarking on the artificiality of the gender norms that organize and regulate sexuality, queer theory has shifted attention away from questions of who is (really) homosexual to questions about how homosexuality is realized and made visible socially, as well as how it runs throughout the culture as a whole—invisibly, inarticulately. (1993, 31)

For queer theorists, pride of analytic place shifts from the text to "notions such as performative identity, gender activism and gender performance" (ibid., 31). Performance draws attention to how we *do* gender as ongoing bodily and linguistic presentation. The concept of performance permits a convergence of the poststructuralist emphasis on discourse with a theorization of the body and therefore of sex and gender. From this perspective, sex and gender are understood as intertwined processes, produced as acts—"on site," as it were, through and with our bodies—and reiterated endlessly. The very reiteration of these acts—these norms, in sociological terms—masks their boundary-creating character. They appear with no history, no rationale; they are "what is." But we are the agents of these reiterations, and by these acts we participate in sustaining and shifting that which the culture permits and forbids.

Queer theory draws attention to these reiterations of gender and sexuality—to the social visibility of sexual differences—but sees them as an ongoing happening, always with the possibility of disruption. The disruptions may be more dramatic in some locations than others. Consider Adams' comments on the lesbian bar scene in Toronto:

> Who hasn't seen or been this: girl who arrives, returning weekly with a new sign (cropped, dread-locked, shaved or dyed hair, new boots, cut-offs, pierces, tattoo), leaving weekly with a new inspiration, a new friend, more certainty and more confusion. The bar is an arena of possibility, a public space in which sexual identity is sought and discarded, and so if we describe it simply in terms of what we do there—dance, talk, drink, have sex—we can lose sight of some aspects of what we are doing there. (1993, 30)

Judith Butler has been in the forefront in developing queer theory's reassessment of sexual and gendered identities. She questions what has usually been assumed in other theoretical (including scientific) perspectives, asking exactly what about the body and sex is given, already there? She is not disputing that we have bodies, but rather she asks, just what can we say about those bodies that falls into the "already there" category? She argues that anything we might say about those bodies has already been taken up by socially constituted discourses on gender, sexuality, race, age and so on. There is no pure discourse through which we can speak about the already given body.

Furthermore, our own sense of who we are—in psychoanalytic terms, our ego—is constituted (in part) through our projections of our bodies. But those projections are thoroughly informed by our participation in cultural (including linguistic) practices. The sense, therefore, that we have of being male or being female cannot be partitioned into biological and social compartments. It's not so much that the social infuses the biological, but that the biological can only be thought of and named through the social, namely through discourses, among others, on gender, race duality, health and illness, religion and ethics, and physiology. These discourses, of course, infuse each other: only for the purposes of a list are they separable.

In Freudian discourse, for example, the significance attached to the presence or absence of a penis mobilizes a huge literature on gender, sex, relationships, neuroses, and psychoses. While some feminist appropriators of psychoanalysis have shifted the importance from the penis to the symbol of the penis—the phallus—there remains the connection between male bodies and power (either because of the presence of the penis or the connection between penis and phallus). But what sustains this connection? Butler argues that it is sustained through reiteration of linguistic practices, practices that, because of the reiteration, become *sedimented*, or materialized. But the sedimentation is an illusion to the extent that what sustains it is in fact the reiterations. The reiteration depends on people engaging in repetitious acts; however, the repetitions are never simply repetitions. Everything that has not been acknowledged in previous repetitions can always make an appearance in the next; that which is desired but unacknowledged always remains, in whatever partial or distorted sense, as possibility. In this sense, then, the connection between penis and phallus is not signed, sealed, and delivered for eternity, but neither will the connection be severed all at once.

Judith Butler seeks to destabilize the connection. For, as long as the connection between penis and phallus is not questioned, all the questions about power and gendered identities will take their cue from the *assumed* differences between men and women. This is Butler's critique of psychoanalysis in both its Freudian and Lacanian versions. Both versions assume that entry into the symbolic order—the social world—is predicated upon already existing, biological, prediscursive differences between the sexes. These theories organize the prediscursive differences hierarchically, with masculine principles constructed as the entry point into the symbolic order. Butler asks why acceptance into this world of meanings should be contingent upon collusion with masculine principles and a dichotomy between masculine and feminine. After all, this hierarchical dichotomy is simply the ongoing product of endless reiterations, including those produced by psychoanalytic theory. Why should the phallus (power) and the penis be assumed to be prediscursively connected and therefore left unquestioned? To put it another way: castration anxiety (the prototypical male problem) and penis envy (the defining characteristic of femininity) would lose their privileged status in psychic and social terms once the connection between power and penis became just one of many (optional) possibilities.

If this sounds unbearably abstract, think for a moment about the underlying messages behind the following oft-heard statements: "All she needs is a man"; "All she needs is a good fuck" (with the implication that only a person with a penis could provide this); "She's a lesbian because she had a bad experience with a man"; "He's gay because he had a suffocating mother"; "Lesbians/feminists hate men"; "He's a wimp, he must be gay"; or "Bisexuals can't commit." One of my (male) students told the following joke: "Why do so many men give their penis a name? Because they don't like to take orders from a stranger." Many feminists have used the word phallocentric to describe society or even civilization itself. The connection is to men via the assumed link between power and penis. Butler questions this connection theoretically and socially. In so doing, it becomes increasingly difficult to take the differences between male and female bodies as given. Accounting for, and deposing, male power becomes implicated with challenges to the privileged status accorded to sex/gender differences.

Feminists have been aware of this for a long time. In offering critiques to the first words said upon the arrival of a newborn—"It's a boy!" or "It's a girl!" rather than "It's healthy!" or "It's small!"—feminists have suggested that there was something problematic about the intense interest in this one aspect of the child. Moreover, it has recently become clear that when babies are born with genitalia that are not categorizable by appearance, the doctors *decide* whether the baby is boy or girl. It seems that a precondition for entrance into a human community is having a body that may be deemed male or female, even though some don't present themselves that way (Findlay 1995).

What is so important about insisting upon this distinction between male and female? In social terms, what is riding on it? Butler argues that this distinction makes possible the discourse and practices that privilege heterosexuality. The founding principle for heterosexuality is the distinction between male and female. But what if the founding principle depends upon reiteration? What if the reiteration brings the founding principle into play—and keeps it in play—rather than the reverse? The enormous range of practices that sustains heterosexuality as normal, preferred, and unremarkable requires and mobilizes another set of practices that are banished, punished, and in other ways declared "outside." The "outside" is, of course, also "inside." What we repress remains; therefore reiterating our desires is never simple reiteration. Indeed, vehement reiteration of desire may indicate the instability of those desires. The old expression "The lady doth protest too much" captures the insight that statements, including statements of desire and aversion, cannot be taken at face value. Consider, for example, the following common statements: "I could *never* love a woman"; "I can't *imagine* being gay"; "I feel sick if a man approaches me in a bar." Virulent expressions of homophobia can be understood as anxiety-creating desires that are articulated as revulsion and projected onto others. Such statements provide evidence that we need to question "both gender binarism and the inside-outside logic that makes homosexual identity seem like heterosexuality's opposite" (Adams 1993, 31).

Homophobic assumptions—that gay men are effeminate and lesbians are mannish, for example—reify both masculinity and femininity as well as the categories straight and homosexual. At the experiential level, it is easy enough to counter such generalizations. But often these generalizations are refuted in ways that redraw the boundaries between acceptable and not acceptable. Consider the (defensive) remark "Of course gays don't 'have to be' wimps" (read they could be as macho as any (straight) man). Or "many lesbians are feminine and even wear make-up and high-heeled shoes" (just like straight women). In these cases, the proof of the normality of (some) gays and lesbians is seen to reside in their conformity to the very gendered roles that are elsewhere undergoing critique.

In such ordinary statements, we see how the categories male-female, masculine-feminine, gay-straight are all used to sustain each other, thereby constantly constraining, modifying, and confirming the sense of the possible and the impossible. From this perspective, conventional masculinity is produced through constant reiteration, and those reiterations aim to approximate some masculine ideal that does not exist prior to the reiterating process. But this ongoing attempt to approximate that ideal represents and produces psychic anxiety and social, political, and economic consequences. How can someone ever know if he is "being man enough"? Man enough for what, we want to ask? If we substitute woman for man in this phrase, we may be trying to demonstrate that woman can never measure up, or we may be parodying the original phrase to display its meaning and its vacuity. The phrase "being man enough" appears both full of meaning and empty at the same time.

Perhaps this is a useful way to apprehend the concepts of masculinity and femininity. There seems little question that they are charged with meaning, used and reused in multiple ways to reward and punish, exclude and include, valorize and undermine. But when we examine them closely, they seem to disappear before our eyes. Women speak of having to become like men to succeed in the corporation. For example, they may dress like men, suited up, briefcase in hand. But few of us think that masculinity actually resides in the clothes. Or do we? Consider the enormous interest, humour, and revulsion generated by those who most obviously flout convention—a man dressed as a woman and displaying feminine mannerisms, perhaps. A man cannot simply get up in the morning and decide to wear a skirt: immediately he is labelled a cross-dresser, with all that term entails. And his mannerisms: Why are such mannerisms seen as feminine, now that they are displayed by a male? But wait, is he a man? Or is he a woman dressed as a man? Is he a woman dressed as a man displaying feminine mannerisms? Is he a woman dressed as a man gazing at a woman dressed as a man who is "acting like" a woman?

At this point, you will probably have thrown up your hands. But consider this poem, written by Mikaela Hughes, when she was six or seven. Her best friend had just moved to Australia, and her cat had just died. At the same time, she had realized that her classmates had assumed that she was a boy.

I seem to be a boy
But really I am a girl.
I seem to be happy
But really I am sad.
I seem to not have a cat
But really I have a cat that is dead. (1996, 146)

Why, then, all this categorization? What on earth does it mean in the end to ask, What is s/he "really"? *Exactly*, say the queer theorists. If you look only at the performance, the categories of sex and gender appear as a chest of halloween clothes and props, a cultural resource for the mis/use of all. But Judith Butler is careful to point out that sex and gender are not garments to be put on in the morning; in the reiteration of acts, the specific materiality of the body is produced. We may feel ourselves to be male, female, masculine, feminine, gay, straight in the depths of our being. In her words, the "activity of this gendering cannot, strictly speaking, be a human act or expression, a willful appropriation, and it is certainly not a question of taking on a mask; it is the matrix through which all willing first becomes possible, its enabling cultural condition" (1993, 7).

Let us return to women who may try to appear like men in their bid to climb the corporate ladder. Dressing the part may be accompanied by attempts to appear unemotional at work. But does that mean that masculinity is coincident with failure to display emotion? These days at least, there is a lot of attention paid to the idea that men can feel too. The "sensitive new-age guy" may not be a passing phenomenon. Or women may behave like men by taking on the corporate goals and culture. But does masculinity reside in the pursuit of profits and the instrumental use of others? Or women may sleep with women, like men (or at least like those men who sleep with women). But the limits for women's being like men seem to have been crossed in this last example. Indeed, women report that they often risk their jobs if they are known to share their intimate lives with women. Gay men in the corporation may well stay closeted. Loving other men—regardless of their other behaviours—may put them across the line of acceptance, promotion, or employment. Is this because they are, in this respect, like women—that is, like the women who love men, not like the women who love women as men (are supposed to) do? Here we see that, just as sexual boundary making draws upon and uses gender markers, so are the boundaries of masculinity and femininity maintained, in part, through sexual boundary making (Ingraham 1994).

Butler goes further in her theorizing, arguing that just as discourses on masculinity and femininity and discourses on sexuality enable each other in the ways we have seen, so too do they both depend upon and enable the continuous reiteration of other social inclusions and exclusions. In particular she points to the ways in which dominant ideas of normative masculinity incorporate and depend upon images of nonracialized men—that is, white men. In fact, we might ask, do we even have a discourse on masculinity (however full and empty we deem the category to be), or do we have discourses on masculinity intricately bound up with whiteness and racialization? If the latter, this would mean that reiterating one's identity as male depends not just upon the identity female but also upon the identities—the excluded identities—of colour, blackness, brownness, and all that those identities, in turn, are taken to mean.

Consider how often media accounts of the activities of the subgroup in the population identified as youth not only include the (assumed) sex of participants but also their race—when they are not white. White usually requires no mention because it is seen to be normative, while "young" "black" "men" are presented as having an identity that distinguishes them from young white men, or old white men, or young black women. Much of their media image partakes of many aspects of normative masculinity: toughness, instrumentality, aggressiveness, refusing to take direction from others (known in other circles as "being one's own boss"). But somehow, in the process of being racialized, such characteristics take on menacing tones. "Boys will be boys," but these boys are threatening and are excluded from the more benign rendition of that cliche. Given all the data on date rape, wife battery, and child abuse, this can't be because there are no "white" "male" "youth" who are menacing anyone. On the contrary. Statistics Canada's 1994 survey found that "the highest rates of wife assault are among young men 18 to 24 years of age" (Rodgers 1994, 46). How is it that masculinity remains, at least in non-feminist discourse, apparently untainted by such findings?

In a study of recent Canadian trial judgments, the researchers found some clues in the language of the judges (Coates, Bavelas, and Gibson 1994). They found that there is no consensus about the courtroom language to describe sexual assault in cases where the assailant is not a stranger to the victim. As a result, judges vacillate between using the language of "stranger" rape and the language of consensual sex. A man who entered a woman's bedroom while she was asleep and inserted his penis into her mouth was described in the judgment as having "offered" his penis (ibid., 189). Words that are common in discussing love making, like fondle, touch, and intercourse, were regularly used instead of the term sexual assault, the legal words for unwanted encounters. A man found guilty of sexual assault was described as having an "impeccable character" (ibid., 196), leading one to wonder just what he would have had to do to rule himself out of this category. Despite evidence such as this, an editorial in the *Globe and Mail* took the Canadian Panel on Violence Against Women to task for "an avalanche of recommendations, some vague, some silly, some worthy." In particular, the editors urged, "mandatory gender-sensitivity training for judges should be quickly rejected" (1993, D6).

Poststructuralism's focus on the text and queer theory's focus on performance permit an analysis of gendered subjectivity in all areas of human literary and artistic production from scientific documents through legislation to comic strips and television programs. The word games that maintain the boundaries between male and female, masculinity and femininity, need constant reinvention, but their reinvention relies on the fixed idea that men and women are different in ways that are known. But there is a trick here, to return to Judith Butler. The trick is that it is these reinventions (reiterations) that maintain the boundaries by presenting themselves as simple reflections of an underlying reality. For example, observers noted that Kim Campbell would "have to be aggressive to fight Liberal Leader Jean Chretien, but when women become aggressive they are often labelled hysterical" (Smith 1993, A4). In an article arguing that "sharing the housework isn't a political gesture, it just makes sense," Ken Mark wrote that he recalled "Peter Gzowski's chat with a naval non-commissioned officer on the proper way to iron a shirt. These men are not wimps or sissies just because they know what is the business end of an iron" (1994, A24). Note how the category wimp and sissy is left untouched, presumably to be filled with some behaviour that *will* bring such opprobrium upon some men's heads. In another story entitled "Handywoman: Powerful new role model is plugged in," the reader is introduced to "icons of a new brand of feminism in the nineties—the handy yet feminine woman" (Williams 1994, A24). These reiterations create the exclusions and the inclusions, the hierarchical arrangements that feminists have variously called patriarchal relations, the sex/gender system, or the racialized sex-gendered system.

POSTSTRUCTURALISM'S FEMINIST CRITICS

The emphasis in this chapter on psychoanalytic and poststructuralist perspectives reflects my view that together they provide new and illuminating insights for understanding subjectivity and representation. In our society, gender makes itself felt early and deeply in all human beings, and gendered understandings inform virtually every aspect of the social world in complex and interrelated ways. Psychoanalytic and poststructuralist perspectives have been the most attentive to this depth and pervasiveness, but they need each other to provide satisfactory accounts of how gender is psychically lodged and linguistically sustained and resisted.

It is not the case, however, that they replace other feminist perspectives in providing explanations for gendered hierarchies. Their utility depends upon the kinds of questions one is seeking to answer. Psychoanalytic theories have not yet been developed in ways that explain how gender interacts with other social hierarchies—those of class, race, age and so on—in the process of psychosexual maturation.[16] Moreover, as most proponents of the theories would concede, these approaches generally make no sustained contribution towards understanding the gendered relations of political economy, including capitalism, imperialism, or racism, or towards strategies for the dismantling of these exploitative systems.[17] Strategies for social change at every level, however, need to include the insights of psychoanalysis, namely, that we are constituted as gendered human beings—as an aspect of deep psychosexual development—in the earliest days of infancy and childhood. To undo the equation of masculinity with domination and femininity with subordination, therefore, not only requires more than one generation, but the willingness of adult men and women to revisit their own past with the unlearning and changing basic patterns of self-perception and desire.

Poststructural approaches have also been challenged by many feminists, generally on two interrelated grounds. By focusing upon the texts or observing the performance, poststructuralism fails to distinguish between subjectivity as the constitution of a self (who we are), representations of that self (how we are portrayed), and activity (what we do). What this means, as some critics have argued, is that there isn't theoretical space for asking questions about *causal* relationships between gendered behaviours and attitudes, the depictions of men and women, and what men and women do. The absence of a causal analysis appears to leave feminists without strategic analyses for transforming oppressive and exploitative relationships. This political concern is related to a second problem that many feminists have with poststructuralism: that an understanding of subjectivity as an outcome of discourse—rather than as a site for the constitution of a self—fails to provide a full account of human agency and the potential of people to act individually or collectively to change the social world.

Neither explanation nor strategic thinking is the strong suit of poststructuralism, and most feminists show little interest in abandoning either. A poststructural approach continues to coexist, then—and I think necessarily—with older approaches and controversies about the interconnections between gendered subjects, gendered representation, and gendered activity.

Conclusion

As we discussed in Chapter 1, different feminist perspectives provide different understandings of what is most important to changing patriarchal society. Let us take an example. A magazine editor accepts advertisements illustrating women who have dieted to produce the "perfect" body. A young girl reads the magazine and starves herself while another looks for alternative images of robust and cheerful women. How are the different responses to be explained? By the ads, by the presence or absence of alternative images, by variations in early childhood development, by what the reader sees women and men doing in her daily life? Why do popular magazines routinely run such images? Because those who produce them share the dominant valuation in the culture? Because they help sell magazines? Because the advertisers realize profit from all the products designed to produce the body beautiful?

Such questions look for causal explanations. Liberal feminists have engaged in many, often successful, campaigns to pressure the popular media into providing alternative images of women and girls (Macpherson 1994, 149). Their belief in the saliency of education for changing laws and attitudes guides this kind of strategic thinking. What is clear—twenty-five years on from those first protests against beauty pageants—is that issues around sexual objectification resonate among subsequent generations of young women. Naomi Wolf's *The Beauty Myth* sold millions of copies; her speeches in the United States and Canada draw packed halls; and young women especially, whether self-described feminists or not, respond to her spirited critique of a culture that induces them to diet their way to oblivion. The protests against beauty pageants appear now as the first salvo in a long feminist challenge to a cultural economy that not only rewards and punishes women on the basis of their appearance but also induces them to spend lots of money on their appearance, to take unconscionable risks with their health, and to spend lives in a spiral of guilt-ridden dieting (Kirsch 1995, A3).[18]

Marxist feminists, by contrast, might begin with questions about profits and the dependence of capitalist relations upon the creation of needs. There are multimillion-dollar industries that depend upon women altering their body size through methods ranging from dieting to surgery. Such industries employ women in Canada, and abroad, at very low wages. From this perspective, therefore, an analysis that began with images of women and dieting would extend to the international political economy. But Marxist feminists would also highlight the continuing situation of women's economic dependence upon men, and how these relations of dependence help create the need for women to please men.

Radical feminists challenge the institutions of heterosexism, partly in order to loosen the hold that men have over women. Women have been coerced by man-made law and masculine violence—physical and representational—into heterosexual marriage, into degrading and oppressive work as models in pornography and as prostitutes, and into conforming with the entire hetero-sexist structuring of society. Why does the young girl looking at the magazine images feel that she should look like them? Does she believe that this will help attract male attention? Radical feminists insist that women must get out from under the power of men, and this involves action on many fronts. They have argued, for example, that men sexually violate women because they absorb violent pornography. Censoring such material, therefore, is justified on grounds that it will diminish the violence that men wreak upon women.

Marxist feminists do not see censoring pornography as central to eliminating male violence, but focus rather on economic coercion in explaining many manifestations of gender. Women do low-paid gendered work because most of the time that is all that is available. From this perspective, women endure violence in the home because of their economic dependence on men, and men are more likely to act violently in the home when they are exploited at work (Luxton 1980). As the economic circumstances of so many people's lives worsen with cutbacks in social services and rising unemployment and underemployment, increasing numbers of women and children will be in growing jeopardy, including danger from physical violence.

The political discourse in the mid-1990s reinvents, with a vengeance, long-standing distinctions between those who are dependent on others and those who fend for themselves. In this rhetoric that provides the fuel for electoral success, increasing numbers of people find themselves with bodies that don't matter, written out of the social and political world. Psychoanalytic understandings of the false distinction between dependence and independence; poststructuralist and queer theory's readings of discourse and performativity; radical feminist insights into men's abuse of women's minds and bodies; liberal feminist insistence on the centrality of education and attitudes—all these, I would argue, contribute to an understanding of contemporary social life and suggest ways to destabilize the late twentieth century's version of the deserving and the undeserving. Finally, as I have indicated in other chapters, Marxist and anti-racist analyses of the contemporary global political economy draw attention to the immense power of those controlling capital to shape the lives of women, children, and men in different ways.

Notes

1 According to Prentice et al., the first public action of the newly formed Toronto Women's Liberation group was a protest against a winter bikini contest (1988, 353).
2 When Colleen Swanson, wife of Dow Corning's ethics advisor, experienced debilitating ill health, neither of them connected this with her recent breast implants, implants produced and marketed by her husband's employer (Byrne 1995). Yet in a CBC radio interview, John Swanson reported that, in the 1970s, he had dis-

counted warnings in *Ms.* magazine about the danger of silicone breast implants as feminist overreaction. An estimated 150,000 women in Canada had breast implants (*Winnipeg Free Press*, 1992a).

3 I am very grateful to Patrizia Gentile for providing me with a copy of her unpublished paper. She convincingly argues that "the beauty contest 'model' was appropriated by the federal service in order to enforce specific codes of femininity, masculinity and heterosexuality" (1995, 1). See also Kinsman 1995.

4 The Kingston Women's Liberation Movement held an elaborate protest against beauty queen contests at Queen's University in October 1969. Six members of the group entered the contest. When they were introduced, each in turn took the opportunity to address the audience (Adamson 1995, 262–63).

5 Beauty competitions could also be the occasion for reflections on competition itself. One of Canada's leading social activists, Joan Newman Kuyek, remembers her reaction to winning the beauty queen title at the University of Manitoba in 1962: "I saw the heartbreak in the faces of all the other contestants, and I realized what a horrible thing competition truly is. I was supposed to be happy at the expense of these other young women and I wondered, 'What kind of system is this'?" (Lowe 1995, 14).

6 Reginald Bibby and Donald C. Posterski's *Teen Trends: A Nation in Motion* (1992) cite a 1988 survey on male-female couples, aged 15–24, who live together. Forty-six percent of the respondents said the female partner did all the cooking, cleaning, and laundry, while only 4 percent said the male did most or all of these jobs.

7 In July 1957 a "weeping Miss USA" lost her title when organizers discovered that she was married and the mother of two children. Leona Gage told pageant officials that she and her cousin Barbara Gates had gambled every cent they had to finance her chance at fame and fortune (*Toronto Star* 1957, 1).

8 See Smith 1992.

9 See also Susan Russell's 1978 research in an Ottawa high school. She discovered that boys reported that their grades were improving even when they had deteriorated, while girls continually underestimated their performance (1987).

10 Statistics Canada has responded to John Fekete's allegations in his book *Moral Panic: Biopolitics Rising* that this was a "fake survey" and that Statistics Canada "traded science for voodoo" (*Statistics Canada* 1995a, 1). Statistics Canada responded that Fekete had made serious errors in his arguments, which led to misinterpretations of the nature and purpose of the survey and the survey results. They carefully refuted all eight of his allegations. In its response, *Statistics Canada* points out that "the Violence against Women Survey has been recognized by international experts as a major achievement and a significant contribution to the science in this area" (ibid., 7).

11 In a letter to *Ms.* magazine, Pam Elliot, co-ordinator of the Lesbian Battering Intervention Project in St. Paul, Minnesota, wrote that she had been "besieged with requests nationwide for setting up support services on lesbian battering" (1991, 5).

12 In July 1994, a group of young Filipino-Canadian men and women protested in Winnipeg against the Maria Clara beauty contest held by the Knights of Rizal, a Filipino cultural group. The protesters argued that Maria Clara, a fictional character in the work of Jose Rizal, was submissive, and that the contest encouraged young women to model themselves after her. They argued that "Filipina women have always been in the forefront of the struggle for national liberation and they should be celebrated without the kind of stereotyping that is so offensive to young women in Canada today" (Nett 1994, A7). My point is that beauty contests, like other cultural events, may carry with them a range of meanings about age, sex, gender, race and nation.

13 See Maxine Tynes evocative poetry and stories about black women "in service" (1987, 11–12, 68–71), which capture the dignity of those who work for others, the complexity of the social relationships, and the resistance to discrimination, especially when it took the form of personal hypocrisy and rudeness (1990, 85–89).

14 Following her double mastectomy, the late Kathleen Martindale wrote: "I've got an invisible disability. I've become a quick-change artist in gyms and other places where there's no or little privacy. Most people cringe when they see my chest. They say I've been mutilated. In place of breasts with nipples I have a scar which extends under my left armpit, goes jaggedly across my entire chest, and then ends up under what used to be my right armpit. My lover and I call it 'the zipper.' That's what it looks like, a long, red zipper" (1994, 12). Martindale also had to deal with the fact that there were no support groups for lesbian cancer patients even in Metropolitan Toronto.

15 In a memoir about her relationship with her sister, Karen, and their coming-out stories, Joy McBride writes that Karen "was involved in long-term relationships with women, though I very naively thought she and her 'roommates' just didn't have enough space or money for two beds. (Honestly)" (1996, 182).

16 There has, however, been some useful work in this area. For an elaboration on this development see Hamilton 1996.

17 But see, for example, the last chapter in Jessica Benjamin's *The Bonds of Love* (1988) for an insightful treatment of the relationship between gendered socialization and bureaucracy.

18 Dr. Ron Davis, a Toronto clinical psychologist, estimated at a seminar on eating disorders that "five per cent of university women have full-blown eating disorders" and that more than 90 percent of those with eating disorders are women (Kirsch 1995, A3).

References

Adams, Kathleen Pirie. "Back to Estrus: Thoughts on Lesbian Bar Scenes." *Fireweed* 38.2 (1993): 29–35.

Adamson, Nancy. "Feminists, Libbers, Lefties and Radicals: The Emergence of the

Women's Liberation Movement." In *A Diversity of Women: Ontario, 1945–1980.* Ed. Joy Parr. Toronto: U of Toronto P, 1995. 252–80.

Archibald, Kathleen. "Men, Women and Persons." *Canadian Public Administration* 16 (Spring 1973): 14–24.

Atwood, Margaret. *Cat's Eye.* Toronto: McClelland and Stewart, 1988.

Batcher, Elaine. "Building the Barriers: Adolescent Girls Delimit the Future." In *Women and Men: Interdisciplinary Readings on Gender.* Ed. Greta Hofmann Nemiroff. Richmond Hill, ON: Fitzhenry and Whiteside, 1987.150–65.

Benjamin, Jessica. *The Bonds of Love.* New York: Pantheon Books, 1988.

Bibby, Reginald and Donald C. Posterski. *Teen Trends.* Toronto: Stoddart, 1992.

Brand, Dionne. "A Working Paper on Black Women in Toronto: Gender, Race and Class." *Fireweed* 19 (1984): 26–43.

Brant, Beth. "Coming Out as Indian Lesbian Writers." In *In the Feminine: Women and Words/les Femmes et les mots.* Ed. Ann Dybikowski et al. Edmonton: Longspoon Press, 1985.

——. *Food and Spirits.* Vancouver: Press Gang, 1991.

Brunswick, Ruth. "The Preoedipal Phase of the Libido Development." In *The Pyschoanalytic Reader.* Ed. Robert Fleiss. New York: International Universities Press, 1948.

Butler, Judith. *Bodies that Matter: On the Discursive Limits of "Sex."* New York: Routledge, 1993.

Byrne, John A. "Informed Consent." *Business Week* 2 Oct. 1995: 104–16.

Carpenter, Mary. "Female Grotesques in Academia: Ageism, Anti-Feminism and Feminists on the Faculty." In *Anti-Feminism in the Academy.* Ed. Vévé Clark et al. New York: Routledge, 1996.

Chase, Gillean. "Strangers, Sisters." In *To Sappho, My Sister: Lesbian Sisters Write About Their Lives.* Ed. Lee Fleming. Charlottetown: Gynergy Books, 1996. 59–68.

Chenier, Elise Rose. "Tough Ladies and Troublemakers: Toronto's Public Lesbian Community, 1955–65." MA thesis, Queen's University, 1995.

Coates, Linda, Janet Bavelas, and James Gibson. "Anomalous Language in Sexual Assault Trial Judgements." *Discourse and Society* 5.2 (1994): 189–206.

De Beauvoir, Simone. *The Second Sex.* New York: Knopf, 1952.

Elliot, Pam. Letter to editor. *Ms.* 1.4 (1991): 5.

Findlay, Deborah. "Discovering Sex: Medical Science, Feminism and Intersexuality." *Canadian Review of Sociology and Anthropology* 32.1 (1995): 22–52.

Firestone, Shulamith. *The Dialectic of Sex.* New York: William Morrow & Co., 1970.

Gaskell, Jane. "The Reproduction of Family Life: Perspectives of Male and Female Adolescents." In *Gender and Society: Creating a Canadian Women's Sociology.* Ed. Arlene Tigar McLaren. Toronto: Copp Clark Pitman, 1988. 146–68.

Gentile, Patrizia. "Defending Gender in the Security State: Beauty Contests and Fruit Machines, 1950–1972." Unpublished paper, Carleton University, 1995.

Globe and Mail. "Violence is not a women's issue." [Editorial]. 31 July 1993: D6.

Hamilton, Roberta. "Theorizing Gender, Sexuality and Family: Feminism and

Psychoanalysis Revisited." In *Feminism and Families*. Ed. Meg Luxton. Halifax: Fernwood, 1996.

Hughes, Mikaela and Catherine Hughes. "The Hughes Family Chronicles." In *To Sappho, My Sister: Lesbian Sisters Write About Their Lives*. Ed. Lee Fleming. Charlottetown: Gynergy Books, 1996. 135–50.

Ingraham, Chrys. "The Heterosexual Imaginary: Feminist Sociology and Theories of Gender." *Sociological Theory* 12.2 (1994): 201–19.

Kaufman, Michael, ed. *Beyond Patriarchy: Essays by Men on Pleasure, Power, and Change*. Toronto: Oxford UP, 1987.

Kinsman, Gary. "'Character Weaknesses' and 'Fruit Machines': Towards an Analysis of the Anti-Homosexual Security Campaign in the Canadian Civil Service." *Labour/Le Travail* 35 (1995): 133–61.

Kirsch, Vik. "Eating disorders plague students: Hundreds now affected by dietary chaos says hospital psychologist." *Guelph Mercury* 27 June 1995: A3.

LaMarsh, Judy. *Memoires of a Bird in a Gilded Cage*. Toronto: McClelland and Stewart, 1968.

Lowe, Mich. "Joan Kuyek vs. INCO." *Canadian Forum* 74 (Nov. 1995): 14–20.

Luxton, Meg. *More Than a Labour of Love*. Toronto: Women's Press, 1980.

McBride, Joy and Karen McBride. "Answering to My Sister's Name." In *To Sappho, My Sister: Lesbian Sisters Write About Their Lives*. Ed. Lee Fleming. Charlottetown: Gynergy Books, 1996. 175–84.

MacKinnon, Catherine A. and Andrea Dworkin. "In Defense of Themselves." *New York Times Book Review* 7 May 1995: 47.

Macpherson, Kay. *When in Doubt, Do Both: The Times of My Life*. Toronto: U of Toronto P, 1994.

Mark, Ken. "Sharing the housework isn't a political gesture, Ken Mark says. It just makes sense." *Globe and Mail* 16 Feb. 1994: A24.

Martindale, Kathleen. "Can I Get a Witness? My Lesbian Breast Cancer Story." *Fireweed* 42 (1994): 9–15.

Messing, Karen. "Do Women Have Different Jobs Because of Their Biological Differences?" In *Women and Men: Interdisciplinary Readings on Gender*. Ed. Greta Hofmann Nemiroff. Richmond Hill, ON: Fitzhenry and Whiteside, 1987. 341–53.

Millett, Kate. *Sexual Politics*. New York: Avon Books, 1971.

Nett, Emily. "Demure no more?" *Winnipeg Free Press* 31 July 1994: A7.

Newman, Peter. *The Distemper of Our Times*. Toronto: McClelland and Stewart, 1969.

Noble, Kimberly. "Being a bad sport about harassment." *Globe and Mail*, 29 November 1991: A18.

Odette, Francine. "Body Beautiful/Body Perfect: Challenging the Status Quo. Where Do *Women with Disabilities* Fit In?" *Canadian Woman Studies/Les cahiers de la femme* 14.3 (1992): 41–43.

Ondaatje, Michael. *The English Patient*. Toronto: McClelland and Stewart, 1992.

Parsons, Talcott. "The Social Structure of the Family." In *The Family: Its Function and Destiny*. Ed. R.N. Anshen. New York: Hayner, 1959.

Pierson, Ruth Roach. *"They're Still Women After All": The Second World War and Canadi-an Womanhood.* Toronto: McClelland and Stewart, 1986.

Phillips, David. "No difference, no deference." *Globe and Mail,* 10 November 1995, A22.

Prentice, Alison, et al. *Canadian Women: A History.* Toronto: Harcourt, Brace, Jovanovich, 1988.

Rodgers, Karen. "Wife Assault: The Findings of a National Survey." *Juristat* 14.9 (1994): 1–22.

Ross, Becki. *The House that Jill Built: A Lesbian Nation.* Toronto: U of Toronto P, 1995.

Russell, Susan. "The Hidden Curriculum of School: Reproducing Gender and Class Hierarchies." In *Feminism and Political Economy: Women's Work, Women's Struggles.* Ed. Heather Jon Maroney and Meg Luxton. Toronto: Methuen, 1987. 229–46.

——. "From Disability to Handicap: An Inevitable Response to Social Constraints?" *Canadian Review of Sociology and Anthropology* 26.2 (1989): 276–93.

Sadlier, Rosemary. *Leading the Way: Black Women in Canada.* Toronto: Umbrella Press, 1994.

Salutin, Rick. "The sexual politics of Kim Campbell's future." *Globe and Mail,* 12 March 1993, C1.

Silvera, Makeda. "How Far Have We Come." In *In the Feminine: Women and Words/les Femmes et les mots* Ed. Ann Dybikowski et al. Edmonton: Longspoon Press, 1985. 68–72.

Smith, Dorothy. "Whistling Women: Reflections on Rage and Rationality." In *Fragile Truths: Twenty-Five Years of Sociology and Anthropology in Canada.* Ed. William K. Carroll et al. Ottawa: Carleton UP, 1992. 207–26.

Smith, Vivian. "Women welcome victory, 'but it's still not an election.'" *Globe and Mail* 15 June 1993: A4.

Statistics Canada. "Response to Allegations Made About the Violence Against Women Survey." Feb. 1995.

Toronto Star "Disqualified: 'Miss USA' Mother of 2." 19 July 1957: 1.

Tynes, Maxine. *Borrowed Beauty.* Porters Lake, NS: Pottersfield Press, 1987.

Valpy, Michael. "Lives of Canadian girls and women." *Globe and Mail,* 12 March 1992, 2.

Weissman, Aerlyn, and Lynne Fernie. *Forbidden Love.* National Film Board, 1993.

Williams, Pam. "Handywoman: Powerful new role model is plugged in." *Globe and Mail,* 10 March 1994, A24.

Winnipeg Free Press. "Passing the buck." 21 March 1992: A6.

Wolf, Naomi. *The Beauty Myth.* Toronto: Vintage Books, 1990.

Yetman, Lori and Julie Yetman. "Peanut Butter and Jam." In *To Sappho, My Sister: Lesbian Sisters Write About Their Lives.* Ed. Lee Fleming. Charlottetown: Gynergy Books, 1996. 211–24.

York, Lorraine. "Whirling Blindfolded in the House of Woman: Gender Politics in the Poetry and Fiction of Michael Ondaatje." *Essays on Canadian Writing* (1994): 71–91.

⇛+ SEX AND RACE +⇚

The texts in this section consistently interfuse sexuality and race, thus complicating both categories by unmooring them from the certainties according to which they are often deployed. For Ian Rashid, sexuality is inseparable from race: "My beauty is branded / into the colour of my skin," he writes. Here the notion of "beauty" unsettles its masculine referent as "colour" does the aesthetic norms that have grown up around beauty, each of these categories further complicated by the (post)colonial context in which they are set. Karen Dubinsky and Adam Givertz are concerned with colonization of another sort. Their article demonstrates how, in a period from the 1880s to the late 1920s, as part of labour's anti-Asian campaign, Chinese men were "monsterized" as sexual predators in such a way that "the strands of masculinity, class identity, and ethnic/racial identity converged." Dubinsky and Givertz focus on the shifting grounds that these categories occupy, whereby the feminized Asian man could safely be employed in Euro-Canadian households, but became sexually dangerous if he were the employer. In *Disappearing Moon Café*, SKY Lee orchestrates themes similar to those emerging from the Jack Kong murder case discussed by Dubinsky and Givertz. In Lee's novel, a Chinese houseboy is accused of murdering a Euro-Canadian woman in a scenario based on the *cause célèbre* of Janet Smith, the greatest unsolved crime in Canadian history. Lee sets this story against the backdrop of the sexual operatics within the Wong family as it seeks to produce a male heir and the political machinations of the state which result in the proclamation of the Chinese Exclusion Act. The theme of (re)colonization persists in Martin Cannon's account of the Canadian state's regulation of First Nations sexuality. Cannon is concerned with the intersections of race, gender, and sexuality put into place by the Indian Act of 1876, which made heterosexuality compulsory in Native communities through its gendered regulation of status and non-status Indians, whereby Native women lost their status if they married non-Native men. This process enforced heterosexual marriage and patrilineal descent. The human cost of these regulated categories is seen in Gregory

Scofield's narrative, which parallels two interrelated identity stories: that of coming out as a gay man and that of asserting pride in his identity as a Native man. The achievement of this life story is Scofield's discovery of himself outside these categories, as two-spirited.

SKY Lee

from *Disappearing Moon Café* (1990)

Ties Overseas—A Ticket In

MUI LAN
1924

Tyrannized by her own helplessness, Fong Mei cowered on the floor in front of her mother-in-law and wept piteously. Mui Lan sat at the secretary in her bedroom and stared at her daughter-in-law, a sneer frozen on her mouth, her plump, slippered feet tucked so neatly under her chair that she gave the appearance of being a cruel court eunuch in an opera. On the dainty desk top, strategically placed, a marriage certificate, a neat stack of immigration papers and miscellaneous receipts. On the four-poster bed, a camphor chest inlaid with mother-of-pearl, full of Fong Mei's wedding gold and jewelry, rested its case. Strategically gone, both the Wong elder and son, to their respective vocations, thus qualifying Mui Lan for omnipotence at home.

A gentle breeze blew through the tulle curtains at the window. Outside, a thick, hazy summer's midmorning, the air unctuous with the cloying scent of overripe fruit. Raspberries oozing sweet juices rotted and dropped from their limp canes, smashing in the dust like the bloodied carnage of a badly executed slaughter.

"Her male offspring guarantees the daughter-in-law's position in the family. You are barren and thus may not be accredited with one!" Mui Lan brought the matter of concern home with a single daggerous plunge! After this, she would no longer have to address the petrified younger woman. As far as Mui Lan was concerned, Fong Mei was a dead person.

"Damned, stinky bag!" she spoke into the air. "We received her into our home in the most flamboyant style. With the costs of hiring the go-betweens and the negotiators; with the costs of her passage and the bribes, never mind the gifts; and of course the cost of the wedding itself—never mind the risks we took with our Wong name and livelihood in a government investigation to secure HER immigration status ..." Her face contorting violently, she screeched out, "Your mother's stinking ... no one, absolutely no one would dispute me if I claimed publicly to have borne you in your flowery sedan chair across the ocean on my own back!"

Mui Lan had escalated to such a brain-bursting pitch so quickly that she had to pause to regather her corporeal forces. It had become stifling hot in the upstairs room. Taking great gulps of air, she started again.

255

"For five years, five long years, we've housed, fed and clothed her. And for what end? So that she could disgrace our ancestors' good name and bring bad luck onto this family, and ultimately risk our future descendants? Where am I to find peace in such a situation? Who do I go to for justice? Damned stinky she-bag!"

Having no face left at all, having lost her standing as a human being, Fong Mei's colour drained away, her neck limp and weak as if broken. She had been expecting a scolding for a long time, but this tirade of raging obscenities left her flaccid with fear. Snot drivelled out of her nose; tears trickled after each blink. Sobs, chokes and mucous muffled into her sleeves. Mui Lan's eyes fixed on her, black as hell, as if yearning to rub her off the face of this earth.

Ha! Mui Lan thought to herself, looking over the results of her exertions, satisfied with the slumped remains of her daughter-in-law before her. That despicable pig-bitch wouldn't dare wrangle with her. Her standing as a human being was all but lost. She might as well die!

Actually, in the beginning, Mui Lan had been afraid that Fong Mei would balk at her. One could never be sure of this younger generation of wild chickens who dared to presume that they had rights. Her daughter-in-law was no simpleton. She could have learnt very quickly to turn against the old ways when they didn't suit her any more. Who knew what she might attempt, from beguiling her husband to turn against his own mother to shamelessly running away to the Jesus-ghosts who would no doubt harbour her?

Mui Lan glanced down at her hands and the small key held in her own unconscious grip. She had stolen the little brass key from her husband's ring of keys while he slept. If the old man were to catch even a whiff of her plans, he would veto them with one big puff of his smelly cigar. Then, where would she be? Still, Mui Lan was willing to risk her old man's ire to play the trump card that she now pushed towards Fong Mei.

"Here, look!" Mui Lan said decisively. "Here are your entry papers, marriage certificate and wedding gold. According to our tang people's customs and laws, they are all meaningless now. Even this marriage contract! Useless too. Take them! Take them and go! Roll your useless female eggs a long way from here!"

Fong Mei gave an agonized shriek and sprang to her knees. "No, no, Nye Nye!" she begged and kowtowed. "Have mercy! Have mercy! Where am I to go?"

"Go back home to your own family! You have more than enough gold here to pawn for a passage." Mui Lan sneered, knowing full well that a spurned daughter-in-law would rather commit suicide than go back to her parents' home, for all the ten generations of everlasting shame that she would cost her family, in fact her whole village.

"No!" Fong Mei gasped as if strangling, and broke down into uncontrolled heaving and sobbing again.

"I don't care where you drag your dead body. You definitely have no right to stay in the way of my son's son. Who's going to speak up on your side? Resist, and other people will hold up your stinky thing for ridicule. Ha! They'll all say Lee Mui Lan has right on her side," she sniffed like a fretful badger, this way and that.

"If we were in the village, not even your father would dare say a thing. Who else would have the patience and virtue to keep a big-eating cow, a downright fraud, in her home for so long." Still shaking with pent-up anger, Mui Lan stopped again, her breathing fast and strained.

After a long sigh for dramatic effect, she fussed: "Haven't I done everything possible?" And her voice cracked with emotion as if she were the one hard done by. "Spared no expense to ensure you 'get happiness' and bear a boy—even a girl—to my son? You've eaten our best food, had all the required medicines. I've sent gifts, and money to have incense burnt at the temples at home, to have amulets made. I've even risked our reputation to send you to that dead, immoral, white doctor-specialist. All without results. You have no future. You're no good!"

I have her now, thought Mui Lan, and waited until the torrential sobs subsided. Confident that her daughter-in-law's life was now entirely in her hands— to have and to hold, to squeeze or to let live—Mui Lan began gently. "Listen, Fong Mei! I'm not so hard-mouthed as to want to disgrace your parents. What is there in it for me? But our customs are clear and practical too. If the first wife cannot bear a son, then she stands aside for another. That way, the family is assured of a yellow, 'lucky' road. Otherwise, who will there be left to honour even you, to sweep your grave? Now if we were in China, A Fuk would simply bring home a concubine. And when she bore a son, he would call you 'first mother.' You know these traditions. It's not as though we are out to strike you in the face!"

By now, Fong Mei was all but cried out. She still kneeled on the floor, covered in a cold sweat, as if drained from some kind of wasted exertion. The funny thing was she didn't know why she should be exhausted. Her life was like that of a work beast. When old and used up, it is bovine and calm, placid about its fate, and does not expect mercies. She had accepted this long ago, and now she tried to fix this image in her mind, if for no other reason than it would give her dignity. But tears quickly oozed beyond control, and fear made her grovel before she could stop herself. Suddenly, she realized that there was rage as well. So, it was rage, pushing her body beyond its limits! Rage that made her body shudder with icy fear.

Mui Lan thought Fong Mei was nodding in agreement, so she went on. "As daughter-in-law, though obviously not flawless, your behaviour is above reproach. A Fuk is fond of you, is he not? As am I and Lo Yeh! The past five years, you have learnt and worked a good deal." Mui Lan's words skidded together, and Fong Mei recognized their insincerity immediately. "But no matter how much you do, you have done nothing until you have given a son to us."

This idea of a baby was a trance-inducing chant that had long ago lost its meaning. Fong Mei was being punished, not for something she had done but for some apparent blank part of her.

"However," Mui Lan continued, "no one can accuse the Wong family of having 'a wolf's heart and a dog's lung.' Here, we are living on the frontier with barbarians. We stick together. Who wants to turn you out?" Adding slyly, "It's more a matter of whether you want to stick with us."

"Living in a land with foreign devils makes it very difficult for tang people. How can we bring another woman into the country without exposing ourselves to another, even more treacherous government investigation? Then, by their laws, concubines are illegal. So A Fuk would need to divorce you first." Mui Lan stole a sly glance at Fong Mei, who stiffened on cue. "And we tang people don't like to subject ourselves to their courts. It would be like placing ourselves in the paws of a tiger."

Each detail flawlessly revealed; every angle precisely designed for Fong Mei's unconditional surrender. Strangely enough, Mui Lan felt a twinge of guilt. She suddenly became aware of the glass wind-chimes that hung on the porch downstairs. Was it an isolated gust of wind, or did she just now hear the thin, incessant tinkling drift in through the window? It made her slightly uneasy.

"Here in this wilderness," she said, more loudly than she'd intended, "there are no Chinese women who are suitable for marriage into a respectable home. What few there are, are no good; but perhaps with the right connections and a sizable sum of money, we can pay off a clean enough woman to have a child for us! In secret of course, if you want! Then, after she brings him forth, the baby is yours. And no one but the four of us will be the wiser."

Yes, her plan did sound very simple after all. Mui Lan looked almost elated after she heard her own words. After all she wasn't the sort who enjoyed this kind of sneaking about. If only she had stayed in the village, none of this would have been necessary. It would have been a simple matter to have Choy Fuk take a wife more of her own choosing. Then, how blissful things would have been!

Dote on her grandsons! Wait for letters and money from an 'old rooster' who might never have come back into her life! Sit around the threshold, splitting melon seeds with her front teeth, chattering with the neighbours to her heart's content. Delighted with herself, Mui Lan began to ramble on, forgetting the presence of her daughter-in-law who observed her very carefully.

"I know a woman's heart! What woman would deny that yearning for a baby son, or even a baby girl to begin with. First-born daughters bring good luck, he, he, he! Do you think that I haven't shared the emptiness which you must have suffered, being childless these long years? Well, now you have the opportunity. All you need to do is give up your old man for a few days, and soon you'll have a son—and with him, security, prestige, honour, and the glowing warmth of a family to look after your old age. What could be easier? And where's the harm in that?" she asked innocently.

Mui Lan wasn't really expecting an answer. And of course there wasn't one.

KAE
1986

I myself was not present, but I've often wondered. What if, maybe just for a second or two during this lengthy monologue, my grandmother's young eyes—albeit puffy, bloodshot and glassy—had raised up to her mother-in-law as if to make bold? What if they had betrayed her innermost thoughts for that instant?

"You ancient she-dog," she might have cursed, very quietly of course, "look at yourself. Frothing at the mouth one moment, grinning dementedly at your own dreams at another! Would you take in another woman's offspring? You old bitch, would you give over your man to some diseased slut?"

Obviously, if such a flash of defiance had happened, my great-grandmother's steely stare would have crushed it in a second. More shrill curses would have rained upon my grandmother's bent back.

"And don't believe for a moment, you foul female stench, with your modern-day thinking about rights and freedom-ah, that you're too good for this bargain. What are you but just a woman!"

But my great-grandmother was a woman too. What did she mean by that? Was she referring to the substance we as women have to barter away in order to live? In order to live with men? In the male order? Then, what was I referring to? How we turn on ourselves, squabbling desperately among ourselves about our common debasement? Branding self-hatred across our foreheads—I wonder how deeply it seared into Fong Mei's flesh. And how willingly we fuel the white fire with which to scar other women. What choices did she have? Like so many hordes of women, didn't my grandmother consent to give away her own destiny? Who but women would do that?

A whole lifetime later, lying prone on a postpartum bed to rest my "female-bag," I still wonder about ... everything, I guess. My mother has gone, and I am alone. I wonder too, about the volatile lunacy that wasn't my great-grandmother's alone, but lurks in our peasant backgrounds, in our rustic language. This craziness that drove many beyond the brink towards self-destruction. Agonizing passion worth more than life itself, then dragging still more along that black road of anguish and guilt after the suicide.

An ache from the depths of my womb pulses through my body as I think back. Sadness washes over me from a deep, dark, secret pool. Staring at the ceiling—such an untouched white—I suddenly remember Morgan.

MORGAN KEUNG CHI WONG
1967

"Do I have a choice?"

I had asked Morgan that over the telephone. Nineteen years ago, I had just arrived home, dripping wet from school, when the phone rang. I was exhausted. I was piqued. My ski jacket hung heavy like lead weights, and my toes were frozen from my long trek through the snow and sludge. Having recently broken up with my steady, Terry Paling, I had lost my cosy ride home every day as well. And at that age, I was always starving, so I was not in a receptive mood.

"Of course not!" he replied curtly. I could hear him crunching potato chips over the receiver. Morgan was actually my uncle, even though I wasn't supposed to know that. The understanding between my parents and me was that Morgan was the notorious skirt-chasing black sheep of another branch of the family. And I was to under no circumstances have any contact with him. That was why he was calling at that particular time of the day. He knew no one would be home except me.

To me, Morgan was quite simply a haunted man. I was seventeen at the time, and of course frightfully sentimental. Now, there is no doubt in my mind that it was Morgan who made normal guys like Terry Paling pale in comparison. "Gee ... Well, I don't know, Morg ..." I tried to squirm out of this commitment as nicely as a nice girl could in those days, "I mean, I don't feel like going out in weather like this just to spend another evening watching you sleuth in the university librarinth, you know!"

How could I have possibly said what I really thought? "Morgan, at twenty-nine years old, you're too old to be a perpetual student, and I don't care how graduate! And besides, I don't feel like push-starting that stupid ancient Morgan you drive when it conks out in the god-damned snow ..." a strong emphasis on "you know what I mean?" Cute! A Morgan driving a Morgan—both wounded, helpless dinosaurs.

I went. My white patent go-go boots hopelessly inadequate against the elements. Miniskirted, with a rabbit-fur minicoat, my ass practically quivering right off the icy leather bucket seats. The Morgan had no heat. Sneaking sidelong glances at the munificently dashing man driving me to distraction. I just couldn't believe that he was my uncle. I couldn't believe his whole sordid story.

"Well, you yourself said that my great-grandfather was supposed to have a reputation for fair dealing," I argued in the library. "How could all this deviousness go on right under the big boss's nose?"

"Aahh yess! Great-grandfather ..." Morgan replied, as if my great-grandfather was his great-grandfather. "The benevolent patriarch of Disappearing Moon. All Chinatown turns to him in times of trouble," he murmured, seemingly to himself, while cranking the roller handle of the microfilm viewing machine. Shadows of old newspapers flew by. The air in the underground library was unbearably dry and hot, permeated with the smell of crumbling literary effort.

He finally answered, "Well, Great-grandfather is as famous as your great-grandmother is infamous. Even after she had gotten the word loud and clear from above, she still went ahead with her secret plot. I mean she really thought she could pull it off."

"Oh, I still can't believe that! There must have been easier ways to come by a baby," I maintained. "Lots of those rich, old Chinatown guys had several wives. You know the Kees and the Chens. They had lots of local-born daughters too. If you ask me, she could have easily gotten rid of my Poh Poh, and good riddance! Even if she didn't, in those days Gong Gong would still have been free to marry any one of them."

"Yeah, well, the old broad was definitely a bit of a cheapskate. Still, the family was nowhere near as rich as the Kee family. Great-grandfather was too public-minded. And what rich little local-born girl would want to be a number-two wife, when she could have had her pick of horny bachelors? Six males to each little girl in those days!" he whistled meaningfully at the impossible odds. "I hear your Gong Gong was no prize either."

Uh oh, another little dig, a less than kindly shove perhaps, and I pretended I was too polite to notice. Of course, I didn't trust Morgan. Him and his sly little pen scratches on paper! Was his story the same as my story? Or should I have said, is history the same as mystery? If I had had any savoir faire at all, I would have headed for the hills, saved my skin, but this kind of scenario is exactly what keeps me glued to my seat, even today.

Too bad for my family that money couldn't buy long life (prosperity couldn't buy posterity either); too bad for me, I could have simply asked. Instead of dead, silent ancestors who kept me hanging by a million possible threads, someone would have told me—I'm sure. Instead of Morgan busy fraying the tapestry, I could have claimed my righteous inheritance to a pure bloodline. I wouldn't have fallen in love/hate with his/my truth and wasted all these years trying to answer him.

"O.K. Now listen!" Morgan cut in. "You want to know what I found out? It's 1924 ... in the heat of summer, the news rips through Chinatown like wild fire! A white woman is murdered! The prime suspect is a Chinese houseboy named Wong Foon Sing! Chopsticks drop and clatter in surprise! Clumps of rice stick in throats ..."

"Morgue, what are you sputtering about?" I couldn't bear to hear any more. I cringed and glanced nervously around the stacks, hoping no one had heard his embarrassing comments. Chineseness made me uncomfortable then.

"Listen!" he repeated. This Janet Smith murder case kicked up a lot of fuss in Vancouver. Don't you want to know more about it?"

"What for?" I was beginning to wonder if this vacuous pursuit of still-life wasn't unbalancing his mind.

"Summer! 1924 ... remember why your great-granny had a free hand at plastering your grandma's face against the floor whenever she felt like it? ... Come in Manila!" Morgan had such an irritating way about him, as though on some subconscious level he was out to punish me. What had I ever done to him? Still, I crumbled like a cupcake in his hands, because I let him go on.

"The old patriarch was too busy becoming a big-shot, muscling in on all the action to worry about daughters-in-law. Hey, when old guys in Chinatown tap you on the shoulder, and say, 'I once shook your great-grandfather's hand. He was a good man,' it's precisely because of those bizarre times. Let me tell you, the whole town went nuts! The Chinese Exclusion Act—the Day of Humiliation—and then this killing."

I smiled ever so sweetly and chose not to tell him that I didn't ever go down to Chinatown except for the very occasional family banquet. And I certainly wouldn't ever let any dirty old man touch me! Those little old men were everywhere in Chinatown, leaning in doorways, sitting at bus stops, squatting on sidewalks. The very thought gave me the creeps.

I looked over at Morgan to see if he had any inkling of me, but he was already in midair, springing into a high-pitched performance. The bitterness of it surprised me.

"People became openly obsessed with splattered brain matter. At dinner tables, they might as well have been eating coagulating blood pudding. Newspapers egged them on at breakfast. More lovesick but banal diary tidbits for tea, dear?"

He flung his arms about and squeaked out a female stereotype, "Inflammatory rumours all over this hot little town! How did our dear little Janet meet her demise? B.C. Telephone operators wore their dear little fingers to the bone, incessantly plugging in first the fantastic, then the freakish, finally the fanatical. They began to swoon on courthouse steps."

Then his voice turned sinister. "The crowds began to get restless and ugly. All over the land, men on soapboxes cried out, 'It is our God-given duty to protect our poor, white, working-class maidenhood from those filthy minded, slant-eyed vermin, even if we have to string a few of 'em up by their ten-inch finger-nails ...'"

"Morgan," I gasped again, my ears burning red-hot. Until then, I had been laughing nervously. I mean what else could I do? He was mad! "Pipe down, will you!" I begged.

He had been scribbling furiously as he talked. He suddenly looked at me and grinned blithely. "How do you know," he asked, "which of the two were going to get strung up? The poor white maidens? Or the slant-eyed vermin?"

Morgan calmed down, but he continued to lecture at me, as though there was an entire classroom full of adoring students (female, I would imagine) behind me. In fact, I had to keep looking over my shoulders to make sure there wasn't.

"You know, there was once a law prohibiting Chinese men from working too closely with white women, and vice versa, I suppose. But it backfired in the end because, given a choice, employers tended to hire the cheaper, more-for-their-money chinamen; and as a result, white women got protected right out of a job. By and large, this masterful bit of law-making was successfully ignored until some of the more upstanding white citizens tried to pursue it again, over Janet Smith's corpse. This time, as you know, it was our very own great-grandfather, Wong Gwei Chang, who had a big hand in stepping in and stopping it."

"It was a historical landmark in British Columbia's usual pattern of interracial relations," said Morgan. "Chinatown fought back the rising tide of virulent hatred headed their way, and for a change they won!"

"The 'murder' itself was a simple, though unsolved 'hole in the head' story, but it told a lot about Vancouver then. The intrigues and plots, the cover-ups and scandal, which flourished as a result of a young female body, clearly revealed the seething hysteria that, up until then, had successfully remained the suppressed sexual undertones of Vancouver's church-goers. The story had something for every kind of righteousness. For those who hated chinese and thought they were depraved and drug-infested. And for those who hated the rich and thought they were depraved and drug-infested."

"And Chinatown in 1924," Morgan continued, "seventeen years after the race riots of 1907, had become quite the thriving, respectable little establishment. The streets were clean. Mostly paved. They even had street lamps. It was a self-contained community of men: sold its own suspenders, had everything from its own water pipes to its own power elite. There were a few things in short supply once in a while, like when registration cards for Chinese were suddenly deemed necessary. So tempers were short, for instance. And only one thing missing—women!"

"Oh," I sighed, "is that all?"

"Yeah," he piped in, "who needs 'em!"

I had been listening, draped over the desk, my chin cupped in my hands, idolizing his face, breathing in his after-shave lotion. It certainly wasn't what Morgan said which interested me. After all, this private inquest could have only impressed him, since he actually lived in the very basement where this murder had taken place. A bright Sani-Queen washer and dryer now blocked the exact spot where illustrious legs once littered the floor. Morgan grew up there, and after his mother remarried, she left him the fading glory of this notorious Shaughnessy address, 4414 Osler Avenue. Ubiquitous irony? Well then, life must be full of vexations! But again, I bet there was a simpler explanation for this too.

Like, I'm willing to bet that Morgan's father, Wong Ting An, who was a pure businessman at heart, really did pick up the house for a song, regardless of its history, when real estate was real depressed towards the end of the Depression. Now, whether he got sentimental about the good old days, who can say?

Yet Morg has always maintained that his dad acquired it from a german family with four children, who couldn't get rid of it fast enough, even to a chinaman, because it was haunted by a willowy, tuneful Scottish nightingale.

I had to ask, "Why didn't she haunt you guys, Morgue?"

"Why?" he echoed, and I waited. By the tilt of his head, I could almost see him pluck a suitable explanation right out of the air. "Because ... ah, because she and the Chinese houseboy were actually friends. And we're Chinese too, you see."

"Your mother's not. She's french-canadian."

"You know, Ying, for a supposedly intelligent girl, your thinking is awfully one-dimensional. No matter where you turn, we're all related in the end."

Morgan implied that since he had both proximal and apparitional insights into this murder, he was going to make "a killing" by naming the person who had committed the most spectacular, unsolved scandal-page murder in Vancouver. Fascinated, I rested my chin on my interlaced fingers and coyly sighed again. He said it was a risky business though. If word got out, there were still plenty of people who'd take drastic measures to keep their grisly secrets.

I wonder if Morgan ever realized that he didn't need to embellish his task with romance to keep me at his side, evening after evening, in that library. It occurred to me perhaps he needed these flights of fancy to keep himself there. But as for myself, I only needed to stand close to a heroic man, with an upturned collar and a burning cigarette, who'd smile down on me tenderly. After all, it's written: "When placed face to face with one's superior, one's ego can do nothing but declare love!"

Ian Iqbal Rashid

"An/other Country,"
from *Black Markets, White Boyfriends and other acts of elision* (1991)

All this new love of my parents' country:
We have bought the videotapes together,
bought the magazines and books,
all the advertisements,
each others' responses.
We watch the slides of your visit.
Your handsome face tanned, surrounded by mango trees,
planted above the poverty,
the moist beauty,
(which you think of blowing up and then framing,
building into your walls)
majesty imposed upon majesty.

Now I watch you watch Sergeant Merrick watch poor
    Hari Kumar.
And follow as the white man's desire is twisted,
manipulated into a brutal beating.
You are affected by the actor's brown sweating
body supple under punishment. What moves you?
The pain within the geometry of the body bent?
The dignity willed in the motions of refusal?
A private fantasy promised, exploding
within every bead of sweat?
Or is it the knowledge of later:
how my body will become supple
for you, will curve and bow to your wishes
as yours can never quite bend to mine.
What moves you then?

My beauty is branded into the colour of my skin,
my strands of hair thick as snakes,
damp with the lushness of all the tropics,
My humble penis cheated by the imperial wealth of yours.

Hari's corporal punishment, mine corporeal:
Yet this is also part of my desire.
Even stroking myself against your absence
I must close my eyes and think of England.

Gregory Scofield

from *Thunder Through My Veins:*
Memories of a Métis Childhood (1999)

CHAPTER FOURTEEN: A LIGHT IN MY HEART

At fourteen
I trusted men
the way a mouse
trusts a snake.
My dreams were phantoms
fluttering
bat's wings, mad cries
of my stepfather
lurching
from back alleys, dragging me
down dark streets
crushing bone, stealing breath.

The next morning as Mom and I drove into Vancouver, an unsettling silence stood between us. I felt as if I was the cause of her life's suffering, yet at the same time I felt completely betrayed, angry at her for her lack of nerve.

A wave of utter panic swept through me as we pulled into the parking lot of the Vancouver General Hospital. Unlike the first time, it appeared over-whelmingly cold and institutional. I thought about making a break for it, but where would I go? There was no escape from the social workers, the doctors, all of the people who controlled our lives. We were at their mercy.

The Adolescent Psychiatric Unit was not at all what I expected. It was con-siderably larger, more like a group home. The living room was spacious and comfortable, decorated with colourful wildlife pictures, a couple of over-stuffed sofas and recliners, and a big-screen TV and VCR, complete with numerous video games and movies. The kitchen and dining room were com-bined into one big room. A large rectangular table and chairs accommodat-ed the unit's fourteen residents and staff. Directly across the way was a small classroom which held desks and bookshelves, correspondence material, vari-ous books, and school supplies.

The reception area was located by the main door and was covered com-pletely by plexiglass, as medication was dispensed there. A long hallway ran throughout the unit and on either side were offices and bedrooms. At the north end of the unit were the offices of the head psychiatrist and ward supervisor. Opposite the main door were two separate washrooms and a small, unfurnished, padded room, which I later discovered was the "time-out room."

After our tour we were greeted by Dr. McQuade, the head psychiatrist. He was typical of the doctors I had seen at PAU: middle-aged and balding, impeccably dressed. Though he seemed friendly and welcoming, I took an instant dislike to him. He led us to his office where we were introduced to the ward supervisor, a petite middle-aged East Indian woman named Nan Sharma. I shook her hand coldly and took my seat. She gave Mom a warm smile, shook her hand, and then directed her to the chair beside mine before introducing the rest of the group.

The two youth-care workers that had been assigned to my case were Michael DuBois and Carrie Smith. Both were in their mid-twenties and appeared friendly and eager to help *too* eager, I thought. Lastly, we were introduced to Ann, the schoolteacher. She flashed us a polite smile, then focused her attention on Dr. McQuade.

Dr. McQuade rambled on for a good hour about the program, stopping periodically to ask if Mom or I had any questions. He finally finished and excused himself, saying that he had other patients to see. I remember thinking, *Yeah, like I signed up to be one of your God damn patients.* I hoped it would be the last I saw of him, and I could tell by the look on Mom's face she felt the same. She had told me numerous stories about her experiences with psychiatrists, none of them good. I resented how everyone in the room seemed to be looking at me and Mom. I was sure they saw us as poor welfare trash, more so Mom, as some sort of whacked-out pillhead who couldn't control me.

After Dr. McQuade left, the atmosphere in the room seemed to change. Nan stood up, smoothed out her lime-green sari and began to explain the ins and outs of the program. "The program," she began, "works on stages of behaviour. All new residents start on stage two, which allows you the privileges of the unit like watching TV or playing video games. You are allowed to wear your own clothes, eat with the other residents, and stay up until ten o'clock."

"The third stage," she encouragingly nodded, clasping her hands together like a saint, "means even more freedom. You are permitted supervised outings, the use of the phone, and are allowed visitors, primarily your Mom and family. Also, you are allowed to smoke, if you do."

"The fourth stage," she continued, "is a little more difficult to achieve, but with hard work and perseverance it can be accomplished. Once this happens, you will be allowed three hours of unsupervised time in which you can leave the unit. You must try," she cautioned, "not to get back-staged, especially to stage one. All of your personal belongings will be confiscated and you will be confined to your room in hospital pyjamas. As well, your phone privileges will be suspended and you will be required to eat in your room, *alone*."

I felt as if she'd stressed the word "alone" as some sort of scare a tactic, as if she was threatening me. I looked at her defiantly. "Well," I quipped, mustering up as much sarcasm as possible, "exactly how hard is it to move between the stages—and *exactly who* makes these *important* decisions?"

Nan cleared her throat and smoothed out the invisible lines from her lap. "The decisions," she said calmly, much too calmly, "are made by myself, Dr. McQuade, and the youth-care staff. We meet once a week to discuss your progress or *lack of* it." Her words hit the intended target, and I could feel the blood rush to my face. Mom reached over and squeezed my hand, but I was just as angry with her. Nan stood up and smiled, signifying the end of the meeting. The rest of the group remained seated. She asked Mom if she had any questions. Mom, looking as defeated as I felt, mumbled no. Nan followed her to the door, assuring her that everything would be fine.

Then like a flash, I suddenly realized Mom was about to leave—without me. They were already halfway down the hallway when I broke into a dead run. I reached the main door and had my hand on the push bar when I felt a powerful grip on my shoulder. I swung my fists wildly, screaming at the top of my lungs. But within a matter of seconds, I was wrestled to the floor by a large orderly.

Mom, Nan, Michael, and Carrie stood over me, silently bearing witness to my futility. I was so angry I couldn't even cry. Mom helped me to my feet and held me closely. She was crying and shaking badly, and I suddenly realized how much I loved her. She hugged me and whispered in my ear, "Greg, I am sorry. Whatever you do, play their games. Act like you don't know anything. Remember that I love you." I was completely astounded. It was the first time she'd ever apologized to me, seemed to comprehend the hopelessness of my life and how I *felt* about it. She kissed me and then disappeared out the door, which to my surprise locked automatically. I was trapped.

The first few days I spent a great deal of time in my room. I had been through a tiring succession of talking to doctors, doing their various tests, and I wanted to be alone. They always asked the same stupid questions, things like, "What do you fantasize about while masturbating?" or "Do you ever hear voices?" or "Have you ever thought about killing someone?" Of course I had thought about it, even felt like it. But I certainly wasn't going to tell them that. They would lock me up and throw away the key.

Yet, strangely enough, their questions left me feeling as if there was something truly wrong with me. I still thought about boys more than I did girls. And sometimes I heard Indian songs on the wind, sometimes voices, too. But they were good voices—voices of the Grandmothers and Grandfathers.

As the weeks dragged on and the tests became more difficult, I became more and more depressed. I kept thinking back to my overdose, wishing more than ever that I'd been successful. It was obvious that no one could be trusted, especially adults.

With a lot of coaxing from Michael and Carrie, I tried to mix more with the other residents. But I had nothing in common with them. Sure, they were just as fucked up as I was, but most of them came from good homes, had nice things and the attitude that went along with it. I viewed them as superior, much the way I thought about the kids at school. To me, they were spoiled white brats who had everything handed to them. They had no clue of the real world, let alone any idea of true pain and suffering.

I wasn't engaging with the other residents as was hoped by Nan and Dr. McQuade. I missed Aunty and the comforting smell of her house, the fresh bannock and apple pie she baked for me. I missed her stories and laughter, all the things that had given me such happiness when I was a little boy. Suddenly I felt small again, needful of her love and steady assurance. How I would have given anything to drift off to sleep to one of her Carter Family tunes!

Then one afternoon I was told that a special worker was coming to see me. She was a Native hospital liaison worker who dealt mostly with elders and people from up north. The following afternoon she came to see me. I instantly liked her. Rachel was Chilcotin from Williams Lake, in her mid-twenties, happy and unassuming, and full of jokes. Her dark eyes sparkled with a playfulness that put me completely at ease. She teased me about looking so white, saying that one side of the toaster must have been broken when I was born.

I gave her a tour of the unit and showed her some of my poems, which she read with great interest and appreciation, especially the ones about being Native. We talked for three or more hours and I told her everything. She didn't say a word or push me to tell her how I really felt, as the doctors had. Instead she listened patiently, encouraging me to keep talking. After our visit, I walked her to the door and she gave me a big hug as if she'd known me for years. She promised to come every week and I was overjoyed, feeling at long last I'd found a soul to confide in.

I recall one occasion when Rachel was unable to visit me. I was disappointed enough, without the added frustration of the unit. I became totally enraged when another resident made a racial comment about Indians being stupid and dirty. I retreated to my room and as usual tore up all of my poems, feeling ugly and worthless. After my fit was over, I slumped to the floor among the shredded paper and cried hysterically until I had nothing left. I pulled myself together and was straightening up when someone knocked at my door. When Michael walked in he was relaxed and smiling, which made me feel all the more embarrassed and stupid. He helped me clean up in silence and asked if I wanted to talk. I felt better, but wanted to be alone. I thanked him for his help and he hugged me, then left.

I thought about Michael that night. He was different from Don and Uncle Tim. He was gentle and kind, not the least bit threatening or intimidating. He had a sincerity, a realness that I could sense. Best of all, he knew when to pull back and give me space. There was also something else that I liked about him, something that I couldn't explain, although I found myself thinking about his blue eyes and rugged face. He was strong and tall, forever smiling with his eyes.

Nevertheless, I stayed clear of him for a couple of weeks. Sometimes I went with the other residents, mostly the girls, to the time-out room and listened to him play his guitar and sing. His voice was so beautiful that I couldn't even look at him. But I felt him watching me, singing loud and clear. By the time he finished the last chorus, my heart would be pounding, inexplicably aching. I would dash off to my room and write a poem about him, trying to capture the emotions he invoked in me, the beauty of his voice and how it had reached out and touched me. I would fly off to an imaginary place far beyond the wire mesh covering the windows, a place where Michael and I could be equals.

I began to feel more and more comfortable around him, and looked forward to his coming on to shift. I started to talk more, feeling safe and secure in his presence. *At last*, I thought, *there's a good man in the world—a man I can really trust.*

Even Rachel noticed a difference in me, commenting on my constant chattering and joking. I spent more time with the other residents, feeling a new and wonderful confidence. I even made a wholehearted attempt to get along with Nan, Dr. McQuade, and the other doctors.

Although I didn't fully understand it at the time, I knew that Michael favoured me. I could see it in his eyes and I could hear it in his voice. Often at bedtime, he came to my room and we would talk. He told me about himself and about his childhood in Quebec. He talked about his travels and his friends, and I thought he had a wonderful and exciting life. Although I missed my own life and freedom, his nightly visits somehow made my incarceration easier. I was amazed by his deep concern and understanding.

Already a month and a half had gone by, and without realizing it, I had adjusted to the flow of the unit. I started to deal with my anger, completely letting my guard down, allowing the doctors more insight into my head and heart. I was moving quickly through the stages, and I was a role model for newer residents. In fact, I was so comfortable with the routine that I dreaded going home, dreaded the thought of losing Michael, I had begun to feel safe, tingling with a new sense of myself—something that had to do with my heart and body.

One night, shortly after Michael came on to shift, something unexpected happened. I was already in bed, lying on my stomach, when I heard the door quietly open. Michael softly called me, and I knew without even looking at him that something was different. He crawled in beside me and started to rub my back. "You're so beautiful," he murmured. "I love the feel of your skin. It's so soft, so tight." He ran his fingers through my hair and nestled into my neck, his breath hot and heavy. I could smell alcohol. "You're so incredibly strong and mature," he groaned, "so different from the others."

Then without warning, he slipped his hand beneath my pyjama bottoms. I was absolutely frozen. He kissed the back of my neck and explored my body without speaking. I felt his body, his penis against me. "I've thought so much about kissing you," he confessed, turning me over so that our mouths met. He pressed his lips to mine and kissed me the way I had kissed my girlfriends, long and deep. I was petrified, and yet I felt joyously alive, pulsing like the blood rushing to my head.

Before Michael left, he told me that he loved me. He made me promise to keep *our secret*, half apologizing for his behaviour. I assured him that I would-n't say a word, convinced it was just as much my fault. After all, I had dreamed about this night and written poems about it. I was older and more mature— at least that's what I wanted to believe. But inside I felt like a kid. I was suddenly afraid of our new relationship, afraid of the things he'd done and said. And I certainly didn't want him to know that. I wanted him to think that I was capable of making adult decisions

Michael never mentioned that night, nor did we speak about it. I started to think maybe it was one of my crazy imaginings. But my body felt different. I felt nervous, yet oddly familiar in his presence. I looked for any reason to be alone with him, even if it meant acting out on purpose. But I also knew these were silly ploys, games that would make me look even more childish. Adults didn't act that way. And here I was, acting as if I was ten years old. I knew that I needed to be careful for Michael's sake. Nan and Dr. McQuade weren't stupid. Neither was Rachel.

As far as I knew, our secret was safe. No one suspected anything. Yet no matter how hard I tried, I found myself acting out in strange ways. I couldn't seem to help myself. I felt confused: destructively angry one minute and so in love the next. I felt as if Michael had tricked me, lied to me. Then again, I was sure that he truly loved me. Of course he couldn't openly display affection or come to me every night. An adult would understand that.

One afternoon, while I was writing, Michael came to my room. It was the first time in weeks that we were alone. He hugged and kissed me and apologized for his absence. He told me that he had a big surprise—he was going to take me out for supper. I was so excited, I threw my arms around him. Although I was on stage four of the program, I hadn't stepped foot outside the hospital, fearful that I might miss an opportunity to be alone with him.

Finally, seven o'clock rolled around and we left. Vancouver seemed like a brand new place. The lights were glimmering all around us and I pressed my face to the window of the car, drinking in the ambience of the city. Michael smiled at my excitement and reached over and kissed me.

We went to a busy cafe in the west end, and for the first time ever I saw men holding hands and kissing openly in the street. After supper we drove through Stanley Park and Michael parked the car near English Bay. We stood on the seawall, watching the lights shimmer and dance on the water. All around us there were high-rises, their windows aglow as if each suite held a party. I wondered where Michael lived—where I would live after I was released. He had promised to look after me.

Sensing my wonder, Michael took my hands and drew me close. "What are you thinking?" he asked, looking into my eyes.

"Oh, nothing. I'm just happy to be away from the unit."

He smiled and tightened his hold. "I think you've got the most beautiful lips—Indian lips," he said. He kissed me again, only this time there was an urgency about him. He pressed into me and I felt his excitement, his hunger. Unlike before, I, too, was excited. How I ached for him to take me home, to touch his naked body the way he had touched me.

On the way back to the unit I recall wondering about sex. I knew how to "do it" with girls, but boys were different. Besides the twins, I had no *real* idea what men did together. I thought about the time I had gone to stay with a friend of mother's when I was eight. I had to sleep with her son, Brian, who was seven years older. He had all sorts of dirty magazines. He was looking at them and touching himself. He wanted me to rub his penis, and so I did. Then he wanted me to put it in my mouth or bum, but I got scared and said no. I knew it was bad and told Mom. I wasn't allowed to go back there and I didn't see Brian until years later when his mother died. Even after all that time, I felt guilty, as if I had caused him a great deal of shame and trouble. And now it was the same with Michael. Only this time I was going to keep silent.

It was almost three months since my arrival at the unit. I was a model resident, doing all that had been asked of me. I had come out of my shell and received glowing reports from the doctors, Michael and Carrie, even Rachel. My anger, so they said, was more constructive and healthy. I was no longer a danger to myself or anyone else.

But secretly I felt terrible inside. I still trashed the love poems I wrote for Michael, ashamed of my feelings and desires, and sometimes, especially when I felt his attention slipping, I hit, scratched, or bit myself in private. I felt as if I deserved it, almost wishing that Don was here to beat me up. Michael seldom came to my room any more and it seemed he was trying his best to avoid me. I couldn't understand why. He'd said that I was beautiful, strong, and mature. He'd promised me happiness.

I began to realize that love was never without cost, that I forever ended up paying a heavy price—my heart and spirit—for a few moments of happiness.

Two weeks after our dinner, Nan told me that I was going home—home to Mom. How could Michael do this to me! I hadn't pestered him or acted out in any way. Most of all, I had kept our secret.

I was crying even before I got to my room. I started to hit myself in the face, disgusted by my own pitiful tears, ashamed of myself for trusting Michael. The more intense the pain, the more I cried, and the more I cried, the harder I hit myself. Then like a tornado, the rage turned outward. I smashed everything in sight, demolishing anything that wasn't screwed down. I tore the drapes down, ripped the blankets and sheets off the bed, and smashed the night-stand and rocking chair to pieces. I ripped up my poems.

The entire unit was buzzing around my door like frantic bees. Before I could do any more damage, I was restrained by two orderlies who gave me a shot and held me down until it took effect. I was losing all sense of time and space, but I knew Michael was nowhere around.

I awoke much later on the couch in the living room. Carrie sat beside me, scribbling notes on a silver clipboard. The unit was dark and quiet, and I wasn't sure if I'd been sleeping a couple of hours or a couple of days. Carrie fixed me something to eat and I ate in silence, trying to recall what I'd done. I wasn't sure if it had actually happened. My face was sore and I noticed my hands were swollen and bruised.

I suddenly remembered my outburst and asked Carrie about Michael. She looked at me for a long moment, offering up a hopeful smile. "Well, kiddo," she began, "he's leaving for Hawaii in the morning and he'll be gone for a month." My heart sank. Suddenly I wanted to tell her everything. But my anger was quickly replaced by emptiness. I retreated to that inner room that was mine alone, where no one could hurt me.

One week later I was released. It was determined, after intense observation, that my outburst was due to the anxiety I felt about going home. But inside I knew the truth and guarded it with my life, secretly hoping that Michael would come back for me. Every day I waited for him to call, even to say goodbye, but he never did.

I had written close to sixty poems in three months and had nothing to show for it, not even the memory of a favourite line, likely inspired by Michael.

CHAPTER FIFTEEN: SPIRIT-KEEPER

an old woman was soothing me in Cree I
cried in her lap   she kept singing   singing
an old man gave me four eagle feathers   four
songs   four stories   then painted my face
divided in two

It took me a long time to get over Michael, to forgive myself for trusting him. I suppose I still carry a certain amount of resentment towards him, as I do with most of the men from my younger life. But many of those long-ago pains are behind me. I have been able to find healing, to grow into the sort of man I so desperately needed as a child.

It disturbs me to think about the teenagers who, like me, experience this kind of introduction to the gay community. Michael not only violated a position of trust, but he scarred me deeply, shaped my image of gay men, myself, and the future. At one point, not so long ago, I believed the ultimate curse in life was to be gay. Sadly, Michael perpetuated the negative myth of gay men as predators, sexual perverts, and pedophiles.

Mom had no idea about Michael, nor was I going to tell her. I just couldn't bear to have her think Don was right about me being a "poofter." I struggled with my feelings in silence, moving through the days so deeply wounded, plagued by thoughts of suicide. Finally I couldn't stand it any more and wrote Michael a long letter, telling him everything I felt. I begged him to take me back, promising to love him until the end of time. The next morning I caught the bus into town and dropped the letter off at the hospital. I stood outside the door, uncertain as to whether I should give it to him personally or just leave it on the doorstep. I was afraid to see him and so I left it outside, hoping that only he would find it.

A few days later the phone rang and Mom answered it. By the look on her face, I was certain it was Michael. But it was Dr. McQuade. He had found the letter and read it. When he questioned me, I denied everything. All I could think about was protecting Michael. I wanted so much to believe that he still loved me. Dr. McQuade never called back, and as far as I knew the whole thing was dropped. Michael, of course, didn't call either. I never saw him again.

Years later I met one of the youth-care workers from the unit (he had restrained me the day of my outburst) who was teaching a workshop on Anger Management. I was working with young offenders, now a youth-care worker myself. After the workshop I introduced myself. He barely remembered me, but then I asked about Michael. His face grew pale and apprehensive and, without elaborating, he told me that Michael had left the unit shortly after I did, that he'd found a job with mentally challenged people. I later discovered (through Rachel) that he'd been bothering another Native boy at the unit.

So much of that time is a blur, but I do remember writing every day, even though I eventually destroyed my work. I wrote numerous poems and stories about being Native, wanting to connect myself to something spiritually nourishing, wanting to find some sort of belonging. The writing kept me alive, kept me somehow connected to an ancient world where I found peace.

While I was in the hospital, Rachel had encouraged me to find out more about my family background. I went to Salmon Arm to visit Aunty Sandra, and while I was there I wrote a letter to my grandfather's sister-in-law, asking if she had any information on the Scofields. She wrote back and told me about Kohkum Otter, the secrecy around Great-grandma Ida and the shame her children felt at being half-breeds. That letter made me feel very ambivalent. On one hand, I was happy to finally know the truth and, on the other, I was disappointed that we weren't *pure* Indians. I recall thinking that maybe Grandpa and his brothers and sisters were right to feel ashamed. Half-breeds were nothing.

After I returned home I showed Mom the letter, then threw it out, deciding to disassociate myself from anything white or mixed-blood. Kohkum Otter was Cree, so I was Cree, too. Oddly enough, I still thought of Mom and my aunts as white. How could I think of them differently? They certainly didn't seem interested in anything Native. I took a new interest in learning about the old ways—the Cree ways—and once again went to Aunty, who continued to teach me Cree and retold my favourite stories from my childhood.

One story was about *We-sak-e-jack*, the Trickster, and how he had tricked the ducks and geese into coming to his lodge for a special ceremony called the Blind Dance. Once the ducks and geese were assembled into a circle, *We-sak-e-jack* told them, "My brothers, this is a very sacred dance taught to me by my grandfather. You must keep your eyes tightly shut while I am singing, for if you open them, the medicine of this dance will be lost." And so *We-sak-e-jack* began to play his drum and sing. The ducks and geese danced in a circle, going round and round, their eyes tightly closed. But every now and then the drum would stop for no apparent reason. One little duck, who'd grown suspicious, decided to take a little peek. To his horror, he saw what *We-sak-e-jack* was doing. "Brothers," he cried, "We-sak-e-jack is killing us for his supper!" The birds took off in every direction, but *We-sak-e-jack* only laughed. "Blind Dance," he chuckled to himself. "Stupid birds!"

Besides going to Aunty for information, I also called Grandma Francis, and she, too, did her best to help me. As always she encouraged me to dance, letting me know where there were powwows and gatherings.

But the most significant thing that happened was a dream that was more like a prophetic vision. Some years later I wrote about this dream in my first book, *The Gathering: Stones for the Medicine Wheel*. The book begins with a story called "*Kiskey-tayew Maskwa Osisima*" (Black Bear's Grandson). I originally changed the story so as not to give away the power of my vision. But I now feel I can share it as part of my sacred journey, a journey predestined by my grandmothers and grandfathers.

Aunty told me that, long ago, young boys were sent out into the wilderness on their first vision quest. They were required to fast and pray for four days, thus cleansing their minds and bodies to receive a guardian spirit that would lead them through life. My dream was much like these vision quests. It began in an old cemetery somewhere in the wilderness. Among the carved headstones and crosses there were totem poles that seemed to reach the sky. Some of them held mortuary boxes where the bones of ancient people had been laid to rest.

There were other boys with me in the dream, all the same age. Some of them appeared anxious and impatient while others, like me, were scared and unhappy. An old man, whom we called Grandfather, gathered us together and began to talk to us. "Grandsons," he began, "today is a very sacred day, for today you are no longer boys but men. Some of you are old in spirit and some of you are still very young. Some of you," he continued, pointing to the mortuary boxes, "do not come from here, but these are the bones of your grandmothers and grandfathers. You are about to embark upon a very sacred journey. If you become scared, think of them, for they will help you. They will give you strength. Some of you will become lost and frightened. Look within your heart and there you will hear a sacred song. Sing it and you will again find your way.

"Grandsons," Grandfather instructed, "you are to go towards the east, the Place Where All Life Begins. Along your journey you will meet a black bear. Do not be afraid of him, for he, too, is your grandfather. Approach him respectfully, and if your heart is good, he will let you pass. He will give you medicine."

As we started out, the sky grew dark and claps of thunder rolled in the distance. Soon we became separated, and I found myself wandering alone in the dark forest. It began to rain, and peals of lightning tore across the sky, illuminating the treetops. I became hopelessly lost, feeling angry and frustrated. I started to cry, thinking that I would never find my way. But then I remembered the bones of the Grandmothers and Grandfathers. I sat down on a fallen tree, closed my eyes, and listened to my heart. Suddenly, I heard the song. How beautiful it was! I could hear the Grandmothers singing high above the Grandfathers, their voices strong and powerful.

I started out again, singing, only this time I felt as if my feet were being led by an invisible force. Soon it was morning. I walked and walked until I reached a small clearing. There in the distance, I saw the black bear. My heart felt as if it was going to stop beating, but I approached him respectfully.

As I stood before him, Grandfather Black Bear stood up on his hind legs and looked deeply into my eyes, and I felt him say to my heart, *Grandson, you have nothing to fear. Your heart is good and you have much work to do. Go now and do not look back.* He fell down on all fours and ambled off into the forest. I began to run and my body suddenly felt light and graceful. As I ran faster, my feet lifted off the ground and I began to fly. I flew above the treetops, looking down upon our little shack and myself sleeping in bed. I awoke with the sacred song in my head.

As I wasn't on a vision quest, at least in the physical sense, I'm not certain why I was given this dream. But this is not for me to ask. I believe *Kee-chee-man-*

itow, the Creator, touched me in a sacred way, gave me power I would need later on. Although I have lived in many places and done many things since my vision, it is still as vivid to me today as it was sixteen years ago. I have been given Bear Medicine—healing medicine—and I honour this medicine by writing. I believe this is what Grandfather Black Bear meant when he said, *You have much work to do.*

I went back to school in May. The Native Education Centre was like heaven compared to public school. It was an adult basic-education program in Vancouver that provided upgrading and cultural/spiritual courses for urban Native people. The entire program, except for math, was taught from a Native perspective using the works of Native writers and spiritual people. As well there were classes in beadwork and leatherwork, hide tanning and drum-making, classes on powwow singing and dancing, and even traditional Native cooking.

Most of the students were older, some of them Mom's age, married or shacked-up with families. At first, I felt awkward because of my age, but I soon realized it didn't matter. Everyone treated me as an equal, more so than I'd ever felt in public school. I was excited to be with my own people and to meet students from tribes from across Canada: Nishga'a, Haida, Salish, Blackfoot, Mohawk, Cree, and Ojibway. To some degree, we were all displaced people, survivors who had either been through foster care, in jail, or on the streets. Some of the students had lost their children to social services or had come out of abusive, drinking relationships. All of us were struggling to heal the past, to find some sort of meaning in who we were.

Most of the teachers were white but sympathetic to the Indian cause, even somewhat radical. I began to learn about people like Anna Mae Aquash, Leonard Peltier, Dennis Banks, and Russell Means, about the political battles and injustices they and other American Indian people suffered at Wounded Knee in the late seventies. I also began to learn about Canadian Native history: the truth behind the government's broken promises and the residential schools—all of the information that was avoided in high school.

I remember one teacher in particular, whom almost everyone admired and respected. Peter was from Chicago and supposedly Native, although it was rumoured he was Jewish. I didn't care either way because he was a good teacher, more so because everything he taught had a political agenda. For English and social studies he encouraged us to debate his opinions, many of which were from a Eurocentric perspective. Of course, he did this on purpose, but some of the students took it to heart, practically coming to blows with him. Nevertheless, his "fire-starter" teaching style hit the mark. Many of us would be close to armed resistance by the end of his class.

Now Mom and I seemed to reach a new level in our relationship. She treated me more like an adult, often talking to me about her feelings and child-hood experiences. She even took an interest in some of the things I was learn-ing, primarily the political struggles of Native people. We would have long conversations about some of the books I brought home. She seemed gen-uinely interested, and I started to see her differently. How, I wasn't sure, although I found myself including her more in my newfound awareness.

A short time later I moved out on my own. I found a small attic suite close to school in the house of an older German couple. They were apprehensive at first because of my age, but I promised to be responsible, clean, and quiet. Because I was too young to get welfare, Mom paid the rent and gave me gro-cery money out of her cheque. The ministry didn't know, and so they con-tinued to pay for my tuition and school supplies, but that was all. If I needed anything else, I went to Mom.

When school let out, I found a summer job with a Native theatre company called Spirit-Song. The program was for Native youth and was meant to teach us theatrical training and work skills. The director was a well-known Native actress, who for some reason disliked me. She made me feel out of place and untalented, as if I was wasting her time.

I became more and more self-conscious of my appearance, doing what I could to fit in. I dyed my hair black and spent every available minute in the sun. Thankfully, my skin had a bit of dark pigment and I was able to turn nut brown. The only thing I couldn't change was the colour of my eyes. Oh, how I hated having grey eyes.

I devoted myself to Spirit-Song, to becoming a great actor. I was excited by our upcoming tour of the legend pieces we'd been rehearsing, various West Coast legends that we had adapted for the stage. I played the Seagull in the Haida legend *How Raven Stole the Sunlight*. The main character was, of course, the Raven, played by an actor whom I secretly envied for being more mascu-line and Native looking. As the story went, he steals the sun and keeps it hid-den in a box. My character, the flamboyant Seagull, somehow tricks him and saves the world from eternal darkness. It wasn't a glamorous role, but it was a funny one.

We were scheduled to perform at a Native theatre festival on Vancouver Island in July. I went to the beach every day after work and studied the seag-ulls for hours. I was determined to upstage the Raven. The Native communi-ty would love me and the director would see that I was talented and worthy of her time.

Martin Cannon

"The Regulation of First Nations Sexuality,"
Canadian Journal of Native Studies 18.1 (1998)

INTRODUCTION

Several aspects of Canadian political reality have led historical sociologists to maintain that race, gender and sexuality are not separate categories of experience and analysis but dynamic sets of social constructions which, as they interconnect, impact upon individuals and their (re)productive activities in distinctive, historically specific ways (Ng, 1993: 50; Parr, 1995: 356–60; McClintock, 1995). Informed by this understanding, any comprehensive analysis of Canada's Indian Act and early Indian policy should examine how configurations of racist, sexist and heterosexist knowledges were manifested in the process(es) of colonization. Such an analysis would seek to document the endeavours toward making (European) heterosexuality compulsory within status Indian communities (Rich, 1993). Such an analysis, in its most ambitious sense, would illuminate the convergent discrimination(s) directed toward those preferring same-sex intimacies, and make a contribution toward an integrated theory of race, gender and sexuality. Such an endeavour, though far from exhaustive, is the primary focus of this paper.

The first part of the paper will provide a critical review of the literature which suggests that a broad range of gender and erotic relationships existed among Aboriginal populations at early contact. Part of this exercise will be to specify homosexuality as an analytic category describing in turn the difficulty with using terms such as "gay" and "lesbian" to describe historic First Nations sexual categories (Whitehead, 1993). The second part of the paper will then document how racist sexism and heterosexism worked together to legislate and define First Nations political reality. Upon illustrating the interactive relationship among these systems of domination, I will conclude that none of the development of class relations, the regulation of sexuality, racism or patriarchy can be explained as mutually exclusive.

SEXUALITY AND GENDER IN NATIVE NORTH AMERICA

Even prior to Confederation and the emergence of the first statute entitled the Indian Act in 1876, the colonial enterprise in Canada had virtually enforced a system of Eurocentric policies, beliefs and value systems upon First Nations. The earliest missionaries, for example, were determined to "civilize" the Indian populations by attempting to indoctrinate a Christian ethos and patriarchal familial structure (Brodribb, 1984). It was within the context of such a conversion mission that same-sex erotic and sexual diversity was negatively evaluated and often condemned (Kinsman, 1987: 71; Katz, 1983: 28). This mission was a project fueled by heterosexism.[1]

One of the often quoted passages related to the views of the early missionaries is that of the Jesuit, Joseph François Lafitau. Speaking of the erotic and gender relations which he observed among Native North Americans from 1711–17, he noted:

> If there were women with manly courage who prided themselves upon the profession of warrior, which seems to become men alone, there were also men cowardly enough to live as women ... they believe they are honoured by debasing themselves to all of women's occupations; they never marry ... (Joseph François Lafitau, quoted in Katz, 1976: 288).

The later diaries of the Jesuit, Pedro Font, resonated with the observations made by Lafitau. Only Pedro Font also identified an impending need to eradicate all such erotic or sexual relations and in their place establish a system of Christian morality. Making an assessment based on his observations taken from the expedition of Juan Bautista de Anza from 1775–76, he noted:

> Among the women I saw men dressed like women, with whom they go about regularly, never joining the men ... From this I inferred they must be hermaphrodites, but from what I learned later I understood that they were sodomites, dedicated to nefarious practices. From all the foregoing I conclude that in this matter of incontinence there will be much to do when the Holy Faith and the Christian religion are established among them (Pedro Font, quoted in Katz, 1976: 291).

Missionary accounts of sodomy were not always so subtly expressed. Jean Bernard Bossu, whose translated journals from the interior of North America between 1751 and 1762 spoke of "perverse" addictions among the Aboriginal nations he observed, expressed it thusly:

> The people of this nation are generally of a brutal and coarse nature. You can talk to them as much as you want about the mysteries of our religion; they always reply that it is beyond their comprehension. They are morally quite perverted, and most of them are addicted to sodomy. These corrupt men, who have long hair and wear short skirts like women, are held in great contempt (Jean Bernard Bossu, quoted in Katz, 1976: 291).

The spectrum of erotic and gender diversity recorded in times of early contact suggests that same-sex relations were considered to be of some moral and political consequence.[2] Labelled as "nefarious," the relations that did exist were seen as illegitimate. Clearly, there is no superior foundation for such "common sense" forms of paternalistic judgement, but we can explain the claims to Euro-Christian preeminence as grounded in the ethos of the historical period.[3] Informed by notions of supremacy, ideologies of racial inferiority and of "civilized" (hetero)sexual behaviour, the early Europeans saw First Nations (indeed all non-Europeans) as subordinate and undeveloped entities (Miles, 1989; Said, 1979).[4] Of pertinent interest in the aforementioned passages is also the way they reveal the interrelated nature of all systems of oppression.

Configurations of racist, patriarchal and heterosexist knowledges worked together to influence the views of the missionaries. Being a "nefarious sodomite," for example, not only meant "debasing" oneself by "cowardly" appropriating the gender and assumed sexual roles of a devalued (in this case) female class, it was an "unproductive" realm that, as I will describe in further detail, required complete refashioning. Salvation (sexual and otherwise) was to rest under the auspices of a religiously superior race, Europeans: a motive that was clearly racist. Salvation was something that required the regulation of a "savage" sexuality thought antithetical to Christian decorum, gendered domestic relations, and moral rationality. There may be reason to suggest, however, that the view toward individuals referred to as "nefarious" by the missionaries was an unshared sentiment among some of the original inhabitants of North America; it has been suggested that the berdache enjoyed an esteemed role within certain communities prior to contact.[5]

Among the Bella Coola Nation located in what is now called British Colombia, Franz Boas noted the special status accorded to the berdache, a status that was central to an origin myth on food (Boas, reprinted in Roscoe, 1988: 84). Toleration of the berdache and even "institutionalized homosexuality" is suggested in more contemporary anthropological literature and Native testimonials (Benedict, quoted in Roscoe 1988: 16–17; Mead, quoted in Roscoe, 1988: 19; Owlfeather, 1988: 100; Kenny, 1988: 153). Sharing a similar perspective, Kenny (1988: 26) has noted that:

> Some tribes, such as the Minois, actually trained young men to become homosexuals and concubines of men. The Cheyenne and Sioux of the plains may not have purposely trained young men to become berdaches but certainly accepted homosexuals more readily than perhaps other tribes.

In short, some have been inclined toward emphasizing the berdache as a recognized and legitimate social institution. Nonetheless, it is necessary to look upon this claim with some scepticism.

First, there is some difficulty in making cross-cultural comparisons like the one made by Kenny (1988) in the above noted excerpt. In his postulation, the tradition of berdache gets conflated with "homosexual" leaving little or no recognition of Native sex/gender systems. Such an interpretation is limited, for as Harriet Whitehead has argued, "sexual practices and beliefs must be understood within the context of the specific gender-meaning system of the culture in question" (Whitehead, 1993: 523; Rubin, 1975: 159). If we take a brief look at Native North American cultures, we grow increasingly familiar with the weaknesses of "homosexual" as an analytic category.

The evidence to substantiate the claim that the Native North American berdache was an equivalent to the modern-day "homosexual" is limited. As Harriet Whitehead explains, such cross-cultural investigations tend to posit a shared sexual identity between the gender-crossing berdache and modern "homosexual": the very place where contradictions start to emerge (1993: 498). Alluding to the importance of sex/gender systems, Whitehead explains:

> Western society foregrounds erotic orientation as the basis for dividing people into socially significant categories, but for Native North Americans, occupational pursuits and dress/demeanour were the important determinants of an individual's social classification, and sexual object choice was its trailing rather than leading edge (1993: 498).

Whitehead does not suggest that the role of the berdache excluded same-sex sexual behaviour (1993: 514). She illuminates instead a sex/gender system that renders one's chosen occupational behaviour of much greater importance than sexual object choice when it comes to social classification (Whitehead, 1993: 511; 513). The role of berdache, according to Whitehead, was more about gender-crossing than it was about sexual relations. In making this point, she alerts anthropologist and social historian alike to the weaknesses of "homosexual" as an analytic category. In an historic or cross-cultural interpretation, modern-day Western categories may be unknown to the culture or past under study. The category's applicability is subsequently limited. This is a position that is broadened by constructionist theorists who are interested in the history of sexuality. Foucault is exemplary.

For Foucault, sexuality is not a natural given, but the name that is granted to a historical construct (1978: 105; 127). Sexuality, in other words, is never more than a set of ever-varying developments tied to the mode of production and prevailing social/political realities (Foucault, 1978: 5–6; Padgug, 1989: 58). In short, sexuality and subsequently related behaviour is socially constructed. Failing to recognize this category as such presents the social historian with conceptual and interpretive difficulties. Kenny's postulation in the above noted excerpt on Native "homosexuals" is again problematic.

The inclination to extract some modern-day notion of "homosexual," "gay" or even "lesbian" Native identity from the missionary statements on "sodomy" cannot be clearly substantiated. Nor can references to Indigenous sexualities be referred to as "homosexual" as this is known in the historical present. There are at least two reasons for this. First and foremost, the history of sexuality does not permit a conclusion such as the second. Foucault, for example, reminded us that the concept of "homosexuality" did not even emerge in western discourse until the 19th century (1978: 43). To be sure, and this is my second point, the missionaries were speaking of "sodomy" and "nefarious practices" as a set of sex related acts. The missionary statements, though they may speak of "morally perverse" behaviour and the outwardly physical attributes of the berdache, make no explicit mention of a specific personality type, sexual sensibility or sexual identity. It is not possible to make such an inference on that basis.

It is necessary to distinguish between behaviour and identity when we apply an analytic category such as "homosexual" to the historic past. We cannot take the sexual acts reported to have been witnessed by the missionaries and convert them to a history of personality or contemporary "gay" identity. For on this question of identity, Robert Padgug insists:

> These identities are not inherent in the individual. In order to be gay ... more than individual inclinations (however we might conceive of those) or homosexual activity is required; entire ranges of social attitudes and the construction of particular cultures, subcultures, and social relations are first necessary (1989: 60).

In sum, while it may be true that homosexual behaviour existed in history, we cannot call those whose behaviour was so inclined either "gay," "lesbian" or homosexual as these are known in the historic present.[6]

The third problem with postulating on and about "Native homosexuality" is in alluding to its prevalence as "institutionalized." This suggestion, as noted by Kenny and others, tends to overshadow any critical understanding of the practice from a culturally-informed point of view. This characterization of homosexuality threatens to foreground the homosexual sex act over and above gender-crossing, occupational choice and the distribution of (cross-gendered) tasks. The effect of this characterization is to suggest that sexual object choice was more important than gender-crossed behaviour in Native social classification systems. A mistaken consequence is thereby afforded to the homosexual or even heterosexual sex act since some berdache "lapsed into anatomic heterosexuality and on occasion even marriage without any loss of their cross-sex status" (Whitehead, 1990: 512; also see Schnarch, 1992: 115). In sum, it is important to recognize when we speak of "institutionalized homosexuality" that:

[H]omosexual acts were not in any way immediately suggestive of an enduring disposition such as that which characterized the gender-crosser (or the "homosexual" in our culture), and such acts were not confused with gender-crossing in the Native mind (Whitehead, 1990: 511).

This brief investigation on sexuality and cross-gendered behaviour in Native North America provides some insight into the diversity of erotic and gender relations that existed among a selection of Aboriginal populations at early contact. Through the use of secondary documents provided by Katz (1976), this investigation also illustrates the missionary response to such interactions. By no means exhaustive, what I have sought to illuminate is merely the care required when using "homosexuality" to describe or interpret the historic past. To that extent, the preceding discussion permits at least three conclusions.

First, missionary statements confirm the existence of "sodomy" following (and likely even prior to) contact and nothing more. While it may be tempting to transform the Jesuit accounts to reveal a history of homosexual identity, we can deduce only that homosexual behaviour existed in a selection of Native communities. Neither homosexual nor heterosexual behaviour was definitive to the classification of social identity under Native sex/gender systems (Whitehead, 1993). On that account, the history of First Nations sexuality may be better thought a history of cross-gendered behaviour.

A second conclusion is that heterosexual behaviour could not have been as "mandatory" for Native North Americans as it was for the Euro-Jesuit newcomers since sexual behaviour did not set into motion an entire process of gender reclassification (see Schnarch, 1992: 111). Contrary to a European sex/gender system that characterized or equated the homosexual sex act with some enduring (cross)gendered disposition, the Native North American could engage in same-sex sexual conduct without necessarily acquiring the recognized status of (gender-crossing) berdache. Later colonial policy would work to alter this system through institutionalizing a structure of power and kinship relations that were both patriarchal and heterosexist. In the next section of this paper, this proposition will be further elaborated.

A third and more central conclusion based on the preceding analysis and evidence is the way that racism, patriarchy and heterosexism are witnessed to have developed in relation to one another. In the selected descriptions, the sexuality of Native North Americans was quite simply racialized and engendered. "Sodomy," for example, was viewed as a practice engaged in by a "morally perverted" and "coarse natured" race of people. By extension, the cross-gendered effeminacy and homosexual behaviour of the male berdache was socially constructed as "cowardly" or effeminate. In short, the dynamic interplay between "racial," sexual and gendered types of knowledge both produced and organized missionary recordings. A similar set of ethnocentric understandings would later translate into a set of policy objectives. These colonial knowledges would influence the contemporary circumstances of Native "gays" and "lesbians," some of whom continue to identify as "two-spirited" people. In the following section I explore the interactive relationship between racism, patriarchy and heterosexism in early "Indian" policy and the Indian Act.

RACISM, PATRIARCHY AND HETEROSEXISM IN THE INDIAN ACT

In this section I will highlight the way in which the Indian Act, in the assumptions that it made about the kinship and social organization of First Nations, assumed homosexual behaviour out of existence. Further research is needed to illustrate more precisely the actual impact, or causal effect that government initiatives and legislation had on the suppression of homosexual behaviour and same-sex intimacies. For an initial analysis of how the berdache tradition is no longer as recognized an institution as it once was in Native communities, see Roscoe (1988, Part II).

For well over 100 years, the Indian Act has been the central legislation governing the affairs of First Nations in Canada. Since its inception in 1876, the Act consolidated earlier policy and appointed the Federal Government in control of all aspects of "Indian" life including education, social services, health care and lands administration. For the purposes of this paper I will concentrate largely upon those sections of the Indian Act that deal with "Indian" status and citizenship. These were the sections that fundamentally reorganized kinship relations and delineated who was, and who was not, eligible to be registered as an "Indian" under the jurisdiction of the Indian Act.[7] While the historical development of these sections are most blatantly patriarchal, I will also illustrate how they combine to reveal an interactive relationship between racism, patriarchy and heterosexism. It is necessary, in other words, to understand patriarchal discrimination in relation to racism and heterosexism. Moreover, these systems of domination cannot be understood outside of the formation of capitalist relations.

The implementation of the Reserve system in 1830s Upper Canada was among the earliest of statutory policies to affect First Nations prior to Confederation. This was a policy intended to resocialize First Nations into recognized "British-agricultural-Christian patterns of behaviour" (Frideres, 1983: 22). To that extent, the agricultural policy of the reserve system revealed underlying ideologies of racism and ethnocentrism. The Reserve system was intended to "civilize" the "Indian" who, in the eyes of the European, would be otherwise susceptible to nomadism and societal decline.

The agricultural component of the reserve system was also among the earliest of policies to commence with the social construction of gendered tasks.

Commenting on the sexual division of labour associated with this policy, Ng has observed that "men were taught farming skills such as how to clear land and hold a plow, [and] women, under the tutelage of the missionaries' wives and daughters were taught 'civilized' domestic skills" (1993: 54). The reserve system policy thus represented a further endeavour toward the re-construction of gender relations among Aboriginal populations. These "common-sense" assumptions about the gendered division of tasks likely impacted upon First Nations women. At the same time, these assumptions likely influenced the position of the berdache discussed earlier in the paper. Had systems that recognized and affirmed an engagement with cross-gendered occupations existed prior to European contact, they would not have been possible during the 1830s.

A continued emphasis toward gender hierarchicalization continued well into the late 1800s. Most notably, it emerged in the status and citizenship sections of "Indian" policy. These were the sections that defined who was, and who was not, entitled to "Indian" status. In the tradition of earlier statutes, these initiatives made invidious distinctions between male and female "Indians."

The status and citizenship sections of the Indian Act have historically excluded Aboriginal women from recognition as status "Indians." As early as 1869, for example, Native women marrying non-Native men lost status, along with their children, as defined under section 6 of *An Act for the Gradual Enfranchisement of Indians* ([S. C. 1869, c. 6 (32–33 Vict.)], reprinted in Venne, 1981: 11.1S).[8] This same loss of status did not apply to Native men or their children. In law, Native men retained their entitlement to status along with an ability to bestow it regardless of whom they married.

The exact motive for making invidious distinctions between Native men and women is not immediately discernable, but as one author has put it: "[T]he 1869 legislation ... was intended to reduce the number of Indians and "half-breeds" living on reserves" (Jamieson, 1986: 113). The surface motivation behind the 1869 Act, then, was doubtlessly assimilationalist. It may also have been about protecting "Indians" from White male encroachment onto Reserve lands (Sanders, 1972: 98). To be sure, the mandate of the 1869 Act was to institutionalize a system of patrilineal descent and heterosexual marriage.

The status and citizenship sections of the 1869 policy carried connotations that were simultaneously racist, patriarchal and heterosexist. As Jamieson (1986: 118) has asserted "the statute of 1869, especially section 6 ... embodied the principle that, like other women, Indian women should be subject to their husbands." At the level of "common sense," in other words, it went unstated that all Native women (and children) take on the "racial" status of their husbands at marriage. It also went unstated that Native women and men ought to be inclined toward the Euro-Christian institution of heterosexual marriage. Had there ever been a time where heterosexual behaviour was not judged "mandatory" in First Nations communities, it was unlikely to have been during the mid to late nineteenth century. By making marriage the only possible avenue through which to convey "Indian" status and rights, the 1869 Act simply legislated European forms of heterosexuality compulsory in First Nations communities.[9] Later legislation would only perpetuate such institutionalized domination.

In 1876, for example, the Federal government passed the first legislation entitled the Indian Act. Like preceding legislation, this Act imposed patriarchal definitions of "Indian" by again emphasizing patrilineal descent. Section 6 of the 1869 statute became section 3(c) of the Indian Act, only later to become section 12(1)(b) in the revised 1951 Indian Act.[10]

Similar to previous legislation, the 1876 legislation did not require a loss of status for Native men. Native men retained their legal "Indian" status and, under section 3, were able to bestow it onto the non-Native women they married. Section 3 of the Indian Act would later become section 11(1)(f) in the revised 1951 Act.[11] Historically, these legislated changes institutionalized descent through the male line and simply "naturalized" the heterosexual nuclear family within First Nations communities.

Major changes to the Indian Act were common following 1876 and several systems of domination were upheld. In 1956, for example, an amendment to section 12(2) of the 1932 Act strengthened patriarchal definitions of "Indian" by enabling individual Band members to contest the status and Band membership of Native children thought to be "Illegitimate." If an individual band member could prove that the father of a child was not an "Indian," then the child would not be entitled to statutory registration or Band membership.[12] "Indian" women's status, henceforth from 1956, ceased to be of any official legal significance in and of itself since only men could bestow legitimacy (Department of Indian and Northern Affairs, 1991: 14). It was by entrenching this system of relations that a discourse of patrilineage was offered to First Nations. At the same time, notions of "illegitimacy" in the 1952 Act privileged heterosexual unions by emphasizing the importance of paternity to the exclusion of non-male partners. In this way, the existence—even possibility—of same-sex relationships in First Nations communities went unacknowledged.

This chronological selection of legislation provides some insight into the early provisions of the Indian Act. What I have sought to illustrate are the colonial assumptions made with respect to gender and sexuality. But, in many ways, this brief explication requires further engagement. At least two considerations might guide this analysis. First, how can the Indian Act be considered a tool through which "Indians" were being "resocialized" to become "productive" members of an emerging Nation? Second, why did racism and (hetero)sexism interrelate as they did within "common-sense" attitudes about kinship organization? To what larger project, or sets of knowledges, was the interrelationship between these systems of domination tied? In short, what is so unique about the regulation of First Nations sexuality?

The historical development of the Indian Act and other "Indian" policy was a process coincident with the building of Canada as a nation. Between 1830 and 1950, for example, most of the Act's central prescriptions were being created. These were the years when Canada was moving toward an urbanized industrial economy. On that account, it is reasonable to speculate that the Indian Act and other "Indian" policies were informed by ideologies congruent with the impending processes of social and economic change. The Indian Act may be reinterpreted as a mechanism fashioning the human infrastructure necessary for the growth of capitalism. Informed by that understanding, the Reserve system of the 1830s may be revisited.

The agricultural policy of the 1830s not only placed emphasis on the state's motivation toward socializing "Indians" into economically viable entities, it also made some fundamental distinctions between the male and female genders. Policy makers of this new legislation, as mentioned, simply presupposed that "Indian" men would learn agricultural skills; and women, domestic chores. In this way, policy makers made "common-sense" assumptions about the gendered distribution of tasks. These assumptions were informed by ideologies of the sexual division of labour and the private and public spheres. It was within the broader context of these knowledges that the State mandated the regulation of gendered behaviour among First Nations. The imperative to divide tasks on the basis of gender must certainly have impacted upon women and also those inclined toward cross-gendered activity.

For women, capitalist and patriarchal knowledges combined to require that their labour be restricted to the private sphere. The implication of capitalist and patriarchal knowledges was to relegate women to the lower strata of the institutionalized gender hierarchy.[13] For those inclined to cross-gendered behaviour, capitalist and patriarchal knowledges relating to the sexual division of labour combined to mandate, even if unintentionally, the loss of gender flexibility. The effect of these knowledges was likely to have intensified gender classification systems making cross-gendered behaviour of considerable consequence. Seen in the 1880s as an implicit threat to the very project of Nation building and economic prosperity, the cross-gendered individual was seemingly confronting legislative regulation if not vigilant policing. A similar concern over discordant individuals inhered within the "Indian" status sections of 1869 and 1876.

The status and citizenship sections of the Indian Act were as much about extending a project of invidious gender distinctions into First Nations communities as they were about the regulation of sexuality. The formulation of these sections were shaped through an historical context that ideologically prescribed the types of sexual behaviour thought most compatible with the mode of production. Capitalist and patriarchal knowledge relating to the (re)productive modes of sexuality combined in the 1800s to require the disavowal of same-sex relationships. Since only heterosexual marriage ensured a form of reproductive sexuality, these would become the only recognized unions through which to convey status in the Indian Act. Later Indian Act prescriptions on "illegitimacy" would reveal a similar influence from the historical period.

The "legitimacy" sections of the Indian Act were just as much inspired by the patriarchal emphasis on paternity as they were by the emerging productive relations of the late 19th century. The imperative of "legitimacy," for example, was tied intimately to capitalist notions of private property. Those status provisions that upheld notions of "illegitimacy" simply reflected a legal and social system which tried to ensure that only men could bequeath wealth onto their own children (Engels, 1942: 76; O'Brien, 1981: 54). The way that wealth was bequeathed was to declare that wives were the sole and exclusive property of their husbands and that subsequently, a man's children were those that his wife bore. It was in the broader context of wealth and the transference of property that the state endeavoured toward the regulation of women's sexuality. The imperative of paternity was largely to bring all First Nations into further congruence with a patriarchal system of private property.

To sum up, the historical development of the Indian Act was a process that coincided with the building of Canada as a Nation. With that in mind it is not possible to consider the Indian Act's development outside of the pervasive ideologies of that period. Engrained within the Act itself are "common-sense" assumptions about the gendered distribution of tasks, the forms of reproductive sexuality and capitalist notions of private property. All of these knowledges were contained within early "Indian" policy.

CONCLUSION

A central conclusion of this paper is that the regulation of First Nations sexuality cannot be explained apart from, or without reference to racist and patriarchal configurations as those that emerged in the Euro-Christian and subsequent colonial contexts.

For the early missionaries, descriptions of sexuality were informed by both "racial" and "gendered" knowledges. "Sodomy," for example was a practice engaged in by a "coarse natured" "race" of people. The cross-gendered behaviour of the berdache was further constructed as effeminate. Informed by knowledges that linked sexuality with "racial" difference along with ideas that linked gender with masculinity and femininity the Euro-Christian missions made the first attempt toward a "civilizing" agenda. In any attempt to reconsider that agenda, the dynamic interrelationship among all systems of domination needs to be recounted.

Racist and patriarchal configurations also influenced the later agenda of nation building. Capitalist and patriarchal knowledges relating to the (reproductive) modes of sexuality, for example, combined to require the disavowal of same-sex relationships in the status and citizenship sections of the Indian Act. By extension, the sexual division of labour intensified gender classification systems in turn requiring the regulation of cross-gendered behaviour. All of these systems combined to deeply affect First Nations.

In short, the dynamic interplay between racist, patriarchal and capitalist knowledges all influenced the regulation of First Nations sexuality. Any account of the history of this regulation, or theory of state formation, needs to illuminate that interrelationship.

Notes

1 By the term "heterosexism," I mean the system of knowledges or "political institution" through which heterosexuality is either implicitly or explicitly assumed to be the only acceptable or viable life option (Rich, 1993: 232; Blumenfeld and Raymond, 1988: 244–45).

2 The actual depth of missionary observation, comment and sentiment about "sodomic practices" cannot be thoroughly discussed in a paper of this size. Testimonies can be analyzed more closely, however, in Katz (1983).

3 I borrow the term "common sense" from Himani Bannerji (1987) who draws attention to the way that systems of discrimination "disappear from the social surface" and become ordinary ways of doing things of which we rarely have consciousness.

4 For a scholarly analysis of the genealogies of imperialist knowledge, see Anne McClintock (1995: 21–74).

5 As Burns has noted (1988: 1), berdache is the word used by early French explorers to describe male Indians who "specialized in the work of women and formed emotional and sexual relationships with other men" (also see Kinsman, 1987: 71).

6 It is worth noting—without delving too far into an analysis of "essentialist" versus "constructionist" theories of sexuality—that the instability of analytic categories such as "gay," "lesbian" or "homosexual" are of some political urgency for communities interested in recounting "minority history" and validating an immemorial existence (Boswell, 1989: 20; also see Sharpe, 1992: 31; 38). This may represent one explanation as to why modern-day notions of "homosexuality" are sometimes conflated with the role of the berdache.

7 The very first attempt to define the term "Indian" and thereby racialize a heterogeneous and diverse group of people was made in 1850 under legislation entitled *An Act for the protection of the Indians in Upper Canada from imposition, and the property occupied or enjoyed by them from trespass and injury* (Indian and Northern Affairs Canada, 1991: 7)

8 As section 6 read: "Provided always that any Indian woman marrying any other

than an Indian, shall cease to be an Indian within the meaning of this Act, nor shall the children issue of such marriage be considered as Indians within the meaning of this Act ..." (*An Act for the Gradual Enfranchisement of Indians* ... [S.C. 1869. c.6. (32–33 Vict.)]; reprinted in Venne, 1981: 11),

9 Resistance to heterosexist status sections may have been possible by securing some alternate arrangement whereby the children of "two-spirited" people could obtain Indian status. However, this did not alter the fundamental effect of the legislation which was to privilege heterosexual over same-sex relationships. Had same-sex relationships ever been recognized and affirmed in First Nations communities—and it seems more than reasonable to suggest they were—the Indian Act would work toward ensuring that the legal and structural means with which to regain such systems were lost.

10 As section 3 (c) of the 1876 Act read: "Provided that any Indian woman marrying any other than an Indian or a non-treaty Indian shall cease to be an Indian in any respect within the meaning of this Act ..." (Indian Act [S.C. 1876, c. 18], reprinted in Venne, 1981: 25). In 1951, this section was amended to read: "The following persons are not entitled to be registered, namely ... (b) a woman who is married to a person who is not an Indian" (Indian Act [S.C. 1951, c. 29], reprinted in Venne, 1981: 319).

11 As section 3 of the 1876 Act read: "The term 'Indian' means, First. Any male person of Indian blood reputed to belong to a particular band; Secondly. Any child of such person; Thirdly. Any woman who is or was lawfully married to such person" (Indian Act [S.C. 1876, c. 18], reprinted in Venne, 1981: 24). In 1951, this section was amended to read: "Subject to section twelve, a person is entitled to be registered if that person ... (f) is the wife or widow of a person who is entitled to be registered by virtue of paragraph (a), (b), (c), (d) or (e)" (Indian Act [S.C. 1951.C.29], reprinted in Venne, 1981: 318–19).

12 As section 12(2) of the 1952 Act read: "The addition to a Band List of the name of an illegitimate child described in paragraph (e) of section 11 may be protested at any time within twelve months after the addition, and if upon the protest it is decided that the father of the child was not an Indian, the child is not entitled to be registered under paragraph (e) of section 11 (Indian Act [R.S.C. 1952, c. 149], reprinted in Venne, 1981: 360).

13 For many settlements, this meant a fundamental reconstruction of gender relations as some communities are said to have been egalitarian and matriarchal prior to contact. For a discussion of the matriarchal kinship organization and egalitarian relations among the Iroquoian Nations see Druke (1986: esp. 305). Also see Native Women's Association of Canada (1992) and Kirkness (1987: 410–13).

References

Bannerji, Himani (1987). "Introducing Racism: Notes Toward an Anti-Racist Feminism." *Resources for Feminist Research* 16(1):10–12.

Blumenfeld, Warren J. and Diane Raymond (1988). *Looking at Gay and Lesbian Life.* Boston: Beacon Press.

Boswell, John (1989). "Revolutions, Universals, and Sexual Categories," pp. 17–36 in Martin Duberman, Martha Vicinus and George Chauncey (Editors): *Hidden from History: Reclaiming the Gay and Lesbian Past.* New York: Meridian.

Brodribb, Somer (1984). "The Traditional Roles of Native Women in Canada and the Impact of Colonization." *The Canadian Journal of Native Studies* 4(1):85–103.

Druke, Mary (1986). "Iroquois and Iroquoian in Canada," pp.303–24 in R. Bruce Morrison and C. Roderick Wilson (Editors): *Native Peoples: The Canadian Experience.* Toronto: McClelland & Stewart.

Engels, Frederic (1942). *The Origin of the Family, Private Property and the State.* New York: International Publishers.

Foucault, Michel (1978). *The History of Sexuality, Volume One: An Introduction.* New York: Vintage Books.

Frideres, James S. (1991). *Indian and Northern Affairs Canada: The Indian Act Past and Present: A Manual on Registration and Entitlement Legislation.* Ottawa: Indian Registration and Band Lists Directorate.

——. (1983). *Native People in Canada: Contemporary Conflicts.* Scarborough: Prentice-Hall.

Jamieson, Kathleen (1986). "Sex Discrimination and the Indian Act," pp. 112–36 in J. Rid Ponting (Editor): *Arduous Journey: Canadian Indians and Decolonization.* Toronto: McClelland & Stewart.

Katz, Jonathan (1983). *Gay/Lesbian Almanac.* New York: Harper and Row.

——. (1976). *Gay American History.* New York: Thomas Y. Crowell.

Kinsman, Gary (1987). "Sexual Colonization of the Native Peoples," pp. 71–74 in Gary Kinsman: *The Regulation of Desire: Sexuality in Canada,* Black Rose Books.

Kirkness, Verna (1987/88). "Emerging Native Women." *Canadian Journal of Women and the Law* 2: 408–15.

McClintock, Anne (1995). *Imperial Leather: Race, Gender and Sexuality in the Colonial Context.* New York: Routledge.

Miles, Robert (1989). *Racism.* London: Routledge.

Native Women's Association of Canada (1992). *Matriarchy and the Canadian Charter: A Discussion Paper.* Native Women's Association of Canada.

Ng, Roxana (1993). "Racism, Sexism, and Nation Building in Canada," pp. 50–69 in Cameron McCarthy and Warren Crichlow (Editors): *Race, Identity and Representation in Education.* New York: Routledge.

O'Brien, Mary (1981). *The Politics of Reproduction.* London: Routledge.

Padgug, Robert (1989). "Sexual Matters: Rethinking Sexuality in History," pp. 54–64 in Martin Duberman, Martha Vicinus and George Chauncey Jr, eds. *Hidden From History: Reclaiming the Gay and Lesbian Past.* New York: Meridian.

Parr, Joy (1995). "Gender, History and Historical Practice." *Canadian Historical Review* 354–76.

Rich, Adrienne (1993). "Compulsory Heterosexuality and Lesbian Existence," in Henry Abelove, Michele Aina Barale and David Halperin (Editors): *The Lesbian and Gay Studies Reader.* New York: Routledge.

Roscoe, Will (1988). *Living the Spirit: A Gay American Indian Anthology.* New York: St. Martin's Press.

Rubin, Gayle (1975). "The Traffic in Women: Notes on the Political Economy of Sex;" pp. 157–210 in Reyna R. Reitar (Editor): *Toward an Anthropology of Women.* New York: Monthly Review.

Said, Edward (1979). *Orientalism.* New York: Vintage Books.

Sanders, Douglas (1972). "The Bill of Rights and Indian Status." *University of British Columbia Law Review* 7(1): 81–105.

Schnarch, Brian (1992). "Neither Man nor Woman: Berdache—A Case for Non-Dichotomous Gender Construction." *Anthropologies* 34(1).

Sharpe, Jim (1992). "History from Below," pp. 24–41 in Peter Burke (Editor): *New Perspectives on Historical Writing.* Pennsylvania State University Press.

Venne, Sharon Helen (1981). *Indian Acts and Amendments 1868–1975: An Indexed Collection.* Saskatoon: University of Saskatchewan Native Law Centre.

Whitehead, Harriet (1993). "The Bow and the Burden Strap: A New Look at Institutionalized Homosexuality in Native North America," pp. 498–527 in Henry Abelove, Michele Aina Barale and David Halperin (Editors): *The Lesbian and Gay Studies Reader.* New York: Routledge.

Karen Dubinsky and Adam Givertz

"'It Was Only a Matter of Passion' : Masculinity and Sexual Danger,"

Gendered Pasts: Historical Essays in Femininity and Masculinity in Canada (1999)

Much ink has been spilled in recent years coming to grips with the stunningly simple insight that 'gender' means 'men', too. Perhaps the most important historical contribution to this discussion was penned by British historians Michael Roper and John Tosh several years ago. Their argument that masculinity 'has been formed in relationship to male social power' has been kept central by too few historians of masculinity in general, particularly those studying the history of masculine sexuality.[1] It seems almost anachronistic to suggest that sexuality—and especially sexual conflict between women and men—also exerts considerable influence in shaping the contours of masculinity. Three decades of feminism have, one would think, taken us at least this far. Still, there have been few historical studies of masculine heterosexuality at all, which, in light of the recent explosion of coterminous interest in the history of sexuality, creates a curious deficiency. Thus, despite decades of activism and research on issues of heterosexual violence, we still know far more about how such conflicts affect women than men.[2]

Recent works in the history of sexuality, in several national contexts, have allowed us to glimpse the internal world of late nineteenth- and early twentieth-century courtship. If one is interested in rural, working-class, and immigrant communities, the records of state and 'state-like' agencies charged with supervising and shoring up lapses in sexual behaviour (such as the legal system and foundling hospitals) are a fruitful, though not uncomplicated source through which to reconstruct what American historian Christine Stansell has identified as the 'system of barter' between the sexes. A compelling portrait of the agonies, ecstasies, and fundamentally unequal status of women in the heterosexual barter system is emerging in the US, Britain, and Canada.[3] But where did men fit? What were the self-perceptions and public representations of the men who abandoned their pregnant girlfriends or were charged with assaulting their neighbours? Such men may well have escaped a set of onerous obligations, or even a jail term, but did they escape completely unscathed? Based on our combined research on the history of heterosexual conflict in Ontario between 1880 and 1929, and preliminary research into one particularly significant sex crime in British Columbia, this paper points to ways in which men explained their own sexual transgressions and how others explained their breaches of respectability. This may then suggest some of the ways that, historically, men have learned the rules, written the script, wielded power, and had power wielded over them in sexual relations with women.

MALE SELF-PERCEPTIONS AND THE COURTS

Between 1880 and 1929, approximately 725 men were charged with sexual crimes against women in our sample of half the counties and districts of Ontario. When they were brought to trial, almost half of these men, 49 per cent, were judged not guilty by the courts.[4] There was no single surefire defence a man could invoke to make his version of events more believable, though we argue strongly that men who were able to harness any number of prevailing stereotypes about women's sexuality and morality had a greater chance of raising doubts about the character, and hence veracity, of the complainant's story.[5]

That the behaviour or character of the woman involved was scrutinized more intensively than the actions of men makes it that much more difficult to write men into the history of sexual assault. A turn-of-the-century rape trial revealed far more about the history, life circumstances, and specific behaviour of the female complainant than the male accused. Thus, this project immediately confronts a vexing political and methodological problem: what we call the irony of the invisible man. In a rape trial, the presumption of innocence of the accused included the assumption of consent by the woman, and therefore the trial was structured in such a way as to force the woman to prove her lack of consent. The more successful men charged with sexual crimes were (and remain) at deflecting attention to their female accusers, the more likely they were to walk away from both the courtroom and the historical record.

When men chose to explain their own actions in court, they told several different kinds of stories. Some issued outright denials. They claimed mistaken identity; they said they were too drunk (or, occasionally, sick) at the time to realize, or remember, their behaviour; they told inventive stories of walking into the wrong hotel room or water closet; they claimed they were being framed or 'put up' on a variety of personal conspiracies. In a handful of cases, outright admissions of culpability emerged; a few apologized. The vast majority of men, however, justified coercive sexual activity in terms of their right as men to 'take' women sexually. In Wentworth County, for example, in all but two of the 103 available cases men did not dispute that sexual contact of some sort had taken place.

The self-perceptions of men who claimed that their sexual involvements with women had not crossed the boundaries of the criminal law were by no means uniform. There was a wide spectrum of male responses to charges of sexual assault, which in turn suggests a variety of cultural frameworks that shaped understandings of masculine prerogatives within heterosexuality. As Karen Dubinsky's work on rape in Ontario during this period has shown, the sharply contrasting positions of power occupied by women and men within turn-of-the-century heterosexuality are often crystal clear.[6] Some men clearly believed that their more favoured position in the heterosexual barter system gave them a right to sexual conquest or ownership. In a similar vein, other men understood their behaviour as part of the 'spoils' of heterosexual competition. Those who claimed to have been 'just as seduced as she was' or who insisted that the woman was a prostitute obviously believed that they were acting properly within the boundaries of a contested sexual arrangement.

Others drew from the same cultural framework but admitted to a certain infraction of the rules, though not as serious an infraction as the criminal law suggested. Ross M. admitted in his 1922 trial that he got 'a little fresh' with 15–year-old Lila W. in his car as he was driving her home from a dance. 'I put my hands up her clothes, but did not pull down her drawers', he claimed. 'I laid up against her but did not have connection. She did not squawk, she only told me to stop.'[7] 'Women and men', notes British historian Françoise Barret-Ducrocq, 'met in a climate of mingled love and mistrust.'[8] There was no such thing as an absolute boundary line between respectability and deviance. How 'fresh' was too fresh? Such negotiations went on in countless back seats of countless vehicles, and just as women were ultimately expected to police the boundaries themselves, some men expected that they had the right to test, once or twice, to make sure the woman had drawn her line firmly. A fascinating set of explanations came forward from men who merged tales of masculine sexual privilege with biological imperatives. American historian Anthony Rotundo's argument that, by the late nineteenth century, male passion occupied a 'new and honoured place in the bourgeois definition of manhood' is well illustrated by the men who claimed passion as a legal defence.[9] 'My passion for women overcame me', claimed one man who raped two young girls at gunpoint in 1922.[10] Male passion was a potent force indeed, but many claimed that women bore some responsibility for inflaming it in the first place. Frederick L., who employed Vera B. as a domestic in his home in Oshawa, told police that he had sex with the 13–year-old because she was constantly 'fooling with him, and *he could not stand it.*'[11]

Men who explained their actions with reference to their passionate nature may have expressed either sorrow or defiance, but all tried to convey that this was a temporary lapse. Frederick L., for example, convinced his banker to testify to his high moral character, which helped reduce his sentence to a fine rather than a jail term. Others were able to convince judges that their actions displayed, as one judge put it, 'weakness, rather than wickedness'.[12] Passionate men failed to exhibit self-control *in the moment*. This was a character flaw, to be sure, and one that diminished—weakened—one's manhood. But this was not a condition that necessarily had lifelong consequences. It was a temporary falter, not equivalent to women's more dramatic 'fall'. The examples of relatively high-profile men who bounced back from sexual scandals suggests a certain elasticity to men's moral characters, which was rarely present for women.[13] 'Passionate men' were still, at the end of the day, 'normal men'.

'FIENDS IN HUMAN FORM': MONSTER MEN AND NORMAL MEN

On 13 April 1883 a 10–year-old girl was sexually assaulted in Hamilton by Theodore F. The next day the story hit the newspaper with the headline: 'A horrible crime was committed and a beautiful girl was ravished by a drunken fiend in human form.' In 1925, another child molester was, because of 'his appearance rather than what he said', labelled subnormal by a medical expert on the witness stand. Such individuals, usually motivated by what the press declared 'inhuman lust', joined a group of men of this era who travelled quickly from the status of 'normal man' to 'monster man'.[14] The category of 'monster men' condemned certain kinds of behaviour (often, but not only, sex with children) by certain kinds of men (usually working-class men). At the same time, of course, the category mystified the way in which these crimes both reflected and reinforced a system of sexual oppression of women and domination by men.

We are not suggesting that all 'normal' men raped their daughters, but rather that the lines between the normal and the abnormal, or deviant, were a subject of constant negotiation in a context in which men simply held more power than women. By placing such men outside the realm of 'normal' masculinity and classifying their actions as deviant, the legal system and the popular press saw to it that these men no longer reflected the relations of a masculine heterosexual order. Indeed, they were barely men at all, they were 'brutes' , 'fiends', and 'animals'. Each crime was at the same time condemned and dismissed as an aberration. By locating sexual violence in the body of one man, or one type of man, everyone is relieved when the villain is found and removed from the larger body: the social.[15]

The creation of 'monster men' has a long history, for it continues, scarcely changed, to the present. For example, British feminist Wendy Holloway argues that debate over the motives of Peter Sutcliffe, England's 'Yorkshire Ripper'—whether he was 'mad' (clinically insane) or 'bad' (a warped product of his environment)—obscured 'garden variety' sexual violence. Thus, even when one man is found guilty, men in general are exonerated.[16] Canadians will likely also recognize the similarity to the case of Paul Bernardo, convicted in 1995 of a series of extremely high-profile rapes and murders in southern Ontario. Bernardo's arrest—and instant monsterization—in February 1993 brought enormous relief to the residents of Scarborough and St Catharines (two communities in which he committed his crimes), indicating that the eagerness to create and condemn one villain flourishes still.

One can detect this process of monsterization of Bernardo even in his police and press-created nickname, 'The Scarborough Rapist'. By associating the crimes with a single individual and a distinct geographic location, the information gatekeepers heightened Bernardo's threat, and the actions of other rapists—in Scarborough as well as other communities—were subtly diminished.

POPULAR SEXUAL VILLAINS

This process of naming or identifying the villain is also a process of locating villainy, of constructing distinct typologies of the sexual villain. Of all men who are seen as sexually threatening, none has an image more pervasively dangerous than the 'stranger'. Whatever the imagined location or the constructed scenario, the villain to be avoided is the stranger, lurking in the shadows, ready to pounce. In the past as in the present, this image of sexual violence looms much larger than its actual occurrence.[17]

Despite being a statistical minority, a number of types of dangerous strangers have been uncovered. Each had his own set of characteristics that made him particularly frightening. One such man was the taxi driver. In her 'exposé' of Canada's drug problem, Judge Emily Murphy, a leading Canadian feminist, suggested that taxi drivers were moral culprits twice over. The majority of these men, she claimed, were 'pedlars of drugs' as well as 'lascivious lechers'. Murphy even produced statistics to support her claim: of all occupational groups in Alberta, taxi drivers were most likely to have fathered illegitimate children.[18]

Another stranger, whose image was more ambiguous than that of the taxi driver, was the tramp. At times he could be seen charitably as a down-on-his-luck fellow, a harmless and lonely ragamuffin. Other times, the image of the eccentric tramp was itself enough to provoke suspicion and fear in women and men alike. Tramps, one police constable noted, were particularly suited to a life of crime since they 'tend to look alike and it is difficult to identify them.'[19] This association of tramps with crime and their status as outsiders often made tramps scapegoats in cases of sexual assault, especially in small communities, where they might be seen as malevolent infiltrators of rural harmony. The urban equivalent of the tramp was the 'street masher', that impolite boy or man who harassed women on the street. While serious physical abuse on the street did happen, such events were rare. Usually, street harassment in cities and towns involved men 'grabbing' women or making 'insolent' remarks. These 'everyday' events were not, however, ignored. In Ontario, the labour press as well as the commercial press took up a campaign against street mashers. Regulating male behaviour by chastising the rude and offering suggestions to the polite was a part of labour's program to foster a moral working-class masculinity.[20]

Moreover, as Dubinsky's work has also shown, events of street harassment were transformed into tales of depraved men and unsafe streets, in particular with the creation of the 'Jack the Hugger' character. Though Jack was a minor character, he was a well-travelled popular villain who roamed the streets of several Ontario communities between the years 1894 and 1916. These narratives about Jack and his wrongdoings contain four significant themes. First, they were urban stories: street harassment by strangers became a socially recognized problem whereas similar incidents in rural settings never engendered like panics. Second, the result of the Jack the Hugger scare was a perception that fear kept women off the street. As well, blame was not levied or moral aspersions cast on 'brazen' streetwalking women, as in so many other tales of urban sexual impropriety. Instead, the culprit was the street masher himself. Finally, Jack remained a villain only as long as he remained a *stranger*. The 'Jack-like' behaviour of a well-known character, such as a neighbourhood bully, was much less alarming.[21] Although Jack never displayed the absolute violence of his English cousin, the suggested relationship to Jack the Ripper seemed to both mock and mirror public fears.

THE ARISTOCRATIC LIBERTINE MEETS THE 'HEATHEN CHINESE': LABOUR'S SEXUAL VILLAIN

The working class had its own cast of sexual villains. While both the labour press and the mainstream press tended to import their villains from England (after all, neither Jack the Ripper nor the aristocratic libertine were home-grown), labour's sexual villains were not simply reproductions of mainstream stereotypes but part of their critique of the relations of labour and capital. Their villains were constructed to counter the charge that urban workers were prone to vice. They argued that lascivious behaviour was one symptom of the disease of capitalism, prevalent among the ruling class but not within the ranks of modest working men. Hamilton's labour newspaper, the *Palladium of Labor*, for example, regularly castigated the social purity movement for failing to recognize that at the root of vice was the wage-labour system.[22]

We can observe a similar process in labour's discussion of the sexual dangers of Chinese men, in which the strands of masculinity, class identity, and ethnic/racial identity converged. The moral panic that used the image of the aristocratic libertine coincided with labour's anti-Asian campaign, which yielded a distinct sexual panic. One illustration will suffice: in October 1884 a *Palladium of Labor* writer, having glanced in the window of a Chinese laundry, reported seeing 'six or seven little girls' in their early teens frolicking with the 'Heathen Chinese'. The newspaper suggested that these girls were not at the laundry to pick up their 'washee' but had been plied with opium and taken advantage of. Along with a cautionary note to parents of girls 'to stay away from John Chinaman', the *Palladium* issued a not-so-subtle threat to

'Wah Lee' to 'give up coaxing little girls' or else.[23] This warning to beware of the exotic wily stranger was consistent with the generally racist campaign against Chinese immigration that dominated the pages of the Hamilton labour press.

The campaign to construct Chinese men as sexual villains involved the interaction of several historical processes, namely, the making and remaking of sexuality and the relatedness of gender, class, and race. The connection between these is illuminated in the fabrication of the Chinese man as simultaneously a degraded labourer and a debaucher of young White girls. Certainly working-class cognizance of the impact that Chinese immigration would have on the labour market must have played a part in the making of labourist racism. But working-class anti-Asian racism was not simply a manifestation of the insecurity of alienated labour. Though it could reflect labour market concerns, it was inconsistent in its application. Making 'Chineseness' a threat to young girls was a distinct typology, and Asian immigrants were regarded as especially threatening to the sexual and gender order.[24] This perceived economic and sexual threat was reflected in royal commissions on Asian immigration and in a series of exclusionary government immigration policies implemented between 1880 and 1923. The result was a predominantly male Chinese community, the presence of which, ironically, intensified the images of Chinese sexual immorality.[25]

Some may propose that the image of the lecherous Chinese male was invented by middle-class reformers and simply reproduced by working-class activists. But the notion of a dangerous sexuality inherent in Chinese men surfaced in the working-class position on immigration long before it became prominent in the discourse of middle-class moral reformers or, as Madge Pon has illustrated, in the pages of the Toronto press.[26] In both cases, the image of Chinese men entrapping White women was crucial to the formation of Anglo-Canadian male identity, and certainly also reinforced already existing concerns among White male labourers about economic competition. While many historians, most recently Gail Bederman, have noted how turn-of-the-century White men drew sustenance (and power) from their common-sense equation of 'whiteness' with civilization, this worked in class-specific ways.[27] Furthermore, as our next case will suggest, the boundary separating the civilized self from the dangerous, foreign other was not always understood with the precision that this binary opposition implies.

A BRITISH COLUMBIA PANIC: THE CASE OF JACK KONG

The Chinese man was by no means the only or even necessarily the most 'dangerous' racialized sexual villain. Newspapers regularly commented on the ethnicity of southern and eastern European men charged with sexual crimes, but found other angles, such as alcohol or 'passion', when the men were

British. Similarly, judges constantly offered stern rebukes about the 'lawlessness' of foreigners, turning 'obedience to the law' into a racial trait possessed by Anglos and lacking in all others. The dangerous foreigner was a villain thoroughly implanted in the Canadian mind. Yet the relationship between race and sexual villainy was not always so direct. In early twentieth-century British Columbia, a highly politicized atmosphere of racial conflict helped shape state and public responses to one particular crime. In this case, the possible sexual threat of the 'Chinaman' was rivalled by his economic and social threat, and mediated by his age.

One spring day in April 1914, Charles Millard, the chief ticket agent for the Canadian Pacific Railway, left his home in Vancouver for a business trip to nearby Victoria. Returning to his Pendrell Street home the next evening he was surprised to discover that his wife, 30–year-old Clara Millard, was not there waiting for him. When he failed to track her through family and friends the following day, he became worried and called the police. Within a couple of days, traces of human remains were discovered in the basement furnace. With this, all attention turned to Jack Kong, the family 'houseboy' who had been in their employ for three years. Kong was instantly taken in for questioning, and the *Vancouver Sun* explained what followed:

> The China boy, who is only 17 years of age, and who has been noted as the brightest scholar in the Lord Roberts school, sat in his stone cell, looking through the bars at his inquisitors and refused to say a word. Question after question was hurled at him by the officers, but the Oriental, who is so slight of frame as to appear almost girlish, simply stared with a sharp eyes [sic] at them and kept his lips tightly closed. His eyes, while unnaturally bright, had dark blue circles under them and he had the appearance of not having slept for several nights.[28]

Kong's 'girlish' frame instantly marked him as something other than a 'normal' man—a process of feminization noted by other historians of anti-Asian racism in Canada.[29] Indeed, as cultural critic Marjorie Garber has recently pointed out, there is a long history, in Western fantasies of 'the Orient', of emasculated, gender-blurred Asian maleness, of which David Hwang's play *M. Butterfly* is one recent example.[30] Yet, when an Asian man was rendered 'girlish', this did not necessarily make him safe, particularly when he was, as this quotation implies, also identified with the twin 'Oriental' evils of 'inscrutability' and drug use. After a day in police custody, and subject to continued questioning that included methods the newspapers straightforwardly termed 'the third degree', Kong confessed to the crime. He hit Mrs Millard accidentally during an argument over burnt porridge: he had burnt it, and she refused to eat it and demanded he cook more. He was late for school and refused, she reacted to his insolence by threatening him with a kitchen knife, and he threw a chair at her. She fell, hit her head, and was killed instantly, and, in panic, Kong hid the body in the fumace.[31]

In a region that had experienced enormous racial conflict, as Vancouver had for decades, the accusation of murder of an Anglo woman by an Asian man would hardly have escaped attention. Kong was certainly monsterized, but in particular ways. He slid, quite easily, into categories made available by decades of British Columbia racial politics: the economic threat, whose presence in the domestic economy became as contested as it had previously been in other industrial sectors, and the social threat, whose place in the school system was as worrisome as the presence of Asian shopkeepers or neighbours. What's missing here is sex, for, unlike other non-Anglo men who killed Anglo women in this era, Jack Kong's sexual habits never became part of the Kong/Millard narrative as it unfolded in British Columbia.[32]

This apparent anomaly can be understood in the context of the particular relationships between Anglos and Asians in turn-of-the-century British Columbia. The idea of Chineseness created by Europeans constructed Asians as lacking in both sanitation and morality.[33] The moral threat posed by Chinese men was more nebulous, but more far-reaching, than that posed by other 'dangerous' men. Behind Jack Kong's 'sharp eyes'—even if they were 'unnaturally brightened'—lurked a 'Celestial' mind, capable of feats of cunning far more dastardly than simple rape or murder; and 'none of us', reminded the *New Westminster News,* 'can fathom the workings of the eastern mind.'[34] In this political climate, the sexual dangers of Chinese men went beyond 'normal' sexual violence. Instead, they were feared for their ability to 'lure': they led women into opium smoking and prostitution, and children into untold vices. Prevailing racial discourses had dehumanized Asians in British Columbia; even the use of police brutality to extract a confession from Kong—the notorious 'third degree'—was defended in the press since 'any method by which can be used to extract the truth from the inscrutable Oriental is justifiable.'[35] It follows, therefore, that Chinese men, in some historical epochs, were not 'normal men' at all: they were 'Chinamen', and Kong, a 'China boy'.

ORIENTALIZING THE 'CELESTIAL': RESPONSES TO KONG

Within days of Kong's arrest, several 'Chinamen' were stopped on the street and assaulted by White men. Chinese employment agents announced that at least 50 or 60 Chinese boys had been discharged from employment in hotels, restaurants, and private homes, and the call went out, from several quarters, for the complete segregation of the provincial school system.[36]

The campaigns against Chinese domestic servants and Chinese children in the school system fit an agenda of anti-Asian racism pre-dating the actions of Jack Kong. The Trades and Labour Congress, for example, used the public clamour about the crime to repeat its request to the Vancouver Board of License Commissioners to bar 'Orientals' from working in hotels.[37] Some in the labour movement felt vindicated. According to the *BC Federationist,* newspaper of the British Columbia Federation of Labour, 'the organized labour movement did not have to see a woman murdered before taking pains to try and secure the exclusion not only of Chinese domestics, but of all kinds of Asiatic labour from Canada.'[38] In an earlier era, middle-class BC ladies regarded their 'China boys' as a precious commodity. Some White women, according to witnesses at the Royal Commission on Chinese Immigration in 1885, employed their 'Chinamen' to 'scrub them whilst in their baths.'[39] By the time of Kong's trial, however, debate raged about the dangers of domestic 'Celestials' : to individual families, to unemployed White female domestics, and to the social and economic health of the province as a whole.

Anne McClintock has written provocatively of one of the paradoxes of Victorian culture, which zealously enforced the boundaries of middle-class self and degenerate other, while simultaneously gathering up thousands of those same others—working-class female domestic servants—into the family hearth. The result, she claims, at least for middle-class male children, was to re-create the contradictions of female sexuality literally from birth. Growing up with two (or more) starkly different mothers helped to dichotomize female sexuality 'distinctly along class lines'.[40] Furthermore, she suggests, Victorian discourse on degeneration served not only to dichotomize the sexuality of women in class terms, but to create racial distinctions as well. 'The more menial, paid work a woman did, the more she was manly and unsexed, the more she was a race apart.'[41]

If, by crossing the thresholds of private and public, home and market, working and middle class, the female domestic servant in England became 'the embodiment of a central contradiction within the modern industrial formation' let us consider the paradox of British Columbia.[42] In this context, one did not need to tax the imagination: neither age nor feminization could completely erase the fact that the Chinese houseboy was a masculine and 'foreign' presence in the domestic sphere. The furore created by the Kong story was thus attributable not only to the grisly death of Clara Millard but to the public exposure of one of the great 'threshold crossings' of turn-of-the-century British Columbia: public/private, male/female, Anglo/Chinese.

This exposure, however, was not limited to the domestic sphere, and here Kong's status as a schoolboy was as problematic as his role as houseboy. The demand to remove Chinese children from the school system had been raised in various levels of government since at least 1910—at which time fewer than 100 Chinese children attended Vancouver schools—and the Kong story gave this campaign fresh impetus. The day after Kong's arrest, the Vancouver city council debated a motion, which later got waylaid over legal technicalities, to separate Euro-Canadian and Asian children in schools. That Kong had spent several successful years in the Vancouver school system—and indeed, if his own confession was to be believed, that his reluctance to be late for school caused his disobedience to his employer—worked not to establish a character advantage for him, but rather to contaminate the entire public school system. The *Vancouver Sun,* for example, noted with dismay that Chinese boys were usually much older than their classmates; 17–year-old Jack Kong was a seat-mate of a 13–year-old White boy. Age difference, when combined with 'Oriental inscrutability', made for a dreadful combination:

> No one knows the moral standard of any Chinaman. A Chinaman's face as a rule is as expressive as a steam radiator. No one can tell by looking at him what is passing in his mind. What the result of contact of this youthful self confessed murderer may have had upon the minds of his more youthful contemporaries no one can tell. But this awful tragedy should teach the school board that their first duty is to segregate the Orientals from white children in all the schools.[43]

Age played a central role in delineating gender in this case. Combined with race, age initially helped to render Kong safe, a houseboy Mr Millard felt no qualms about bringing into the family hearth or leaving alone with his wife. After the crime, however, Kong's 'advanced' age, relative to his schoolmates, was portrayed as yet another source of danger.

Such were some of the ways in which Kong's villainy was framed. It is equally revealing, however, to consider what was not said. Kong was not, as he might easily have been, turned into a hypersexualized masculine object of peril to female employers, schoolteachers, or students. References to his 'girlishness' never triggered public speculation or innuendo about homosexuality or other 'lust-driven' diseases.[44] This raises interesting possibilities regarding regional and racial variations in the discourse of masculine sexuality. And this is even more apparent when we contrast the local reaction to the crime with reactions in other Canadian centres.

Clara Millard's murder received prominent press attention in Toronto, particularly when her southern Ontario roots were traced. A more sensational local connection, however, was that a bill to prohibit the employment of White women by 'Oriental' businessmen was being debated in the Ontario provincial legislature just as Kong was arrested for the crime. This heated up the debate considerably, and helped to reinforce pre-existing sexualized images of the Chinese man in Ontario. 'The people of the Orient do not consider human life by the same standards as we of the white race', declared the bill's sponsor, Dr Forbes Godfrey, MPP from West York. 'Witness the recent deplorable murder of a white women by a young Chinese in Vancouver.'[45]

The British Columbia example certainly added an impetus to the debate on this bill in the provincial legislature—a debate that resulted in the passage of the bill, conditional on the legality of similar legislation in Saskatchewan being contested before the Judicial Committee of the Privy Council.[46] But the Ontario debate had a distinctive flavour, captured in one Toronto newspaper headline: 'Chinese and Our Girls'.[47] There were, it was estimated, 120 'white girls' working for 'Chinamen' in Toronto, primarily in restaurants.[48] In 'socially purified' 1914 southern Ontario, however, these 120 girls had the same effect as the 98 Chinese children in Vancouver schools: they were a powerful metaphor for the dangers of racial mixing. The political discourse in southern Ontario, steeped as it was in the heavily racialized sexual anxieties of the social purity movement and the labour movement, determined that the debate would be framed in the familiar terms of the protection of 'White womanhood' from the 'degraded' Oriental male.

Gender identities, like racial identities, are created in the social world. We would not suggest that citizens of BC were 'more racist' in this era, or that those in southern Ontario were 'more sexually uptight'. Different communities, at different times, take up these issues in varying ways. The limitations of this comparison are obvious, and we can say little conclusively about the way racial and sexual panics came together in British Columbia based on one high-profile case. Further research in the history of sexual crime in British Columbia will help to determine whether the tenor of the reaction to Kong was representative of, or anomalous to, other men, Asian and non-Asian.[49] At this point, however, we would argue that these examples amplify Linda Gordon's contention that social definitions of violence and sexual antagonisms are products of political conflicts and struggles.[50] As the political home of the social purity movement and, before that, the Canadian stronghold of the Knights of Labor, early twentieth-century southern Ontario possessed a particular set of lenses through which to view racial and ethnic relations, which magnified the gendered and sexualized dimensions of non-Anglo 'others'. In this instance at least, the specifically feminist racist discourse of social purity did not resonate in BC in exactly the same fashion as Ontario, perhaps because of the way the 'frontier' muted Euro-Canadian women's political voices.[51] Jack Kong was monsterized in a manner that emerged from local conditions, particularly the long-standing provincial politics of economic and social exclusion of Asians. He did not become the hypersexualized masculine foreigner so familiar on the social landscape in other parts of the Victorian world.

The criminal justice system does not, as Angus McLaren has recently reminded us, 'simply-rubber-stamp public prejudices'.[52] Nowhere is this more apparent than in Jack Kong's case. Agreeing with the defence's contention that Kong had hit Clara Millard accidentally and that she had died before dismemberment and cremation, the jury found him guilty of the lesser charge of manslaughter, rather than murder, for which the sentence would have been hanging. This was a tremendously unpopular verdict, which was only rectified somewhat by the imposition of the extraordinary sentence of 'natural life' in prison. This sentence, which could only be imposed for manslaughter where 'the character of the accused makes it appear that reform is not to be looked for', was used in this case for the first time in Canadian legal history.[53]

CONCLUSION

The fevered pitch of anti-Asian racism in early twentieth-century Canada is obviously well illustrated in the Jack Kong case. Moreover, and especially when compared to stories that could have been (but were not) regarded as similar in Ontario, it reinforces the way in which race, class, and region shape the contours of gender. Masculinity is not a property unto itself. In this case, Kong's 'Chineseness' and his status as a houseboy form the content of his masculine persona. This case also provides a useful example of the complex relationship of signifier (or event) and signification (or meaning). Chineseness could mean different things. It made Jack Kong a general public threat in British Columbia and, simultaneously, a specifically sexual threat in Ontario. It is also striking, as historian Constance Backhouse has pointed out, that while the apparently harmless, feminized Asian man was permitted into the households of middle-class Euro-Canadians, he became an exceedingly dangerous character if he employed White women in his own establishment. Two years before the Kong case Saskatchewan passed legislation to prohibit the employment of White women in Asian businesses and quickly convicted two Chinese restaurant owners for this offence.[54] That Jack Kong, Asian men, or men in general did not present a unified or solitary image, but had distinct regional characteristics, reinforces the point that the relationship between knower and known varies from place to place and subject to subject.

What is common, however, to all of these tales, is how communities could define the boundaries between insiders and outsiders: between harmless tramps, passionate if misguided lovers, or even innocent victims of vengeful females and those villains who were 'truly' deserving of legal or social condemnation—the monster men or the lecherous, deceitful Chinese 'Celestial'. As this comparative analysis of sexual and racialized villains in British Columbia and Ontario reveals, outsiders could be defined by their sexuality or by their 'race' or by both, but the particular interplay was neither predictable nor predetermined. The boundaries between normal men and monsters were shaped and reshaped within the class, racial, and sexual contexts of their time and place. The task of sorting out who was who makes historical inquiry into the history of male violence a challenging and complicated enterprise.

Notes

We would like to thank Kate McPherson and Cecilia Morgan, as well as Annalee Golz, Atina Grossmann, Angus McLaren, and Bay Ryley, for their comments.

1 Michael Roper and John Tosh, 'Historians and the Politics of Masculinity', in Roper and Tosh, eds, *Manful Assertions: Masculinities in Britain since 1800* (London and New York, 1991), 2.
2 Recent works on the history of masculinity, which address masculine heterosexuality, include Angus McLaren, *The Trials of Masculinity: Policing Sexual Boundaries, 1870–1930* (Chicago, 1997); Lesley A. Hall, *Hidden Anxieties: Male Sexuality, 1900–1950* (Cambridge, 1991); Kevin White, *The First Sexual Revolution: The Emergence of Male Heterosexuality in Modern America* (New York, 1993); E. Anthony Rotundo, *American Manhood: Transformations in Masculinity from the Revolution to the Modern Era* (New York, 1993); Jonathan Katz, *The Invention of Heterosexuality* (New York, 1995).
3 See, for example, Christine Stansell, *City of Women: Sex and Class in New York, 1789–1860* (New York, 1986); Françoise Barret-Ducrocq, *Love in the Time of Victoria* (London, 1991); John D'Emilio and Estelle Freedman, *Intimate Matters: A History of Sexuality in America* (New York, 1988); Beth Bailey, *From Front Porch to Back Seat: Courtship in Twentieth-Century America* (Baltimore, 1988); Joanne Meyerowitz, *Women Adrift: Independent Wage Earners in Chicago, 1880–1930* (Chicago, 1988); Kathy Peiss, *Cheap Amusements: Working Women and Leisure in Turn-of-the-Century New York* (Philadelphia, 1986); Carolyn Strange, *Toronto's Girl Problem* (Toronto, 1995); Steven Seidman, *Romantic Longings: Love in America, 1830–1980* (New York, 1991).
4 For further details about our methodology and the history of sexual crime in the Ontario court system in this era, see Karen Dubinsky, *Improper Advances: Rape and Heterosexual Conflict in Ontario, 1880–1929* (Chicago, 1993); Adam Givertz, 'Sex and Order: The Regulation of Sexuality and the Prosecution of Sexual Assault in Hamilton, Ontario, 1880–1929', MA thesis (Queen's University, 1992).
5 Ibid. Further historical analyses of rape prosecutions in the courts include Marybeth Hamilton Arnold, 'The Life of a Citizen in the Hands of a Woman: Sexual Assault in New York City, 1790–1820', in Kathy Peiss and Christina Simmons, eds, *Passion and Power: Sexuality in History* (Philadelphia, 1989), 35–57; Constance Backhouse, *Petticoats and Prejudice: Women and Law in Nineteenth-Century Canada* (Toronto, 1991), 81–111; Anna Clark, *Women's Silence, Men's Violence: Sexual Assault in England, 1770–1845* (London, 1987); Barbara Linemann, 'To Ravish and Carnally Know: Rape in Eighteenth-Century Massachusetts', *Signs* 10,1 (Autumn 1984): 63–82; Guido Ruggiero, *The Boundaries of Eros: Sex Crime and Sexuality in Renaissance Venice* (New York, 1985).
6 See Dubinsky, *Improper Advances*.
7 Criminal Assize Indictment (CAI), case M., Peterborough County, 1922.

8 Barret-Ducrocq, *Love in the Time of Victoria,* 110.

9 Rotundo, *American Manhood,* 232.

10 CAI, case M., Lincoln County, 1922.

11 Provincial Archives of Ontario (PAO), RG 22, County Court Judges Criminal Court (CCJCC), L., Ontario County, 1903; emphasis added.

12 *Oshawa Daily Reformer,* 27 Nov. 1926.

13 On sexual scandals in this era in Ontario, see Dubinsky, *Improper Advances,* 86–112.

14 *Hamilton Spectator,* 14 Apr. 1883; CAI, case R., Wentworth County, 1925; *Hamilton Spectator,* 1 Oct. 1925.

15 Jack the Ripper, of course, remains the most enduring example of this phenomenon. Judith Walkowitz, *City of Dreadful Delight* (Chicago, 1992).

16 Wendy Holloway, 'I Just Wanted to Kill a Woman: Why? The Ripper and Male Sexuality', in Feminist Review, ed., *Sexuality: A Reader* (London, 1987). See also Walkowitz, *City of Dreadful Delight;* Angus McLaren, *A Prescription for Murder: The Serial Killings of Dr. Thomas Neill Cream* (Chicago, 1993).

17 Assaults by strangers account for approximately one-third of our sample.

18 Emily Murphy, *The Black Candle* (Toronto, 1922; reprint, 1973), 134.

19 *Stratford Evening Beacon,* 29 Oct. 1894. For a discussion of the murder trials of transient men convicted of sexual assault and murder, see Dubinsky, *Improper Advances,* 99–103.

20 On the sexual politics of the Knights of Labor, see Karen Dubinsky, 'The Modern Chivalry: Women and the Knights of Labor in Ontario, 1880–1891', MA thesis (Carleton University, 1985); Givertz, 'Sex and Order'; Robert B. Kristofferson, '"True Knights are We": Unity, Conflict and Masculine Discourse: The Knights of Labor in Hamilton', Major Research Paper, York University, Sept. 1992. This labour program of self-regulation is an interesting counterpart to the way the American bourgeoisie defined itself at the same time by advising women to look to middle-class male protectors in case of trouble from working-class men. See John P. Kasson, *Rudeness and Civility: Manners in Nineteenth-Century America* (New York, 1990).

21 For an extended discussion of Jack the Hugger, see Dubinsky, *Improper Advances,* 39–43.

22 *Palladium of Labor,* 10 Oct. 1885.

23 Ibid., 11 Oct. 1884.

24 The extreme exploitation of Italian navvies was alluded to ibid., 6 Sept. 1884. In addition, the racism of the Knights of Labor was not consistently directed at all non-Whites. For example, according to Deborah King the Knights encouraged the organization of Black men and women workers. 'Multiple Jeopardy; Multiple Consciousness: The Context of a Black Feminist Ideology', in Micheline R. Malson et al., eds, *Feminist Theory in Practice and Process* (Chicago, 1989), 99. Similarly, David Montgomery notes that the Knights were affiliated with unions of domestics in Black communities in the southern US: *The Fall of the House of Labor: The Workplace, the State and American Labor Activism, 1865–1925* (Cambridge,

1987),147. Thus, labour's racism was contingent. Still, Blacks were not immune from working-class racism. One article, picked up from the *Bobcaygeon Independent,* told the story of a 'colored' woman 'enticing white girls to evil ways' and warned that 'All Christian lands are reeking with immorality, are rotten with vice.' *Palladium of Labor,* 1 Aug. 1885.

25 See, for example, Patricia Roy, *A White Man's Province: British Columbia Politicians and Chinese and Japanese Immigrants, 1858–1914* (Vancouver, 1989); Edgar Wickberg, ed., *From China to Canada: A History of the Chinese Communities in Canada* (Toronto, 1982).

26 Valverde found that the intersection of sexual purity, national purity, and the advocation of stricter control over immigration in middle-class reformers' discourse only became prominent during the second and more forceful wave of the White slavery panic, 1909–14. Mariana Valverde, *The Age of Light, Soap, and Water: Moral Reform in English Canada, 1885–1925* (Toronto, 1991), 53, 92, 186–87 n. 70. See also Madge Pon, 'Like a Chinese Puzzle: The Construction of Chinese Masculinity in *Jack Canuck* ', in Joy Parr and Mark Rosenfeld, eds, *Gender and History in Canada* (Toronto, 1996), 88–100.

27 Gail Bederman, *Manliness and Civilization* (Chicago, 1993).

28 *Vancouver Sun,* 4 Apr. 1914.

29 Kay J. Anderson, *Vancouver's Chinatown: Racial Discourse in Canada, 1875–1980* (Montreal and Kingston, 1991), 56; Constance Backhouse, 'The White Women's Labor Laws: Anti-Chinese Racism in Early Twentieth-Century Canada', *Law and History Review* (Fall, 1996): 315–68.

30 Marjorie Garber, *Vested Interests: Cross-Dressing and Cultural Anxiety* (New York, 1993), 234–66. In Hwang's play, the Judge presiding over René Gallimard's espionage trial asks Song Liling, Gallimard's cross-dressed lover, how he had been able to trick Gallimard into believing that he was really a woman. Song Liling answers: 'One, because when he finally met his fantasy woman he wanted more than anything to believe that she was, in fact, a woman. And second, I am an Oriental. And being an Oriental, I could never be completely a man.' David Hwang, *M. Butterfly* (New York, 1989), cited in Garber, *Vested Interests,* 240.

31 This account of Kong's story is drawn mainly from newspaper reports. See *Vancouver Sun, Vancouver Daily Province, Victoria Daily Times,* 3, 4 Apr. 1914, and during Kong's preliminary hearing and trial, 16, 17 Apr., 18, 19, 20, 21, 22 May 1914. See also Roy, *A White Man's Province,* 14–15; Anderson, *Vancouver's Chinatown,* 90–91. Kong had the historical misfortune to come to trial just as the *Komagata Maru* was making its way to the Vancouver harbour—a boat carrying immigrants from India that was prevented from landing in Vancouver by an angry mob and, eventually, turned around. This simply exacerbated what was destined to be an enormous anti-Asian panic throughout the province. For days, headlines such as 'Boatload of Hindus on its Way' fought for space alongside 'China Boy's tale of Killing is Denied by Medical Expert'. On the *Komagata Maru,* see Hugh Johnson, *The Voyage of the Komagata Maru: The Sikh Challenge to Canada's Colour Bar* (Vancouver, 1988).

32 On the moral panics surrounding Black and French-Canadian men charged with murder in this era in Canada, see Dubinsky, *Improper Advances,* 98–104.

33 Anderson, *Vancouver's Chinatown,* 92–95.

34 *New Westminster News,* 6 Apr. 1914. See also the discussion of Kong in the *Vancouver Sunday Sunset,* 11 Apr. 1914, which asserts that 'the Chinese are as different from Canada and Canadians as nature and traditions can make them. Their minds do not run in the same channels.'

35 *Vancouver Sun,* 6 Apr. 1914.

36 Ibid.; *New Westminster News,* 6 Apr. 1914.

37 *Vancouver Province,* 9 Apr. 1914.

38 *BC Federationist,* 10 Apr. 1914. The paper also pointed out that, 'owing to the large number of unemployed women now seeking jobs in Vancouver, they can be hired cheaper than a Chinaman.'

39 Jean Barman, *The West Beyond the West: A History of British Columbia* (Toronto, 1991), 134; *Report of the Royal Commission on Chinese Immigration* (1885), cited in Backhouse, 'White Women's Labor Laws', 337.

40 Anne McClintock, *Imperial Leather: Race, Gender and Sexuality in the Colonial Context* (New York, 1995), 86.

41 Ibid., 103.

42 Ibid., 164.

43 *Vancouver Sun,* 6 Apr. 1914.

44 Another intriguing example of a lust-driven 'monster man' is the case of Vachar the Ripper, a serial killer who stalked the countryside in nineteenth-century France. See McLaren, *Trials of Masculinity,* 158–81.

45 *Toronto Evening Telegram,* 8 Apr. 1914.

46 In fact, the bill never received royal assent but remained amidst the statutes of that year as an unproclaimed bill. But when Ontario's statute law was collected and rationalized in 1927 in a single bill, the *Revised Statutes of Ontario,* the unproclaimed bill, because of a technical error, became law. Perhaps more interesting is the fact that several communities, shortly after proclamation, called on the Attorney-General to enforce the law. In a letter from Dr J.W. MacMillian of the Minimum Wage Board to Attorney-General W.H. Price (30 Aug. 1928), MacMillian reported that though the Board had corrected wages in a number of Chinese restaurants, it had 'received no evidence of misconduct on the part of the Chinese proprietors toward this class of help' (White female waitresses). Nevertheless, MacMillian reported it was his 'feeling that the law in question was a good one'. In addition to the desire for enforcement, Attorney-General Price also received a letter from the Chinese Consul-General (1 Sept. 1928) protesting the Act and asking that the government act 'in a manner most creditable to Christian civilization as well as Western democracy, and conducive to the best interests of Canada and China.' In the midst of all this the City of Toronto commenced prosecution of a restaurant owner named Ing, apparently at the insistence of Mayor McBride who was generating momentum for his fall campaign for re-election. At

the same time, a group of 69 waitresses petitioned the Lieutenant-Governor of Ontario requesting that he rescind the legislation, stating that they were well satisfied with their present employment. Ultimately, the Act was amended under the *Statute Law Amendment Act* (1929) to return it to its unproclaimed state. PAO, RG 4–32, 1928–916.

47 *Toronto Evening Telegram,* 8 Apr. 1914.

48 Ibid., 14 Apr. 1914.

49 In 1924 and 1931, for example, two other high-profile British Columbia cases, in which a White woman was murdered and a Chinese male the suspect, triggered a panic about sexually dangerous Chinese, including attempts to bar White women from working in Chinese-owned establishments. There are interesting parallels and convergences in the case of Wong Foon Sing, another Chinese domestic servant charged with the murder of a White woman in Vancouver in 1924. The death of Scottish nurse-maid Janet Smith, Sing's fellow employee in the household of F.L. Baker, raised many complications: party rivalries, rumours of drug trafficking on the part of the prominent Baker family, and an incredible kidnapping and six-week torture—by police—of Sing. While there were certainly several possible explanations for Smith's death (including suicide), many—particularly the Scottish community and Smith's domestic servant friends—were instantly suspicious of Sing. In this case, the 'sexually threatening Asian man' became a plausible and readily understood character. See Edward Starkins, *Who Killed Janet Smith* (Toronto, 1984). According to Kay Anderson, the 1931 murder of Mary Shaw, a White waitress in Chinatown, allegedly by her Chinese admirer Lee Dick, renewed civic campaigns through the 1930s to bar White women from working in Chinese establishments. Anderson, *Vancouver's Chinatown,* 158–64.

50 Linda Gordon, *Heroes of Their Own Lives: The Politics and History of Family Violence* (New York, 1988), 3–6.

51 On this point, see Adele Perry, 'Oh, I'm just sick of the faces of men: Gender Imbalance, Race, Sexuality and Sociability in Nineteenth-Century British Columbia', *BC Studies* (1995). On how the construction of White femininity has played an important historical role in maintaining racial hierarchies, see Antoinette Burton, *Burdens of History: British Feminists, Indian Women and Imperial Culture, 1865–1915* (Chapel Hill, NC, 1994); Vron Ware, *Beyond the Pale: White Women, Racism and History* (London, 1992); Nancy MacLean, *The Making of the Second Ku Klux Klan* (New York, 1994).

52 McLaren, *Trials of Masculinity,* 111.

53 *Vancouver Province,* 30 June 1914.

54 Backhouse, 'The White Women's Labor Laws'.

⇒+ SEX AND RELIGION +⇐

As Leonard Cohen suggests in *Beautiful Losers*, the relationship between sex and religion goes back to the origins of Canada: the colonization of Native peoples that ultimately issued in Confederation was also a sexual colonization. Cohen sees this scenario as repeating itself in the colonization of Québec and represents it through the interactions (just prior to Canada's centennial) of the unnamed Anglo narrator ("I"), the French-Canadian "F.," and Edith, a Native woman. Their story is juxtaposed with that of Catherine Tekakwitha, converted by the Jesuits in the seventeenth century and the first Native woman to take an Oath of Virginity. While the liberation movement for a "Québec libre" promises an end to this series of colonizations through a resexualization of politics, it does so by excluding Edith, with whom the two men have had sexual relations, and by negating the homosexual experiences of the Anglo "I" and his friend "F." thus placing in question (allegorically) the identities of both English and French Canada. Timothy Findley's concerns are similar, but he casts his net much wider, incorporating the history of the New World itself. The action that takes place on board Dr. Noyes's ark parodies that of the Flood story and revisits the darkest moments of the twentieth century, when national aspiration coincided with sexual—and racial/religious—regulation. In Dr. Noyes's Manichean universe there is no place for the sexual response elicited by the massage Hannah gives Emma or for beings such as Lotte, who are halfway between the animal and the human worlds. Margaret Atwood extends this vision of a dystopic theocratic state, where only a few "handmaids" remain fertile. Heterosexual relations (the only kind permitted) have been transformed into The Ceremony, a form of sexual interaction without "passion or love or romance" or "sexual desire." This vision contrasts with Nancy Christie's account of the role played by the Protestant church in Canada's sexual liberation movement. When the federal government instituted Family Allowance cheques in the 1940s, there was a fear among Protestants that Québec Catholics would seek to gain large incomes by producing huge families, thus threatening the political power of Anglo Canadians (as well as Protestants). By promoting intra-familial sexuality, the

Protestant Church sought to address not only this threat of political imbalance but also that of increased divorce brought on by the large number of women entering the workforce. These shifting grounds of moral terrain have resonance with Iain Barrie's narrative of sexual abuse in the Catholic Church. The implications of the abuse at Mount Cashel extend from the domain of religious morality to the media's representation of Newfoundland as the homespun heart of our national consciousness.

from *Not Wanted on the Voyage* (1984)

"Mother!"

Mrs Noyes almost tumbled from the steps. "MOTHER!"

It was Shem, the Ox.

"MOTHER!"

He was alarmingly close, and Mrs Noyes had to work so fast at hiding Mottyl and the kittens and at retrieving her lamp that she inadvertently used her fingers and cried out in pain.

Shem came around the corner and almost collided with her.

"What are you yelling about?" he said—ignoring the fact that he had been yelling, too.

"I banged my arm," said Mrs Noyes. Just as she spoke she heard, to her alarm, the sound of Mottyl's kittens. Shem, though dense, was not so dense that he could not tell the sound of kittens and Mrs Noyes leapt to their defense by suddenly bursting into song.

"*O Rock of ages, cleft for me!*" she bellowed. "*Let me hide myself in thee!*"

"Mother ..."

"Why don't we step down the hall?" said Mrs Noyes. "We don't want to wake the animals ..." and then she went on singing at the top of her voice; "*let the water and the blood ...*"

Mrs Noyes gave Shem a push with her elbow and urged him back along the gangway towards the stairs.

"Now, tell me what it is," she said—once they were on the steps, and the kittens safely out of hearing. "Why have you come down to bother us this time?"

"I want Emma," said Shem.

"Well—you can't have her," said Mrs Noyes. "She belongs to Japeth."

She pushed him in the ribs and made him walk up in front of her.

"All you and father ever think about is sex," said Shem. Mrs Noyes stopped in her tracks. "I beg your pardon?" she said.

"All you and father ever think about is sex," said Shem again.

"Never mind about me," said Mrs Noyes. "Why do you say that about your father?"

"I don't mean his own sex," said Shem. "I mean other people's. Seems to me it's all he talks about these days."

"Oh, really ..." Mrs Noyes tried to remain calm. "And now you want Emma? ..."

"Yes."

They got to the top of the steps and turned towards the galley, where Emma—more than likely—would be found.

"*Why* do you want her?"

"Not allowed to tell," said Shem. "Only meant to come down here and get her."

Mrs Noyes was about to throw up another defense when all was lost through the sudden appearance of Emma herself.

"Did someone call?" she said. "I heard my name."

Indeed you did, thought Mrs Noyes. *Alas.*

"You're to go with Shem," she said aloud. And then, to Shem; "isn't there time to let her change her dress, at least?"

"Meant to take her straight up," said Shem.

"Won't you even let her brush her hair?"

"Straight up," Shem said—unfolding his Oxen arms and giving Emma his tight little smile that was meant to be a pleasant greeting.

Mrs Noyes saw how clean her son was. The hairs on his arm were shining in the lamplight and the back of his neck was clean and his toenails were clean. It made her feel quite odd, when she realized she hadn't been clean herself for days and possibly weeks. The civilized parting in the centre of Shem's sandy hair and the smell of his tunic almost made her weep.

"Well," she said to Emma. "You'd best go with him. Don't be afraid."

She passed Emma on towards the stairs to the upper deck and kissed the top of her head as she let her go. And then she said; "here. Wait ..." and took a few quick steps in Emma's direction. "Take this," she said—and handed Emma her handkerchief. "Wipe your face as you cross the deck. And do up the bow at the back of your dress."

"Yes'm."

Emma took the handkerchief and smiled. It was wrong. Whenever she should have been in tears, she never was.

"I'll take a good deep breath of fresh air for you, Mother Noyes," she said. "Goodbye."

Mrs Noyes gave a wave—and instantly regretted it. A pain shot through her arm.

"Goodbye," she whispered.

And smiled, for Emma's sake.

When the door above her opened, Mrs Noyes thought she saw a star—but it was only a lantern, hanging from the portico.

The sound of the bolts being shut was worse than any sound she could imagine.

Turning back, she saw that Lucy was standing in the gloom below her. Her eyes were strangely luminous.

"What's the matter?" she asked.

"I don't really know," said Mrs Noyes. "I only know I wish I believed in prayer."

"So there you are," said Noah, as if the child Emma had wilfully absented herself. "Let me see you—let me see."

Emma had managed to make a circle of cleanliness right in the centre of her face, so that her eyes shone brightly out of a moon. Her hair was restrained with several ratty bits of cloth that were tied here and there and no two pieces of one colour. Her dress was severely torn and her aprons covered with grease and soap stains. Bird droppings and straw dust were matted on her shoulders. Her arms, with the sleeves of her dress rolled up in order to save them from the dish pan, were brightly and inappropriately pale and unspotted.

Noah stood up and gave the nod to Shem, who retired against his will. He was leery of his father now, and dreaded what might be going to happen—though not for Emma's sake. Shem's dread had all to do with the mood his father would be in if events unfolded against his will.

"Send Sister Hannah," Noah said—just as Shem had made it to the door. "Tell her I want her."

Once Shem had gone, Noah smiled—though his smiles were difficult to find in all that beard. And his wooden teeth were troubling him: locking shut when he wanted them open—and remaining open when he wanted them shut. He put his hand to his mouth and pushed the rows of teeth together, almost biting his finger as he did so.

"Well, well, then. Say hello," he said.

Emma bobbed.

Noah coughed.

"We have been concerned," he said.

Emma waited.

Noah had nothing more to say about "concern," apparently. Or at least as far as Emma understood the word.

"You are looking fat and sassy," the old man said, with his eyes very bright and his fingers in his beard. "How old are you now. Tell me the truth."

It did not occur to Emma to lie about her age. "I don't know," she said. "I think I'm twelve."

"You cannot be twelve," said Noah. "You were twelve a year ago, at least. I was rather hoping you'd tell me you were fourteen."

"I might be. I don't know."

"Well—whatever age you are," said Noah; "you are not a child any more."

Emma knew that.

Hannah appeared—dressed entirely in white and wearing a heavy cardigan over her long and voluminous gown. The child inside her might be twins, Emma thought. She's huge.

"Yes, yes. And good," said Noah. "Here's your young friend, Sister Hannah." Noah coughed and waved Hannah forward in Emma's direction. "She—ah—she perhaps—ah—she ..."

Hannah said; "perhaps she could do with a bath, Father Noyes."

"Precisely," said Noah. "Yes. A bath. A good, hot bath. Yes."

Emma sniffled and drew Mrs Noyes's handkerchief beneath her nose. A bath, she thought, would be lovely, but ... why?

"Come along, Em," said Hannah—putting out her hand and smiling.

They were being so friendly.

What did it mean?

"I'll be waiting," said Noah. "Right here."

Hannah led Emma towards the galley.

Not more pots and pans, thought Emma—already drawing back.

Recognizing Emma's reluctance from long practice, Hannah said to her; "the bath house is through here."

Oh.

"Sister Hannah ..." said Noah.

Hannah turned back and Noah leaned in towards her ear—"You might consider a little of that almond oil you use."

Hannah nodded.

Emma wondered what all the whispering might be about. But it did not concern her greatly. She could see that all the pots and pans and all the dishes in the galley had been cleaned and put away—and she could also see the bath towels warming by the oven.

A bath, she thought; a bath ... I hope it's nice and deep, so I can soak.

The bath house was already full of steam, the sponges set out in their bucket and the birch switches hanging down from their pegs on the wall above the bench. Hannah was well prepared for Emma's arrival and could have bathed an army. If there had been an army. (No more armies, she thought, pouring another bucket of scalding water into the tub. All our terms of reference have been changed forever. Now, everything will be "*before the flood*" and "*after the flood*." And "*she could have bathed an arkful....*")

Hannah went away, locking Emma in. She had forgotten the almond oil.

Emma went and stood by the tub and stuck her finger into the water. Hot. Too hot to climb into yet. She took off her shawl and stood there—mesmerized—with her shawl in one hand and the buttons of her blouse, one by one, in the other.

The birches looked like animal tails, hung up the way that Shem used to hang them in the slaughterhouse on earth—the long ones like cows' and the short ones like calves'. Emma put her buttoning hand out to touch them: dead as tails, with their withered leaves curled in tufts.

The smell of the soap and the warmth of the steam were so comforting they made Emma drowsy. Everything here reminded her of her parents and her brothers and the bath house at home, where everyone sat together once a week while her father told stories. Steam and stories were forever linked in her mind—and the feel of her mother's fingers massaging the back of her neck. Her brothers, like her father, had all been giants with pale hair and woodsman's arms and they spoke, like her father, with the low, gentle voices of animals. Some of them had moustaches that curled towards their chins—and the steam would gather at the ends of these moustaches in big, pearly drops that Emma was allowed to gather on her finger and fling against the stones, where they sizzled like insects. Her mother had been quite the opposite of all these quiet, blond men—being small and dark and excitable. She had been a gay and playful woman, whom all her children had adored. Her eyes had been a shade of brown that only Lotte's had imitated—and her hand was always out to touch you.

Lotte had been everybody's favourite—spoiled by all the brothers, carried by her father in his arms and on his back and her arms were so strong, he could swing her up to his shoulder while she did a somersault. Lotte had hardly ever been out of her mother's sight and the only time she had ever been unhappy was when she got left behind if the family went on a shopping excursion—everyone piling into the democrat except Lotte and one person (always someone different) who was chosen to stay behind with her. The hiding was different. Every time a stranger came to the door, Lotte had to be hidden from sight and the bath house was where she was hidden. It had been chosen as the hiding place especially because the bath house was a place where everyone was always happy. Sometimes, it was Emma's turn to hide with her and they would play at being woodsmen like their brothers—cutting down birch-switch trees and piling them all in the centre of the floor, crisscrossed in stacks of miniature lumber and firewood.

What Emma remembered most of Lotte, though, was how soft she had been and how lovely it had been, in their big straw bed in the loft, to lie up close to her and stroke the long, thin downy arms and, in the wintertime when they were cold, to creep down into the centre of the bed and curl up together underneath the covers while the wind had howled around them and the owls on the rafters had flown down to sit at the foot of the bed....

"What are you doing? You're not even undressed." It was Hannah, returning with the almond oil. She filled the open doorway briefly with her great height and bulk—and all the steam rushed out towards her and made a great cloud around her head.

"I was thinking," said Emma.

How unusual, Hannah thought—and closed the door. At once, all the steam fell away from her and she was revealed in a high flush of colour that made Emma think of Hannah sitting in the sun, her face pressed eagerly towards the light.

"Oh, my," Hannah said as she crossed the floor to the stove and began to shake out the towels she had previously brought from the galley. "I'm out of breath. I tire so easily, these days...."

Emma said; "you're carrying such a big child in there. No wonder. Do you think it will be twins?"

"I hope not," said Hannah.

"Oh," said Emma. "If I was going to have a baby, I'd want it to be twins."

"Yes—*you* would. Hurry up now. We haven't got all night."

Hannah had already removed her cardigan and was rolling up her sleeves. White—white—white: every bit of her clothing was white.

Emma stared at Hannah's belly.

"May I touch the baby?"

"No," said Hannah. "Take off your clothes."

The tub was so deep a person had to climb up over the top and drop down through the water, reaching for the bottom with her toes. Emma was so round and tiny, she almost filled the tub and the water rose around her neck and spilled out over the rim and onto the floor.

The first thing Hannah did was cut away the bits of cloth that served as ribbons in Emma's hair and then she pushed her all the way under so that her hair would be soaked.

Spluttering and squawking, Emma resurfaced and clung to the edge of the tub with every ounce of strength she could muster. Being drowned was everything she had feared it would be, with everything turning black and making a great ringing noise in her ears.

"Don't," she said. "Don't!"

Hannah applied a thick bar of soap—of the strength that Japeth had used in his desperate bid to remove the blue from his skin. It was the strongest soap that Mrs Noyes could manufacture and it smelled so heavily of lye that Emma was driven further into a state of stupor.

Hannah's fingers were very strong and as they worked the soap through Emma's hair, they sent deep messages of pleasure all across the top and back of Emma's head and down her neck.

The fingers worked their way down the skull and paused at the nape of the neck to massage the muscles there, spreading the message further down the spine and across the shoulders....

Emma gave up her grip on the edge of the tub and simply stood there, breastbone high in the water, head bowed and mouth open.

Hannah was working her way—vertebra by vertebra—down the child bride's back, pressing with her thumbs at the centre and spreading her fingers out across the flesh on either side . Emma had never felt so relaxed or warm or confused.

"Turn around," said Hannah.

Emma managed an almost balletic turn, rising up on her toes and spinning slowly in the water until she was facing Hannah.

Hannah said; "dunk."

Emma, her mouth still open, bent her knees and sank. Hannah stood up and went across the room to the stove, where she removed the lid and began to throw in Emma's clothes: her stockings full of holes and tears, her half-melted cardboard shoes, her skirts and her bloomers, her underblouse and her overblouse and her shawl.

It was just at this moment that Emma rose from the water and wiped her eyes and saw what Hannah was up to.

"What are you doing? ..." she said—only half aware of what she was seeing.

"I'm burning your clothes. What does it look like?"

"But—you can't! You mustn't! Not my shawl! My mother made that for me...."

A wail began to rise.

"Emma."

Emma bit her lip—and the shawl fell into the fire Next—and linally—Hannah, using a stick, picked up the filthiest of all of Emma's clothes—her apron—and held it out to the flames.

"Not my apron! NO!"

But the apron was already gone. And with it, all of Emma's feathers.

Emma had half-clambered out of the tub and one of her fat little legs was hanging over the edge. "My feathers ..." she said. All the feathers so patiently collected during her bird feeding duties—the feathers with which, in day-dreams, Emma manufactured wings. Wings for Mrs Noyes. Wings for Ham and Lucy. Wings for Mottyl and wings for the Unicorn—so that one day they could all take off and fly away with Crowe and leave the ark forever.

Emma sank back—her leg flopping helplessly over the edge.

After the bath, Emma stood quite silent—thinking of her apron and her shawl—while Hannah dried her all over. Finally, Hannah sat down on a three-legged milking stool and drew the almond oil from her placket.

"Come and stand here," she said.

Emma went and stood before her sister-in-law.

"Put your hands up on top of your head," said Hannah. Emma—assuming she was about to be inspected for any surviving lice, in the way that her Mother had always inspected her children after a bath—did as she was told and locked her hands in place on top of her head, gathering fistfuls of hair to hang onto. She also closed her eyes.

"What's that?" she said.

"You just be quiet and don't move," said Hannah, whose voice sounded oddly excited.

The smell of almonds floated up to Emma's nostrils and she felt Hannah's fingers touch the sides of her breasts.

"Oh my," she said. "Oh my ..."

Hannah's fingers were capable of much more gentleness than Emma would have suspected. Round and round they flowed—spreading the oil up over her breasts and down between them and underneath them, caressing them with oil and working—very slowly—towards the nipples.

"Oh my, oh my ..."

Emma pressed forward.

Hannah stopped.

Emma opened her eyes—but Hannah was only spilling more of the almond oil in the palms of her hands and rubbing her hands together, preparing for another assault.

"Be still."

"I can't be still. I don't know what you're doing...."

"Never mind what I'm doing. Be still."

Emma re-locked her hands on top of her head and waited. Where would the fingers touch her next? This was not at all like Japeth, whose hands were all fingernails and fists and thumbs.

The fingers landed—light as butterflies—and began moving down across her belly and up across her thighs.

"Just be still. Just be still ..." Hannah whispered.

But that was impossible.

When Emma was returned to Noah, she was wearing one of Hannah's white shifts and she was almost in a trance. Her hair had been dried and brushed and pulled back loosely—tied with a single ribbon on her neck.

"Well, well," said Noah. "What have we here?"

"Clean from stem to gudgeon," said Hannah.

"Everything?"

"Everything."

Noah sat forward in the great chair and his eyes were glittering. His voice, when he spoke, was not like any voice that Emma remembered his having used before: thick and wet with a quaver in it.

"Come and stand here, in front of me, child."

(He had gone back to calling her a *child* again. Why did he keep on changing what he called her? "*You're not a child any more*" and then, "come here, child....")

As Emma shuffled forward, afraid of tripping on the shift, Hannah went and sat on the far side of the table—one arm resting over her belly. Her hair was damp from having been in the bath house so long and she looked very beautiful sitting there in the lamplight, apparently at rest.

"Now," said Noah—giving the shift a twitch with his fingers. "I want you to raise this above your hips."

Emma just stared.

"Up, up," said Noah—as if he was doing no more than asking her to raise a window blind. "Come along."

Emma looked at Hannah for help—but Hannah was not even watching and, perhaps, not even listening. She was simply sitting there across the table—staring into space.

Emma reached down and took the folds of cloth in her hands and drew them to her thighs—but could go no further.

"Up," said Noah. "All the way."

Emma closed her eyes and lifted the shift all the way to her waist, where she held it tightly, like a girdle.

Noah muttered; "yes, yes ..." and she could feel his breath on her legs.

The ark heaved up and down and the rain could be heard on the roof of the Castle—but nothing more.

Noah reached out with his fingers.

Emma shivered.

"You cold, girl?"

"No, sir."

The fingers rode up her thighs towards her centre, soft as tongues in the oil. Emma pulled away.

"Stand still!"

The fingers of one hand reached the mark and the fingers of the other— seeking entrance—gently pulled to one side.

Emma wept. "That hurts," she said. "That hurts."

But one of Noah's fingers was already inside her—exploring.

"That HURTS!" Emma screamed—and pulled away so violently that she fell against the wall behind her.

But neither Noah nor Hannah seemed to be concerned with her hurt. All that Noah said was; "no wonder the poor boy can't get in. She's so thick and tight, a pin could hardly enter."

Hannah said nothing.

Emma sank down to the floor and pulled her knees to her chin.

And Noah just went on talking—not as if she was being harmed, but as if she was being helped. As if they were being kindly.

"I want to go back now," she said. "I want to go back."

But she might as well not have uttered. Noah, with his back to her, was bending forward—leaning across the table to Hannah.

Emma heard: "... something sufficiently firm ... something sharp ... I should hate to use ..."

Emma moaned and put her hands across her ears.

What they brought (it was Hannah who brought it)—was the Unicorn.

Emma's screaming lasted for an hour.

In the bowels of the ark, Mrs Noyes could hear it, but she could not guess what it meant. Emma's whole life, it seemed, had been spent, since she had been married to Japeth, either wailing or sobbing or screaming. And all that went through Mrs Noyes's mind was; "good for her! Resisting him to the end."

On the other hand ...

If Japeth succeeded ...

But, no. She must not allow herself to think of that.

Just as Noah was withdrawing the Unicorn's horn, Japeth—who had also heard the screaming as far away as the Armoury—came bursting through the door to the saloon. He was armed to the teeth, quite literally, since he carried a knife between his lips and his lips were bleeding.

The scene before him was meaningless at first. His father holding the dog-sized beast with the horn—Emma held in an angular embrace by his brother, Shem—while Sister Hannah crouched at Emma's feet, with a small red towel, and dabbed at something there that seemed to be a wound. Emma was screaming, still, and stamping the floor with her feet like someone trying to kill a snake.

It took a whole minute for all these images to come together and deliver a single meaning which—even then—Japeth could not believe.

But the Unicorn's horn was covered with blood and that said everything left unsaid by the rest of what he saw.

"We were just ..." said Noah.

Japeth drew his sword.

Noah stood his ground—a gesture he knew from long experience would intimidate his son. A single step back—and all might be lost. But Japeth could not bear a man who did not move. It confused him. Especially if that man was unarmed.

Noah's hand was on the Unicorn's back—and the Unicorn had collapsed to its knees, already very nearly unconscious. The only voice it could manage could not be heard by human ears. There was blood all over its face, as well as its horn, and its horn had been almost torn from its brow. Some of the blood was its own—and it was bleeding to death on the table. But no one paid it the slightest attention—and the weight of Noah's hand was so heavy that the Unicorn could not breathe.

Hannah stood up and went away with the dark red towel. Shem let go of Emma's arms and—at once—she ran to the darkest corner of the room and turned her face to the wall and was completely silent and completely still.

Noah spoke to Japeth in a monotone—his voice the very sound of reason—and he pacified his son by saying; "we have solved all your problems: the ones you could not solve. She is able to take you, now. It was not your fault, before—but hers. This was necessary ..." he gestured at the Unicorn. "Nothing more than a midwife would have done: nothing more than the apothecary would have advised her mother to do, if her mother had taken half the responsibility that any decent mother takes and had gone to the apothecary for advice in the first place. Your *own* mother should have seen to this...." Here, Noah took that always wild and unpredictable turn that was meant to save him from any kind of blame: that turning which even convinced himself that he was blameless and—more than blameless—that he and he alone was saving the entire situation by salvaging everyone and everything from certain ruin: that wrenching that began with his arm extended and his finger reaching out through the air to find the true and absolute culprit: the inevitable cause of all that was threatening, all that was dangerous; all that was foolish; all that was madness. That finger of reason that always found someone *else*—and most usually, his wife.

"Blame your mother—but don't come at me with that sword drawn. I have only done my duty as a father. Nothing more."

Japeth slowly lowered the sword and withdrew the knife from his mouth and—for a moment—it looked to Noah and to Shem that he was going to leave them without a word, since he half turned away and took one step that seemed to be leading to the door. But all at once he turned again so quickly that neither Shem nor Noah could truly see what he was doing.

The sword went up through the lamplight—and came down hard, two-handed, on the table, where it severed the Unicorn's horn from its head.

from *Beautiful Losers* (1966)

46.

—I am sick, but I am not too sick, said Catherine Tekakwitha's uncle.

—Let me baptize you, said the Black-Robe.

—Do not let any of your water fall on me. I have seen many die after you have touched them with your water.

—They are in Heaven now.

—Heaven is a good place for Frenchmen, but I wish to be among Indians, for the French will give me nothing to eat when I get there, and the French women will not lie with us under the shadowy firs.

—We are all of the same Father.

—Ah, Black-Robe, were we of one Father we should know how to make knives and coats as well as you.

—Listen, old man, in the hollow of my hand I hold a mystic drop which can snatch you from an eternity of woe.

—Do they hunt in Heaven, or make war, or go to feasts?

—Oh, no!

—Then I will not go. It is not good to be lazy.

—Infernal fire and torturing demons await you.

—Why did you baptize our enemy the Huron? He will get to Heaven before us and drive us out when we come.

—There is room for all in Heaven.

—If there is so much room, Black-Robe, why do you guard the entrance so jealously?

—There is little time left. You will surely go to Hell.

—There is much time, Black-Robe. If you and I should talk until the weasel befriends the rabbit, we would not break the rope of days.

—Your eloquence is diabolic. Fire waits for you, old man.

—Yes, Black-Robe, a small shadowy fire, about which sit the shades of my relatives and ancestors.

When the Jesuit left him he called for Catherine Tekakwitha.

—Sit beside me.

—Yes, Uncle.

—Remove the blanket which covers me.

—Yes, Uncle.

—Look at this body. This is an old Mohawk body. Look closely.

—I am looking. Uncle.

—Do not weep, Kateri. We do not see well through tears, and although that which we see through tears is bright it is also bent.

—I will look at you without tears, Uncle.

—Remove all my garments and look at me closely.

—Yes, Uncle.

—Look for a long time. Look closely. Look and look.

—I will do as you say, Uncle.

—There is much time.

—Yes, Uncle.

—Your Aunts are spying through the spaces between the bark but do not distract yourself. Look and look.

—Yes, Uncle.

—What do you see, Kateri?

—I see an old Mohawk body.

—Look and look and I will tell you what will happen when the spirit begins to leave my body.

—I cannot listen, Uncle. I am a Christian now. Oh, do not hurt my hand.

—Listen and look. What I tell you cannot offend any god, yours or mine, the Mother of the Beard or the Great Hare.

—I will listen.

—When the wind is no longer in my nostrils my spirit body will begin a long journey homeward. Look at this wrinkled, scarred body as I speak to you. My beautiful spirit body will begin a hard, dangerous journey. Many do not complete this journey, but I will. I will cross a treacherous river standing on a log. Wild rapids will try to throw me against sharp rocks. A huge dog will bite my heels. Then I will follow a narrow path between dancing boulders which crash together, and many will be crushed, but I will dance with the boulders. Look at this old Mohawk body as I speak to you, Catherine. Beside the path there is a bark hut. In the hut lives Oscotarach, the Head-Piercer. I will stand beneath him and he will remove the brain from my skull. This he does to all the skulls which pass by. It is the necessary preparation for the Eternal Hunt. Look at this body and listen.

—Yes, Uncle.

—What do you see?

—An old Mohawk body.

—Good. Cover me now. Do not weep. I will not die now. I will dream my cure.

—Oh, Uncle, I am so happy.

As soon as smiling Catherine Tekakwitha left the long house her cruel Aunts fell on her with fists and curses. She fell beneath their blows. "Ce fut en cette occasion," writes P. Cholenec, "qu'elle déclara ce qu'on aurait peut-être ignoré, si elle n'avait pas été mise à cette épreuve, que, par la miséricorde du Seigneur, elle ne se souvenait pas d'avoir jamais terni la pureté de son corps, et qu'elle n'appréhendait point de recevoir aucun reproche sur cet article au jour du jugement."

—You fucked your Uncle! they cried.

—You uncovered his nakedness!

—You peeked at his tool!

They dragged her to the priest. Le P. de Lamberville.

—Here's a little Christian for you. Fucked her Uncle!

The priest sent away the howling savages and examined the young girl stretched bleeding on the ground before him. When he was satisfied he drew her up.

—You live here like a flower among poison thorns.

—Thank you, my father.

47.

Long ago (it seems) I awakened in my bed with F. pulling my hairs.

—Come with me, my friend.

—What time is it, F.?

—It is the summer of 1964.

He wore a curious smile on his face which I had not seen before. I cannot explain it, but it made me shy, and I crossed my legs.

—Get up. We're going for a walk.

—Turn around while I get dressed.

—No.

—Please.

He pulled the sheet from my body, still heavy with sleep and the dreams of a lost wife. He shook his head slowly.

—Why didn't you listen to Charles Axis?

—Please, F.

—Why didn't you listen to Charles Axis?

I squeezed my thighs tighter and laid the nightcap across my pubic hair. F. stared at me relentlessly.

—Confess. Why didn't you listen to Charles Axis? Why didn't you send away the coupon on that distant afternoon in the orphanage?

—Leave me alone.

—Just look at your body.

—Edith had no complaints about my body.

—Ha!

—Did she ever say anything to you about my body?

—Plenty.

—Such as?

—She said you have an arrogant body.

—What the hell is that supposed to mean?

—Confess, my friend. Confess about Charles Axis. Confess your sin of pride.

—I have nothing to confess. Now turn around and I'll get dressed. It's too early for your cheap koans.

With a lightning flash he twisted my arm in a half-nelson, twisted me off the nostalgic bed, and forced me to confront the full-length mirror in the bathroom. Miraculously the nightcap had adhered to the wiry growth of my pubic hair. I shut my eyes.

—Ouch!

—Look. Look and confess. Confess why you ignored Charles Axis.

—No.

He tightened his expert grip.

—Oh, oh, oh, please! Help!

—The truth! You disdained the coupon because of the sin of pride, didn't you. Charles Axis wasn't enough for you. In your greedy brain you cherished an unspeakable desire. You wanted to be Blue Beetle. You wanted to be Captain Marvel. You wanted to be Plastic Man. Robin wasn't even good enough for you, you wanted to be Batman.

—You're breaking my back!

—You wanted to be the Superman who was never Clark Kent. You wanted to live at the front of the comic. You wanted to be Ibis the Invincible who never lost his Ibistick. You wanted SOCK! POW! SLAM! UGG! OOF! YULP! written in the air between you and all the world. To become a New Man in just fifteen minutes a day meant absolutely nothing to you. Confess!

—The pain! The pain! Yes, yes, I confess. I wanted miracles! I didn't want to climb to success on a ladder of coupons! I wanted to wake up suddenly with X-ray Vision! I confess!

—Good.

He turned the half-nelson into an embrace and drew me to him. My fingers were very skillful there in the porcelain gloom of my prison bathroom. As I undid the top clasp of his beltless Slim Jim slacks, I flicked away the nightcap. It fell between my toes and his shoes like an autumn figleaf in a Utopia of nudists. The curious smile hadn't left his luscious mouth.

—Ah, my friend, I have waited a long time for that confession.

Arm in arm, we walked through the narrow harbor streets of Montreal. We watched great showers of wheat fall into the holds of Chinese cargo boats. We saw the geometry of the gulls as they drifted in perfect circles over center points of garbage. We watched great liners shrink as they hooted down the widening St. Lawrence, shrink into shining birch-bark canoes, then into white-caps, then into the mauve haze of distant hills.

—Why do you smile like that all the time? Doesn't your face get sore?

—I'm smiling because I think I've taught you enough.

Arm in arm, we climbed the streets that led to the mountain, Mont Royal, which gives its name to our city. Never before had the shops of Ste. Catherine

Street bloomed so brightly, or the noon crowds thronged so gaily. I seemed to see it for the first time, the colors wild as those first splashes of paint on the white skin of the reindeer.

—Let's buy steamed hot dogs in Woolworth's.

—Let's eat them with our arms crossed, taking risks with mustard.

We walked along Sherbrooke Street, west, toward the English section of the city. We felt the tension immediately. At the corner of Parc Lafontaine Park we heard the shouted slogans of a demonstration.

—Québec Libre!

—Québec Oui, Ottawa Non!

—Merde à la reine d'angleterre!

—Elizabeth Go Home!

The newspapers had just announced the intention of Queen Elizabeth to visit Canada, a state visit planned for October.

—This is an ugly crowd, F. Let's walk faster.

—No, it is a beautiful crowd.

—Why?

—Because they think they are Negroes, and that is the best feeling a man can have in this century.

Arm in arm, F. pulled me to the scene of commotion. Many of the demonstrators wore sweatshirts inscribed with QUEBEC LIBRE. I noticed that everyone had a hard-on, including the women. From the base of a monument, a well-known young film maker addressed the cheering assembly. He wore the scholarly thin beard and violent leather jacket so commonly seen in the corridors of L'Office National du Film. His voice rang out clearly. F.'s judo pressure cautioned me to listen carefully.

—History! the young man called over our heads. What have we to do with History?

The question inflamed them.

—History! they shouted. Give us back our History! The English have stolen our History!

F. pressed deeper into the mass of bodies. They received us automatically, like quicksand swallowing up the laboratory monster. The echoes of the young man's clear voice hung above us like skywriting.

—History! he continued. History decreed that in the battle for a continent the Indian should lose to the Frenchman. In 1760 History decreed that the Frenchman should lose to the Englishman!

—Booo! Hang the English!

I felt a pleasant sensation at the base of my spine and jiggled ever so slightly against the thin nylon dress of a fanatic, who cheered behind me.

—In 1964 History decrees, no, History commands that the English surrender this land, which they have loved so imperfectly, surrender it to the Frenchman, surrender it to us!

—Bravo! Mon pays malheureux! Québec Libre!

I felt a hand slip down the back of my baggy trousers, a female hand because it had long fingernails smooth and tapered as a fuselage.

—Fuck the English! I shouted unexpectedly.

—That's it, F. whispered.

—History decrees that there are Losers and Winners. History cares nothing for cases. History cares only whose Turn it is. I ask you, my friends, I ask you a simple question: whose Turn is it today?

—Our Turn! rose in one deafening answer.

The crowd, of which I was now a joyful particle, pressed even closer about the monument, as if we were a nut on a screw to which the whole city we longed to possess wound us tighter and tighter like a wrench. I loosed my belt to let her hand go deeper. I did not dare turn around to face her. I did not want to know who she was—that seemed to me the highest irrelevance. I could feel her nylon-sheathed breasts squash against my back, making damp sweat circles on my shirt.

—Yesterday it was the Turn of the Anglo-Scottish banker to leave his name on the hills of Montreal. Today it is the Turn of the Québec Nationalist to leave his name on the passport of a new Laurentian Republic!

—Vive la République!

This was too much for us. Almost wordlessly we roared our approval. The cool hand turned so now her palm was cupped around me and had easy access to the hairy creases. Hats were jumping above us like popping corn, and no one cared whose hat he got back because we all owned each other's hats.

—Yesterday it was the Turn of the English to have French maids from our villages in Gaspé. Yesterday it was the Turn of the French to have Aristotle and bad teeth.

—Booo! Shame! To the wall!

I smelled the perfume of her sweat and birthday presents, and that was more thrillingly personal than any exchange of names could be. She herself thrust her pelvic region hard against her own trouser-covered hand to reap, as it were, the by-products of her erotic entry. With my free hand I reached behind the both of us to grab like a football her flowery left cheek, and so we were locked together.

—Today it is the Turn of the English to have dirty houses and French bombs in their mailboxes!

F. had detached himself to get closer to the speaker. I snaked my other hand behind and fastened it on the right cheek. I swear that we were Plastic Man and Plastic Woman, because I seemed to be able to reach her everywhere, and she traveled through my underwear effortlessly. We began our rhythmical movements which corresponded to the very breathing of the mob, which was our family and the incubator of our desire.

—Kant said: If someone makes himself into an earth-worm, can he complain if he is stepped on? Sekou Touré said: No matter what you say, Nationalism is psychologically inevitable and we all are nationalists! Napoleon said: A nation has lost everything if it has lost its independence. History chooses whether Napoleon shall speak these words from a throne to a throng, or from the window of a hut to a desolate sea!

This academic virtuosity was a little problematical for the crowd and provoked only a few exclamations. However, at that moment, out of the corner of my eye, I saw F. lifted on the shoulders of some young men. A wildcat cheer went up as he was recognized, and the speaker hastened to incorporate the spontaneous outburst into the intense orthodoxy of the whole crowd.

—We have among us a Patriot! A man the English could not disgrace even in their own Parliament!

F. slid back into the reverent knot which had hoisted him, his clenched fist raised above him like the periscope of a diving sub. And now, as if the presence of this veteran conferred a new mystic urgency, the speaker began to speak, almost to chant. His voice caressed us, just as my fingers her, just as her fingers me, his voice fell over our desire like a stream over a moaning water wheel, and I knew that all of us, not just the girl and me, all of us were going to come together. Our arms were tangled and squashed, and I did not know if it was I who held the root of my cock or she who greased the stiffening of her labia! Every one of us there had the arms of Plastic Man, and we held each other, all naked from the waist, all sealed in a frog jelly of sweat and juice, all bound in the sweetest bursting daisy chain!

—Blood! What does Blood mean to us?

—Blood! Give us back our Blood!

—Rub harder! I shouted, but some angry faces shushed me.

—From the earliest dawn of our race, this Blood, this shadowy stream of life, has been our nourishment and our destiny. Blood is the builder of the body, and Blood is the source of the spirit of the race. In Blood lurks our ancestral inheritance, in Blood is embodied the shape of our History, from Blood blooms the flower of our Glory, and Blood is the undercurrent which they can never divert, and which all their stolen money cannot dry up!

—Give us our Blood!

—We demand our History!

—Vive la République!

—Don't stop! I shouted.

—Elizabeth Go Home!

—More! I pleaded. Bis! Bis! Encore!

The meeting began to break up, the daisy chain began to fray. The speaker had disappeared from the pedestal. Suddenly I was facing everyone. They were leaving. I grabbed lapels and hems.

—Don't go! Get him to speak more!

—Patience, citoyen, the Revolution has begun.

—No! Make him speak more! Nobody leave this park!

The throng pushed past me, apparently satisfied. At first the men smiled when I seized their lapels, attributing my imprecations to revolutionary ardor. At first the women laughed when I took their hands and checked them for traces of my pubic hair, because I wanted her, the girl I'd come to the dance with, the girl whose round sweat fossils I still wore on the back of my shirt.

—Don't go. Don't leave! Seal the park!

—Let go of my hand!

—Stop hanging on my lapels!

—We've got to go back to work!

I implored three big men wearing QUEBEC LIBRE sweatshirts to hoist me on their shoulders. I tried to get my foot hooked on the top of a pair of trousers so I could scramble up their sweaters and address the disintegrating family from the height of a shoulder.

—Get this creep off me!

—He looks English!

—He looks Jewish!

—But you can't leave! I haven't come yet!

—This man is a sex pervert!

—Let's beat the shit out of him. He's probably a sex pervert.

—He's smelling girls' hands.

—He's smelling his own hands!

—He's an odd one.

Then F. was beside me, big F., certifying my pedigree, and he led me away from the park which was now nothing but an ordinary park with swans and candy wrappers. Arm in arm, he led me down the sunny street.

—F., I cried. I didn't come. I failed again.

—No, darling, you passed.

—Passed what?

—The test.

—What test?

—The second-to-last test.

from *The Handmaid's Tale* (1985)

The Ceremony goes as usual.

I lie on my back, fully clothed except for the healthy white cotton under-drawers. What I could see, if I were to open my eyes, would be the large white canopy of Serena Joy's outsized colonial-style four-poster bed, suspended like a sagging cloud above us, a cloud sprigged with tiny drops of silver rain, which, if you looked at them closely, would turn out to be four-petalled flowers. I would not see the carpet, which is white, or the sprigged curtains and skirted dressing table with its silver-backed brush and mirror set; only the canopy, which manages to suggest at one and the same time, by the gauziness of its fabric and its heavy downward curve, both ethereality and matter.

Or the sail of a ship. Big-bellied sails, they used to say, in poems. Bellying. Propelled forward by a swollen belly.

A mist of Lily of the Valley surrounds us, chilly, crisp almost. It's not warm in this room.

Above me, towards the head of the bed, Serena Joy is arranged, outspread. Her legs are apart, I lie between them, my head on her stomach, her pubic bone under the base of my skull, her thighs on either side of me. She too is fully clothed.

My arms are raised; she holds my hands, each of mine in each of hers. This is supposed to signify that we are one flesh, one being. What it really means is that she is in control, of the process and thus of the product. If any. The rings of her left hand cut into my fingers. It may or may not be revenge.

My red skirt is hitched up to my waist, though no higher. Below it the Commander is fucking. What he is fucking is the lower part of my body. I do not say making love, because this is not what he's doing. Copulating too would be inaccurate, because it would imply two people and only one is involved. Nor does rape cover it: nothing is going on here that I haven't signed up for. There wasn't a lot of choice but there was some, and this is what I chose.

Therefore I lie still and picture the unseen canopy over my head. I remember Queen Victoria's advice to her daughter. Close your eyes and think of England. But this is not England. I wish he would hurry up.

Maybe I'm crazy and this is some new kind of therapy.

I wish it were true; then I could get better and this would go away.

Serena Joy grips my hands as if it is she, not I, who's being fucked, as if she finds it either pleasurable or painful, and the Commander fucks, with a regular two-four marching stroke, on and on like a tap dripping. He is preoccupied, like a man humming to himself in the shower without knowing he's humming; like a man who has other things on his mind. It's as if he's somewhere else, waiting for himself to come, drumming his fingers on the table while he waits. There's an impatience in his rhythm now. But isn't this everyone's wet dream, two women at once? They used to say that. Exciting, they used to say.

What's going on in this room, under Serena Joy's silvery canopy, is not exciting. It has nothing to do with passion or love or romance or any of those other notions we used to titillate ourselves with. It has nothing to do with sexual desire, at least for me, and certainly not for Serena. Arousal and orgasm are no longer thought necessary; they would be a symptom of frivolity merely, like jazz garters or beauty spots: superfluous distractions for the light-minded. Outdated. It seems odd that women once spent such time and energy reading about such things, thinking about them, worrying about them, writing about them. They are so obviously recreational.

This is not recreation, even for the Commander. This is serious business. The Commander, too, is doing his duty.

If I were to open my eyes a slit, I would be able to see him, his not-unpleasant face hanging over my torso, with a few strands of his silver hair falling perhaps over his forehead, intent on his inner journey, that place he is hurrying towards, which recedes as in a dream at the same speed with which he approaches it. I would see his open eyes.

If he were better looking would I enjoy this more?

At least he's an improvement on the previous one, who smelled like a church cloakroom in the rain; like your mouth when the dentist starts picking at your teeth; like a nostril. The Commander, instead, smells of mothballs, or is this odour some punitive form of aftershave? Why does he have to wear that stupid uniform? But would I like his white, tufted raw body any better?

Kissing is forbidden between us. This makes it bearable.

One detaches oneself. One describes.

He comes at last, with a stifled groan as of relief. Serena Joy, who has been holding her breath, expels it. The Commander, who has been propping himself on his elbows, away from our combined bodies, doesn't permit himself to sink down into us. He rests a moment, withdraws, recedes, rezippers. He nods, then turns and leaves the room, closing the door with exaggerated care behind him, as if both of us are his ailing mother. There's something hilarious about this, but I don't dare laugh.

Serena Joy lets go of my hands. "You can get up now," she says. "Get up and get out." She's supposed to have me rest, for ten minutes, with my feet on a pillow to improve the chances.

This is meant to be a time of silent meditation for her, but she's not in the mood for that. There is loathing in her voice, as if the touch of my flesh sickens and contaminates her. I untangle myself from her body, stand up; the juice of the Commander runs down my legs. Before I turn away I see her straighten her blue skirt, clench her legs together; she continues lying on the bed, gazing up at the canopy above her, stiff and straight as an effigy.

Which of us is it worse for, her or me?

Nancy Christie

"Sacred Sex: The United Church and the Privatization of the Family in Post-War Canada," *Households of Faith* (2002)

> Christianity looks upon sex as one of the basic factors in human experi-
> ence. The Word became flesh in Christ, thereby manifesting the truth that
> the physical can be the vehicle of the spiritual ... Sex is God-given and as
> such we must seek to understand its meanings and manifestations in phys-
> ical development, physiological reactions and spiritual potentiality.[1]

This remarkable statement by the Board of Evangelism and Social Service of
the United Church of Canada suggests that what has come to be known as the
"sexual revolution" was not simply the product of the liberal youth culture of
the 1960s, as some historians have maintained.[2] As this essay will argue, mainstream institutions such as the Protestant churches, which otherwise have
been mythologized as the vessels of the conservative social mores so characteristic of the 1950s, were in fact agents of cultural change and were at the
forefront in redefining the nature of the family and the purpose of sexual
relations, as well as more relativistic conceptions of morality. Between 1945
and 1966 the United Church's perception of sex changed radically from epit-
omizing original sin to symbolizing the highroad to the Kingdom of God, a
transformation that calls into question the easy generalizations about the
1950s as a somnolent and conservative era that have been offered by the snap-
shot analysis of generational historians.[3] Their emphasis upon mega-trends
and their propensity to juxtapose the domestic ideology of the post-war era
against the liberal aspirations of 1960s youth have masked the complex
undercurrents of cultural change that percolated beneath the surface. Moreover, their descriptive narrative, which rightly points out that the family was
re-conceived as a haven of emotional and psychological retreat, rather than
primarily as an economic unit, during this period, fails to explain why there
was a heightened emphasis upon the centrality of the domestic sphere during these post-war decades.

   Indeed, one of the striking lacunae in the historiography of the baby-boom
generation is the virtual absence of any lengthy discussion of Canada's Protestant churches, institutions that traditionally have seen marriage, children,
and family as crucial to sustaining evangelical faith. By focusing upon an institution that had for generations spoken about the theme of family, separate
spheres, and sexual conduct, we can more precisely discern what was indeed

novel about the discourse on family after World War II, and more importantly, we can discover some of the reasons why the Canadian family was reinterpreted as occupying a distinctly private realm, and why sex became elevated
from an act circumscribed by prohibitions to the centrepiece of religious
experience, the development of a healthy personality, and the hallmark of
individual liberty, especially for women. The idea of domesticity, I argue, was
not consensual; rather, it was a contested terrain and thus a receptacle for a
multiplicity of ideological perspectives. While it may be said that the Protestant churches participated in the general discourse on the family, their preoccupation with it was not simply a consequence of concerns over wartime
instability and fears regarding the rise of delinquency; nor were they concerned with the containment of the sexual energies of modern teenagers in
the face of the Cold War threat. Rather, their elevated concern for the family was a response to uniquely Canadian events, such as the emergence of the
welfare state—most notably, the Family Allowances Act of 1944—the consequent spectre of the political power of Roman Catholicism in Quebec, and
the realization that, by entering the workforce in ever larger numbers, married women were transgressing traditional gender categories. Though the
impulse of Protestantism to resist these disruptive social forces was an essentially conservative one, the very attempt to control and contain what were
viewed as direct challenges to the authority of the Protestant churches had
peculiarly liberal results and were instrumental in establishing the cultural
preconditions for modern sexual mores. In the years immediately after World
War II the problem of how to stabilize the family was under discussion, a
debate well documented by several historians, including Annalee Golz, Doug
Owram, and Elaine Tyler May. Post-war commentators fretted over normalizing gender relations within the family and thus directed their attention to the
problem of whether married women would choose the workplace over the
home, or whether returned soldiers would rejoin their families and once
again take up their responsibilities to work and support their dependents. As
well, a host of social commentators saw in the escalating divorce rate and the
increase in juvenile delinquency and illegitimate births distinct signs of moral
and social decay.[4]

Although the notions that the family was merely a microcosm of society
and that home and nation were interdependent were not new ideas,[5] the
public insistence that domestic values determined social stability and economic progress reached a fever pitch in the first few years after the war.
Indeed, the idea that domestic economic prosperity, the upholding of gender
boundaries between the workplace and the home, and a stable family life
were all interdependent variables was frequently evoked during the public
debate on family allowances between 1942 and 1944.[6] However, the heightened focus upon the importance of marriage and family to the social order
was not simply a response to the supposed instability of family life during the

war; many of the concerns voiced at the conclusion of war found their provenance in social trends which had emerged during the thirties. Thus, while the
Canadian Youth Commission, one of the most concerted efforts to study the
interconnection between employment, women's work, Christian belief, and
family relations, was established in 1943, the actual impetus behind its existence hearkened back to concerns arising out of the Depression, when social
scientists first uncovered the troubling connection between youth unemployment, the postponement of marriage, and the development of deviant sexual behaviour.[7]

Like many other commentators at the time, the authors of the various
reports of the Youth Commission adumbrated a decidedly public conception
of family, viewing it as the most fundamental cell of all social relationships. In
Young Canada and Religion, published at the end of the war in 1945, the commission concluded that the home promoted "unselfishness and a sense of
responsibility," and because of its singular ability to establish "Christian principles," the family was the outstanding institution and the most powerful
influence in society."[8] In drawing a direct connection between the character
of the family and national well-being, the *Youth Commission* echoed a set of
beliefs that had been frequently articulated in Canada since the turn of the
twentieth century, when industrialization and the apparent increase in poverty and social inequality, together with the assertion of women's rights, were
seen to be potent forces creating family disarray. In this way the statement
offered by the United Church that the "life of the nation cannot rise above
the level of life in its homes"[9] was not a novel one. Indeed, the Protestant
churches were but one among a host of voices that stressed the home as a
nursery for the development of notions of thrift, work, and responsibility
which were so crucial to sustaining national economic progress and that
placed an overwhelming emphasis upon the moral economy of the family
with its important "emotional or personality functions."[10]

If the church's insistence that the primary function of the stable, Christian
family was to forestall social collapse replicated a conservative ideological
position indistinguishable from the broader culture, its preoccupation with
the interconnectedness of marriage and nationalism was a direct response to
the anti-Catholicism that was unleashed by the implementation of the Family
Allowances Act of 1944. While anti-Catholicism has always simmered just
beneath the surface of the Protestant creed, it was catapulted to the centre of
public debate with the implementation of government family allowances.
Old-style conservative nationalists erroneously believed that this social legislation would reward large Catholic families, and it had, in their estimation,
the potential to trigger a birth explosion in Quebec of such enormous proportions that not only would the balance of political power within the dominion be irreversibly altered, but Protestantism would be overcome by the sheer
numerical preponderance of Catholics.[11] Whereas Mackenzie King and the

Liberals argued that welfare measures would bring about national unity by creating equal opportunities for all, Conservative thinkers such as the Reverend Edwin Silcox, Charlotte Whitton, and Premier George Drew adhered to an older vision of nationalism which conceived of the nation in terms of linguistic and religio-cultural traditions and thus saw in family allowances the spectre of destabilizing the balance between French and English Canada. Birth control, observed Silcox, would allay Protestant fears and create national unity, for it would "obviate the suspicion that one ethnic group was trying to outbreed the other." Family allowances, on the other hand, simply inflamed a pre-existing "cultural incompatibility" between Protestant and Catholic.[12] While he recognized that tension existed between the pervasive natalist propaganda, which equated family reproduction with economic prosperity and the necessity to combat Roman Catholic "totalitarian sacerdotalism"[13] perceived by mainline Protestantism, he nevertheless proclaimed the Malthusian argument that overpopulation was the main source of poverty and that an alternative to government relief and family allowances would be a rigorous system of birth control for all families, Protestant and Catholic.[14]

For Protestant leaders, family limitation and the containment of sex even within marriage had distinct social and political consequences. Not only would a national—preferably, government—commitment to birth control solve the problem of the supposed fecundity of the Roman Catholic family, but by permitting families to relate the number of children they produced to the family budget, it would obviate the need for government intervention in family welfare. Social conservatives such as Whitton and Silcox abjured any state intervention in the family because, in their estimation, it allowed governments to tamper with the "natural" responsibility of the male breadwinner to support his dependents. Removing the state from the sphere of family self-sufficiency, Silcox also believed, would eliminate the modern emphasis upon economic over moral imperatives not only from the family circle but also from public discourse and national policy. Moreover, by conveniently demolishing what he castigated as the false god of economic security, he promoted birth control as the true prophylactic against the "acids of modernism," for it would inhibit the need and desire for married women to enter the workforce; not only would it serve to remove the spectre of want and the "lust" for material possessions, but at the same time it would tend to elevate the spiritual and emotional relationship between husband and wife by alleviating the burden of reproduction.[15]

What is compelling about the Protestant churches' response to the threat of Catholic ascendancy is that they did not simply recapitulate the nexus of family and nation which has come, in the common coin of historical discussion, to denote the conservative, complacent culture of the 1950s. Rather than reaffirming the long-held notion that the family was a public institution, anti-Catholicism was in fact the catalyst that decidedly shifted the whole bias of evangelicalism and the very question of the survival of the church towards the issue of reproduction and sexuality. By so doing, the United Church began to carve out a new sensibility in which the family looked inward to the private relationships of its members, rather than outward to the world of public duties and ideologies. By 1945 this movement from public to private was in its incipient stage, for leading commentators in the United Church began explicitly to proclaim that the family was a "divine institution" based on love and fidelity. However, some continued to maintain that personal values and individual rights must be preserved and exalted in the interests of sustaining democracy. The high-water mark of this congruence between family and society, private and public values, and the sacred and the secular, which formed the foundation of social evangelism, was represented by the wartime United Church Committee on Mixed Marriages, one of whose architects, the Reverend Hugh Dobson, reported that the "Family to a far greater degree than the State determines the shape of things to come and the nature of the civilization which is on the way ... If we can produce a democratic and Christian family life—Democracy and a Christian civilization to that degree is on the way!"[16] In this statement, Dobson unwittingly identified what would become the catalyst for the privatization of the family—namely, the modern state.

His insistence that an individual's experience within the family was a more direct route to achieving the Kingdom of God than her or his participation in the wider society represented a crucial break with the tradition of social Christianity which had formed the core of the United Church's outlook since the turn of the twentieth century. What was especially remarkable about this abrupt about-face undertaken by Dobson at the end of World War II was that he was one of the principal exemplars of the ideal of a full-orbed Christianity, in which evangelicalism and social reform constituted a seamless whole. In this formulation the state was perceived as part and parcel of a broader Christian culture and was thus regarded as an institution both complementary and subordinate to Protestant church authority.[17] This equipoise between church and state, in which both institutions functioned amicably within an interdependent culture and society characterized as "an organic whole," was breached with the launch of the Liberal government's social security legislation in 1943–44. In the view of conservative clergymen such as Edwin Silcox, by defining familial security and stability wholly in terms with economic well-being, the Beveridge and Marsh reports threatened to re-conceive society as "an economic machine."[18] With the emergence of a social security state, not only did church leaders suddenly recognize that the goals of government were singularly economic and thus amoral in their attitudes in that they gave little recognition to the spiritual and emotional contexts of family life, but the weakening authority of Protestantism within the realms of government and social reform were forcefully brought home by the fact that the Liberal reconstruction and social security proposals had been devised by university-trained economic experts such as Leonard Marsh, F. Cyril James, A.E. Grauer, and George Davidson, who were indifferent to the United Church's traditions in the field of family social policy.

Not only had Protestant church leaders been excluded from the inner circles of government policy-making during the war, but—more disturbingly for the influence of Protestantism in Canadian society as a whole—clergymen believed that, although in practice the creation of a cadre of elite experts, the modern security state had garnered such a large degree of mass support that, from their point of view, the emergence of the welfare state had been transformed into a broad cultural movement. It was this aspect of the welfare state that most threatened the cultural edifice of Christianity and prompted the United Church Committee to Arrange for a Forward Movement after the War to declare that "this is what makes the real crisis of our time a cultural as well as a moral one."[19] In many ways, the Liberal government's own propaganda that the very essence of the nation grew out of its offer of social security to the masses was immensely successful. What induced clergymen such as Silcox to equate family allowances with the demise of Protestantism and to rail against the "doctrinaire apotheosis of the common man,"[20] an attitude that ran directly counter to Protestant traditions of incorporating the aspirations of the Canadian working class, was that public debate over the Liberal welfare initiative reinterpreted human personality and identity wholly in terms of government provision of material security. Indeed, much of the public commentary on social security involved finding the intellectual means by which to directly link the ideal of individual self-determination with the drastic expansion of government authority. Thus Paul Martin, himself a former labour activist in Windsor, observed that the true realization of "man's personality"[21] lay with government welfare schemes. Not only did he maintain that the idea of "liberty for all"[22] was derived from economic variables, but he, like other defenders of the new social security state, postulated that, because the government was the only institution in modern society which could provide equal access to economic abundance, it alone defended the "democratic way of life."[23]

The way in which the crucible of welfare discussion redefined democracy as an economic creed was anathema to the principles of Protestant belief.[24] The emphasis that social security now placed on the rights of the masses to economic prosperity threatened the very essence of Christian endeavour. By rejecting the idea that individuals had a responsibility to society, it not only nullified the Christian ideal of social service, but it eviscerated the notion that all social relations flowed from an inherently moral core. Under this new dispensation, the individual had a prior right to government assistance irrespective of any obligation to society, a modern idea of citizenship that totally expunged any necessity for a moral community. It was for this reason that Silcox denounced "the arms of the paternal state" and its privileging of economic security, for not only had this virus of materialism begun to infect "even religious people," but it threatened "to take the place of salvation as the highest good."[25]

The creation of social security profoundly unsettled the Protestant mindset, not simply because legislation such as the Family Allowances Act appeared to diminish the conservative ideal of family self-sufficiency, but because post-war welfare, in identifying the state and economic security with the totality of social and cultural experience, seemed to the beleaguered leaders of the United Church completely to eradicate Christian ethics from Canadian culture. Unprecedented wartime state growth redefined the boundaries between church and state and compelled the United Church to retreat from culture into the precincts of a narrowly defined institutional church, guarded by the ramparts of a neo-orthodox theology which insisted upon a radical disjuncture between the secular and the sacred. The modern welfare state thus destroyed the concept of a full-orbed Christianity which had so well sustained the authority of Protestantism for four decades. In January 1943, the very month in which Leonard Marsh began to write his famous *Report on Social Security*, the United Church attempted to stave off the forces of economic materialism by establishing a Commission on Church, Nation and World Order. The stated objectives of this Protestant commission were to establish "the RIGHT of the Church to speak on political, economic and social problems."[26] However, that the church felt compelled to enunciate reasons why it had a claim upon the public sphere was telling evidence of the rapidity with which its broader cultural authority had been eroded during wartime.

The commission ultimately failed miserably in its attempt to temper the implications of Marsh's conclusions, for in their desire to counter what they termed "modern economic thinking"—"modern Beveridgian philosophy"[27]—church leaders were forced into an increasingly conservative bunker. In final analysis, the commission's report was feeble and merely restated the verities of nineteenth-century moral philosophy, which exalted the doctrine of self-help, and its remedy for the deficiencies of modern, mass culture was to retreat into a parody of Matthew Arnold's Oxbridgean elitism, in which the quest for high art and culture would evoke "the deep moral undertones"[28] of society. While church leaders hoped to deploy the commission as a means of propping up its message of social evangelism in order to deflate the popular movement for government social security, the commission's backlash against modernism propelled it into an ultimately defeatist attitude, in which its members declaimed against environmentalist explanations of poverty, concluding that the ills of society were the result of disobedience to God, a position unheard of in mainstream Protestantism since the palmy days of the age of atonement in the mid-nineteenth century.[29] In attempting to assuage the impact of "secular and materialistic" forces, one of its prominent lay advisers, Arthur Lower, who taught at United College, Winnipeg, actually protested against any intervention, whether by private or by public means, which might raise the general standard of living, claiming that "a facile materialism is no answer to life's problems," because history had taught that only through tragedy and struggle did individuals find spiritual awakening.[30] The increasingly conservative direction of the United Church was not merely a temporary aberration, but gained force throughout the decade following the war. Indeed, by 1950 the Commission on Culture, a precursor to the Massey Commission, replete with a similarly elitist bias, released a report entitled *The Church and the Secular World*, in which it defined our modern cultural crisis "as the result of forces that had divorced religious faith from all other matters pertaining to human life." Although at specific junctures throughout the report the commission's members, who included Mary Q. Innis, John Irving, Northrop Frye, Professor John Line (a former member of the left-leaning Fellowship for a Christian Social Order), Lorne Pierce, and Principal Graham of United College, spoke of their desire to reintegrate science and religion, the secular and the sacred; but so completely had modern, conservative theologies such as neo-orthodoxy come to define the United Church's identity that the commission could only declare that, because "in modern thinking God has been dethroned," the church's survival depended upon its standing "over-against the world."[31]

The fact that United Church leaders now maintained that there existed an unbridgeable gap between the secular and the sacred and had effectively relinquished the wider culture of politics, social reform, and education as a sphere of Christian influence constituted the intellectual watershed which was instrumental in compelling the Protestant churches to seek out a new relationship between the institutional church and the family. If the wellspring of the church's sustenance and the means of finding the Kingdom of God could no longer be ensured through an individual's participation in the larger society a new vessel for Christian renewal must be sought. Since the symbol of modernism, according to Protestant thinkers, was the erosion of "personality"— this word occurs again and again throughout their perorations against the palliative of economic security, state control of marriage laws, the overweening demand for emotional stimulants, the increasing dependence upon the machine, economic and psychological definitions of history, and the growing depersonalization and alienation of modern urban living[32]—then it followed that the family must be exalted as the supreme focus for Christian endeavour. Indeed, if the solution to all modern ills rested upon the recovering of what was "uniquely personal,"[33] Protestant leaders concluded that the home was the haven for protection against secularization for it was the only institution that emulated personality, freedom, and spiritual values, and only there were individuals free from the tyranny of utilitarian concerns.[34]

In 1946 the United Church's Commission on Christian Marriage and the Christian Home reported that "the life of the family is being threatened at its source by secularism and materialism, and that the Church has a great responsibility in combatting the disintegration of the home."[35] The preoccupation with marriage, family, and the domestic sphere and the tendency throughout the 1950s to reinterpret these as a private realm in which spiritual and emotional values flourished were not, as recent historians have suggested, a merely secular response to war and international instability; rather, the re-conceptualization of the home as the "plumbline of those ultimate [spiritual] values"[36] was a creation of mainstream Protestantism, and its provenance lay in concerns peculiar to problems of religious faith in a secular world. If the supposed "acids of modernity" and the "secularization of modern social services"[37] were acting primarily upon the family, it was imperative that the United Church capture the domestic sphere and transform the cultural attributes of family life into the central redemptive force in society.

In the United Church discourse the family—and with it, the rights of personality—was commonly juxtaposed against the "absolute value of the state."[38] Increasingly, the family was seen as the singular pathway to faith, superior to even church worship itself. Having relinquished the public sphere to modern "barbarism,"[39] Protestant church leaders felt compelled to elevate the home to a position equivalent with the divine. Thus they concluded that the answers to all ultimate spiritual questions could be found only "through our own hearths,"[40] and homes were celebrated in terms of "domestic ties" that bound its individuals together with God.[41] As never before, the Kingdom of God was understood solely in terms of the home: Christ was the exemplary family-builder; the earthly family mirrored divine domesticity, in which heaven was the ideal home; God was the Father; the church was called the "Mother Church."[42] In short, spiritual efflorescence no longer occurred in the nexus between individual and community; rather, one's whole personal development and the accretion of piety occurred through one's personal fulfillment and emotional satisfaction within the domestic sphere. Domestic security, however, was not the fruit of either maternal morality or the work ethic of the male breadwinner, the traditional gender divisions within the family. Rather, the idea of the world becoming a "household of faith"[43] was guaranteed by sexual intimacy. Increasingly, the ideal Christian and the wellspring of spirituality came to be wholly identified with the sexual act itself, for as Edwin Silcox concluded in his lecture "Toward a Philosophy of Christian Marriage," sex was the "most dynamic and constructive force in the building of personality and in the integration of society."[44]

Immediately after World War II the identification of sex as the central dynamic of society had not as yet taken hold in the United Church. As Arthur Lower, one of the prominent lay leaders of the Commission on Church, Nation and World Order, declared, marriage was still primarily a social act, and for this reason he adamantly opposed divorce on any grounds. Preoccupied with the growth of materialism and hedonism, Lower maintained that the ultimate test for divorce "must be social utility and the spiritual health of society rather than the fate of individuals."[45] Indeed, the report of this commission offered reluctant support to the principle of family allowances because at the very least they reinforced the notion that the family—and more particularly, parenthood—was important to the commonweal.[46] In the years immediately after the war the Protestant conception of the family studiously emphasized the production of children. Lower himself recommended that, at the very least, Protestant families should have three children and preferably five in order to keep abreast of the natural fecundity of Catholics.[47] Moreover, the moral education of children was seen as the centrepiece of evangelical renewal and the primary means of fighting "secular attitudes of life" during wartime.[48] The crucial role played by children in the conversion of adults was evoked in a Mother's Day poster for the Christian Education Advance movement which showed a young girl standing with her parents on their front doorstep and beseechingly asking, "Why don't you come with me to Sunday School?"[49]

This emphasis upon Christian nurture had, since the late nineteenth century, formed a large dimension of evangelical theology, wherein the primary relationship of faith was seen to be between God and his children.[50] In this traditional conceptualization of the Christian home, the family cleaved to the central figure of the moral mother, whose primary role was to use her maternal instincts to promote Christian values throughout society. In turn, the sexual needs of both men and women were considered to be antithetical to the development of spirituality and thus destructive of the Kingdom. This attitude generally held sway within the mainline Protestant denominations until World War II. Thus in 1940 Edwin Silcox protested against the growing tendency throughout society "to minimize procreation or the rearing of a family as the end of marriage, and to consider the question of sex-adjustment as a matter to be solved wholly by the individual according to his own tastes and with little or no sense of social responsibility."[51] Indeed, during wartime, Protestant commentators were somewhat preoccupied with the problem of sex containment for youth,[52] but this never formed a dominant theme even during the 1950s, when popular attitudes regarding sexual discipline were believed to be at their height. Certainly, Silcox, whose wife had recently died, did exclaim, after seeing a "bevy of buxom young girls" passing by with "their skirts swishing rhythmically with the vital abandon of their walking," that if "it weren't for the women, we could extend the Kingdom of God almost indefinitely."[53] And the 1939–40 United Church Committee on Mixed Marriages did warn against the modern emphasis upon "sex gratification" outside of marriage.[54]

What is remarkable about even these conservative commentators is that the concept of original sin occupied an increasingly minor place in their thought. While Silcox may have castigated Freudian psychology for insisting that sex was indispensable to an individual's psychological health,[55] he at the same time called upon the United Church to advance a new sex morality, one that would extoll sex as the primary "spiritual agency," and to re-conceive marriage, not as a social unit of reproduction, but as the personification of personality, in which the physical sharing of husband and wife would in and of itself be symbolic of "Creative love itself." Thus, while marriage was deemed to be the means by which to regulate and channel these dangerous sexual appetites, the libido, thus constrained, was regarded as a determinedly spiritual force, while sexual union itself was re-conceived as even "sacramental in its nature."[56]

What then prompted the leaders of opinion within the United Church to so drastically reinterpret the functions of marriage and family and the relationship between sex and spirituality? Male leaders in the church were driven to reconceptualize the purpose of marriage in terms of sexual satisfaction largely because they recognized that the future of the institution of marriage now centred upon the attitudes of women. While it is true that in the past the church had been receptive to feminist demands for the ideal of a companionate marriage where, through the use of birth control methods, women could exert control over male sexual passion,[57] the impetus to convert the home and family into a haven of emotional and sexual satisfaction for women reached its apex during the 1950s and was directly related to new patterns of women's work. Indeed, the creation of the United Church Commission on Marriage and Divorce in 1957 coincided with a drastic upsurge in married women's work. Although its stated aim was to find a means to reform the divorce laws and at the same time preserve the institution of marriage, its real intent was to reinstate the gender boundaries, which the commission's members believed had been transgressed by the modern, materialistic woman. Women's economic independence could be circumscribed, they believed, if their sexual freedom could be enhanced within the family. Post-war sexual containment was thus not an end in itself, as many have argued; rather, it was a means to the economic containment of married women. As married women began to enter the workforce in increasingly large numbers by the late 1950s, churchmen recognized that the economic independence which work conferred on women created a vast potential for the option of divorce. Declarations such as that issued in 1954 by the Reverend Harriet Christie to the effect that her colleagues would just have to accept the fact that 20 per cent of the working population of Canada now consisted of women did little to allay the rising anxiety within the ranks of the United Church clergy.[58] Apart from a few references to the fact that families with working mothers could potentially produce more homosexuals,[59] the United Church objected to mothers working, not because this would detract from their moral and educative role, but because the fact of married women's work directly challenged the authority of their husbands. The reaction of the United Church during the 1950s contrasted volubly with the immediate post-war mentality as articulated by the Canadian Youth Commission, which inveighed against married women's work primarily because it caused delinquency and diminished the religious function of family life.[60] By the fifties the primary focus of concern was no longer the family as a unit, but the nature of the marital relationship itself.

That the authority of men was thought to reside in both the public sphere of the workplace and the private sphere of the home may be explained by a massive cultural shift which occurred in Canadian society following the Depression. Even though Protestant clergymen may have protested against the concentration that the modern welfare state appeared to place upon economic security, they nevertheless accepted the reinterpretation of the ideal of separate spheres that came about during the thirties. As I have argued in *Engendering the State*, the traditional notion of separate spheres, in which the home was dominated by the moral mother and the workplace by the bread-winning father, was irrevocably transformed. By the end of the Depression, both the workplace and the home had been re-conceived as legitimate domains of the breadwinner; but more significantly, where the borderlines between gender spheres had previously allowed some space for women's work, following the crisis of the thirties the ideal male head of the household was intended to be the sole bread-winner in the family.[61] But what made the economic and social trends of the 1950s even more problematic for defenders of this patriarchal home was that for the first time married women were directly challenging the exclusivity of this male domain, which transcended both the public and the private. It is not without significance then that the United Church's Commission on Marriage and Divorce began to solicit reports from clergymen across the nation in 1958, the very year that witnessed the beginning of one of the severest economic recessions since the war.[62] But because male dominance in the family had become so thoroughly identified with a man's dominance in the workplace, any assaults on his status in the workplace were thought to automatically undermine his status in the home. Thus one submission to the Commission on Marriage and Divorce concluded that, because of the recent explosion in married women's paid labour, a man could not "carry his 'role' as earner in the home."[63]

What the convenors of the Commission on Marriage and Divorce feared therefore, was the end of the patriarchal family, which had hitherto been guaranteed by the pre-eminent status of the husband. Between 1958 and 1966 the commissioners launched a massive research program in order to find ways to deflect the impact of women's work upon male authority in both the workplace and the home. As early as 1950 the report of the United Church Commission on Culture, *The Church and the Secular World*, had identified the problem of "a modern matriarchy,"[64] and by 1957 the spectre of "the difficult masculine wife"[65] had become a reality, as statistics indicated the awful truth that fully one-half of all women in the workforce were married.[66]

Even female commissioners, such as Dr Patricia White, concluded that the fundamental problem posed by "modern society" revolved around the question of gender relations: "In today's society man has lost his former place of authority because, one by one his sources of authority have been taken over by other people and organizations. With the development of Government, Religion, Education and other things man has not the authority that he once had."[67]

While White praised the modern recognition of women in industry and extolled the work of sociologists and anthropologists because they concluded that women were indeed the stronger sex, her male colleagues reached very different conclusions. R.S. Hosking, for example, penned an article in the Toronto *Star Weekly* in 1959 called "What's the Matter with Father." In it he presented an analysis of modern social trends similar to White's. However, he blamed the changing status of men on the changing role of women. In fact he, like other United Church clergymen, conceived of the post-war juggernaut of secularization as a decidedly gender-specific process. Indeed, Edwin Silcox equated modernity with matriarchy. In his peroration "The Menace of Modernity to Christian Life," he concluded that the battleground between the secular and the sacred, between material and spiritual values was merely a reflection of a deeper warfare between biology and economics. That pagan ethics were in the ascendancy Silcox attributed to the disturbing new reality of the working "Magna Mater."[68] For the United Church clergy then, there was no greater symbol of the modern excesses of materialism and the consequent loss of spiritual values than the trend towards married women's work.[69] The increasing depersonalization of life, the obsession with material things, birth control, and the emphasis on personal satisfaction were attributed to women—in particular, their temptation to enter the workplace. The congruence many believed existed between women's desires and modern materialism was clearly enunciated by Hosking. He contended that the primary culprit in the post-war disequilibrium of traditional gender spheres was the modern domestic appliance. Not only did the purchasing of these appliances fuel the desire for more consumer items, but the consequent pressure upon the family budget caused friction between husband and wife. Moreover, in saving women's labour in the home, appliances produced an abundance of leisure time for them, which caused wives to become bored and dissatisfied with their homes, thus propelling them to seek personal satisfaction in the workplace.[70]

It followed from these assumptions that women's sexual gratification was the key to overcoming the temptations of material gratification and the desire for economic independence. What better way to ensure that the sexes are once again "clearly defined" than through the experience of sex itself.[71] Male clergymen believed that establishing an ideal of equality through difference within the sexual relationship would solve the problem of the economic disequilibrium between the sexes outside the home. Thus, while the United Church Commission on Marriage and Divorce addressed the issue of sexual containment among single young people, both heterosexual and homosexual,[72] its real focus was upon the "fundamental satisfactions"[73] experienced by adults within marriage. The enunciation of the modern democratic family, in which husbands and wives were equal but separate in their sexual and emotional temperaments, thus became the means by which the patriarchal family could be defended and the status of the sole, male breadwinner preserved. Ideally, if women were treated as equals within the sexual relationship, thus completing their sense of personal achievement and individuality, male clergymen were convinced, the need to seek economic independence would be negated. This was what was meant when contributors to the Commission on Marriage and Divorce such as R.S. Hosking and Leonard Marsh stated that a new balance had to be found between freedom and discipline within the Canadian family: women were to be given unlimited personal freedom in terms of sexual and emotional satisfaction so that men could regain their role as sole provider and thus rediscover their own sense of authority.[74]

Because the family no longer nourished traditional gender divisions between work and home, sex became the only means for men and women to "discover the meaning of the manhood and womanhood through the various relations in which they fulfill one another."[75] The modern Canadian family was no longer united by the economic contribution of all its members; rather, its interdependent nature flowed from the "personal fellowship" of the husband and wife alone, in which sex was the dynamic for "creating a new union between man and woman."[76] What the members of the Commission on Marriage and Divorce wished to make abundantly clear, however, was that the personality of each partner was not diminished, for in the modern theology in which "sex is sacred," sex became a substitute for evangelical faith in so far as it accentuated "personality and self-realization."[77] Nevertheless, sexual intercourse was believed to be the highest sacramental act, where through "self-abandonment"[78] one found a higher "spiritual integrity"[79] with God. Churchmen, anxious to proffer a new prescription for marriage that would salve women's desire for equality and independence and did not involve economic competition with men, declared that sexual relations must reflect the notion that a woman was a "person with rights."[80] They adamantly rejected the traditional master-servant concept of the marital relationship and maintained that henceforth the basis of marriage must be sexual intercourse, not for procreative purposes, but as an activity in which the consent of the wife was imperative and which would ideally lead to "personal satisfaction"[81] and amplify her sense of individuality, freedom, and creativity. Sexual containment within marriage was an avenue of woman's assertiveness and equality because she, and not the husband, determined the sexual relationship. However, the personal gratification she derived from an equal sexual relationship within marriage was also touted as a relief from the cultural poverty of the modern, technologically driven home and as the spiritual counterpoint to the alienation of modern industrial automation. Sex was thus the surest pathway that would lead the modern woman back to the welcoming family circle.

The novelty of such a positive revalorization of sex, especially a new concern with the importance of female sexuality, within the official thinking of the United Church should not be underestimated. It did not simply constitute an extension of pre-war ideals of "companionate marriage" or the interest of certain clerics such as Edwin Silcox in the question of birth control, evident in the 1930s. While a number of American historians began in the 1980s to insist that, within the wider culture, positive views of female sexuality became the mainstream in the 1920s and 1930s, reversing the nineteenth-century association of sexuality with maleness,[82] a more nuanced revisionism has suggested serious qualifications to this chronology. Indeed, it would seem that in both Britain and the United States any severing of female sexuality from reproduction did not permeate the social strata beyond rather limited segments of upper-middle-class, urban bohemians or Ivy League college youth before the 1940s. Working-class attitudes firmly condemned casual sex, and there was little evidence for a widespread culturally accepted notion that marriage was based solely on sex.[83] Likewise, the historical definition of "companionate marriage," promoted by the Protestant churches in the era before World War II, is itself the subject of considerable misunderstanding.[84] Companionate marriage had its origins in an insistence on egalitarian and emotional compatibility, and it was only in the 1930s that sexual compatibility was added to this equation,[85] a view that did not reach Canada until after World War II. More significantly, a commitment to birth control, usually regarded as the harbinger of more positive notions of female sexuality, seems not to have fulfilled this function in the Canadian Protestant churches. Until 1932 the United Church remained officially committed to large families, and although by the later 1930s the church could speak in terms of "voluntary parenthood," there seems to have been little connection between birth control and acceptance of sexual pleasure. In the immediate post-war period there was something of a backlash against the idea of birth control in some sections of the United Church, and although clearly liberal views prevailed by the early 1960s, with the United Church well in advance of the Anglican Church on such matters, the impetus from Anglicans and other Protestants seems not to have stemmed from the need to accommodate the notion of female sexual desire but, rather, from concerns over global overpopulation.[86]

While the impetus behind the United Church's Commission on Marriage and Divorce to regularize the concept of the "two-sex society"[87] was decidedly conservative, the underlying implications were much more liberal in orientation and led rapidly to the jettisoning of traditional standards of morality and a new sexual ethic for Canadian society. Where old-style evangelicals continued to associate the sins of the flesh with the devil,[88] the younger cadre of United Church clergymen asserted the view that sexual intercourse itself was a sacred act. If sexual behaviour was reinterpreted as an actual positive force, "especially but not exclusively within marriage,"[89] it was difficult to maintain the older view that sex was immoral. Moreover, because this new theology of sex was so identified with female desire for emotional satisfaction, personal development, and the woman's very sense of individuality, it was likewise impossible to sustain the conception of woman as the temptress. In 1958 United Church clergymen began to warn against sermons that superficially drew an equation between "sin and sins of the flesh."[90] By 1960 the whole Protestant tradition of moral theology had been recast. "Christianity at its best," commented one clergyman, "has never considered the human body evil ... Sex, being part of the order of God's creation, is good and not evil."[91] By conceiving of sex as a divine gift and the body as a thing to be enjoyed, clergymen were compelled to abandon the very concept of original sin and to maintain that the real message of Genesis was that Adam and Eve had simply disobeyed God.[92] Thus promiscuity and homosexuality were now deemed to be merely symptoms of "a disturbed personality," which could be easily forgiven and remedied through Christian counselling.[93] Even the very notion of monogamy came under scrutiny by clergymen such as the young John Webster Grant, who castigated the first drafts of the report of the Commission on Marriage and Divorce for their "pious spirituality" and called for the Scriptures to be reinterpreted in terms of "the newest discoveries in the social sciences," which postulated that the concepts of monogamy and sexual chastity were not eternal moral verities but merely cultural constructs relative to time and place.[94]

By 1960 moral relativism had become the watchword of the new theology of the United Church. Driven by the increasing emphasis that Protestantism placed upon "the freedom of the individual,"[95] church leaders in turn dropped the traditional moral sanctions against divorce. By 1966, in their landmark submission to the Special Joint Committee of the Senate and House of Commons on Divorce, United Church leaders were no long arguing that divorce was a "social disease"[96] but, rather, that the inability to dissolve a marriage was the main source of "festering sores in our society and a threat to the sanctity of marriage."[97] The very basis of the church's argument for widening the grounds for divorce rested upon two fundamental beliefs: that sexual incompatibility was the primary cause for marital breakdown and that marriage was a private and not a social contract. As Dr Thomas G. Donnelly noted in 1958, "Certainly, marriage is increasingly being regarded as an area of private choice where the *collective* concern that marriage as an institution be stable is yielding to the *individual* that marriage be rich, rewarding and fulfilling to each of the two participants separately."[98] Some clergymen may have been more comfortable with the accepted view that marriage was a public matter for the state, but as the Reverend R.C. Chalmers hastened to add, neither Calvin nor Luther had envisioned "our secular state."[99] Marriage was now the arena of "personal and domestic morals,"[100] a position lent a scriptural gloss by the work of the neo-orthodox theologians Karl Barth and Emil Brunner, who insisted that marriage was a covenant between two individuals before God and thus a matter wholly outside the purview of public legal sanctions.[101] From this position, clergymen were easily led to the conclusion that all marriages could be dissolved by mutual consent. But more problematical still, the overwhelming preoccupation of the United Church with shoring up the institution of marriage and the increasing need to assert the relevance of the church to those who had been separated and divorced[102] led them to eviscerate the concept of sin from sex and marriage. This development in turn ineluctably propelled the United Church to evacuate the core of Protestant evangelicalism, which rested upon the notion of universal moral principles and the ever-present reality of sin from which the individual must be redeemed, and to embrace Protestant modernism, in which "the conscience of the sincere individual"[103] remained the fundamental anchor of Christian commitment. By 1966, after two hundred years of forming the core of Methodist and Presbyterian theology, evangelicalism in mainline Protestantism foundered upon the rock of modern gender identities and human sexuality.

The discourse on family that occurred immediately after World War II, in which domestic ties were believed to mirror the broader social order, was not emblematic of cultural attitudes throughout the 1950s. But as the debates about family within the United Church reveal, there was a perceptible disjunctive between the concerns of wartime culture, which had focused upon the problem of juvenile delinquency and the sexual containment of teenagers and had celebrated the family as a primarily reproductive unit, and those of the mid-1950s, in which the family had been reinterpreted as a distinctly private entity, bereft of any public significance, in which the personal emotional and sexual relationship between husband and wife was the central pillar. Not only has this essay called into question the prevailing historical characterization of the 1950s in positing that it was a period of considerable cultural variegation and considerable social flux, but it has also challenged the notion that Canadian discussions on family life were but an echo of American trends. The retreat towards the sexually charged, private family was not hastened by the threat posed by international Cold War politics in a nuclear age, nor was the sexual revolution the consequence of youth culture, feminism, or a lifestyle defined by the Kinsey Report.[104] Rather, the reformulation of the Canadian family as a haven of spiritual and moral nourishment occurred within the context of the precipitous growth of the "secular" welfare state, while the exaltation of sex as a primarily sacramental act was intended to offset the transgression of gender boundaries caused by the new social reality of married women's work in the rapidly expanding consumer economy of the late 1950s.

Although the motivation underlying the position of the United Church regarding marriage and sex was a conservative one, its preoccupation with reasserting the status of the sole, male breadwinner led to a paradoxical view that equated personal freedom with sexual fulfillment, thus unleashing a dynamic which created a mindset in mainstream culture that actually facilitated something of a groundswell of sympathy for the radical youth culture of the 1960s, with its open celebration of sexuality.[105] Cultural change was thus not simply the reflection of the baby-boom generation, as Doug Owram has contended, for cultural innovation also occurred in the more traditional corridors of mainstream Protestantism. Our contemporary cultural attitudes did not suddenly appear on the scene in the 1960s, but were the by-products of a peculiar alchemy of conservative reaction to modern bureaucratic collectivism, secularization, and consumerism, questions that revolved around the issue of rapidly changing gender identities between adults within marriage. This response, in turn, precipitated a new theological construct whose emphasis upon sex as the preserve of individual identity was distilled into a clearly modernist sensibility.

Notes

1 United Church of Canada, *Report of the Commission on Christian Marriage and the Christian Home* (Board of Evangelism and Social Service, 1946), 132.

2 See, for example, Doug Owram, *Born at the Right Time: A History of the Baby Boom Generation* (Toronto: University of Toronto Press, 1996), 262.

3 Ibid., 90; Elaine Tyler May, *Homeward Bound: American Families in the Cold War Era* (New York: Basic Books Inc., 1988); Wini Breines, *Young, White and Miserable: Growing Up Female in the Fifties* (Boston: Beacon Press, 1992); Veronica Strong-Boag, "Home Dreams: Women and the Suburban Experiment in Canada, 1945–60," *Canadian Historical Review* 62 (December 1991) 5–25; Strong-Boag, "Canada's Wage-Earning Wives and the Construction of the Middle Class, 1945–60," *Journal of Canadian Studies* 29 (1994); Valerie J. Korinek, "Mrs. Chatelaine vs. 'Mrs. Slob': Contestants, Correspondents and the *Chatelaine* Community in Action, 1961–1969," *Journal of the Canadian Historical Association* 7 (1996): 251–76. For a more nuanced perspective on this period, see Neil Sutherland, *Growing Up: Childhood in Canada from the Great War to the Age of Television* (Toronto: University of Toronto Press, 1997); and Joan Sangster, *Earning Respect: The Lives of Working Women in Small-Town Ontario, 1920–1960* (Toronto: University of Toronto Press, 1995). See also the essays in Joy Parr, ed., *A Diversity of Women: Ontario, 1945–1980* (Toronto: University of Toronto Press, 1995); John Murphy, "Shaping the Cold War Family," *Australian Historical Studies* 26 (October 1995): 566; and

Gaile McGregor, "Domestic Blitz: A Revisionist History of the Fifties," *American Studies* 34 (spring 1993): 5–33. For a critique of the views of those historians who have adopted Betty Friedan's evaluation of post-war domesticity as a conservative phenomenon, see Joanne Meyerowitz, "Beyond the Feminine Mystique: A Reassessment of Postwar Mass Culture 1946–1958," *Journal of American History* 79 (March 1993): 1455–82.

4 For a discussion of these themes, see Annalee Golz, "Family Matters: The Canadian Family and the State in the Postwar Period," *Left History* (1993): 9–49; Owram, *Born at the Right Time*, 31–53; May, *Homeward Bound*; Mariana Valverde, "Building Anti-Delinquent Communities: Morality, Gender, and Generation in the City," in Parr, ed., *A Diversity of Women*, 19–45; Nancy Christie, *Engendering the State: Family, Work, and Welfare in Canada, 1900–1945* (Toronto: University of Toronto Press, 2000), chapter "Reconstructing Families"; Owram, "Canadian Domesticity in the Post-war Era," in Peter Neary and J.L. Granatstein, eds. *The Veterans Charter and Post-World War II Canada* (Montreal and Kingston: McGill-Queen's University Press, 1998), 205–23.

5 See, Christie, *Engendering the State*, chapter 3.

6 For a discussion of this theme, see Christie, *Engendering the State*.

7 H.A. Weir, "Unemployed Youth," in L. Richter, ed., *Canada's Unemployment Problem* (Toronto: MacMillan, 1939), 159–60. See also United Church Archives UCA, Silcox Papers, 8: 36, "Youth's Eye View of Some Problems of Getting Married," YMCA, 1936, in which Silcox connects the "sublimation of the sexual impulse" caused by delayed marriage in the thirties to the kind of mass psychosis that gave rise to fascism. By the end of the war he was arguing that democracy and national unity depended upon the containment of sex.

8 Canadian Youth Commission, *Young Canada and Religion* (Toronto: Ryerson Press, 1945), 72.

9 E. Gilmour Smith, "The Christian Home," *United Church Observer*, 1 July 1945, 9.

10 Canadian Youth Commission, *Youth, Marriage and the Family* (Toronto: Ryerson Press, 1948), 28. See also Owram, *Born at the Right Time*, 134.

11 Silcox had been an advocate of Catholic-Protestant cooperation prior to the Family Allowances Act of 1944. See Silcox, "Religious Peace in Canada," *Food for Thought* 11 (October 1941). For the Protestant backlash against the Catholic church, see UCA, Inter-Church Committee in Protestant-Roman Catholic Relations (which equated Catholicism with communism), Watson Kirkconnell to Rev. Dr H.H. Bingham, 10 November 1945. See also UCA, United Church Committee on Mixed Marriages, 1939–40. Mixed marriages were castigated as hastening secularization, loss of faith, and an anti-religious climate within the home. See also UCA, Commission on Marriage and Divorce, 2:21, Rev. John Shearman, "Mixed Marriages in Quebec," April 1959.

12 UCA, Silcox Papers, 11:5, Silcox to Arthur Maheux, Archives de Séminaires de Québec, 8 July 1942; 9:20, Silcox, "Will Canada Split," 10 September 1944.

13 Ibid., 11:5, Philip Quebec to Silcox, 17 November 1941; Silcox to Rev. Carring-
ton, 8 December 1941. On the economic necessity for post-war population
growth, see Silcox, "Population Problems," Anglican Church of Canada, Council
of Social Service, *Bulletin*, 15 October 1941. Silcox was a great advocate of British
immigration.

14 Silcox, "Family Allowances and the Population Question," *Saturday Night*, 23
October 1943. Silcox was a frequent contributor to this popular journal largely
because the father of its editor, B.K. Sandwell, a Congregational minister, had
worked alongside Silcox's father in Toronto.

15 Silcox, "Birth Control: Bane or Blessing," *New Outlook*, 15 January 1937, 29; Silcox, "What is Wealth and Poverty?" *Mentor*, 1938; UCA, Silcox Papers, 8:45,
"Transcript of Mr. Silcox's Testimony during the Eastview Trial, 1937," 17.

16 UCA, United Church Committee on Mixed Marriages, 1939–40, 1:1, Hugh Dobson to J.R. Mutchmor, 20 June 1939.

17 Nancy Christie and Michael Gauvreau, *A Full-Orbed Christianity: The Protestant
Churches and Social Welfare in Canada, 1900–1940* (Montreal: McGill-Queen's University Press, 1996), 197–223.

18 UCA, Silcox Papers, 13:16, "Private Enterprise and Social Ownership of Control,"
in *Private and Public Enterprise* (Church of England publication), no. 113 (10
April 1944): 5.

19 UCA, Committee to Arrange for a Forward Movement after the War, 1:2, *Report
of Committee* (n.p).

20 Silcox, "Family Allowances and the Population Question," *Saturday Night*, 23
October 1943, 1.

21 Paul Martin, *Labour's Post-War World* (Toronto: Canadian Institute of International Affairs and Canadian Association for Adult Education, 1945), 3, 7–8, 12–13.

22 Ibid.

23 Advertisement for lipstick, *Canadian Home Journal*, October 1943, 25. For a larger
discussion of the modern democratic state, see Christie, *Engendering the State*,
chapter "Reconstructing Families."

24 UCA, Silcox Papers, 13:i, Silcox, "Why Anti-Semites Hate Christ: A Study in
Hitleresque Pathology," *Churchman*, 1 January 1941,13; 13:8, Silcox, *The Atlantic
Charter and Christian Concern* (Church of England pamphlet, 14 February 1942),
4.

25 Ibid., 5:15, "Living Dangerously," CBC Radio Pulpit, 27 March 1937.

26 UCA, United Church Commission on Church, Nation and World Order, i:3, C.E.
Silcox, "Memorandum," 11 October 1943, 1.

27 Ibid., 1:8, Hugh Wolfenden to Gordon A. Sisco, 2 September 1943.

28 Ibid., 1:3, Silcox, "Memorandum," 11 October 1943, 3.

29 For a discussion of social and economic attitudes typical of this older evangelicalism, see Boyd Hilton, *The Age of Atonement* (Oxford: Oxford University Press,
1988).

30 UCA, Commission on Church, Nation and World Order, 1:10, Arthur Lower,

"Memorandum re: the Basic Memorandum," 9 August 1943; 1:7, Lower to Sisco, 25 March 1943.

31 United Church, Commission on Culture, *The Church and the Secular World* (Board of Evangelism and Social Service, 1950), vii, 34, 70.

32 UCA, Silcox Papers, 9:28, Silcox, "The Interest of the Christian Churches in Marriage and the Home," *Home and School Review* (n.d.), 2.

33 Commission on Culture, *The Church and the Secular World*, 70.

34 United Church, *Report of the Commission on Christian Marriage and the Christian Home* (1946), 116; Anglican Church, *Social Service Annual Report* (1958), 18; UCA, Silcox Papers, 9:19, Silcox, "Canadian Churches and Postwar Reconstruction," *Religion and Life*, 1943, 3.

35 United Church, *Report of the Commission on Christian Marriage and the Christian Home*, 106.

36 Ibid., 111.

37 UCA, Commission on Christian Marriage and the Christian Home, 1.1, "Untitled Memorandum," 1946.

38 UCA, Silcox Papers, 9:19, "Canadian Churches and Postwar Reconstruction," *Religion and Life*, 1943, n.p.

39 Commission on Culture, *The Church and the Secular World*, 70.

40 UCA, Silcox Papers, 9:29, "Toward a Philosophy of Christian Marriage," 22 January 1946, 4.

41 Ibid., "The Menace of Modernity to Christian Life" (n.d.), 11.

42 Anglican Church of Canada, *Social Service Annual Report*, 1958, 17; UCA, Silcox Papers, 9:28, "The Interest of the Christian Churches in Marriage and the Home," 2; United Church, *Report of the Commission on Christian Marriage and the Christian Home*, 118.

43 UCA, Silcox Papers, 9:28, "The Interest of the Christian Churches in Marriage and the Home," 2.

44 Ibid., 9:29, "Toward a Philosophy of Christian Marriage," 22 January 1946, 3.

45 UCA, Commission on Church, Nation and World Order, 2:15, Lower, "Comments and Suggestions on the Ninth Draft," 2.

46 United Church, *Church, Nation and World Order: A Report of the Commission on Church, Nation and World Order* (Board of Evangelism and Social Service, 1944), 25, 28. Although it was a minority perspective by the 1950s, a few Protestant clergymen still linked the family with the creation of national values. See UCA, Commission on Marriage and Divorce, 4:38, F.W.L. Bailey, "Why Divorce," 1953.

47 UCA, Commission on Church, Nation and World Order, 2:15, Lower, "Comments and Suggestions on the Ninth Draft," 2.

48 "Backing Up the Sunday School," *United Church Observer*, 1 November 1940; "Prayer for the Children," *United Church Observer*, 15 January 1941.

49 "Mother's Day Poster," *United Church Observer*, 1 May 1942, 5.

50 See Marguerite Van Die, *An Evangelical Mind: Nathanael Burwash and the Methodist Tradition in Canada, 1839–1918* (Montreal and Kingston: McGill-Queen's Univer-

sity Press, 1989); Neil Semple, *The Lord's Dominion: The History of Canadian Methodism* (Montreal and Kingston: McGill-Queen's University Press, 1996); UCA, Commission on Marriage and Divorce, 4:39, "The Meaning and Responsibility of Christian Marriage," 1932.6.

51 UCA, Silcox Papers, 9:13, "Some Moral Aspects of Birth Control," 1940, 5.

52 Muriel Jacobson, "The Church and the Teenage Girl," *United Church Observer*, 1 August 1942, 15, 18. There were very few examples of a discourse regarding sexual containment, and most of these were written during wartime and not into the 1950s. Indeed, one later article, "Should Teen-Agers Go Steady?" (*United Church Observer*, 1 July 1958), argued that early teenage dating made for healthier and happier marriages. For a contrasting view on the fifties discourse on teenage sex, see May, *Homeward Bound*, 94, 101.

53 UCA, Silcox Papers, 5:12, "Possibilities and Limitations of Social Planning in a Dynamic World," speech to Winnipeg Central Council of Social Agencies, 21 October 1935.

54 UCA, Committee on Mixed Marriages, "The Meaning and Responsibilities of Christian Marriage," 1940; Social Service Council of Canada, "The Trend of Family Life and Marriage in Our Times," n.d., 27. By war's end the United Church, though generally supportive of the concept of birth control, also feared that it would unleash a popular emphasis upon sex.

55 UCA, Silcox Papers, 9:4, Silcox, "The Oxford Group Movement," 31 July 1934. Silcox opposed this movement because he believed that it led to public declarations of sexual improprieties.

56 Ibid., 9:13, Silcox, "Some Moral Aspects of Birth Control," 1940, 5–6; 5:22, Silcox, "Constructive Birth Control and Tomorrow's Children," January 1940, 14–15.

57 Ibid., 9:13, "Some Moral Aspects of Birth Control," 18; UCA, Committee on Mixed Marriages, 1:4, "Birth Control and Sterilization."

58 UCA, Rev. Harriet K. Christie Papers, 1:23, "Men and Women in the Church," 1954. See also "Canada's Working Women," *Globe and Mail Magazine*, 20 May 1961; United Church, *Married Women Working: Report of the Commission on the Gainful Employment of Married Women* (1962); and Canadian Association for Adult Education, *The Real World of Women* (1967).

59 UCA, Commission on Marriage and Divorce, 3:35, J. Alex Edmison, National Parole Board, to Rev. Frank Morgan, 15 February 1961, 3, 2:20, WE. Boothroyd, "Homosexuality in Marriage," 3.

60 National Archives of Canada (NA), MG28 111, Canadian Youth Commission, series C-7, vol. 42, file "Family Report," Margaret S. Davis to Dr S.R. Laycock, University of Saskatchewan, 12 April 1946; R.E.G. Davis to Eugene Forsey, director of research, Canadian Congress of Labour, 1 February 1946; ibid., file "Effects of War on Family Life," L.W. Skey to R.E.G. Davis, 21 March 1947; "Findings of the Youth and Family discussion held in Budge Hall, Central Y.M.C.A., Westmount," 21 October 1944; "Brief Submitted by Winnipeg Group on Family Life," 26 September, 1944.

61 Christie, *Engendering the State*, chap. 6, "'Not Only a Living Wage, but a Family Wage."

62 On the connection between women's work and unemployment among men, see Jean Shilton, "Prudence in the Parsonage," *United Church Observer*, 1 May 1957; R.B. Craig, "A Married Woman's Place Is in the Home," *United Church Observer*, 1 November 1957; "On Unemployment," *United Church Observer*, 15 March 1959.

63 UCA, Commission on Marriage and Divorce, 3: 28, Canadian Welfare Council, "Family Desertion," May 1961, 3. On post-war North American concerns to define a domestic, rather than a purely economic, role for fathers, see Jessica Weiss, "Making Room for Fathers: Men, Women and Parenting in the United States, 1945–1980," in Laura McCall and Donald Yacovone, eds., *A Shared Experience: Men, Women, and the History of Gender* (New York: New York University Press, 1998), 359; Robert L. Griswold, *Fatherhood in America* (New York: Basic Books, 1993), 189; and Robert Rutherdale, "Fatherhood, Masculinity, and the Good Life during Canada's Baby Boom, 1945–1965," *Journal of Family History* 24.3 (July 1999): 351–73.

64 Commission on Culture, *The Church and the Secular World*, 33.

65 United Church, *Report of the Secretaries of the Board of Evangelism and Social Service* (1957), 8. This phrase was coined by the Reverend J.R. Mutchmor.

66 United Church, *Married Women Working* 9. See also Canadian Association for Adult Education, *The Real World of Women*, 119, 128, which reported that in 1961 fully 47 per cent of married women were in the workforce and that wives had become at the very least "partial breadwinners." Significantly, this publication noted that there was no significant increase in juvenile delinquency as a result, showing the length of the route travelled since World War II.

67 UCA, Commission on Marriage and Divorce, 2:22, Dr Patricia White and R.S. Hosking, "The Changing Role of Women in Modern Society," 2 November 1959.

68 UCA, Silcox Papers, 9:39, "The Menace of Modernity to Christian Life," 1946, 17.

69 Since the war there had been a constant campaign in various United Church commissions against the increasing trend of married women in the workplace. See UCA, Commission on the Ministries of Women, which aimed to undo the ten-year experiment in women's ordination. There was considerable response from women in the church on these questions. See ibid., 1.2, Sisco to Marion Hilliard, 18 January, 1947; Gerturde L. Brooks to Gordon Sisco, 15 February 1947; UCA, Commission on Church, Nation and World Order, 1.9, Mary A. Endicott to Sisco, 11 March, 1944.

70 R.S. Hosking, "What's the Matter with Father," *Star Weekly*, 21 November, 1959; UCA, Commission on Marriage and Divorce, 1.6, Dr R.S. Hosking, "The Family in Modern Society," 12 January 1960, n.p.; 2:22, Dr W.G. Scott, "The Changing Role of Women"; 3:28, "Family Desertion," 4.

71 UCA, Commission on Marriage and Divorce, 2:25, James Anderson, "Charts on the Psycho-Sexual Differences between Men and Women"; College of Worcester, Department of Sociology, "Preparation for Marriage," Course 366.

72 The issue of homosexuality formed a central point of departure, but the emphasis placed by some of the members of the commission upon this theme was not without controversy, since many clergymen did not believe this was a crucial dimension of the modern issue of marriage and divorce. See UCA, Commission on Marriage and Divorce, 1:2 "Minutes," 16–17 June 1959. The reorientation from marriage for reproduction towards an ideal of personal fulfillment did at the very least move the church towards the conclusion that homosexuality was not immoral. See ibid., 1:7, "A Christian Understanding of Marriage and Sex," 2.; 2:20, W.E. Boothroyd, "Homosexuality and Marriage." This position caused great controversy; see ibid., 3:35, J. Alex Edmison, National Parole Board, to Rev. Frank Morgan, 15 February 1961.

73 UCA, Commission on Marriage and Divorce, 2:18, Morrison Kelly, "Marriage and Divorce," 9 October 1958, 4.

74 Ibid., 1.6, R.S. Hosking, "The Family in Modern Society," 12 January 1960; 1:4, Minutes, 11–12 April 1961, 150. For the view that the patriarchal family was in decline, see C.W. Topping, "The Egalitarian Family as a Fundamental Invention," *Canadian Journal of Economics and Political Science* 8 (1942); 598.

75 UCA, Commission on Marriage and Divorce, 1:7, "A Christian Understanding of Marriage and Sex," 8 January 1958, 7; 2:17, E.S. Lautenslager, "A Re-Study of Christian Marriage and Divorce," n.d., 3.

76 Ibid., 3:28, "North American Conference on Church and Family," 30 April-5 May 1961; 1:7, "A Christian Understanding of Marriage and Sex," 8 January 1958, 7.

77 United Church, *Report of the Commission on Christian Marriage and the Christian Home*, 108; UCA, Commission on Marriage and Divorce, 2:17, Rev. R.H.N. Davidson, "Christian Marriage and Divorce," July 1958, 11.

78 UCA, Commission on Marriage and Divorce, 1:7, "A Christian Understanding of Marriage and Sex," 7.

79 Ibid., 1:6, "First Draft of Report," 29 March 1960, n.p.

80 Ibid., 2:20, R.S. Hosking "The Changing Role of Women," 28 January 1959, 2; 2:17, Hosking, "Standards of Morality," July 1958.

81 Ibid., 2:19, Patricia White, "Men and Women in Society," January 1960, 1; 1:7, "A Christian Understanding of Marriage and Sex," 8 January 1958, 7–8; 1:7, Dr W.E. Boothroyd, "Marriage and Interpersonal Relationships," 125–26; 4:39, David W. Gauike, "A Christian Approach to Sex in Marriage," 1959, 1.

82 Christina Simmons, "Modern Sexuality and the Myth of Victorian Repression," in Barbara Melosh, ed., *Gender and American History since 1890* (London and New York: Routledge, 1993), 17; Carroll Smith-Rosenberg, "The Body Politic," in Elizabeth Weed, ed., *Coming to Terms: Feminism, Theory, Politics* (New York: Routledge, 1989), 109; Anita Grossman, "The New Woman and the Rationalization of Sexuality in Weimar Germany," in Ann Sitow, Christine Stansell, and Sharon Thompson, eds., *The Politics of Sexuality* (New York: Monthly Review Press, 1983), 158; Barbara Epstein, "Family, Sexual Morality, and Popular Movements in Turn-of-the-Century America," in Sitow, Stansell, and Thompson, *The Politics of Sexuality*.

On nineteenth-century notions of female sexuality, see Nancy Cott, "Passionless: An Interpretation of Victorian Sexual Ideology, 1790–1850," *Signs* 4 (1973); Carl Degler, *At Odds: Women and the Family in America from the Revolution to the Present* (New York: Oxford University Press, 1980); and Judith Walkowitz, *City of Dreadful Delight: Narratives of Sexual Danger in Late-Victorian London* (Chicago: University of Chicago Press, 1992).

83 John D'Emilio and Estelle B. Freedman, *Intimate Matters: A History of Sexuality in America* (New York: Harper and Row, 1988), 271; Mary Jo Maynes, *Taking the Hard Road: Life Course in French and German Women's Autobiographies in the Era of Industrialization* (Chapel Hill and London: University of North Carolina Press, 1995), 136–41; Ellen Holtzman, "The Pursuit of Married Love: Women's Attitudes toward Sexuality and Marriage in Great Britain, 1918–1939," *Journal of Social History* 16 (Winter 1982); 42; Gate Haste, *Rules of Desire: Sex in Britain, World War I to the Present* (London: Chatto & Windus, 1992).

84 A misunderstanding perpetuated most recently in Canada by Mary Louise Adams in *The Trouble with Normal: Postwar Youth and the Making of Heterosexuality* (Toronto: University of Toronto Press, 1997), 9.

85 D'Emilio and Freedman, *Intimate Matters*, 266. In the Canadian context, it is significant that even the lectures of Beatrice Brigden to groups of young women and married women were less celebrations of female sexuality than expositions on reproduction. Indeed, Brigden never overtly referred to human sexuality, preferring to draw her examples from the animal kingdom. On this point, see Christie and Gauvreau, *A Full-Orbed Christianity*, 49.

86 For a survey of the principal shifts in Canadian opinion and legislation on birth control, see Brenda Margaret Appleby, *Responsible Parenthood: De-criminalizing Contraception in Canada* (Toronto: University of Toronto Press, 1999), 31, 62, 70.

87 UCA, Commission on Marriage and Divorce, 2:19, Patricia White, "Men and Women in Society," January 1960, 1.

88 UCA, Crusade for Christ, 1:2, J.R. Mutchmor to Rev. Moorehouse, 16 November 1944.

89 UCA, Commission on Marriage and Divorce, 1.7, "A Christian Understanding of Marriage and Sex," 7.

90 "Evangelism in Our Time," *United Church Observer*, 15 March 1958, 7.

91 UCA, Commission on Marriage and Divorce, 2:19, Frank H. Morgan, "Responsible Parenthood," 20 January 1960, 1.

92 Ibid., 1:7, "A Christian Understanding of Marriage and Sex," 8; 2:19, National Council of the Churches of Christ in the U.S.A., Carson McGuire, "The Cultural Sources of Our Sex Attitudes and Behavior," 7.

93 Ibid., 2:21, "A Christian Understanding of Sex and Marriage," April 1959, 8.

94 Ibid., 3:32, John Webster Grant, Ryerson Press, to Frank Fidler, 16 November 1959; 1:3, Minutes, 25–27 April 1960, 117.

95 Ibid., 1:7, "A Christian Understanding of Marriage and Sex," 41.

96 Ibid., 3:35, Milton Weber to Rev. Berry, 20 April 1961.

97   Ibid., 2:16, "Brief of United Church of Canada to the Special Joint Committee of the Senate and House of Commons on Divorce," 22 January 1966, 2. Whether the submissions presented by organizations such as the United Church or the "'plot' element" of life stories presented in personal letters to Prime Minister Lester Pearson were more effective in altering the divorce law remains an open question. See Christina Burr, "Letters to Mike: Personal Narrative and Divorce Reform in Canada in the 1960s," in Lori Chambers and Edgar Montigny, eds., *Family Matters: Papers in Post-Confederation Canadian Family History* (Toronto: Canadian Scholars' Press, 1998), 396.

98   UCA, Commission on Marriage and Divorce, 2:18, Dr Thomas G. Donnelly, Untitled submission, 28 August 1958, 7.

99   Ibid., R.C. Chalmers, "A Brief on Divorce," August 1958, 3–4.

100 Ibid., 2:16, Mervin Bury, "The Meaning and Responsibilities of Christian Marriage," 13 May 1958, n.p.

101 Ibid., 1:7, Rev. Professor David Cairns, Christ's College, Aberdeen, "The Teaching of Brunner and Barth on Marriage and Divorce," 171–73. A host of Scottish professors were consulted by the United Church commission because its secretary, Frank Fidler, a Scotsman, had himself written a similar report for the Church of Scotland in May 1957.

102 Ibid., 2:16, Rev. E. Gilmour Smith, Timmins, "Common-Law Partnerships and Morals," 2; *Toward a Christian Understanding of Sex, Love and Marriage* (1960), 121–22.

103 UCA, Commission on Church, Nation and World Order, 2:15, Lower, "Comments and Suggestions on the Ninth Draft," 2. Lower intended this focus to serve conservative purposes, but by 1960 the implications of this priority of the United Church were very different.

104 United Church clergymen read and reacted to the Kinsey Report, but its findings regarding female sexuality were not the primary engine behind the church's exaltation of sexual relations. See UCA, Commission on Marriage and Divorce, 4: 38, Richard E. Lentz, "The Challenge of the Kinsey Report," n.d.

105 On this development within the broader framework of Western society, see Arthur Marwick, *The Sixties: Cultural Revolution in Britain, France, Italy, and the United States, ca. 1958–1974* (Oxford and New York: Oxford University Press, 1998), 19, 111. Marwick notes that "many of the exciting developments in the sixties, and much of its unique character are due to the existence of a genuine liberal tolerance and willingness to accommodate to the new subcultures, permitting them to permeate and transform society" (19). He observes that simultaneously with the youth revolution there was considerable activism also among young married—and indeed, middle-aged—individuals throughout Western society, especially on issues regarding sex and personal behaviour. "The liberation of the sixties," concludes Marwick, "affected, and was participated in by, majorities: it was not the prerogative of ultimately frustrated revolutionary minorities" (694).

Iain A.G. Barrie

"A Broken Trust:
Canadian Priests, Brothers, Pedophilia, and the
Media," *Sex, Religion, Media* (2002)

Alfred, Ontario, sits on the edge of an escarpment 70 kilometers east of Ottawa, Canada's capital city. This little town, with a population of slightly more than 1,000, is bisected by Highway 17, a two-lane blacktop that parallels the Ottawa River, connecting Montreal and Ottawa. The main landmark if you approach from the west is Alfred's huge, Quebec-style, silver-spired, Roman Catholic Church—St. Victor. It dominates the landscape. Motorists passing through the town cannot miss it or the adjacent rectory. The rest is architecturally non-descript—a small hotel that still features nude dancing, a gas station, a hardware store, a funeral home that also provides an ambulance service, an outdoor hockey rink, the Miss Alfred Motel, and a small liquor store. The town's major attraction for travelers is the more than a dozen mom-and-pop snack bars that feature hot dogs, hamburgers, and french fries. Some people call it the french fry capital of eastern Ontario.

Down a side street, a few meters to the south of Highway 17, sits an old, unremarkable, grey, stone-block building currently being used by the Ontario Ministry of Agriculture. The building is not hidden; it is just not particularly dominant. What was hidden from public view for decades was the horribly commonplace sexual and physical abuse that went on unchecked behind the closed doors of what was then called St. Joseph's Training School.[1] This tale of emotional and physical cruelty against young men, wards of the Crown, eventually became known as the Alfred scandal.

Between 1931 and 1974, members of a religious lay order known as the Brothers of the Christian Schools ran St. Joseph's. The province took over the reform school in 1974 and ran it until it was closed in 1981.

On November 28, 1990, 16 years after the lay brothers had left Alfred, the Canadian Press (hereafter CP) ran an unbylined, 15–paragraph story on its national general news service. The lead paragraph implied this was essentially a police story: "Criminal charges could be laid against Roman Catholic lay brothers who allegedly sexually and physically abused boys at a reform school at Alfred, Ont., police said Wednesday." The story quoted an Ontario Provincial Police (OPP) detective who said despite a 7–month investigation into allegations of abuse "there is still lots of work for us to do" and no charges would be laid until after consultation with the Crown and others.[2]

A review of CP's coverage of this scandal between March 1990 and November 1993 revealed that the news gathering cooperative ran 41 separate stories dealing directly with the unfolding drama and subsequent court actions. These stories were made available to CP subscriber newspapers and its radio news wire, Broadcast News. CP relies heavily on its member newspapers for copy. As *The Canadian Press Stylebook* suggests, the organization is "the national news-gathering not-for-profit co-operative owned and operated by the daily newspaper industry. The newspapers ... are members of the co-operative and ... [must] contribute news of its area to the common pool."[3]

An examination of CP's database on this story reveals that CP's editors did not regard the religious dimensions of the scandal as very important. Of the 41 stories analyzed, only 2 received a religion slug. One story, 13 paragraphs long, dealt with a 6–day conference of Roman Catholic bishops held in Ottawa in August 1990. The conference chairman, Robert Lebel, bishop of Valleyfield and president of the Canadian Conference of Catholic Bishops, told reporters that the issue of child sexual abuse would be dealt with. The conference was not open to the public. The other brief story ran in the religion roundup file that CP makes available to subscribers for their weekend sections. That story relied extensively on copy generated for the *Catholic New Times* magazine where an Alfred abuse victim said, "The problems we suffer today are problems that began in the church and they have to get resolved in the church."[4]

CP's attitude probably originated with its major source of copy, the *Ottawa Citizen*. Sean Upton, the *Citizen*'s lead reporter on the Alfred scandal, recalled, "I saw it as a police story, not a religious story. Religion is what you see on the religion pages of the *Citizen*."[5] With this observation, Upton was doing what most reporters at a secular newspaper would do: he relegated the religious questions and implications raised by this type of scandal to a lesser status.

There were plenty of reasons to report it as a cops and courts story. The abuse of the boys led to more than 180 separate criminal charges being laid against "19 members and former members" of the order that ran St. Joseph's and a smaller juvenile detention home in Uxbridge, north of Toronto. Eventually, 25 people were charged. "Investigators, who spent more than a year on the case, believe that at least 177 former students—some as young as seven— were victims between 1941 and 1971." The stiffest sentence handed out in the trials that followed the police investigation went to Lucien Dagenais, 67. Dagenais was convicted of 15 of the 18 charges filed and was sentenced to five years in jail. "Known as 'The Hook' to former students ... because his left hand only has a middle finger and the stump of a thumb" an apparently unrepentant Dagenais listened as Judge Hector Soubliere said: "We built walls around that school—not of brick and mortar, but of much stronger material: walls of silence and indifference. I'm even tempted to say walls of ignorance. [The judge said] Dagenais had abused the trust placed in him."[6] Reporters covering the trial practiced conventional court reporting. Upton asked to be assigned to the trials of several of the brothers to see the story through to its logical conclusion. He is fully bilingual and was versed in the case's lurid background. The *Citizen*'s religion editor, Bob Harvey, said "the story was getting a lot of ink and I saw it as a cop story. Maybe it would have been worth the try to look more seriously at the religious dimensions." Harvey suggested, with the benefit of hindsight, that "the religious dimension was ignored. I would have liked to sit down with the people involved and talk with them about their struggle with conscience ... how the abuse affected their spiritual lives."[7]

If the story had been approached from a religious angle, some of the dimensions that could have been probed include: how religious communities cope with a group of people who violate their ethic of belief, how a religious community—living a vocation with prayerful and financial support from a larger community—could countenance the horrible actions of abusers, and what this story says about the church. Jim Travers, the editor at the *Citizen*, said in an interview that "in retrospect we should go back and check [the religious aspects] of this story. The story touched a core value in society ... it was a story about a breach of trust ... the religion dimension was implied and ran through the story as a sub-text."[8]

Since the Alfred scandal, the Roman Catholic Church has established a $16–million fund to compensate victims of abuse who were in its care at Alfred and Uxbridge. The fund in a sense is a secular response by the church to a secular crime and has been reported as such. But the journalists who covered this story generally ignored the religious dimension, and in doing so probably failed their readers, readers who will never understand that the horror experienced by children the Roman Catholic Church was charged with looking after has a spiritual as well as social or psychological dimensions.

A spokesperson for the OPP "called the investigation of abuse at St. Joseph's and St. John's [in Uxbridge] the biggest sex-crimes [case] in Canadian history."[9] In the late 1980s and early 1990s, even a casual newspaper reader could not have been blamed for thinking that Catholicism was riddled with priests and brothers who practiced buggery and other severe forms of physical, mental, and even spiritual abuse. What was less apparent was why this was happening so often. If the reporting had analyzed the patriarchal structure of the Roman Catholic Church and its deep-rooted powers over people and other institutions, perhaps the media would have served the community better.

What made the crimes at Alfred so appalling was that the church, which sets itself as a moral authority for close to 12 million Canadians, was guilty of duplicity. The public had not been hearing only about Alfred and Uxbridge. Another residential school, this one in Newfoundland, Mount Cashel, had become infamous. For decades, a Roman Catholic lay order, the Irish Christian Brothers, had been charged with looking after boys and teenagers who were wards of the Newfoundland government. These youngsters—some orphans, some from broken families that could not offer proper care— became residents of the Mount Cashel orphanage. The Newfoundland department of child welfare assumed they would get the care needed to make them healthy, educated, and contributing members of society. Instead, as it was later revealed in news reports and at a public inquiry into the management and operation of the Mount Cashel orphanage, many of the boys in the brothers' care would be treated violently, sexually abused, controlled, degraded, exploited, and wounded emotionally.

Dereck O'Brien was just one of Mount Cashel's victims. He arrived at the gloomy institution after a dreadful childhood. His earliest memories of home were of his one-legged grandfather "drunk all the time. The floor of [my] room was littered with urine and rum bottles that toppled over when I opened the door ... I slept with my clothes on and never changed them ... being dirty was just another part of life for me ... I begged people for food and money."[10] By 1964, the four-year-old was on the path to Mount Cashel, via a series of foster homes where the abuse and neglect continued. Eight years and countless foster homes later, O'Brien and one of his younger brothers found themselves at Mount Cashel on Torbay Road in St. John's.

Rumors of mistreatment at Mount Cashel had been circulating since the early 1970s. Very late in the story, in 1989, the Newfoundland government set up a Royal Commission, chaired by retired Ontario Supreme Court Justice Samuel H. S. Hughes, which discovered there had been a long-time cover-up involving the police, the justice system, and the Christian Brothers.[11]

As O'Brien recalled it, the lid lifted slightly in 1975 when, "something unexpected happened. It was early Sunday morning and we had just finished breakfast. Brother [Douglas] Kenny [the orphanage superintendent] came into the dining hall and told several of us that we would be going out. He didn't say where. Myself and about six other boys piled into Kenny's station wagon. Kenny explained that we would be going to the police station and that they would be asking us some questions. 'Don't say anything about me or Brother English' [the brother in charge of dormitories], he said. 'Don't mention our names.' When he said this he squeezed my hand hard."[12] But at this point, despite the stories of abuse, neither the police nor other authorities took any action.

It was later revealed that two of the boys interviewed by the police that day "identified Brother English as a violent pedophile who had tormented them during their stays in Mount Cashel." Another boy interviewed was John Pumphrey. His father, "Ron Pumphrey, was the host of a popular talk show on radio station VOCM in St. John's." Although the topic of Mount Cashel was raised on the show by several callers, "they were cut off, in keeping with the station's policy of not permitting criminal allegations to be made on air." At the Hughes inquiry years later, "Ron Pumphrey would ... say that the police had downplayed the whole affair and that he had no idea of what was really happening [in 1975] at the orphanage."[13]

The Christian Brothers knew that the allegations and facts, if exposed, would create a crisis, so they quickly posted Kenny and English to other parts of the province. Michael Harris, in his book *Unholy Orders* (1990), was able to show clearly that police, senior bureaucrats in various government agencies, the Newfoundland church hierarchy, and the brothers' international administration all knew about the gravity of the suspicions—yet they chose damage control over revelation and action, a tawdry cover-up at the expense of innocent children. The church's tentacles reached as far as the media. In 1975, the *St. John's Evening Telegram* had a couple of reporters who knew about the instances of sexual abuse at the orphanage. The stories "were suppressed by the paper."[14]

The actions that the government, police, and brothers had taken held for three years. In 1978, as a result of the separate Soper Inquiry into allegations of police cover-ups, word of the abuse at Mount Cashel slowly surfaced to again be suppressed. "The first public reference to the 1975 Mount Cashel investigation ... ever ... made, [happened] on May 17, 1978 when *The Daily News*" reported a few sketchy details about

> the case of three Christian Brothers alleged to have sexually assaulted two children.... CBC Radio [Canada's national radio service] gave the same coverage as *The Daily News*, broadcasting the bare fact of an alleged 1975 cover-up of a sex scandal at Mount Cashel. The *Evening Telegram* ... took a different approach, perfectly in keeping with the paper's 1975 decision to suppress the story that two of its own reporters had unearthed. All references to the Brothers were expunged from the copy, an editorial decision whose impact the Christian Brothers themselves quickly realized was to their advantage. The *Telegram* story was conveniently vague.[15]

The decision to play down the story was taken by the paper's publisher, Stephen Herder, who died in 1993. Bernie Bennett, a 26-year veteran of the *Telegram*'s police and court beat, who covered all the Mount Cashel trials, said, "the reason was never given but I guess it was because the clergy [in Newfoundland] were seen to be so Almighty. The publisher took the reason to his grave and the newspaper has never released the reason."[16]

In the late 1970s and into the following decade, several instances of child sexual abuse by priests occurred in other parts of the island province. Most of these were quickly settled by the Roman Catholic Church co-opting the police and criminal justice system, playing down the problem, and reassigning the guilty priests to other church jurisdictions—often off the island. Newfoundland media reported details of these cases but the full impact of Mount Cashel and the cover-up of the scandal would not be felt until early 1989.

Several forces involving the media coincided that year to guarantee that the Mount Cashel story would blow wide open. "A television documentary about the spate of Roman Catholic priests and Brothers who had been charged with sexual offenses" led to calls to radio station "VOCM's morning talk show, *Open Line*."[17] Those calls prompted certain listeners, including a judge's wife, to action. Phone calls to the province's justice department asking about Mount Cashel could not go unheeded. The investigation that had been hidden from public view for so many years was reopened. Shane Earle, 23, a victim of Mount Cashel, took his story to the media. The unravelling began in earnest.

There is some confusion as to what media outlet really broke the story first. Michael Harris was editing the *St. John's Sunday Express* and he interviewed Earle extensively. His first story ran "on Easter Sunday 1989 [sending] shock waves across the country."[18] Some media observers including CBC commentator Rex Murphy claimed that the "corporation's [CBC] local radio morning show and supper hour television show were instrumental in getting the story of abuse out before the *Express* hit the newsstands."[19] Bernie Bennett of the *Telegram* suggested that both media took credit for breaking the story. "One thing for sure is that, around the same time, Shane Earle called the *Telegram*—and I don't know why—but the interview didn't materialize." In the spring of 1989 the floodgates were open. Bennett, a practicing Roman Catholic, schooled by the Irish Brothers from grade 1 through 11, watched the story unfold and was assigned to cover the court cases. Eight Christian Brothers were charged, convicted, and sentenced. "We approached the entire story as a cover-up. We didn't get into the religious dimensions. It was simply a story of men who abused children. It didn't matter if they wore a backwards collar."[20]

O'Brien, one of the Mount Cashel boys who had signed a police statement back in 1975, said watching the media in 1989 was like "watching a feeding frenzy—they went in feet first. What broke this story wide open was Shane Earle came [to the media] and then I came. Michael [Harris] can't take the credit for blowing this up." O'Brien felt the Mount Cashel story was about "crime and abuse with a big helping of the church in there somewheres [*sic*]." O'Brien shared the common Newfoundland attitude that the church was omniscient, omnipresent, and untouchable. He did not blame the media for his fate or for not uncovering the scandals earlier. "I can tell you sure as I'll die that the media ... the government couldn't have stopped the abuse before it stopped. The Catholic Church could put the squeeze on the media and even the social workers couldn't do anything. How can you fight more than 100 years of good work" by the church in Newfoundland?[21]

Rex Murphy, a Newfoundlander, Rhodes scholar, and later an acerbic columnist for CBC TV's *Prime Time* news show, also has hosted *Cross Country Checkup* on CBC Radio. In 1989, he was in Newfoundland and the Maritimes broadcasting commentaries for the St. John's CBC stations. In his commentaries on the scandal, he analyzed how Mount Cashel might affect the cultural and spiritual fabric of the province and in doing so covered an aspect of the story neglected by most reporters. He suggested Mount Cashel "posed questions that were absolutely fundamental to Newfoundland's self-image ... we have such shocking politics and economics—I think we clung on to the idea that we had a bit of decent domestic or personal virtue and this thing just blasted that all to hell.... So it was yes, at the core, a story with a religious dimension, but it had an awful lot more wings ... than just religious."[22]

Murphy said the reporting contained "a tremendous amount of relish ... because it was [done by] the kind of people who grew up in the 60s, who fell off church more or less, and went the kind of high secular route giving them a chance to get back at what they regarded as their petty miseries in the classrooms with the nuns and the brothers." O'Brien's view that the media were on a feeding frenzy when the story really took off was echoed by Murphy, who questioned coverage that was "so relentless and so particularized that the overly specific, continuous, unremittent reporting of who was dangling penises" turned off many news consumers. The point that Murphy was making was that the media were playing catch up with a story many realized they had missed. Murphy also says there were "certain reporters [who] ... had a chance to take a smack at the bishop and at the church. There should have been more of a clean take here.... What is the equally glaring story of this era that isn't being touched now that we are so busily congratulating ourselves on moving out these fiendish priests?"[23]

In 1984, Jason Berry, a freelance writer from New Orleans, began an epic journey that revealed a frightening side of the North American Roman Catholic Church. The product of his research into sexual misconduct by priests and brothers was a 1992 book, *Lead Us Not into Temptation: Catholic Priests and the Sexual Abuse of Children*. In his foreword to the book, Father Andrew Greeley, an author, sociology professor, and parish priest, said Berry "dug into what may be the biggest scandal in the history of religion in America and perhaps the most serious crisis Catholicism has faced since the reformation." Berry discovered: "In the decade of 1982–1992, approximately 400 priests were reported to church or civil authorities for molesting youths, and the vast majority of these men had multiple victims. By 1992, the church's financial losses—in victims' settlements, legal expenses, and medical treatment of clergy—had reached an estimated $400 million."[24]

Berry met with several of the boys who had been abused at Mount Cashel and devoted a chapter to their story. Two observations Berry makes about the Canadian experience are valuable. First, televising the Hughes Commission inquiry helped to alert Canadians to the depth of the church's problem and it may have made people think about how to prevent more of the same. He alludes to comments made by Canadian Archbishop James M. Hayes saying, "first in our compassion must be those who have been sexually abused." Second, Berry said he believes the Canadian church may be leading the way in North America in dealing with such scandals: "No such candor has emanated from the U.S. [church] hierarchy."[25]

Before his book was published, Berry tried to sell a number of articles on sexual abuse by priests to U.S. news magazines. "I would say that on the whole, newspapers have a strong secular bent and they just don't like stories like this. It was depressing material to deal with ... people didn't want to go near it." He took advance payments from magazines who failed to publish the resulting articles because "they just didn't want to tangle with the Church. You know when you get paid $4,000 or $5,000 from the *Los Angeles Times Magazine* ... and they sit on it and finally the assignment chief says: 'we are asking ourselves why should we publish this' ... do I have to lobby the guy to tell him, you know, the public has a right to know?"[26]

Berry's experience illustrates that mainstream media have trouble dealing with society's central institutions like the churches. There was the perception that these organizations should be treated with the same kind of deference that other elite organizations get from the media. The special religious dimension that makes this kind of scandal even more vivid is ignored. Book publishers shied away from Berry's text even though it had been rigorously checked by lawyers. He approached more than 30 publishers. "I wanted to understand how corrupt the church was. Probably I never thought of the church in those terms, but when you have bishops proclaiming the sanctity of life in the womb and being so cavalier in their dismissal of the rights of children ... I came to see the bishops as a bunch of politicians."[27]

When considering the media's seeming preoccupation with sin, sex and sleaze, it seems unfathomable that Berry could have faced so many problems getting his stories published. The same sort of question may be asked about Mount Cashel. How did the story stay hidden for so long? As Howard Kurtz, the press critic for the *Washington Post,* notes: "Nothing in the media business spreads faster than a hot rumor. And nothing creates more headaches for editors and reporters. The line between news and third-hand gossip has become badly blurred in recent years, and our moral compass increasingly erratic. The most titillating rumors often involve sex and public officials, which only add to the growing sense of unease in the nation's newsrooms."[28]

One reason these stories were not dealt with when they first arose was alluded to earlier: the media just did not want to tangle with the ecclesiastical power structure. Moreover, the church and the media keep their distance from each other. Few reporters have ever learned about the intricacies of the Christian church—the complexities of its structure, its absolute moral stands, its internal politics, and its 20 centuries of mystique. It would be difficult to find a general assignment reporter who understands the doctrine of papal infallibility, the rule of celibacy, or the power of a bishop. As the Right Rev.

Bruce Stavert, the Anglican Bishop of the Diocese of Quebec, said in an interview: "We in the church often get cynical about the lack of knowledge in the media about our business. There's an obsession with scandal. Yet, overall there seems to be very little interest in the secular media about what we do."[29]

In her book, *Scandal: The Culture of Mistrust in American Politics,* Suzanne Garment says "today's scandals have devastating effects on the people involved in them." Writing about current American political scandals, Garment asserts: "if we want to learn about political scandal we must look beyond the malefactors themselves, for their evil deeds alone do not constitute scandal. A scandal is created not only by the individual who scandalizes his community, but just as important, by the community that is scandalized when it learns what the miscreant has done."[30]

The secular media, although providing a massive public service by reporting directly on the scandals, does a great disservice to the community of faithful when it ignores the implications of these stories. Newfoundland, with its large Roman Catholic population, will never be the same. There has been a crisis of confidence in the church and many are disillusioned with the people they trusted to help them with their most precious attribute—their faith. Bernie Bennett, the *Telegram* reporter who listened to every word spoken in court during eight trials, will never be the same. "My faith has been shaken ... the only time I now go to church is for weddings and funerals ... it has brought an element of doubt ... suspicion is there. When the priest stands at the altar I wonder what's going on in his mind and I wonder what he's done. I can't help it."[31]

If Bennett is relying on his paper to cover those issues and questions he may be out of luck. The *Telegram,* with only a part-time religion editor, has had few resources to devote to developing the religion beat. Megan Johnston, the reporter responsible for religion, said in an interview that "we basically rely on wire copy ... we have one page a week when we have the space ... [the beat] is not given high priority."[32] Johnston said she could not remember when religion or its impact on the larger community were reported in an analytical way.

So, the spiritual story remains untold. Dereck O'Brien sounds tired and disillusioned. "Brothers have received counselling, legal fees, and even their pensions from the church—that should be reported. I've left the church, the priests and brothers—they make me sick, sick to my stomach when I see one of the bastards. The Roman Catholic Church is so corrupt it looks after its pedophiles ... the hell with them."[33]

Evidence of just how turbulent life has been recently in the Roman Catholic Church has slowly crept into the public's consciousness. It could be argued that the Mount Cashel and Alfred scandals in Canada and the litany of child sex abuse stories that appear regularly in the North American media were but one aspect of the larger story of a church suffering its own brand of purgatory. One of the more devastating indications that this is an institution in serious trouble is illustrated by the decline in seminary enrollments. In 1965, there were "10.6 enrollments in seminary per 10,000 U.S. Catholics ... in 1990 that had dwindled to 1.1 per 10,000." This reduction has struck at the heart of the church and led to a loss of vitality and leadership. The current projections indicate that the loss of priests in North America will continue unabated well into the twenty-first century. "Reduced attendance ... the frequency of going to confession, participation in church activities, even daily prayer fell sharply"[34] in the 1960s and 1970s and continues to this day.

To this day, religious news receives short shrift in many newsrooms. Although "the generalization is less true now than it was 20 years ago, the journalistic community is not very comfortable with religion. Some editors view religion stories as soft, irrelevant, and non-objective."[35]

Jim Travers, the editor of the *Ottawa Citizen,* said in an interview that newspapers should be asking: "What does religion mean in people's lives? How does it affect people's lives?" He suggested that religion today should not be ghettoized like so-called "women's news" was in the past. With 75 beat reporters and one religion specialist, Travers acknowledges that the religious dimensions to stories are sometimes neglected. "We haven't made the progress we should have."[36]

CTV's (the Canadian Television network) principal news anchor, Lloyd Robertson, was critical about both newspaper and television coverage of religion. Robertson said in an interview that he would like to see "more stories of the human spirit,"[37] but he qualified his remarks by mentioning the time constraints on television journalists.

Canadian community college and university schools of journalism in the mid-1990s still offered no reporting religion courses. A new (and so far the only) Canadian introductory text on reporting, *The Canadian Reporter* by Carman Cumming and Catherine McKercher, published in 1994, contains no references to reporting religion or the religion beat. McKercher said when the text was put together the authors "start[ed] with the [reporting] basics. We did not get into some of the more specialized beat areas, so we don't have one on ... social affairs reporting, we don't have one on international, we don't have one on religion ... it's only the first edition. We can't do everything." McKercher suggested that if journalism students are taught well and learn the basics "how to conceive of news, how to structure stories, how to look at story ideas, how to think...about issues" they should be able to apply their acquired skills to almost any assignment or beat. McKercher added that her generation is "kind of secular,"[38] and she had not noted any heightened interest in religious questions or issues.

When the Jim Bakker PTL scandal broke, followed by the Jimmy Swaggart scandal, the international media were all over the stories. News is preoccupied with power and authority and it found the abuse of power and misuse of authority in both these stories. The Canadian religious scandals were different and the Canadian media were asleep at the switch for over a decade. The boys of Mount Cashel, Uxbridge, and Alfred, and the countless children who have been victims of physical and mental abuse in residential schools and orphanages were certainly overlooked. Realistically, the media may only be partially blamed. In the late 1950s and through to the 1980s, when the scandals were unfolding, the Roman Catholic Church wielded extreme power and the media understandably backed off. But the result was that these helpless children were let down by the governments and church that were supposed to protect them. The *Washington Post* ethics code has one tenet that stands out—to listen to the voiceless. It speaks volumes about the role the media should have played.

These boys were voiceless. Rumors had been circulating for years, particularly in Newfoundland, about priestly and institutional sexual abuse. The cover-up, undertaken by the Newfoundland government and the Roman Catholic Church, held for years until the crisis at Mount Cashel could not be ignored. Interviews with reporters and commentators who covered the scandals and the subsequent trials revealed that the media, at their highest levels, had been steered away from the developing story by church and state complicity. Part of the explanation lies in the fact that Newfoundland is an insular community with a large Catholic population. The Roman Catholic Church had generations of good works to its credit. Coziness between the church and the media made conservative reporters, editors, and publishers hesitant to probe deeply into ugly rumors about the church.

Media silence rested on an apprehension of resistance or public disbelief—the public appetite for scandal drew the line at the Roman Catholic Church. When respect for the church weakened enough to allow coverage, most of it focused on the secular story—sex, greed, avarice, power, abuse, exploitation, and/or tragedy. There was little on the religious dimension, the story of a trust broken and loss of virtue, loss of innocence and loss of simple dignity, so valued by the Newfoundland community.

The church's slow response to help the healing process has damaged its position irrevocably. The victims of abuse at Mount Cashel did not receive compensation, and the church, despite its vast financial resources, dragged its heels in court. The stories of lost faith, pain and suffering, angst and anger, have been let lie in a community that just wishes the story would go away. There has been no retrospective analytical reporting to help reconciliation. The church in Newfoundland will not be going away. It is difficult to comprehend that the religious dimensions of life and the impact of the church have not been taken more seriously by the Newfoundland media. Faith is as much a part of the Newfoundland community as the fishery, and as abundant as the fish once were. As the memories of Mount Cashel fade, the story that remains is the future of the faithful, the priests, and the church hierarchy. It looks as if this story will not be fully covered.

In Ontario, justice officials knew as early as the late 1950s that there were rumors of abuse at St. Joseph's Training School in Alfred. It is reasonable to conclude that Ontario, in that period, was no more open to tackling the Roman Catholic Church than was Newfoundland 20 years later. And most Ontario media simply would not have known of any such rumors, given the isolation of Alfred, a francophone backwater in eastern Ontario.

When the Alfred story broke in the late 1980s, CP used *Ottawa Citizen* copy extensively. The wire service ran the story as general news and only slugged the story with a religious designation twice. The *Ottawa Citizen* regarded the story as essentially one of abuse and violence and the religious pages stayed away from any in-depth treatment of the religious issues that swirled around the main story. It again may be suggested that a secular paper chose to ignore or downplay aspects of the story that would have required comprehensive analysis by someone skilled at understanding religious matters. Interviews with several *Citizen* editors suggest that the paper is looking again at its coverage of religious news and issues. Editor Jim Travers said he regarded interviews for this study as a wake-up call. This is some proof that this newspaper is certainly not antireligious, but that is only a starting point in improving religion reporting.

Notes

1 The story of child abuse by clergy and other religious figures recently has begun being told with increasing frequency, with this essay focusing primarily on only one story. The growing body of literature includes books such as Thomas G. Plante, ed., *Bless Me Father for I Have Sinned: Perspectives on Sexual Abuse Committed by Roman Catholic Priests* (Westport, Conn.: Praeger, 1999); Stephen J. Rossetti, *A Tragic Grace: The Catholic Church and Child Sexual Abuse* (Collegeville, Minn,: Liturgical Press, 1996); Philip Jenkins, *Pedophiles and Priests: Anatomy of a Contemporary Crisis* (New York: American Philological Association, 1996); Chris Moore, *Betrayal of Trust: The Father Brendan Smyth Affair and the Catholic Church* (Dublin: Marino, 1995); Anthony Okaiye, *The Story of an Abused Priest* (Ann Arbor, Mich.: Proctor Publications, 1995); Elinor Burkett and Frank Bruni, *A Gospel of Shame: Children, Sexual Abuse, and the Catholic Church* (New York: Viking, 1993); Stephen J. Rossetti, *Slayer of the Soul: Child Sexual Abuse and the Catholic Church* (Mystic, Conn.: Twenty Third Publications, 1990); and Eamonn Flanagan, *Father and Me: A Story of Sexual Abuse at the Hands of a Priest* (North Blackburn, Australia: HarperCollins, 1995). Numerous similar articles have been published in theological, public policy, cultural studies and other journals. For more insight into news coverage, see James Lull and Stephen Hinerman, *Media Scandals: Morality and Desire in the Popular Culture*

Marketplace (New York: Columbia University Press, 1997); David Hechler, "The Source You Shouldn't Talk To," *Columbia Journalism Review,* March-April 1992, 48; and David Hechler, "Danger Ahead: Sex Abuse Cases," *Washington Journalism Review,* September 1991, 37–40.

2 "Abuse," Canadian Press (hereafter CP) database, 28 November 1990.

3 Peter Buckley, ed., *CP Stylebook* (Toronto, Ont.: The Canadian Press, 1993), 3.

4 CP Database, 15 October 1990.

5 Interview with Sean Upton, November 1994.

6 CP Database, 4 June 1992; 23 January 1993; 19 March 1993.

7 Personal interview with Bob Harvey, November 1994.

8 Personal interview with Jim Travers, November 1994.

9 CP Database, 18 April 1991.

10 Dereck O'Brien, *Suffer Little Children* (St. John's, Newfoundland: Breakwater, 1991), 19–22.

11 For further information see *The Hughes Inquiry Report* and Michael Harris, *Unholy Orders* (Markham, Ont.: Penguin Books, 1990).

12 O'Brien, *Suffer Little Children,* 143.

13 Harris, *Unholy Orders,* 95–96.

14 Harris, *Unholy Orders,* 95–96.

15 Harris, *Unholy Orders,* 180.

16 Personal interview with Bernie Bennett, September 1994.

17 Harris, *Unholy Orders,* 260.

18 Harris, *Unholy Orders,* flyleaf.

19 Personal interview with Rex Murphy, August 1994.

20 Interview with Bernie Bennett.

21 Personal interview with Dereck O'Brien, November 1994.

22 Interview with Rex Murphy.

23 Interview with Murphy.

24 Jason Berry, *Lead Us Not into Temptation* (New York: Doubleday, 1994), xiii, xix.

25 Berry, *Lead Us Not,* 305.

26 Personal interview with Jason Berry, August 1994.

27 Interview with Berry.

28 Howard Kurtz, *Media Circus* (New York: Random House, 1994), 151.

29 Personal interview with the Right Rev. Bruce Stavert, Anglican Bishop of the Anglican Diocese of Quebec, November 1994.

30 Suzanne Garment, *Scandal* (New York: Doubleday, 1992), 14.

31 Interview with Bennett.

32 Personal interview with Megan Johnston, November 1994.

33 Interview with O'Brien.

34 Roger Finke and Rodney Stark, *The Churching of America 1776–1990* (New Brunswick, N.J.: Rutgers University Press, 1992), 260.

35 Benjamin J. Hubbard, "The Importance of the Religion Angle in Reporting on

Current Events," in *Reporting Religion,* ed. Benjamin J. Hubbard (Sonoma, Calif.: Polebridge Press, 1990), 1.
36 Interview with Travers.
37 Personal interview with Lloyd Robertson, August 1994.
38 Personal interview with Catherine McKercher, August 1994.

⇒+ Sex and Law +⇐

The interface of sexuality and the law takes the form of regulation. As Gary Kinsman demonstrates, legal discourse *produces* the categories that it regulates through a set of assumed norms, such as the institutionalized heterosexuality summarized by the slogan "No Baby—No Nation." These norms impinge on our everyday lives through legal definitions of obscenity and pornography and the related issue of freedom of speech. Lynn Crosbie is concerned with the way in which legal discourse produces its subjects. Focusing on the sexual predator and murderer, Paul Bernardo, her text takes the form of a letter to Bernardo in which she imagines him, his motives, and his desires. She thus uneasily pushes her piece toward pornography while decrying the crimes she writes about, thereby forcing her reader to experience the agony of drawing the line between freedom of expression and censorship. For Michael Turner's protagonists—an unnamed narrator, who is being (self?) interrogated for his pornographic activities, and his closest friend, Nettie—pornography is a central factor in growing up. What Turner emphasizes, however, are the ways in which pornography—and sexuality itself—shift territory in this process of *Bildung* and the concomitant need for an ethical compass (what he terms elsewhere in the novel a "bullshit detector"). Dixon and Persky take us into the public dimension of the regulatory process, providing a detailed analysis of how the 1993 child pornography bill came into being. The historical specificity of their analysis reminds us how moral standards are not absolutes but are themselves in history and thus contingent upon a vast range of factors. Jane Rule's testimony at the 1994 Little Sisters trial (which sought to determine the right of Canada Customs to censor shipments of books destined for Canadian bookstores) addresses the issues of pornography and obscenity through the optic of freedom of expression. Rule argues that her books were stopped at the border not because their content was obscene but because she is a lesbian, thereby suggesting that censorship was at the heart of the case. The Little Sisters case is still before the courts.

from *The Pornographer's Poem* (1999)

4.11

The railroad tracks ran through the west side of the city in pretty much a straight line. There were exceptions, of course. One of which was the half-mile length of track that ran through our neighbourhood, just north of the school, a winding S shape that curved along a bluff overlooking a lane, a row of rooftops, then the northwest portion of Vancouver proper. The first major bend was where the blackberry bushes were at their thickest, fifty yards west of the Cypress crossing where we said our hellos and goodbyes to John McKinney.

We were just about to cross when Nettie motioned for me to stop. "Look!" she said. "Isn't that Billington's car?" Indeed. About a hundred yards down the tracks, idling in the lane, was Billington's white Rolls-Royce. And climbing up from the lane, carrying a white plastic Safeway bag, was my next-door neighbour—Billington. "Hide," said Nettie, and the two of us ducked into a ditch. Nettie poked her head up and gave the play-by-play: "I see the toupee ... the tweed coat, the tan slacks ... he's looking right, he's looking left ... he's taking a couple more steps ... he's stepping over the tracks ... he's looking around again ... he's swinging the bag once, twice ... he's let go! Billington has let go of the bag! It's in the air, folks. It's falling into the blackberries. He's looking around again. He's turning back. He's going down. Down, down, down. He's gone! Mr. Billington has left the building!" Nettie settled back into her crouch and giggled. "What's so funny?" I asked. "Mr. Billington's a space polluter," she said, cracking up. I got the reference. It was total Smith-Gurney. We shared the joke: Billington as alien. His door opened and shut. Billington drove slowly past, oblivious. Nettie turned to me: "Race you there. On three. One, two—"

Nettie cheated, of course. Bolting on the two-count. Why she did stuff like that I'll never know. She was, by a mile, the fastest Grade Seven I'd ever met. Boy or girl. "So what's the deal?" I shouted after her. "It's only a bag of fuckin' garbage." But Nettie didn't answer. She ran hard till she hit the bushes, where she picked up a switch and hacked her way into the tangle.

I was really impressed with the way she went at it. The way her face tightened up, intensified, her little mouth puckering above her dimpled chin, her strokes swift and decisive. Obviously she had the same determination for bushwhacking as she had for baseball. But of course this was different. There was no field, no arena—no ball or bat. I began to feel a tingle for Nettie, a new sensation. As she whipped her way deeper into the brambles I began to

notice, with each swipe, the jiggle of her ass—and that she had an ass—and
how that ass was a little bigger, proportionately, than the rest of her body, and
how she might one day have an ass like her mother's, which looked good in
a swimsuit the one time I saw it. Nettie called out, but I didn't catch what she
said. Too caught up in this new sensation.

Nettie turned around. Her face was flush, her stick limp and ragged. "Why
are you just standing there, shit-for-brains? I told you to get a bigger stick. We
can't reach this thing until we get *a bigger stick,*" she said, tossing the spent
switch. I shook off my thoughts and went looking. When I returned—I'd
found an old car antenna—Nettie was on her stomach, beating up the bush,
just her feet sticking out. "I've almost got it," she said, her voice strained and
creepy. I was about to ask her for a second time why we were going through all
this effort over a lousy bag of garbage, when I realized it didn't matter. Sometimes it was enough just to be around Nettie's enthusiasm. She always had a
way of making something out of nothing. But she answered me anyway, as if
she knew what I was thinking. "If ... it was only ... a bag of garbage ... why
wouldn't he ... throw it ... into ... his ... own ... garbage can?" I stretched the
rusty antenna as far as it would go and crawled in beside her, passing up the
tool.

Nettie was on fire. Her body writhing, jerking, banging against me. At one
point she had herself turned in such a way that her ass was rubbing right up
against my groin. But the weird thing was, it had nothing to do with retrieving the bag. In fact, from where I could see, Nettie wasn't making a very good
attempt at snagging the bag at all. She certainly had enough antenna to work
with. Yet her arm was only half-extended. I looked down at Nettie's ass as it
arched into me—grinding, clenching, retracting, withdrawing. Then she'd
roll over on her stomach, take a few swipes, then repeat the whole thing all
over again. Clearly, a pattern was emerging.

I decided to test my theory. The next time Nettie rolled over onto her stomach I'd inch away and wait.

Nettie's back arched, thrusting her butt into nothing. She froze for a
moment. I was about to laugh, but then she startled me with a loud grunt,
lunging forward, announcing for the tenth time that she'd "just about got
it." I looked up. I could see through the brambles that the antenna was now
waving back and forth over Billington's bag. Nettie let out another grunt,
before pushing her ass towards me, into me, hard this time, winding me.
She did a quick little shimmy, then lunged forth for yet another lame swipe.

I could feel the heat off her body now. And this heat seemed infectious,
shooting down my thighs and up under my arms, a gyro, convincing me of my
own heat. Again, she ground into me. But this time when she clenched her
ass I could feel the squeeze of each cheek tighten. I'm not clear on what happened next. I think it went like this: I reached between her legs, dug in my
heels, and slid her deeper into the bush, where she rolled onto her stomach,

pushed her pelvis into the ground, and thrust the antenna forward. At that point, of course, she could've grabbed the bag with her teeth.

Nettie collapsed, exhausted. She was breathing quite heavily now. And this worried me. Her mother was always going on about how Nettie was born with a heart murmur, and how she disapproved of Nettie's tomboy behaviours if only, she claimed, because of the strain sports put on her delicate condition. Not that you'd notice, given what she was capable of on the playing field. But still. "Nettie? Are you okay?" A breathy yes. I reached up and pulled the bag between us. I was about to open it, then changed my mind. What did I want with a bag of garbage? Besides, it wasn't about that anyway. So I touched her shoulder instead. "Do you wanna look inside?" I said. Nettie shivered. I watched her ass slowly unclench, relax over the mud we'd made. We lay there for quite some time, just breathing.

It was getting dark. The cold air was making plastic of our sweat. Nettie rolled over and started fiddling with the twist-tie. I'd kinda forgotten about the garbage. "Whoa!" she said, quickly closing the bag. "What?" She opened the bag again. I tried to peek in, but she closed it tight against her chest. Her face a strange shape, that place where horror meets delight. "C'mon, lemme see," I said, gesturing towards the bag. But Nettie rolled away. She kept going, "Whoa, whoa, whoa—this is unreal." I reached over and grabbed her shoulder, pulling her towards me, playfully. Nettie rolled over on her own strength, opening the bag in my face. I was speechless.

4.11a
The Contents of Mr. Billington's Garbage

1 copy of *Garçons de Maroc* magazine
1 copy of *Big Boys on Bikes Illustrated*
1 copy of *Hot Rod Hunks* magazine
1 8–oz. jar of Vaseline petroleum jelly
1 roll of Scott toilet paper
3 or 4 crumpled tissues, shit-streaked with flecks of blood
1 condom wrapper
1 condom, fully extended over ...
1 Schneider's beer sausage

4.12
—Why is this so important?
—It's important because it's something that happened right after John and Penny dropped us off.
—Yes, but what does it have to do with John and Penny?
—I don't know. I mean, it might make sense later on—but you're just gonna have to trust me. I've already figured out that this line of questioning is, for

the most part, not so much to do with what I think is important but why I think it's important. Am I right?

—Continue.

—Not until you tell me what you were going to ask me.

—What if we told you that we weren't going to ask you anything, that we're finished with you?

—Then you'd be lying.

—Well, in that case, we were going to ask you if Nettie ever told anyone about what happened to Mr. Gingell.

—She didn't.

—And did Penny keep up her end of the bargain?

—I don't know. The Gingell affair never came up again. Besides, Nettie had moved onto other causes.

—One more thing.

—Sure.

—Do you think John and Penny had something to hide?

—No. I just think they were worried about us stirring up trouble. They were applying for citizenship, so that might've had something to do with it.

5.1

Nettie and I finished our films the following Saturday. Although John and Penny were really pleased with the results, I must admit I was getting a little bored with the project by then. Nettie, on the other hand, was super-excited—and once again it was Nettie's enthusiasm that brought me back to the moment: the first screening of our brand new films. John made a big bowl of popcorn and Penny closed the drapes. We watched Nettie's film first, since it was what Penny kept referring to as a "lyrical work." John thought it would make more sense to end with a narrative.

After the films were over—we watched them twice—John gave us his critique. He told Nettie he liked her film a lot—even more the second time—especially after Penny suggested we view it without the Vera Lynn. John particularly liked the metric montage sequence in the middle of the film. He thought that the relationship Nettie established between the ninety-six frames of rain falling on the aluminium watering can, intercut with the stillness of the sunlit mud puddle, at forty-eight frames, was an "effective rotation." He also remarked that the reflection of the watering can in the muddy puddle was a "nice opposition." The weak link, however, lay in the flowers. John felt that the flowers, which inexplicably appeared near the end of the film, seemed unnecessary, gratuitous even. He suggested Nettie either rethink that section or just cut the flowers altogether and go with the out-of-focus clouds she used in her intro. Penny added that a looping effect would keep the film open-ended, cyclical. Nettie agreed. The three of them looked at me with such determination that I had no choice but to go along.

The first thing John said to me was that he liked my film a lot more than what was originally scripted. I smiled when he said that, but a second later felt a twinge of hurt. A backhanded compliment? Penny was quick to ask John what he didn't like about the writing. John pursed his lips. "Well, I felt it was a little too TV," he said—to Penny. Nettie agreed. Traitor. I was beginning to feel ganged up on. "But that was the point," I blurted, not quite sure what I meant yet. John raised an eyebrow. "I wanted to make fun of TV. I wanted to do something that would remind people of TV, but then twist it into something unexpected, something you wouldn't see on prime-time." John's eyes lit up. Penny's, too. "You mean by having Joe and Ken run off together?" she said excitedly. Exactly, I guessed. And then Nettie made this face.

After watching *Joe and Barbie* a third time, John and Penny seemed won over to my ad-lib way of thinking. "I must say, I had no idea you put so much thought into this," John said. And Penny agreed. "Yes, now I know why you opened with Joe sitting before a cluster of lilies," she said, before turning back to John, "long a symbol of male homosexuality." I looked to Nettie and smiled, well aware that the misplaced symbolism in her film involved those very same lilies. Nettie was so pissed off. She didn't have to say anything. The raves continued to pour in. "And that scene in the end, where Barbie alludes to Joe's abandoned weapon collection, as if those discarded guns and bazookas were symbols of Joe's violent past, and how violence was just a symptom of Joe's repressed sexuality; and then cutting to the very last scene where Joe and Ken walk into the lavender together—brilliant!" John said, before turning it back to Penny, who liked the fact that "the relationship between Barbie and Skipper was no longer sororal but sexually ambiguous as well," before turning it over to Nettie, who said that we should probably get going soon because soccer ended an hour ago.

We were at the exact same spot on the tracks where Nettie told me to stop the week before when she told me, this time, that I was nothing but a bull-shitter. "You didn't intend to do any of what you talked about during the critique, did you?" she said, her head down, kicking a rock against the clang of track. All I could do was shrug. "Then it's not fair," she said, stepping onto the rail, steadying herself "What's not fair?" I asked, as if it were no biggy. Nettie ignored me in an effort to balance. The silent treatment. "A lot of my shots didn't turn out so I had to improvise," I said. "A lot of the writing came in the edit." Nettie took a couple of shaky steps. "I guess I stumbled onto something," I said, almost ashamed, as Nettie lost her balance and jumped off. "It's interesting, though, isn't it?" she said, remounting. "It's interesting how sometimes we set out to do things one way, but then once they're done they often take on a completely different meaning." I agreed, then reminded Nettie of that day in class when Penny used the example of *Reefer Madness,* how it was originally intended to be an anti-marijuana film, but how, over the years, it became a cult film frequented by marijuana smokers. "That wasn't the example she used," Nettie said, rebalancing. "That was the example she used for irony." Nettie took three steps on the rail and told me the example Penny used for intent was *Triumph of the Will*.

5.2

—How did you and Nettie discuss the contents of Mr. Billington's garbage?
—I didn't think you were interested in talking about that.
—Why?
—I don't know. I sensed you were trying to get at something and—
—So you changed the topic in order to find out if we would try to get you to go back to it later?
—That's right.
—Just like you're doing right now.
—Right.
—Well, then?
—Well, I suppose I *could* tell you about what we talked about regarding Mr. Billington's garbage. But I don't see the point. We were able to figure out what he was up to just from what was in the bag. And sure, we talked about it. We were curious. We had imaginations. But it didn't change our lives or anything. In fact, it quickly became a segue into something else: Nettie wanted me to come over to her house because she wanted to show me something related to Billington's garbage, something that would really blow my mind. I mean, I could tell you how she made me guess what that might be. I could tell you how she refused to tell me, and how I got bored guessing. I could also tell you about seeing Mr. and Mrs. Billington out walking their poodles after we crawled out of the bush and how Nettie said extra loud how she was glad they replaced the teeter-totters at the park because the old ones made her *bum hurt* and would I like to come over for lunch tomorrow for *beer sausage* sandwiches and—*ouch*—her lips crack if she forgets to put *Vaseline* on them when reading *Garçons de Maroc* in her room overlooking *the lane* and how that was infinitely more interesting than our reactions to a complex bag of garbage. So why don't I just tell you about what happened after that.
—Continue.

5.3

We walked down Cypress from the tracks, turning left at Quilchena Crescent, the street where Nettie lived, just around the corner from me. All of a sudden Nettie bolts towards the Galts' driveway. She saw it first: Bobby and his older cousins, Mitch and Donal, had a pissed-off Timmy Waite up and out of his wheelchair. They were leading him towards the giant bear trap that usually hung from the ceiling of the Galts' garage but which was now spread open in the middle of the lawn. Totally bizarre. I couldn't believe my eyes. To this day a very strong image, much stronger than the contents of Billington's garbage:

the three Galts laughing their heads off, barely able to contain themselves, Timmy spazzing out in all directions, and looming six feet away, this rusty trap, its steel jaws yawning, everyone oblivious to the full-tilt Nettie.

She arrived swinging, corking Donal, the biggest of the three, right on the side of the head, knocking him out. Then she went for Mitch, grabbing his shoulder, swinging him around, ripping the sleeve clean off his Edgar Winter T-shirt. Bobby, meanwhile, took off down the side of the house. He kept screaming, "No way, no way am I gonna hit a girl." Nettie followed. Within seconds you could hear Bobby's laugh, then his plea, his cries of "Uncle, uncle, uncle ..."

5.4
—Stop.
—Why?
—You're lying. This never happened.
—Sure it did. It just didn't happen that day. This was something that happened years before. See, I'm just trying to get a handle on the way you're set up to recall the facts of my life.
—So you can continue your lying ways?
—Naturally.
—And what would be the point of that?
—To protect myself.
—From what?
—From whatever's coming next.

6.1
I awoke to my name, my mother's voice calling up from the kitchen. "It's Nettie!" I shut my eyes and took a deep breath, all set to let go with something just as loud, something about my being asleep. But of course I was too late: the shush of Mom's slippers, the receiver rocking gently on the sideboard, Nettie's mouth pressing on the other end. And as for all that air? My big inhalation? I yawned instead. Then I put on some gaunch and stumbled down to say hi.

That's what it was like when I was a kid. Whenever the phone was for me— and if I was around, and if I wasn't sick or grounded—my mother always made me answer. Never made excuses, never took a message. No help that way at all. And what a piss-off, too! I used to love sleeping in. All those warm thoughts. And to this day I hate waking. I remember calling her on it once. But she played tough: Why should I be your social secretary? Why should I lie for you? I mean, in a way she was right. After all, I was the man of the house now. I had to be responsible. But whatever. Nettie always called early on a Sunday. And my mother was always glad to see me up. She liked Nettie for that reason. My mother always had stuff for me to do after she kicked my dad out.

Nettie wanted me to come over to her place—which was new, because usually we'd just meet in the park and do something sporty depending on the season. "Well, for what?" I asked her. "Whaddaya wanna do?" There was a pause. Somewhere in the background James Taylor and Carly Simon were singing "Mockingbird."

"I have an idea for a new film," she said. And then she went on to say that she'd done up some storyboards and had written a voice-over and she was really excited about it and she wanted to know what I thought. I reminded her that she'd just finished a film, and that maybe she should take a break before launching into a new one. "Asshole!" she said, sounding more dejected than menacing. Still, I felt menaced enough to tell her that I'd come over in a couple of hours, and that she shouldn't get her hopes up because, to be quite honest, I was sick of anything to do with film. But really, though, I just hated to see Nettie dejected. And I guess I felt a bit guilty, too. I think she was still pissed off over how I wrangled genius out of *Joe and Barbie.* So I guess I owed her.

There were no cars in the Smarts' driveway—which was odd, because usually at least one of her folks was home when I was over. I think that was a rule. Also, I began to sense that what Nettie and I were about to do was wrong, especially since she'd told me to come around the basement way. But whatever. I walked down the back steps and was just about to knock when suddenly the door swings open, sucking me into the rec room. "Good. You're here," said Nettie, grabbing my hand, leading me towards a paper-strewn table. "These are some of the boards I've done up. I'm working with the title *A Bird and a Worm,*" she said, carefully arranging the pages in numerical order. I checked out the drawings, most of which consisted of stiffly drawn robins. Only the worms had any life to them. "Well, whaddaya think?" she said, hands on hips, a gesture she'd picked up from her mom. "Well," I began, "it looks like the story of a bird catching a worm." Nettie gave me a hard nod. She was very serious. "Or," I continued, "it could also be the story of a worm being caught by a bird." Nettie smiled. "Exactly," she said. "It's from the worm's point of view."

Nettie sat down at the table and opened a brand new notebook, entitled: NETTIE SMART: FILM IDEAS: MARCH 15, 1975. She pushed a chair towards me, then began flipping, stopping on a page, making a mental note, then flipping back to something else, then flipping forward a couple more. I remarked on how her jagged writing looked like fish hooks, but the comment went unnoticed. "I've written some narration and I want you to help me with it," she said, slowing down on her flipping, then looking up for an answer. I think I made a discouraging face because Nettie responded as if I'd said no. "It'll be really easy if we work on this together," she said, going back to her flipping, before stopping on a neatly printed page. "Here," she said. "This is how I'd like it to start."

The lowly worm. It crawls through the dirt on a daily basis, tilling the soil for whatever the people are growing. Tomatoes, roses, lilies, trees.

Up in the cedars the robins chirp. They watch for a wriggle in the people's compost. They watch for the worms that crave the bright light. The robins swoop down and pull the worms from the ground.

The worms are carried in the beaks of the birds. They are fed to the robins' squeaky children. They die in the darkness of the robins' young tummies.

"That's all I've got so far. What I need is some help on the edit," she said, sliding the notebook over to me.

I reread the text. In my head. I even pretended to read it twice. Because I needed time. I needed to think of something to say. I didn't want to tell her that worms don't crave the sun, and that they're actually digested by adult robins who then regurgitate them back to their chicks. No point in telling her all that. And besides, I sort of knew what Nettie was getting at: narration, this time, as opposed to a wash of images, what Penny would call "the lyrical." "Well, I think the story's fine. Maybe drop a word or two. But other than that, it's fine. Great even!" I said, looking up from the notebook. But Nettie had stopped listening. She was drawing a thought bubble above a "lowly worm." In the bubble she wrote the word *help*.

So was that it? Was that all she wanted to show me? Not likely. I was about to ask her if I could go, but thought otherwise just as quick. I knew better. Something was on her mind. And I knew my leaving would only piss her off. What we needed was a change. Nettie was acting really hyper, super-fidgety, like she needed to burn something off. So I suggested we go to the park and kick field goals. Nettie scrunched her face, shook her head no. Now she was being a baby. What was her fucking problem? Why was she being so ... *evasive*. That's when I noticed the heat.

"Have you got the thermostat cranked or something?" I said, taking off my sweater. "Nope," said Nettie, shading the underside of her worm. I went over to the window and pulled back the curtains. The driveway lay in wait. "Where're your parents?" I asked her. "Mom's in Seattle shopping and my dad's giving a speech at some lawyer thing," she replied. Oh. "And my brother's with my mom," she added. "He's getting an electric guitar. They're cheaper in the States, y'know." Thank you, Nettie. I did not know that. "Besides," she continued, "he didn't want me watching him rock out in the music store, so"—Nettie's chair creaked; I refocused on the window and caught her reflection, her approach—"so I guess that just leaves the two of us."

I could feel the heat off her body, just like the day before, in the brambles. But this time was different. This time something was going to be acknowledged. I could tell. I brought my arms up to rest on the sill, let my breath smudge the pane. Nettie came to rest beside me, and her breath did the same—but her smudge was huge. "Know what I found in my dad's study?" she said, fingering a bird shape into her section of the vapoured pane. "What?" I said, happy to break the silence. "Some pictures," she said, making a worm shape with her nail. "Oh yeah? Pictures of what?" I said quickly, hoping she'd get to the point. "Pictures that Mr. Billington might like," she replied matter-of-factly, dotting a sight line between the bird's eye and the worm. So that's what this was all about. "Yeah, they were in a folder under some of his court notes," she added. "That seems like a pretty funny place to put them," I said, not knowing what else to say, wondering whether all men that age shared something that I, a boy of twelve, knew nothing about. Nettie smiled. I could feel her staring at me, studying me for some kind of reaction. "I bet your mom would flip out if she found them, huh?" I said, hoping to get her talking again. "Nope. She'd know they were just evidence in some case," she replied, unfazed. I laughed like it was funny or something. Nettie made a strange face, said nothing. I watched the corner of her mouth curl. "So let's go look at them," she said, pushing off from the sill. "Unless, of course, you're chicken."

Judge Smart's study was dark and sinister and smelled like a pipe. I'd never actually been inside before, having only walked past it twice in my life. Once to use the washroom; another time when I helped Nettie and her mom carry up a carpet. Both times the door had been ajar, and all I could make out was the back of the judge's silver head, the emerald-green desk lamp that glowed like a lantern.

Nettie flicked on the lamp, deepening the grain in the woody room. "You've never been inside here before, have you?" she said, knowing full well that I hadn't. "Duh?" I said, just for something to say, just to be cool. Nettie went up on her tiptoes and withdrew a binder from one of the judge's mighty shelves. Her bum flexed as she did this. "We'll start with the white one first," she said, plopping the binder down over the judge's leather blotter.

The binder had a title: CROWN VS. WHITLOCK, STOKES, AND MAR-SHALL. "This doesn't feel right," I said, frightened by the detail in the provincial court logo. "Aren't you interested in what my dad does for a living?" she said, flipping open the binder to reveal an eight-by-ten glossy of a freckle-faced boy sitting on a tree stump, naked but for a pair of oversized gumboots. "This isn't what he does for living," I said to the boy in the photo. "This is just evidence in a case."

Nettie turned the photo over to reveal another photo. Once again, the freckle-faced boy. But this time he had his legs spread, and crouched before him was a girl, also about our age, looking over her shoulder at the camera. She had big dark eyes and loopy brown curls and her little mouth was smooched towards whoever was taking the picture. Between the thumb and forefinger of the girl's right hand was the boy's penis. She was pulling it towards her, stretching it into something thin, like an elastic band. The boy had a surprised look on his face, like Alfalfa from *Little Rascals*. Nettie turned the photo over. This time the boy was standing sideways, and the girl, who was still crouched before him, still pulling on his penis, had her tongue extended so that it was just touching the underside of the boy's scrotum. Nettie turned the photo over to reveal yet another photo: a close-up of the little girl's mouth stretched over an adult penis. The strain in the little girl's face made me weak. "There's tons like this," Nettie said, fishing for something near the back.

Nettie removed a folder marked STOKES. She opened it over the binder. The first photo was of a playground. Children on swings, climbing monkey bars, teeter-totters. "These belong to a different series, so we can't get them mixed up," she said, turning the photo over. The next photo was a medium-shot of three boys, maybe fourteen or fifteen, sitting in front of a tree. The boys were all wearing cut-offs and one of them, a bigger boy with a faint moustache, was shirtless. "I like his chest," Nettie said of the young moustache. I agreed. I wanted pecs like that, too. Nettie flipped through the pile and withdrew two photos. The first photo showed the three boys in what looked like an old garage. They were huddled together, naked, mugging for the camera, each one holding rulers up to the other's erections. "Do you think his penis is bigger because he's older?" Nettie said, pointing to the young moustache. I didn't know, so I just said maybe, "Well, is your penis that big yet?" she said. "I don't know. It's hard to say," I said, suprised by her candour. Nettie nodded. "Yes," she agreed. "There's nothing in the photo to give a sense of scale. I mean, the numbers on the rulers are totally out of focus." Nettie lingered for a moment, then showed me another.

6.2
—Mr. Billington?
—Either Billington or someone who looked just like him.
—So you weren't sure?
—No, but that's the first thing I thought.
—Did Nettie say it was Billington?
—Not really. I mean, I think she knew that I might think it was him. I think she was waiting for me to ask.
—Continue.
—What for?
—We need a description.
—You have the photo.
—Yes, but we need your description.

6.3
I guess Nettie already had her mind-blowing moment. So I guess that's why she was more interested in getting my reaction than she was in revisiting the

photo. And she certainly must have gotten what she was looking for, because I just couldn't believe what I was seeing. *I could not believe it!* There before me were the three teenagers, all in various stages of sexual activity. And who should they be working on? Who should be lying there—on his back, legs in the air, his face and chest covered in ejaculate—but Billington! Or someone who looked a hell of a lot like him. So yeah—I couldn't believe it. It was super-heavy—way heavier, of course, than what we'd found in the guy's garbage the day before. In fact, now that I think about it, I remember the moment so well if only because of the way the photo seemed to animate that garbage, how each item—the Vaseline, the beer sausage, the tissues, the magazines—came to life, leapt from the page, how they danced about my neighbour like something from *Fantasia.* That was really the moment: Billington twirling like a rotisserie pig, the condom jumping out of its wrapper, opening wide, receiving the sausage, then dipping itself in the Vaseline, before going to work on Billington's ass, while the mothy tissues dabbed at his spunk and the magazines hovered like birds in a gale. Total Disney. I could not believe it!

Nettie nudged me. "Ironic, huh?" I agreed. Then I asked her if that's why she was so eager to chase the bag down in the first place. "Duh?" she said, careful to replace the photo in the exact same spot she took it from. "Do you want to see more?" she said. "One more," I said. "You won't like it," she said. "It couldn't be any more fucked than the last one," I told her.

The next folder we looked at was the one marked MARSHALL. Nettie opened it up, lay it before me. A woman, about forty, stared back. She looked like somebody's mother. "This is the woman who took those first pictures, the ones with that kid in the gumboots," Nettie said, pushing the photo aside to reveal another photo of the same woman. But this time she was being accompanied by a man. They looked like some average middle-aged couple stepping out of a McDonald's. "That man she's with—he's the boy's legal guardian," she said, handing me the photo. I took the photo and examined it closely. There was nothing out of the ordinary. But then again, what was I looking for anyway? I guess that's what made this photo the creepiest one of all. "They look so normal," I said. "Exactly!" said Nettie. "That's why it took so long for the cops to catch up to them." Nettie went on to say that the man and the woman were part of a ring.

Nettie shelved the binder, then plunked herself down on the judge's chair. She tested the swivel with her hips, her feet firmly planted. Her top half seemed relaxed, but her knees were knocking wildly. She stared at me kinda weird, like she was trying to be sly or something. "I don't know," I said, scratching my head. "I mean, I don't know how I feel about all this. Do you look at your dad's stuff often?" Nettie smiled. "All the time," she replied. "But I figure it's okay as long as I don't tell anyone." Hmm. "Well, you kinda told me by showing me, didn't you?" I said. Nettie spun a three-sixty. "Yeah, so?" she said, slamming her feet down. I was confused. I decided to go on the offensive. "Does this stuff do anything for you?" I asked her. Nettie laughed out loud. "Yeah, it does. *Sometimes*," she said, almost giggly. "Some of it makes me feel kinda ... *sexy*." Nettie cocked her eyebrow, effectively turning the question around. I shrugged. Nettie's smile gave way to a scowl. She looked away. "But some of it does the opposite," she added, spinning again, this time stopping with her back to me. "Some of it," she began, "makes me feel sorta ... *sad*." And with that, Nettie jumped ftom the chair and returned to the shelf. She removed the binder a second time.

A car was slowing. I glanced at the window. "Our brakes don't squeak," Nettie said, miles ahead. Once again, she opened the binder over the judge's desk. "Why do these photos make you feel sexy?" I asked, curious about Nettie's mixed feelings. She gave me a I puzzled look, which scared me, took me back. For now I had to account for my own feelings. And the only thing I was feeling at that moment was the fear of being caught. "Well, what I mean is— these little kids are being used, right?" I said, aware of the quiver in my voice, but happy just to get something out. Nettie gave me a withering look. "You are *so* repressed," she said. I wasn't sure what she meant by that. But it was too late to ask. She was leading up to something. I could tell. "What if I told you that the boy and the girl liked each other—*a lot*," she said, her tone too serious, almost defensive. I shrugged. Maybe she was right. I guess you'd really have to like someone in order to do what those two were doing—especially with people taking pictures and stuff. "I mean, what if I told you those adults never went to jail, that the Crown had no case, and that the whole thing never even made it to court?" she continued. I shrugged again. I wasn't sure what we were talking about any more. "And what if I told you that in the eyes of the law none of these people have done anything wrong, and how that therefore makes none of these photos illegal?" she said, flipping to the back, stopping on a section of text, tapping it with her finger for emphasis. "I mean, that's basically what it says in the report."

I adjusted the desk lamp. I was all set to start reading when Nettie flipped back to the beginning. "I like this one the best," she said, removing a five-by-seven colour snap, a low-angle shot of the boy in the gumboots and the girl with the big eyes. They were both on their sides, in the sixty-nine position, over a fuzzy pumpkin-coloured rug. The boy had his finger in the girl's anus, while the girl's kissy lips pressed against his testicles. The photo did nothing for me. "What's so great about this one?" I asked, leaning a hand on the desk, steadying myself. "I just think it's beautiful. They both look so happy. I think they love each other a lot, don't you?" Nettie said, picking up the photo, holding it out between us. "Is that what it says in the report?" I asked. "I haven't read everything yet," she replied, absently, as she set the photo down.

I felt Nettie's hand brush the small of my back, the twist of her thumb in my belt loop. I was still concentrating on the photo. "Looks like they used a wide-angle lens," I said, my voice dry. Nettie ignored me, tugging gently on the loop, pulling herself closer. I could feel the heat off her body, her coloured scent curling up and under my nose. Nettie tilted her head into the flesh of my shoulder. From the corner of my eye I could see that she was no longer interested in the photo. She seemed to be looking off, towards the black hole of the judge's waste-paper basket. I wasn't sure where this was going, so I continued my critique: "The POV is odd, though. Don'tcha think? I mean, the person taking this photo had to be lying on their stomach. Pretty weird, huh? With all that going on?" Nettie responded by pushing closer. I could feel the calf of her leg squish against my shin. Her breath seemed to hiccup. I lifted my arm over hers and let it slide down her back, to where the heel of my hand came to rest on her ass. I wasn't sure why I did this, but I did. "The lighting's a bit bad, too. I don't think they should've used a filter," I said, stuttering on the *f* in "filter." Nettie began to sway—slowly, gently. I lowered my eyes. I could see where the corner of the desk met her groin. Then the leg I was sharing with Nettie suddenly began to shake. I shifted my weight. Nettie moved with me. Now *that* leg was shaking. Again, she pulled on my belt loop. It felt like she was trying to turn me. So I let her. I opened my mouth. Our teeth clicked. Our tongues met. We were kissing. It was my first wet kiss. Not like those other dry puckers I'd known in the past. And it felt great, too. But it wasn't what I wanted. Not like this. Not with Nettie.

It was as if something exploded between us. Nettie jumped back. Her face went wide. "It's my dad!" Somewhere in the distance: an emergency brake engaging. "Don't just stand there," she said, all frantic. "Go down to the basement." I tore out of the study, ran down the stairs, through the kitchen, then down the short flight to the rec room. I leaned against the door and quietly caught my breath. I could hear the tinkle of keys, the crunch of the opening door. Nettie's faint "Daddy!" Then the judge's low cough, his grumble. I scanned the room for hiding spots. The house shook with footsteps. I listened as they went from carpet to hardwood, finally coming to rest on the kitchen tile, just above my head. The rec room was cold now. I grabbed my sweater and strained to listen. All I could make out was the chirp of Nettie's high notes. My heart was beating like a bass drum. A couple of footsteps, then the shuffle of the judge's slow retreat, the tamp of his feet up the stairs. Nettie's descent seemed in counterpoint. She walked in spinning a football.

from *Paul's Case* (1997)

I. FEAR

Paul Bernardo
Kingston Penitentiary
King Street West
Kingston, Ontario
K7M 2E7

We shall therefore star the text, separating, in the manner of a minor earthquake, the blocks of signification of which reading grasps only the smooth surface ...
—Roland Barthes, *S/Z*

You, reader, know the delicate monster.
—Baudelaire

August 27, 1996
Dear Paul,
I was in Fire Island the day the verdict was announced. I hadn't seen the Atlantic since I was nine years old. Then, I would run in right away. My first taste of salt, the ocean tossing me up. I swam like a shark, tireless, and blind. When I arrived, David and Ira brought me to the beach. They dove into the surf with bright red boards. I hesitated, then moved in slowly, feeling the undertow shift the sand. The water darkened, crested, and knocked me over. When I tried to stand up I was pulled under and thrown into another wave. I ran, choking and falling, to the shore, and wouldn't go back.

The first day of September. You were pronounced guilty of nine charges: two counts each of first-degree murder, kidnapping, forcible confinement and aggravated sexual assault, and one count of committing an indignity to a human body. Your wife, Karla Homolka, was already serving time for two counts of manslaughter—twelve years for her role in the murders of Leslie Mahaffy, Kristen French, and Tammy Homolka.

I had followed the trial. The composite pictures of the Scarborough Rapist (who turned out to be you). The disappearance and discovery of two teenage girls: one found in a lake, cut into pieces and placed in concrete blocks, the other found naked in a ditch with her hair cut off. Both of them raped and beaten. The arrest of Homolka. The deal she cut to testify against you before the videotapes were found. Your arrest. The discovery of videotapes, films of these girls. Your trial, which I attended, shaking, because I did not know what I would feel when I saw you both.

Feeling nothing, watching Homolka testify. Watching the back of your head. Nothing.

Leaving for New York as the jury deliberates, arriving at Fire Island. The woods are dry and brittle. There has been no rain and there are caution signs in the laneways: fire. That night we walk the dog on the beach and he finds a crab-shell. When he shakes it seven baby crabs fall out.

We wrench it from his mouth and they creep into the darkness. The sky is red and orange, burning.

I am staying in a stranger's study, behind the house. It is designed like a ship-captain's room; small and unventilated. I look up at a school assignment tacked to the wall. For a creative writing course. Write a List Poem, it says. There are examples, involving tangerines, lemons, pomegranates and black-berries. I see that I am bleeding: squadrons of mosquitoes have appeared, vectorial. I can't sleep and I try to write—why do I always feel this way I can't stay here I can't—a list poem:

> Fire Island
> Pitch black, pitched back
> Unlocked window, killers
> Vampire bugs; crabs' legs
> Tinderbox, seething
> Sleepless, Fear

I am thinking of murder and I run back into the main house and leave the lights on. I wasn't thinking about you, I hadn't heard. I had to call to find out. Men who look through windows, who have wanted me dead. I had stopped sleeping months before.

There were things I wanted to say, about the way I felt, about how little I felt until I would begin. Afraid and appalled. Wanting to face you.

Ira took my arm the next day. He pulled me out past the breakpoint. One wave fell, and crashed around me. I left this water, feeling safe. And blessed and other things I had forgotten.

Crumpled miserably on the bed the day I went under. David sat with me and read a poem by Anne Sexton. About a time she was scared in the ocean and ran away. It was the end of the poem he wanted me to listen to, and now I'm writing to you, listening:

> There is no news in fear
> but in the end it's fear
> that drowns you.

You showed no signs of remorse, I would read. There is no news in that; your remorse doesn't concern me. I have been anxious about myself, what is missing. Intent on invention, I am writing you a letter in fifty-two sections. Simple cartomancy between a young fair-haired man who is the Jack of Spades, a young dark-haired woman who is the Queen of Clubs. Interfaced, I will assist you, although you are dangerous, and not worth the effort. According to the *Little Book of Fortune Telling*.

Which also suggests that you attach small stars to the cards. These stars are useful when, arranged in an archway, the cards *begin to contradict each other.*

(These patterns are referred to as The Doors—you know the day divides the night, night divides the day.)

You cap shuffle and cut these letters, crayon them with constellations. Peculiar combinations will foretell misfortune, death, the assistance of friends.

Or play fifty-two pickup. Just throw them in the air and gather them randomly. Stacking love on injury, on fear and mystery. This is up to you: a way to pass your time. Fold, spindle and mutilate them; make an exquisite corpse. A picture we will draw together, oblivious of each other's intentions.

This letter begins again with an aside. It could be meaningful: *a woman you do not know well has deceived you. She is trying to hide this from you.*

The rest follows: A woman of ill repute who is disheartened, and curious: Beware of her. She is not fond of you.

Silence is usually the preferable surrounding for the reading of cards.

Sharin Morningstar Keenan died the year I came to Toronto. She was a little girl and her killer is still out there. His name is Dennis. He raped and strangled her, left her in his refrigerator. The neighbours heard the noise, but were too frightened to call for help. He is balding, a large man with broad features. He is missing part of one of his fingers; at bars, he arranges his loose coins in a circle around his glass. I think about them both, now and then. Of seeing him and calling the police, while nailing his hands to a table with ice picks. Of her, without fetish, though her small body bends like a swan against the metal racks. I think of how terror is consumed. As if she is a python, swallowing an elephant. I will imagine her parents, a mother's head crowned in peacock feathers, painting a mandala around her navel: morningstar. Her father who shuffles through dim hallways at night, listening.

The killer's hair is thin and dark. He fills me with disgust; and she, beatified, has risen. Her cygnet limbs streaming, beyond my sight. Even so, I think of him more often, with great agitation. The two-boned digit rapping against formica, his corona of coins: clues. I think of his father, torturing him, and try to envision an illness I cannot occupy. But understand in small stabs. The desire, as an adult, to inhabit two subject positions. At one time, you were defiled and powerless: the tall shadow of the monster, the way you curled into a ball and waited for the blows. When you inflict these blows on others later, it is a lot like acting. There is this and simple cruelty. A thrill, like stepping, simply, from a ledge. Your carelessness supports you. Falling with a rattle to the ground, you rise. And perversion. A sick sensation, like swooning: our entire capacity. You want to throw up when you think about it, your breath becomes shallow. Forcing your tongue through a child's kiss, laying bare and breaking the covenant. Innocence makes you ill and angry.

Dennis is overweight and has a wide sloping forehead. He is not visible. It has been over ten years and he is sitting somewhere now, feeding money into a jukebox until "Summer Wind" drops into place. His eyes close in revery: two sweethearts (I live just across the park—be quiet be quiet be quiet) and the summer wind.

I lost you, he thinks, or doesn't. But still the days live on and on, and I need to know you. Pieces of my own life lost in you: *Just stand still and be quiet.* A girl's eyes narrowing, white slits. Thick fingers closing them, with coins.

> *If one calls bricolage the necessity of borrowing one's concepts from the text of a heritage, which is more or less coherent or ruined, it must be said that every discourse is bricoleur.*
> —Jacques Derrida

By now you've stopped reading Paul (*tacco et video*); you have torn this letter to shreds or let it slide to the floor, more or less coherent or ruined. You are tired all the time. I followed your trial closely, in my own way. *Bricolage.* Some makeshift repair of the event, clippings I kept close at hand: I Was Enjoying Myself, Sir.

Newspapers I cut out and stapled together randomly, their headlines like pulp paperbacks I have always wanted to own (*Make My Bed in Hell*). I have made you over with these materials, differently. A lurid flipbook—Paul jumps from Hawaii to prison in one deft shuffle—inured to you, I touch your picture, goodbye, when I leave this desk to buy one pint of milk/sugar/envelopes. Think of setting you on fire, tarred and feathered, a soiled dove. Return, disgusted, and withdraw the sheaf of yellowing packrat papers, absent-mindedly folding them into shapes. A sugar cone; a grass pyre; a burial shroud.

I look around for something you like, thinking how obtuse you are, how you lie. Beyond good and evil, in a region that is simulated. (You watched *Wall Street* to discover, *And when you gaze long into an abyss the abyss also gazes into you,* then pasted this aphorism to your wall.)

If Nietzsche was an invalid and his Fascist sister re-arranged his work for her own purposes, he never meant to say *Te amo* Mussolini, Hitler, *liebling*.

He may have heard the gunshot; delirious, he may have seen the hanged body, burned and mutilated, swaying. At the end of his rope, he thought of woman's nature, her capacity for revenge: *the tiger's claws beneath the glove and inner savagery. This dangerous and beautiful cat woman.*

He refers to me as a *beast of prey,* when I borrow from him also, and asks that I do not erase the line, but examine each region. An orthographic projection that reveals hidden points and corners. I am cornering you, and I am getting closer, closer than I was when I came to your trial. When I wrote to you in January and asked you to explain something to me. I detest your crimes, I said, parenthetically. But I know that you have been punished To The Full Extent Of The Law.

My flower of evil, hypocrite Lector:

> *Comme d'autres par la tendresse,*
> *Sur ta vie et sur ta jeunesse,*
> *Moi, je veux régner par l'effroi.*

You see that I have made a girl of you and you are afraid. In French everything is gendered, my glue, *chérie,* darling scissors: a scissoresse, sorceress. You liked to cut and paste things too, I read; and it was disgusting, you said, dismembering a corpse. Locked in antitheses and disinterested, in what makes things work. I wrote a nice polite letter to you without spelling errors (it occurs to me I have never taken a clock or a radio apart) and you didn't write back. That was something like love, what I have known in the past. Reaching out, and my beloved recoils. Dogs get killed that way, trying to get away from you. You tend to make people uneasy, revolted. What—was I saying? I know that you are barely alive, that your partner is almost through. It is possible that I should be writing to her. But she is not the captive audience I require.

She does love to read so it's unfortunate. Karla enjoys mysteries; her IQ is formidable. When she is not busy with her schoolwork, she devours true-crime novels. Please send me that book about the Monsters of the Moors, she wrote to a friend. Twice, on flower-bordered paper, perfumed with Poison

a potion in plum-coloured glass
Myra Hindley's atomizer of Tabu.

Myra also killed children, and she kept things clean and simple. A striking blonde in black; Ian Brady photographed her, in high boots and mesh stockings. Long red nails shining, whiphand. Riding on the back of his Triumph, her arms wrapped around his waist, screaming Faster, and while he dug the graves she walked out farther in the mist. She looked up at what moon there was, milky above the scrim of her long lashes. She has since become a model prisoner and her tastes are no longer catholic; her lips move carefully, with humility, at mass (bodies of matter of indefinite shapes).

Martha Beck and Raymond Fernandez, an obese nurse with a gigolo husband who practiced voodoo (the dead walk the earth). Executed for multiple murders on March 9, 1951, Beck remarked that theirs was a love story that only those tortured by love could understand. Tortured by Love. This is a misprision, which Karla would recognize, shifting the words around into a more logical sequence.

Folie à deux: a clinical term for the lunacy or madness of one and another. These four and you two make three. As an accountant, surely you understand the figures. You are not like anyone else either, please don't misunderstand me.

I do not want to confuse you any further, although I was wondering if you think of weakness and strength in adversative terms. Because I will examine you, with affection and loathing, bend and break you.

The play within this play is performed with shadow puppets: as Minerva, I call out to you in a thin and ruthless voice, Hades, leave your dark realm and show yourself.

This morning I thought about heaven, that it is not an assembly but a retreat into dreams. Dreams I write unbidden, within a traversal, the milky way between each hemisphere. John Rosen, your lawyer, showed Karla a photograph of her sister's dead body and she looked away. Look at it, he commanded. This satisfied many, though I will carve out her eyes instead. She has become the blonde starlet of my Senecan drama. Like Vendice (and you my Gloriana), I'll make the bad bleed and the tragedy good.

Deploying stichomythia, repeating and opposing myself, repulsing you. Speaking all the while in inherited tropes: falling angels, the spherical cycle of violence and consolation. I'll be the entire chorus, sliding across the stage in strophe, antistrophe, and epode, standing still. Just looking at you again as I have and will, your immutable face the place you reside: where no birds sing. I visited the Kingston Penitentiary last Sunday, walking past the gun towers, sensors and guards. Toward the lake, passing by your little window, toward you. Sitting on your mattress, one foot is hooked beneath you as you fold and refold a towel.

The sun razing the water, the rotunda of silver and gold. You heard me approach, as you did in court last July when I was late and dressed like an assassin. Detained by the police, I had just arrived when you were led through the door. In a forest green suit and tie (paler bars of green), your head averted, from me.

I could see your mouth moving, your lips pulling at the corners. It's that tremor that gives you away, that would arouse my suspicion, if you had ever asked me to accompany you to your car or hotel room in Fort Lauderdale. Maybe feeling good, the sand circled from the rim of a tequila glass leaving olympian symbols, the lost weekend inflamed with your profile or poetry: *Poor soul, the centre of my sinful earth.* My body still pale but burning, watching your mouth calculate how easily my arms can be bound behind my back, the crack of the blade (dislocation occurs when the arm is abducted). But I was never young. Waiting always, looking at the prim curve of your white collar, the tenderness of your neck. Still against the bulletproof glass, even my eyes which

> *Like comets shine through blood*

you resist. Laughing once with your lawyer (the lesser one, who still fields calls), pulling at his robes in a gesture of contempt while he play-hits you and you shrink. And shaking your head when Karla says, Ask Paul. He knows the truth.

Already this letter has become intimate. I have included an appendix because this is all so factual and specific and does not flow like lyrical fiction: gibson riverrun, past paul and karla. The surfeit of information and documentation has freighted my imagination: it is sinking, like a cement casket, into the mud and green water of the serpentine stream.

The prose is inelegant. What I mean is it is prosaic, the way you try to speak.

Also I am overdressed: white lab coat, stethoscope, book-strap, pick axe, magnifying glass, fossil-brush, latex gloves, razors, black hood. I could write a horrifying poem about you: I am stabbing you over and over and you will not die. Something detached, or smooth true-crime: The sun burned unusually bright that day, although Port Dalhousie residents would remember feeling a chill in the air. I could pin you down and dissect you, or care for you in my own nervous illness. Split your atoms in a chamber, tear you to shreds until I am greeted

> *avec des cris de haine*
> (Burn in Hell You Bastard.)

Instead I will examine each element. There is no consolation in elegy: I have not been well. When the ambulance arrived there was smoke everywhere. The policeman reached out to me and held my hand, examining the incisions. He asked, Do you want to come with me?

Revision—writing redemption, benedictions, untruth. In dejection, I have turned to you: come with me.

Because I have so many questions, because you have nothing else to do. Unfolding, then folding the towel into shapes: a triangle, a sailor's hat, a crescent moon. There is a woman who visits you, who compares herself, with some indignation, to a nun. She mentions her Bible, how she sticks it with pins and counsels you, swings low singing the Song of Solomon as you bow your head and your kiss, remembered, is sweeter than wine. You have mentioned, unsuccessfully and in your own defence, how film is often imported into life; you have tried to unravel deceptions: you have failed. I suggest to you that, like me, your little nun knows a dead man walking when she sees one. Things have a habit of reverting to form, a square, a stone, an apron.

Among the many things you said in court: that you did not beat and throw Karla into a mud puddle; that Kristen French's last words were not "There are some things worth dying for." Among the things you did not say: that Homolka is a grifter, who borrowed much of her testimony from television, books, and film. Paul knows the truth, she said on several occasions, nodding at you. *Toronto Sun* posters all over the city during the trial: your face framed with the legend THE TRUTH THE WHOLE TRUTH.

(My mistress's eyes, you remarked & I hold this picture now, looking into yours.)

If you could be more logical in the assembly of your ideas they might acquire a critical contour, the edges of the towel gathered to produce *Illuminations*.

Your opponent is dangerous, one who told the police you were too stupid to hold onto someone captive; one who was playing with a Hardy Boys crime-fighting kit (matching her prints with those of Alice Crimmins, Mary Flora Bell, Diane Downs) while you were walking silently through your Scarborough home, staring into space.

You did not speak until you were five, merely pointed and grunted, a fact which your lawyer did not mention. By the age of two and a half the average child has at least a 200–word vocabulary. If he does not, he may develop a grimace or facial twitch. He may be hearing or speech impaired; or he may be *giving his concentration and energy to acquiring some other skill.*

While the lack of oxygen in your brain during your birth is thought to have caused this protracted aphasia, your speaking skills, curiously, developed in direct correlation to your skill as a voyeur (creeping under night windows as a boy, your hands crossed over your pants, listening for Eros's first snap and click). Your father preoccupied, more interested in girls, gentle with them, easing their skirts up, navigating. Rosen, like the Metro Police, forgets to extract your DNA from the electrophoresis gel; he does not see the way its strands bend, in small pirouettes.

He's not my real father, you would say. Your mother claims to have had an affair. You think of her as a whore. And wonder about what is learned, what is encrypted (The Bad Seed).

Karla dressed in pink and white, her blonde hair loose as she hung out the window to see the hamster fall to the lawn. Alight on the wind, bound to a pillow case, it tumbled to the grass, stunned.

She loved dolls and admonished children who killed insects.

Encountering a child in a schoolyard with tiny arms (which ended like flowers where elbows should be), she cornered the girl's brother and said his sister was a freak, a seal who belonged in the zoo; creepy looking, is what she called her, as she combed her doll's yellow hair.

After the hamster died, she dug it up to look at it, sepulchral with maggots and worms, its limbs rigid, gesturing to the stars. I'm going to be famous, Karla said.

You are standing in a schoolyard also, smiling. As a group of
children surround you in a circle. Calling *barnyard barnyard*
what a smelly barnyard. You cried and wondered
why is everyone so mean to me?

Learning fast to meet evil with evil: "Out of every adversity comes the seed of an equal or greater benefit." One of many quotations you organized in columns along your bedroom wall.

It's just evil, writing to you this way.

Someone wrote this graffiti on newspaper boxes all over the city: Stop Profits From Bernardo. In black.

I don't know if you know this, but people hate your guts. Your best friend keeps ratting you out and collecting money. He was devoted to you (although he always thought there was *something unusual* about you).

One woman saw your lookalike in an advertisement for a CD player and went nuts, writing to magazines. The whole thing pains me, she said.

Or someone will say, out of the blue: He has a television in his cell. It's disgusting.

Sometimes I wonder if you're watching the same thing I am.

When I'm alone and hear strange noises: the gang in the alley (known as The Apostles). I worry about things. I have worried your case like a handkerchief. All the loose ends.

My doubt is reasonable, passed on to you on azure sheets of paper, with a black rat insignia. Slinking through the events of your trial, drawn to the smell of what is concealed, possibilities. Putrefaction.

Suspicion, torments my heart. I sing to you, when I remember—

I heard the defence attorney yell, This is the face of a killer! Pointing to a frozen video frame. Spectators were not able to see these images. I imagine you looked furious, your features contorted with rage.

Not at all benign. The way you looked when you came to the stand and waved your arms expansively. People, you said. I've done some terrible things. But I did not kill these girls.

Killers look very angry and ugly. They should always begin their testimony by impersonating a politician. Their attorneys should never, under any circumstance, introduce relevant psychiatric evidence.

Killers are not pretty. When Karla took the stand, she was lovely. Exceptionally polite and well-groomed. I want Paul to drool when he sees me, she said.

Pretty girls are not killers. Please pass me a tissue. Thank you. Yes sir, that is the truth, Paul killed them all, I have never hit anyone in my life. I merely stopped my sister's breath.

No I cannot explain why the victim had small knee cap-shaped bruises on her back, or why her face was bruised. It is true that Paul didn't hit her, but I never used that mallet. I've never hit anyone in my life! Yes I am aware that women invariably strangle with a ligature, not their bare hands. I suppose it makes it easier for them, but what you are proposing is a lie. Paul used that ligature, ask him.

May I be excused? Thank you.

The semiotics of women and violence: THE GUN WENT OFF, SHE STOPPED BREATHING.

The spectre of Lizzie Borden: Just look at this woman. Does she look like a murderer?

I think about these things and write them down. I am writing you an essay. It is experimental, analogous to your case. Your sex trial, where female sexuality was never mentioned. An experiment involving burial and decomposition, the essence that attracts rats who mistake it for perfume.

Paul, you are a sick and hateful man but you might as well be dead. Even if you aren't a murderer, you'll never see the light of day. The light of day you once watched breaking through the blinds and illuminating Karla's beautiful face.

The same sun that rose as she lay in a psychiatric ward, nodding on anti-psychotics, anti-depressants and tranquilizers. Enthralled by the attention, her doctor, Mesmer, drawing out untruths from the point of a needle.

While you languished, unexamined. Withholding your pathologies, all this deviance stonewalled: this cat has your tongue.

Pretty cat, who had her wrists slapped after playing rock paper scissors: the long arm of the law covered her briefly, a white sheet on a stone.

(I would never write to Karla because she might write back.)

I only mention all this because I have talked about these letters to a friend. He was disquieted although he liked all the mean things I said I would write, especially the part about sticking a knife right down your throat. But so does anyone who saw the Stones live, playing Midnight Rambler. Right here in Toronto at the El Mocambo—on that recording some girl screams Paint it Black. Paint it Black, You Devil.

Just like my friend.

I cannot erase your baby's face with black marker any more than I can Love You Live. You're doing something dangerous, he said. And I said, coldly, as I left, Danger Is My Business.

To return home and feel ashamed. And wish I was the avenger he wants me to be. The contract killer, the girl who was frightened of you my whole life.

Maybe you have read the three books about you, though I doubt it. I mean, I don't think you're allowed to read pornography in jail. This is irony, which you may or may not know. I have read them all and I'm tired of the story. It never changes, and I want to mix things up with you.

You will become confused and uncertain. Never knowing who I am. All of these voices and false/true documents. As if you are in court again, drawing question marks on a legal pad. Or worse, as if you are desperately unhealthy: you have begun imagining things. Everything I am asking you to absorb or swallow.

Because you don't say a word your purpose is certain. A cold seed, unhooked from its nidus, a pure object of study. Your value, however, cannot be determined. Unearthing you, I may discover what you have entombed (archaeologists hold up ropes of jewels, stepping over the bodies of the sentries, buried alive); I may stand, filled with fear, in a derelict cave. Where bats whisper and cling, high among the charred rocks and cold stalactites.

Either way, I will present you in fragments. And make a figment of you. With one bone or sunken footprint, scientists have built killers: I see them, as I think of you, in the golden light of the museum, craning their vicious heads as if advancing. When I draw away, I see the wooden ligatures and pegs, their hollowed eyes. They are harmless, but I have never moved closer, to touch them.

Jane Rule

Detained at Customs:
Jane Rule Testifies at the Little Sister's Trial (1995)

In December 1986, Canada Customs detained the first books and magazines destined for Little Sisters Book and Art Emporium in Vancouver, British Columbia. In 1990, the bookstore, B.C. Civil Liberties and owners Jim Deva and Bruce Smyth filed their Statement of Claim in B.C. Supreme Court instigating a constitutional challenge to Canada Customs' practice of seizing materials destined specifically for a gay and lesbian bookstore. The case would tackle the federal government on the issue of freedom of expression. It also challenged Canada Custom's power to seize a book at the border and force the bookstore that was ordering it to prove that the publication was not "obscene." In October of 1994, after many adjournments, all precipitated by the government, the trial between Little Sisters and Canada Customs finally began.

The following pages are the testimony of Jane Rule in the Supreme Court of British Columbia on October 24, 1994 at the trial. The transcript has been edited for grammar and sense in order to make it easier to read. The initial questions, establishing Jane Rule's credibility as an expert witness by listing the titles of her books and her academic credentials, have been deleted. The questions are asked by Little Sister's lawyer Joseph Arvay, and answered by Jane Rule.

The Court: Then I rule that Ms. Rule is qualified to express opinions in the field as you've described.

Q: Before we turn to the books, Ms. Rule, can you tell his lordship the criteria that you consider to be important if one is going to judge a book, and particularly if the ultimate result might be that the book is to be judged banned from circulation in Canada?

A: It seems to me that there is no set of rules that you can apply generally in a circumstance of this sort because literature is so various. As scholars and critics, we try to read a book and let the book dictate how we will deal with it. That is, we do not deal with what is said to be a stage drama as if it is a novel. We read it as a script for a play. If the writer makes it clear to us that it's a comedy, we don't treat it like a tragedy. We try to ascertain the intent of the novelist if we're dealing with a novel, not only the artistic intent, but often the social intent, the insights that the novelist calls to our attention. Therefore, we don't, if we're good critics, fault Jane Austen for not dealing with the French Revolution.

We, on top of that, have to be very good at reading tone because writers are notorious, if you like, in delivering their message in various tones, and irony is one of the most difficult ones to deal with. It is, however, a favourite of writers. Swift's *Modest Proposal* to cook Irish babies to deal with a famine is a book, or a proposal that some people thought he was offering seriously.

I think great errors in judgement can be made when a person who is judging a work for perhaps banning reasons is missing the cultural context of the book because books are not born out of nothing. They live inside the traditions of our culture and our culture is not only a North American culture, a contemporary culture, but it also reaches back into the literatures that we have studied and modeled our own upon.

Therefore, if we were going to deal with questions of humiliation, of sexual explicitness, we would have to know that we are dealing with Dante's *Inferno,* the Marquis de Sade's work as well as dealing with writers of our own time, recognizing that there have always been writers who have been preoccupied with the darker sides of human experience, who are perhaps best equipped to give us insights into those very troubling and often horrifying things that go on in the world today where in Bosnia women are routinely raped and children are molested, where in almost every case there is a sexual component which, if we don't finally come to understand in all its complexity, we are in great danger of not knowing how to live our lives.

Q: I want to bring you back to the question of what skills you would bring in assessing and judging a book or what qualities or criteria you would consider to be important. As a reviewer, what qualities and criteria you would apply to a book in considering whether it has merit. You've considered a couple of matters. You've talked about tone, and talked about an understanding of the cultural context in which a book arises. Is there anything else you want to add along those lines?

A: I think in our training and our experience, we learn how to read the different elements in balance. For instance, it's common for me to say plot is the moral agent of a book. So you could assume that anybody who got killed was a bad guy and anybody who lived was a good guy, if the writer's morality is functioning in terms of plot. But of course most of our writers use plot ironically, sometimes with tragic irony, so you'll end up with all the good guys dead. So you cannot simply have a formula for a plot as a moral statement and not read it with a subtlety of the climate of the book.

Q: As a writer and a literary critic, do you draw distinctions between the artistic purpose or intent of a book and its merit and value?

A: I think it's quite easy to draw a distinction between the artistic purpose and the artistic merit. Let me give you an example of *Moby Dick*. It is probably the worst built novel ever written in terms of what [Melville] should have done. He started out to write a novel, he ends up writing a play, and then he's writing an essay; he's all over the map. It's probably one of the greatest failures of our inheritance, and [at the same time] a better book than most well-made books.

Q: And so that would be a book that you would say failed insofar as artistic merit is concerned?

A: On certain levels, yes. As a structure it fails, but it's a brilliant brilliant book. It breaks all the rules.

Q: And just to stay on *Moby Dick* for a moment. Since Herman Melville I don't think is with us any more, you can speak freely. If it failed with respect to artistic quality or merit, what does it do with respect to artistic purpose or intent?

A: The intent is so enormous. To understand and manifest even in the words and to do it, to come at it from every angle you can think of, is revelatory.

Q: I see. Thank you. Now, have you had any personal experience, Ms. Rule, with the Customs process, or the training that Customs officials might have had prior to assuming the responsibilities in deciding whether books should be allowed entry into the country?

A: I don't know the process by which they're selected, and I don't know in detail the training that they're given. I have had the experience of knowing one Customs officer because he was in a class of mine at UBC, English 100, the freshman English class.

I had been assigned a special class, a particularly small class of students, all of whom had failed English 100 once and some of them had failed it twice, and as many of you may know, if you fail English 100 three times, you're out of the university. So these were fairly desperate students. Some of them were foreign students doing brilliantly well in other courses, a few were simply marginal students, possibly because they weren't terribly bright, but also because they were shingling off into the fog. The young man in question had failed it twice, and if he was going to fail again, then he was out of the university. He did marginal work, and I think if he had worked very hard he might have gotten a gentleman's C and gotten through, but he only did half of his assignments. In the spring, he came to me and said, "I'm really being frivolous. It's time for me to go out in the real world and earn a living and stop being a silly child." I thought that was a very sensible decision for him to come to.

Shortly after that, he came to me, and asked me if I would give him a letter of recommendation to be a Customs official for Canada Customs. I thought at that time that he was a personable young man, he's good with people and probably he would make a good Customs officer, so I was perfectly willing to give him a letter of recommendation. I was not aware at that time that such a person would be given the responsibility of censoring books coming into Canada.

Q: In preparing for your testimony, Ms. Rule, I asked you to compare two books, one which was entitled, *Tell Me What You Like*, by Kate Allen, which I advised you had been detained by Customs but ultimately released, and another was a book entitled *Bushfire* [edited] by Karen Barber which had been detained at Canada Customs and prohibited entry into Canada. First of all, tell [his lordship] something about *Tell Me What You Like*, and whether you can see any principled reason for releasing one book and prohibiting the other.

A: The first book, which was allowed through, is a book in which S and M relationships are explored by a curious and rather titillated female policeman. The [plot revolves around the fact that] some of the people who are involved in the sex trade and involved in sado-masochistic behaviour are being killed, and they're trying to pin the murders on someone inside the field. Finally it turns out that the person who is doing the harm is a young man who has been raised to be a bigot, and so there is a kind of moral twist to the plot; it is the bigot, the homophobic person who is the murderer, not any of the people involved in S and M.

It's, I suppose, an entertaining enough book, a book even that has the mild virtue of turning the moral tables and saying that violence comes from those who are bigoted, rather than from those who are engaging in sexual fantasy. There is not a great deal of violence in the book, there's not a great deal of vivid description. You do get some passages of it. It would certainly not occur to me that it would be a book to ban.

Q: Is it in fact a book that may find a place in any curriculum?

A: Yes. I think it could. Its literary quality isn't high, but I think the moral problems that it poses would be interesting in the debate about cultural pressures that produce judgemental attitudes.

Q: So you're not in disagreement with the Customs' ultimate assessment that the book should be released.

A: No.

Q: How do you then compare that book, and the decision with respect to that book, to the book *Bushfire?*

A: I was really startled and cannot figure how a Customs official could let the first book go, and prohibit *Bushfire,* which is a collection of short stories by lesbian writers, all of which focus on the erotic in one way or another. The blurb on the cover says this book is fun, this is fun sex, take this to bed with your girlfriend and you'll have a lovely time. It's offered as a masturbatory fantasy as a way of selling the book. I see nothing to object to in this. If there is some undue exploitation of sex involved, we would have to debate whether stories that take a lot of their time being erotic are unduly exploitive of sex.

But what I'd like to say about this book is that it may not be something as clearly understood for a heterosexual audience as it is to, say, a lesbian audience. A great many lesbians discovering that they are lesbians in this homophobic culture, feel bad enough about how they feel to think maybe they're the only person in the world who feels like this. They're young and coming into their own sexuality, or they find other people who are, they're all ashamed together, and sex is not a happy or fun thing, but a thing that is hungered after and shamed. [The audience is] people who are very ambivalent about their own sexuality [and this book is] a series of stories which deal not only positively with eroticism for lesbians, but bring up a lot of the issues that trouble lesbians in their sexual lives.

For instance, there is a story of the seduction of a woman who up to now has refused to play a passive part in her sexual experience. She will only give pleasure to others. ["A True Story."] In this story, it seems it would give insight to a fairly inexperienced lesbian about one of the myths about the butch-fem [relationship], the stone butch, the woman who never ever gets involved in sexual feelings but only controls another. This is a myth and it is a repression.

There is another story which is called "Sweat." It is about a woman who has just had breast surgery for cancer, and she's feeling perfectly awful about her body and feeling that perhaps, she will never get a sense again of being erotically alive, and so the erotic experience she goes through in this story is an enormously life-affirming assertion for her.

Q: Can you refer to some of the other stories?

A: "Past Lives" is a story that deals with an older and a younger woman. The younger woman has been sexually abused, and is very fearful of being in a relationship. The older, wiser woman is able, through erotic behaviour, to teach that young woman to trust her body and to celebrate her own sexuality with the older woman. Over and over again we deal with circumstances that lesbians actually go through. [In "A True Story"] there is a woman who is living in a very small town and she knows that everyone knows that she's a lesbian. She's ostracized, and so the erotic experience that she has is an affirmation that she's maybe not the only one, maybe there is a life to be lived even in this very homophobic, very narrow place.

The last story is called "Spelunking." I didn't know what spelunking was; it's apparently a term for exploring caves which is used, as you might imagine, with erotic overtones. It's great fun to read. It is about a young woman who has not had much sexual experience and every time she gets into a relationship with somebody, that somebody is politically totally correct. [One person says] "No penetration. No good lesbian ever gets involved in penetration. We don't do that." No this, no that. So she goes through one relationship after another feeling that she is just confined by rules when she really thinks that she probably is a speluncker and finally finds someone who is, too. It's fun. It's also, I think, very healthy in the exploration of sex as a creative and exploring and loving activity between women rather than a rigid exercise proving you're a real this or a real that or a real anything. I would be really, really glad to have this book around, particularly for quite young lesbians who know very little in their own experience.

There are black people in this book, there are working-class people, handicapped people, there are overweight people. It's interesting to me how often in the book the characters are said to be not really beautiful, and I think this is a kind of affirmation of women saying, "You do not have to be a poster, a male-imagined woman, to be attractive and to have these wonderful adventures." It seems to me from the sweep of the book [that I can't imagine] anyone not wanting to read it. Except, I suppose, if you were heterosexual, you might find the specific details of lesbians making love to each other not to your taste, though the sexual acts are not all that different. But I can imagine people being offended as we all are offended in our tastes by our narrow definition of appetite.

Q: Just before we leave this book, can you tell his lordship a little bit about some of the other stories. I don't believe you've referred to "Underground Fame."

A: "Underground Fame" is a more complex story, and certainly one that gives a kind of added power to the book because it is exploring a relationship which is obsessive and which must come to an end. It has to do with damaging people in an ego circumstance, and the resolution of the story is that this couple acknowledges the damage they're doing to each other and they separate.

Q: What about "Down-Home Blues"? You mentioned race earlier.

A: The exercise in the story is very simple. The exercise is to incorporate those we associate with Bessie Smith and the great lesbian singer of the blues,

Ma Rainey, into the culture of black women at this time. The story itself is of a woman recovering from the death of an older lover, attached to a woman that she isn't really interested in. She comes out of that relationship into another one that's going to be much more fully realized and loving, so that it's a happy ending story. But all the way through it there are refrains to call up the whole tradition of the blues. And this again is a wonderful way to give lesbians, and particularly black lesbians, a sense of their culture because it hasn't been said out loud that Ma Rainey and Bessie Smith were lesbians, as they were.

Q: I see. If this was a film, you'd obviously give it two thumbs up, but I have to ask you the question in legal terms. What is your opinion with respect to whether the portrayal of sex in the book is designed to advance serious literary or artistic or similar purpose?

A: I think it has a very strong purpose of making a positive statement about lesbian sex and lesbian experience, and this seems to me to be good. And the calibre of the stories is quite good. They're not all equally good, but many of the writers here are writers who are well-established and who publish novels and short stories; some of them are academics. The standard of writing is quite high.

Q: The third novel I asked you to look at was the novel, *Doc and Fluff* by Pat Califia. Can you tell his lordship what your assessment of that novel was?

A: This I found a much more difficult book to deal with. It is a dystopia futuristic book about the world being taken over by violent bikers and of women trying to protect themselves against these violent bikers by setting up rather dubious camps to protect themselves. There's a great deal of violence, there's a great deal of degradation, and it seems to me finally you have to look at this book, and this is a book where the whole notion of purpose must be concentrated on.

I think it is a moral book. I think if we do not come to terms with power, if we do not come to terms with hatred, if we do not come to terms with our murderous blundering, we will in fact end up slaughtering each other, and this is not a book that is prophetic in any way that should baffle us. All around us we see this going on in the world as it is. I think the purpose that Pat Califia has in writing the book is to make this very moral point, and if I talk about plot as moral, this is a very vengeful book. We really do get the bad guy, he really does get murdered in a quite disgusting way, and nobody could be unclear that the worst of these people has been destroyed and has paid the debt. Whether or not this is a resolution that satisfies some of us who have other solutions than vengeance, certainly vengeance is a morality that we all understand and a morality that has functioned from the time of the Greeks through Shakespeare.

I don't think there's any question that this book has serious intent in its moral vision of the world.

Q: Is that a legitimate literary or artistic purpose?

A: Yes.

Q: You mentioned earlier about the importance of knowing one's culture and literary history. Do those comments apply to the context of *Doc and Fluff*?

A: Yes. And for me, *The Story of O*, and a number of books that go back to the masochistic, sadistic explorations of sexual need and desire, the connection between pain and pleasure, Eros and Thanatos. These are the tensions that we have in our psyches from classical times to now. We have writers who are called to do this work, and some of them have great literary talent as well. In my opinion, Pat Califia is not a fine stylist, she's very crude. She can be sentimental, she can be over-simplistic. But she is asking all the right questions. She is asking about the nature of power, she is asking about the nature of bondage, she is asking us about the darkest things in ourselves. And if we don't agree with some of her answers, we have to admit that the questions are the right ones.

Q: Now, Ms. Rule, you mentioned that you were the author of two books. One is entitled *The Young in One Another's Arms*. I'd ask the registrar to show you that book. You can identify that as your book, I take it?

A: Yes, it is. Through and through all the way.

Q: Now, I understand that book was detained by Canada Customs in approximately 1990 and subsequently released?

A: Yes.

Q: And as well I'm going to show you a book which is called *Contract with the World* by Jane Rule. I take it that's your book as well.

A: Yes.

Q: With respect to *Contract with the World*, Ms. Rule, were you aware that the book was detained by Canada Customs and subsequently released in April or May of this year, or in 1993?

A: Not until yesterday.

Q: As a writer in Canada, and particularly one whose books have been detained—not prohibited, but certainly detained—by Canada Customs, what are your concerns and what's the implication for you of having Canada Customs detain your work on the grounds that it may be obscene?

A: Some cynics have said, "Isn't it nice to get all that attention." But in fact it's the kind of attention that would, if it attracted readers, find readers who would be very disappointed in the books, since they aren't pornographic. It is a kind of attention that would very possibly cut me off from the general audience for whom I write. It is the kind of statement or implication that does not simply last for that week or that month, but labels me for the rest of my professional life as someone who is probably a pornographer because, you know, if they held the books, there must be something in them that they don't like.

Now there are quite a number of people in Canada who do know that *The Young in One Another's Arms* won the Canadian Author's Association Award for the best novel of 1978. There are a great many more people in Canada who know that *The Young in One Another's Arms* was detained by Customs. And that is what I have to carry. I have to carry a reputation created by this charge from which I have no way of defending myself. Every time this issue comes up, whether I were testifying in this trial or not, my name would come up over and over again as that woman whose books are seized at the border, and I have no defence against it. And I bitterly resent the attempt to marginalize, trivialize and even criminalize what I have to say because I happen to be a lesbian, I happen to be a novelist, I happen to have bookstores and publishers who are dedicated to producing my work. The assumption that there must be something pornographic [in my writing] because of my sexual orientation is a shocking way to deal with my community.

Of course we have writers who are writing erotica, and so we should. I celebrate that. But we are not a community churning out sex tracts. We are a community speaking with our passion and our humanity in a world that is so homophobic that it sees us as nothing but sexual creatures instead of good Canadian citizens, fine artists, and brave people trying to make Canada a better place for everybody to speak freely and honestly about who they are.

Gary Kinsman

"'These Things May Lead to the Tragedy of Our Species': The Emergence of Homosexuality, Lesbianism, and Heterosexuality in Canada,"
The Regulation of Desire: Homo and Hetero Sexualities (1996)

FOUNDATIONS OF CANADIAN STATE FORMATION

From the mid-1800s to the early twentieth century, Canada was becoming increasingly industrialized and urbanized, with its own State and ruling relations. Some of these changes were pre-figured in developments concerning the Upper Canadian school system. Bruce Curtis points out that educational reforms in the late 1830s and 1840s were made with a view to the construction of political subjects and a "proper" political socialization in the wake of the 1837–1838 popular democratic rebellions. The school system played an ever more important role as it was extended to more and more young people in making "citizens" and a Canadian "public."[1] Central to the concerns of the school promoters, says Alison Prentice, were questions of gender, sex, and the body: "How to deal with the growing gap between childhood and manhood was greatly complicated, if not entirely governed, by the whole question of sex."[2]

A more specific concern with relations of sex and gender emerged in the context of political "socialization" and construction of "character" through various practices of moral regulation and governance.[3] In the first half of the nineteenth century in both Upper and Lower Canada, the conditions for industrial development were being laid with the formation of internal markets and the intentional creation of an urban working class. By the 1840s, access to the land was restricted, forcing many farm families onto smaller plots and new immigrants into wage-labour.[4]

A number of new concerns were generated through these social changes: the decline of the older Family Compact or Chateau Clique-type colonial elites; the emergence of a clearly defined capitalist class and middle class; increasing urbanization (although Canada would only become more than fifty percent urban in 1926[5]); and the formation of an urban working class. Previous paternalist forms of social authority were gradually replaced by more centralized State and ruling relations. The old colonial elite gave way to a new capitalist class that developed an alliance with male middle-class professionals managing and regulating society. Canadian State formation facilitated the formation of these professional groups. The Canadian Medical Association was founded in 1867, the same year that Confederation took place.[6] This was all part of a shift from community regulation to "national" and increasingly centralized forms of bureaucratic and professional organization.

Confederation came about through the conjunction of British and developing Anglo-Canadian bourgeois interests to block integration with the U.S. giant to the south. There emerged a particular Canadian system in which there was a division of jurisdiction and tasks between the central federal State and the provinces. Canadian State-and nation-building strategies in the late nineteenth and early twentieth centuries combined railway expansion in the West—and the development of a wheat commodity on which it could depend for freight—with land settlement through extensive white immigration.[7] In Canada, perhaps more integrally than elsewhere, the development of capitalist relations and State formation went hand-in-hand.[8] In the late nineteenth century, "frontiers" were being settled (after the indigenous people had been expropriated), new agricultural communities were opening up along the railways, towns were emerging, immigration was increasing, and an East-West transportation and communications system was dramatically altering the landscape, the social fabric, and the lives of Canadians.

NEW FORMS OF SOCIAL REGULATION

The new elite and their ruling agencies, along with middle-class moral reformers, searched for ways to regulate and administer the social organism in the new urban setting.[9] Older means of moral and social regulation were no longer working. "Traditional" social boundaries were rapidly eclipsed with the emergence of new social spaces and sites and the development of class relations. A fundamental feature of this process was the reorganization of sex and gender relations:

> The market economy, the capitalization and mechanization of production, the partition of home and workplace, of producer and consumer, were transforming life in farm and city, separating and increasingly differentiating the material and social circumstances of men and women.[10]

The middle class increasingly became interested in the life of the "lower orders." As early as 1816 (and probably earlier), in Upper Canada, concern had been generated over the living arrangements of mechanics in Kingston. Bryan Palmer reports that "it was suggested that the establishment of a church and individual homes for workmen" would solve this problem.[11] Craftsmen were encouraged to marry local women as a way of promoting social stability.[12]

By the late nineteenth century, urban poverty came to be defined by State agencies and middle-class moral reformers as a perplexing problem. The poor were now to be classified and administered as the professionals sought to comprehend and contain them. The "poor," as a social category, were a creation of these early philanthropic and welfare agencies.[13] Middle-class women played an important role in organizing class relations through their volunteer welfare work, in the process classifying the surplus labour pool in the cities and further defining the boundary between the middle class and the "lower orders." In Toronto, "increasingly the 'poor' lived apart from and unconnected to 'respectable' society in a way unprecedented in the city's history."[14] The poor were considered either reformable or beyond redemption—as worthy or unworthily—that would later become integral features of the policies of the Welfare State.

By the 1890s, social order seemed to be in crisis as the "underside of industrial capitalism"—poverty, unregulated homeless children and young people, prostitution, non-Anglo-Saxon and non-Christian immigration, and crime— was the subject of numerous reports.[15] The legal term "juvenile delinquent" was used to classify the "waifs and strays" appearing on city streets. The increasing visibility of ill-clad, undisciplined and unschooled working-class youth symbolized for middle-class reformers a breakdown of the family contract and a threat to moral order itself.[16] This street culture was seen as a breeding ground for immorality, vice, and crime. Control of the streets meant control of the city as "public" social space emerged. Emerging social agencies policed the "surplus" population, intervening directly in working-class social life. Young who did not belong to a "proper" family were considered a social problem. Unsupervised youths were shepherded into schools or reformatories. The school system became a crucial agent of discipline and "socialization."[17]

These agencies began to fear that the "foreign" culture of the working class and poor would "pollute" and "corrupt" society as class cleavages deepened and as working-class struggles emerged. Some of these concerns were focused on the morality of working-class women.[18] Female workers were seen as suffering from both poverty and lack of morals. This anxiety informed the work of the 1886 Royal Commission on the Relations of Labour and Capital:

> The commissioners searched diligently for immorality, assuming it to be a necessary consequence of the mingling of the sexes in the factories.... Their questions indicated an overwhelming concern about whether overhearing "immoral" language in the factories would cause them to become immoral.[19]

In different ways, both pro-capitalist members of the Commission and the worker representatives constructed women workers as raising troubling "moral" questions. While working-class representatives (largely male) defended the virtue of women working outside the home, they also constructed them as at risk for moral dangers. Male workers testified that women working in large mills would be exposed to "immoral words which could lead them to become immoral." The Commissioners agreed: "... morally corruptible women [have] to be protected from the ill effects of words."[20] Female workers were considered both physically and morally weak. Dr. T.A. Morre, Secretary of the Temperance and Reform Department of the Methodist Church, carried out an investigation of women's wages. He was far more interested, however, in maintaining the "innocence" and "purity" of working women than in their low wages.[21] Alice Klein and Wayne Roberts explain: "Their often compulsive concern for the working women's purity was rooted in profound anxiety about the changing roles and endangered status of women."[22]

State agencies, religious leaders, and many male workers all played a role in creating the image of the immoral woman who worked outside the home. This provided justification for "protective" legislation—keeping women from competing with males in certain job categories, usually in the skilled and better-paid areas.

> Protective legislation placed the parameters of reform well within their traditional notions of womanliness and femininity. Through factory inspection, the state acted as watchdog ... over the morality and cleanliness of the environment of women workers.[23]

Within the working class, patriarchal family relations were organized by class pressures and the pressures of industrial capitalism and State moralization. The Canadian Trades and Labour Congress had an avowed aim, early in this century, of eliminating women—particularly married women—from the wage-labour force.[24] Working-class social and political life came to be dominated by men. The emergence of the skilled trades was intrinsically tied to notions of social respectability, which, in turn, was equated with economic independence and the family wage paid to the male worker. Working-class men could thereby avoid the stigma associated with charity. Further, this sense of social respectability linked skilled workers with the middle class, establishing a cross-class alliance around certain social and moral "norms."[25] The division of the working class into "respectable" and "rough" was just one more distinction dividing workplace and society: skilled/non-skilled now joined masculine/feminine and adult/child.

Concerns were also generated about the morality of middle-class women. Women who rode bicycles clad in pant-like bloomers were likened to prostitutes.

> The essential costume for women cyclists, pant-like "bloomers," scandalized education trustees who charged that women teachers thus attired

resembled prostitutes. Unchaperoned riders were "exposed at the road houses to the most dangerous temptations," warned evangelist Methodists. Fantasies of blazing saddles flashed before the editor of the *Dominion Medical Monthly*, who condemned [bicycle riding] as the latest outlet of carnal passion. "Bicycle riding produces in the female a distinct orgasm," he wrote. Already, he continued, "Toronto's scorching thoroughfares make the streets of Sodom and Gomorrah appear as pure as Salvation Army shelters."[26]

There was also official concern about "race suicide" as the birth rate among Anglo-Saxons in Ontario dramatically declined; it was feared that Anglo-Saxon stock was being submerged by "inferior" races through immigration and a higher birth rate among Irish-Canadian and French-Canadian Catholics. During much of this time, Catholics were almost seen as a separate race by many Protestants.[27] English Protestant social character was considered necessary to the ruling class. Yet, more middle-class Anglo-Saxon women were staying single.[28] There was a particularly low marriage and birth rate among college-educated women. Furthermore, Canada had a high infant and maternal mortality rate, and this was seen as indicative of "race degeneration."[29] Immigrants from China, Japan, and southern Europe were considered a particular threat to the "physical and mental superiority of the native white Anglo-Saxon-Canadian."[30]

In the West, alcohol and opium were associated with immigrants while "proper" religion, morality and good character were associated with Anglos. Native and mixed-women and their families found themselves outside the "newly forming respectability."[31] Opium use was prohibited except for medicinal purposes. The image of white women being "seduced" by Chinese men helped to instigate riots against the Chinese.[32] The Criminal Code sex legislation was used to discriminate against Asians. Black males were considered by official white society to be long on sex drive and short on mental ability.[33] All this demonstrates connections between sexuality, sexism, racism, and Canada's roots as a class, gender, and race-divided society.

Thus were fuelled the campaigns for the regulation of immigration and for the "Canadianization" of immigrants. People were denied entry if they were of "bad character" or if they were physical or moral "degenerates." The churches and the Women's Christian Temperance Union tried to teach immigrants to be good Christians, and to assimilate them to middle-class Anglo-Protestant respectability. This was all part of broader attempts to establish social rule over a stable, efficient, disciplined work force made up increasingly of non-English immigrants. A key aspect of this project of moral regulation reformation was to create a particular kind of Canadian "citizen."[34] Campaigns against alcohol and opium consumption were linked to campaigns against the "secret vice," the "social evil" and promiscuity.[35]

The emergence of eugenics, the study of improving the "quality" of the "race" through selective breeding, led to proposals for the segregation and sterilization of "inferior" immigrants so that "Canada would forever remain white, Anglo-Saxon and Protestant."[36] In 1928, the Alberta government enacted Canada's first legislation for the sterilization of the "mental defective," which lasted until 1972. Under the terms of this Act thousands were sterilized. Similar legislation in British Columbia was also repealed in 1972.[37]

DEFENDING MARRIAGE AND FAMILY

There were campaigns to defend and shore up patriarchal family and gender organization. Initiatives were launched against birth control and to get women out of the paid work force and into the home and institutionalized motherhood. The feminist and suffrage movements were blamed for the decreasing birth rate among middle-class women, the growing divorce rate, the growing numbers of middle-class women who were not marrying, women's economic independence, and for involving women—horror of horrors—in the "public" world of production. These campaigns, in a number of ways, were a response to feminism—an attempt to shore up the institutions of marriage and motherhood. In 1908 Rev. C. Sharp told his Toronto congregation:

> God abhors the spirit so prevalent nowadays which condemns motherhood. How it must grieve Him when He sees what we call race suicide; when He sees the problems of married life approached lightly and wantonly; based on nothing higher and nobler than mere luxury, and gratification of passion.[38]

Concerns over motherhood had been developing throughout the late nineteenth century.[39] By the early twentieth century, the surveillance of motherhood had led to the generation of the concept of the "inadequate mother"— usually immigrant or working-class women without enough time to spend with their kids according to middle-class standards. The anxiety over race suicide and infant mortality was exacerbated by losses in World War I. The war heightened the emphasis on patriotism and maternity and the interdependence of cradle and sword. These national and "racial" concerns led to the introduction of domestic-science training for girls.[40] By the "early twentieth century, motherhood, now a burden of State, a sacred office and a scientific practice could be none other than a full-time occupation."[41] And as Beth Light and Joy Parr also point out:

> The ideological sanctity of motherhood as the fount of and essence of female nature grew stronger as the need to bear many children decreased and the choice to raise large families became less common.[42]

These social trends led to concerns over sexual morality, particularly sex out-side marriage. There had already been considerable middle-class and "respectable" working-class concern over family instability in the years before World War I due to the social strains of industrialization and urbanization. Divorce had been difficult to obtain: in Ontario and Quebec, there was no provincial divorce law, which meant divorce had to be granted through a pri-vate-member's bill passed by federal Parliament—a process which took a year and cost at least $1,000, and was thus not available to the working class.[43] The divorce rate, however, seemed to be doubling every decade. Desertion, mean-while, "the poor man's divorce," was defined by moral reformers as a serious problem.[44]

> Marriage and the family were perceived to be weakening, undermined by general causes such as urbanization, but also by increasing immorality as demonstrated by such "sins of the flesh" as prostitution, adultery and cohabitation outside marriage and by a diminishing sense of responsibility on the part of individuals as shown by non-support, desertion and divorce.[45]

Marriage, home, and the family were considered by ruling social agencies as the essence of a "healthy" community. In the words of Ontario Conservative Member of Parliament E.A. Lancaster, if divorces were granted freely, "the whole social fabric of the country would go to pieces." Moral reformers, the social-purity movement, and politicians pushed the State to play a stronger role in defending marriage and discourage sex outside its confines. Prostitu-tion, the "social evil," symbolized all forms of sexual immorality and perver-sion, and all women's sexual activity outside marriage was thus identified.[46]

> Marriage breakdown operated as a similar, negative symbol. Marriage rep-resented a code of moral and sexual behaviour which was felt to have long ordered society: marriage breakdown, on the other hand, symbolized a wide variety of conduct that was considered immoral, anti-social and unac-ceptable.[47]

The link between marriage breakdown and sexual conduct was only rein-forced by adultery being the main grounds for divorce. Marriage was the only State-sanctioned terrain for sex. Laws were passed to "protect" marriage, to inhibit the social process of breakdown. With the formulation of the Crimi-nal Code in 1892, it became clear that Parliament, and not the courts, would be the main agent of legal change.

The Society for the Protection of Women and Children, under the leader-ship of D.A. Watt, made use of social-purity literature from England and the United States. Young girls and women must be protected from seduction, they said, and the brothels and the "white slave trade" must be crushed. Use of the term "white slave trade" had racial connotations informed by social purity's symbolic emphasis on whiteness, cleanliness and purity.[48] They attempted to make an analogy between the black slave trade and white female prostitution. Social-purity agitation ignored the plight of Native women and women of colour and focused on an image of the virginal white girl being led astray by moral perverts.[49]

Watt wrote lengthy tracts on "morals legislation" between 1889 and 1892.[50] As a result, the 1892 Criminal Code included a comprehensive system of offences designed to "protect" young women and girls.[51] The Criminal, Code also included "gross indecency," referring to all sexual acts between men not already covered under "buggery." These sex offences were codified as part of an attempt to establish the patriarchal family as an unshakeable institution.

Within the House of Commons social purity activists like Watt often supported the campaigns of Norfolk County MP, John Charlton, for morals legislation to censor "obscene" literature, to criminalize sexual acts outside marriage and to oppose abortion and birth control. For Charlton there was a close relationship "between a strong morality and a strong state."[52]

Charlton became especially associated with new legislation against "seduction," which he argued was necessary to protect women, especially young women, from moral danger. He first introduced such legislation in 1882, and by 1886 a version of it became law. This criminalized "seduction" as opposed to coercive or forcible sexual attack. In these cases, consent was not an issue since the law proclaimed that in certain situations consent to sexual relations could not exist. The law applied only to younger women who were "of previously chaste character" and were between the ages of fourteen and sixteen, or were under twenty-one when sex was tied to a promise of marriage, or were twenty-one and their employer or guardian had "seduced" them.[53] Throughout the 1880s and 1890s, Charlton attempted to raise the age limits for the protection of women from "seduction." In her study of the use of these laws in the late nineteenth and early twentieth centuries in Ontario, Dubinsky found that criminal "seduction" laws were often used by parents to regulate consensual different-gender relationships.[54]

Social-purity activists continued their campaigns in the succeeding decades in the belief that "the state had a clear right and duty to intrude into the bedrooms of the nation."[55] Their work, however, was only one aspect of a broader effort to coerce working-class men into accepting their responsibilities as "proper" husbands and breadwinners and to force women to be "proper" wives and mothers. The imposition of these middle-class standards onto the working class was, in turn, only one part of the establishment of the family wage system and patriarchal family relations within the working class.[56] One way in which this was established was through an intensification of the regulation of non-matrimonial different-gender sex and same-gender sex.

Social-purity arguments influenced both "public" opinion and State policy. This public discussion, meanwhile, also produced a form of secular and popular consciousness of sexuality and sex "education."

SOCIAL PURITY

The Canadian social-purity movement was a main force behind the increasing regulation of sexuality, including same-gender sexualities. In social-purity discourse, the "social evil," and sex itself, were a metaphor for concerns about sexual violence, gender, and racial and class morality.[57] The social evil became a symbol for national and social degeneration. In England, the social-purity movement emerged partly out of feminist protests against the sexual double standard and the "victimization" of female prostitutes. However, given that feminists did not control the institutions and discourses which were coming to define and regulate erotic life, and given the prevailing notions of male sexual lust and female lack of sexual passion, the movement took a morally conservative direction, led by organizations which not only tried to control male lust and violence, but also tried to stigmatize and criminalize such female sex-linked activities as prostitution. The movement which had initially rejected aspects of women's subordination and attempted to challenge male sexual violence, now moved in a repressive and anti-feminist direction, arguing for much of the sexual legislation that continued to shape the policing of sexuality until recently: higher age-of-consent-laws for engaging in sexual activities, the criminalization of prostitutes, and "gross indecency."[58] Jeffrey Weeks describes the movement's views on homosexuality:

> In their minds, homosexuality was barely differentiated from prostitution. For the morality crusaders ... both were part of the continuum of undifferentiated lust, products of man's selfishness. Let one crack appear in the order and floods of lustfulness would sweep society away. In their minds the syndromes of schoolboy masturbation, public school "immorality" (meaning homosexuality) and prostitution were closely intertwined.[59]

The weakness of a progressive radical or socialist feminism in the Canadian suffrage movements rendered them less resistant to the social-purity trend. Feminism based on equal rights for women was often subordinated to a maternal feminism that advocated women's rights as a way of protecting and extending the institution of motherhood in the home and in society.[60] Canadian women, unlike their U.S. sisters, did not have the same radicalizing experiences of the antislavery movement, and only a "small minority suggested that women be freed from familial ties to allow them to pursue careers of their choice."[61] Canadian feminists like Flora MacDonald Denison, Agnes Deans Cameron, and Carrie Derick were exceptions to this trend.[62] Indeed, several movement and suffrage leaders belonged to social-purity groups.[63] At that time, mainstream feminism in Canada had a white, largely Christian character, and was concerned about non-white and non-Christian immigrants.

> In order to understand the suffragists' social attitudes we have to understand the values of the group with which they identified. As Anglo-Saxon, Protestant, middle-class, such women shared the anxieties and expectations of this group. They saw women's problems through glasses tinted with values shaped by this allegiance.[64]

At the same time, African-Canadian women were beginning to organize, but these were excluded and marginalized from the mainstream of Canadian feminism.[65]

The social-purity movement was led for a number of years by Reverend J.G. Shearer, the secretary of the Toronto-based Social and Moral Reform Council of Canada—"a federation of the social and reform departments of the leading churches and temperance and reform organizations of Canada" and the strongest force in the Dominion for the advancement of social purity. The Social and Moral Reform Council was affiliated with social-purity organizations in the U.S. and England. *The Light*—the official organ of the International American Purity Federation—reached a reported 75,000 in the U.S., Canada, Mexico, and elsewhere.[66] The Canadian Purity Education Association, staffed by medical doctors, existed in Toronto from 1906–1915.[67] The pre-mentioned Society for the Protection of Women and Girls, led by D.A. Watt, played a crucial role in law reform and was an important part of this movement.

The purity movement—moral reformers, clergymen, doctors, and members of the National Council of Women—focused their campaigns on the "social evil," usually referring to female prostitution but often referring to sexual immorality in general—masturbation, possibly same-gender sex, sex outside marriage, as well as male sexual violence against women. Their definitions could include "self-abuse," or masturbation, and same-gender sex with "perverse" practices. For example, *Jack Canuck*, the Canadian equivalent of the *Police Gazette* in its sensationalizing of the underworld, once warned in an article of the white slave trade "of boys being led astray by moral perverts."[68] It is not clear who the "moral perverts" are here, but there is a suggested linkage between female prostitution and boys engaging in masturbation or same-gender sex. In 1912 the social purity-inspired Vigilance Committee listed in a pamphlet as one of its objectives to support "efforts to aid in preventing boys being led astray by moral perverts."[69] Here the mobilization of this expression against male same-gender sex was part of a broader social purity campaign against prostitution, immoral plays, and indecent pictures.

Many women engaged in casual forms of prostitution as a means of survival.[70] The social purity campaigns, in alliance with business interests and the police, took advantage of middle-class fears about the character of "public" space to stigmatize and criminalize prostitutes. Yet at the same time they created an image of the prostitute as a "victim" in the white slave trade.

> Belief in the essential vulnerability of women precluded recognition of the fact that a woman may not have been duped at all, but may have acted on her own evaluation of her position and alternatives.[71]

The social purity perspective ignored women's financial reasons for involvement in the trade, simply calling for State "protection" rather than looking at women's social, economic, and sexual situations. They also ignored many young working class women's desires to actively explore and experience the pleasures of city life.[72]

Social purity helped establish a number of commissions to investigate and survey the "social evil." In 1913 a Social Survey Commission was set up in Toronto at the request of the Toronto Local Council of Women.[73] The Commission was made up of members of the Young Men's Christian Association, the Toronto Local Council of Women, the Roman Catholic Archbishop, the Salvation Army, the city's medical health officer, other religious figures, and academics. Their report, released in 1915, relied on various other vice commission reports, including the report of the Chicago Vice Commission. While noting that they found little evidence of the white slave trade in Canada, they criticized police indifference to prostitution and recommended the "total suppression" of prostitution. They also generated a new concept of the "occasional prostitute," referring to women who went out on dates with men to parks and ice cream parlours and may have had sex with their male companions.[74] Among the causes of the "social disease," they listed poverty, overcrowding, boarders—"which necessarily lead towards immorality"—and the great tide of immigration which brought with it "foreigners" with different standards of sexual morality and the growth of "feeblemindedness." There were 5,000 unmarried men in Toronto with no living quarters except a bedroom, said the report.

At the same time, their major focus was on young, white, unregulated working women who were tempted by the amusements of the city to engage in occasional prostitution. Poverty itself was not seen to be the cause of this since some working women survived on low wages and managed to protect "their virtue," but was seen instead as a moral failing. The report associated feeblemindedness with "sexual immorality" and pronounced that prostitution was caused by "abnormal sensual propensities and lack of moral perception." "Feebleminded" women (often including unwed mothers) were linked with low morals. The report also linked the increase in infant mortality and sexual diseases like syphilis with prostitution and "promiscuous sex relations." A sexual appetite was natural in men, it said, but in women "... the desire for motherhood [was] the primary factor ... The abnormal development of sex desire when it does occur, is, however, more pronounced in women than in men."[75] The report recommended social purity education to deal with the "perversion of natural instincts by bad social environment" and also suggested raising the age of consent for sexual acts to sixteen.

While "social evil" generally meant female prostitution, there were also references to sexual immorality and perversion. "Perversion" in social purity discourse usually referred to non-reproductive sex but was sometimes used in a broader sense. In the Chicago Vice Commission report, a section entitled "Sexual Perversion" noted an increase in same gender sex and referred to "colonies of these men who are sex perverts," but who did not often come into contact with the police or physicians.[76] These men adopted the "carriage, mannerisms and speech of women," were "often people of a good deal of talent," and had a "vocabulary and signs of recognition of their own." The report also referred to "female impersonators" and men who dressed as women and solicited other men for "perverse practices." It recommended the "practical ideal of a straight and pure sexual life both before and after marriage" and tougher legislation. Another section of the Chicago report discussed "pervert methods" in the higher-priced prostitution houses, apparently referring to oral sex. The Toronto study included no such exploration of pervert practices.

Social purity rhetoric combined notions of "feeblemindedness," moral degeneration, and race degeneration, from the language of Social Darwinism, with the Christian terms of "immorality," "vice" and "evil."[77] The social purists advocated the prohibition of all non-matrimonial and non-reproductive sex, but they also proposed and indeed instituted a particular form of sex "education."[78] J.S. Shearer called for educating boys and girls

> in the purpose and problems and perils of sex, including information as to the awful penalty nature imposes in the forms of social diseases, such as syphilis and gonorrhoea, well designated the Black Plague upon those who violate her laws of sex.[79]

SEXUAL ADVICE: SEX EDUCATION FOR PURITY

During the late nineteenth and early twentieth centuries, social purity advice literature was widely available, and lectures were heard by thousands. In the early 1890s Reverend W.J. Hunter was reportedly lecturing to as many as 1,500 men a night at St. James Methodist Church in Montréal. He addressed such topics as prostitution, masturbation—the "solitary vice"—and puberty. He defended sexual purity as necessary to the vigour of the race, since "loss of semen is the loss of blood."[80]

According to the Methodist Church, the best selling sex advice literature in Canada between 1900 and 1915 were the eight volumes of the *Self and Sex* series.[81] These books were based on the "spermatic economy" theory of a limited energy model of sex and development. "Self-abuse" was equated with waste and with moral and physical degeneration. Two Canadian doctors had in their respective 1865 and 1877 reports supported this "self abuse" scare. *The Dominion Medical Monthly* and the *Ontario Medical Journal* had both concluded that in single men, masturbation led to insanity. The *Self and Sex* series was favourably reviewed in the *Canadian Journal of Medicine and Surgery*, and leading Canadian doctors supported this sexual discourse. Dr. Maurice Bucke, who we will meet again in another context, not only linked masturbation with insanity, but operated on the "insane" to correct the "problem."[82]

There also began to develop a sense that something was wrong with close, same gender intimacies. This affected friendships and emotional support networks among both men and women. "Proper" non-erotic friendships were promoted, in contrast to the horrors of same gender perversion. In *What a Young Woman Ought to Know*, part of the *Self and Sex* series, Dr. Wood Allen warned:

I believe in reserve even in girl friendships. Girls are apt at certain periods in their lives to be rather gushing creatures. They form the most sentimental attachments for each other. They go about with their arms around each other, they loll against each other, and sit with clasped hands by the hour. They fondle and kiss until beholders are fairly nauseated, and in a few weeks, perhaps they do not speak as they pass each other, and their caresses are lavished on others. They are a weakening of moral fibre, a waste of mawkish sentimentality. They may be even worse. Such friendship may degenerate even into a species of self-abuse that is most deplorable.

When girls are so sentimentally fond of each other that they are like silly lovers when together, and weep over each other's absence in uncontrollable agony, the conditions are serious enough for the consultation of a physician. It is an abnormal state of affairs, and if probed thoroughly might be found to be a sort of perversion, a sex mania, needing immediate and perhaps severe measures.

I wish the friendships of girls were less sentimental, more manly. Two young men who are friends do not lop on each other, and kiss and gush. They trust each other, they talk freely together, they would stand by each other in any trouble or emergency, but their expressions of endearment are not more than the cordial handgrasp and the unsentimental appellation, "Dear old chap."

I admire these friendships in young men. They seem to mean so much, and yet to exact so little.[83]

Josephine E. Young, M.D., warned that the affection of a girl for an older woman is abnormal and unwholesome and should be positively dealt with as a "manifestation of sex perversion."[84] Social purity was now applying the notion of perversion more specifically to same-gender erotic activities, although here it seemed tied to age distinctions as well.

The Women's Christian Temperance Union (WCTU) and evangelical churches hired purity reformers such as Beatrice Brigden, William Lund Clark, and Arthur W. Beall to tour the schools warning young people against self-abuse and promiscuity and educating them for a "pure" life and character. It was felt that a proper Christian upbringing required proper sex education, not an ignorance of sex. Ignorance, it was thought, left young people without the fortitude to resist temptation. Brigden and Clark were hired by the Canadian Methodist Church.[85] Brigden spoke to girls and women from 1913 to 1920. After being hired in 1913, she was sent to the home of American purity leader B.S. Steadwell for three weeks of intensive training and reading on sex. She specialized in "The Girl and Her Problems" and argued for pure living and citizenship.[86] Brigden was also influenced by currents within feminism and later became involved in supporting working-class activism.[87]

Clark, as we have seen, had already been busy giving lectures to boys and it was apparently he who urged Brigden to "take on a similar task among girls, to lecture and counsel on sex hygiene and social problems."[88] He was much more influenced by masculinist and patriarchal writings on sex than Brigden.[89] A Methodist report commended Clark for having "given careful and long study to the life problems of boys and young men."[90] He urged boys to avoid degrading influences, wrong thoughts and wrong pictures, and the company of "immorally clothed young women." He recommended that they drink neither tea nor coffee and refrain from dancing, and that they seek improved ventilation and take frequent baths.[91] Through these means they could produce a strong character and a pure self. Clark toured Canada and the United States with this message.

Beall lectured between 1905 and 1911 to a reported 13,463 schoolboys on behalf of the Ontario WCTU.[92] Lesson Nine of Mr. Beall's classes in sex education instructed the boys to repeat after him, "The more you use the penis muscle the weaker it becomes; but the less you use the penis muscle the stronger it becomes."[93] This would likely have been the boys' first introduction to this naming of their genitals and would surely have led to erotic experimentation and play as well as the intended self-repression. Beall stressed the national importance of sex hygiene and its importance in producing the "character" needed for Canada. Beall was hired by the Ontario Department of Education in 1911 and he worked there until the 1930s.[94] Rather than social purity opposing sex education, it actively promoted its own form of sex education and, at least in Ontario, had some success in introducing it into the schools.

VENEREAL DISEASE: "POLLUTING THE RACE"

In the years preceding World War I, the social purity movement made much of the reported increase in venereal disease. VD was seen as a challenge to the health of the Anglo Saxon "race."[95] As Lucy Bland explains when discussing the mood in England, VD stood as a metaphor,

> condensing and "carrying" many of the fears of the period—the concern with the falling birth rate ... concern with national efficiency and physical deterioration of troops and civilians.[96]

By 1912 the Canadian Methodist Church was demanding that all cases of VD be reported to medical health officials. Its association with "feeblemindedness" was made perfectly clear with the naming, in 1918, of the Ontario Government's Royal Commission on Venereal Disease and Feeblemindedness.[97] World War I and a push by public health agitation around venereal disease provided the basis for the establishment of a Canadian Department of Health in 1919. State regulation now took the form of "public health" legislation and management of sexual disease, prostitution, sexual "promiscuity," and "deviance."[98] Laws were directed against prostitutes and "loose women."

In Canada, in the late nineteenth and early twentieth centuries, there were a whole series of measures, often social purity inspired, to try to wipe out the "social evil." In 1918 the Canadian government moved to further regulate prostitutes. It stipulated that "no woman who is suffering from Venereal Disease in a communicable form shall have sexual intercourse with any member of His Majesty's forces or solicit or invite any member of the said forces to have sexual intercourse with her."[99] Notice that in this discourse there was no responsibility placed on the men involved. Government educational pamphlets during these years included such statements as—"Practically all prostitutes and loose women are diseased," and "Prostitution cannot be made safe."[100] Prostitutes and "loose" women were constructed as the "problem" in the spread of VD. Clearly embedded in this official and professional discourse were sexist or patriarchal double standards. The regulatory focus was on the women and not the men, as women's "sexual deviance" came increasingly to be defined as "promiscuity" and prostitution. The precedent was set for more State intervention into the realm of bodies, desires, and pleasures.

THE EMERGENCE OF SEX PSYCHOLOGY

It is within this social context that the psychiatric and medical professions began to import the sex-scientific knowledge being developed in Europe and the U.S. As Xavier Mayne put it, "The topic of simisexuality is taboo in the United States and in Canada except through observation by and for medical

428 Sex and Law

students and physicians."[101] An article entitled "Perversion," for instance, by Ezra Hurlburt Stafford, M.D., First Assistant Physician at the Asylum for the Insane in Toronto, was published in 1898 and read before the Toronto Medical Society.[102] The article discusses the degree to which perversions are a disease and the degree to which they are a product of evolution, explaining that long suppressed characteristics may appear and take hold of isolated members of the species. "Many cases of sexual perversion," Stafford argues, "may be set down as a reversion or a miscarriage in the chain of evolution."

Stafford uses most of his article, however, to deal with two different types of perversion:

These cases of perversions form not a distortion of a natural instinct, but an excrescence apparently completely foreign, and not so often of the nature of a physical defect as of a mental aberration, and therefore a form of insanity.

These perversions referred to prostitution and sex between men (he never uses the word "homosexual"). He refers to the work of Krafft-Ebing, in naming and describing the sex perversions, but he also calls Krafft-Ebing's work the "bible of the bawdy house." Here Stafford exhibits an understanding of the potentially two-sided dynamic of sex-scientific theories. On the one hand, the perversions are named so that they can be identified and contained. On the other hand, the very naming of the perversions provides the opportunity for people to identify with them and to develop resistance to sexual rule. Stafford explains that there exist forms of perversion other than prostitution "which occupy a place of their own in the lives of nations—forms of perversions long familiar to readers of the late classical writers." After an examination of the writings of Ancient Greece and Rome, he tells us that "even in Corinth, a thoughtful man would surely have been forced to admit that these usages constituted a woeful and mischievous trifling with the laws of nature."

He associates this perversion with "periods of racial degeneration." He uses the work of Cesare Lombroso to justify his position that the sexual overuse or misuse of an organ leads to an imbalance of the nervous system and degeneration. Society exists in a rather artificial situation of highly structured relations between the sexes, Stafford contends, of intense religious sentiments and the repression of "natural" physiological inclinations, and this has led the race into "an abnormal condition" whereby perversions are acquired. "These things [prostitution and sex between men] may lead to the tragedy of our species." He links these perversions to an "insidious process of degeneration which is taking place in the inmost structure of modern civilization."

Stafford's analysis is rabidly anti-Catholic: he even suggests that the Roman Catholic Church itself led to abnormal lust, associating perversion with conversion to the Catholic faith—all this in the context of middle-class Anglo-

Saxon anxieties over increasing birth rates among Irish and French Canadian Catholics. While there was always a tendency in sex-scientific literature to blame "foreign" cultures for perversions, Stafford's analysis takes on a particular Anglo-Canadian character with its anti-Catholic fervour.

Stafford's work is rooted in the popularization among Canadian doctors of the works of Lombroso and Krafft-Ebing. The main themes of European sex-scientific debates are reproduced in his article, such as the debate over whether same gender sex practices are innate or acquired, whether congenital or representative of moral degeneracy.[103]

RESOURCES FOR QUEER CULTURES

The literature of forensic psychiatry regarding sex perversion and later sex psychology began to be taken up in professional circles in Canada as networks of men who engaged in sex with each other became more visible in the larger urban centres. Some of these networks grew out of earlier urban networks of men who had sex with men within the military and the interactions between younger men and boys and elite men. Sex-scientific classifications of "perversion" and "inversion" began to be used against these men.

Some of these networks were associated with cross-dressing. In Montréal it was reported in *La Presse* in 1886 that she-men (*hommes-femmes*), would gather in the evening behind the Court House. There they were reported to "hold their filthy revels" and to treat "passers-by to the spectacle of their vile pastimes." Police constables apparently entrapped some of the men but *La Presse* complained that light sentences allowed them "to slip quickly back to the pleasures of their kind." Here we get a sense of these gathering places, organized through the cultural practices of "gender inversion" and cross-dressing. There was also a certain awareness of these networks as a "social threat" generated through the media and police action.[104]

Steven Maynard reports on the 1894 arrest of Mary Cullen in Halifax, Nova Scotia:

> Mary, a tailoress, was arrested at her home when several of the men she had been dating discovered that—as the newspaper put it—"Mary was not all she pretended to be." When Mary, who was in fact Thomas Cullen, was asked why he dressed as a woman, he replied he could fool the "chappies" and "nearly every evening" he could "stroll down Hollis Street and be sure to make a pick up."[105]

These examples suggest the development of networks that had some similar characteristics to the "fairies" that George Chauncey describes in New York City from the 1890s into the early twentieth century. These working-class fairy cultures were defined by taking up certain aspects of "effeminacy" and sometimes cross-dressing.[106] Maynard suggests that, in Toronto, by 1912, some of the men were being referred to as "sissies" and "fairies."[107] This may have been one of the ways in which a distinct group of men who had sex with other men were referred.

In the nineteenth century, there were also many reports of passing or cross-dressing white women in Canada.[108] They cross-dressed to gain access to the economic privileges enjoyed by men, and perhaps also to establish intimate and erotic relationships with other women.[109] A woman who dressed in men's clothes was described in 1872 as follows: "... her demeanour was so masculine as to put in doubt her sex. Was she man or woman or hermaphrodite?"[110] Before the emergence of specific homosexual or lesbian categories, these women were seen as odd for challenging gender practices but were not necessarily considered sexually suspect. By the 1880s, there were already, in some professional circles, "two distinct types of womanhood."[111] On the one hand, there was the "timid, confiding, trusting woman" who "comes to realize that her mission in this world is a domestic one." On the other, there were "the self-confident, self-asserting, self-reliant, fearless, masculine women" for whom "domestic duties have but a secondary attraction." With the emergence of the "homosexual" and the "lesbian," same-gender passionate friendships became suspect. Cross-dressing now became associated with sexual inversion; the history of gender-crossing women formed one of the foundations for lesbian cultures.[112]

A number of men who were influential in the formation of homosexual "identities" visited Canada in the late nineteenth century. Oscar Wilde visited English Canada in the 1880s, prior to the homosexual scandals in which he was involved in England in the 1890s.[113] Newspaper coverage of Wilde's trip reflects an ambiguous and hostile response to a (pre homo) English dandy.[114] Walt Whitman visited Canada in the summer of 1880 and kept in close contact with Dr. Maurice Bucke, who he met earlier as superintendent of the Mental Hospital in London. Whitman influenced not only Dr. Bucke and Edward Carpenter (who himself visited Canada in 1884), but also Upper Canadian intellectuals such as the feminist activist Flora MacDonald Denison.[115]

Denison, one of the few Canadian suffragists to call herself a feminist, was profoundly influenced by Whitman, as well as by the American feminist Charlotte Perkins Gilman, Victoria Woodhul, August Bebel, Olive Schreiner, and Edward Carpenter.[116] Denison was involved in the Canadian Theosophical Society, whose early publications included many poems by Whitman. She held quite progressive views for her day on questions of divorce, prostitution, and sexuality, although she certainly mobilized racism against immigrants.[117] She believed that prostitution was fundamentally an economic rather than a moral issue. She was opposed to violent punishment and flogging. Denison's ideas about sexuality itself were influenced by her Whitmanite spiritualism. In her view "sex was not only necessary for both men and women, it was an exalted function."[118]

In 1910 Denison bought a cottage at Bon Echo in southern Ontario as a combination summer hostel and avant-garde spiritual community dedicated to Whitman. In 1916 a Walt Whitman Club was formed at Bon Echo. The club published a magazine, *The Sunset at Bon Echo*, from 1916 to 1920, a consistent theme of which was male friendship.[119]

> It seems likely that this group would have attracted gays and provided a supportive community as they tried to come to terms with coping with the hostile world outside.[120]

This development also suggests possible overlaps between early progressive feminist, socialist, sex-radical, lesbian and male homosexual networks, especially among the white intellectual middle class. On Denison's death, *The Canadian Theosophist* concluded that "... no one in the present generation of Canadians has done more for the 'institution of the dear love of Comrades' than Flora MacDonald Denison."[121] Her funeral service was sponsored by the Whitmanite Fellowship of Toronto.

The Greek "ideal" may also have played an important role in the making of homosexual identifications among middle- and upper-class and intellectual white men,[122] although the effect of classical literature on the identity formation of white middle-class homosexuals in Canada has yet to be explored. It was apparently feared by some that classical literature might inspire "self abuse." Reverend James Carmichael, writing in 1877, refers to Socrates:

> He faced the most disgusting and abhorrent lusts, thank god, almost unknown by name to western civilization, with a joking nod of recognition ... Fancy our handsome boys listening to the great Athenian. Our girls would be safe but for the sake of pure boy life we would raise and fling the teacher from our ruddy hearthstone.[123]

Elsa Gidlow's account of the formation of her lesbian identification in the years 1914–1919 in Montréal gives us a rare and precious glimpse into the formation of the lesbian and male homosexual worlds in the early twentieth century.[124] In those days, before the demarcation of a specific lesbian identity, male and female homosexual identity formation had shared features. Gidlow tells us of her early sense of being an "outsider" as she struggled to survive as an independent woman. By now, many young women were challenging convention by getting jobs and taking rooms in boardinghouses, which became possible as some women gained more economic independence. Gidlow heard another woman labelled a "mofredite" (slang for "hermaphrodite," a word that could then be used for people involved in same-gender sex). This gave Gidlow an introduction to the naming of another sexuality.[125] Through a writer's group she met a young homosexual man, Roswell George Mills, whom she describes as follows:

> He was beautiful. About nineteen, exquisitely made up, slightly perfumed, dressed in ordinary men's clothing but a little on the chi-chi side. And he swayed about, you know. We became friends almost instantly because we were both interested in poetry and the arts.[126]

Through Roswell, she was able to begin exploring and naming her sense of difference. He introduced her to the writings of Sappho and Wilde. Together they read Havelock Ellis, Edward Carpenter, and the works of Krafft-Ebing, Lombroso, and Freud.[127] She describes how the "trial and jailing of Oscar Wilde were not far in our past and very real."[128] Gidlow and Mills delved "into the mores of Ancient Greece" and the writings of "homosexuals" throughout history, which gave them "reasons for loving ourselves and each other."[129] Here we see a process through which Gidlow and Mills were able to name their difference through the sex-scientific category of homosexuality, and were able to transform it into an affirmation of their desires against social denial. The various influences in this identity making included the sex scientific literature itself, media portrayals of the Wilde trial, a clear homosexual cultural influence on Roswell, as well as a certain reading of the classical Greek tradition.

Mills was given a "Four-F—physically, mentally, emotionally and morally incompetent"—rating, and hence was not drafted into the armed forces during the war,[130] perhaps because of his "gender invert" characteristics. Such military labelling may have helped to create early homosexual networks, by cutting some homosexual men out of "normal" social interaction, as it did on a more extended scale during and after World War II.

These experiences of Gidlow and Mills offer valuable insights into the formation of white lesbian and homosexual identities among intellectuals and artists during the World War I era. The white, European-derived character of much of this construction of "homosexuality" (and perhaps "lesbianism") is important to stress. The reading they produced of sexuality in Ancient Greece, the sex-scientific literature they read, and the references to Oscar Wilde all referenced them to "traditions" within white, European "civilization." Carpenter was a limited (and only partial) exception. Men and women with different cultural, intellectual, and social experiences may not have been able to identify their experiences and desires with this image of homosexuality. For them other "traditions," literatures and experiences may have been drawn upon to define their experiences of sexual and gender differences.

MEN OF THE "OSCAR WILDE TYPE"

References to same gender sex began to appear in Canadian literature during these years. Toronto journalist C.S. Clark's *Of Toronto the Good*, published in 1897, makes a number of references to sex among "boys" (adolescent males it seems) and men.[131] Clark's major purpose in his book was to demonstrate that Toronto was not "the good" but rather was one immense house of ill-fame. He charged that "loose" women could be found everywhere. Clark was also concerned about the lives of unregulated, often homeless poor boys. This was part of a broader social construction of concern over street youth and urban space that was then being generated. Clark argues that the repression of male/female prostitution through bawdy house raids has led to cases like that of Oscar Wilde in England, and to the blackmailing of these types, many of whom, he says, are of "wealth and high standing."

> If saintly Canadians run away with the idea that there are no sinners of Oscar Wilde's type in Canada, my regard for the truth impels me to undeceive them. Consult some of the bellboys of the large hotels in Canada's leading cities ... and find out what they can tell from their own experiences. A youth of eighteen once informed me that he had blackmailed one of Canada's esteemed judiciary out of a modest sum of money by catching him in the act of indecently assaulting one of the bellboys connected with a hotel in that city. This is one case only, but they are countless. Some of Canada's leading citizens could be implicated just as Oscar Wilde was implicated, if some of these bellboys chose to make public what they knew. I know two different merchants in the city of Toronto who have a similar reputation ... Both these men are so well known in Toronto that there is scarcely a boy who does not know of their reputation. I have no doubt that, notwithstanding the positions they occupy, both would be punished to the full extent of the law, could the police catch them. But this fact serves to demonstrate how little is actually known to the police of what is taking place ... while these very men and their acts of indecency are the talk of boys all over the city. Where under heaven people ever learned such appalling things God only knows and humanity can only conjecture that the people in the places I mention appeal to the degraded tastes of their patrons simply because they are paid for it ... Houses of ill fame are blots on the morality of a country ... because everyone knows of them, and the fact of their being public is what constitutes the sin ... These other places [sites of same gender sex] are not usually known to the public, and consequently they thrive, and no effort is made to suppress them, as far as I am aware.[132]

The "Oscar Wilde type," given meaning by coverage of the Wilde trials, was of the wealthier classes and seems to pay for sex with bellboys and working-class street youths. The emergence of this "type" is an important part of the transition to a more defined homosexual category, but it also constructs this "type" with a particular class character. References to the Oscar Wilde type were common around the turn of the century in Canada.[133]

Clark's highly ideological account suggests the existence in Toronto of subterranean networks, involving elite and middle-class men and working-class boys and young men. Although less developed, they shared a number of features with emerging homosexual networks in England—the importance of male prostitution, for example, and the existence of sexual relations between middle-class men and working-class youths. While some of these youths took advantage of the social and legal prohibitions to blackmail the men, most never went to the police, which suggests that they participated for either pleasure or money, or both. This suggests that, within the constraints of the class and social relations in which these young men found themselves, they acted to try to get benefits from their erotic relations with this "type" of man. And even though Clark dismisses this possibility, reading against the grain we can see that many of these working-class young men and boys did get erotic pleasures from these encounters. What Clark does not tell us is whether these boys and young men also had sex among themselves.[134]

These activities were not very visible to the police, says Clark, and therefore could not be suppressed. He may be lamenting the lack of a major public scandal which would direct police activity against these networks; police surveillance of city streets and hotels was not yet very extensive, but it was growing, and Criminal Code classifications were beginning to direct the police against men who had sex with other males.

WORKING CLASS MEN AND QUEER SEX

Maynard's pioneering research, which has been critically examining court, police and reformatory records from 1880–1930 in Ontario—especially Toronto—is very useful here. He reports that his research has turned up clerks, barbers, shoemakers, porters, painters, carpenters, peddlers, machinists, plasterers, and numerous labourers who were charged with offences relating to sex between males.[135] The majority of the men charged were working class, both "skilled" and "unskilled." Among skilled workers there were tailors, butchers, printers, and illustrators, reflecting the significance of the clothing, food, and printing industries in Toronto. Among the unskilled, labourers were the most numerous. There were also clerks, bookkeepers, sales workers, and other office employees.[136] Most of these men were white Anglo Saxons but there were also Italian, Jewish and eastern European men involved.[137] The middle-class men involved in these activities often travelled from the suburbs into the more working-class areas of the city core for sex.[138] Many working-class men also had sex with other working-class men.[139]

As new and more social spaces opened up with urbanization and industrial capitalism in Toronto, more men began to seize some of these spaces to meet other men for sex, and this in turn provoked a response from moral reformers, social purity advocates, the law, and the police. These men met for sex not only in commercial establishments, homes, and the rooms they rented or boarded in, but also in parks, laneways, and lavatories. Many of these working-class men, even if they did live apart from their families, would have been residing in boarding houses or in other working-class households.[140] This would have restricted these men's access to any sort of "private" or intimate space, leading some of them to search for sexual contacts in more "public" spaces.

Men who had sex with other men seized certain urban spaces for their activities. Parks that were frequented during these years included Memorial Square (at the corner of Portland and Wellington Streets), Allan Gardens and Queen's Park, and parks associated with amusement areas such as Sunnyside Beach and the Exhibition Grounds.[141] Men took advantage of the city's maze of laneways to seek out other men for sex.[142] Men also used the lavatories of Queen's Park, Allan Gardens, Union Station, Sunnyside Amusement Park, certain hotels, and the YMCA.[143] In some of these lavatories, men used "gloryholes" (holes in the partitions between cubicles) to facilitate their erotic encounters.[144]

According to Maynard, "it was the park that figured most prominently in the sexual struggle over urban space."[145] City authorities attempted to regulate the use of parks by working-class youth, as well as the young women and men who sometimes resorted to parks to have sex.[146] More lighting and policing was proposed as ways of tightening regulation.

New spaces were also being opened up in this period. Toronto, according to Maynard, "embarked upon something of a lavatory building boom" in the early 1900s.[147] The opening of these spaces unintentionally increased the number of places men could meet other men for sex. Maynard points out:

> Aspects of the city building process, along with the spread of wage labour, established some of the material conditions for the emergence of a subculture, while class and ethnic differences structured sexual relations between men and shaped their journey to sex.[148]

Public-health campaigns were mobilized to regulate outhouses and lavatories. These campaigns raised both health and moral questions.[149] Park attendants were urged to report any holes made in the partitions between cubicles in the lavatories. In response to sexual activity, some of these were covered over.[150]

Many of the men who participated in these activities may have begun to see themselves as homosexual, while others rejected this labelling. Others may have seen themselves more as fairies or queers.[151] This was during a period before "homosexual" had secured its uncontested hegemony as a definition for men who had sex with other men.

Partly in response to the emergence of these networks, and given legal developments in England, there was an intensification of the regulation of same gender sexual activities between men.

LEGAL CATEGORIES: GROSS INDECENCY, SEXUAL SURVEILLANCE, AND THE MAKING OF CRIMINAL PERVERTS

It is in the context of these changing social relations and the initial emergence of same gender erotic networks in Canada that a homosexual "type" began to emerge, partially shaped by the development of legal discourse, judicial institutions, and police organization and activity. Legal and police administration in Canada followed the English model in the nineteenth century.[152] In the Consolidated Statutes of Canada, drawn up in 1859, "buggery" with man or beast was punishable by death.[153]

The need for a new Criminal Code after Confederation was met "principally through the wholesale borrowing, with minor adaptations, of English statutes."[154] Stephen's draft code, which had not been accepted in England but had been made available for export to the colonies, was used in proposals for Canada's first Criminal Code in 1890.[155] Alex Gigeroff wrote:

> One can trace back the sex offences in the present Criminal Code of Canada to our earliest criminal legislation in 1869 only to find that most sections had been borrowed almost word for word from the earlier English statutes.[156]

The social relations in which English legal history and practice had developed were thereby integrated into the foundations of the Canadian State. Confederation also divided responsibility between Parliament, which enacted criminal law, and the provinces, which administered it. The Canadian statute governing buggery varied very little from the English until the early 1950s.[157] In the 1869 Act respecting offences against the person, buggery was classified as an "Unnatural Offence"; in 1892, it was placed under "Offences Against Morality," where it stayed until the 1950s. In 1886, the legal category of "indecent assault" was restricted to males, thus creating the "first distinct male homosexual offence" in Canada only one year after the Labouchere Amendment in England had defined "gross indecency" between men.

Gross indecency was introduced into Canadian statute law in 1890 and entered into the first Criminal Code when it was adopted in 1892. It covered all sexual acts between males not already covered by buggery and applied to anyone

> who in public or private is a party of the commission of or procures or attempts to procure the commission by any male person of any act of gross indecency with another male person.[158]

Punishment was set at a maximum of five years with provisions for whipping.

The introduction of gross indecency as an offence occurred in the midst of agitation for social and sexual purity. D.A. Watt, the driving force behind the Society for the Protection of Women and Young Girls, had responsibility for some of the fundamental changes in the first draft of the bill. Watt was strongly influenced by W.J. Stead's social purity campaign in England.[159] Stead's campaign had culminated in the passage of the Criminal Law Amendment Act of 1885, which raised the age of consent for sexual acts from twelve to fourteen years, and in the Labouchere Amendment, which included the offence of gross indecency. Sir John Thompson, the originator of the Canadian code, supported the inclusion of gross indecency. In 1890, while moving second reading, he said:

> The third section of the Bill contains a penalty for acts of gross indecency committed in reference to a male person. We have upon that subject very little law, and we have no remedy for offences which are now notorious in another country, and which have made their appearance in this country. It will, therefore, be necessary, I think, that a clause of that kind, which is in the English Act, shall be adopted here. I propose, however, in committee to enlarge the maximum term of imprisonment from two years. In this class of offences which, as I said, have obtained notoriety in the mother country, and which have made their appearance here in one or two places, the maximum of two years imprisonment, I think, is entirely inadequate.[160]

Thompson suggested that a five-year sentence be substituted for the original proposal of two years. Sir Richard Cartwright asked whether

> the words he has used, "gross indecency," are not sufficiently precise, and might lead to consequences he does not intend? ... I am quite aware that the particular crime which he has in mind is one which, I very much fear, has been on the increase in certain sections of society, and can hardly be punished too severely. In my opinion the words are not legal words, and it strikes me that consequences might flow from the phraseology which the honourable gentlemen does not contemplate.

Thompson responded:

I think it is impossible to define the offences any better. The provision is the same as the English provision ... It is impossible to define them any better, for the reason that the offences aimed at are so various. The notorious cases I mentioned a few moments ago are not the same in their characteristics and the description which would cover them would not apply to these cases which have been brought to my attention as occurring in Canada within the last few months. I think it is better to leave it in this form. It is no more vague than the English Act.

Mr. Blake, who doubted "very much whether there is any other class of cases in which there is more danger of brutalizing people than in the class of cases dealt with in this clause," argued that the penalty of whipping be added to the clause. Mr. Charlton, who we met earlier, and Mr. Mitchell argued that gross indecency be specifically defined so that, in Mr. Mitchell's words, "there may be no mistake about it."

During final reading in 1892, after discussion of the vagueness of what constituted an "indecent act," the following exchange took place in the House of Commons:

> *Mr. Laurier.* What makes the objection stronger is that in the next section you make a gross act of indecency an indictable offence. It is difficult to know what is a gross act of indecency and what is not.
> *Sir John Thompson*: You get the higher judge for an indictable offence.
> *Mr. Mills (Bothwell)*: All these offences against morality have crept into the common law from the earlier ecclesiastical law, and they were rather sins than crimes, not being attacks upon property or life, or upon any other members of the community. The offences are wholly subjective and altogether different in that respect from the other crimes embraced in the Statute book; and it is a question whether crimes of this sort should be punished by long terms of service in the penitentiary. I do not think they should. I think that flogging, or something of that sort, and the discharge of the prisoners is preferable, and a far better deterrent than anything else.
> *Sir John Thompson*: There is a distinction, I think. We only punish them as crimes when they are offensive to people, or set a bad example. As to Section 178, relating to acts of gross indecency, I have no objection to reducing the term of imprisonment, considering that whipping accompanies it. It is impossible to define these cases by any form of words.[161]

While Thompson argued that this new legal category was necessary because certain offences notorious in England were now becoming common in Canada, he did not cite any specific Canadian cases.[162] The English Act, and the scandals surrounding it, were enough to justify adoption of the new offence.

Through this process legal categories relating to sexual offences became more specific, defining specifically homosexual offences and helping to define the "homosexual" as a criminal suspect and subject. The new legal definitions moved beyond "sodomy" and "buggery," which were retained as well, grouping together various kinds of non-reproductive sex and instructing the police to clamp down on emerging homosexual networks. Not only were medical and psychiatric definitions important in the emergence of knowledge about "the homosexual," but so were the police and the courts.[163] The offence of "gross indecency" encouraged the police to direct their attention against sex between men.

Between 1880–1930 in Ontario, Maynard reports that there were 313 reported cases of sexual "offences" between men. Of these, 113 were from the City of Toronto.[164] Both Carolyn Strange and Steven Maynard report that the numbers arrested for "buggery" and "gross indecency" were low until 1900 and began to increase in the 1910s and 1920s.[165]

In order to detect these activities, new means of surveillance were required. Some men having sex with other men were discovered by constables on the beat in working-class and poor neighbourboods. Others were captured by park caretakers who patrolled the parks. The police also conducted surveillance operations in and around the men's lavatories in Queen's Park and Allan Gardens from 1918 to 1922.[166] The police used a hole in the wall in the back of the lavatory, ladders, light, and photography (to establish the scene of the sexual crime) to survey men and to construct the "facts" or "particulars" of the case against the men who were charged. This defined the reported activities as sexual offences as they were classified in the criminal law; in this case, as "gross indecency."[167] This evidence could then be used against the men in court.[168]

The policing of sex was under the jurisdiction of the Morality Department. As Maynard reports:

In 1886, Toronto mayor and moral reformer William Howland appointed David Archibald to the position of staff inspector of the new Morality Department. Variously described by historians as "an ardent moral reformer" and the "city's moral watchdog," Archibald is a key figure in the history of homosexuality in Toronto ... Archibald made it clear from the beginning that police action against men having sex with other men would be one priority of his department. In his first report in 1886 Archibald made reference to "several cases" involving sex between men.[169]

Maynard reports that police concerns with public lavatories began by the 1880s. In 1887 a committee of Toronto City Council recommended that the police inspect the various urinals two to three times a day "to prevent persons from using them for any other purpose than that for which they are intended."[170] The powers of the Morality Department to police same-gender sex between men was greatly expanded with the enactment of "gross indecency," which led to an increase in the charges laid. However, this increase was gradual and uneven until an intensification of policing of same-gender sex between men beginning in 1913 and reaching its peak in 1917 and the two years following the end of the war. The intensification of sexual policing led to the collection and production of statistics that moral reformers and social purity activists could use in their campaigns against sex between men and also produced the basis for print media reports of same-gender sex offences between men. These were both new and more extensive forms of social surveillance and new forms of power/ knowledge relations.

Maynard reports that this escalation of sexual policing was shaped by the social purity agitation focusing on "white slavery" and the "social evil" that also seemed to produce an intensification of police surveillance of same-gender sex in "public" places and by the wartime conditions that motivated increased police action between 1917–1922.[171] In the first period, this concern was generated by social purity groups, the Toronto Social Survey Commission (mentioned earlier in this chapter) and local clergy, the Toronto Vigilance Committee, and Morality Department campaigns against "sexual immorality." These campaigns were largely directed against "public" activities on city streets, in parks, in lavatories, and in commercial establishments and theatres. They were not largely directed to what went on in "private" households. The Vigilance Committee tended to single out sissies, fairies and "moral perverts" as part of its broader purity campaign.[172] This suggests an important linkage between social purity agitation, the municipal State response, a heightened media focus, and stepped up police activity.

The second period of escalation was shaped by wartime conditions and mobilization. The large number of soldiers in training in the city led to a focus of concern on female prostitutes. But soldiers were also involved in sex with civilian men and with other men in the military. This included soldiers propositioning men for sex on the street. The large numbers of military men in the city increased some of the possibilities for erotic interaction between men, and sexual policing also focused on these interactions.[173] Heightened policing of sex between men was related to concerns over prostitution and sexual purity.

Some men attempted to resist arrest by running away; others made up explanations for their activities even though many of these attempts failed.[174] Even in these circumstances men tried to resist suggesting the growth of networks that made these forms of non-cooperation possible.

Sexual policing, organized through the categories of the Criminal Code,[175] develops in response to the visibility of networks of men having sex with other men as well as social purity agitation, concerns by municipal authorities, and through concerns generated regarding wartime mobilization. As Maynard suggests, this social process brings together concerns over social spaces that could be used for queer sex, the activities of men who had sex with men, as well as the response of the legal system and the police. This brings together analysis of ruling sexual discourse and the emerging regime of sexual regulation and the emergence of cultures and networks constructed by men who had sex with other men. Maynard refers to the interaction between these men who had sex with men and policing as a reciprocal process—"the dialectics of discovery." In this dialectic, the men were surveyed by the police, but it was also through this policing that a certain popular consciousness regarding the existence of "homosexuality" was created, which played a part in the emergence of a distinct homosexual consciousness and identification.[176]

There were also concerns generated over "unnatural practices" in prisons. An official from the Central Prison for Ontario wrote in 1885 that:

> Owing to the crowded state of the Prison, scores of cells have two convicts in each. On moral grounds this is most undesirable; the practice of Sodom's sins did not die with the fiery destruction of that city.[177]

And from a number of years later:

> Another common belief of that period ... is that inmates of prisons were particularly prone to homosexual behaviour. On March 23, 1912, the newspaper [*Jack Canuck*] complained that "unnatural practices" were common among the inmates of the city's gaol, with the facility's greenhouses providing the requisite "shelter and opportunity" and with the result that a great deal of disease was being transmitted among the inmates.
>
> While there is no reason to believe that such practices became more common throughout the period in question, the authorities became more sensitive to the idea. While the rules of the prison system in Ontario in 1903 had forbidden only "indecent behaviour and language," by 1922 "unnatural" intercourse between prisoners had been specifically added to the list of impermissible activities.[178]

During these years of transition in sex/gender relations, the same general features discerned for England and the U.S. can also be uncovered for Canada. The emergence of capitalist social relations led to increasing urbanization and created the opportunity for men, and later women, to live at least partly outside family relations or on its margins. A new regime of sexual classification and policing took shape, rooted in legal and policing changes, medical and scientific discourse, and State formation. Networks of homosexuals and, later, lesbians adopted the category of "homosexual" to identify their own needs. The specific character of the Canadian experience lies in the derived nature of Canadian legal and professional developments in relation to England and to a lesser extent the U.S. The major missing dimension in this work of historical recovery are the voices of those who themselves engaged in same gender pleasures, especially those who were not middle class and not white. With the formation of many of the contemporary institutions of the Canadian State and with the generation of social and family policies, the assumption of heterosexuality would now become institutionalized in State policy.

HETEROSEXUAL HEGEMONY AND THE WELFARE STATE

World War I left Canada with an ever-increasing corporate concentration of capital and with a hierarchy of finance, business, Parliament, the judiciary, the civil service, and various professional groups and agencies forming riding institutions and relations that were constructed in opposition to working-class and other social struggles.[179] The war brought with it increasing State intervention in the realms of social and economic life and introduced "scientific management" techniques.

American companies were now doing more and more business in Canada, bringing with them the social relations found south of the border. Agriculture, however, did not lose its leading economic role until the 1930s, and because of its dependence on other powers, Canada did not develop a strong industrial base. The 1920s and 1930s were the years of monopoly capital's boom and bust. It was only in this environment of corporate capitalism and the initial creation of the Welfare State that heterosexual hegemony became fully established in Canadian social formation.

Beginning with the federal Department of Health and the Division of Child Welfare in 1919, the institutions of State social regulation were put firmly in place. Dr. Helen MacMurchy, first chief of the Division of Child Welfare, who had earlier been Ontario's Superintendent of the Feebleminded, felt that "the decent wish for a true woman is to be a mother"[180] and used her position to "educate" women in the areas of reproduction and motherhood. Her widely circulated "Little Blue Books" signalled motherhood as the highest form of patriotism, for if "No Baby—No Nation."[181]

In the 1930s and 1940s, the foundations of the Welfare State were laid after protracted social and political struggles for family allowances and unemployment insurance.[182] But the form these benefits took was not always that which the social and union activists had been demanding. For instance, the original struggles for unemployment insurance saw it as a fund that only the employers should pay into. The provision of services in many cases also served to justify extended State and professional surveillance and regulation of working-class and poor people's lives.

Women's social, economic, and sexual dependence and institutionalized heterosexuality were cornerstones of these State social policies, so that the heterosexual family unit became the only legally and socially sanctioned way of life.[183] The State enacted legislation

> constitutive of a family in which dependence of women and children ... became legally enforceable and ... progressively incorporated into the administrative policies of welfare agencies, education, health care, etc. ... The man as breadwinner and the woman as dependent become the legally enforceable and administratively constituted relation.[184]

At the same time, the corporatist perspective of the Mackenzie King government attempted to integrate the unions into the workings of the State with government management of negotiations and collective bargaining.

All this transpired in concert with the emergence of mass heterosexual culture and the 1920s' "companionate marriage." This cultural revolution had a dramatic effect on the lives of ordinary people. Sexual intercourse between women and men was defined as "normal" and "natural," and women who were not erotically turned on by men, whether they were labelled "spinsters" or "lesbians," were considered a "social problem." The mass media, with its advertising, the entertainment and amusement industries, and the opening up of new consumer markets all led to the proliferation and eroticization of heterosexual images. The new heterosexual culture was also produced socially in dance halls, movie theatres, ice cream parlours, and among young women and men in factories and schools. Some young men and women developed relationships including erotic ones that broke away from the previous conventions of different gender sex that had been regulated by families and reproduction.[185]

Mass consumer culture helped bring about the fragmentation of working-class cultures. Associational life outside the factory was increasingly replaced by privatized family activities and by commercialized leisure activities.[186] The family, ever more separated from community and kinship networks as it became an even smaller consumer unit, was no longer at the centre of production for the household.[187] By the 1920s, it was actually possible for a minority of male workers in the manufacturing sector to live up to the ideal of the family wage and earn enough income to support an economically dependent wife and children.[188] Later there was the construction of national consumer markets and the development of department stores, especially for middle-class women.[189]

The English-Canadian media was influenced, if not dominated, by U.S. economic interests and advertising. This brought to Canada social relations in which American gender and sexual images were being reproduced. The nascent Canadian film industry was eclipsed by the development of the U.S. industry. Homosexuality was generally denied by its exclusion from films. However, Vito Russo describes the "sissy" as a presentation of male homosexuality according to the model of gender inversion—an image of improper masculinity. As such it was a humorous presentation of what a man should not be. At the same time, some queer influenced images did enter into films and plays during these years. Homosexuality and lesbianism in films was banned from the screen under the U.S. film industry's Motion Picture Production Code in 1934.[190] This was part of what George Chauncey describes as the exclusion of homosexuality from the public sphere in the 1930s in response to the previous visibility of queer networks and was part of constructing the relations of "the closet."[191] This had an important impact in Canada as well.

More than three hundred American mass circulation magazines entered the Canadian market in the 1920s, led by *Ladies Home Journal, Saturday Evening Post* and *McCalls.*[192] This was a period of both change and continuity in white middle-class women's magazines.[193] More women were being schooled and entering into the wage-labour force. By the 1920s it was assumed that a woman would work outside the home for a few years before marriage, while a husband's social status continued to be measured by his ability to keep a wife at home. The magazines clearly opted for marriage as opposed to a career, but they also expressed the tensions which women felt in having to choose. On the subject of child rearing, biology was no longer enough: women had to be trained for motherhood.

> [It was] no longer assumed that natural instinct, trial and error, or practice with young siblings taught a woman to be a mother. Now a professional approach must be taken: women must be trained for the task.[194]

Not only was the middle-class housewife expected to be "educated," the modern woman was also expected to have some business experience before marriage in order to be socially competent and to properly oversee the "socialization" and schooling of her children. The magazines attempted to maintain patriarchal sex/gender relations while also endorsing contemporary ideas of capitalist rationality and efficiency.

By the late 1920s, neo-Freudian ideas, including the notions of "proper" and "deviant" mother/child relations and heterosexuality as the norm, began to enter into popular discussion.[195] These ideas would later be propagated through the marriage, sex-advice, and child rearing manuals that would reach their heyday in the post World War II period.[196]

The household was further reorganized by State-provided compulsory schooling and everything that went with it. This led to the lengthening of the socially organized period of adolescence. Schooling led to a reorganization of working-class women's labour so as to prepare children for school. This set new standards for children's health, cleanliness, and "character."[197] In the middle-class family, the mother provided the communicative skills which would help the child do well in school, and, if it was a boy, to advance into a professional career (doctor, lawyer, manager, executive). The work of the housewife/mother was organized, in part, by the imperatives of the school system.

Adolescent peer-based cultures now emerged, often seizing or moving into the new social spaces opened up by consumer-capitalist relations. These were not simply a reflection of dominant trends; indeed, they often faced stiff opposition from parents and other authorities. But although teenagers did rebel against adult restrictions, their cultural forms were generally heterosexual and male defined. Sexuality was central to teenage social interaction and culture but in a patriarchal and heterosexual context, including sexual coercion and violence against women. Adolescent forms of rebellion and resistance against rigid forms of reproductive marriage relations ironically helped create some of the basis for the new heterosexual "norm."

Despite the construction of heterosexual hegemony and the enforcement of institutionalized heterosexuality, there were those who resisted. They sought out others of the same gender for pleasure and companionship, establishing some of the resources for the subsequent formation of gay and lesbian communities. For instance, in Toronto in the 1920s, homosexually-inclined men picked up soldiers in Queen's Park and in the 1930s cruised the Bay Theatre at Bay and Queen.[198] Many Canadian women who loved or had sex with other women were profoundly affected by Radclyffe Hall's *The Well of Loneliness*, published in 1928. This book and the controversy surrounding it provided a naming for their sexual desires and also provided the media with an image of "the lesbian." In a review written by journalist S.H. Hooke in *The Canadian Forum* in 1929, the censorship of *The Well of Loneliness* was criticized, and Hooke, despite using the language of "abnormality" in relation to lesbians, took up a relatively tolerant view. He ended the review with the following insight:

> But by the irony of life, society's blind reaction in the censorship to certain facts of life defeats itself. As a result of the ban upon *The Well of Loneliness*, thousands upon thousands of people have read the book and become aware of the facts of inversion who would ordinarily never have seen the book, nor become cognizant of the facts which it deals with.[199]

Women inspired by Hall's novel and men who picked up sailors and cruised theatres would open up some of the spaces for the expansion of queer networks in the 1940s and 1950s. It is to these stories and the conservative social responses to them that I now turn.

Notes

1   Bruce Curtis, "Preconditions of the Canadian State ..." in *Studies in Political Economy*, No. 10, Winter 1983, pp. 103–07; Bruce Curtis, "The speller expelled: Disciplining the common reader in Canada West" in *Canadian Review of Sociology and*

Anthropology V. 22, No. 3, 1985, pp. 346–68; his *Building the Educational State: Canada West, 1836–1871* (London: Althouse Press, 1988); and his "'Illicit' Sexuality and Public Education, 1840–1907" in Susan Prentice, ed., *Sex in Schools, Canadian Education and Sexual Regulation* (Toronto: Our Schools/Our Selves, 1994), pp. 101–30.

2 Alison Prentice, *The School Promoters* (Toronto: McClelland and Stewart, 1977), p. 40.

3 See Mariana Valverde, *The Age of Light, Soap and Water: Moral Reform in English Canada, 1885–1925* (Toronto: McClelland and Stewart, 1991); Bruce Curtis's work already cited; and the new Foucault-derived literature on governance including Graham Burchell, *et. al., The Foucault Effect, Studies in Governmentality* (Chicago: The University of Chicago Press, 1991) and Mike Gane and Terry Johnson, *Foucault's New Domains* (London and New York: Routledge, 1993).

4 Bryan D. Palmer, *Working Class Experience* (Toronto and Vancouver: Butterworth, 1983), pp. 9–10.

5 Angus McLaren, "Birth Control and Abortion in Canada, 1870–1920" in *Canadian Historical Review*, Sept. 1978, p. 320; also see Angus McLaren and Arlene Tigar McLaren, *The Bedroom and the State: Changing Practices and Politics of Contraception and Abortion in Canada, 1880–1980* (Toronto: McClelland and Stewart, 1986); and Angus McLaren, *Our Own Master Race: Eugenics in Canada, 1885–1945* (Toronto: McClelland and Stewart, 1990).

6 Heather MacDougall, "Public Health in Toronto's Municipal Politics: The Cardiff Years, 1833–1890" in *Bulletin of the History of Medicine*, V. 55, 1981, pp. 186–202.

7 Dorothy E. Smith, "Women's Inequality and the Family" in Allan Moscovitch and Glen Drover, eds., *Inequality: Essays on the Political Economy of Social Welfare* (Toronto, Buffalo, London: University of Toronto Press, 1981), p. 163.

8 Palmer, *Working Class Experience, op. cit.*, p. 61.

9 See Joey Noble, "Classifying the Poor: Toronto's Charities, 1850–1880" in *Studies in Political Economy*, No. 2, Fall 1979, pp. 109–28; and Susan E. Houston, "The 'Waifs and Strays' of a Late Victorian City: Juvenile Delinquents in Toronto" in Joy Parr, ed., *Childhood and Family in Canadian History* (Toronto: McClelland and Stewart, 1982), pp. 129–42; and Mariana Valverde, *The Age of Light, Soap and Water*, op. cit.

10 Beth Light and Joy Parr, eds., *Canadian Women on the Move* (Toronto: New Hogtown Press and OISE, 1983), p. 2.

11 Palmer, *Working Class Experience, op. cit.*, p. 55.

12 *Ibid.*, p. 14,

13 On the social construction of poverty, see Mitchell Dean, *The Constitution of Poverty: Toward a Genealogy of Liberal Governance* (London and New York: Routledge, 1991). Also see his "'A Social Structure of Many Souls': Moral Regulation, Government, and Self Rule" in *Canadian Journal of Sociology*, V. 19, No. 2, 1994, pp. 145–68.

14 Noble, "Classifying The Poor," *op. cit.*, p. 113. This paragraph is based on infor-

mation in Noble's article. For later years, see Margaret Hillyard Little, "'Manhunts and Bingo Blabs': The Moral Regulation of Single Mothers" in *Canadian Journal of Sociology*, V. 19, No. 2, 1994, pp. 233–47.

15 Wayne Roberts, "Rocking the Cradle for the World: The New Woman and Maternal Feminism, Toronto, 1877–1914" in Linda Kealey, ed., *A Not Unreasonable Claim: Women and Reform in Canada, 1880s-1920s* (Toronto: Women's Educational Press, 1979), p. 30.

16 T.R. Morrison, "Their Proper Sphere: Feminism, the Family and Child-Centred Social Reform in Ontario, 1875–1900," Part II, *Ontario History*, June 1976, p. 73.

17 See Houston, *op. cit.*, p. 136; and Livy Visano, "Tramps, Tricks and Troubles: Street Transients and Their Controls" in Tom Fleming and Livy Visano, eds., *Deviant Designations* (Toronto: Butterworth, 1983), p. 21. Also see the previously cited work of Bruce Curtis.

18 See Carolyn Strange, *Toronto's Girl Problem: The Perils and Pleasures of the City, 1880–1930* (Toronto: University of Toronto Press, 1995), pp. 27–37.

19 Constance Backhouse and Leah Cohen, *The Secret Oppression: Sexual Harassment of Working Women* (Toronto: Macmillan, 1978), p. 57. Also see G. Kealey, ed., *Canada Investigates Industrialism* (Toronto: University of Toronto Press, 1973).

20 Susan Trofimenkoff, "One Hundred and Two Muffled Voices: Canada's Industrial Women in the 1880s" in Cross and Kealey, eds., *Canada's Age of Industry, 1849–1896* (Toronto; McClelland and Stewart, 1982), p. 220.

21 Alice Klein and Wayne Roberts, "Besieged Innocence: The 'Problem' and Problems of Working Women—Toronto, 1896–1914" in Acton, *et al.*, eds., *Women at Work* (Toronto: Canadian Women's Educational Press, 1974), p. 216.

22 *Ibid.*, p. 218. Also see Jane Ursel, *Private Lives, Public Polity: 100 Years of State Intervention in the Family* (Toronto: Women's Press, 1992), especially pp. 83–99.

23 Klein and Roberts, *ibid.*, p. 222.

24 Smith, "Women's Inequality ..." *op. cit.*, p. 182.

25 Palmer, *Working Class Experience, op. cit.*, pp. 31, 33, and 80.

26 Roberts, "Rocking the Cradle," *op. cit.*, p. 16. This reference to Sodom and Gomorrah seems to refer to a notion of masturbation leading to a life of prostitution and immorality and not to the legal offence of sodomy or same-gender sex between women. In the United States, Piver reports, some people "imagined the bicycle as a social vehicle for transporting girls into prostitution. Alarmists even feared bicycle seats might cause women's moral downfall." David J. Piver, *Purity Crusade: Sexual Morality and Social Control, 1868–1900* (Westport, Conn., and London: Greenwood Press, 1973), p. 176.

27 On the shifting historical and social character of constructs of race and ethnicity, see Roxana Ng, "Sexism, Racism and Canadian Nationalism" in Himani Bannerji, ed., *Returning the Gaze: Essays on Racism, Feminism and Politics* (Toronto: Sister Vision Press, 1993), pp. 184–85.

28 Angus MacLaren, "Birth Control and Abortion in Canada," *op. cit.*, pp. 321–22; and Linda Kealey, "Introduction" in *A Not Unreasonable Claim, op. cit.*, pp. 1, 4.

29 Between 1891 and 1901, the number of Canadians born of British stock declined while the number of Europeans and Asians born in Canada almost doubled. Non-British immigrants were considered by State officials and moral reformers as being mentally and physically inferior to Anglo-Canadians and of a lower sexual morality. They were associated with "feeblemindedness" and "mental deficiency." See Carol Lee Bacchi, *Liberation Deferred? Ideas of the English Canadian Suffragists, 1877–1918* (Toronto: University of Toronto Press, 1983), pp. 89, 97, 109; Suzann Buckley, "Ladies or Midwives? Efforts to Reduce Infant and Maternal Mortality" in Kealey, ed., *A Not Unreasonable Claim, op. cit.*, pp. 131–34; Light and Parr, eds., *Canadian Women on the Move, op. cit.*, p. 5; Suzann Buckley and Janice Dicken McGinnis, "Venereal Disease and Public Health Reform in Canada" in *Canadian Historical Review*, V. 63, 3, 1982, p. 346; and Chapman, "Sexual Deviation in Western Canada, 1890–1920," unpublished conference paper given at the Northern Great Plains Conference, Winnipeg, 1979, p. 9.

30 Terry Chapman, "The Anti-Drug Crusade in Western Canada, 1885–1925" in Bercuson and Knalfa, *Law and Society in Canada: Studies in History*, University of Calgary, No. 2, 1979, pp. 89–90.

31 Light and Parr, *op. cit.*, p. 2.

32 Chapman, "The Anti-Drug Crusade," *op. cit.*, pp. 90–94; and Marie Campbell, "Sexism in British Columbia Trade Unions, 1900–1920" in Latham and Kess, eds., *In Her Own Right* (Victoria: Camosun, 1980), p. 174. It is interesting that there was no focus on same-gender sex among Chinese men who were denied access to Chinese women. This comment comes from a conversation with Richard Fung.

33 Terry Chapman, "Early Eugenics Movement in Western Canada" in *Alberta History*, V. 25, 1977, p. 12; and Indiana Matters, "Unfit For Publication: Notes Towards a Lavender History of British Columbia," paper presented at the Sex and the State Lesbian/Gay History conference, Toronto, July 1985, for some suggestions on the racial character of sex offence legislation. Also see Karen Dubinsky, *Improper Advances, op. cit.*, on how race/ethnicity entered into sex offence legal proceedings.

34 See the work of Bruce Curtis, *op. cit.*, and Mariana Valverde, *op. cit.*

35 See Nancy M. Sheehan, "Women Helping Women: The WCTU and the Foreign Population in the West, 1905–1930" in *International Journal of Women's Studies*, V. 6, No. 5, Nov./Dec. 1983, pp. 395–411; Wendy Mitchinson, "The WCTU: For God, Home and the Native Land" in Kealey, ed., *A Not Unreasonable Claim, op. cit.*, p. 163. Also see Barbara Roberts, "Ladies, Women and the State: Managing Female Immigration, 1880–1920" in Roxana Ng, Gillian Walker and Jacob Muller, eds., *Community Organization and the Canadian State* (Toronto: Garamond, 1990), pp. 108–30.

36 Chapman, "Early Eugenics Movement in Western Canada," *op. cit.*, pp. 9, 10. Also see Angus McLaren, *Our Own Master Race: Eugenics in Canada, 1885–1945* (Toronto: McClelland and Stewart, 1990), especially pp. 99, 159, and 169.

37 Chapman *op. cit.*, p. 9. Also see McLaren, *op. cit.*

38 Angus McLaren, "Birth Control and Abortion in Canada," *op. cit.*, p. 319.

39 Constance C. Backhouse, "Shifting Patterns in Nineteenth-Century Canadian Custody Law" in David H. Flaherty, ed., *Essays in the History of Canadian Law*, V. I (Toronto: Published for the Osgoode Society by the University of Toronto Press, 1981), p. 228; also see other Backhouse articles on Canadian legal history: "Nineteenth Century Canadian Rape Law" in Flaherty, ed., *Essays in the History of Canadian Law*, V. 2, 1983, pp. 200–47; and her "Nineteenth Century Canadian Prostitution Law: Reflection of a Discriminatory Society," unpublished paper, Oct. 1982. Also see her *Petticoats and Prejudice: Women and Law in Nineteenth Century Canada* (Toronto: Women's Press, 1991).

40 See Suzann Buckley, "Ladies or Midwives?" *op. cit.*, p. 131; Light and Parr, *op. cit.*, pp. 5–6, 154, 112; and Bacchi, *Liberation Deferred? op. cit.*, pp. 89–94.

41 Light and Parr, *op. cit.*, p. 112.

42 *Ibid.*, p. 5. Also see Joy Parr, *The Gender of Breadwinners: Women, Men and Change in Two Industrial Towns, 1880–1950* (Toronto: University of Toronto Press, 1990).

43 This section is based on James G. Snell, "The White Life for Two: The Defence of Marriage and Sexual Morality in Canada, 1890–1914" in *Histoire sociale—Social History*, V. 16, No. 31, May 1983, pp. 111–29. Reprinted in Bettina Bradbury, ed., *Canadian Family History: Selected Readings* (Toronto, 1992). Also see Snell, *In the Shadow of the Law: Divorce in Canada, 1900–1939* (Toronto 1991), and with Cynthia Comacchio Abeele, "Regulating Nuptiality: Restricting Access to Marriage in Early Twentieth Century English Speaking Canada" in *Historical Perspectives on Law and Society in Canada* (Toronto, 1994). Thanks to Chris Burr for these references.

44 "The White Life for Two," *op. cit*, p. 113.

45 E.A. Lancaster quoted in Snell, "The White Life for Two," *op. cit.*, p. 115.

46 Chapman, "Sex Crimes in Western Canada, 1880–1920," *op. cit.*, p. 41.

47 Snell, "The White Life For Two," *op. cit.*, p. 112.

48 On this see Mariana Valverde, *The Age of Light, Soap and Water, op. cit.*, especially pp. 77–128.

49 See Deborah Brock, "'Unwholesome Truths': Reforming Turn of the Century Urban Ontario," unpublished paper, April 1986, p. 12–13. Also see Mariana Valverde, *The Age of Light, Soap and Water: Moral Reform in English Canada, 1885–1925, op. cit.*, especially pp. 77–103.

50 See Brock, *op. cit.*, p. 12–13, and Snell, "The White Life for Two," *op. cit.*, pp. 117–18, 122. Also see D.A. Watt, "The Canadian Law for the Protection of Women and Girls, with Suggestions for its Amendment and for a General Code" in Aaron M. Powell, *The National Purity Congress* (New York: Arno Reprint, 1976), pp. 437–51.

51 Historical investigation reveals that "protective" legislation usually constructs certain legal or social incapacities in the "protected" group, and all too often comes to be used against the very groups it was designed to protect, whether it be women or young people.

52 Dubinsky, *Improper Advances, Rape and Heterosexual Conflict in Ontario, 1880–1929* (Chicago and London: The University of Chicago Press, 1993) p. 66.

53 *Ibid.*, pp. 68.

54 *Ibid.*, especially pp. 66–71.

55 Snell, "The White Life for Two," *op. cit.*, p. 119.

56 On the family wage system, see Michelle Barrett and Mary McIntosh, "'The Family Wage': Some Problems for Socialists and Feminists" in *Capital and Class*, V. 2, Summer 1980, pp. 51–72. As a result of this defence of marriage, the possibilities for conviction on sex related offences increased as arrest rates increased. See Snell, "The White Life for Two" *op. cit.*, p. 127. Only in 1926 would the first major divorce legislation be passed in Canada, and only in 1968 would a general liberalizing divorce law be passed. Snell, "The White Life for Two," *op. cit.*, p. 115.

57 See Valverde, *The Age of Light, Soap, and Water, op. cit.*

58 See Judith Walkowitz, *Prostitution and Victorian Society* (Cambridge: Cambridge University Press, 1980); and Mariana Valverde, "Sex versus Purity: Conflicts in the First Wave of Feminism" in *Rites*, V, 3, No. 2, June 1986, pp. 10–11.

59 Weeks, *Coming Out* (London, Melbourne, New York: Quartet Books, 1977), pp. 16.

60 Linda Kealey, "Introduction" in Kealey, ed., *A Not Unreasonable Claim, op. cit.*, p. 9.

61 Bacchi, *Liberation Deferred? op. cit.*, p. ix.

62 See Bacchi, "Race Regeneration and Social Purity: A Study of the Social Attitudes of Canada's English Speaking Suffragists" in *Histoire sociale–Social History*, V. 11, No. 22, Nov. 1978, p. 467; Deborah Gorham, "Flora MacDonald Denison: Canadian Feminist" in Kealey, ed., *A Not Unreasonable Claim, op. cit.*, pp. 47–70; and Roberta J. Pazdro, "Agnes Deans Cameron" in Latham and Kess, eds., *In Her Own Right, op. cit.*, pp. 101–23.

63 Bacchi, *Liberation Deferred?, op. cit.*, p. ix.

64 Bacchi, "Race Regeneration ..." *op. cit.*, p. 474.

65 For African-Canadian women's experiences, see Peggy Bristow, *et al.*, *We're Rooted Here and They Can't Pull Us Up: Essays in African Canadian Women's History* (Toronto: University of Toronto Press, 1994); Dionne Brand, "A Working Paper on Black Women in Toronto: Gender, Race and Class" in Himani Bannerji, ed., *Returning the Gaze* (Toronto: Sister Vision Press, 1993), pp. 220–42 and Dionne Brand, *No Burden to Carry: Narratives of Black Women in Ontario, 1920s to 1950s* (Toronto: Women's Press, 1991).

66 G. Roe, *The Great War on White Slavery* (Clifford G. Roe and B.G. Steadwell, 1911), p. 446.

67 Bacchi, *Liberation Deferred? op. cit.*, p. 112; and Roe, *op. cit.* 445.

68 Geoffrey Egan, "These Things May Lead to the Tragedy of Our Species: Notes towards a History of Homosexuality in Canada, 1890–1930," unpublished paper April 1980, p. 7, quoting from an article in *Jack Canuck*, Nov. 25, 1911.

69 Quoted in Steven Maynard, "Through a Hole in the Lavatory Wall: Homosexual Subcultures, Police Surveillance, and the Dialectics of Discovery" in *Journal of the History of Sexuality*, V. 5, No. 2, 1994, p. 234.

70 See Walkowitz, *op. cit.*, for England. For Canada, see Judy Bedford, "Prostitution in Calgary, 1905–1914" in *Alberta History*, V. 29, No. 2, Spring 1981, pp. 1–9; Deborah Nilson, "The Social Evil: Prostitution in Vancouver, 1900–1920" in Latham and Kess, eds., *In Her Own Right, op. cit.*, pp. 205–228; and Lori Rotenberg, "The Wayward Worker: Toronto's Prostitutes at the Turn of the Century" in Acton, *et al.*, eds., *Women at Work, 1850–1930* (Toronto: Canadian Women's Educational Press, 1974), pp. 33–69.

71 Nilson, "The 'Social Evil' ..." *op. cit.*, p. 207.

72 See Carolyn Strange, *Toronto's Girl Problem, op. cit.*, especially pp. 116–43.

73 *Social Survey Commission Report* (Toronto: Carswell Company, 1915). References in the next two paragraphs are to this text, unless otherwise mentioned. On the Social Survey Commission, also see Carolyn Strange, "From Modern Babylon to a City upon a Hill: The Toronto Survey Commission of 1915 and the Search for Sexual Order in the City" in Roger Hall *et al.*, eds., *Patterns of the Past: Interpreting Ontario's History* (Toronto, 1988), 225–78 and also *Toronto's Girl Problem, op. cit.*, especially pp. 102–15.

74 See Valverde, *The Age of Light, Soap, and Water, op. cit.*, p. 83.

75 Social Survey Commission Report, *op. cit.*, p. 136.

76 The Vice Commission of Chicago, *The Social Evil in Chicago: A Study of Existing Conditions* (Chicago, 1911), p. 296. The following references are from pp. 73, 297, 73.

77 On this, also see Valverde and Strange, *op. cit.*

78 Again see Mariana Valverde, *op. cit.*

79 J.S. Shearer, "Introduction" to Roe, *op. cit.*, p. 23.

80 W.J. Hunter, *Manhood Wrecked and Rescued* (Toronto: William Briggs, 1894), p. 71; and Bacchi, "Race Regeneration and Social Purity," *op. cit.*, pp. 469 and 471.

81 The Methodist Church is not necessarily the most "objective" of sources. See Bliss, "Pure Books on Avoided Subjects" in *Historical Papers* 1970 (Ottawa: Canadian Historical Association, 1970), pp. 89–108; Dick in his paper "Heterohegemonic Discourse and Homosexual Acts: The Case of Saskatchewan in the Settlement Era," presented at the "Sex and the State" history conference, also lists a number of other Canadian sex-advice titles, including J.E. Hett, *The Sexual Organs: Their Use and Abuse—The Subject Upon Which Men and Women Know the Least* (Berlin, Ontario, 1899); B.G. Jeffries, *Search Lights on Health: Light on Dark Corners—A Complete Sexual Science and a Guide to Purity and Physical Manhood, Advice to Maiden, Wife, Mother; Love, Courtship and Marriage* (Toronto: J.L. Nichols, 1899); and Reta Gray, *Queer Questions Quaint Answered, or Creative Mysteries Made Plain to Children* (Toronto: J.L. Nichols, 1899).

82 Bliss mentions the reports of Drs. Joseph Workman and Daniel Clarke, *op. cit.*; on Bucke, see Wendy Mitchinson, "Gynecological Operations on Insane Women, London, Ontario, 1895–1901," Dept. of History, University of Windsor, unpublished paper, 1980, pp. 6, 13. Also see her *The Nature of Their Bodies: Women and their Doctors in Victorian Canada* (Toronto: University of Toronto Press, 1991).

83 Dr. Wood Allen, *What a Young Woman Ought to Know* (Philadelphia: VIR Publishing, 1894), pp. 173–74.

84 Josephine E. Young in Roe, ed., *The Great War on White Slavery, op. cit.,* p. 433.

85 Valverde, *op. cit.,* p. 46.

86 Strange, *Toronto's Girl Problems, op. cit.,* p. 126.

87 Valverde, *op. cit.,* pp. 72–74.

88 Bacchi, *Liberation Deferred? op. cit.,* pp. 113, 171; Chapman, "Sexual Deviation in Western Canada, 1890–1920," *op. cit.,* p. 11; and Gigeroff, *Sexual Deviations in the Criminal Law* (Toronto: Published for the Clarke Institute by University of Toronto Press, 1968), p. 39. Also Beatrice Brigden, in Light and Parr, *op. cit.,* p. 210.

89 Valverde, *op. cit.,* pp. 69–70.

90 Dept. of Evangelism and Social Service, Dept. of Temperance and Moral Reform, Sixth Annual Report, p. 131.

91 Clark, *Our Sons* (Ontario: W.L. Clark, 1914), pp. 153, 155.

92 Bliss, *op. cit.;* and Bacchi, *Liberation Deferred? op. cit.,* p. 171.

93 Bliss, *op. cit.*

94 Deborah Brock, "Unwholesome Truths," *op. cit.,* p. 36. Also see Arthur W. Beall, *The Living Temple: A Manual on Eugenics for Parents and Teachers* (Whitby, Ont.: The A.B. Penhale Publishing Company, 1933) and Valverde, *op. cit.,* 70 71.

95 VD was linked with feeblemindedness and fear of non-Anglo immigrants, and with concerns over military efficiency given its rate of incidence among troops and recruits. It was feared that VD threatened national defence by "incapacitating Canadian manpower." Buckley and McGinnis, "Venereal Disease and Public Health Reform in Canada," *op. cit.,* p. 338. Also see Jay Cassel, *The Secret Plague: Venereal Disease in Canada, 1838–1939* (Toronto: University of Toronto Press, 1987), especially pp. 122–44.

96 Bland, "Guardians of the Race" ... in Elizabeth Whiteleg *et al.,* eds., *The Changing Experience of Women* (Oxford: Martin Robertson, 1982), p. 381.

97 Buckley and McGinnis, *op, cit.,* p. 343.

98 *Ibid.* This points to the ambiguous and contradictory character of "public health" legislation. While it has brought about real gains, it has also extended state and medical surveillance of sexual life and has been used to brand certain sexual activities as deviant or "sick." On this, see my review article, "Which Public, Whose Health?" in *Rites,* V. 3, No. 1, May 1986, pp. 16–17; "Their Silence, Our Deaths: What Can the Social Sciences Offer to AIDS Research?" in Diane E. Goldstein, ed., *Talking AIDS: Interdisciplinary Perspectives on Acquired Immune Deficiency Syndrome* (St. John's: Institute for Social and Economic Research, 1991); and "Managing AIDS Organizing" in William K. Carroll, ed., *Organizing Dissent* (Toronto: Garamond, 1992), pp. 215–31. Also Lucy Bland and Frank Mort, "Look Out for the 'Good Time' Girl: Dangerous Sexualities as a Threat to National Health" in *Formations of Nation and People* (London: Routledge and Kegan Paul, 1984), pp. 131–51 and Frank Mort, *Dangerous Sexualities* (London: Routledge, 1987). On the U.S. experience see Alan M. Brandt, *No Magic Bullet:*

A Social History of Venereal Disease in the United States Since 1880 (New York, Oxford: Oxford University Press, 1985).

99   Quoted in Jay Cassell, *The Secret Plague: Venereal Disease in Canada, 1838–1939* (Toronto: University of Toronto Press, 1987), p. 141.

100 *Ibid.*, p. 216.

101 Edward Stevenson (real name Xavier Mayne), *The Intersexes* (Rome: privately printed, preface dated 1908; reprinted New York: Arno Press, 1975), p. 638.

102 Ezra Hurlburt Stafford, "Perversion" in *Canadian Journal of Medicine and Surgery*, Toronto, V. 3, No. 4, April 1898, pp. 179–85. The following references and quotes are all drawn from this article.

103 Krafft-Ebing himself moved from his 1887 position that homosexuality is a disease with a biological basis to his 1901 position, that some varieties of homosexuality are congenital anomalies. The emerging Canadian medical and psychological discourse regarding sex must be studied in much more detail: it affected State policy, newspaper reports, popular culture, and homosexual consciousness.

104 See Ross Higgins, "L'Association Nocturne: A Montreal Cruising Story from 1886" in *Canadian Lesbian and Gay History Network Newsletter*, No. 3, December 1987, pp. 5–7. The article was from *La Presse*, June 30, 1886, p. 4. The article was rediscovered by Cyrille Felteau, a journalist at *La Presse*. It was reprinted in that newspaper, April 19, 1982, and, later in Felteau's *Histoire de la Presse* (Éditions La Presse, Montréal) 1983, Vol. 1, p. 170.

105 Steven Maynard, "In Search of 'Sodom North': The Writing of Lesbian and Gay History in English Canada, 1970–1990," pp. 127 128.

106 See Chauncey, *Gay New York*, *op. cit.*

107 Maynard, "Through a Hole in the Lavatory Wall," *op. cit.*, p. 234.

108 Light and Prentice, *Pioneer and Gentlewomen of British North America*, *op. cit.*, pp. 1–204, 214–15.

109 See Katz, *Gay American History* (New York: Thomas Y. Crowall, 1976) and *Gay/Lesbian Almanac* (New York: Harper and Row, 1983).

110 Light and Parr, *Canadian Women on the Move*, *op. cit.*, p. 24. For use of the term "hermaphrodite" in a later period, see the section on Elsa Gidlow's experiences later in this chapter. At least one cross dressing woman fought in the American Civil War. Katz, *Gay/Lesbian Almanac*, *op. cit.*, p. 191–194. Also see Steven Maynard's critical review of Don Akenson, *At Face Value: The Life and Times of Eliza McGormack/John White* (Kingston and Montréal: McGill Queen's University Press, 1990) in *Rites* V. 8, No. 4, Sept./Oct., 1991, p. 13.

111 See "The Higher Education of Women" Medical and Surgical Reporter, in the *Canadian Lancet*, May 1893, p. 285. The relationship between this initial distinction and the later emergence of the "lesbian" remains to be explored more fully.

112 Other early experiences of female friendships that may have influenced the emergence of lesbian networks are explored by Frances Rooney in "Edith G.

Watson, Photographer, and Victoria Hayward, Writer" in *Fireweed*, Lesbiantics issue, No. 13; and in Frances Rooney, "Loring and Wyle, Sculptors" in *Pink Ink*, V. 1, No. 1, July 1983, pp. 18–20.

113 The scandals involving Wilde were to have an important effect on Canadian debates. Dick, for instance, refers to an 1895 editorial in the *Regina Leader*. Referring to Wilde's activities as "effeminating, debilitating and immoral," it describes his "vile companionships," "scandalous associations.... spiritual corrosion," and "moral leprosy" and calls for Wilde to be jailed for life. See Dick, *op. cit.*, p. 8, quoting from "Oscar Wilde in jail" in *The Leader* (Regina), Apr. 11, 1895, p. 4.

114 On Wilde, see Kevin O'Brien, *Oscar Wilde in Canada: An Apostle for the Arts* (Toronto: Personal Library, 1982).

115 On Whitman, see Michael Lynch, "The Lovers of His Friends and Hot Little Prophets: Walt Whitman in Ontario" in *The Body Politic*, No. 67, Oct. 1980, pp. 29–31 and "Walt Whitman in Ontario" in Robert K. Martin, ed., *The Continuing Presence of Walt Whitman: The Life After the Life* (Iowa City: University of Iowa Press, 1992), pp. 141–51; and Robert K. Martin, *The Homosexual Tradition in American Poetry* (Austin, University of Texas Press, 1979). For Carpenter, see Canadian Gay Archives Publication No. 5, "Lesbian and Gay Heritage of Toronto" in Toronto, 1982.

116 Deborah Gorham, "Flora MacDonald Denison: Canadian Feminist," *op. cit.*, p. 55, 62, 67.

117 See Dubinsky, *Improper Advances, op. cit.*, p. 140.

118 Gorham, *op. cit.*, p. 66.

119 Gorham, *op. cit.*; Lynch, *op. cit.*; and Egan, *op. cit.*, p. 16.

120 Egan, *op. cit.*, p. 16.

121 "A Comrade Passes" in *The Canadian Theosophist*, V. 11, No. 4, Toronto, June 15, 1921.

122 Weeks, *Coming Out, op. cit.*, p. 52, and *Sex, Politics and Society* (London and New York: Longman, 1981), p. 111.

123 Rev. James Carmichael, in *Balfard's Monthly Magazine*, Toronto, 1877. Reference from the *Gay Archivist*, published by the Canadian Gay Archives, No. 4, Sept. 1981.

124 Elsa Gidlow, "Casting a Net: Excerpts from an Autobiography," in *The Body Politic*, No. 83, May 1982, pp. 27–30, and "Elsa Gidlow: Memoirs," introduced by Rayna Rapp, *Feminist Studies*, V. 6, No. 1, Spring 1980, pp. 103–27. Also see Elsa Gidlow, *Elsa: I Come with My Songs, The Autobiography of Elsa Gidlow* (San Francisco: Bootlegger Press, 1986). Elsa Gidlow died on June 8, 1986.

125 "Elsa Gidlow: Memoirs," *op. cit.*, p. 115.

126 "Elsa" in Adair and Adair, *Word is Out: Stories of Some of Our Lives* (New York: New Glide/Delta, 1978).

127 Gidlow, "Casting a Net," *op. cit.*, p. 30. This included Ellis's *Psychology of Sex* and Carpenter's *The Intermediate Sex* and *Towards Democracy*.

128 *Ibid.*

129 *Ibid.*

130 Gidlow, "Casting A Net," *op. cit.*, p. 30. A 4–F classification was also used to stigmatize homosexual draftees in World War II in the U.S. See Allan Berubé, "Coming Out Under Fire" in *Mother Jones*, Feb./Mar. 1983, p. 24 and Berubé, *Coming Out Under Fire* (New York: The Free Press, 1990).

131 C.S. Clark, *Of Toronto the Good: A Social Study, the Queen City of Canada as It Is* (Montreal: The Toronto Publishing Company, 1898). Toronto as a social study was brought before the world by the remarks of Canadian delegates to the Social Purity Conference in Baltimore and the World's Convention of the Women's Christian Temperance Union held in Toronto in 1897. The following is based on my reading of this book, particularly pp. 89–90.

132 *Ibid.*, pp. 89–90.

133 For instance, a Swift Current, Saskatchewan, doctor refers to another doctor as "an Oscar Wilde type" in a 1913 letter to the province's Attorney General. This reference comes from Terry Chapman's research reported in the *Lesbian/Gay History Researchers Network Newsletter*, No. 5, Dec. 1981, p. 14. Also see Terry Chapman, "'An Oscar Wilde Type': 'The Abominable Crime of Buggery' in Western Canada, 1890–1920" in *Criminal Justice History*, No. 4, 1983, pp. 97–118. Another term then used was "third sex." In 1913 an article entitled "Toronto Skating Club Carnival" refers to a "third sex" costume at a costume party. From *Toronto Saturday Night*, Mar. 8, 1913, p. 38, quoted in Egan, *op. cit.*, p. 10.

134 On this, see Steven Maynard's work examining court and police records, as well as training school and reformatory records for his Ph.D. thesis, especially his chapter called "Boys and Their Men: The Homosexual World of Working Class Youth in Urban Ontario," given in a preliminary fashion at the "Out of the Archives" conference, York University, 1994.

135 Steven Maynard, "In Search of 'Sodom North,'" *op. cit.*, p. 127.

136 Maynard, "Through a Hole in the Lavatory Wall," *op. cit.*, p. 216.

137 *Ibid.*, p. 219.

138 *Ibid.*, pp. 217–19.

139 *Ibid.*, p. 220.

140 *Ibid.*, p. 217.

141 *Ibid.*, pp. 211–12.

142 *Ibid.*, p. 212.

143 *Ibid.*, p. 213.

144 *Ibid.*, P. 213.

145 *Ibid.*, p. 235.

146 On this, also see Carolyn Strange, *Toronto's Girl Problem*, *op. cit.*.

147 Maynard, "Through a Hole in the Lavatory Wall," *op. cit.*, p. 214.

148 *Ibid.*, p. 240.

149 *Ibid.*, p. 215.

150   *Ibid.*, p. 237.

151   See Chauncey, *Gay New York, op. cit.*

152   Philip C. Stenning, *Legal Status of Police*, Criminal Law Series Study Paper (Law Reform Commission of Canada, July 1981), p. 7.

153   Referred to in James Edward Jones, *Pioneer Crimes and Punishment in Toronto and the Home District* (Toronto, 1924), p. 7.

154   Gigeroff, *op. cit.*, p. viii.

155   *Ibid.*, p. 36; also see remarks quoted in Gigeroff by Thompson on the importance of this new Criminal Code, pp. 69–70.

156   *Ibid.*, p. 3.

157   *Ibid.*, p. 39. The following section is based on Gigeroff's account, particularly pp. 39–46, unless otherwise cited. Also see Graham Parker, "The Origins of the Canadian Criminal Code" in Flaherty, ed., *Essays in the History of Canadian Law*, V. 1, pp. 249–77; and R.C. Macleod, "The Shaping of Canadian Criminal Law, 1892–1982," *Canadian Historical Association Paper*, 1978.

158   Chapman, "Sexual Deviation in Western Canada," *op. cit.*, p. 13.

159   On Stead's campaign, also see Judith R. Walkowitz, *City of Dreadful Delight* (Chicago: The University of Chicago Press, 1992), pp. 81–134.

160   Debates, House of Commons, Canada, April 10, 1890, V. 2, pp. 3161–62. Other references in this session quoted below are from pp. 3170–71.

161   These exchanges reveal the imprecise character of the official language of the day and the heterogeneous offences apparently included under the heading of "gross indecency." Debates, House of Commons, Canada, May 25,1892, pp. 2968–69.

162   See Gigeroff, *op. cit.*, p. 46–47; the following case may have influenced this law reform process. This story was reported in the *San Francisco Call*, Jan. 29, 1890, under the headline "Canadian Scandal."

> Government has been acquainted with the facts of a most revolting story in which a young clergyman in the Province of Ontario figures conspicuously. Sir John Thompson admitted that the charges have been made, and says that it will, in his opinion, ensure the passage of the purity bill, which provides for the flogging of persons found guilty of such crimes.

It is unclear whether the "offence" is same or different gender in character. From Toronto Lesbian and Gay History Project, "Proposed History Projects," No. 10, 1981.

163   Maynard, "Through a Hole in the Lavatory Wall," *op. cit.*, p. 210.

164   *Ibid.*, pp. 207–08.

165   *Toronto's Girl Problem, op. cit.*, p. 224, and Maynard, "Through a Hole in the Lavatory Wall," *op. cit.*, p. 230.

166   Maynard, "Through a Hole in the Lavatory Wall," *op. cit.*, p. 222.

167   See George Smith, "Policing the Gay Community: An Inquiry into Textually

Mediated Social Relations" in *International Journal of the Sociology of the Law*, V. 16, 1988, pp. 163–83.

168 Maynard, "Through a Hole in the lavatory Wall," *op. cit.*, pp. 224–29.

169 *Ibid.*, p. 222–23.

170 *Ibid.*, p. 223, quoting from Toronto City Council, Minutes, 1887, app., item 1061, p. 1030.

171 *Ibid.*, pp. 232–36.

172 *Ibid.*, p. 234.

173 *Ibid.*, pp. 234–35.

174 *Ibid.*, p, 237–38.

175 See George Smith, "Policing the Gay Community" *op. cit.*, and Gary Kinsman, "Official Discourse as Sexual Regulation," Ph.D. thesis, Department of Educational Theory, University of Toronto, 1989.

176 Maynard, "Through a Hole in the Lavatory Wall," *op. cit.*, pp. 238–42.

177 Cited in Steven Maynard, "Saturday night in the bunkhouse: Prospects for gay history" in *Rites*, Mar. 1990, p. 12.

178 Egan, *op. cit.*, p. 8.

179 Dorothy E. Smith, "Women's Inequality" in Allan Moscovitch and Glen Drover, eds., *Inequality: Essays on the Political Economy of Social Welfare* (Toronto, Buffalo, London: University of Toronto Press, 1981), p. 168; and Palmer, *Working Class Experience* (Toronto and Vancouver: Butterworth, 1983), p. 137.

180 Veronica Strong-Boag, "Canada's Women Doctors: Feminism Constrained" in Kealey, ed., *A Not Unreasonable Claim* (Toronto: Women's Educational Press, 1979), p. 124; and Katherine Arnup, "Education for Motherhood: Government Health Publications, Mothers and the State," unpublished paper delivered at the Canadian Sociology and Anthropology Association annual meeting in Winnipeg, June 1986. Also see Mariana Valverde, *The Age of Light, Soap and Water: Moral Reform in English Canada, 1885–1925* (Toronto: McClelland and Stewart, 1991), p. 53.

181 Also see Katherine Arnup, *Education for Motherhood: Advice for Mothers in Twentieth Century Canada* (Toronto: University of Toronto Press, 1994).

182 Palmer, *Working Class Experience, op. cit.*, p. 234. Also see Jane Ursel, *Private Lives, Public Policy: 100 Years of State Intervention in the Family* (Toronto: Women's Press, 1992).

183 See Smith, "Women's Inequality," *op. cit.*; and Brigitte Kitchen, "Women's Dependence" in the Sexuality and the State issue of *Atkinson Review of Canadian Studies*, V. 1, No. 2, Spring 1984, pp. 11–16.

184 Dorothy E. Smith, "Women, Class and Family" in *Socialist Register*, 1983, pp. 31–32.

185 Also see Strange, *Toronto's Girl Problem, op. cit.*, especially pp. 116–74.

186 Palmer, *Working Class Experience, op. cit.*, pp. 189, 195.

187 Beth Light and Joy Parr, eds., *Canadian Women on the Move* (Toronto: New Hogtown Press and OISE, 1983), p. 49.

188   Palmer, *Working Class Experience, op. cit.*, p. 192.

189   See Cynthia Wright, "'Feminine Trifles of Vast Importance': Writing Gender into the History of Consumption" in Franca Iacovetta and Mariana Valverde, *Gender Conflicts: New Essays in Women's History* (Toronto: University of Toronto Press, 1992), pp. 229–60.

190   Palmer, *Working Class Experience, op. cit.*, p. 194. For a fun and intriguing exploration of American films, many of which would have been seen in Canada, see Vito Russo, *The Celluloid Closet: Homosexuality in the Movies* (New York: Harper and Row, 1981). Also Chauncey, *Gay New York, op. cit.*, p. 353.

191   See Chauncey, *Gay New York,* pp. 331–54.

192   Palmer, *Working Class Experience, op. cit.*, p. 94.

193   This is from Mary Vipond's "The Image of Women in Mass Circulation Magazines in the 1920s" in Susan Trofimenkoff and Alison Prentice, eds., *The Neglected Majority* (Toronto: McClelland and Stewart, 1977), pp. 117–22. Much of the next two paragraphs draws on this article.

194   *Ibid.*, p. 121.

195   Strong Boag, "Canadian Women's Doctors: Feminism Constrained," *op. cit.*, p. 129.

196   See Katherine Arnup, *Education for Motherhood, op. cit.*

197   See Dorothy E. Smith, "Women, Class and Family" in *The Socialist Register* (London: Merlin, 1983), p. 31.

198   See John Grube, "Queens and Flaming Virgins: Towards a Sense of Gay Community" in *Rites,* V. 2, No. 9, p. 16.

199   Quoted in Steven Maynard, "Radclyffe Hall in Canada" in *Centre/Fold,* No. 6, Spring 1994, p. 9. This is quoted from S.H. Hooke, *The Canadian Forum,* Apr., 1929.

Stan Persky and John Dixon

from *On Kiddie Porn* (2001)

Canada's child pornography law was far more a product of political expedience than pressing national need or even a desire to protect children from exploitation and abuse. What's more, although the proposed law received the assent of all political parties in the Canadian House of Commons, it was primarily designed to address the political needs of an ideologically fractured Progressive Conservative Party as it neared the end of a long period of tenure in government.

...

In a February 1990 cabinet shuffle, less than a year and a half after Prime Minister Brian Mulroney's re-election, an unusual politician from British Columbia was appointed as the first woman to hold the powerful post of minister of Justice. For the then forty-four-year-old Kim Campbell, the promotion from a junior ministerial portfolio to minister of Justice and attorney general of Canada was but the latest step in what was truly a meteoric political career.[1]

...

It was no accident that Campbell was concerned with the pornography issue. For the previous two decades, intellectual North America had been preoccupied with "porn wars" that divided venerable allies—feminists and civil libertarians—into opposing philosophical and legal camps.[2] Campbell had read widely in this area and had a natural interest in using her new role to respond to and advance the feminist agenda. Besides, this was an area in which there was an intriguing correspondence between the interests of women and the concerns of the moral and religious Right, as exemplified by the Family Caucus in her party. Women in the United States had already discovered—often uneasily—a common cause with the Republican Party exponents of traditional "family values." This group had never faltered in its war against "dirty" books and pictures, and rather enthusiastically welcomed women joining it in its tireless struggle for "decency."

Such an alliance was inherently unstable, however. Where the Right held to a notion of morality that claimed to discover a perfect and inviolate coinci-

dence between the boundaries of heterosexuality and decency, this moral revelation was not shared by the majority of feminists, whose inclusive philosophy had led them to a liberal acceptance of the many lesbians in their ranks.
Besides, feminists attacked pornography on the modern legal basis of the
alleged social scientific evidence of the harm it caused women, while their
allies on the Right stuck to the older position that "filth" should be expunged
on the simple ground of its immorality.

Campbell saw all of this, but was still intrigued by the potential legislative
initiatives on the porn front. For one thing, as we've already noted, she faced
a very specific political problem in the form of the Family Caucus, and she
needed to solve that problem as a condition of advancing her full legislative
agenda. Could the smouldering pornography issue provide some badly needed common ground for her with the Family Caucus? Could well-conceived
legislation in this area offset some of the unavoidable divisiveness guaranteed
by the Justice agenda?

Along with Campbell's own interest in the pornography question, there
were also institutional pressures for attention to the issue. Although the government had tried and failed, as recently as 1988, to pass new pornography
legislation, commitment to such legislation was still alive in various governmental quarters. As well, a June 1990 report on child sexual abuse by Rix
Rogers, a special adviser to the minister of Health and Welfare, had recommended "that the federal minister of justice introduce legislation that will
address the protection of children from the harmful effects of pornography."

It was not an accident that Campbell's initial memo to her adviser directed
him to look at pornography law in terms of a conflict between individual and
group rights. The most prominent anti-pornography feminist thinker—and
the one who pioneered a legal approach to anti-porn sanctions based on a
notion of the collective or group rights of women—was an American law professor, Catherine MacKinnon.[3] Among other things, MacKinnon was providing advice to an important group of Canadian women lawyers, the Legal Education and Action Fund (LEAF). LEAF had intervened in several judicial
actions, the most significant of which was the pending case (to be heard in
June 1991) of *R. v. Butler*, in which the Supreme Court of Canada would
determine the constitutional validity of the country's obscenity law and,
equally important, the grounds on which it would be upheld or struck down.

There were two other reasons for Campbell's and, as well, Deputy Minister
Tait's interest in the line of argument about collective rights. The first had to
do with the issue of national unity. There was a perceived need for a creative
approach to reconstituting the country, and the current thinking in Ottawa
leaned towards some form of "asymmetric federalism" in which different
rights and powers would be conferred on different provinces on the basis of
their distinctive needs within Canadian confederation. If Catherine MacKinnon provided a "group rights" approach with respect to women, there were

similar theorists about, such as Canadian philosopher Charles Taylor and a contingent of political thinkers interested in "communitarianism," who were being eagerly read in the Justice department for what they had to say about federalism.[4]

The idea was that the "collective rights" notion might provide some intellectual ground that could be used to balance the emphasis on individual equality in the Charter of Rights and Freedoms. The question at issue was: What does the constitutional principle of equality under the law demand? Does it bar "unequal" treatment of different provinces, as contemplated in asymmetric federalism? Perhaps not, went the thinking of some analysts. Perhaps the equality guaranteed in the constitution could be interpreted or extended to include a range of group or collective rights, as was already explicitly the case in terms of aboriginal rights and some language rights.

Beyond this philosophical interest in group equality rights, the Department of Justice had a second and more pragmatic interest in such rights, stemming from its practical experience with Charter litigation. Justice lawyers were responsible for representing the Government of Canada in all lawsuits, and they were becoming swamped by Charter challenges to laws and policies of the government. Perhaps, suggested some lawyers within Justice, setting group rights against individual rights might relieve the pressure. After all, it might be argued that the laws and policies of the government were a means of securing the most general interests and public goods of Canadians. What better way to characterize those general interests and goods than as what Canadians as a collectivity have the right to expect from their government? If individual rights were being advanced to trump, or override, law and policy, one way to protect the government's agenda might be to promote law and policy to the status of group rights. This would give Justice a new range of legal weapons to deploy in defense of its clients, and might provide a means to contain and control the seemingly open-ended threat of Charter challenges to government action.

...

As the option of a child pornography law advanced to the stage of a public commitment, advice on the group rights approach was provided in a series of memos, culminating with one on March 14, 1991, that took the question of whether Canada's individual equality rights were an obstacle to developing policies that addressed national collective interests.[5] At this point the collective rights route was rejected. The bottom line was that "beyond the extent to which some such collective rights (as in the case of aboriginal and language rights) are already entrenched in our Constitution, it would be legally and philosophically awkward, as well as politically dangerous, to attempt to fashion a much more expansive and ambitious role for them." The reason for rejecting a more "ambitious" role for such collective rights had to do with the danger of unleashing genies from bottles.

Positive rights (as contrasted to negative ones), went the argument, are extremely difficult for courts to adjudicate. It's far easier to tell a government to stop doing "x" (as in the Supreme Court abortion decision, where the court told the government to stop relying on overly restrictive therapeutic abortion committees) than to tell a government what it should do.

Further, group rights bring large, organized forces into the policy-making arena with the potential to acquire equally large, novel powers. A notion of "inclusive justice" that brought previously unrecognized groups to the table for genuine consultations was one thing; carving their powers into constitutional stone was another. Self-consciously creating a big role for positive group rights in the scheme of governance could set loose new powers and players that might undermine the authority of the courts as they got more involved in policy adjudication, and could potentially render government itself irrelevant as just one more player in a court-adjudicated policy area. While those were the very reasons that some people supported group rights as a broadening of democracy, it was this argument that quickly cooled the fervour of group rights enthusiasts inside government. In any case, it was argued that collective interests (as distinct from rights) could be accommodated without the necessity of entrenching collective rights.

...

If Justice Minister Campbell could be persuaded that collective rights were too practically cumbersome and too intellectually insubstantial to pursue (and that, in any case, individual rights weren't a bar to accommodating group interests), the same was not true of pornography. The idea of a pornography initiative was now on the table.

However, from the point of view of her advisers, there were considerable problems. First, the existing obscenity provisions of the Criminal Code (Section 163) very clearly covered child pornography. Indeed, there were no decisions extant in any Canadian court that threw any doubt whatsoever on the proposition that pornographic materials involving the use of children would be viewed as the most serious form of obscene expression targeted by the Criminal Code. Second, there was no child pornography controversy abroad in the land, crying out for legislative clarification or governmental response. Child porn was, simply and unequivocally, obscene, and anyone making, distributing, selling, or publishing it would be subject to prosecution wherever and whenever they were detected in Canada.

Finally, there was the crucial related matter of the extreme rarity of child pornography. In 1991 there was virtually no market in child pornography in Canada. At least, there was none that could be detected by officials in the research division of the Department of Justice, who had been charged with the task of going out and finding it. Campbell's advisers met with those officials, who reported that among the very few instances of child pornography found in Canada, the greatest number of them came from misdirected mailings by the U.S. Postal Service as part of an American sting operation against kiddie porn. That is, what market there was in Canada had been inadvertently created by U.S. authorities.

A Justice department study dutifully documented all of this, notwithstanding occasional counterclaims by Canadian police officials that kiddie porn was indeed a problem.[6] For example, in an almost five-year period between 1986 and 1990, only 1.3 percent of more than 38,000 seizures of pornographic material by Canada Customs involved child pornography. Similarly, statistics for Customs' seizures in Ontario from 1987 to 1989 showed that child pornography accounted for only 0.5 percent of some 6,500 "enforcement actions." The marked increase in the availability of child pornography as a result of Internet technology developments had not yet occurred. For the moment, however, there wasn't compelling evidence that there was a genuine need for legislation.

If a principle of sound government is that law should only be enacted when there is real need, then contemplating unnecessary legislation brought with it the danger that the expansion of legislative activity and the multiplication of statutes could damage both the administration of laws and respect for them. Further, if a criminal law had no real target, the danger increased that its impact would be on the wrong people. Such a result in the criminal law context is called injustice.

...

While the ministry was still far from a consensus on child pornography legislation, in February 1992 the Supreme Court of Canada rendered a landmark decision on the constitutionality of Canada's existing obscenity law. The case, *R. v. Butler,* which was heard in June 1991, was the first major Charter test of pornography in the country, and the judgment would have far-reaching consequences, substantially affecting the course of all subsequent debate about the censorship of obscenity, as well as the child pornography legislation.

The decision unanimously upheld the central provision of the existing law, Section 163, which decrees that "any publication a dominant characteristic of which is the undue exploitation of sex, or of sex and anyone or more of the following subjects, namely, crime, horror, cruelty and violence, shall be deemed to be obscene." The decision also explicitly and repeatedly declared that any representation of sexual activity involving actual children in its production is obscene. This meant that only an extension of criminal prohibition to include simple possession of child porn would represent a legislated advance on the case law.

The reasons for judgment make the *Butler* decision—whether one approves or deplores it (we're in the latter camp)—a vital one for the crafting of the kiddie porn law, which was conceived as simply an extension of Section 163.[7] First, we'll provide a bit of historical context concerning Canadian pornography law; then we'll look at what the court decided and why; and finally we'll offer our criticisms.

"As in many other countries, initial attempts to regulate sexually explicit materials in Canada stemmed from traditional notions of government responsibility for societal decency and morality," legal scholar Jodi Kleinick observes in her review of the *Butler* decision. It's a tradition that goes all the way back to mid-seventeenth-century England. In twentieth-century Canada, moral standards changed gradually but dramatically. Before the Second World War, the general view of pornography, consistent with that of the other major Western democracies, was that graphic or textual representations of sex, or even frank discussions of it in a publication, were obscene because they were immoral. Although an otherwise obscene publication might be "redeemed" if its sexual content was coincidental to some more acceptable purpose, for the most part it was not thought either politically or legally necessary to go beyond the identification of a publication as immoral in order to establish its obscene nature and justify its censorship. If it was about sex, it was dirty.

The "archeological" remnants of this idea can be seen in the Criminal Code of Canada, where the obscenity provisions are still posted under the heading "Offences tending to the corruption of public morals." That is, the obscenity provisions sit squarely within the section of the criminal law that literally codifies the sexual morality of Canadian society.

However, after the Second World War a series of court decisions and parliamentary initiatives showed the judiciary and legislatures moving away from the standard that had been set by a nineteenth-century English case, *R. v. Hicklin*, where the test for obscenity was "whether the tendency of the matter charged as obscenity is to deprave and corrupt those whose minds are open to such immoral influences." Legal and legislative thinking turned towards the liberal principles that British political philosopher John Stuart Mill enunciated in his classic *On Liberty*. The core of Mill's principle of liberty was that the only legitimate reason for which a state could limit the freedom of one of its members was to prevent harm to others. This principle, in its turn, is grounded in the more general principle of utility, which held that actions or laws were good insofar as they produced the greatest amount of happiness for the greatest number of people.

On Liberty develops a comprehensive argument that there are very few forms of human freedom more conducive to the production of human happiness than the freedom of what Mill called "thought and discussion." So if there was to be censorship, or interference with the thought and discussion of the citizenry, there must be a justification of such censorship in terms of showing an actual harm to others—harm that, if censorship took the same view as the rest of the Criminal Code, would eventually be defined as direct and measurable, rather than indirect, such as the harm caused by mere offensiveness.

Notions such as these, along with the American tradition of free speech rooted in "natural law," provided the intellectual underpinnings of the expression rights entrenched in Canada's 1982 *Constitution Act.*

Even before that, the accelerating sexual liberalization of Western cultures had an impact on Canadian obscenity standards. Discussions in the Canadian Senate in 1952 led to a series of recommendations that resulted in the House of Commons establishing a new standard in law in 1957: that obscenity is "any publication a dominant characteristic of which is the undue exploitation of sex, or of sex and anyone or more of the following subjects, namely, crime, horror, cruelty and violence ..." This became the core of Section 163 of the Criminal Code.

The new definition raised an obvious question. How do we tell whether the "exploitation of sex" in a publication is "undue"? The measure that Canadian courts developed is what's known as the "Canadian community standard of tolerance" test. In this test, the courts measured a purportedly obscene publication against what the Canadian community, taken as a whole, would "tolerate"—not what it would tolerate seeing or reading itself, but what it would tolerate others seeing or reading. As Chief Justice Brian Dickson put it in a 1985 case, *Towne Cinema v. R.*, "It is a standard of tolerance, not taste, that is relevant. What matters is not what Canadians think is right for themselves to see. What matters is what Canadians would not abide other Canadians seeing because it would be beyond the contemporary Canadian standard of tolerance to allow them to see it." Further, as Justice John Sopinka wrote in the *Butler* decision, "It is the standards of the community as a whole which must be considered."

There are several obvious difficulties with this test. First, if the court is to adopt the perspective of the "Canadian community as a whole," there's the logical conundrum of who, precisely, are the "other Canadians" whose reading and viewing habits will or won't be tolerated. Isn't the notion of the "community as a whole" merely a means of imposing the "tyranny of the majority"? Second, how is a court to determine what the Canadian community standard of tolerance is? The tolerance test was declared to be "objective" and so easy to apply that there was no burden on the Crown to advance any evidence concerning it. But how is the obvious subjectivity of a test of "taste" escaped when the issue is rephrased as one of "tolerance," given that tolerance and intolerance are notoriously matters of taste rather than the product of some dispassionate deliberative process? Further, if the court isn't to make use of some social science or public opinion poll measure of tolerance, won't the "objective" judgment of the community standard simply be a guess?

As if the fundamental concept isn't muddled enough, there's an even larger difficulty. The notion of tolerance evolved as a sort of halfway house between "taste" and "harm." But once rights have been entrenched in a constitution, as happened in Canada in 1982, how can they be subjected to the whims of tolerance? That was exactly the problem Justice Bertha Wilson foresaw in the *Towne Cinema* decision, referred to above. She wrote, "The test of the community standard is helpful to the extent that it provides a norm against which impugned material may be assessed, but it does little to elucidate the underlying question as to why some exploitation of sex falls on the permitted side of the line under [the obscenity law] and some on the prohibited side. No doubt this question will have to be addressed when the validity of the obscenity provisions of the Code is subjected to attack as an infringement on freedom of speech and the infringement is sought to be justified as reasonable."

As feminism matured into a political movement during the 1970s, thinkers such as Catherine MacKinnon also anticipated this difficulty. The solution developed by anti-pornography activists was not to deny Mill's principle that the only justification for state interference in individual free speech was harm to others, but to turn the harm principle back on its proponents. Calling upon the resources of the developing social sciences, feminist theorists advanced the view that the harm done by obscene publications was the incitement of men to the commission of criminal sexual assaults on women.

If it turned out that a notion of direct and measurable harm couldn't be fully supported by social science findings, anti-porn theorists offered an alternative approach that invoked the equality rights guaranteed by Section 15 of the Charter. This approach can be clearly seen in the intervenor's brief submitted in the *Butler* case by the feminist Legal Education and Action Fund. LEAF introduced the idea, inspired by Catherine MacKinnon, that the harm caused by pornography should be determined by asking what effect its existence has upon women's rights to equal treatment before the law. In this way, the legal question becomes an issue of balancing one right—freedom of expression—against another Charter-protected right, the Section 15 right to "equal protection and equal benefit of the law without discrimination."

This radically alters the problem of attempting to justify the limitation of the fundamental right of freedom of expression solely on the basis of evidence that pornography causes men to commit criminal acts of sexual aggression. The old approach pitted a right against a public interest, and the status of that interest was problematical in that there was no objective proof that pornography caused—in the strong sense of "incited"—men to commit acts of violence against women. The new approach recast the pornography issue as one of "sexual discrimination against women." But whatever the approach—social-science-supported proof of harm or an interpretation of equality rights—feminist thinking was underwritten by a long-held tenet of belief summed up in the slogan "Porn is the theory, rape is the practice."

At this point, along came Donald Butler. He was the owner of Avenue Video Boutique in Winnipeg, Manitoba, a shop that sold "hard core" video-tapes. On August 21, 1987, police raided Butler's shop and he was charged with numerous counts of violating the obscenity law. Butler was subsequently convicted by the Manitoba Court of Queen's Bench, and that decision was reinforced by the Manitoba Court of Appeal, which dismissed Butler's appeal of his conviction. Both of the lower courts considered the question of the obscenity law's possible infringement of free speech rights, and the corollary question: If free speech was infringed, could the infringement be justified under Section 1 of the Charter (which says that rights and freedoms are sub-ject to "reasonable limits prescribed by law as can be demonstrably justified in a free and democratic society")? While the trial court decided that the infringement of free speech could be justified under Section I, the Manitoba Appeal Court went further and ruled that the porno tapes at issue were not protected by freedom of speech and, therefore, there was no need to consid-er whether an infringement of freedom could be "saved" by Section 1.

Some four years after Butler's initial arrest, the Supreme Court of Canada "seized the opportunity to address the three main questions that have arisen in the obscenity debate since the Canadian Charter of Rights was enacted: first, whether Section 163 infringes on the right to free expression under Sec-tion 2(b) of the Charter; second, which approach should be used to deter-mine whether a particular publication is obscene under the statute; and final-ly, whether Section 163 is a reasonable and demonstrably justified limitation on freedom of expression under Section 1 of the Charter."[8]

Unlike the Manitoba Court of Appeal, the Canadian Supreme Court deter-mined that pornography, even of a violent or degrading sort, is protected under free speech provisions because it "can convey, or attempt to convey meaning, and thus is not without expressive content."[9] Therefore, the court held that Section 163 infringes on the right of free expression and, conse-quently, must satisfy the requirements of Section 1 of the Charter.

Before deciding on whether the obscenity law is a justified limit on free speech, the Supreme Court of Canada offered a new interpretation of Sec-tion 163's core prohibition of "undue exploitation of sex." The judgment, said the Court, should not be made on moral grounds—and the community standard test should not be regarded as a measure of the community's moral tolerance—but rather on the basis of harm. The court defined "harm," in the context of obscenity, as meaning that exposure to the obscene material "pre-disposes persons to act in an anti-social manner as, for example, the physical or mental mistreatment of women by men, or, what is perhaps debatable, the reverse." The court admitted that "while a direct link between obscenity and harm to society may be difficult, if not impossible, to establish," nonetheless "it is reasonable to presume that exposure to images bears a causal relationship to changes in attitudes and beliefs."[10] In defining obscenity, the court concluded that the community standards and the harm-based approach "are necessarily linked, requiring lower courts to determine what the Canadian community would tolerate based on the degree of harm that may flow from exposure to these materials."[11]

The court further linked the community tolerance test and harm by providing an explicit measure in the form of a spectrum of "violence, degradation and dehumanization." The stronger the inference of a risk of harm, the less the likelihood of tolerance. Applying this measure, the court concluded, "The portrayal of sex coupled with violence will almost always constitute the undue exploitation of sex. Explicit sex which is degrading or dehumanizing may be undue if the risk of harm is substantial. Finally, explicit sex that is not violent and neither degrading or dehumanizing is generally tolerated in our society and will not qualify as the undue exploitation of sex unless it employs children in its production."[12] Thus, if material "is perceived by public opinion to be harmful to society, especially to women," that is sufficient for finding the material, through the community tolerance test, to be obscene.

After establishing its new interpretation of obscenity and harm, the court turned to the Section 1 question and held that Section 163 is a justified limitation on freedom of expression.[13] The court concluded both that the objective of Section 163 was sufficiently pressing and substantial to warrant a limitation on the right to free expression, and that the infringement on free expression was "proportional" to the good sought by the limitation. The most important conclusion of the court in its discussion of Section 1 was that "the harm caused by the proliferation of materials which seriously offend the values fundamental to [Canadian] society is a substantial concern which justifies restricting the otherwise full exercise of the freedom of expression."[14]

At the heart of the *Butler* decision is a notion of harm—one that will be relevant, if not central, to the kiddie porn law and the constitutional challenges to it. Both the concept of harm and the means for determining its presence, as interpreted by the Supreme Court, are highly unusual.

...

At the end of the day, the law of the land in Canada read that a sexual representation is obscene if it is perceived to cause bad attitudes about women that could possibly lead to bad acts. Given such shaky reasoning, it is little wonder that analysts like Kleinick would conclude that "morality is probably the *Butler* court's real justification for upholding Section 163," or that the authors of *Bad Attitude/s* would charge that "the *Butler* decision and its discourse of harm against women is really just sexual morality in drag."[15]

The Butler decision had an immediate impact upon the Justice Department. The day after the Supreme Court's ruling upholding the federal obscenity law, the media eagerly sought out the Justice minister for her reactions to the judgment. Campbell praised the decision for balancing the need for society to protect itself from harmful varieties of pornography and the rights of those who want erotica available for their own purposes.

"The Supreme Court recognizes certain kinds of sexually explicit materials really do communicate a message that is inherently dangerous to women. On the other hand," said Campbell, the decision "is not a prudish view." Campbell also took the occasion to reannounce her intention to introduce a child pornography bill, hopefully by fall 1992.[16]

The fact that the *Butler* decision specifically mentioned child pornography was one of the factors that bore on the fortunes of the nascent child pornography legislation. The identification of pornography that "used children in its production," even if it had no elements of violence or degradation, was, in a sense, unwelcome to the Justice department because it meant that the Court had probably garnered a large share of the available credit for protecting children. If a court that was seen as notoriously liberal by groups like the Family Caucus had certified the criminality of any publication involving the sexual use of children in its production, the government would have to go further if it were to gain any credit for itself. This confirmed the wisdom of crafting a statute making it an offence to merely possess, as distinct from producing or publishing, child pornography.

Given renewed impetus by the *Butler* decision, Justice officials focussed their energies on putting together the actual child pornography bill during March and April 1992. They wrestled with several key problems, the most important of which were age definitions, whether to include those "depicted" as children, whether to include a prohibition of written materials, and the absence of any pressing need for legislation. As noted earlier, Justice department research had failed to turn up a child pornography problem in Canada, and the government could be criticized for making empty political gestures with its criminal law-making authority. This was perhaps the least worrisome of the issues, since it could always be handled by simply insisting that numbers were irrelevant where the safety of children was involved.

The questions of age definition and the inclusion of written materials were more difficult, since both went to the political heart of the legislative enterprise. If the definition of "child" was set at the high end—eighteen to twenty years—it would be vigorously attacked as overbroad by the same civil rights and artistic groups that had successfully scuttled the attempted pornography legislation of 1988. Conversely, if the definition was at the low end of the scale—under the age of consent of fourteen years—it might serve to anger the groups, such as the Family Caucus, that the legislation was designed to please.

Similarly, if the legislative target was restricted to photographic and video representations of the sexual use of actual children, excluding works of the imagination not involving harm to children in their production (such as stories, essays, drawings, etc.), it would displease religious and "pro-family" groups as a weak gesture. But if works of the imagination were included in the legislation, a storm of protest could be expected from the cultural and political left. This political split held for the "depiction" issue as well. Those on the right would want a prohibition on child sex that was acted out or depicted by adult models, whereas those on the left would want such depictions treated as a form of expression and hence legitimately protected by the Charter.

How could the policy objectives of the legislation be balanced with the principles of the Charter of Rights and Freedoms? Or to put the problem another way, how could the government be seen to improve on the protection for children provided by the *Butler* decision while staying within the confines of the Constitution? Justice officials were still entangled in the search for this elusive pivot point months later.

...

On January 3, 1993, Campbell was called to Ottawa and informed by the prime minister that in a cabinet shuffle the next day he would name her to the dual post of Minister of Defense and Veterans' Affairs. The new Justice minister was Quebec MP Pierre Blais. Although Mulroney denied rumours that he was contemplating resignation, less than two months later, on February 24, 1993, he announced his departure, and speculation immediately focussed on Campbell as a potential leadership candidate at the June 1993 convention that the Tories called to select a new prime minister.

On June 25, 1993, Campbell defeated MP Jean Charest in the leadership contest and became Canada's first woman prime minister. In naming her cabinet, she retained Pierre Blais, who had been her leadership campaign co-chair, as Justice minister. Three months later, Prime Minister Campbell set October 25, 1993, as the date for the next federal election.

Between the January 1993 cabinet shuffle and the October 1993 election, Justice Minister Blais introduced and passed the child pornography law that became Section 163.1 of the Criminal Code. Blais, it was generally agreed in Ottawa circles, was no ideologue, but rather a pragmatic politician with an eye on party unity and the forthcoming election. While he, like most other parliamentarians, no doubt supported a child pornography law on its intrinsic merits, both his introduction of the kiddie porn bill as well as his decision to allow the CHRA amendments to die on the Order Paper have to be seen as primarily political moves aimed not only at positioning the Conservative Party for an impending election, but also at maintaining the loyalty of Family Caucus Conservatives and forestalling their defection to the rival Reform Party.

The Family Caucus had been grievously unhappy with the actions of the Department of Justice while Campbell had been in charge. It didn't like her abortion bill, it chafed under the new gun control legislation, it was offended by the feminist preamble to the revised rape shield law, it was unhappy with the department's handling of a series of court cases involving the extension of spousal rights and benefits to gays, and it positively detested the provision for the protection of gay rights in the CHRA. The presence of a new minister who, while not necessarily an ally of Family Caucus views, didn't share Campbell's activist agenda offered the ultra-conservative wing of the Conservative Party a last opportunity to secure some satisfaction before the present mandate expired.

Blais launched his first trial balloons on the kiddie porn issue in March 1993, telling a Toronto audience that he was "considering amendments to the [Criminal] Code to provide better protection to children against their exploitation through child pornography." In a radio interview in Hamilton, Ontario, the same month, the Justice minister admitted that the legislation he was pondering might not go as far as some people wanted. He may have been thinking of Saskatchewan NDP MP Chris Axworthy, who had put forward a private member's bill to outlaw child pornography. The government's plan, Blais conceded, wouldn't cover certain publications, such as the newsletter of the North American Man-Boy Love Association (NAMBLA). "So far we're not contemplating legislation on that, but I'm following it very closely," Blais said.[17]

So was the parliamentary Standing Committee on Justice, which held one of a series of public hearings on child pornography in Vancouver on January 20, 1993. It was there that Vancouver Police detective Noreen Waters (or Wolff, as she was then) brought up the subject of NAMBLA. The officer had previously been in contact with MP Tom Wappel, a "family values" Liberal and a member of the standing committee. She had informed Wappel about the *NAMBLA Bulletin* and was subsequently invited to testify at the justice committee hearings.[18]

The legal problem with the *Bulletin*, Waters explained, was that it wasn't obscene. Although it "advocated" sex between men and boys, she said, neither the photographs nor the articles it published were pornographic. Nonetheless, as she told the *Vancouver Province* a month before, "It's a textbook for pedophiles. It tells them how to seduce children and not get caught."

The standing committee held further hearings in Ottawa in April and May 1993, inviting testimony from a series of experts including academics, mental health professionals, law enforcement officers, and child advocates such as Rix Rogers, who had written the 1990 report for the federal Department of Health recommending child pornography legislation. Rogers was among those concerned about pornography where adults dress as children. On April 27, Justice Minister Blais appeared before the committee. Blais told the committee that he was preparing a "surgical intervention ... addressing child pornography." When MP Tom Wappel asked him about the NAMBLA publication, Blais said that he didn't yet have a "straight answer" but was looking into it.

Both Detective Waters of Vancouver and Detective Robert Matthews of Toronto's Project P, an anti-pornography squad of the Ontario Provincial Police, were committee witnesses on May 10, 1993, in Ottawa. The Toronto officer urged the committee to define child pornography as more than just explicit sex and suggested that the definition include nude photos that showed children's genital areas. Perhaps the tenor of the discussions was best captured when the committee's most vocal member, Wappel, fervently declared, "I say that the sexual exploitation of children is so serious that the very existence of our society as we know it is threatened."

The next day in the House of Commons, MP Chris Axworthy's private member's bill on child pornography failed to get the unanimous consent necessary for it to be further considered, but MP Rob Nicholson, parliamentary secretary to the Justice minister, promised that the government would soon introduce legislation of its own and pleaded for patience.

The legislators didn't have long to wait. The following day, May 13, 1993, Blais rose in the House to table a child pornography bill. Its central feature was the one proposed by justice officials during Kim Campbell's ministry: the criminalization of simple possession of child pornography, which was now a crime punishable by up to five years in prison. Blais described the move as the closing of a "terrible loophole" in the law. As well, maximum sentences for existing crimes, such as production and distribution of child pornography, were "dramatically increased" from two years to ten. The media described the bill as "tough legislation."[19]

The proposed law—again as had been urged during Campbell's tenure—focussed on visual materials, since "the major element of what is child pornography is visual," Blais argued. The definition of child pornography in this section of the law read, "'Child pornography' means a photographic, film, video or other visual representation, whether or not it was made by electronic or mechanical means." Although this definition closely resembles the original narrow focus on photographic or video materials, in fact it had been significantly expanded to include "other visual representation"—thus presumably including drawings, paintings, and computer simulations—a clause that would quickly prove to be relevant.

With Campbell gone, Blais was content to acquiesce to those of his justice officials who had been pressing for the most expansive definition of age available. The law said that child pornography was any visual representation "that shows a person who is or is depicted as being under the age of 18 and is engaged in or is depicted as engaged in explicit sexual activity." Blais opted not only for age 18 as a demarcation line, but also accepted the inclusion of adults who were "depicted as being under the age of 18." Thus the definition—which now included any visual representation and people who were not children—defeated the intention of earlier drafters that the law be strictly limited to capture only sexual representations whose creation required the criminal sexual use of children. Now child pornography could include visual products of the imagination (although the bill included a defence grounds of "artistic merit") or representations not necessarily involving children. Still, the bill was narrowly enough conceived that Blais's officials could assure the minister that the legislation was consistent with the Charter of Rights, a certification of constitutionality required by law. What's more, the proposed law did not proscribe written materials and required that engagement in "explicit sexual activity" be present for a visual representation to be illegal.

However, as Campbell had been repeatedly cautioned during her attempt to craft such legislation, "control of the agenda" could easily be lost. It soon would be.

Several factors now came into play. The most urgent ones were timing and internal party politics. Parliament was scheduled to adjourn the following month, in mid-June, and it was likely that an election would intervene before its next sitting. If Blais intended not merely to table legislation as a symbolic gesture but to actually ensure its passage, the complicated process by which a bill becomes law—legislative hearings, clause-by-clause consideration, proposals for amendments, and all the rest—would have to be drastically telescoped. Doing so would mean that Blais would have to give up considerable leverage in terms of "controlling the agenda." He would have to agree to compromises, most likely in the form of amendments enlarging the scope of the law, which under normal circumstances the government might resist. The danger here was not from opponents of the legislation, but from right-wing partisans of it who would insist that the bill be expanded to cover more ground.

In fact, the immediate criticism offered by opposition parties was not opposition to the bill itself, but the charge that its introduction was simply a pre-election gambit. "This is showcase legislation in its worst form," complained Liberal justice critic Russell MacLellan, who supported the bill but worried about whether it would receive sufficient public scrutiny. "They're bringing legislation forward to show people they're bringing it forward. If it doesn't pass, they'll blame the opposition," he charged.[20]

The second complicating factor for the legislation was the state of affairs in the Conservative Party. Even as Blais tabled his kiddie porn bill, the party leadership convention, in which Blais was the busy campaign co-chair for one of the leading candidates, was scarcely a month away. Presumably, passage of the legislation by the minister campaigning on behalf of Kim Campbell would improve his candidate's *bona fides* in the eyes of convention delegates closest to the views of the Family Caucus. A further irony of the situation is that the one person best positioned to offer advice on and criticism of the proposed child pornography bill, Kim Campbell, was effectively immobilized on this question by her own political ambitions. If she had any objections to the measure, she was in a double-bind, unable to alienate either her campaign co-chair or the Family Caucus.

The final hearings of the Standing Committee on Justice were held on June 15, 1993, a day before the summer adjournment of the Commons, and only hours before the House was scheduled to debate and pass the kiddie porn bill. The main witnesses were representatives of the arts and media—groups ranging from the ACTRA Performers Guild to the Canadian Broadcasting Corporation—who were primarily worried about artistic productions depicting teenage sexuality and child sexual abuse. Recent films such as *The Boys of St. Vincent*, a docudrama about child sexual abuse in orphanages, and current television programs like *Degrassi Junior High*, a teen coming-of-age series, might conceivably fall afoul of the new law, the arts representatives feared.

But it was clear that most of the committee's attention was on finishing the task at hand—producing an amended bill for passage that afternoon—rather than debating what seemed to them to be marginal artistic concerns. Not even the appearance of Allan Borovoy, representing the Toronto-based Canadian Civil Liberties Association, would delay the justice committee for long.

The objections of civil libertarians, both within and outside the political arena, had been curiously muted throughout the whole truncated, hasty process. Only one member of the committee, NDP justice critic Ian Waddell, a B.C. MP, had really raised the issue. In the course of declaring his party's support for child pornography legislation, Waddell nonetheless said that, as a civil libertarian, he was particularly worried about freedom of the press as well as the hastiness of the process. He cited former Justice minister Campbell's "inclusive justice" slogan. "Inclusive justice means that people from all sides come in and discuss the bill, and ... then we will get the best bill possible," he said, presciently adding, "Then it will hold up in the courts and will not be thrown out as unconstitutional."

Once the witnesses were out of the way, the committee got down to clause-by-clause inspection of the legislation and the all-important matter of amendments. There were two crucial additions made to Blais's bill, both of which were accepted by the minister. The first amendment vastly expanded the range of visual materials that could be considered pornographic by adding a clause in the definition of child pornography that included any visual representation, "the dominant characteristic of which is the depiction, for a sexual purpose, of a sexual organ or the anal region of a person under the age of

18 years." Although there would eventually be considerable debate about what that ambiguously worded phrase actually meant, *prima facie* it suggested that any nude photo of anyone under eighteen might be illegal.

A second amendment completely undercut the notion of a law narrowly focussed on photographic visual materials involving children engaged in sex. An additional clause in the definition of child pornography now included "any written material or visual representation that advocates or counsels sexual activity with a person under the age of 18 years that would be an offence under this Act." For example, an essay calling for revision of the law prohibiting people under eighteen from engaging in anal intercourse could now conceivably be seen as "advocacy" or "counselling" that amounted to child pornography. Perhaps worse, written material that contained representations of children engaged in sex could be interpreted as constituting advocating or counselling.

The changes meant that not only had a new offence been created—simple possession of child pornography—but the definition of what that pornography might be had also been drastically expanded. For many in the House of Commons who debated the child pornography bill during its third and final reading that afternoon, such an expansion was precisely what they believed in and wanted. Family Caucus MP John Reimer was pleased to be the lead-off speaker.

Blais's parliamentary secretary, Rob Nicholson, rhetorically addressed NAMBLA, declaring, "This is one bad day for you because ... we are zeroing in on publications like yours." Liberal Tom Wappel told the House how he had been alerted to NAMBLA by Detective Waters. The omission of written material was a serious flaw in the bill as it had been initially presented, but "I was instrumental in having that provision included."

Only Liberal MP George Rideout, a justice committee member, expressed some constitutional doubt. "My concern is that by adding the written word we may find ourselves vulnerable to a Charter challenge," he said. "I guess that in these circumstances one says ... if it does not pass the test then we will try to correct it later on."

On June 15, 1993, the House of Commons passed the child pornography bill. A week or so later the bill received Senate approval, notwithstanding repeated objections by Liberal Senator Richard Stanbury that the bill would not stand up in court.

Two days after parliamentary passage of the kiddie porn law, Kim Campbell became prime minister of Canada, completing the political trajectory that the media had described as her "rise and rise." The child pornography law was officially proclaimed the law of the land by the time Campbell took her party to the polls for an October 25, 1993 federal election.

Although the Tories, during the final days of their administration, had brought in a law-and-order package, of which the child pornography law was

a part, it would have little effect on the outcome, irrespective of whatever favourable impact it might have on party unity. At the end of a seemingly endless rise in the fortunes of Kim Campbell and her party, there wasn't merely a fall, but a catastrophic crash. In the 1993 election, Liberal leader Jean Chretien became prime minister with an overwhelming majority. Not only was Campbell defeated in her riding, but so were Conservatives across the country. The Reform Party and the Bloc Québécois became the leading opposition parties, and the Tories were reduced to a two-member caucus, facing possible extinction as a major Canadian political party.
...

Notes

1 We should note that we're friends and colleagues of former Justice minister and former prime minister Kim Campbell, though neither of us are associated with any of the political organizations or parties that she's represented.

   John Dixon worked for the Department of Justice when Campbell was minister. Stan Persky and Campbell worked together as "friendly rival" B.C. political correspondents on Peter Gzowski's *Morningside* radio program in the 1980s. In addition, Campbell served as an honorary board member of the non-partisan B.C. Civil Liberties Association, where we were also members of the board, and she's been a guest lecturer in college classes we've taught.

   In this chapter, in addition to our own and other sources, we make use, naturally, of Campbell's well-written and informative political memoirs, *Time and Chance* (Seal Books, 1996). Curiously, however, Campbell makes no mention whatsoever of child pornography legislation in her account, and we've had to rely on internal documents and memos produced within the Department of Justice, principally those of adviser John Dixon.

   One of this book's authors has also been a participant in the events described here, which naturally poses a slight technical problem for our narration. Although any solution is bound to be arbitrary, we've chosen to represent John Dixon in the third person, as an actor in the story, and to rely primarily on written materials he produced during the period under review to minimize the vagaries of memory.

2 We'll do no more than briefly refer to the general debate about pornography, except where it impinges on the thinking and actions of the Justice department in the context of child pornography legislation. We will, however, subsequently examine in some detail an important Supreme Court of Canada decision—*R v. Butler* (1992)—about pornography that has direct relevance to the development of the kiddie porn law.

   There is, for interested readers, a rich literature on the general pornography question. Works that we've found useful are primarily those written by feminists and include: Catherine MacKinnon, *Only Words* (Harvard, 1993); Judith Butler,

Excitable Speech (Routledge, 1997); Drucilla Cornell, *The Imaginary Domain* (Routledge, 1995); Lynn Hunt (ed.), *The Invention of Pornography: Obscenity and the Origins of Modernity, 1500–1800* (Zone, 1993); Varda Burstyn (ed.), *Women Against Censorship* (Douglas and McIntyre, 1985); Walter Kendrick, *The Secret Museum: Pornography in Modern Culture* (University of California, 1996); and James Weinstein, *Hate Speech, Pornography and the Radical Attack on Free Speech Doctrine* (Westview, 1999).

3 MacKinnon's publications include *Sexual Harassment of Working Women* (Yale, 1979); *Feminism Unmodified* (Harvard, 1987); (with Andrew Dworkin), *Pornography and Civil Rights* (self-published, 1988); *Towards a Feminist Theory of the State* (Harvard, 1989); and *Only Words* (Harvard, 1993).

4 See Charles Taylor, *Multiculturalism: Examining the Politics of Recognition* (Princeton, 1994); and Michael Sandal, *Democracy's Discontent* (Harvard, 1996).

5 John Dixon, "Memorandum re: individual rights vs. collective interests: equality in the Canadian federal setting," March 14, 1991.

For those with a specific interest in philosophy or philosophy of law, we should note that in our discussion of rights that follows, and in our reference in the previous chapter to the distinction between words and acts, we are not proffering a metaphysical position in the current philosophical debates between "new-pragmatism" and forms of philosophical "realism." While we're attentive readers of Richard Rorty's *Contingency, Irony and Solidarity* (Cambridge, 1989), nothing said here, as far as we can tell, very much hangs on whether one prefers Rorty to John Searle's *The Construction of Social Reality* (Free Press, 1995). In distinguishing between words and acts, or in referring to a theory of self-governance as central to democracy, we are making no claims about whether or not such distinctions have a transcendent character. Rather, our usage is limited to the current standard of usage of such terms within a theory of "political liberalism," as the philosopher John Rawls refers to such a framework. Insofar as political liberalism is assumed as the background theory for our discussion, our claims about words and acts, rights, and concepts of harm are simply meant to be coherent with that framework. See John Rawls, *Political Liberalism* (Columbia, 1996).

6 Sharon Moyer, "A Preliminary Investigation into Child Pornography in Canada," The Research Group, March 1991.

7 The *Butler* decision has generated a considerable legal literature about the case. In what follows, in addition to our own reading of the judgment, we rely on Jodi Aileen Kleinick, "Suppressing Violent and Degrading Pornography to 'Prevent Harm' in Canada: *Butler v. Her Majesty the Queen*," *Brooklyn Journal of International Law*, 1993, v. 19, pp. 627–75, as a characteristic sound critique of the ruling. Other sources for our reading range from Ronald Dworkin's *Freedom's Law* (Harvard, 1996) to Brenda Crossman, Shannon Bell, Lise Gotell, and Becki Ross's *Bad Attitude/s on Trial: Pornography, Feminism, and the Butler Decision* (University of Toronto, 1996).

8 Kleinick, "Suppressing," p. 645.

9 Ibid.

10 *R v. Butler* (1992).

11 Kleinick, "Suppressing," p. 646.

12 *R v. Butler.*

13 In determining whether Section1 requirements are met, Canadian jurisprudence
    has developed the *Oakes* test, so named from *R v. Oakes* (1986), where this inter-
    pretive scheme was first established. "Under the *Oakes* test, two central criteria
    must be met for a limitation on a Charter right to be valid: first, the government
    objective for limiting the Charter right must be sufficiently important to warrant
    the limitation of that right; and, second, the limitation on the Charter right must
    be 'proportional' to the government's objective. A determination of proportion-
    ality involves three separate inquiries: (1) whether a rational connection exists
    between the limitation on the individual right and the government objective; (2)
    whether the limitation only minimally impairs the Charter right; and (3)
    whether the effects of the limitation so severely infringe the protected Charter
    right that the legislative objective is outweighed by the limitation" (Kleinick,
    "Suppressing," p. 633). The *Oakes* test is not only relevant to the *Butler* case, but
    will be invoked by all the courts involved in *R v. Sharpe.*

14 *R v. Butler.*

15 Crossman et al., *Bad Attitude/s.*

16 Jeff Sallot, "Ruling paves way for child pornography bill, minister says," *Globe and
    Mail,* February 28, 1992, p. 1.

17 "Child porn leaking through loopholes," *Vancouver Sun,* April 20, 1993.

18 Cited in Sharpe, *Personal Account,* as is much of the following material on the par-
    liamentary committee hearings.

19 Sean Fine, "Ottawa proposes to outlaw child smut," *Globe and Mail,* May 14, 1993;
    Anthony Johnson, "Tougher sentencing proposed," *Vancouver Sun,* May 14, 1993.

20 Sean Fine, "Ottawa proposes."

≡+ SOURCES +≡

We are grateful for permission to reprint the excerpts in this book, as follows:

Margaret Atwood, from *The Handmaid's Tale* (1985), used by permission of McClelland and Stewart Ltd.

Patricia Baird *et al.*, *Proceed with Care: Final Report of the Royal Commission on New Reproductive Technologies: Summary and Highlights* (1993), with permission of the Minister of Public Works and Government Services and Courtesy of the Privy Council Office.

Iain A.G. Barrie, "A Broken Trust: Canadian Priests, Brothers, Pedophilia, and the Media," from *Sex, Religion, Media* (2002), reprinted with permission of Iain A.G. Barrie. Iain A. G. Barrie, M.J., is professor of broadcasting in Media Studies at Algonquin College (Ottawa, Ontario, Canada).

Persimmon Blackridge, from *Prozac Highway*, used by permission of Raincoast Press.

Michael Bliss, "Pure Books on Avoided Subjects: Pre-Freudian Sexual Ideas in Canada," *Journal of Canadian Studies* (1970); reprinted with permission of Professor Michael Bliss.

Martin Cannon, "The Regulation of First Nations Sexuality," from the *Canadian Journal of Native Studies* (1998); reprinted with permission of the *CJNS* and Martin Cannon.

Nancy Christie, "Sacred Sex: The United Church and the Privatization of the Family in Post-War Canada," from *Households of Faith* (2002), reprinted with permission of McGill-Queen's University Press.

Leonard Cohen, from *Beautiful Losers* (1966), used by permission of McClelland and Stewart Ltd.

John Colapinto, from *As Nature Made Him* (2000), with permission of HarperCollins Canada.

Ivan E. Coyote, "Just Like My Dad," from *Boys Like Her*, used by permission of Raincoast Press.

Lynn Crosbie, from *Paul's Case* (1997), reprinted with permission by Insomniac Press.

Karen Dubinsky and Adam Givertz, "'It was only a matter of passion': Masculinity and Sexual Danger," from *Gendered Pasts: Historical Essays in Femininity and Masculinity in Canada* (1999) ed. K. McPherson *et al.*; copyright© the University of Toronto Press Inc.; reprinted with permission of the publisher.

Timothy Findley, from *Not Wanted on the Voyage* (1984), reprinted with permission of Pebble Productions, Inc. and Westwood Creative Artists Ltd.

Roberta Hamilton, "Representation and Subjectivity," from *Gendering the Vertical Mosaic* (Copp Clark, 2004) 181–222, reprinted with permission by Pearson Education Canada Inc.

Gary Kinsman, "'These things may lead to the tragedy of our species': The Emergence of Homosexuality, Lesbianism, and Heterosexuality in Canada," reprinted from *The Regulation of Desire: Homo and Hetero Sexualities* (1996) with permission of Black Rose Books.

Irving Layton, "The Improved Binoculars," from *Collected Poems* (1971), used by permission of McClelland and Stewart, Ltd.

SKY Lee, from *Disappearing Moon Café,* published 1990 by Douglas and McIntyre; reprinted by permission of the publisher.

Nicole Markotić, from *Yellow Pages: A Book of Intentions,* with permission of Red Deer Press.

Daphne Marlatt, from *Ana Historic,* copyright © 1988 by Daphne Marlatt; reprinted with the permission of House of Anansi Press.

Derek McCormack, "Stargaze" from *Dark Rides* (1996), with permission of Gutter Press and Westwood Creative Artists.

Marshall McLuhan and George B. Leonard, "The Future of Sex," from *Look Magazine,* with permission of the Estate of Marshall McLuhan.

Katherine Monk, from *Weird Sex and Snowshoes,* with permission of Raincoast Books.

Lyndell Montgomery, for "Border Crossing: On the Edge," from *Boys Like Her* (1998), reprinted with permission of Raincoast Books.

Alice Munro, "Family Furnishings," taken from *Hateship, Friendship, Courtship, Loveship, Marriage* (2001). Used by permission of McClelland and Stewart Ltd.

Stan Persky and John Dixon, from *On Kiddie Porn* (2001), reprinted with permission of New Star Books.

Ian Iqbal Rashid, from *Black Markets, White Boyfriends, and other elisions* (1991), reprinted by permission of TSAR Press.

Jane Rule, for "The Killer Dyke and the Lady," copyright © 1981 by Jane Rule and reprinted by permission of Georges Borchardt, Inc., on behalf of the author; and for "Detained at Customs," copyright © 1995 by Jane Rule and reprinted by permission of Georges Borchardt, Inc., on behalf of the author.

Trish Salah, "Surgical Diary" from *Wanting in Arabic*, with permission of TSAR Press.

Gregory Scofield, from *Thunder Through My Veins: Memories of a Métis Childhood* (1999), reprinted with permission of HarperCollins Canada.

Michael Turner, from *The Pornographer's Poem* (1999), reprinted with permission of Westwood Creative Artists Ltd.

Mariana Valverde, "Families, Private Property, and the State: The Dionnes and the Toronto Stork Derby," reprinted with permission of the *Journal of Canadian Studies*.

The author of the book and the publisher have made every attempt to locate authors of copyrighted material or their heirs and assigns, and would be grateful for information that would allow them to correct any errors or omissions in a subsequent edition of the work.